Transformations

TRANSFORMATIONS:
a memoir by Jubal Jepson

"Edited" by

JAMES A. WARREN

Published by

VERITAS PUBLICATIONS

Bringing Hidden Truths to Light

ISBN 979-8-9861351-8-2

This is a work of fiction in the form of a memoir by a fictional character, in which real-life historical events and personages are discussed. With the exception of well-known public figures, names and characters are products of the author's imagination. Any resemblances to actual persons, living or dead, are entirely coincidental. Incidents in which characters interact with well-known public figures are likewise products of the author's imagination.

Published by Veritas Publications, LLC.
jimwarren1000@proton.me.
Cary, North Carolina.

Published October 10, 2024
Sixth printing, August 8, 2025

For Donald W. Miller, Jr., MD,
who changed my life

Jubal Jepson's MS. as given to the editor on September 11, 2023.

Editor's Introduction

I'd known Jubal Jepson in high school but hadn't had any contact with him during the nearly forty years since then. So it was quite a surprise when he showed up recently at Veritas Publications, the publishing company I'd founded a few years ago and whose motto is "Bringing Hidden Truths to Light."

He presented me with a paper manuscript. "It's reminiscences, written down a few years after the events recounted," he told me. "It's not a diary or a daily journal. It's my attempt to recapture how certain experiences during a stupendous nine-month period transformed my life. It's a story that might be of some interest to others." Later in that one and only conversation we had, he added that he excluded from the memoir all aspects of his life—and all persons, including family, friends, and former Foreign Service colleagues he remained in touch with—that didn't relate directly to the transformations described in it.

Jubal didn't stay long, or provide any other details of his life, saying only that the manuscript was self-explanatory. He provided me with full authorization to edit it as I saw fit.

I received it from him only in printed form, the computer on which it had mostly been written having been stolen and there were no backups. It was printed mostly on letter size paper, but some pages were A4 size, showing that Jubal had travelled through or lived in at least one country where that paper size was used. Many pages had handwritten emendations on them, clearly made after the text had been printed. And, stuck into the MS. were scores of pages of varying sizes on which additional text had been inserted.

"I don't have a final Word version," Jubal explained when I commented on the scraps of paper whose ends stuck out. "I often wrote in places where I didn't have my computer, such as while camping, and had to write on whatever paper was available. I stuck the additions into the approximate places in the manuscript. You can add them into the right places—that's what an editor does, right?"

Examining the MS. after Jubal left, I saw that he'd written the memoir as one continuous document, with no chapter breaks or headings. Occasionally he'd added a date, which showed that the "nine stupendous months" began in September 2019 and ended in May 2020. Most of the scraps of paper he'd inserted were dated, but with the date he written them, not the date on which the events described had taken place. I have inserted them into the text where the fit seemed best.

Seeing that Jubal's MS. fell naturally into three sections, I have organized the memoir into three parts, and within them into nine sub-sections, one for each of the nine "stupendous" months. That adjective isn't inappropriate, given the nature of the events that occurred and the beliefs that Jubal came to hold as a result of them; however, I dropped it when I changed the title.

Jubal's original title, *WTF?: A Memoir of Nine Stupendous Months*, wouldn't do, I felt, particularly the vulgarity in it. The new title reflects the transformations that he went through and that are, in fact, the experiences that the memoir had been written to document. Jubal had, as he stated, changed so radically during those months—changed his understandings of so many things about himself and his country and, indeed, about his very soul—that he had become almost a different person. The new title reflects that.

At the end of the MS. Jubal provided a list of books and articles he'd read and websites he'd visited, which are the sources of the information that transformed his understanding of important events in recent American history. To help readers appreciate the substantiveness of Jubal's research, I have ferreted out the cited works and passages in them and added appropriate citations at the end of the book. I have also reorganized and added to the lists of books, articles, videos and websites he provided.

The images on the cover and interspersed throughout the memoir were stuck between the pages of the MS. I have obtained better quality copies of the same, or nearly the same, images, and, where necessary, secured the rights to reprint them.

Jubal's manuscript ends rather abruptly, and I'm publishing it that way, just as he intended. That wasn't the end of his story, though. Just a few days before the release of this book I received by mail a second MS. from Jubal, equal in length to the first, with instructions that it should be published separately. It appears to pick up his story after a gap of several years. Although I haven't yet read it in its entirety, I expect to publish it in full at some point in the future.

Editorial Notes

In passages quoted from English publications, such as books by C. S. Lewis and Aldous Huxley, I have changed British English spellings and punctuation to current American English practices: "standardisation" has been replaced with "standardization" and "behaviour" with "behavior," for instance, and punctuation marks have been moved from outside to inside quotation marks. Obsolete spellings, such as "co-ordinated" and "to-day" have been modernized.

Passages quoted from American publications have sometimes been slightly edited for consistency: US has been changed to U.S., for instance, and president is not capitalized unless it is followed by the name of a president.

Acknowledgements

Passages from Paul Craig Roberts' columns are reprinted with permission. Links to each of them on www.paulcraigroberts.org are provided in the end notes. Permission to reprint portions of Dr. Roberts' columns does not imply that Dr. Roberts endorses the media organizations that republish his columns or that he approves of the content of the books that republish them.

> The individual has always had to struggle to keep from being overwhelmed by the tribe. If you try it, you will be lonely often, and sometimes frightened. But no price is too high to pay for the privilege of owning yourself.
>
> Friedrich Nietzsche

> The individual is handicapped by coming face-to-face with a conspiracy so monstrous he cannot believe it exists. The American mind simply has not come to a realization of the evil which has been introduced into our midst. It rejects even the assumption that human creatures could espouse a philosophy which must ultimately destroy all that is good and decent.
>
> J. Edgar Hoover
> Director of the FBI
> *Elks Magazine*, August 1956

Editor's Note: These quotations were handwritten on scraps of paper stuck into the MS. As they capture important aspects of Jubal Jepson's mindset after the transformations described in his memoir, I am reprinting them here.

CONTENTS

LIST OF IMAGES

AUTHORIZATIONS TO REPRINT IMAGES ARE ON PAGES 503-507.

Aldous Huxley

John F. Kennedy

C. S. Lewis

PRELIMINARY

August 2019

⸙ 1 ⸙

"Tell. Don't ask. Tell her what you want; don't ask, like a child."

I was in Subway, the sandwich shop, and the girl ahead of me in line had said to the staff taking orders, "Can I have the Subway Club?"

After I spoke, she turned and looked at me as if asking herself, "Who is this man, and why is he saying this to me?"

"Sorry," I replied to her unspoken question. "I'm tired of hearing adults ask permission for something when a simple statement of what they want would be more appropriate."

She continued looking at me a second longer and started to speak, but then stopped and turned to look at her friend briefly before returning her attention to the girl behind the counter, to whom she said, "I'll have the Subway Club, six inch, on wheat bread, no cheese, not toasted." She then stepped to the left, still facing away from me, while her friend ordered. After they completed their orders and paid, they walked to a booth near the windows, both casting a quick glance at me as they moved away.

At that time, I didn't know that her name was Gina de Larrocha and she didn't know that mine was Jubal Jepson. Nor did I know that she was from The Philippines. I knew only that she had an air about her I found intriguing. After ordering, I remained at the counter while waiting for my sandwich, glancing at the two of them occasionally and wondering if I might ask to eat lunch with them. But the one I had spoken to had her back to me, and they seemed to be deep in conversation. So, after picking up my tray I found an appropriate table, opened a book I was in the middle of, and ate by myself. When I looked up a while later, they had already gone.

I had recently returned to live in the Raleigh area in North Carolina, near where I'd grown up, after having lived abroad for nearly thirty years. I'd retired only ten days earlier from a career working in half a dozen countries, mostly in Asia. My wife, Diana, had died suddenly a month before the date already set for my retirement. The memorial service for her—my wife and the mother of our two children—had been held soon after my return to the United States.

Those three events—Diana's death, the memorial service and my retirement—together served to mark the end of one part of my life and the beginning of another. Rarely had a transition been marked with such complete shifts of place and circumstances, and never before with such finality, leaving me with no set activities, something I was looking forward to, but, unexpectedly, without the spouse with whom I had planned to enjoy my post-retirement freedom. With our two children recently graduated from college and off building their own lives without much support needed from me, I was at loose ends.

Something I'd always wanted to do, but which I'd had to set aside during the hectic years when a demanding career and raising a family filled almost all waking hours, was investigate the lives of three famous men who died on November 22, 1963, the same day I was born: Aldous Huxley (b. July 26, 1894), John F. Kennedy (b. May 29, 1917) and C. S. Lewis (b. November 29, 1898). I'd ordered a number of books about and by each of them, which had recently been delivered to the furnished apartment I was living in temporarily while waiting to move into my own house after the tenant's lease expired at the end of the month, only three weeks away.

Returning to the apartment, I looked over the three dozen or so Huxley, Kennedy and Lewis books that filled the entire top two rows of the bookcase in the living room. I decided to continue reading the collection of speeches by President

Kennedy that I was already in the middle of, because it was reading his "Peace" speech and seeing a video of it decades ago that had inspired me to pursue a career in the U.S. Foreign Service—a career as a diplomat—which had come to an end 28 years after it had begun with my retirement two weeks ago at age 55. Kennedy's speech, delivered at American University on June 10, 1963, at the height of the Cold War, had shocked many with his call for peaceful coexistence with the Soviet Union. The key phrases expressing his desire for peace—"the kind of peace that makes life on earth worth living—the kind that enables men and women to grow and to hope and to build a better life for their children—not merely peace for Americans but peace for all men and women—not merely peace in our time but peace for all time"—had filled me, a young man in his early 20s when I'd first heard them, with an elevated desire to do all I could to help make Kennedy's vision a reality. Reading those words, more than any other single event or memory I can recall, had steered me down the path I'd followed for more than three decades of university study and work as a Foreign Service officer.

For most people, Kennedy's life and presidency have been overshadowed by the fact of his assassination. I'd looked into that event years before, eventually coming across what appeared to be a credible account of what had happened. That account, presented by Vermont Royster in the *Wall Street Journal* in 1988 (and originally proposed by James Reston), had made a convincing case that Lee Harvey Oswald had been aiming not at Kennedy but at John Connally, governor of Texas, who was seated just ahead of Kennedy in the same car. Connally had been Secretary of the Navy at the time Oswald's discharge from the Marines had been changed to "dishonorable" following his defection to the Soviet Union in 1959. Her husband was angry at Connally, Marina Oswald said later, because he had written several times to Connally to try to get the "honorable" discharge restored without receiving a response. Royster's account was credible also, I believed, because it explained how Oswald had been able to hit his target at such a distance—he hadn't, as his target had been Connally, not Kennedy—and it explained

Oswald's statement after his arrest that he hadn't shot the president. Apparently at the time he made the statement he hadn't known that two of his bullets had struck the president, one of which then entered Connally's body. And with that seemingly reasonable account in mind, I'd dismissed the assassination question.

Looking over the books on the shelves, I figured I'd better learn more about C. S. Lewis, who of the three men was the one I knew least about. At that point I knew only that he was English, that he'd written the Narnia books, several of which I had read to my kids when they were small, and that he was best known for his books explaining Christianity to those who were Christians and to those who, like me, weren't. I decided to begin with a book about Lewis: George Sayer's *Jack: A Biography of C. S. Lewis*.

Aldous Huxley, I knew, was an English novelist and explorer of altered states of consciousness. I'd read only one book by him, the dystopian *Brave New World*. Wanting to know more about his life, I picked up Dana Sawyer's biography. As I did so I recalled that Lewis's and Huxley's places in American and English cultural life had been so substantial that newscasters reporting on Kennedy's assassination on November 22 had repeatedly broken into their broadcasts with news that the two of them had also died that day.

PART I

September 2019

2

Skipping ahead several weeks and passing over the visits by my two children—the first since Diana's memorial service—that aren't part of this memoir, we come to my second encounter with Gina de Larrocha. But first some background.

Upon returning to the United States, I'd set out not only to engage in activities I hadn't had time for earlier—such as exploring the lives and writings of Huxley, Kennedy and Lewis—but also to become a different person. Having retired from the diplomatic service, I no longer had to support policies of the government that I disagreed with, and I no longer had to suppress those aspects of my personality not suitable for success as a diplomat; that is, I could live as the more introverted person I actually was, rather than acting as the extrovert that the position required. And I could return to my interests in history, anthropology and literature that I'd probably have built a career in if I hadn't joined the Foreign Service. The common thread running through all of them was my interest in understanding how other societies and cultures, past and present, had and have organized themselves to meet the needs and wants of their people.

Literature, especially, provides windows into the dispositions and sensibilities of people of all times and places, I thought. It can present life from angles other than that of contemporary American society more convincingly than any non-fiction historical or sociological study. I was quite fortunate,

I thought, in stumbling onto a newly formed book club that seemed custom made for my interests. Timeless Classics, as it called itself, had announced its intention to hold discussions on works of literature from around the world that were of particular importance in the cultural life of the countries in which they'd been written. The first meeting was held early in September.

I arrived early at the Barnes and Noble in Cary, near the Cary City Center mall, just north of Raleigh, where the meeting was to be held. After browsing through the shelves of fiction and literature, I found my way to the public meeting room. It was on entering the room that I saw the girl I'd encountered several weeks earlier at Subway.

After a short pause during which we both overcame our surprise, I said, "Hello. Timeless Classics? She nodded in a puzzled way, and I asked quickly, "Aren't you the girl I spoke to at Subway last month?"

She nodded again and glanced at the list of members on the table, apparently wondering which of them I was. "I'm Gina de Larrocha, the organizer," she said. "This is our first meeting, so we're all getting acquainted for the first time." It occurred to both of us that that wasn't quite true in our case, and she started to ask, "How is it that . . .?" but two other members entered the room before she finished. I was able to observe her more closely while she spoke to them.

I could see that she was Asian—not American born—of some indeterminate country. I ran through the list of Asian countries I was familiar with—Thailand, Malaysia, Singapore, Laos, Vietnam, Indonesia—and concluded that she wasn't from any of them. Nor was she Korean or Japanese, nor Chinese or Taiwanese. I was stumped. She had black hair and brown eyes, was a bit taller than average for an Asian, and was quite slim for someone of her height. She was wearing a yellow dress that seemed almost deliberately dated. It reminded me of the summer dresses that young women might have worn half a century or more ago—around the time I was born. She wasn't overtly beautiful, perhaps, but the stylish and seemingly purposely vintage nature of her dress gave her such a striking appearance that she could have been a model. I thought of pictures of models I'd seen, pictures before and after they'd applied makeup and how striking was the change. This girl resembled the before pictures.

While I was pondering all this, several more members had arrived, making seven of us altogether, three men and four women of varying ages. I appeared to be the oldest. We all sat down and looked expectantly toward the organizer, who sat at one of the narrower ends of the large table.

"Welcome to the first meeting of the Vintage Classics book club," she said. "I am Gina de Larrocha." She explained the purpose of the club, and then asked us to introduce ourselves and the book or books we'd brought.

We'd all brought a book or two that we thought might be appropriate for discussion by this particular book club and went around the table introducing ourselves and our books. Gina introduced her book before herself—José Rizal's *Noli Me Tangere* (*Touch Me Not*)—and explained that it was a novel of special importance in the cultural life of The Philippines because it portrayed how powerfully Spanish influence affected the life of the people in what at that time was a colony of Spain.

"This is the most famous Filipino novel ever written in English, inside or outside The Philippines," she said. "It's considered to be the quintessential Filipino novel. It's often referred to as *The Noli*."

This was just what I wanted. Having spent much of my career working in countries in the British Commonwealth—that is, in countries that are former British colonies—reading this book would be like entering a whole new world, the world of Spanish Catholicism rather than English Anglicism, and of Spanish, rather than English, cultural influence.

But even then I didn't get it. It wasn't until Gina introduced herself that I realized she was Filipino, or a Filipina, to use a term I would soon learn. Given my background working in countries that had been British or French colonies, The Philippines was almost completely outside my range of experiences. No wonder I'd overlooked it in trying to place her home country.

Gina went on to explain that she'd recently completed a master's degree in literature, and that after graduating she'd founded a company that provided tutoring to high school students in English and Spanish language and literature, as well as in grammar, vocabulary, reading comprehension and related skills.

When my turn came, I explained that I'd brought Mark Twain's *Adventures of Huckleberry Finn*, which I had read decades ago and wanted to reread. I described briefly its importance in American literary history, noting Ernest Hemingway's statement that "All American literature derives from one book—*Huck Finn*." I then introduced myself as recently retired and interested in reading books from cultures around the world.

The 14 books proposed by the members of the group provided a good cross section of world literature, with books from, in addition to The Philippines and the United States, England, France, Italy, Japan, Peru and Russia. I was happy to see that these included *Brave New World* by Aldous Huxley and *That Hideous Strength* by C. S. Lewis. By the end of the meeting, we decided to read first Rizal's *Noli Me Tangere* because it had been proposed by the group's founder. Robert Louis Stevenson's *Dr. Jekyll and Mr. Hyde* would be discussed the month after. Gina was quite pleased, telling us, "I am excited that we've selected *The Noli*! Nothing makes me feel more elated than discussing the rich culture of my country."

As we stood up to leave, Gina remarked that she was happy to see that everyone had brought printed copies of the books they proposed the group read. "So many people read books on their computer or phone," she lamented, before explaining that she herself had only 70 books, but that she treasured each one and occasionally rearranged them with loving care. That explanation hit home with me, as I felt the same way about each of the thousands of books I owned.

I remained in the room after the discussion ended. Gina did too, and I think for the same reason: so that we could talk together.

"How is it," she started to say, before I interrupted. "Do you believe in coincidences?"

"Not usually," she said.

"Me neither. But we should, this time."

"But what was all that 'Tell, don't ask,' stuff at Subway?"

"It's a bit complicated," I said. "Why don't we get a coffee while I explain."

Once we were seated at the coffee shop inside the bookstore, I explained the idea of Principality that I'd become obsessed with in recent months. Over the final year of my career, it had been borne in on me more and more that as a diplomat I was acting as an agent for the U.S. government. I'd been pursuing its interests almost as a lawyer pursues the interests of his clients. My employer was the principal, I was only a mere agent acting on its behalf. But I wanted to be a Principal, acting on my own behalf. That was one of the reasons why I'd opted for retirement earlier than I might have.

"The idea of 'Principality' is leading me to reconsider all aspects of my life, big and small," I concluded. "Ordering at restaurants is of course one of the smaller ways that the principal could be effected."

There was much more to the concept than this, and more complicated factors had led me to it than I'd mentioned to Gina. One was the way in which Diana had died. She'd been unconscious and I'd had to decide on the course of treatment. The doctor had told me that the procedure he recommended was risky. I should not have accepted his recommendation without investigating further to find out how risky and what the other options were, perhaps also getting a second opinion. But I hadn't. With the demands of my job pressing on me, I did the simplest thing. I accepted the doctor's recommendation blindly. I had acted as a Principal in form only, but not in spirit. I'd been the decision maker, but I hadn't made an *informed* decision. I had, therefore, failed to act as a true Principal. Ever since then I hadn't been able to shake the feeling that I was partly to blame for my wife's death during the possibly unnecessary surgery.

Gina of course was unaware of these things and responded

only to what I'd told her. "Perhaps it was a similar thought that led me to start my own tutoring company after graduating," she said. "Or perhaps I'm just following the example of my father, who had a small store of his own in Manila. He probably could have made more money working as the manager of a branch of a large chain, but he valued his independence. And now I do, too. It's still only just me and two others, who are part-time contractors. I'm the owner and only full-time employee of the company. But little by little parents are noticing that I'm helping their kids, and word of the value of my services is spreading.

"The exciting thing at the moment," she continued, "is that I'm about to offer courses for students who are home-schooled. I'll teach group classes in the home of one of the students; other home-schooled students who live nearby will join the class. We'll meet just before lunch, so that the students can eat lunch with friends before returning home. So, the class offers a partial solution to the isolation of home-schooled students, especially when combined with lunch."

"That's brilliant," I said. "You've found an important niche for yourself and your company." There was much more I could have said to her, about how intrigued I was by her, by how smart and educated she appeared to be, by her ability to express herself so clearly, by her knowledge of literature, and by her forwardness and courage in founding her own company. And about her lively beauty, which shown like the sun once she began talking about subjects she was interested in. But I kept quiet about all that as we parted.

3

Once home, I found Gina's company online: "Gina's Tutoring Services: Specialists in English and Spanish Languages and Literature, Grammar, Vocabulary, Rhetoric and Reading Comprehension."

Then, in searching for the short videos she'd posted to YouTube explaining the tutoring services her company offers, up popped a link to the Zapruder film, the film of the Kennedy assassination made by Abraham Zapruder. The link was perhaps triggered by my recent searches for books by and about JFK.

I knew of course that Kennedy's assassination had taken place in Dallas as the presidential motorcade had passed through Dealey Plaza. It was in the middle of that stretch of Elm Street, so the story goes, that Lee Harvey Oswald had shot him from a sixth-floor window in the Book Depository just after the motorcade had passed by the building.

When I'd first seen the film, decades ago, I had been as shocked as everyone else who has seen it, which these days is just about everybody. The version I'd seen had been rather low resolution and very jerky. The version I watched now, however, was crystal clear and had been stabilized to keep the vehicle at the center of the image. I watched it several times. Each time anomalies jumped out at me more and more insistently. One was that the people in the background, on the grass on the far side of the road beyond the limo, during the seconds surrounding the assassination, appeared to be larger than the people in the limo, which was much closer to Zapruder. How could that be, I wondered? Was I the only one who saw this?

I also noticed that the shadows didn't seem right. Kennedy was killed just after noon, local time. Dallas is located in the middle third of the time zone, so the sun should have been pretty much directly overhead. And indeed, the shadows cast by the limo were nearly vertical, as expected. Yet the shadows cast by the people on the lawn were long, almost horizontal, as though they had been filmed early in the morning, when the sun was still low in the sky. It didn't make sense that the shadows cast by the vehicle and those cast by the people on the lawn should differ so radically. This oddity was even more pronounced near the end of the film. It seemed almost as though the limo on the road and the people beyond it were two different videos that had been combined. The background video had, for reasons not apparent to me, been enlarged, which accounted for the larger size of the people farther away than those in the limo.

"WTF?" I wondered, for the first of what was to be innumerable times over the following months. Had I discovered things no one else had observed before?

I decided to contact retired Ambassador Russell Fletcher, who had been one of my bosses early in my career and who I'd kept in touch with. I knew that since retiring a decade ago he'd filled much of his time by studying various aspects of American history and occasionally teaching courses on American diplomacy at the University of North Carolina, Chapel Hill. I wanted to see what he thought about the oddities I'd noticed in the Zapruder film.

We met for lunch later that week.

After expressing his condolences on Diana's passing, he asked what I'd been doing since retiring. "It's important to stay busy during retirement, Jubal" he said, "which is why I'm teaching a course or two each semester as Ambassador in Residence."

I explained about my Huxley-Kennedy-Lewis project and mentioned how important Kennedy's Peace speech had been in motivating me to pursue a career in the Foreign Service. Then I mentioned the Zapruder film and the oddities I'd seen in it.

"Ah," he said, his eyes lighting up. "Many people have long suspected that the film has been manipulated, that the version available to us today isn't the original."

It turned out I'd pushed the right button with Russell, or one of them, for he was a man of many interests. The Kennedy assassination was a topic of special importance to him.

"I've read a lot about various aspects of the assassination and the film," he continued. "I don't recall anyone ever commenting on the shadows, though I did read something, somewhere, about the relative sizes of the people in the limo and on the grass beyond."

I explained the theory that Vermont Royster had written about, but he waved it away, saying, "No, Oswald wasn't the shooter. The assassination was organized by elements within the U.S. government, particularly the CIA and the military, with assistance from the FBI and the Secret Service." I'd heard variations of that idea years before, of course, but hadn't paid much attention to them after, as I've noted, seeing Royster's article.

"But why would the CIA and the military want to kill the president?" I asked.

"It's quite complicated," Russell replied. "Rather than try to explain it all in the short time before my class begins, I'll recommend a few books that address that very question." He wrote down three titles and passed the list to me. On it were *JFK and the Unspeakable: Why He Died and Why It Matters*, by James W. Douglass; *Brothers: The Hidden History of the Kennedy Years*, by David Talbot; and *An Encounter with Evil: The Abraham Zapruder Story*, by Jacob Hornberger.

"The last one draws on information in the first two, and also provides much information on the Zapruder film. I think you'll enjoy it," he added.

I didn't know it at the time, but that conversation was the moment that this story really began. It was to change my life.

4

Back at my computer, after ordering those three books and a few others on the assassination, I turned to a closer examination of the Zapruder film. I slowed it down and watched it at one-quarter speed to study it more closely. As I did so, other oddities I hadn't noticed before jumped out at me. One was that throughout the first third of the film (through frame 132, I later saw), the people waiting for and watching the motorcade, on both sides of the street, appeared to be frozen—almost as if they were photographs that had been pasted in behind and in front of the motorcade.

The scene changed in frame 133. The motorcade was suddenly in the center of the frame, whereas only the advancing motorcycles had been seen before. It was as though the camera had been stopped or frames had been cut out of the film. Or perhaps, given the frozen appearance of the first images, the film didn't actually begin until frame 133.

Beginning in that frame the people on the far side of Elm Street began moving normally for the first time. They waved to the motorcade, backed up as it approached, and one young girl ran alongside it on the grass. But the people on the closer side of the street remained frozen. And so did those beyond Houston Street, behind those moving normally on the far side of Elm Street. In other words, the closest and farthest people appeared to be photographs; only the motorcade and the people directly behind it appeared to be moving normally as in a video. It was quite odd. Had no one noticed this before?

I then turned to slides of each of the individual frames that I had obtained earlier but hadn't yet looked at. Going through them one by one I noticed something even weirder, something that confirmed that the frozen people were indeed a photograph that was moved along little by little to give the impression of motion. In some of the frames one and only one person moved, and did so in an artificial way. In frames 56-64, for instance, all people remained frozen except one woman in brown on the closer side of the street, standing on the right. Her head appeared to move slightly from frame to frame, giving the appearance of motion. But the movement was unnatural: only the position of her head changed from one frame to the next, with no change in the position of her shoulders or arms, and with all others around her remaining completely frozen.

Something similar happened in frames 84-88. All spectators remained frozen except for one woman in black on the close side of the street, whose hands appear to clap even though the rest of her body doesn't move. Her arms and shoulders remain frozen; it's only her hands that appear to move.

In frames 96-101 all people on the close side of the street remain frozen except for one woman in gold. The coloring of her head changes, which gives the appearance of movement. Yet her shoulders and the rest of her body don't move at all. And in the same frames, all people on the far size of the street remain frozen except for one man near the wall, who moves his left arm, but in an unnatural way with no movement in his shoulder, neck and head, or the rest of his body.

Especially bizarre were frames 117-126, in which the legs of a woman in white on the left end of Houston Street move, giving the effect that she's walking. But neither her body nor her position relative to those standing near her change at all.

And in frames 136-165, although the people on the far side of the street move normally, the people on the closer side remain motionless, except for the scarf of a woman standing next to the sign and the white head scarves of two other women standing next to each other, which move slightly from frame to frame, giving the appearance of waving in the breeze.

Similarly, in frames 161-167, in which the people on the far side of Elm Street move normally and the people on the closer side remain frozen, the people in the distant background, along Houston Street, continue to remain frozen, except for one man in yellow who moves his arm even though his shoulders and the rest of his body remain frozen. And in frames 172-185, there is no movement among anyone on the close side of the street, except for a woman near the sign and a woman in a purple dress whose hands appear to clap even though there is no movement in their shoulders or the rest of their bodies.

I envisioned those who made the alterations thinking up these ridiculous changes over a glass or two of scotch while laughing themselves silly about how they are going to put one over on the American people. On second thought, though, perhaps they'd been deadly serious about what they were doing. Such an extensive effort had been made to insert the alterations—whose fraudulent nature became visible only when toggling between adjacent frames or when viewing the film at a very slow speed—that they must have been inserted for some serious purpose.

Farther on, I noticed that in frames 279-280 and 325-336, and again in 340-345, the people standing on the grass are very blurry, as though the camera had been moving quickly, tracking the movement of the limo, but their shadows are crisp. How is that even physically possible, I wondered. Shouldn't the shadows have been as blurry as the people who cast them? And, I noticed, as have others, that the back of Kennedy's head in the frames just after the most serious head wound occurred in frame 313 appears to have been blacked out, as though a piece of black paper had been used to cover the wound on the back of his head and then the frame reshot with a camera. Whatever was used to cover the back of the head moved from frame to frame as though it had been sloppily placed before the frames were reshot.

In frame 302, the limo is crisp but the people on the grass beyond it are very blurry, as though the camera had been tracking the movement of the limo. But in the very next frame, 303, the people on the grass and the limo are both clear and crisp. Could it be that the limo had stopped? That's the only explanation I could come up with. Similarly, in frame 315 the people on the grass and the limo are both clear, but in 316 the people on the grass are blurry while the limo remains clear. Had the limo been stopped in 315 but it and the camera began moving in 316?

And what's with the guy in the middle of frames 344-358? The way he moves from standing to sitting gives the appearance that the film is being shown in reverse.

I noticed many other instances of unnatural movements, and of apparent cuts and splicings in the film—too many to detail here. I'll note, though, that the splicings coincide with the nearby sprocket areas being blacked out, even though they should have been visible before and after the frames cut.

I was now convinced that the first third of the Zapruder film was fake. Most of it was compiled from photographs that had been altered slightly, then refilmed in slightly different positions to give the impression of movement to convince the viewer that he was viewing a video; serious flaws were apparent in much of the rest of the film as well.

That day was the beginning of my investigation into the assassination of President Kennedy that for several weeks would largely overshadow my examination of the lives and writings of Huxley, Kennedy and Lewis.

5

A few days later, however, needing a break from my absorption in the Kennedy assassination, I turned to C. S. Lewis's *Mere Christianity*. Selecting that book from among the dozens of Lewis and Huxley books on the shelves surprised me. It was at that moment that I became consciously aware that I in fact had a growing interest in learning more about religion, Christianity in particular.

As a child I had hated going to church and Sunday school—we were Presbyterian—so much that I used to hide under the bed to try to avoid having to go, only to be dragged out by dad and forced to put on a shirt with buttons, which was always too tight in the neck, and a tie.

Later, in my teens and early adulthood, as an avid reader of history, I came to regard Christianity as the cause of the wars and barbarity that had existed throughout much of European history. Who could read about the motivations of Philip II and the Inquisition he launched without reaching such a conclusion? Later, after decades of reading more books on history, including the history of societies outside of Europe and the West, I came to see that the cause of wars and barbarity and the like was not Christianity or religion *per se*; the cause was the very nature of human nature. It's human beings everywhere who start wars and engage in the most barbarous cruelty. "Homo homini lupus," as they said in ancient Rome, or, as Freud translated the phrase in *Civilization and Its Discontents*, "Man is a wolf to man." Religious differences were only the proximate cause; the deeper cause was the "fallen" or barbarous nature of man himself.

Still later I began to realize that Christianity, far from being the ultimate cause of war, was often a moderating influence on the darker aspects of human nature from which wars arose. It was Christianity that had inspired the religious art of the last two millennia in the West. And it was Christianity that was the source of the idea that all people are equal in the eyes of God, which led eventually to the idea that all people should have equal rights before the law.

As I reached for Lewis's book, it struck me what a great intellectual distance I had travelled in my opinion of religion over the course of my life. I realized also that if the distance from regarding Christianity as harmful to regarding it as useful and inspirational was long, the distance from regarding it as useful and inspirational to believing that its core beliefs were true was infinitely longer. Yet it is a journey that could be completed in the blink of an eye. It was a journey that I didn't think I'd ever make. But who knew? Decades ago, I'd have adamantly denied that I'd ever hold the benign if not favorable view of Christianity that I now realized I did in fact hold.

And what were Christianity's core beliefs? Maybe I was already a Christian without even knowing it? *Mere Christianity* answered my questions almost at once. Setting aside the differences between individual churches, Lewis explained that beliefs common to all Christians, whether Catholics, Anglicans, Lutherans, Presbyterians, Methodists, Baptists, or any others, are that there is one God and that Jesus Christ is his only son. Christians accept the teachings of the apostles, who accept Christian doctrine. The core belief is in the ascension of Jesus from earth into the presence of God 40 days after the resurrection. "The central Christian belief is that Christ's death has somehow put us right with God and given us a fresh start," Lewis wrote. "We believe that the death of Christ is just that point in history at which something absolutely unimaginable from outside shows through into our own world. . . . We are told that Christ was killed for us, that His death has washed out our sins, and that by dying He disabled death itself. That is the formula. That is Christianity. That is what has to be believed."[1]

So, no, I wasn't a Christian. I believed, to the slight extent that I'd thought about the subject at all, that God must exist. Some power had created the universe; why not call it God? But, I'd assumed, we couldn't know anything about that power with our limited human brains. Lewis, I could see from a quick look at the book, rejected that conclusion. He established, or so it seemed at a glance, that God existed, that the God that existed was the Christian God, and that the Christian God was not just the best of all possible Gods, but the only possible God.

But how could that be, I wondered. If God is all powerful, and if God is good, how to explain the cruelty and misery in the world? Lewis nailed that question, too. There is a Good Power and a Dark Power at work in the world, he explained, and both were created by God. The Dark Power was good when it was created, but it went wrong. Then came this jaw-dropping idea:

not just the idea that the war between the Good Power and the Dark Power "is a civil war, a rebellion," but that "we are living in a part of the universe occupied by the rebel. . . . Enemy-occupied territory—that is what this world is. . . . Christians, then, believe that an evil power has made himself for the present the Prince of this World."[2]

No wonder it's so hard to live a good life! We are living in enemy-occupied territory! We must battle the Dark Power when trying to understand how to live a good life, and then again when trying to live such a life in the face of a power seeking to lead us astray.

Mere Christianity, I'd learned from the foreword, was one of half a dozen books reprinting, in revised format, radio talks that Lewis had given during 1942, 1943 and 1944. As the Second World War raged during those years, England was being bombarded by 400 planes a night—"the infamous 'blitz' that changed the face of the war, turning civilians and their cities into the front lines."[3] Lewis's broadcasts provided a ray of hope to listeners inundated with reports of death and destruction that filled the radio waves. As I glanced through the book, and also at the other collections of his talks lined up on the bookshelves, it occurred to me that Lewis's thoughts during that dark period could provide a ray of hope to all, even non-Christians, living in difficult times.

I could see that *Mere Christianity* was filled with astute observations about human life, morality and Christianity, and that I'd need to give the book much more careful attention than I'd given it in this first brief look through it.

6

After lunch, eager to return to investigating the Kennedy assassination, I put *Mere Christianity* aside.

I recalled that Lee Harvey Oswald, arrested soon after the assassination, denied having killed the president and described himself as a "patsy." I knew that President Lyndon Johnson had convened the so-called Warren Commission, headed by Chief Justice Earl Warren, to determine the facts of what had happened. The Commission's conclusions, stated in the so-called Warren Report, were that Oswald, acting alone, had fired three shots, two of which had struck the president. One of them, after passing through Kennedy's body, had also struck Texas governor John Connally, who was seated directly in front of the president. The Report's conclusions were widely accepted by the media and its investigations widely praised for their thoroughness and accuracy.

I'd thought that doubts about the Report's conclusions had arisen only years later, but now learned that one investigator had expressed doubts soon after the Report was published—something I learned from the first of the books about the assassination to arrive, *History Will Not Absolve Us* by E. Martin Schotz. I'd ordered it simply because its title intrigued me, but it turned out to be one of the most important books I'd read about the assassination.

Schotz highlighted the work of Vincent J. Salandria, particularly three articles he'd published at the end of 1964 and early in 1965, soon after the Warren Report had been released. In them Salandria showed that information presented in the Report itself contradicted and undermined the Report's own conclusions. Salandria's articles, Schotz explained, "established, using the government's own evidence, that without a doubt there was a conspiracy, and that the Warren Commission was clearly and consciously cooperating with the cover-up."[4] These articles, he concluded, "proved much more than a conspiracy to kill Kennedy, for they demonstrated that across the entire spectrum of our governmental establishment there was a systematic involvement of the civilian authorities (either actively or through acquiescence) in covering for the murderers."

In the first article, Salandria had shown that the Warren Report provided no evidence placing Oswald on the 6th floor of the Book Depository behind the motorcade from which the shots had supposedly been fired, and cited considerable evidence placing him elsewhere. Salandria showed that more than three shots had been fired, which meant that Oswald could not have been the only shooter (if he had been a shooter at all), because the shots had occurred too close together to have been fired by the bolt action rifle supposedly belonging to him found in the book depository.[5] Furthermore, Oswald had not only denied killing Kennedy or anyone else; paraffin tests showed he had not fired a rifle that day.[6] And, more than 150 witnesses thought that shots had been fired from the so-called grassy knoll to the front right of the president's limo. A hole in its windshield also showed clear evidence of a shot fired from the front.

Those points, and many others laid out in Salandria's first article, led him to conclude that the Commission's Report was a conscientiously prepared fabrication. "The evidence offered by the Commission indicates there was more than one rifleman firing on November 22, 1963. There were more than three shots. If Oswald was one of the gunmen, then with that gun, from that vantage point, in that timespan suggested by the Commission, he could not have been alone in the performance of the terrible work that destroyed our president and wounded two other men."[7] To reach its conclusion of a lone gunman, Salandria showed, "the Commission ignored all of the above in so far as the evidence reveals auditory, visual, and olfactory stimuli reception incompatible with the source of shots exclusively from the Book Depository Building."[8]

In his second article, published in January 1965, Salandria showed that one bullet could not have caused five injuries to two men. The hole in the president's jacket and shirt showed that the bullet that entered his back had entered far too low to have exited through his throat and then hit Connally. "The evidence of the Zapruder film, the testimony of Governor and Mrs. Connally, the impossible course or courses of the bullet, . . . the contradictory ballistics testimony, the problem of the alignment of the president and the governor, and the resort to logical fallacy on the part of the Commission spell out at least one separate shot hitting the governor after the President had been hit by a different bullet. To conclude otherwise would be to grasp at not only the improbable but what photography, all the eyewitness testimony, logic, the laws of physics, and geometry tell us is impossible."[9]

Salandria's third article, published in March 1965, discussed statements by Dr. Malcolm Perry, one of the doctors who attended to Kennedy at Parkland Memorial Hospital in Dallas, confirming the large blowout on the back of the president's head that he and nearly all medical personnel at Parkland who attended to the president saw, but which does not appear on the official x-rays taken during the autopsy.

He also noted the puzzling statement in the Report that the testimony about the head wounds by the witness closest to him, Jacqueline Kennedy, who held her husband's head in her lap, was omitted from the Warren Report. "In the midst of her testimony appears the cryptic note: 'Reference to wounds deleted' (V, H-180)."[10] The Warren Commission "appears to have involved itself wittingly or unwittingly in fabrication and withholding of vital evidence."[11]

In sum, Salandria concluded, "The Commission chose to ignore the mass of witnesses who heard shots from the knoll, smelled gunpowder and saw smoke in the locale, . . . the Zapruder film, the intact bullet, [and] the testimony of Bethesda's Dr. Humes, and Parkland's Drs. Shaw, Gregory and Shires[, which] solidly support the view that a separate bullet or bullets struck Governor Connally. It was the Commission that conjectured to draw a conclusion that one bullet struck Kennedy and Connally. This inference is contradicted by overwhelming evidence."[12]

Salandria's evidence and reasoning, and his conclusion that the Warren Report was flawed if not fraudulent, was published in the American media within a year of the assassination. His second and third articles appeared soon after. Yet all three appeared only in periodicals with limited circulation; neither the articles nor the information and reasoning in them had been picked up by the mainstream media, either print or broadcast.

I soon learned that Salandria wasn't the only early investigator to uncover and try to report on what they had uncovered. Harold Feldman, in January 1964, only ten weeks after the assassination, reported on connections between Oswald and the CIA and FBI.[13] Yet that information, too, not being reported in national newspapers or on television news broadcasts, was effectively buried.

Most prominently, Mark Lane had published a 10,000-word piece even earlier than Feldman, on December 19, 1963, less than a month after the assassination, in which he identified disturbing holes in the official version of the crime. After his work had been rejected by major print publications, including *Life, Look*, the *Saturday Evening Post* and the *Nation*, he published his findings in the little-known *National Guardian*. The American people were thirsty for information, and, David Talbot reported, Lane's article "created a sensation. When the issue promptly sold out on the newsstands, the [*National*] *Guardian* printed thousands of extra copies of the article in pamphlet form."[14]

"Blacked out by the American media," Talbot continued, "Lane found an eager audience in the European press. He also formed a Citizens Committee of Inquiry, which began interviewing Dealey Plaza witnesses, and he rented a New York theater, where each evening for many months he presented his case against the lone gunman theory." In 1966, Lane published his findings in *Rush to Judgment*, among the first of many books published to challenge the findings of the Warren Commission.

Fred J. Cook, also, I learned, in a piece written for *The Nation* in the spring of 1965, showed that the Warren Commission Report "was a tissue of rationalizations in which the most credible testimony . . . had been discarded because it did not fit the lone-assassination hypothesis, and the most suspect word was accepted as valid and ultimate truth because it did." "The most credible evidence seemed to me to point to a conspiracy," he concluded in the article, "and if conspirators could get away with murdering a president as popular as Kennedy, there was no guarantee that they would not repeat the deed any time a leading politician's program posed a threat to their interests."[15]

"I felt the hair prickle on the back of my neck with excitement at this discovery," he later wrote. His editor, however, rejected the article, "telling me that [although] he and others could find no flaw in my reasoning, . . . *The Nation* didn't want to criticize the Warren Report." The piece eventually appeared in the *Nation* on June 13 and 20, 1966, more than a year after it had been written.

Learning all this, I was filled with questions. Why had the Warren Commission presented conclusions so at odds with the evidence documented in its own Report? Why hadn't it interviewed witnesses who heard or saw evidence of shots fired from the grassy knoll? Why hadn't the mainstream media—those with the largest viewership or readership—discovered these anomalies themselves or reported on them once Salandria and others had exposed them? Their findings should have been headline news. I wanted to know why the American people accepted an investigation so flawed in its methodology and a Report so flawed in its conclusions.

And most of all I wanted to know who, if not Oswald, had assassinated the president, and why.

7

I was thinking about Gina as I walked through the Cary City Center Mall on Saturday morning. Several times I'd mistakenly thought I'd seen her, but each time it turned out to be only another girl who looked somewhat like her. So when I actually did see her, I thought it was just my imagination again. I would perhaps have walked right by her if she hadn't recognized me and called out.

"Jubal!"

"Gina!" I responded.

An observer might have concluded that we were two old friends glad to have unexpectedly met, not two people who hardly knew each other.

As we walked through the crowded mall together, I thought of telling Gina about my investigations into the Kennedy assassination, but what she had to say about herself and her activities pushed all thoughts of that subject from my mind.

"After I graduated, I set myself up as a tutor," she told me. "I informally called myself Gina's Tutoring Services, because at first it was just me, not a real company. Now I rarely have fewer than

20 hours a week of tutoring, including some hours on Saturdays. I can only tutor one student at a time during the peak afternoon hours and would have had to turn others away if I hadn't brought in two university students I know to tutor the others.

"Demand is continuing to be so high that I've decided to start a real tutoring company, not just the informal tutoring service I have now. I'm seeking to rent space and buy tables and chairs and other equipment I'll need. I hope to open the studio in January, after the holidays. I have three university students lined up to provide tutoring in addition to myself. I know all of them and know that they are capable and have suitable personalities."

I was impressed and said so.

It was getting on toward noon, so I suggested that we have lunch. Once we were seated in a noodle restaurant, I spoke first.

"Might I be able to ask you a somewhat personal question? After our brief conversation after the book club meeting, I left saying to myself, 'She has had a first-class education.' It wasn't just that you're smart that struck me, but that you're smart *and educated*. Every Asian person I have ever known who seemed to have had a good education was educated by nuns. Might you perhaps have had your early education at a convent school?"

"Thanks for such a compliment, Jubal!" she said brightly. "I'm proud to say that I never attended any private institution or school managed by any religious institution. I had my early education from regular public schools in my hometown."

"And what about college or university study? It clearly shaped your innate intelligence, raising your ability to think and organize your thoughts to a very high level."

"I got my degree from the top state university in my country, which is by the way known in Asia for providing high-quality education to students from poor socio-economic backgrounds. It's the Polytechnic University, in Manila.

"My family did not have the income to send me to college, but I got admitted through a scholarship and by God's grace, finished my degree in Linguistics and Literature as Magna Cum Laude. It is a shame that Philippine universities are so underrated as they have been doing a great job for centuries, teaching my countrymen how to think and to make them genuinely love learning."

I was glad she was in such an expansive mood, willing to share information about herself that answered questions I'd had.

"You far outshone me as a student, Gina," I responded. "What most impresses me is that you are able to think things through for yourself and have the courage to express your own thoughts. Those are rare qualities. Treasure them. Safeguard them at all costs from the pressures of the world toward mediocracy and blind acceptance of what everybody else thinks. Sometimes we have to be a Dr. Jekyll and Mr. Hyde in the sense of having a public face and a private soul. In heaven, perhaps, the two can be the same; here we must take special care that outside pressures do not corrupt our inner qualities."

"Wow, thank you so much for those encouraging words," she replied. "I don't really have a lot of people who tell me such things. There aren't a lot of people who can relate to me, and who I can relate to. You're absolutely right, the struggle against mediocrity is real. I literally work hard each day in protecting my sense of identity as my ways are often different from others, and I get invalidated a lot by people who don't get me or think that their way is better than mine. It can be seriously damaging to self-esteem and self-image if the person being criticized cannot handle the outside noises properly."

"One way I try to handle the difficulties of dealing with other people," I said in response, "is to remind myself that half of all people have an IQ below average, that they're doing the best they can. That's kind of shocking when you think about it, just as it's shocking to realize that only three percent of people read books. Only a tiny minority of people have a life of the mind, or want to, or even understand what that means. I remember when it suddenly hit me as a teenager that every book I read separated me more and more from everybody else around me. With most people their brains are turned on but not active, like a motor that's running but only idling. The gear is not engaged."

I was again about to mention the Kennedy assassination, but Gina spoke first.

"I think you nailed it perfectly, that reading or having a life of a mind indeed separates a person from others. When a person has that kind of lifestyle, it becomes difficult to have decent and profound conversations with most people, let alone make friends. I now know that having a cultured lifestyle can be alienating at some point since most people don't choose to live that way. A cultured person's circle is smaller because it is filled only with people of quality. As I grew up, I realized that being cultured protects me from crappy and toxic people. A person with a life of the mind, I believe, has a very low tolerance for bad behaviors and can't stand shallow conversations. When I reached my 20s, I started to feel that 'separation' from my peers, from other girls, from other Filipinos and from most Asians in general. Not animosity, just separation. Superficial conversation gives me a kind of dizzy and heavy feeling, because the topics are so very limited."

Before we parted I gave Gina the two articles on literature that I'd read while having a coffee just before running into her. I thought she might enjoy them. One was about Jane Austen, the other about G. K. Chesterton and C. S. Lewis.

She glanced at them as we walked back toward our cars parked near the bookstore.

"That's funny," she said. "The coincidence of both Chesterton and Lewis being referred to by their initials rather than having their names spelled out! T. S. Eliot is the only other writer I can think of who is regularly referred to by his initials." She laughed as she spoke, and we both laughed at another coincidence when we noticed it: We'd parked next to each other.

8

The following morning, I returned to the questions of who, if not Oswald, had assassinated the president, and why. If the official story of Oswald as assassin hadn't been correct, then some other person or persons must have organized it and carried it out.

In the early weeks after the assassination, the American media—and Americans themselves—had almost unanimously accepted that Oswald was guilty and not the "patsy" he claimed to be. In the following weeks, months and years, the American press continued to repeat the official story, avoided pointing out anomalies in the evidence and failed to investigate who might really have been behind it all.

And yet, I learned from Schotz's book, one person had presented a very different account. In a speech broadcast only thirty hours after the assassination, Cuban leader Fidel Castro provided a credible if horrifying alternative explanation as to who had been behind it and why they had carried it out. His remarks, like the information in Salandria's, Cook's, and Lane's articles, received little if any coverage in the American media.

In his speech, "Concerning the Facts and Consequences of the Tragic Death of President John F. Kennedy," broadcast on Cuban TV and radio on Saturday evening, November 23, Castro provided a persuasive account of forces within the United States—within the U.S. government—that had organized the assassination. He identified an "internal struggle for power in the United States," between two groups. Those in one supported a policy "much more reactionary [toward Cuba], . . . a policy much more aggressive, much more warlike." Those in the other were "not constantly thinking in terms of force, but were thinking along lines of diplomacy; . . . [they] have a less aggressive policy—a more moderate policy."[16]

Kennedy, in Castro's view, was representative of and the leader of the more moderate group and was working to restrain the worst elements of the more aggressive. "Unquestionably when [there] is a recognized, accepted, strong authority in the United States, the dangers that arise from the struggle of a whole series of reactionary currents within the powerful organizations of the United States are much less than when this authority does not exist. And without any shadow of doubt, Kennedy had this authority in the United States."[17]

The more aggressive group had benefited from the assassination. "[W]hat happened yesterday can only benefit those ultra-rightist and ultra-reactionary sectors, among which President Kennedy or some of the men who worked with him cannot be included."[18]

Surely, Castro suggested, questions—such as "What is behind the assassination of Kennedy? What were the real motives for the assassination of Kennedy? What forces, factors, circumstances were at work behind this sudden and unexpected event that occurred yesterday?—ran through the minds of most people, . . . and this was only logical." Surely many wondered if "President Kennedy's assassination was the work of some elements who disagreed with his international policy; that is to say, with his nuclear treaty, with his policy with respect to Cuba—which they did not consider aggressive enough, and which they considered weak—with his policy with respect to internal civil problems of the United States."[19] "Was there perhaps some kind of plot? . . . Was there perhaps in certain civilian and military ultra-reactionary circles in the United States, a plot against President Kennedy's life?"[20]

Castro concluded by noting that "[I]t is necessary for all people of the United States themselves to demand that what is behind the Kennedy assassination be clarified. It is in the interest of the U.S. people and of the people of the world, that this be made known, that they demand to know what is really behind the assassination of Kennedy, that the facts be made clear: whether the man involved [Oswald] is innocent, sick or an instrument of the reactionaries, an agent of a macabre plan to carry forward a policy of war and aggression, to place the Government of the United States at the mercy of the most aggressive circles of monopoly, of militarism, and of the worst agencies of the United States."[21]

Although the American media, with very few exceptions, confined itself to supporting the U.S. government's "Oswald" line, coverage of the assassination outside the United States was much more varied and inquisitive. "While American pundits still chortle over the idea of a wider conspiracy to assassinate the president," one analyst later observed, "in any other country this is not an absurd idea at all, particularly in nations targeted by American intelligence agencies. Understanding the international reaction, and the thoughts of other world leaders in 1963, helps put the unresolved assassination into context."[22]

"Governments overseas saw the assassination as the work not of a lone nut, but of a right-wing conspiracy," Peter Dale Scott observed. In Mexico City, President Lopez Mateos believed that "Kennedy had died at the hands of 'extremely right-wing elements that did not like his policies, especially his policy toward Cuba,'" and the French representative to the United Nations believed that "the assassination was a 'carefully organized act' by a determined group on the far right of American politics.'"[23]

French president Charles De Gaulle commented that "the security forces were in cahoots with the extremists." When asked specifically about Oswald, he replied, "they got their hands on this communist who wasn't one, while still being one. He had a sub par intellect and was an exalted fanatic—just the man they needed, the perfect one to be accused." De Gaulle "explained the necessity of Oswald's death at the hands of the conspirators, and how Ruby had been tasked to silence Oswald forever." He then offered a "remarkable insight on how the United States would bury the coup: 'America is in danger of upheavals. But you'll see. All of them together will observe the law of silence. They will close ranks. They'll do everything to stifle any scandal. They will throw Noah's cloak over these shameful deeds. In order to not lose face in front of the whole world. In order to not risk unleashing riots in the United States. In order to preserve the union and to avoid a new civil war. In order to not ask themselves questions. They don't want to know. They don't want to find out. They won't allow themselves to find out.'"[24]

As I was to see over the coming weeks, truer words were never spoken.

9

I'd intended to return to *Mere Christianity*, to see what Lewis had to say about free will and morality, and about how Christians could use their faith to strengthen their ability to choose well—an idea in alignment with Principality—in a world often hostile to Christian values. Instead, in leafing through another collection of his wartime broadcasts and speeches, *The Weight of Glory*, I came across a piece that grabbed my attention: "Learning in Wartime," a talk given at Oxford University on October 22, 1939, that fleshed out the idea of living in "enemy-occupied territory."

Living in such territory, he implied, is similar to living in wartime. In such circumstances should we devote all our efforts to combatting the enemy, he asked, or does space still exist to engage in learning, cultural endeavors and intellectual work? Is it necessary "to exclude entirely from our lives those interests and pursuits which, in peace time, make life worth living?" as someone else once asked.[25]

My answer was that we should sacrifice these activities only to the extent that we must. Until conditions force such a sacrifice, we should continue them to the fullest extent possible, while still doing what we can to battle the forces hostile to them. To abandon them sooner than necessary is to give the enemy an unearned victory.

I was relieved to see that Lewis's answer was similar to mine. The real issue is not learning in wartime, he stated, but learning at any time. "The war creates no absolutely new situation; it simply aggravates the permanent human situation so that we can no longer ignore it. Human life has always been lived on the edge of a precipice. Human culture has always had to exist under the shadow of something infinitely more important than itself. If men had postponed the search for knowledge and beauty until they were secure the search would never have begun. We are mistaken when we compare war with 'normal life'. Life has never been normal."[26]

Lewis then raised the larger question of whether "it is right, or even psychologically possible, for creatures who are every moment advancing either to Heaven or to Hell to spend any fraction of the little time allowed them in this world on such comparative trivialities as literature or art, mathematics or biology."[27] "Is there any legitimate place for the activities of the scholar? . . . We have always to answer the question: 'How can you be so frivolous and selfish as to think about anything but the salvation of human souls?'"[28]

In answering these questions, Lewis noted that "Neither conversion [to Christianity] nor enlistment in the army is really going to obliterate our human life. Christians and soldiers are still men. . . . If you attempted, in either case, to suspend your whole intellectual and aesthetic activity, you would only succeed in substituting a worse cultural life for a better. . . . [I]f you don't read good books, you will read bad ones. If you don't go on thinking rationally, you will think irrationally. If you reject aesthetic satisfactions, you will fall into sensual satisfactions."[29] All that made sense to me.

"Christianity does not exclude any of the ordinary human activities," Lewis continued. "All our merely natural activities will be accepted, if they are offered to God. . . . Christianity does not simply replace our natural life and substitute a new one; it is rather a new organization which exploits, to its own supernatural ends, these natural materials. . . . There is no essential quarrel between the spiritual life and the human activities as such."[30] Lewis had provided, I saw, an explication of what J. S. Bach meant when he said his aim was to create "well-regulated church music to the glory of God."

There is, Lewis continued, inherent value in intellectual and artistic work. In history, for instance. "We need intimate knowledge of the past. We . . . need something to set against the present, to remind us that the basic assumptions have been quite different in different periods and that much which seems certain to the uneducated is merely temporary fashion. A man who has lived in many places is not likely to be deceived by the local errors of his native village; the scholar has lived in many times and is therefore in some degree immune from the great cataract of nonsense that pours from the press and the microphone of his own age."[31]

Lewis's thoughts were making Christianity a more understandable and human world for me. They were reinforcing my view of Christianity as a force for good in the world even though I didn't feel at all closer to becoming a Christian.

October 2019

⸙ 10 ⸙

The book club's first discussion, of José Rizal's *Noli Me Tangere*, was held in early October. The discussion was rather perfunctory, as though the book hadn't resonated with the club. Most members seemed rather puzzled by it; and Gina and I, I felt, had held back our most personal thoughts about it, though why we'd done so I couldn't say.

Afterwards, Gina and I both hung back, looking forward to another interesting conversation between just the two of us.

During the short walk to a nearby restaurant, I finally mentioned my study of the Kennedy assassination and my surprise at the idea—introduced to me by Fidel Castro and supported by much I'd read since—that it had been orchestrated by elements within the U.S. government.

"I'm not surprised at all, given the sorry history of the United States in The Philippines during the decades of American colonial rule," Gina responded, catching me by surprise. At that time, I knew little about U.S. involvement in her country, other than its misguided support for the Marcos regime in the 1970s and 1980s.

"Kennedy was one of the good presidents," she continued. "He understood countries that had been colonized by the Europeans and that were in the process of becoming independent nations after the end of the Second World War." She mentioned how The Philippines had suffered under U.S. rule both before and after it achieved its independence in 1946. This was the first time I'd heard a Filipino's take on U.S. rule of the islands, and I jotted down a note to learn more about it.

"That's one reason why *The Noli* that we read is so important. It shows what the country was like under foreign domination. It's a narrative record of the lives of our people during that time. Almost nothing in it is fictional and it's not meant to be read as fiction.

"At my university there was a one-year compulsory course on Rizal's biography and his works that everyone needed to pass. That's how revered he is back home. There are countless movies and plays about his life and works. The best movie is *José Rizal*, made in 1999. I've watched that film more than 20 times in my life, I guess, and it's one of the highest grossing films in The Philippines. It's one of the best movies I've ever seen because it gives an even better sense of what life under Spanish rule was like than the book does."

I felt embarrassed that I'd never heard of someone so important in the history of The Philippines before reading the book and said so. "It's not a country that is ever taught about in the American school system, nor is it a country where I've ever worked," I explained apologetically.

"We Filipinos know that our history isn't taught or even talked about outside our borders, and it's a real shame. We are so proud of our ancestors, as other Asian nations during that time weren't able to produce such brilliant minds. Even our politicians during the '70s and before were insanely intelligent. History books in other countries, when they mention my country at all, say things that aren't nice and that are extremely biased.

"I also recommend a movie, *General Luna*, about a Filipino general who was also educated in Europe and who was Rizal's contemporary," she continued. "He founded the Philippine Army during the Filipino American War. It may interest you to see a movie portraying actions by the American military in my country."

I made notes about about both movies, then turned the conversation to *The Noli*.

"It's odd that the young man, Chrisostomo, and the young woman, Maria Clara, hardly knew each other—hardly even had a private conversation together at any time in the book," I said. "Who knows if they'd have had a good marriage. They certainly didn't know, and we the readers don't either. The bonds between them might have been greatly strengthened if they'd ever spent some time alone together, without a chaperone. Some light physical intimacy might have strengthened the bonds between them enough that they'd have withstood all the external pressures pushing them apart. Or not. It's hard to know how people might have behaved in a time and place so different from the world I grew up in."

"When we read *The Noli* at school," Gina replied, "we read it as a historical text, not as a fiction. The reason there's not much interaction between Maria Clara and Ybarra [Chrisostomo] is because Rizal based their love story on his own early experience. The inspiration for Maria Clara was Rizal's cousin and sweetheart before he left for Spain, Leonor Rivera. They also were pushed apart by outside circumstances."

That made sense to me; literature suffers when it mirrors real-life situations too closely, which might explain why the book club had had such a cool response to the book.

Driving home after we'd wrapped up our conversation, it occurred to me that I had probably already conversed more with Gina than Chrisostomo had with Maria Clara in the entire *Noli*. Yet whereas those two felt as if they knew each other intimately, I felt as if I hardly knew Gina. I liked her, sure, but felt there were hidden currents in her that I couldn't even guess at now.

Back home, I continued to think about her. Impressed by the intelligence she showed during the book club discussion, her obvious education and common sense—and her loveliness in body and spirit—I got to thinking about what life with someone like her would have been like, would be like. Beautiful, poised, with a strong and delightful personality, smart, educated, interested in literature. I could get inspiration and energy from such a person. I felt a surge of pride from even the thought of introducing her as my wife.

But of course that would never happen. I knew that nothing could come of any relationship with her or anyone else now. I was too old to start a new family, and I was enjoying my new freedom to explore my Huxley-Kennedy-Lewis project—and my research into the Kennedy assassination—too much to think of placing any restrictions on it. And, having been married for 28 years, I was enjoying being free of external constraints, being able to move to my own rhythms, without having to take someone else's desires and moods into account every minute.

At the same time, knowing all that didn't stop me from enjoying thoughts of what it would be like if I were twenty years younger and could get to know Gina as fully as she'd allow me.

11

When I'd been inspired by Kennedy's Peace speech 30+ years ago, I'd known only that the Cold War was in full swing and that it took great daring and confidence for him even to suggest peace with the Soviet Union. That speech, I now knew from my research, was one of the many events powering the iceberg heading his way. I want to record here the details of Kennedy's clash with the U.S. military and intelligence agencies because it's among the most important factors resulting in the transformation of my thinking about events in recent U.S. history and the state of the country today recorded later in this memoir.

Castro's intuition had been right on target. In the decades since 1963 historians have established that Kennedy faced many powerful persons within his own administration determined to bring him down—the very persons and institutions that Castro had intuited were behind the assassination. Among then were Allen Dulles and the CIA, General Lyman Lemnitzer, Chairman of the Joint Chiefs of Staff and Air Force General Curtis LeMay.

Conflict between these men and their institutions and the new president began almost immediately after Kennedy was sworn in. Early in 1961 he faced pressure from the Joint Chiefs to invade Laos with up to sixty thousand soldiers empowered to use tactical nuclear weapons. Kennedy resisted their pressure and negotiated a political solution.[32]

In April 1961, only three months after his presidency began, the Bay of Pigs invasion of Cuba took place. 1,400 U.S.-trained paramilitary, mostly Cubans, were transported to Cuba in American ships with the intent of overthrowing Castro. The invasion was a fiasco, with all invaders killed or imprisoned, due to, I'd just learned, CIA duplicity. Kennedy had repeatedly told Dulles and others that under no circumstances would he approve U.S. Air Force cover for the invasion, something that would have made U.S. involvement in the invasion obvious. Dulles and others had repeatedly assured Kennedy that no U.S. air support would be needed, all the while believing that it was an essential component of the invasion, confident that they could pressure Kennedy into changing his mind once the event was underway and going to fail without it.

They had misjudged their man. Kennedy held firm and allowed the invasion to fail rather than authorize involvement by the U.S. Air Force. In response to what he saw as its betrayal of him, he swore he'd "splinter the CIA in a thousand pieces and scatter it to the winds." By the end of the year, Kennedy had forcibly retired three top men in the Agency: Allen Dulles, Director, who would later run the Warren Commission, Deputy Director Charles Cabell, whose brother was the Mayor of Dallas on the day of the assassination, and Deputy Director for Plans Richard M. Bissell, Jr.

The CIA and military hadn't given up on invading Cuba and forcing Castro from power, though. Ten months later, on February 2, 1962, General William H. Craig, on behalf of the Joint Chiefs of Staff, submitted plans for a number of false flag scenarios that could be blamed on Castro, including riots and sabotage to simulate attacks on Guantanamo, the U.S. naval base on the Cuban island,[33] thereby justifying an American invasion.

A month later, on March 13, 1962, the military urged Kennedy to approve Operation Northwoods in a memo approved by Chairman of the Joint Chiefs of Staff General Lyman Lemnitzer and every member of the Joint Chiefs. The operation consisted of five plans, all designed to make it appear that Castro had murdered American citizens and therefore an invasion to remove him from power was justified. One plan called for the U.S. military to shoot down a plane full of American students and blame it on Cuba. Others called for Americans to be shot on American streets with their deaths blamed on Castro, "for boats carrying Cuban refugees fleeing Cuba to be sunk on the high seas, and for a wave of violent terrorism to be launched in Washington, D.C., Miami and elsewhere. People would be framed for bombings they did not commit. . . . Using phony evidence, all of it would be blamed on Castro."[34] All this was new to me.

The Joint Chiefs also urged Kennedy to launch a nuclear first-strike against the Soviet Union. At a National Security Council meeting on July 20, 1961, "the Joint Chiefs of Staff and CIA Director Allen Dulles presented a plan for a preemptive nuclear attack on the Soviet Union 'in late 1963, preceded by a period of heightened tensions.'"[35] Kennedy walked out of the meeting, saying to Secretary of State Dean Rusk, "And we call ourselves the human race." The Joint Chiefs repeated their call for a nuclear first-strike at a National Security Council meeting on September 12, 1963, with a projected date of 1964 to 1968.[36]

After rejecting Operation Northwoods and the first proposal for a nuclear first-strike against the Soviet Union, Kennedy commented, "The first advice I'm going to give my successor is to watch the generals and to avoid feeling that because they were military men their opinions on military matters were worth a damn."

Kennedy's tensest moment with the CIA and military came at the tensest moment with the Soviet Union during the so-called Cuban Missile Crisis in October 1962, triggered by the U.S. discovery that the Soviets had placed offensive nuclear weapons in Cuba. After 13 tense days, Kennedy resolved the crisis by negotiating a settlement with Soviet Premier Nikita Khrushchev in which the Soviet Union would withdraw the missiles in return for a U.S. promise not to invade Cuba. Kennedy also agreed, secretly, to withdraw U.S. offensive nuclear missiles from Turkey.

I'd known about the Cuban Missile Crisis, of course. What was new to me now was the extent of the anger that Kennedy's solution triggered among senior U.S. military officers. Air Force General Curtis LeMay, who believed that the crisis should have been resolved by a U.S. invasion of Cuba, called the blockade tactic "almost as bad as the appeasement at Munich." He later denounced the settlement that ended the crisis as "the greatest defeat in our history."[37] One close observer of the military leadership stated that "there was virtually a coup atmosphere in Pentagon circles, . . . a mood of hatred and rage. The atmosphere was poisonous, poisonous."[38]

Kennedy himself recognized the danger of opposing policies supported by the military. At the peak of the crisis in 1962, his brother, U.S. Attorney General Robert Kennedy, "told the Russian ambassador, Anatoly Dobrynin: Even though the president himself is very much against starting a war over Cuba, an irreversible chain of events could occur against his will. . . . If the situation continues for much longer, the president is not sure that the military will not overthrow him and seize power. The American military could be out of control."[39]

By 1963, Kennedy believed he knew the lay of the land and was ready to go beyond merely opposing actions urged by the military to introducing new policies to benefit the country even though doing so, he knew, would stoke the military's anger further. He had seen that his secret personal communications with Khrushchev in Moscow helped ease tensions and resolve the Cuban Missile Crisis. Perhaps that success indicated a way forward, even if, as Peter Dale Scott recognized, "It is possible that U.S. intelligence services became aware of this private diplomacy; if so, some must have thought it no less than treasonable."[40]

In his so-called Peace speech, delivered on June 10, 1963, Kennedy announced an immediate unilateral suspension of nuclear weapons testing in the atmosphere, a move that was followed a few months later by a formal Test Ban Treaty with the Soviets. In that speech, which had so inspired me as I've noted, Kennedy called for reduced tensions with the Soviet Union, announcing in effect the possibility of ending the Cold War by moving to a policy of mutual coexistence.

The ideas introduced in that speech were so far out of line with those of the CIA and the military that Kennedy had the speech drafted by writers outside the national security bureaucracy. "In preparing the address, Kennedy had limited the discussion to a handful of White House advisers. . . . McNamara, Rusk, and [his new Joint Chiefs Chairman Maxwell D.] Taylor were only told about the speech two days before Kennedy delivered it. He did not want predictable quibbling from the principal national security bureaucracy officials. . . . His caution was borne out by instant objections from Taylor that the Joint Chiefs could not endorse a unilateral suspension of atmospheric tests."[41]

The Joint Chiefs and others in the intelligence field had been shocked not just by the policies proposed in the speech, but also because it had been prepared without their knowledge or input. Time and again in it Kennedy emphasized his commitment to establishing a peaceful relationship with the Soviet Union, thereby undermining the military's and intelligence agencies' prestigious place in American life. If he succeeded, their budgets could be severely cut, their power threatened, and their worldview shown to be not only misguided but actually harmful to the United States.

Just one day later, on June 11, 1963, Kennedy delivered another bombshell speech, this one on civil rights. Although the Peace speech had received little coverage in the U.S. media (though it made quite an impact on Khrushchev and others abroad), the Civil Rights Speech was televised live. In it he called for civil rights legislation to ensure that all Americans had equal rights protections and opportunities. In Scott's assessment, "Given America's divisions in 1963, such strong affirmations of American ideals reached outside the usual constricted limits of political discourse, and courted disaster."[42]

Two final actions perhaps sealed Kennedy's fate.

In a speech at the University of Maine on October 19, 1963, he laid out specific steps that the United States could take to implement the ideas broached in his Peace speech four months earlier. "While the road to peace is long and hard, and full of traps and pitfalls," he said, "there is no reason not to take each step that we can safely take. It is in our national self-interest to ban nuclear testing in the atmosphere so that all of our citizens can breathe more easily. . . . For without our making such an effort, we could not maintain the leadership and respect of the free world. Without our making such an effort, we could not convince our adversaries that war was not in their interests. And without our making such an effort, we could never, in case of war, satisfy our hearts and minds that we had done all that could be done to avoid the holocaust of endless death and destruction."[43]

Commenting on Kennedy's speech, *The Nation* stated "That he had brought us this far—and the polls would seem to show that he had struck a responsive chord—was the president's finest achievement."[44] The positive response in the polls to these proposals—to policies adamantly opposed by the CIA and the military—may have convinced them that Kennedy was likely to win reelection a year later and that drastic steps had to be taken to stop that from happening.

The final action, one not known to the public at the time, was Kennedy's signing National Security Action Memorandum (NSAM) 263 in October 1963, which made it official policy to begin withdrawing U.S. advisors from Vietnam later that year and to have all of them out by the end of 1965. Yet behind his back, on November 20, two days before the assassination, senior military officers held a conference in Honolulu to begin planning a program of escalating U.S. attacks on North Vietnam. "A preliminary draft of this plan, later known as OPLAN 34A, had been approved by General Maxwell Taylor of the Joint Chiefs of Staff."[45] "As far as is known, Kennedy never saw either the plans for the 34A Ops or the draft NSAM 273 of November 21, 1963."[46]

On November 26, 1963, only four days after the assassination, President Johnson signed NSAM 273, "which authorized planning to begin for graduated offensive operations against North Vietnam," reversing NSAM 263 that Kennedy had signed a month earlier. NSAM 273, together with the Tonkin Gulf incident, "led in August 1964 to the first bombing of North Vietnam with U.S. planes, something which 'President Kennedy for two and one-half years had resisted.'"[47]

In other words, the military moved with great speed to reverse Kennedy's policy toward Vietnam, showing just how important the issue was to them. The advance planning suggests that the military was well aware of the assassination plans; why else hold a planning session in Hawaii for military action directly contrary to the president's policy? Why else draft a National Security Action Memorandum reversing the one Kennedy had signed only a month earlier and that he certainly would not have authorized, unless it was to have it ready for Kennedy's successor to sign at the earliest possible moment?

With my new understanding of things, I saw that that change in policy was of critical importance to the orchestrators of the assassination because Vietnam was a critical component of their plan to combat Communism in Southeast Asia—a component so important that they couldn't let Kennedy disrupt it. As David Neal explained this point, "The war in Southeast Asia, as part of the Cold War Strategy, had been in the works during Eisenhower's presidency, and since JFK had begun to show he was not going to go along with that plan, a cabal of powerful U.S. officials, businessmen and intelligence people in collusion with military leaders, and some foreigners, decided to remove him."[48]

They got away with the assassination, Neal explained, because so many powerful entities in what President Eisenhower had called the Military-Industrial Complex supported it. "They did it surreptitiously, criminally, and with sophisticated planning, and covered their tracks with the help of compliant media. Since the assassination involved so much of the hierarchy of the government and private business, particularly prominent individuals associated with the Texas oil industry, intelligence, defense communities, and powerful political figures, it was essentially a 'government' decision—an official act of the State. This is the basic and honest reason why, if there are papers in the archives that prove this, they cannot be released."[49]

Of everything I learned over the past month of intense research, one factor stood out above all others because it was personal: Kennedy's Peace Speech—the very speech that had inspired me to enter a career in the Foreign Service that had filled nearly three decades of my life—had been one of the key triggers of the assassination. Occurring on the very day I was born, that tragic event was personal to me in ways that are hard to describe.

12

While researching Kennedy's assassination I came across repeated references to a remarkable book and movie, *Seven Days in May*, which was inspired in part by the conflict between Kennedy and the CIA/military. The authors of the book, Fletcher Knebel and Charles Bailey, both seasoned political reporters, wrote the book after interviewing General Curtis LeMay in the wake of the failure of the Bay of Pigs invasion early in Kennedy's presidency. During the interview LeMay accused Kennedy of "cowardice;" investigating further, Knebel and Baily discovered to their surprise that the military and the intelligence community despised Kennedy, and that he returned their sentiments.

In their suspenseful novel, top generals seek to remove the president from power after concluding he is a risk to the security of the United States because he signed a treaty with the Soviet Union. The plot was not dissimilar to the CIA/military's removing Kennedy, though not through a coup but through assassination, a few months after he signed the Nuclear Test Ban Treaty with the Soviets.

The generals in the book acted as they did, honorably in their eyes, because they feared the political process would move too slowly to remove at the next election a president who promised to destroy the country's entire nuclear arsenal in exchange for a mere promise that the Soviets would do the same. Kennedy's military and CIA opponents were far less honorable than the president's opponents in the book, with the CIA having lied to Kennedy about the need for air cover in the Bay of Pigs invasion and the generals having pushed Kennedy to authorize false flag attacks on American citizens that could be blamed on Castro, not to mention their urging him to approve a nuclear first-strike against the Soviet Union.

Seven Days in May was released before the Cuban Missile Crisis in October 1962 and was listed on the *New York Times* best seller list for a lengthy period beginning two weeks after the Crisis erupted.

What I found most intriguing was Kennedy's own connection with the book and movie based on it (directed by John Frankenheimer and staring Burt Lancaster, Kirk Douglas, Frederic March and Ava Gardner), which was released in

February 1964, less than three months after the assassination. Having read an advance pre-publication copy of the book in the summer of 1962, Kennedy remarked "it could happen" here, and "some generals might hanker to duplicate fiction."

If only Kennedy had followed the lead of the president in the book, who had removed the generals from power before the coup took place! Kennedy had ample justification for relieving the Joint Chiefs from active duty after they had demonstrated themselves to be morally unfit for command by urging him to authorize false flag attacks on American citizens and a nuclear first-strike attack on the Soviet Union. How different the course of his presidency would have been! Instead, Kennedy supported production of the movie by allowing the director to film part of it in the White House during the summer of 1963. Perhaps he'd thought that by alerting the public to the possibility of a coup the film would make one less likely.

Soon after I learned all this, I had lunch with Russell Fletcher, so I was primed to express my surprise at the parallels between *Seven Days in May* and real-life events during Kennedy's presidency.

"What's even more surprising, Jubal," Russell responded, "is that the book was published in 1962, long before the Test Ban Treaty outlawing atmospheric testing was even a gleam in Kennedy's eye. Perhaps it was the book that gave him the idea of a treaty with the Soviets.

"And perhaps the book gave the CIA and the generals the idea of removing Kennedy from office," he continued, "not by a coup as in the book but by assassination. The Test Ban Treaty was viewed favorably by the public and ratified by the Senate, though opposed by most of the military. British Prime Minister Alec Douglas-Home deemed it 'the beginning of the end of the Cold War.' In the military's eyes the possibility of an end to the Cold War would be a disaster and had to be stopped by whatever means necessary."

I nodded, and said, "The popularity of the Test Ban Treaty, possibly leading to an end of the Cold War, gave them the motive, and the coup in the book showed them the means. Their actions followed only one year later."

Smiling his wry smile, Russell observed, "The president in *Seven Days in May* and President Kennedy in real life, once in office, changed their views and adopted and espoused policies that would have put the CIA and the military largely out of business. Kennedy wanted to seek peace with the Russians. He wanted to get along with the Cubans. He wanted to pull out of Vietnam. He was determined to dismantle the war machine. And, I think, he had an active partner in much of that with Soviet Premier Nikita Khrushchev. Kennedy's Peace Speech that you've mentioned, was 'like waving a big, red flag in front of a bull. Khrushchev, though, was so impressed by it that he had it broadcast on Soviet TV."[50]

Russell was quiet for a moment, then added, "I vaguely recall that those who ordered the assassination used the same phrase as the generals in the book. They called Kennedy a 'threat to the national security of the United States.' Orders were issued to one of the assassins in the form of a flash cable printed on thin paper that would normally soon dissolve in the air. The assassin, however, stuck it between the pages of a book, where it apparently survived. I don't remember where I learned that, though."

I made a mental note to find the source of that story, then described to Russell the research I'd done into the early days of investigations into Kennedy's assassination. I mentioned Salandria's findings and that they'd been confirmed by later scholars, including those whose books he had recommended.

I also commented on how striking the photographs were of medical personnel who had been in the operating room with Kennedy in Dallas shortly after the assassination. Nearly all of them had indicated that a large part of the back right of Kennedy's head had been blown out by holding their right hand to the back of the right side of their head, as seen in photographs taken during their interviews. [See Image 7, p. 57.]

"It's really amazing that their testimony was so consistent, and right in line with the 152 witnesses who stated that shots had come from behind the fence at the back of the grassy knoll in front of the president.

"It's saddening, even disturbing, that all this information, from such a large number of medical folks and other witnesses, had been kept out of the Warren Report because it conflicted with the government's Oswald-as-lone-gunman theory."

"You know, Jubal," Russell replied, "for a detailed account of the role in the cover-up played, under duress, by two doctors who examined Kennedy—Admiral George G. Burkley, Kennedy's personal physician, and Dr. Malcolm Perry, who performed the tracheotomy on him—you should see the articles by Donald W. Miller, MD, who knew both of them. In fact, you should see all of Miller's articles on the assassination, especially 'Pursuing Truth on the Kennedy Assassination" and 'Reflections on the Assassination of President John F. Kennedy, 50 Years Later.' They're an ideal starting point for anyone becoming interested in the subject. They might bring to your attention aspects of the assassination, especially the medical angle, that you're not yet aware of."

I made another mental note to find these articles as soon as I got home.

As we walked out of the restaurant, I remembered something interesting.

"Hey Russell," I said, "what do Presidents John F. Kennedy and Donald Trump have in common, besides being president and wanting to reduce tensions with the Russians?"

Russell shook his head and waved his hand for me to continue.

"Both were elected on November 8th!"

13

Although it might sound ridiculous or contrived, Gina and I encountered each other entirely by accident a second time, this time in the Barnes and Noble where the book club met.

As we strolled through the bookstore together, I mentioned my most memorable encounter with Filipinos in the United States. "It was in San Jose, when I worked in Silicon Valley before joining the Foreign Service," I began. "I bought a car from one of them, and later sold it to someone else in the same group. While drinking beer with them to celebrate the sale/purchase—all of us passing around and drinking out of the same large bottle, something I'd never done before!—they taught me a phrase I have never forgotten: 'Easy to get, easy to forget.'"

Gina smiled halfway before responding. "That phrase 'easy to get, easy to forget' had been always told to us Filipinas since we were kids. I am not sure if the Filipinos you met were talking about the same thing but for us it is about the value of courtship, something that I personally believe and practice as well."

The word "courtship" caught me off guard. It's a word Americans rarely use these days, a concept that seems as dated as the Eisenhower era. Young people don't court any more, do they? From what I've seen, they don't even date. Too many decades had gone by, and I'd been out of the country too long to know how things really work today. But it seemed to me that young adults merely congregate, without either sex attempting to dress or act in any way designed to impress or attract the other. The idea of courting appeared to be as foreign to them as a foreign language.

Memory of a book stirred in me. "Twenty years ago," I said to Gina, "Ellen Fein wrote a book called *The Rules*, which laid out steps that young women should follow when courting, when dating, if they want to determine whether a man's interest in them is for a lifetime or for only a nighttime or two. Like traditional courtship, which no longer exists in America, adhering to the rules would force men to reveal their true intentions and the strength of their commitment."

Since we were in a bookstore, I steered us over to the section where that book would be, if the store stocked it. It did, and I bought a copy for her. We then headed to the coffee shop inside the store. As we drank our coffee, Gina glanced through it with a puzzled look on her face. Then she spoke.

"This book is both interesting and appalling at the same time. Back home we don't have books on dating like this, and it's sad that the things that, for me, are common sense and only demand the bare minimum from a man have to be written as a book—things such as not inviting a guy to our place or not sleeping with a guy during the dating phase. Almost everything in the book is very basic. It also reminds me how this view of courtship is now starting to die back home because of the mainstream media, so this practice is also getting rarer in The Philippines these days. Anyway, each person has his own ways of doing things, and traditional courtship is just something that has helped me so much."

As she was speaking, I'd once again been daydreaming about what my life would have been like if I'd been able to spend the last several decades with someone who had only 70 books but who treasured each one, occasionally rearranging them with loving care, rather than with someone who had never read a book in her life. What would life be like now with such a person?

"If circumstances were different, I would court you to the moon and back," I thought. Except that I'd spoken the thought out loud.

"What do you mean, if circumstances were different?" Gina asked, alerting me to my having vocalized my thought. Her dark brown eyes looked directly into mine, blue green in color, as she asked.

"Come on," I said, standing up. "Let's get some lunch." I needed time to organize my thoughts and decide what exactly to say before responding.

Once we'd ordered in the Thai restaurant nearby, I began by noting that I still knew very little about her from which to try to form explanations for the things about her that intrigued me. So my imagination had gone to work to try to explain her to myself.

"Among the many things that have puzzled me about you, three stand out. One I already asked you about—how you came to be so well educated, in addition to being smart and interested in literature.

"The other two things seem to be interconnected; I can't separate them clearly. One is the influences from your Spanish Catholic heritage. My experiences have been mostly in countries influenced by English speaking Anglian culture, but I'm now intrigued by that Spanish Catholic heritage because it's something I know so little about. So I'm glad that we've read *Noli Me Tangere*, and I might read two other books proposed by book club members that shed light on this heritage, Alessandro Manzoni's *The Betrothed* and Shusaku Endo's *Silence*. The first, as I'm sure you know, takes place long ago in Catholic Italy, and the second deals with the experiences of Catholic missionaries in Japan during a time when such activity was illegal and punishable by torture and death.

"The other intertwined factor is that from things you've said during the book discussions I gathered that you have not had a lengthy intimate relationship with a man; that is, you have never lived with a man, never been married. You have, I concluded, theoretical knowledge about such relationships but not that type of knowledge that comes from personal experience. How that could be I found almost inexplicable, and my imagination went to work to try to explain it.

"At first I considered whether you were gay, but rejected that idea almost immediately."

Gina laughed gaily at that.

"Another idea was that in the Spanish Catholic world girls remain un-*tangere*-d until marriage. So perhaps that part of your life had been influenced by the Spanish and Catholic aspects of your heritage. And maybe that would be an aspect of traditional Filipino culture, too, even apart from the colonial influence. I was intrigued by that idea, but concluded that it could not be the whole story, not even if you had stronger religious beliefs than the typical person, as I think you do."

She nodded, listening attentively.

"What that something more was, my imagination came up with, was that you are an only child—and that you have no brothers and sisters because your mother's hips were so narrow—as are yours—that she died in childbirth, while giving birth to you. And as a result, you have—or the person in my imagination has—a possible fear of pregnancy and childbirth. That fear, reinforced by your Catholic beliefs and heritage, has led you to avoid certain experiences that most women have had by age 25.

"Of course, my imagination may be wildly off base. I hope you aren't offended by such personal comments. They result from my pondering something, well, someone, who has intrigued me beyond words."

I hadn't meant to lay out my thoughts in such detail, and in fact I was as surprised by some of them as Gina appeared to be.

Her first response was to laugh—and to my relief to laugh in a light way, as though someone had gently tickled her. Then she said, "Be assured that I am not offended by anything you came up with. I would say that most of it is funny, albeit shocking. Nonetheless, I take your efforts to imagine those things as flattering even if they may have not been intended to be such. It means you let thoughts about me fill your head for some time and that's really sweet.

"As for my mom, she is still young and alive, and despite her petite frame like mine, she gave my dad four healthy and happy daughters. I'm the oldest.

"It might look like my choice of saving myself for the right man is borne out of fear or naiveté, but it's not. I call it fortitude, prudence, and sanity. I am not afraid of childbirth either, in fact I know it will come to me one day, that's why I make sure to stay fit and healthy. My experiences with men are always very positive, too. But that's all I can say, just like how I didn't burst their bubbles of intrigue, I won't burst yours, too. I will let your active imagination go wild to no end.

"Now that I have addressed your imaginings," she continued, "I think it will only be proper if you do me the favor of telling me the reason behind you sparing time to be intrigued by me. I am baffled because from what I've gathered about you, you are currently married." She nodded at the ring I was wearing.

Here I explained what I've already recorded—that my wife had died four months ago, and that I felt some degree of responsibility for her death, because as the decision maker for someone unconscious I hadn't done everything I should have to understand the risks involved in the surgery recommended by the doctor before agreeing to it on her behalf.

I mentioned again the idea of Principality, this time explaining in more detail the manner in which I had acted on Diana's behalf in a less than fully informed way. "That's where I failed my wife," I said. I hadn't taken the time to get the information I needed to make an informed decision. I simply relied on the advice of one doctor."

"I'm so sorry to hear all this, Jubal," she said. "It must have been awful to lose her."

"Yes, it was, and still is. I'm still not recovered from the shock." I then explained more about my situation, the retirement soon after Diana's death, and my relocation to the Raleigh area. And about the marriage having lasted 28 years, and about our two children, who aren't part of this memoir.

"When I was 16 my dad passed away because of cancer," Gina said, "so I know how devastating it can be to lose someone close to you, someone irreplaceable. On his last day, I will never forget the things he told me while I was praying the rosary next to him. He told me that I can go wrong in anything in life but I should never let myself go wrong in choosing a husband or else I will be miserable my entire life; that the greatest gift I can give to my husband is saving myself for him; that I should honor and always respect my husband; that my children will not be able to choose their father so I must be wise in choosing him for them; and that I should only choose a man who will take care of me and our future children.

I nodded silently as she continued.

"Those words are so ingrained in my head that they're serving me really well in my personal life. My experiences are always positive because I've learned how to vet a guy and let guys court me. I am not wanting a perfect man. I know he will be flawed but I know the key qualities that I want in a man, and as a young woman, I am always doing all the work to be deserving of such a man, so I also have much to offer to him."

This was unexpected information, and I didn't know quite how to respond to it. I'd never before met a woman who had thought so carefully about courtship, about vetting a potential spouse, about life after the wedding ceremony. My goals when her age had hardly extended beyond the short term, and as regards marriage, if I ever thought about it, I thought not much beyond the ceremony launching it. Americans in general, I thought, spent more effort investigating the qualities of various models of refrigerators before making a purchase than they do those of prospective spouses before agreeing to marry one of them.

Gina then smiled, and related happier details about her parents and family life when she was younger.

"Your reading so many books reminds me of my dad when he was still alive. He used to have reading as a hobby, but it became the bottom of his focus because he got a new hobby after getting married: my mom! He always rushed from work to home, just because he couldn't wait to see my mom and spend time talking to her. My dad didn't even allow my mom to work or do heavy household chores like laundry or even washing the dishes, because he said, she's the wife, not a maid.

"We were always involved in everything he did. In return, my mom and us, their kids, treated my dad like a king. All my dad's personal belongings were handled by us as if they were owned by royalty and we respected him as if his every word was the law. My mom is 44 now and didn't remarry. My dad treated us as if we were princesses; we were very poor, yet it's in the family to look classy, nonetheless. I saw the exact same relationship pattern with my grandparents. Now I see the pattern manifesting itself in my life, too. That's why when I hear stories about unhappy or toxic marriages, it makes me ponder, and at the same time, I feel like no matter what I do I can't wrap my head around it because I didn't see those when I was growing up."

I nodded, and laughed, because it was the same with my parents. "My dad also used to get home from work as quickly as he could, to be with my mom. They'd known each other in college, but hadn't dated until after they'd graduated, and didn't marry until he'd gotten out of the Air Force. The draft was still in effect in those days. With four kids born in less than five years, we were chronically short on money, yet they somehow saw to it that all of us had birthday parties, presents for Christmas, and three good meals a day, every day. I don't know how they did it. Now, having raised a family of only two children, in much better financial circumstances, I'm exhausted just thinking about all the difficulties my parents faced and overcame."

And with that I stood up and prepared to leave. I needed time to mull over all that I'd learned from Gina. While driving home I realized that I hadn't answered her question about "if circumstances were different." And, I saw, if I'd seen that, she'd already realized it, too.

14

During the past several weeks I'd become so interested in the Kennedy assassination and in the early efforts to uncover the truth about it that all thoughts of the Huxley-Kennedy-Lewis project had vanished from my mind. I'd already read a dozen books and many articles that provided a mass of evidence substantiating the contradictions in the Warren Report identified by Vincent Salandria. Other researchers and scholars had also uncovered much evidence confirming early suspicions that the CIA and the military had been behind the assassination and the cover-up.

The House Select Committee on Assassinations, for instance, found in 1976 that a fourth shot had been fired, this one from the grassy knoll in front of the president's limousine. There had, therefore, been a second shooter and a conspiracy to assassinate President Kennedy. Yet this fact is usually omitted whenever the Oswald-as-lone-gunman story is put forth in the media and in textbooks of American history.

I also learned that the Pentagon had destroyed its files on Oswald and the Secret Service had destroyed its records for Kennedy's trip to Dallas, both claiming that it was standard procedure to destroy records. Having had a career in government service, I knew full well that destroying records is not standard practice, and as a human being with common sense I knew there'd be no legitimate reason for destroying records related to the assassination of the president.

Jacob Hornberger, drawing on eyewitness accounts and the work of other scholars and investigators, especially Douglas Horne's *Inside the Assassination Records Review Board*, provided two examples of actions undertaken by the CIA and the military in the hours after the assassination that showed conclusively, to me at least, that they had played leading roles in organizing and covering up the murder.[51] Playing supporting roles were the FBI (which intimidated witnesses; altered, lost and planted evidence; and stage-managed the evidence and witnesses presented to the Warren Commission); and the Secret Service (which withdrew much of its protection for the president on that day and approved a route that violated its own protocols in several ways at just the point where the assassination occurred).[52]

The evidence that convicts the CIA beyond a reasonable doubt of criminal complicity in the JFK assassination, Hornberger explained, consists of "the altered, fraudulent copy of the famous Zapruder film that the CIA secretly produced . . . on the weekend of the assassination."[53] Drawing on Horne's work, Hornberger recounted "the secret transport of the original Zapruder film on November 23, 1963 to the CIA National Photographic Interpretation Center (NPIC) in Washington, D.C. . . . [and] then to its top-secret photographic operation Hawkeyeworks in Rochester, where it was copied and altered. The altered, fraudulent copy of the film was then shipped back to NPIC in Washington, where it was presented as the original film."[54]

Among the alterations that Hornberger cited are the cutting out of the film of the extremely wide turn onto Elm Street that the motorcade made in violation of Secret Service protocols,[55] the complete stop or near-complete stop that the president's limousine made after the first shots rang out in Dealey Plaza as attested to by 59 witnesses,[56] and the patch that had been added to the back of JFK's head beginning in frame 313 to hide the large gaping hole, which could have been made only by a shot from the front. Hornberger cited a film expert who described the patch as "crude," and who pointed out that "if you run the film, you'll see that it moves—differently than his head does, as well. So, it's an optical, some sort of an optical [effect] that they put on there, to not show the back of his head." And, he observed, they've "added in the pink splash, the pink water-balloon—whatever it is that's supposed to be the blood—it's just not even believable. . . . Maybe fifty years ago that might have passed muster, but for anybody—I mean—my impression is if I showed it to a 12-year-old kid, they would say it was a cartoon."[57]

The key point, Hornberger explained, is that "There is no innocent explanation for an altered, fraudulent copy of the film of the assassination. Once one concludes that the famous Zapruder film is an altered, fraudulent copy of the original Zapruder film, one has automatically concluded that the CIA was criminally complicit in the assassination of President Kennedy. There is no way around that."[58]

The evidence that Hornberger presented convicting the military of involvement in the assassination is the fraudulent autopsy that it conducted on the president's body on the evening of the assassination. "A fraudulent autopsy doesn't just happen on the spur of the moment as some sort of spontaneous act. It had to be [a] pre-planned part of the cover-up of the assassination itself, especially given that the fraudulent-autopsy scheme was actually launched at Parkland Hospital in Dallas at the moment that the president was declared dead. That was when a team of armed Secret Service agents, brandishing guns and stating that they were operating under orders, declared that under no circumstances were they going to permit the Dallas County Medical Examiner, Dr. Earl Rose, to conduct an autopsy on JFK's body, notwithstanding that Texas state law required it."[59]

Drawing on evidence uncovered by Horne and others, Hornberger showed that "there were actually two separate brain exams as part of the JFK autopsy. . . . The brain at the first brain exam almost certainly was JFK's brain. The brain at the second exam was not. . . . There can be no innocent explanation for perjury and two separate brain exams, especially when they involve brains belonging to different people. That is conclusive evidence of autopsy fraud."[60]

As with the altered Zapruder film, "it necessarily equates to criminal culpability in the assassination itself. There is no way around that."[61]

More than 60 people who witnessed the assassination or who worked to save the president's life at Parkland Hospital in Dallas stated that they saw a massive hole in the back of Kennedy's head.[62] [See Image 7.] And yet the official autopsy photos show little damage to the back of the president's head. [See Image 8.]

All this had convinced me that the autopsy photos in the official records today are fake even before I came across FBI Director Herbert Hoover's statement to President Lyndon Johnson on November 29, 1963, that one of the bullets "tore a large part of the president's head off."[63]

After digesting these two definitive pieces of evidence showing that elements in the U.S. government had orchestrated and covered up the assassination, I came across a third. It again came from Douglas P. Horne, who established that the windshield of Kennedy's limousine had been pierced by a bullet that had struck it from the front. He provided statements by six eyewitnesses as to the existence of the hole. Two of whom "were absolutely positive that the bullet causing the damage had been a shot from the front, which had entered the front surface of the windshield, and exited the inside surface."[64] He also provided definitive photographic evidence of the holes, which established that at least one shot was fired from the front.

Horne documented the process through which the original windshield was replaced with a new one, and that "the windshield in the Archives today, which exhibits cracks but not a bullet hole, was intentionally damaged [in that condition] by the Secret Service."

Adapting Hornberger's statements regarding the faked Zapruder film and faked autopsy to the windshield, I came up with, "There is no innocent explanation for an altered, fraudulent replacement of the windshield. Once one concludes that the windshield in the Archives is an altered, fraudulent replacement

Image 7. Twelve of the medical personnel at Parkland Hospital in Dallas who saw the gaping hole in the back of President Kennedy's head.

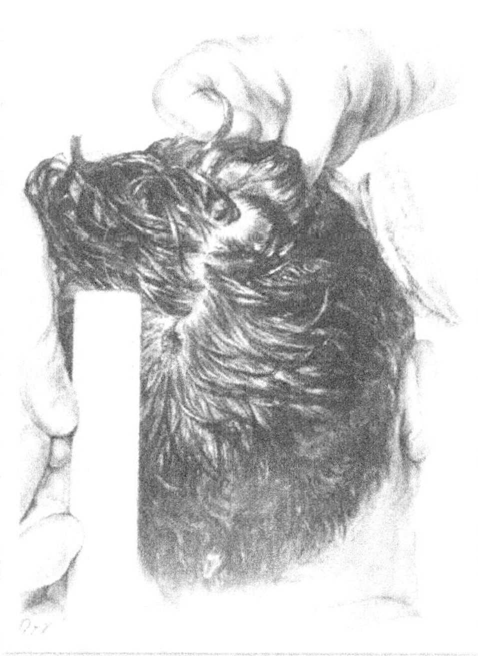

Image 8. Faked JFK autopsy photo.

of the original windshield, one has automatically concluded that the Secret Service was criminally complicit in the assassination of President Kennedy. There is no way around that."

Reviewing all these facts and many others, investigator Noel Twyman concluded that "no one except the president of the United States, acting in concert with a few high military and government officials, could have caused these things to happen and to dovetail."[65] Phillip F. Nelson and other researchers reached the same conclusion: Lyndon Johnson knew of the plot in advance and played a leading role in the cover-up.[66]

Even after having accepted all this evidence, I still hadn't gotten the key point and was thus startled to read Hornberger's statement that "the assassination was a highly sophisticated regime-change operation orchestrated and carried out by the U.S. national-security establishment. . . . It was no different in principle from other regime-change operations, especially ones that involved state-sponsored assassinations based on 'national security,' such as those operations that targeted Iranian leader Mohammad Mossadegh, Congo leader Patrice Lumumba, Chilean Gen. Rene Schneider, Cuban leader Fidel Castro, and Guatemalan president Jacobo Arbenz."[67]

That statement shook me. I'd been aware that the CIA had orchestrated coups in other countries throughout the 1950s and 1960s. And I'd become convinced that it had been behind Kennedy's assassination, too. But I'd never connected the two; I'd never thought of the assassination as a coup, perhaps because I had in mind coups as they had taken place in other countries, with open involvement by the military. There were no tanks on the streets of Washington, yet a coup had in fact taken place, a secret coup perpetrated by certain elements within the government against the rest: the CIA and the military against the Kennedy faction, just as Castro had intuited.

I was startled, too, when learning that Lee Harvey Oswald had warned us of the possibility of a coup a year before the assassination: "Americans are apt to scoff at the idea that a military coup in the U.S. . . . could ever replace our government. But that is an idea that has grounds for consideration."[68]

15

I was up early the next day, eager to try to understand how they—the perpetrators of the assassination, of the coup—the CIA and the military—had gotten away with it.

One large part of the explanation must be that in the years just after the assassination the American people, including government officials not involved in it, didn't know many things that are known today. They didn't know that the FBI and Secret Service had provided extensive support for the assassination and cover-up. They didn't know, for instance, that the FBI had secretly obtained Oswald's belongings from the Dallas Police several days before it official took possession of them, during which time "it altered, destroyed and planted evidence before returning them to the Dallas Police earlier on the day on which it officially received them."[69]

They hadn't known of the security irregularities ordered by the Secret Service. They hadn't known that, as Phillip F. Nelson, explained, all "local, state and federal law enforcement officers, were removed in Dallas, unlike any other motorcade. Except for several motorcycle patrolmen, the last vestiges of President Kennedy's protection stopped at the corner of Houston and Elm Streets as the limousine entered Dealey Plaza, [and] . . . that the only remaining motorcycle escorts—which were supposed to be flanking the rear quarter-panels of the limousine—had backed themselves completely away from the presidential limousine and began riding alongside the Secret Service car after the turn on[to] Elm Street."[70] They didn't know that "the planning for that particular motorcade—and only that one—was managed entirely by Vice President Lyndon Johnson and his sycophantic assistants." They hadn't known, as I only recently learned, that the new president, Lyndon Johnson, had been involved in planning the assassination and had taken charge of the cover-up from the first moments after Kennedy's death.

Nor did they know that the Zapruder film had been altered, or that two autopsies had been conducted, with the official autopsy and the photos from it being faked.

In the years just after the assassination, most Americans

believed what government spokesmen and the media told them: that the Warren Commission had investigated the assassination. They hadn't known that the Commission had merely jotted down what the witnesses selected by the FBI told it, and that the Commission itself was guided away from sensitive areas by Allen Dulles, the senior member of the Commission who had been fired by Kennedy two years earlier.

Nor had they known that Lee Harvey Oswald's defection to the Soviet Union from 1959 to 1962 had been faked, that he had been a spy whose "defection" had been organized by the U.S. Office of Naval Intelligence, or that he had a lengthy and continuing relationship with both the CIA and the FBI before and at the time of the assassination, as documented separately by John Armstrong, John Newman and others.

They didn't know that the photographs of Lee Harvey Oswald holding a rifle in his backyard had been faked, with his face pasted in. Once I learned about this, I looked at the two photos again with a magnifying glass, trying to see if that was indeed true. At first, I couldn't tell for sure. But then I noticed that Oswald's face is exactly the same size and facing exactly the same way in both photos, even though his body had shifted slightly between the two, and is smaller in one of them, as though the photographer had stepped back between shots. I also noticed that the shadows on the face differed from those on the body and on other things in the backyard.

I recalled, as the American public wouldn't have known at the time, that when Oswald was presented with the photos during interrogation, he studied them silently for a moment before saying that they were fake, that he knew something about photography and could easily have prepared similar photos. I suspected it was at that moment that he realized that he hadn't been arrested by mistake, that a real plot had been organized to frame him, that he was indeed a patsy.

They didn't know that a file containing similar photos with Oswald's face cut out of them would later be found in the records of the Dallas Police Department, indicating that the falsification had been done by it—by a Department under the control of

Mayor Earle Cabell, who had been a CIA asset since 1956 and who was the brother of Charles Cabell, who had been Deputy Director of the CIA until fired by Kennedy after the Bay of Pigs fiasco.

Nor had they known the thousand and one details of planning, execution and follow-up to the assassination later documented by researchers such as Jim Fetzer, Jim Marrs, Noel Twyman and so many others whose work is well-known today.

They didn't know, for instance, of the unnatural deaths of large numbers of key witnesses to the assassination. Richard Charnin documented 71 unnatural deaths among the 104 JFK assassination witnesses who died in the following three years. The probability of so many in that small population dying unnatural deaths in that short a span of time was, he calculated, "less than 1 in 700 million trillion trillion."[71]

They didn't know that a decade later many more witnesses would die in mysterious circumstances after being called to testify before the House Select Committee on Assassinations (HSCA), including "in 1977, seven top FBI officials [who] died in a six-month period just before they were scheduled to testify."

The American public then hadn't known, as I hadn't and was only just now beginning to understand, how extensively the U.S. media, print and broadcast, was influenced by the CIA. I'd heard, vaguely, of Operation Mockingbird, the program launched in 1948 through which the CIA influenced the media, or through which the media had cooperated with the Agency.

I'd discounted rumors of the extent of the operation's influence because as a Foreign Service officer I'd known that the Smith-Mundt Act prohibited government officials from distributing within the United States the materials we used to educate officials and the public in other countries about American history, government, and society. These materials had always seemed to me straightforward and accurate accounts of these subjects, but to avoid even the appearance of influencing American citizens in support of the government, we could not distribute them in our own country. I had, therefore, believed that the media was the objective source of information that it presented itself as being.

But, I was now learning, the Smith-Mundt Act did not apply to the CIA—either that, or the Agency illegally and secretly violated it. Through Operation Mockingbird, I now learned, the CIA had "infiltrated more than 25 newspapers and wire agencies . . . to promote the CIA viewpoint."[72] I learned that "during the 1950s, an estimated three thousand salaried and contract CIA employees were engaged in propaganda efforts, . . . that whenever the CIA wanted a news story slanted in a particular way, it got it."

Having done more in-depth analyses of the media in the countries I'd worked in than I'd ever done of the media in my own country, I was astonished to learn of this subversion of one of the most important institutions in a country that prided itself on being a model of democracy. I was especially dismayed to learn that Philip L. Graham, publisher and owner of the *Washington Post*, which I'd read daily for several decades, was "one of the CIA's biggest initial supporters." I'd soon learn much more about how the CIA's extensive influence over the American media resulted in its support for the Warren Report's conclusions and its failure to expose the Report's flaws uncovered by Vincent Salandria, Mark Lane and others.

16

Saddened by what I'd learned about Kennedy's assassination and the complicity of the media in the cover-up, I wanted to talk to someone about it. I called Russell to see if he was free for lunch, but he didn't answer. I thought of calling Gina, but had never called her before, and didn't know what she'd think of an invitation for lunch out of the blue and at the last minute. I called her anyway and was relieved that she sounded glad I'd called and was free for lunch.

After we sat down—we were at the Subway shop where we'd encountered each other for the first time—I surprised myself by launching into a continuation of our last conversation rather than telling her about my Kennedy research.

"I don't think I've ever heard that idea stated so powerfully:

that children can't choose their father, so their mother must choose wisely on their behalf," I told her. "I've been thinking about that a lot. That truth, combined with another idea your father passed on to you, that you can make many mistakes in life and recover from them, but that a mistake in the selection of a spouse can result in untold misery nearly impossible to escape from, leads me to regard your father as a very wise man."

Gina nodded, then told me something startling. It seems I was being startled a lot lately, first about the Kennedy assassination, now about Gina.

"As you know I have been here for a couple of years now," she began. "There have been times that I almost got into nasty troubles because of women attacking me for some things that were beyond my control. I don't usually have traumatic experiences in life, but now I will count my experiences with these women as very traumatic. Last year, I lost a job and went through hell just to jump back financially because some woman was not happy about me at work. She harassed me to the point of me calling the police when she hollered at me outside my school threatening to throw acid in my face—and these don't even include the mini nasty encounters I had, all with women from countries where throwing acid in a woman's face is apparently not an uncommon means of solving a problem; I am just glad that for the bigger fiascos the guys involved sorted it out for me.

"That's one of the reasons why I am very selective of people I associate with, and that's why I like the book club so much, because there are very nice people in it, and it makes me feel safe."

I didn't quite know how to respond to all that, but finally said something about being glad to know that she'd been able to bounce back from those difficult situations.

"Now tell me more about yourself," she said.

I'd already told her about Diana's death. Now I gave her a fuller account of my diplomatic career, my retirement after 28 years of service, the death of Diana after a marriage of a slightly longer length, and about our two kids, who were building good lives for themselves.

"That 15-year period when I had a young family," I told Gina with a wistful smile," when I had young children so eager for my return from work each day, when I was raising a family and building a career, was the high point of my life. I wonder what it would be like to do it all over again, this time without the pressure of trying to build a career in a stressful field at the same time. And when I now have some experience in how to raise a family."

Gina was silent after hearing this, so we both had a chance to eat.

I was about to tell her about my Kennedy research, but she spoke first, and on a different subject than either of us had spoken on.

"The reading and comprehension abilities of American kids have been declining for years," she said. The problem was already recognized as severe in 1983, when *A Nation at Risk*, an assessment of kids and their abilities, raised the alarm."

She pulled a copy of the report out of her bag as she spoke. This surprised me, but shouldn't have, because I'd already observed that she always carried a bag large enough to hold papers and a book or two. It pleased me no end to see that, because I did the same thing.

"This study found that about 13 percent of all 17-year-olds and some 23 million American adults are functionally illiterate," she continued. "The U.S. Navy found that one-fourth of its recruits cannot read at the ninth-grade level, and business leaders stated they must spend millions of dollars on costly remedial education and training programs in such basic skills as reading, writing and spelling. I don't think anyone thinks things have improved in the 35 years since that report was issued."

"I remember reading to my kids almost every night," I recalled with a smile. "They loved being read to, even after they were beginning to be able to read simple books for themselves."

"The problems are far greater than merely reading comprehension," Gina continued. "All that makes my tutoring work so important."

I loved it when she spoke about subjects she was enthused about. It was the enthusiasm as much as the subject matter that caught me.

Gina then mentioned the two articles I'd given her, and pulled them out of her bag, too. "Thanks for sharing this article on Jane Austen with me, "Jane Austen's Vision of a Happy Marriage," by Eleanor Bourg Nicholson. I have read some of Austen's works, but not yet *Emma*. I can see now that it's of special interest to me at this point in my life."

"It's my favorite of all her novels," I said. "I thought of you immediately when I read the article, as it shows just how important courtship and good sense are in determining who would be a suitable spouse for ourselves and for others. And about how hard it is to judge situations objectively when we are personally caught up in them."

"I like both Chesterton and Lewis, . . ." Gina said, moving on to comment on the other article I'd passed to her, "Walking with Chesterton and Lewis" by Joseph Pearce.

I recalled that I'd been particularly struck by Pearce's observation that the differences in the writing styles of these two famous authors were mirrored in their approach to a country walk. "Lewis goes from A to B as the crow flies," Pearce had written, "getting straight to his point and making it with succinct precision. Chesterton wanders off from the designated route, pursuing some secondary thought or path of reasoning; he takes his time, enjoying the walk at a leisurely pace and in no great hurry to reach his destination."[73]

". . . so I can't choose one over the other," Gina continued, "though as a child I read more Lewis, as there aren't a lot of books by Chesterton in the libraries and shops back home. We hadn't learned much about Lewis in school either, but several of his books were in the school library. And of course, many more were in my university's library.

"This article was so timely, as a few days ago I read something about a similar subject which made me feel incredibly uneasy and sad, and reading that article you shared brought me to good spirits again."

I'd thought that I might be introducing Gina to Chesterton, not imagining that a young woman who grew up in The Philippines had already known of him and might have already read a book or two by him. I then realized that I, too, knew little of his work, having read only two of his novels.

While thinking these thoughts, Gina began to speak again, and I made a mental note to ask her later what she'd read that had so troubled her.

"I've been meaning to read Chesterton's *The Everlasting Man*, ever since I read in Lewis's *Surprised by Joy* that it had shown him how much sense it made to view history through a Christian lens, though without making him a believer in Christianity."

"Oh, I know *Surprised by Joy*," I said. "Or rather know of it. It's his account of how he became a Christian. I intend to read it soon."

"When you do," Gina replied, "you'll see that Christianity is the best expression there can be of the moral principles that should govern human life. Be sure to note his statement that "You must not do, you must not even try to do, the will of the Father unless you are prepared to 'know of the doctrine.'"

What she'd said surprised me for several reasons. One was that she had apparently quoted Lewis verbatim. Another I expressed to her.

"What? I'd always thought that even if one wasn't a Christian—because one didn't believe in the religion's core beliefs—one could still try to live by Christian ethics. If we do that, or try to, does the rest of Christian faith really matter?"

"It matters tremendously," Gina said, "because without faith we do not have the strength we need to live by those ethics. Christian moral principles are not so different from those professed by other religions. The real problem is that living by them is not easy. Only Christian faith gives us the strength we need to do so.

"In fact, living by Christian ethics without Christian belief is not possible because without Christian belief one is drawn to another way of life completely, one characterized by 'the pursuit of happiness.' That phrase is often used to justify any and all actions, even those that Christian ethics deem immoral. These are the two poles that exist; to try to live in the middle, between them, by obeying Christian ethics without Christian belief to support that effort, is to leave oneself vulnerable to the lure of the pleasures of the moment inherent in the so-called pursuit of happiness."

"I'd never thought of it like this before," I said.

"People don't choose Hell," she continued, almost talking over my comment, "but they choose those actions that place them there. All actions are choices. Yes, there are pressures on us, but God gave us freedom of choice. We can choose to do what is right, or the opposite. I can't imagine ever being successful in choosing to do what is right without the strength that comes from Christian faith."

The impact of all this was disconcerting. Gina's intelligence and fluidity in expressing herself, her liveliness and energy, her knowledge of literature and the firmness of her religious nature—I was dazzled by it all. I was so dazzled that it was hard to look directly at her.

Have I mentioned that she was again dressed in a manner that was provocative and chaste at the same time? She wore trousers, but also wore on top what could have been a blouse if it had been shorter, but it extended below her knees. The bottom of the hem on both sides was slit. Both pieces were of lightweight material and of an eye catching blue and silver pattern. It reminded me of clothing I'd seen in Pakistan and India.

And on her lips was bright red lipstick. She knew how to make herself not just attractive but provocative, without there being anything inappropriate one could point to, such as a low neckline or an ultra-short skirt.

She was a puzzle I doubted I'd ever figure out.

17

In the morning, I continued examining why the American people had remained silent in the face of the nonsensical Magic Bullet Theory—the idea that one bullet had changed direction in mid flight twice in order to inflict five wounds on two people, Kennedy and Connally, break several bones in the process, yet end up in pristine condition. There had to be more to it than that they didn't have the full story in the early years after the assassination. Enough was known then to cast serious doubt on the official story of a lone gunman.

Americans might have been more inclined to face whatever unspoken doubts and fears they had if members of the Kennedy family and administration had spoken up about theirs. Many of them certainly had knowledge or suspicions about what had really happened, yet to a man and woman they kept silent in public.

The family and administration were in shock initially, and by the time they recovered their sensibilities the new president was firmly in control. They were locked in. Cabinet members and close family, insiders all, were not inclined to rock the boat, even, apparently, in the face of the murder of the president.

Although Jacqueline Kennedy and Robert Kennedy remained silent publicly, they suspected what had really happened, and sent JFK's close friend, William Walton, to Moscow with a private message to explain their real beliefs to Nikita Khrushchev in order to calm relations between their country and his. Walton met with Georgi Bolshakov, the man who had been the secret link between Kennedy and Khrushchev at the time of the Cuban Missile Crisis, to explain the Kennedys' belief that a political conspiracy lay behind the assassination.[74]

Kennedy aides Kenneth O'Donnell and Dave Powers also remained silent in public. Both had been in the follow-up car, only 10 feet behind Kennedy. Both had seen shots coming from behind the picket fence on the grassy knoll in front of the president—and both had seen the blowout of the back of the president's head—yet both testified before the Warren Commission that the shots had come from the book depository behind them after having been persuaded by the FBI to lie under oath.[75]

John Connally, the governor of Texas who was in the limousine with Kennedy and had been wounded by the so-called

Magic Bullet, also kept quiet. When asked later whether he believed that Lee Harvey Oswald had fired the gun that killed Kennedy, he replied, "Absolutely not. I do not, for one second, believe the conclusions of the Warren Commission." When asked why he remained silent, he said, "Because I love this country and we needed closure at the time. I will never speak out publicly about what I believe."[76]

The same silence pervaded the entire Kennedy administration. Not a single cabinet secretary or aide resigned from the government or made his or her doubts or suspicions public. In E. Martin Schotz's assessment, "Maybe all these people didn't know the CIA did it, but certainly . . . no honest person could ever accept the 'single bullet theory.' So then we have a situation in which all these people basically kn[ew] the Warren Report [wa]s a fraud. . . . Virtually the entire establishment kn[ew] that there was a conspiracy to kill the president but cho[se] not to find out who did it and why. What does that say? It says that a conspiracy to kill the president and its cover-up [were] acceptable. Not legal, mind you. Nor moral. Upsetting? Of course. But, in the end, acceptable."[77]

From one perspective, continuity of government during a crisis is a strength. The assassination showed that the American democratic system was so strong that it could absorb a shock on the magnitude of the murder of the president and keep functioning. Of course, that would be a strength only if the president had died from shots fired by a lone gunman. It would be a weakness if the murder had been orchestrated by officials within the government itself.

"The assassination of JFK was . . . a wound against certain political forces in our democracy, but not to the democracy itself,"[78] Schotz reasoned. "But how is it possible? How can you have a democracy in which there is a coup and literally no one, not a single person in power, protests by resigning?"[79]

I could see three possible explanations.

Schotz presented the first by asking and trying to answer the question, "What would have been the effect on the government and the country and the American people if it had been revealed that elements within the government had assassinated the president?" We'll never know the answer, he observed, because the information didn't come all at once, but seeped out bit by bit over the following decades. Kennedy's family and cabinet had presumably considered the situation and concluded that the shock to the country of exposing the CIA and the military and the FBI and the Secret Service would have been too great. No one knew how they would react if confronted publicly with evidence of their guilt. So, members of the Kennedy family and cabinet, along with other insiders, kept their suspicions and doubts to themselves in order to protect the democratic system from possible collapse.

"At first glance this idea may seem disorienting, shocking, even bizarre," Schotz realized. And yet it is understandable. The need to protect the system itself required that the actions of the CIA and the military be swept under the rug. "The entire spectrum of the governmental establishment, the entire spectrum of the university establishment, the entire spectrum of our media establishment,"[80] Peter Dale Scott explained, didn't want to know for sure. Better to only suspect than to have suspicious confirmed. Better to absorb the smaller harm, as shocking as it was, and move on.

The second answer, again suggested by Schotz, is that Americans had too deeply absorbed the Cold War mentality, the mentality "which pursues anti-communism and the Cold War above all else, a mentality which will subordinate any crime, including the threat to annihilate mankind, in pursuit of defeating this supposed enemy." "What did Kennedy in," he explained, "was his effort to depart from this insanity, and on this score, in deciding to handle the assassination as they did, the left/liberal establishment revealed that when push came to shove, when they had to make a choice, this left/liberal establishment was more addicted to the military and the CIA than to the Constitution. And by and large the American people are part and parcel of this addiction."[81]

Many officials in the Kennedy administration, not just in the CIA and military and other security agencies, had so thoroughly absorbed the anti-Communism mindset that they were of two minds about Kennedy's peace feelers and the lessening of tension with the Soviet Union. One mind supported the turn toward peace. The other was in agreement with the fierce anti-Communism of Allen Dulles and the generals. They too feared the Soviet threat to Europe and America; they too supported the extraordinary steps needed to repel and contain it. If the assassination had been conducted by Dulles and the generals—something they only suspected, not knew—it had been an act carried out by those who were willing and brave enough to do what they thought had to be done to protect the United States.

And so, as Schotz concluded, "Dulles and the CIA didn't take over the government, because they didn't have to. The CIA reasoned quite correctly that basically the balance of forces would be on its side if Kennedy were removed."[82]

And yet, if Kennedy was out of step with the mindset of the military and intelligence agencies in his own cabinet, he was, I saw, in tune with rising possibilities for a newer, less tense, more peaceful world. It was a world with great appeal for the American people who were perhaps beginning to see how warped their society had become. Imagine having children practice hiding under their desks for protection against nuclear bombs! Imagine the absurdity of frequent nationwide tests of the emergency broadcast system that regularly interrupted TV and radio programs!

It was Kennedy, not the CIA or generals who saw the possibilities for a saner world and who had the strength to stand up to the generals when they unanimously urged him to authorize false-flag attacks on the United States and nuclear first-strikes against the Soviet Union. It was Kennedy's vision, not theirs, that was gaining favor with the American people, who, the generals suspected, would re-elect him, giving him from the fall of 1963 another five years to implement his policies.

It wasn't just that Kennedy had expressed a desire for peace in his Peace speech that was dangerous to the generals—anyone could do that. And it wasn't just how eloquently he expressed the type of peace he envisioned: "world peace . . . genuine peace, the kind of peace that enables men and nations to grow and to hope and to build a better life for their children; not merely peace for Americans but peace for all men and women, not merely peace in our time but peace for all time."

It was that he outlined practical steps through which such a peace might be attained: peace "based not on a sudden revolution in human nature but on a gradual evolution in human institutions—on a series of concrete actions and effective agreements which are in the interest of all concerned. There is no single, simple key to this peace—no grand or magic formula to be adopted by one or two powers. Genuine peace must be the product of many nations, the sum of many acts. It must be dynamic, not static, changing to meet the challenge of each new generation. For peace is a process—a way of solving problems."

It was a way of solving problems based on concerns and interests common to both Americans and Russians: "In the final analysis, our most basic common link is that we all inhabit this small planet. We all breathe the same air. We all cherish our children's future. And we are all mortal." It was a way that called for a greatly reduced role for the CIA, the military and the security and intelligence agencies and the companies associated with them.

It was a way that inspired many people of that generation and, in a later generation, me. Though Kennedy's words had been spoken half a year before I was born, I wanted to help bring about the peace he'd envisioned. I felt he'd spoken to me as well as to the students graduating from American University that day when he said, "let us examine our attitude toward peace and freedom here at home. The quality and spirit of our own society must justify and support our efforts abroad. We must show it in the dedication of our own lives—and many of you who are graduating today will have a unique opportunity to do so."

After considering all this, I recalled *Profiles in Courage*, the book Kennedy had written in the mid 1950s while recuperating in bed from a severe back injury. In it he had examined moments in the lives of twenty U.S. senators who had resisted pressure from powerful interests, who had rejected the path that would have been most politically expedient for themselves, to do what was best for their country.

I jotted down a reminder to see the book again.

As I turned to considering the third reason why administration officials and the American people largely accepted the official explanation, I realized how hungry I was, and got up to prepare dinner. I'd get back to this later.

18

In spite of the distress I felt when I'd made arrangements for lunch with Russell, I was in good spirits when we met.

I opened our conversation by pointing out a humorous aspect to the cover-up.

"It's ironic that the Warren Commission was forced into contortions like the Magic Bullet theory because of the fabricated Zapruder film. If the film hadn't been shortened by cutting out several sections to eliminate the stopping or near stopping of the limousine, the span of time in which the shots occurred might have been much longer, making it possible for the cover story of Oswald as the lone assassin to have included four or more shots. Their cleverness in one way created great problems for them in others!"

We both laughed at that. Russell, too, was apparently in a jocular mood, and he responded with another absurd but true fact. "Woody Harrelson, the actor—you must know of him, a great actor—his father was one of the three men found in a railway car and apparently arrested in Dallas on that day. There are photos of them with Edward Landsdale walking in front of them in the opposite direction. Landsdale worked with the CIA in 1963, after retiring from the Air Force as a major general. But get this, Woody's mother's maiden name was Oswald! How's that for a coincidence!"

We laughed some more, but then I changed the tone a bit.

"There's still so much I don't know, Russell, even after reading so many books and articles. Perhaps these are merely loose ends that no one has addressed yet. One of them is that apparently neither Marina Oswald nor Oswald's brothers ever spoke to Oswald's mother—the brothers' own mother—again after November 1963.[83] What's that all about?

"And get this: George de Mohrenschildt, Oswald's CIA handler in the year before the assassination—his wife was Abraham Zapruder's business partner. There are so many oddities about what happened that still need to be investigated.

"Here's another one: The lights went out and the phones went dead in the School Book Depository just as Kennedy's motorcade approached the building. There were no blackouts or phone outages in any other part of Dallas at the time.[84] And here's another: The telephone system in Washington D.C. broke down one minute *before* the shooting in Dallas. The official explanation of overloaded lines makes no sense, and it was almost an hour before full service was restored.[85] And, after the first shots were fired the Dallas police radio channel used by motorcade security was blocked for more than eight minutes by an open microphone."[86]

Russell looked thoughtful before commenting. "Imagine the power needed to coordinate all those things happening nearly simultaneously, in different places."

I nodded in agreement. "And get this," I continued. "Nearly the entire cabinet was out of the country on the day of the assassination. The Secretaries of State, Defense, Agriculture, Treasury, Interior, Commerce and Labor, as well as the National Security Advisor and the press secretary—all had attended a conference in Honolulu the day before the assassination. It was unprecedented for so many senior members of the government to be away from Washington, D.C. at the same time.[87]

"And not just out of town," Russell added, "but out of the country. "Most of them were on the same plane, over the Pacific on their way to a conference in Tokyo at the time of the assassination. They turned around immediately on hearing the news, of course."

"You know, Russell, in all the books I've read I've never come across even one that offered an explanation for why so many members of the government were out of the country at the same time. Not one. Surely not more than a few of them knew of the impending assassination, so it's not like they all together decided to absent themselves from Washington to escape any responsibility for what was about to take place. There are still mysteries that scholars need to investigate and explain, and that's one of the most intriguing.

I then mentioned the Stemmons Freeway sign that blocked Zapruder's view of the limousine at the time the "first" shot hit Kennedy.

"In the Zapruder film the sign appears to have several marks on the back that could have been holes or indentations where bullets had struck it, an idea supported by a report that the sign was taken down the night of the 22nd because it doesn't appear in photos taken on the 23rd. By one account, the sign was damaged during the shooting and removed within thirty minutes.[88] No official explanation for the removal of the sign was given, but some folks in Dallas remember a local news segment explaining that the sign was taken down because it had a bullet hole in it.[89]

"And get this: a copy of the Zapruder film with the four missing frames that *Life Magazine* officials said had been damaged during processing recently surfaced. Those frames show a small hole in the Stemmons freeway sign that computer experts have confirmed is a bullet hole.[90]

"And here's another oddity: In the Zapruder film, the version that is supposedly the original, but isn't, to my eyes the sign, like the lamp post later, do not move relative to the background as they should as the camera angle changes as it follows the motorcade. Neither have the right size or shape. They appear to have been pasted into the film after the other alterations had been made."

"The deeper I look into the film, the more oddities I see. Two films taken by spectators show other spectators standing three feet into the street as the motorcade approaches, yet none of them appear in that location in the Zapruder film.[91]

"And here's one more, Russell. All photos that I've seen showing Zapruder standing on the pedestal are darkened so much in the upper half that he can't be identified. The pedestal itself is in direct sunlight and easily seen; it was, after all, just after noon and the sun was nearly directly overhead. And there's even one photo that shows no one at all standing on the pedestal even though the limo is directly in front of it. Other photos show persons of varying heights standing on it. The pictures are dark, so their faces and bodies can't be clearly seen, but their heights can be gauged. There's more afoot here than researchers have yet explained.

"Another strange story is that fifty-four crates of Robert Kennedy's records at the JFK Presidential Library and Museum are so sensitive that even the library's director doesn't know what's in them."[92]

"All that's fascinating, Jubal. There's clearly still much work to be done to clear up the puzzling gaps in our knowledge and inconsistencies in what we think we know. One area that has become clearer, though, is just who within the CIA was behind the assassination. The Agency, as you know, is even more highly compartmentalized than the State Department. As I see it, Allen Dulles probably came up with the idea of assassinating JFK, after Kennedy fired him as Director of the CIA following the Bay of Pigs debacle.

"James Jesus Angleton, Chief of Counterintelligence, was most likely its architect, employing Oswald as pawn in the plot. Both Richard Helms, Deputy Director for Plans and later Director of the CIA, and Angleton had worked closely with Dulles in the World War intelligence agency Office of Strategic Services, which predated the CIA."

"John Newman came to the same conclusion about Angleton," I said. "In his view, no one else in the Agency had 'the access, the authority, and the diabolically ingenious mind' to design and carry out such a sophisticated plot.[93] So it does appear that scholars and researchers are reaching a consensus about what really happened and who specifically was behind it."

"David Atlee Phillips and E. Howard Hunt started working together in 1954," Russell continued, "when they plotted and engineered the overthrow of Guatemalan President Jacobo Arbenz. Phillips and Hunt were in Mexico City when Oswald allegedly visited the Russian and Cuban consulates there; and they were in Dallas the day JFK was killed.

"Angleton has been recorded saying, 'It is inconceivable that a secret intelligence arm of the government has to comply with all the overt orders of the government.' And it was Angleton who promoted the idea that Oswald was a Soviet agent.

"It has been said that many people holding high-level positions in government are sociopaths, people with no conscience who are as cold, unemotional and predatory as reptiles. That would fit the five CIA conspirators who killed Kennedy."

"But not everyone who became ensnared in their plot was a willing participant," I said. "Their machinations ruined the lives of many people involuntarily caught up in it. Douglas Horne, in *Inside the Assassination Records Review Board*, wrote that Admiral Burkley's behavior—he was, as you know, Kennedy's personal physician—'can only be understood as that of a man who was filled with deep and profound guilt about the massive cover-up he'd participated in.'"

"Yes, Burkley's plight is deeply moving," Russell responded. "It's a real human story that everybody can relate to even apart from its connection with such a tragic event in American history. Donald Miller, MD—I've mentioned him to you before—lamented to me that 'Admiral Burkley's plight was akin to that of the old Bolsheviks, who were airbrushed out of Soviet history books and the national narrative after they fell victim to one of Stalin's purges.' That JFK's death certificate, which Burkley signed, was not reprinted in the Warren Report, and that Burkley himself was not called to testify before the Warren Commission are, along with so many other facts, why the assassination continues to be an open wound that won't heal. That the State of Texas won't convene the examination of the murder required by the state's own laws, and that the media refuses to examine the case, are all causes for shame. And the longer it goes on the more shameful it becomes because the less excusable it becomes."

"I'm a sadder man now than I was two months ago, Russell,"

I said after another moment of silence.

"As a counter to the negative and upsetting information you're immersed in, you need something worthy of admiration and respect to counter it, Jubal," Russell suggested.

I surprised myself when thoughts of Gina immediately filled my mind. I thought, too, of my kids and my Huxley-Kennedy-Lewis project, but didn't mention any of these to Russell.

"You might consider reading Jordan Peterson's new book, *12 Rules for Life: An Antidote to Chaos*," he continued. "Jordan is a professor of clinical psychology at the University of Toronto and is a trenchant critic of neo-Marxist identity politics and post-modernism. I've just finished reading it. Following his rules we can cope better with the awful things happening in our government and the world, and with the tragedy of existence."

I made a mental note to get a copy of the book.

After signaling to the waitress for the check, Russell told me a poignant story.

"I just read an interesting article by Jeffrey Hart," he said, "about a lunch he had with Lionel Trilling—both were literary and cultural critics—after Kennedy had been elected in November 1960. Kennedy had run to the right of Eisenhower and even of Nixon—recall the missile gap he repeatedly referred to in the closing months of the campaign. Hart was thus surprised when Trilling told him, 'You have no idea how far left this administration is going to go.' Hart reported that 'I was puzzled by that then and I still don't know what to make of it.'[94] He went on to say how wrong Trilling was, given that he retained J. Edgar Hoover as head of the FBI and Allen Dulles as head of the CIA. He explained Trilling's comment to himself by concluding that Trilling must have been referring to the way that a leftward move in the culture as a whole would push Kennedy left. But Trilling was far more insightful than Hart ever realized, wasn't he?"

I nodded, recalling how Kennedy's Peace speech, the Test Ban Treaty and other actions he'd taken in the middle months of 1963—all of which could be called "left-leaning"—had resulted in his death.

November 2019

❦ 19 ❦

The book club held its second discussion on the first Monday in November. We discussed Robert Louis Stevenson's *Dr. Jekyll and Mr. Hyde*, which was the first of many books we would read centered on the main characters' efforts to try to understand a puzzling situation by uncovering and interpreting clues. Caught up in my Kennedy research, I was glad the book was on the short side. Somehow even after retirement, with my time fully my own, the days were still too short.

After the discussion, as Gina and I were walking toward an Asian restaurant nearby, I said to her, "There are several really interesting people in the book club, but only one who really stands out—that girl from The Philippines. What was her name?"

She laughed, as I'd hoped she would.

Once we were seated and had ordered, I started to tell her about my latest Kennedy research, but all that got swept away by her eagerness to talk about the status of the tutoring business that she was setting up.

"Would you like to see it?" she asked with a lilt in her voice that reflected her animated spirits.

"Sure. I'd love to see your business. Your shop." I wasn't sure what to call it.

"My studio, I call it. I should show it to you in the daytime. You can see it better in the light. More furniture is being delivered tomorrow morning," she said proudly. "Why don't you come by later in the morning."

I wrote down the address as she gave it to me.

We met at the studio the next day, in the late morning. She saw me walking from the parking lot and came out and waved as I approached. I couldn't help noticing the sign, in large red letters, above the studio:

WORDS, WORDS, WORDS: TUTORING IN ENGLISH AND SPANISH LANGUAGE AND LITERATURE

"That's quite a sign," I said. "It's sure to be noticed by everyone coming to any of the surrounding shops."

The studio was located in a shopping center that had a grocery store at the left end, a dozen shops in the middle, and two restaurants at the other end. Her store was near the middle, between an ice cream parlor and a small school for young ballerinas. She saw me looking at it and said, "I was worried at first that the sound of music from the ballet school would be too loud. But we can't hear it at all. They must have put insulation behind the mirrors."

As we entered, I noted the reception and waiting area in the front that spread the width of the studio. In it were some two dozen boxes containing newly delivered tables and chairs.

Behind them, in the middle, was a walkway that opened into six cubicles, three on each side. At the back end were three rooms: Gina's office, on the left; a storeroom straight ahead; and a larger conference room on the right. I was impressed, both by the ambitious nature of the business and by the sensible layout of the studio.

"But Gina," I said, turning to her, "where did you get the money for all this?" My right arm swept around to indicate all the chairs, tables and room dividers. "Not to mention the lease and the sign?"

"I borrowed from my uncle. He really wanted to help me, in part because my father, his brother, died when I was so young, only 16. But he's not rich, and it really is a loan. I'll have to pay him back as soon as I can." She sighed as she wiped her brow with the back of her left hand, revealing the stress she was under in setting up the business.

With noon approaching, lunch was in order, and we walked to the Mexican restaurant at the end of the row of small businesses.

"I'm so glad the furniture was delivered today," she said, over lunch. "That gives me the rest of the week to get everything in place." I offered to help her unpack and move the furnishings to their appropriate places, but she said that she had three people coming to help her in the afternoon.

"The same three who will be tutoring here?" I asked.

"No, these are three Filipino friends, undergrads, who I've met since arriving here. We Filipinos help each other out whenever we can. Some of them might end up tutoring in the future."

"My biggest worry now," she continued, "is the bookkeeping end of things. As you can see from the name of the company, my strengths are in words, not numbers. My father had a bookkeeper, Milee, who kept track of things for him, so that he could focus on buying and selling the books and on getting to know his customers. He used to throw all receipts in a box. Milee would then magically turn them into accounting records and financial statements. I'm looking for someone who can do that for me."

I thought for a moment before saying, "I could perhaps set up an accounting system up for you. Then turn it over to you or someone else to process receipts and payments as they occur."

"But you were a diplomat!" she said, frowning, perhaps wondering how a diplomat had acquired knowledge of accounting sufficient to set up the system for her.

"Yes, nominated by the president and confirmed by the Senate," I said. "But in college I took some accounting courses. Of course, computerized systems are different now than 30 years ago, and I'd have to bring myself up to speed on the latest programs. But I've been thinking about doing that anyway, now that I have the time to do whatever I want, with the idea in mind of perhaps opening a business of some kind in the future. Perhaps a rare book business."

I'd surprised myself by making the offer, as I valued having a life with few commitments for the next year at least. But I was glad that I'd done so.

She thought for a moment, before saying, "I couldn't pay you much. The expenses have been so high just to get the doors open."

"No," I said forcefully. "I don't want any salary. I don't want the commitment or obligation that a salary implies. I'd just be doing this to help out a friend. You could consider me an honorary member of the Filipino community, like those students who are coming in to help you this afternoon."

We left it at that, but I really was interested in bringing my knowledge of computerized accounting systems up to date. Who knew when such a skill might be needed in my own life, whether I opened a business or not.

Later, back home, I sorted out the financial documents Gina'd given me, which was easy, and tried to sort out my thoughts about Gina herself, which wasn't. What kind of relationship did we have? What kind did I want? I knew we were friends. I thoroughly enjoyed our conversations, and thought she did, too.

I wanted more than that, though. She was so charming and enthusiastic, earnest and even ardent, filled with ideas and energy. Seeing her go about her business was like watching a fine athlete in action, or a lioness chasing its prey, every muscle responding in sync. I wanted to possess her, in bed and every other way. But at the same time didn't want anything to disrupt our conversations.

I knew that a sexual relationship with Gina was out. Whatever fleeting thoughts I'd had in that direction were gone. Her Filipino Christian beliefs about preserving the purity of her body, combined with her promise to her father on his deathbed, made for an impregnable fortress. Sleeping with her would be the wrong thing to do even if in a moment of weakness she consented.

The only way to sleep with her would be to marry her, and marriage was the last thing I wanted right now. It had been only four months since Diana died, and I was enjoying too much being disconnected, moving to my own rhythms as I've said, without having to take another person into account every minute.

Putting aside all thoughts of sex with Gina actually made things much easier. She could be like a younger sister. Or a niece. Yes, that's what I must aim at, at having acquired a friend and a niece.

20

Needing another break from the distressing aspects of my Kennedy assassination research, I turned again to C. S. Lewis, to one of his books about reading and literature—*An Experiment in Criticism*. In one part he contrasted people who have a literary sensibility with those who don't. The majority, he observed, when they read at all, read a book once and then toss it away, and often accompany their reading with listening to the radio. Or they confine their reading to railway journeys and other odd moments of enforced solitude. But, he stated, "those who read great works . . . will read the same work ten, twenty or thirty times during the course of their life. . . . Literary people are always looking for leisure and silence in which to read and do so with their whole attention. When they are denied such attentive and undisturbed reading even for a few days they feel impoverished."[95]

All that described me to a T, I felt, though I'd change "even for a few days" to "even for a day." What surprised me was how quickly my thoughts turned to Gina when reading that passage. I knew she was literary, of course; she had, after all, started a book club dedicated to reading great works of literature from around the world. What surprised me even more was my realization that it didn't seem to matter what subjects I'd been thinking about recently, or what I observed when I was out and about, I somehow found a connection between those thoughts and observations and Gina. But I put that thought away and went back to reading Lewis's book.

To appreciate literature, Lewis wrote, "we must begin by laying aside as completely as we can all our own preconceptions, interests, and associations. . . . After the negative effort, the positive. We must use our eyes. We must look, and go on looking till we have certainly seen exactly what is there. . . . The first demand any work of any art makes upon us is surrender. Look. Listen. Receive. Get yourself out of the way."[96]

Yes, that is exactly what I'm trying to do not just when I read a book of literature, I thought, and also in my Kennedy research. I'm trying to clear away all preconceptions and stay objective in my examination of the evidence that researchers and scholars have already uncovered.

Then, if a work of art is deemed worthy of further attention, Lewis continued, imagination comes into play. Using music as an example, he explained that "The direct emotional impact of this or that passage is of very minor importance. When [listeners] have grasped the structure of the whole work, have received into their aural imagination the composer's (at once sensual and intellectual) invention, they may have an emotion about that. It is a different sort of emotion and towards a different sort of object. It is impregnated with intelligence."[97]

Reading that passage, I immediately thought of Gina, of my "at once sensu[ous] and intellectual" appreciation of her various qualities. That wasn't quite the thrust of what Lewis had in mind, though, and his use of the word "impregnated" in the final sentence led my thoughts further astray.

I put Lewis's book down and turned to Aldous Huxley's novel *After Many a Summer Dies the Swan*. Perhaps his story about a Hollywood millionaire and his desire to live forever would be far enough afield that thoughts of Gina wouldn't come creeping in.

21

With my spirits restored by the visit to Gina's studio and a break of several days to read books by Lewis and Huxley, I was ready to return to examining the Kennedy assassination. I knew there was more behind the American people's acceptance of the official explanation than I'd considered so far, but didn't quite know what it was. Something was still missing from my understanding of why Americans had accepted a story that didn't hold together and a Warren Report so obviously flawed. Something beyond the limited amount of information was holding them back from acknowledging their doubts, something beyond the silence of the Kennedy family and cabinet, something beyond their fear of Communism.

And then I had it. The American people had such confidence in their country and its government that they simply could not even consider the idea that elements in their government might have murdered their president.

In the days, months and years after the assassination, they faced a dilemma. On one hand they could see the absurdity of the so-called Magic Bullet theory. At the same time their faith in the United States government was so deep that they simply couldn't believe the evidence of their own eyes and minds. There had to be an explanation that reconciled the Magic Bullet theory with their faith in the American system even if they couldn't see what it was. The other option—that their own government had killed their president—was too horrible to contemplate, so it must be wrong. With no reconciliation of these two opposed views forthcoming, they simply turned their attention away from the horrible, suspected reality they couldn't bring themselves to face.

The spark that led me to this conclusion—that Americans' faith in their government and country was so strong that it outweighed the evidence presented by their own eyes and minds—was recalling a book I'd read years before, *Americanism: The Fourth Great Western Religion*, by David Gelernter. "America is not only a nation;" he'd written. "America is a religious idea."[98]

It's the fourth great Western religion, the book's subtitle proclaims, following Judaism, Christianity and Islam. "The idea that liberty, equality, and democracy were ordained by God for all mankind, and that America is a new promised land richly blessed and deeply indebted to God—that is Americanism."[99] Elsewhere Gelernter explained that "[t]he central tenant of the American religion was . . . that American democracy is good and right, for America and for the whole world, and is destined ultimately to supersede tyranny everywhere."[100]

Most Americans in 1963 believed in America, deeply, and accepted the duties that Americanism imposed on them. Their country had saved Europe, twice, in the Great War and in the Second World War. It was continuing to defend Western Europe against invasion by the communist Soviet Union. And it had saved South Korea, going to its defense after invasion by communist North Korea in 1950. It had done all this at great cost, not just financially, but by the sacrifice of hundreds of thousands of Americans killed and permanently injured. That made it personal.

These sentiments were deeply and widely held in the world I grew up in. I now saw that the famous words and phrases Kennedy spoke in his Inaugural Address—"Ask not what your country can do for you; ask what you can do for your country" and "We shall pay any price, bear any burden, meet any hardship, support any friend, oppose any foe, in order to assure the survival and the success of liberty"—were moving expressions of them. These sentiments had inspired and challenged a generation of Americans to civic action and public service, to contributing in some way to the greatness of their country.

Kennedy's words had inspired me, too. Along with his Peace Speech in June 1963, those words at his inauguration had inspired me throughout my early life and led, twenty years later, to a career in diplomacy, to bringing American experience and practices and beliefs to the countries in which I worked. I'd been not only religious without realizing it, but evangelical.

And Kennedy himself, even apart from the Peace Speech, was inspirational. He'd been a war hero. Founder of the Peace Corps established to share American knowledge with newly independent countries. He'd launched the effort to reach the moon—to land a man on the moon and bring him back safely. And he'd stood firm against Communism and against his own security, intelligence and military agencies as he sought to lessen world tensions. All these gave me as a young man reasons to admire him and to opt for a career in government service. I was proud to serve in America's diplomatic corps and to help promote "the American way of life."

Returning to the United States after having spent nearly three decades representing my country overseas, I still believed in Americanism. The more I'd seen of the horrendous conditions that exist in much of the world outside the United States, the prouder I was of the achievements of my country and of my service on behalf of it. We had avoided the passions that had torn many other countries apart. We had established a system of civilian government elected by the people that served their interests. We had kept the military in check and avoided the rule by strongmen that existed in so many countries around the world. America, I believed, was the freest and most secure, the fairest and most prosperous country the world had ever seen.

Sure, the country was far from perfect—the Kennedy assassination being a glaring example—but that was to be expected in any system designed and staffed by flawed human beings. There was messiness in its politics, but that's just democracy in action, I thought. That's the way things are when people and parties work out their different views in public. Far better that than secret deals made by powerful forces behind closed doors followed by scripted public theater. The democratic institutions are fundamentally sound—that's what I believed throughout my career, and that's how I explained things to people in the countries to which I'd been posted.

In fact, Americanism made me proud that my life overlapped with so many accomplished Americans whose major achievements had largely been completed before I was born. Realizing this, I paused in my research to compile a list of great Americans from the past who had influenced me in my early years and with whom my early life overlapped. These were Americans I had admired when young and who I still admired, and who I am proud to have shared the planet with in my first years. The following list is in order by how long our lives overlapped. [Editor: See nearby text box.]

Of course, there were others—non-Americans—who I also admired when young and whose lives I was proud my life overlapped with. I made a list of some of them, too. Too bad, I thought, that I couldn't add to that list two others who I was intrigued by now but who I hadn't been aware of when young: C. S. Lewis (1898-1963) and Aldous Huxley (1894-1963).

Two anecdotes show the nature of the society that I was pleased and proud to have been born into. The first involved Aldous Huxley. As recounted by Dana Sawyer in his biography, in the autumn of 1960 Huxley was scheduled to give a lecture titled "What a Piece of Work is Man" at the Massachusetts Institute of

Americans Whose Lives Overlapped with Mine Who I Admired as a Child and Youth and Still Admire Today

John F. Kennedy, 1917-1963 (only a few hours)
Cole Porter, 1891-1964 (11 months)
T. S. Eliot, 1888-1965 (13 months)
Edward Hopper, 1882-1967
Helen Keller, 1880-1968
Judy Garland, 1922-1969
Louie Armstrong, 1901-1971
Duke Ellington, 1899-1974
Charles Lindbergh, 1902-1974
Walter Brennan, 1894-1974
Lionel Trilling, 1905-1975
Elvis Presley, 1935-1977
Will Durant, 1885-1981
Cary Grant, 1904-1986
Benny Goodman, 1909-1986
Fred Astaire, 1899-1987
Richard Feynman, 1918-1988
Leonard Bernstein, 1819-1990
Aaron Copland, 1900-1990
Isaac Asimov, 1920-1992
Audrey Hepburn, 1929-1993
Mortimer Adler, 1902-2001
Jacques Barzun, 1907-2012
Kirk Douglas, 1916-still living in 2019
Willie Mays, 1931-still living in 2019

Non-Americans

Winston Churchill, 1874-1965
Albert Schweitzer, 1875-1965
Bertrand Russell, 1872-1970
Igor Stravinsky, 1882-1971
Pablo Casals, 1876-1973
Dmitri Shostakovich, 1906-1975
P. G. Wodehouse, 1881-1975
John Lennon, 1940-1980
Glenn Gould, 1932-1982
Karl Popper, 1902-1994

Technology. "The hall was packed with an eager audience. Latecomers were sitting in the aisles. Loudspeakers had been placed outside in the corridor, and in two large rehearsal halls where five hundred others . . . [could] listen. Many more, caught up in the traffic jams Huxley's appearance had set off, never made it in time to hear him."[101]

Huxley's lecture had been given three years before I was born, but a similar incident, involving the psychologist Carl Rogers, took place a few years after my birth. My father, who had attended the event, described it to me a decade later. Several hundred people had arrived to hear Rogers speak, far too many to fit into the hall. Many people had arrived hours early to get seats near the front. So many people showed up that the talk was moved to a larger hall. My father described his amazement at how so many in the audience, especially those who had been seated in the front, leaped from their seats, rushed from the hall and then ran to the new venue, so eager were they to sit as close as possible to Rogers. These weren't teenagers at a rock concert, he observed, but sober professional psychologists, professionally dressed, who leaped, rushed and ran to the new venue.

These two events—and I recall reading about a third similar event when Albert Camus gave a talk, "The Crisis of Man," in New York not long after the Second World War ended—show just how seriously so many people regarded the intellectual life of their country at the time. I still smile whenever I think of those events, so characteristic of the world into which I'd been born. Are there any intellectuals today who inspire such eager attendance at their public lectures? None spring to mind.

Redirecting my thoughts to the Kennedy assassination, I saw again that Americanism beliefs and sentiments had made it exceedingly difficult for Americans in 1963 to accept the fact that their own government had murdered their president. And for me, too. Only now, nearly 56 years after the assassination, was I ready to examine the evidence objectively. I realized that I could now do so in large part because the pressures of a demanding career and raising a family had ceased. I understood why those whose lives were still so hectic as they sought to meet the demands on them remained unaware of how elements within the U.S. government had betrayed their country. Still, I wished that some way could be found to draw their attention to the facts of one of the most important events in their country's history, one still within living memory.

22

I stopped by WORDS, WORDS, WORDS, ostensibly to pick up more financial documents, but really because I wanted to see how Gina was doing amidst the flurry of activity to prepare for the opening of WORDS.

She surprised me by having cupcakes with candles on them ready when I arrived. I'd wondered if she'd remembered that it was my birthday. She had, and said if I hadn't dropped by in the morning, she'd have called to ask me to stop in later. Two of her tutors were there, Maja Mindanao, who I recognized as the girl who'd been with Gina at the Subway shop during our initial encounter, and Mike Ramos, a young man I hadn't seen before. He was Filipino, so Mike was clearly a nickname. The four of us had a merry time polishing off a dozen cupcakes while waiting for the Filipino food we'd ordered to arrive.

While the other two went to the grocery store to get drinks, I commented to Gina on how stylishly she was dressed. She had on a sleeveless print dress that she said was designed in Italy.

"It's a knock-off, of course," she told me. "I can't afford the real thing but do want to appear stylish whenever I go."

"If you continue to think like that, Gina, you'll never become a real American." I motioned to two women visible through the window who were dressed, in a typically casual American manner, in jeans with holes in the knees and shirts, untucked, with writing on them.

Seeing them reminded me of something that G. K. Chesterton had written nearly 100 years ago and that I'd read since our discussion of him and C. S. Lewis a month or two ago. I happened to have the book with me, and pulled it out to show Gina the passage, which I read to her.

> To put it shortly, the evil I am trying to warn you of is not excessive democracy, it is not excessive ugliness, it is not excessive anarchy. It might be stated thus: It is standardization by a low standard. This [is] the chief danger confronting us on the artistic and cultural side and generally on the intellectual side at this moment.

I also showed her the book in which I'd read the passage, *Literary Converts* by Joseph Pearce, which I was reading to understand the process through which Lewis and other writers had become Christians. I then read to her Pearce's comment on Chesterton's statement.

"'It was this aspect of Chesterton, his defence of culture and civilization in the face of uncultured vulgarity, which lay at the center of Lewis's admiration for his work.''[102]

Gina shook her head as she continued looking at the two women walking toward the grocery store. "I don't know how they can dress down like that," she said. "Don't they know they're out in public, not at home in their living room? How will they ever attract suitors, dressed like that?"

Maja and Mike returned with the drinks, and I noticed that they, too, were dressed a cut or two above the usual American standard. Maja was dressed in a flowing print dress that would have hidden her figure if not for a sash tied around the middle. Mike was dressed like me, wearing jeans without holes in the knees and a long-sleeved shirt with buttons.

The food then arrived, and the two girls unpacked it and set about organizing it on one of the small tables in the foyer.

"Are all Filipinas as charming as these two girls?" I asked Mike, knowing that they would overhear me.

Mike, catching the flirtatious nature of my comment, replied, "Oh yes, all girls in The Philippines are beautiful, but Maja and Gina are two of the loveliest."

They smiled in return, and as we sat down around the small table, Gina explained to me what the food was. Fried chicken I recognized, of course, and pork, but they had an unusual flavor that was hard to describe, at least for me, with my limited knowledge of cooking.

I mentioned that I'd read *Dusk*, a novel by Sionil José and had learned from it a lot about the life of ordinary Filipinos under Spanish and American rule. They looked puzzled for a moment, until I recalled that the book's original title in The Philippines was *Po-on*, the name of the village where the family lived. Then they all started to talk at once.

Gina explained that "Everyone back home knows José's books. Many of them, like *Dusk* or *Po-on*, portray how the Spanish colonial masters oppressed the people in my country for more than 330 years. They never accepted us as equal to themselves or allowed us to rise to positions above a rather low level in the government or the Church."

Maja noted that "Most people at the time *Po-on* takes place, at the end of the 1800s, were very poor and uneducated, as were people in most other countries in that part of the world at that time. But the Spanish domination held most of our people back long after they had begun to become more educated and more prosperous in other countries in the region. The Philippines had been a colony of Spain, and held back by Spain, for more than 300 years before the French even entered Vietnam."

Mike added two thoughts. "The Philippines wasn't a unified political entity before the Spanish came, and not even under Spanish rule. Filipinos live on 7,000 islands and include hundreds of different groups that speak scores of different languages. These groups were often hostile to each other, which made travelling dangerous for Istak and his family in the novel, a condition that would have existed even if the Spanish had never set foot on our islands."

"And, Istak wonders if the lives of the poor would have been any different under rich Filipinos than they had been under the Spanish. The wealthy always use their power to increase their wealth, he observed, and noted that virtue and wealth seldom go together."

"The Filipino spirit for independence is portrayed very well in the book," I commented. "I hadn't known much about the famous battle at the mountain pass of Tirad before reading the book."

Gina nodded, and added, "The book shows very clearly that the revolution was held back because the country was divided into so many small groups, often hostile to each other, as Mike said. And it shows that some of the leaders of the revolution, especially Apolinario Mabini, recognized that the task for their generation was to establish unity among the various groups, to create a strong foundation on which their continuing struggle for independence could be based, so that it could be achieved in the future."

"Few Americans know anything about the American colonialization of the Philippines," I said. "It's not a part of our history that we're taught in school. I knew almost nothing about it before reading a few books recently. I had no idea how brutal the American occupation was, or that more than 250,000 Filipinos were killed when they fought the Americans,[103] who had stepped in to dominate the country after it had nearly won its independence from Spain."

No one spoke for a few seconds, until I jumped back in with, "I especially liked how Istak's mother called his father "Old Man," and his father called her "Old Woman," and then Istak and his wife did the same thing after they had children, ten years later, even though they were only in their 30s."

We all laughed at that, and Gina said, "It's still that way today. My parents did that, too!" And we all laughed some more.

A while later I noticed Gina frowning as she looked out the window. Following her gaze, I saw several young Americans, men and women, dressed in a manner that merited the adjective "shabby."

"You know what, Gina?" I said. "You could design a new class on how to present oneself in public. On how to dress, act and speak to make a positive impression."

"What a great idea!" she responded, and then added, "And another course on how to carry on a conversation, how to give a speech, how to prepare for an interview, and how to behave and speak during an interview."

"What Americans need is Charm School," Maja said, and we all laughed. But I could tell that she was serious when she added,

"Remember, Gina, that all of us girls had to take such a class in school?"

We all laughed again at Mike's next comment. "You could use one of those girls as the 'before' picture," he said as he motioned toward the window, "and Maja as the 'after' picture to show the perfect model of feminine beauty, poise and charm."

I'd have thought Gina merited that distinction, though I could see that Maja would be the choice of those who preferred a more voluptuous figure.

We broke up soon after, and as I was leaving I gave Gina another article that I'd read recently, "Reading," by Mortimer J. Adler, which was to have pleasant consequences some months later.

Back home, I read and thought further about the American war to dominate the Philippines from 1899 to 1902, which lingered on until 1912 or so. Of course it wasn't called that. It was billed, in the words of President McKinley, as a selfless effort to "uplift and civilize and Christianize" the people of The Philippines, a comment that could have been made only by someone ignorant of the fact that Filipinos had already been mostly Christian for twice as long as the United States of America had been in existence.

As I read more about that American effort to subdue resistance to its rule, which involved herding entire villages into concentration camps, indiscriminate killing of civilians, and torture used on Filipinos trying to defend their country from domination by an alien force, I never felt more ashamed of my country. That shame was deepened on learning that that torture included the use of water torture,[104] a method nearly identical with the water boarding torture the U.S. inflicted on suspected terrorists after September 11. No wonder any but the most cursory mention of the war is avoided in the textbooks used in American schools.

Two ironies of the American war in The Philippines stood out. One was that whereas the American colonies had defeated the far stronger British through the use of guerrilla tactics, it was now the Filipinos who were using those tactics against the far stronger Americans—leading the Americans, like the British, to complain about the use of such "unfair" tactics. The second was a comment that F. Sionil José, the author of *Dusk*, made when lecturing before committees of the Council on Foreign Relations at the height of the Vietnam War, around 1970: "If the Americans did not suffer from historical amnesia, they would never have gone to Vietnam,"[105] where, as I now knew, they fought a similar war in similar conditions using similar tactics to those used in The Philippines 60 years earlier.

Ignoring black spots in our own history leads us to repeat them, I observed. At least, I told myself, the wars in the Philippines and in Vietnam were two isolated instances, distinctly different from the usual American practice of sharing the country's experiences and expertise with others—a sharing inspired by Americanism—the area of my specialization during my career in the Foreign Service.

23

Having established—to my own satisfaction, at least—who was behind the assassination of President Kennedy and why, and how and why the cover-up had succeeded, I now wanted to understand the effects the assassination—the coup—had on the United States—on the American government and on the American people.

I noted first that power flowed to the perpetrators. The CIA and the military, assisted by the FBI and the Secret Service, had gotten away with it, and everybody who mattered in the government knew it. That couldn't help but increase their influence and reduce everybody else's. The perpetrators weren't shy about using their power to further cover their tracks. I've already noted the 71 witnesses who died unnatural deaths in the first three years and the seven top FBI officials who died unnaturally after being called to testify. There were many others.

Robert F. Kennedy, who had vowed to reopen the investigation into his brother's death if he became president, was assassinated after winning the California primary in June 1968, which had made it all but certain he would be the

Democratic Party's candidate for president that year and likely the next president. I found credible reports that law enforcement officials in several agencies were heavily involved in his murder. Tim Tate's and Brad Johnson's account in *The Assassination of Robert F. Kennedy* was particularly convincing. I also came across credible evidence that John F. Kennedy, Jr.'s death in 1999, just before he was set to launch a political career, was an assassination. Donald Jeffries, for one, recorded that "[Kennedy's] high school girlfriend and others told me that he had a real 'quest' to find out who really killed his father, behind the scenes."[106]

The domestic regime-change operation, or coup, like those the CIA orchestrated abroad in the decades before and after 1963, was designed to effect changes in government policies. Perhaps no change was more radical than the reversal of Kennedy's intention to withdraw all U.S. advisors from Vietnam by the end of 1965, as already noted. The new policy, enacted only four days after Kennedy's assassination, would lead to the deaths of 58,000 young Americans and severe injuries to another 350,000. Not to mention the 3.8 million Vietnamese who died as a result of the war.

It was in the context of that U.S. involvement in Vietnam that further assassinations took place. Malcolm X was killed on February 21, 1965, and Martin Luther King, Jr., on April 4, 1968. Both were prominent activists in the civil rights movement, but neither was assassinated until after becoming active in the anti-war movement. "King was killed at the point he was joining our civil rights movement to our anti-war movement,"[107] E. Martin Schotz explained. William F. Pepper, in *The Plot to Kill King*, convinced me that the FBI was behind King's assassination and that James Earl Ray, the supposed assassin, was as much a patsy as Lee Harvey Oswald had been.

Other policy changes were less visible. The U.S. Treasury currency that Kennedy had introduced was withdrawn. His Executive Order 11110 had authorized the U.S. Treasury to issue a new public currency called the United States Notes. This new currency, issued by the U.S. government and backed by silver, broke the monopoly on currency held by the Federal Reserve, a private organization. Nearly $5 billion of the new notes was in public circulation at the time of the assassination [$50 billion today], but all was pulled from circulation and destroyed after Kennedy's death. According to one report, "John J. McCloy, president of Chase Manhattan Bank and president of the World Bank, [was] named to the Warren Commission . . . to cover up what was going on, . . . to make sure the American public never got even a hint of the financial dimensions behind the assassination.'"[108]

Kennedy's assassination also resulted in greater CIA influence over the American media. In 1976 Carl Bernstein documented in "The CIA and the Media"—a 25,000-word exposé in *Rolling Stone*—just how extensive CIA influence was. During the past 25 years "more than 400 American journalists . . . have secretly carried out assignments for the CIA,"[109] he stated. Some were "full-time CIA employees masquerading as journalists abroad." Others were eager to perform tasks for the CIA "with the consent of the managements of America's leading news organizations. . . . Reporters shared their notebooks with the CIA. Editors shared their staffs."

Among the most valuable media providing support to the CIA were the *New York Times*, CBS and *Time*, Inc. "From 1950 to 1966, about ten CIA employees were provided *Times* cover" as "part of a general *Times* policy . . . to provide assistance to the CIA whenever possible,"[110] Bernstein revealed. "CBS was unquestionably the CIA's most valuable broadcasting asset. . . . Over the years, the network provided cover for CIA employees; supplied outtakes of newsfilm to the CIA; established a formal channel of communication; gave the Agency access to the CBS newsfilm library and allowed reports by CBS correspondents to the Washington and New York newsrooms to be routinely monitored by the CIA."[111] "Henry Luce, founder of *Time* and *Life* magazines, readily allowed certain members of his staff to work for the Agency and agreed to provide jobs and credentials for other CIA operatives."[112]

As skepticism about the official story of a lone assassin

grew—as independent investigators began to uncover what had really happened on that day in Dallas—the CIA realized it needed to take action. In January 1967 CIA officials issued guidance to its media assets on how to respond: Label and dismiss the reports as mere "conspiracy theories" and the investigators as misguided "conspiracy theorists" who were borderline crazy and so could be and should be ignored.

Schotz's account of how this strategy played out in the media is worth noting. Because the work of Salandria, Lane, Weisberg, Meagher, Groden and other early independent researchers had "provided proof of a conspiracy that was simple and obvious," the media couldn't present their work accurately; "it had to distort [it] in order to rescue the government's good name."[113] Through the use of the phrases "conspiracy theory" and "conspiracy theorist," "the media were able to take *proof* of conspiracy and turned it into *theory* of a conspiracy. With *proof* turned into *theory*, *knowledge* was turned into *belief*, and the government was able to retreat to the position that perhaps the Warren Commission was mistaken, but of course no one would be 'so extreme' as to claim that Earl Warren and the other Commission members were anything but honorable men. Thus was launched the . . . debate over the Warren Commission."

"Since the Warren Report was an obvious fraud," Schotz continued, "so was the pseudo-debate over whether there was or wasn't a conspiracy, a debate over a question which had long ago been answered definitively. . . . Unwittingly many honest citizens, tricked into participation [in the pseudo-debate], became part of the cover-up, because the debate gave legitimacy to the notion that there was doubt and uncertainty when there really was none."

In short, "the public is allowed to think anything it wants, but is not allowed to know, because the case is shrouded in supposed uncertainty and confusion. This was and is the big lie, that virtually no one is sure who really killed President Kennedy or why."[114] If the truth can't be known, then the solid facts that the most substantive researchers and scholars have uncovered and presented can be dismissed as of no more validity than the wildest fantasies presented by others.

This was all highly sophisticated psychological manipulation, I recognized. The perpetrators' success was admirable, in the sense of being worthy of admiration, in a way. E. Martin Scholtz's perceptive exposing of it was worthy of admiration in every way.

This cloud of supposed "uncertainty and confusion" was in place in 1977 when the House Committee on Assassinations released its Report, giving the media cover to present as no more than theories or opinions its findings that "both the JFK and MLK murders were conspiracies. Acoustic evidence indicated a 96% probability that at least four shots were fired. At least one came from the grassy knoll, indicating at least two shooters." "That," Richard Charnin observed, "should have closed the book on the Warren Commission's physically impossible, irrational Magic Bullet Theory, but this 50-year-old work of fiction is still presented as gospel by the mainstream media while the overwhelming scientific ballistic, acoustic, video, medical, eyewitness and mathematical evidence of suspicious deaths is ignored."[115]

Although Operation Mockingbird might have been shut down after being exposed in the mid 1970s, the CIA's effort to control the American media continued. "Plenty of evidence," Joseph Mercola reported, "suggest[s] it's still in operation. If anything, the system has only gotten more efficient and effective, as the number of major media outlets has shrunk over these past decades, and a vast majority of journalists and news anchors simply parrot what's reported by the three global news agencies."[116]

The assassination and successful cover-up also resulted in increased surveillance of American citizens. "Somewhat illogically," Peter Dale Scott observed, "the Warren Report concluded both 'that Oswald acted alone,' . . . and also that the Secret Service, FBI, [and] CIA, should coordinate more closely the surveillance of 'organized groups.'"[117] These recommendations were implemented, and "helped inaugurate a new era of domestic intelligence operations which, as one Nixon official conceded, 'would have been unthinkable, and frankly, unattainable from Congress in a different climate.'"[118]

That day in Dallas was the moment when Americans began to lose trust in their government and confidence in the American enterprise. One reporter at the time who uncovered FBI duplicity and intuited what had really happened unknowingly spoke for many of his fellow Americans when he stated that his "faith was forever shaken"[119] in his government. In the pre-assassination world I was born into, Monika Wiesak showed, "there was general trust in government and trust in John F. Kennedy himself. When he entered office, trust in government was at around 70 percent and grew to 77 percent during his time in office. After his assassination, trust in government declined precipitously, to 26 percent by 1980 and today sits at an abysmal 24 percent."[120]

The subtle but constant pressure in the media to accept the conclusions of the Warren Report, and the attacks in the media on anyone who presented solid evidence that the Oswald-as-lone-gunman story was false, have inflicted incalculable harm on the American people. The pressure to deny the testimony of our own eyes and the judgment of our own minds resulted in a rip, a tear, in the American soul. To accept the Warren Report is to accept the validity of the absurd Magic Bullet theory. Yet to doubt it is to accept an idea even more disturbing, the idea that elements in the U.S. government had murdered our president—in cold blood, in broad daylight, in front of our eyes. Better, many thought, to close their eyes and minds and accept the official story. Yet accepting the official story set the precedent for accepting future official stories that conflict with the testimony of our eyes and the judgment of our mind.

The American people's trust in government, at 70 percent when Kennedy entered office, rose to 77 percent during his time in office, as Monika Wiesak has shown. "JFK was trusted, not by asking the public to trust him," she explained, but "by asking the public to question him and to question those in power."[121]

"No president should fear public scrutiny of his program," Kennedy stated, "for from that scrutiny, comes understanding.

And from that understanding comes support or opposition, and both are necessary. Without debate, without criticism, no country can succeed, and no republic can survive."[122] "His brother Robert urged the same: 'We have the right to ask questions and we must ask questions, of our own government and of ourselves.'"[123] We must, in short, be Principals.

"JFK's world is unrecognizable today," Wiesak continued in a passage highlighting how our world differs from the world I was born into. "We went from a culture of asking questions, and a general trust in government that resulted from our ability to ask questions, to a deep chasm where some of us fell into paranoia, distrustful of everything and much of the rest of us slipped into a comfortable delusion, not wanting to believe we were living under the system that had murdered our president, needing to believe the official stories we were told."[124]

"This cultural shift is not natural. It was the direct result of John F. Kennedy's assassination,"[125] she stated. "We let our democracy die. . . . We, as a society, have lost the spirit we held when John F. Kennedy was our president. . . . The spirit of asking questions and seeking truth in our society died when John F. Kennedy died.'"[126]

If we fail to resurrect that questioning spirit that not only asks questions but demands answers, we will be condemned to living in the world of force and corruption created by his murderers. And we will do worse than that: we will betray the spirit of the man who was "dedicated to the common good above his own interests, . . . who [was] incorruptible amid intense pressures, [and] who ha[d] the courage to stand up to powerful interests."[127] "He did what he must for us," Wiesak said in concluding her book. "Let us channel his spirit and courage, carry the torch, and honor him by doing what we must for those that follow us."[128]

Monica Wiesak's book—*America's Last President: What the World Lost When It Lost John F. Kennedy*—is one of the most moving and insightful accounts of Kennedy's life that I've ever come across. There's so much of interest and of value in it that I had to set it aside for now, until I'd have the time needed to absorb her account of Kennedy's embodiment of the ideals of Americanism early in his political career, of his interest in and support for the sovereignty of the newly formed nations in the post-colonial world as a young Congressman, and of his efforts later in his career to create a world of peace and prosperity in the face of opposition by powerful men with other goals in mind.

The most moving chapters, I saw in my first all-too-quick look through Wiesak's book, are the final ones, in which she lays out in detail what's expressed so succinctly in the book's subtitle: "what the world lost when it lost John F. Kennedy."

24

Over lunch with Russell Fletcher at his home a day or two later, I summed up my findings—already laid out in this memoir—about how the CIA and Joint Chiefs had orchestrated the assassination with support from the FBI and the Secret Service, why they'd done it, and how and why the cover-up had succeeded. I also laid out a quick version of the effects of the assassination on American society.

"That's pretty much how I see things, too, Jubal," Russell responded, "which isn't too surprising, given that we've read many of the same books and absorbed the same information. I'd only change assassination to assassinations, and cover-up to cover-ups. I'm thinking here of the murders of Robert Kennedy and Martin Luther King, Jr., too. I'm old enough to remember clearly each of those events. In fact, I watched the live TV coverage of Robert Kennedy's assassination at the Ambassador Hotel in Los Angeles, just after he'd won the California primary."

I was relieved that someone who'd risen to the rank of ambassador agreed with my take on things.

"It's all very upsetting," I told him. "Not just the assassinations themselves, but that so many of my fellow Americans continue to accept as true the absurd Oswald-as-lone-gunman story and the stories of the patsies on whom the other assassinations were pinned. And that the media blithely ignores the mountains of evidence that have been uncovered about all of those murders."

"I take heart from the dedication, sometimes for decades, that private individuals have put into their investigations into that really happened," Russell said. "The first generation of early researchers—Vincent Salandria, Mark Lane, Sylvia Meagher, Josiah Thompson, Harold Weisberg, Robert Groden, Cyril Wecht, Gary Shaw, Richard Sprague, Larry Harris, Penn Jones, Jerry Policoff, John Judge, Paul Hotch, Marry Ferrell, Ray Marcus, Maggie Field, Jim Garrison—I have great respect for all of them."

Russell clearly knew far more about the early years of investigations into the assassination than I did. I'd never heard of half of those names.

I nodded, and added, "I'm sure that every president since 1963 knew the real story. It's puzzling, and distressing, that they didn't reveal what they knew. During their terms of office, they were the one person in the country elected to represent the country as a whole, the one individual tasked with doing what was best for all of us, not just for constituents in specific states or districts.

"Why haven't any of the presidents since Kennedy revealed who did it? Why did they not attempt to clean house? Lyndon Johnson, I understand; the evidence is pretty strong that he was one of the plotters. And look where that got him. He had to give the military the war in Vietnam it wanted in order to become president. Yet the war destroyed his presidency. He'd made a bargain with the devil, and in the end, it destroyed him.

"Gerald Ford, I understand, too. As a member of the Warren Commission—as 'the FBI's man on the Commission,' as he's sometimes called—he was in on the cover-up from the get-go, so he'd have kept quiet later, too.

"But what about the others—Nixon, Carter, Reagan, Clinton and so on?"

"Jubal, if you were one of the presidents after Kennedy and Johnson and you knew that the CIA and the Joint Chiefs, with assistance from the FBI and the Secret Service, had murdered Kennedy, wouldn't you think twice, or three times, before you revealed what you knew?"

"Huh! So even the most powerful man in the world lives in

fear? Let's examine each of them.

"Nixon . . ." I started to say, but Russell cut in.

"Nixon's a special case, and quite complicated. Let's look at the others first."

"OK," I agreed. "What about Carter? Why didn't he reveal what he knew?"

Russell had some ideas. "Carter initially continued the effort to reform the legislation governing the security agencies. But his popularity and effectiveness took a hit when the energy crisis resulted in oil shortages, high prices and long lines at gas stations. His ability to govern was hampered further with the failure of the attempt to rescue American diplomats held hostage by Iran. And then, after the Soviet invasion of Afghanistan, he was distracted and largely ineffective during the final year of his only term in office."

"Reagan, I know something about," I said. "He was reportedly fascinated by the assassination, but there's no indication as to whether he discovered what had really happened. In any event, he wouldn't have allowed any side issues to deflect from his primary goals of resurrecting the U.S. economy and defeating the Soviet Union.

"The first president George Bush, formerly Reagan's vice-president, had earlier been head of the CIA," I continued. "Rumor and some evidence have it that he was associated with the Agency since the early '60s, if not before, and that he had been in Dallas on that day in 1963. If so, he would have kept quiet to protect his old Agency. The younger Bush would have kept silent to protect his father."

"Clinton is an interesting case," Russell said. "I'm sure you've seen the photo of a teenaged Bill Clinton meeting Kennedy at the White House in the early '60s. His awe and respect for the president was obvious in his body language and his eyes."

"Right," I said, "Fast forward 30 years: I was in the Foreign Service by then and Clinton was president. I recall hearing that he refused to meet CIA officials alone, that he met the Director of Central Intelligence alone only once during his two terms. I thought at the time it was because he felt the CIA had dishonored

America by engaging in coups and other mischief overseas, but now I think it was because he blamed the CIA for the assassination of the president he had idolized.

"In fact, once Clinton became president, one of the first directives he issued, to Associate Attorney General Webster Hubbell, was to find out who killed JFK. Hubbell reported back that he wasn't satisfied with the answers he was getting."[129]

"Yet Clinton, too, kept silent about whatever he'd eventually learned. Perhaps he calculated that revealing what had really happened, 30 years after the assassination, would harm the country and its standing in the world for no useful end.

"That leaves only Obama and Trump. I don't recall reading anything about Obama on the assassination. Trump, though he has released some documents, hasn't ordered the CIA to release all those it's still holding. I'd bet my bottom dollar that Trump knows exactly what happened but is being held back from telling us by threats to his life.

"But why is Nixon so special?" I asked.

"Nixon," Russell began, "as Eisenhower's vice-president for eight years and as an arch anti-communist, was at the extreme end of the anti-communism mindset so prevalent in the United States during the 1950s and early '60s. Recall also that Nixon had been Kennedy's Republican Party opponent in the 1960 election. He understood politics as well as anyone.

"He knew very well what had really happened in Dallas and described the Warren Report as 'the greatest hoax that has ever been perpetuated.'[130]

"You've probably heard the story that Nixon once told his Chief of Staff, Bob Haldeman, that the Watergate break-in would open up the whole Bay of Pigs thing, that being the phrase by which he referred to the Kennedy assassination.[131] In other words, Nixon saw a connection between the assassination and Watergate.

"The evidence is very strong now that Nixon was forced from office by the CIA. Several CIA operatives were involved in the Watergate scandal that brought him down, including E. Howard Hunt and Frank Sturgis, who had been involved in the assassination a decade earlier. They set him up."[132]

"But why would the CIA want to bring Nixon down," I asked, "if he had been a staunch anti-Communist, and his thinking in line with those who organized the assassination?"

"Because his thinking changed," Russell replied. "Once president, Nixon moved not only to end American involvement in the war in Vietnam, something any president at that time would have been forced by domestic pressures to do, but also to normalize U.S. relations with the Soviet Union and China. The CIA and the military needed those countries as enemies to justify their own existence, to keep the funding flowing to their institutions."

"Recall that lessening tensions with the Soviet Union was one of the main reasons the security organizations killed Kennedy. Nixon was doing what Kennedy had started to do a decade earlier, and the response from the military was similar. Admiral Elmo R. Zumwalt, Jr., came close to accusing Nixon and Kissinger of treason, and retired admiral Chester Ward charged that Kissinger was not just a Soviet sympathizer but a conscious Soviet agent.[133]

"And, adding fuel to the fire, Nixon's two CIA directors, James Schlesinger and William Colby, sought to reform the CIA and to demand explanations for its past illegal activities. The Agency was desperate to stop that investigation.[134] It couldn't kill Nixon as it had Kennedy, but it could take him out another way. It drove him from office. So we see that these two presidents, both resented by the military and the CIA, had their presidencies ended prematurely.[135]

"There's another reason why others might have wanted to see Nixon gone," Russell continued. "His agenda for his second term, what he called a 'New American Revolution,' would return government power back to the states and bring federal agencies more directly under the authority of the White House. Some scholars see this plan and the bureaucracy's response to it as the real story behind Watergate.[136]

"After his landslide win in the 1972 election, Nixon wrote in his diary, 'This is . . . probably the last time, that we can get government under control before it gets so big that it submerges the individual completely and destroys the dynamism which makes the American system what it is.'"[137]

"I had no idea," I said. "That's the first I ever heard of that. My opinion of Nixon is on the rise."

"That part of the story has been buried," Russell explained, "What was of critical importance was that just as the Kennedy assassination instilled fear for their lives in all future presidents, so too Watergate established the precedent of ending a presidential administration 'through nonpolitical means,' including 'the media and especially the investigative and prosecutorial powers of the Justice Department. Accusing political adversaries of lawbreaking and threatening criminal indictment has become the new form of waging political warfare.'"[138]

This was an astonishing new version of the Watergate story, very different from those I'd ever heard before.

It then occurred to me that it wasn't just presidents after Kennedy who had kept silent, it was also the two living former presidents, Harry S. Truman and Dwight D. Eisenhower. Truman, 79 at the time of the assassination, lived another nine years after it. I recalled that he had, in fact, tried to warn the nation about the CIA after the assassination by writing an op-ed calling for the CIA to be reigned in.

Russell must have read my thoughts, or perhaps I'd spoken them aloud, because he walked over to the shelves that housed his Kennedy books, and found the text of the op-ed: "There is something about the way the CIA has been functioning that is casting a shadow over our historic position and I feel that we need to correct it," he read, and explained that the op-ed had been published in *The Washington Post* on December 22, 1963, exactly one month after the assassination.

"Yet his warning was buried. The *Post* didn't carry it in later editions that day. It wasn't picked up by other major papers, nor was it mentioned on any national radio or TV broadcasts.[139] And the cover-up of his warning has continued, even decades later. Not even David McCullough's biography of Truman mentions it."

"Unbelievable," I said. "Did every editor in America independently regard a statement by a former president, the one who had overseen the founding of the CIA, on the most important public event in recent memory, as totally unworthy of notice or comment? Or does this show that the CIA's control of the media was already so strong that it could order publishers and editors to ignore the former president?

"Eisenhower," I continued, turning to Kennedy's immediate predecessor, "was 73 at the time of the assassination. I haven't found any evidence that he'd made any public comment whatsoever about his understanding of what had happened, other than a statement of condolence on the day of the event. In that statement he said,"—I said, reading from the paper Russell had just handed me—"that he shared 'the sense of shock and dismay that the entire nation must feel at the despicable act that took the life of the nation's president.' He spoke of his confidence that 'the entire citizenry, the nation, will join as one man in expressing not only their grief . . . [but in standing] behind the government. The American nation is a people of great common sense, and they are not going to be stampeded or bewildered.'"

"Eisenhower probably felt he couldn't reveal what he knew or suspected," Russell said. "He was up to his neck in developments that led, eventually, to the scenario in which the CIA and the military became convinced that Kennedy's assassination was best for the country. He'd appointed Dulles as Director of the CIA, and General Lyman Lemnitzer as Chairman of the Joint Chiefs of Staff, both of whom Kennedy had retained in those positions when he became president.

"Eisenhower thought like they did, or at least deferred to them. While president, he approved CIA actions to overthrow governments in several countries, including Iran, Guatemala and Nicaragua. The first operation, the overthrow of Mohammad Mosaddegh, prime minister of Iran, occurred in August 1953, seven months into Eisenhower's first year in office. Such events occurred throughout his presidency. The final event that I know of was the assassination of the first independent prime minister of the Congo, Patrice Lumumba, just weeks before the end of

Eisenhower's second term.

"He also approved plans for false flag events, telling Lemnitzer during the final month of his presidency that 'if Castro failed to supply a reason for invading Cuba, perhaps, "The United States 'could think of manufacturing something that would be generally acceptable.'" He was suggesting an attack of some kind by the United States against the United States that could be blamed on Cuba.[140]

"At the same time, Eisenhower apparently came to believe that the military had become too powerful, too out of control, yet felt constrained from taking steps to reign it in. Instead, on January 17, 1961, only three days before the end of his term as president, in his oft-quoted Farewell Address, he finally expressed opposition to the power the military folks had acquired during his two terms, saying that 'we must guard against the acquisition of unwarranted influence, whether sought or unsought, by the Military-Industrial Complex.'

"It's less well known that 'the text of Eisenhower's speech was prepared outside his own bureaucracy,"[141] Russell added.

"Huh! Just like Kennedy's Peace speech," I interjected.

"Right," Russell continued. "'Ike turned instead to his brother Milton, who directed the drafting of the speech. Eisenhower knew very well he was challenging forces at work in his own government.'"

"Sadly, it was all too little, too late," I said. "Eisenhower was still in his 60s throughout all but the final months of his eight-year presidency, and he lived another eight years after it ended. He had the good health and energy to have brought the military and CIA into line. I know that many people have the image of him as a kindly grandfather figure during his presidency. But he'd been Supreme Commander of the Allied Forces in Europe during the Second World War. He surely had the spine of steel needed for command. Yet he didn't command, not in any effective way. It was a failure of will on his part that he didn't, and it was Kennedy who paid the price for it."

We were both silent for a moment, and then I added, wistfully, "All that's needed is for one prominent person—just one!—in a high political position—President Trump, for instance—to call for a new investigation. He'd need to do it unexpectedly, before he is stopped. One sentence would do it: 'I am ordering the Justice Department to investigate the assassination, as urged by the Congressional Committee in 1992 when it turned its files over to Justice.'"

"I can't disagree," Russell said as I stood up to leave. He then said something that was to affect me even more profoundly than had learning the real story of the Kennedy assassination.

"Now that your investigations have given you the main points of the murder of JFK, Jubal, you might consider looking into the events of September 11. You might be amazed by what you find."

PART II

December 2019

✿ 25 ✿

Gina and I both arrived early for the discussion of Natsume Soseki's *Kokoro*, in which a young man investigates the life of an older friend in hopes of understanding puzzling aspects of his beliefs and actions.

Gina always spoke directly and freely about whatever was on her mind—a trait that I was trying to copy. Tonight, it was that the idiosyncrasies of her computer had become more numerous and more frequent, with problems ranging from the hard drive to the battery, which didn't work at all, to bugs in the operating system, which sometimes caused it to shut down altogether.

"Sounds like you need a new one, Gina."

"I'd hate to replace it," she said. "My computer and I have gone through a lot together. It's been my companion since I was in college back home. The cost of repairing it is close to the cost of buying a new one and I was told that even a repair will not guarantee optimal results. So it looks like I'll have to, somehow. But the loan from my uncle is gone. I used it all to get the studio ready."

Her scrunched-up face told me that she really was distraught.

"Gina, might you allow me to buy a computer for you? We could consider it an early Christmas present."

She hesitated before responding and glanced at my face a couple of times while thinking. Finally, she said, "I recognize your genuine kindness and I will accept your early Christmas gift with humility and grace as long as it will not give you any inconvenience. I am truly happy and grateful. Such an offer will help me a lot to move forward with the business more efficiently. Thank you so much, Jubal."

I appreciated her words but could see she was still concerned that there might be an ulterior motive behind the gift. So I explained my thinking. "I know it's a bit unusual for someone to make a large gift to someone he doesn't know all that well. Especially if it's a man making the gift to a girl. The short explanation is that I have been poor in the past and know what it's like to have to repair a car or a computer and not be able to do so without great difficulty. Now that I am not poor, I am happy to be able to help others from time to time. I could give you a longer explanation after the discussion, if you want to hear it."

An hour and a half later we were seated in the coffee shop inside the bookstore. We'd substituted juice for coffee because neither of us wanted caffeine to keep us awake half the night. Although Gina hadn't said anything about my offer of a longer explanation, the expectant look on her face told me she was waiting to hear it.

I began by recalling the idea of Principality that I'd mentioned to her several times before.

"There are two lines of thought that form my longer explanation, Gina. The first concerns Principality. As Principals, we are the decision makers in our lives; others are only advisors. Doctors give us information and advice, but we make the decision about what treatment to undergo. Lawyers advise us, but we decide how to proceed. Financial advisors make recommendations, but we make investment decisions. Yet there are some situations in which people must make decisions on behalf of others. Parents on behalf of children, high government officials on behalf of the country as a whole, and so on. But where do we draw the line? When is it inappropriate to make decisions on behalf of others?

"The second line of thought concerns my own situation. You know that my wife died, five months ago, only a few weeks before I retired. I'm still absorbing the impact of those two changes in my life and considering what I want to accomplish in the years ahead. Of course, my two children will remain a big part of my emotional life no matter what course it takes, even if I don't see them often.

"These thoughts about the rest of my life and those of Principality have become intertwined recently because I've been wondering what I'd do if I met someone new, someone who intrigued me enough to consider beginning a serious relationship with her. What would it be like to do it all over again: to get to know someone new, to date her, court her, fall in love with her, marry her, begin a new family—to build a life with her? This time with someone who shares my interest in books and literature."

"Have you met such a person?" Gina asked.

I didn't answer her directly, but said, "Now, I don't know much about you, Gina. But, somehow, meeting you has triggered thoughts like these—perhaps not about you personally, but about a situation I might face in the future. What should I do? Should I try to build a new life with her, with this hypothetical woman?

"But, I've said to myself, I can't build a life with anyone new. I can't spend my thirties with her because my thirties are gone. Same for my forties and half my fifties. I am too old to build a new life. It would not be right for her, assuming this hypothetical woman to be younger than I am, perhaps three decades younger than me, because she would not be able to build a life with me either, for the simple fact that I would die several decades before her. We would be able to build only half a life together. We would have only a couple of decades and then she would be left alone with children to raise on her own, without a husband, and they without a father."

Gina was listening quietly and intently.

"This is the first time in my life that it's hit me that I'm older than I'd once been, that age is now a factor I'll have to take into account in all my decisions from this time forward. That's a sobering realization."

Gina started to speak, but I continued quickly.

"Principality enters my thoughts because, as I asked myself,

'To what extent can I make decisions on behalf of others? Do I tell this hypothetical woman of the increasing seriousness of my feelings for her when I can see that any relationship between us would ultimately be harmful for her, in spite of how right it might feel for the next decade or two? Or do I keep quiet? I can't see how such a relationship could possibly have a happy ending for her. But if I don't share my feelings, am I in effect denying her Principality? Am I not making a decision on her behalf without her knowing that a situation that might require a decision by her even exists? If I did that, would I not be violating my belief in the importance of Principality for all persons?

"As I said, Gina, I hardly know you, but having met you has given rise to these thoughts. You have brought to the fore things I need to think about to clarify the course of the rest of my life. So that is the long explanation for why I offered to buy a computer for you. It is in gratitude for your having, inadvertently and without realizing it, helped me to think more clearly about the rest of my life."

Gina was silent when I finished. When she eventually spoke, she said, "I am deeply humbled and, yes, flattered by all of this, Jubal. I think I should not say anything more now. I'll keep the rest of my thoughts on this to myself." She stood up and I did, too. We said our goodbyes and walked separately to our cars.

26

Back home, I intended to look into the events of September 11, 2001, as Russell as suggested.

But something was at the back of my mind that I couldn't place. I thought it might be the words of warning through which several past presidents had tried to alert us to potential dangers. Thinking that was the case I assembled warnings from Truman and Eisenhower. Eisenhower, I knew, in his Farewell Address on January 17, 1961, had tried to warn the country about the dangers that arose when government power and corporate power merged, particularly when combined with the power of the military. "In the councils of government," he'd stated, "we must guard against the acquisition of unwarranted influence, whether sought or unsought, by the Military-Industrial Complex. The potential for the disastrous rise of misplaced power exists and will persist. We must never let the weight of this

Alerts and Warnings from Harry S. Truman

"Once a government is committed to the principle of silencing the voice of opposition, it has only one way to go, and that is down the path of increasingly repressive measures, until it becomes a source of terror to all its citizens and creates a country where everyone lives in fear. We must, therefore, be on our guard against extremists who urge us to adopt police state measures. Such persons advocate breaking down the guarantees of the Bill of Rights in order to get at the Communists. They forget that if the Bill of Rights were to be broken down, all groups, even the most conservative, would be in danger from the arbitrary power of government."

August 8. 1950
Special Message to the
Congress on the Internal
Security of the United States.

"I think [the creation of the CIA] was a mistake. And if I'd known what was going to happen, I never would have done it. . . . Now, as nearly as I can make out, those fellows in the CIA don't just report on wars and the like, they go out and make their own, and there's nobody to keep track of what they're up to. They spend billions of dollars on stirring up trouble so they'll have something to report on. . . . It's become a government all of its own and all secret. They don't have to account to anybody. That's a very dangerous thing in a democratic society, and it's got to be put a stop to. The people have got a right to know what those birds are up to. . . . And when you can't do any housecleaning because everything that goes on is a damn secret, why, then we're on our way to something the Founding Fathers didn't have in mind. Secrecy and a free, democratic government don't mix. . . . And if what happened at the Bay of Pigs doesn't prove that, I don't know what does. You have got to keep an eye on the military at all times, and it doesn't matter whether it's the birds in the Pentagon or the birds in the CIA."

Quoted in Merle Miller,
Plain Speaking (1974), p. 285.

combination endanger our liberties or democratic processes. We should take nothing for granted. Only an alert and knowledgeable citizenry can compel the proper meshing of the huge industrial and military machinery of defense with our peaceful methods and goals, so that security and liberty may prosper together."

Truman had issued similar warnings on at least two occasions, in addition to the piece he'd placed in *The Washington Post* on December 22, 1963. [Editor: see text box.]

That wasn't it, though. Then, reading through the full text of Eisenhower's Farewell Speech, I realized what it was. My comments to Russell about Eisenhower had sold him short. I was more than impressed—I was moved—by his farewell remarks. Rarely had I read a statement of more wisdom, probity and love for our country and people. Rarely had I seen a clearer statement of the country's successes combined with such astute recognition of the dangers it faced even at that moment when its power and prestige were unrivaled.

I printed out the entire speech and made a note to find a frame suitable for a document of its length. I wanted to have Eisenhower's words of insight and wisdom readily available to read, ponder, and serve as a source of guidance and inspiration in the years to come.

27

A few days later I followed up on Russell's suggestion and turned to examining the events of September 11, 2001. I did so with some reluctance because I wanted to get back to my investigations into the lives and writings of Aldous Huxley, C. S. Lewis and John F. Kennedy (apart from the assassination).

I was also averse even to looking into the issue because I suspected how painful doing so could be. With Kennedy's assassination, I'd had the alternate story provided by Vermont Royster that had helped ease my way into the subject. With September 11 I had no such alternate theory. It was either 19 Muslims hijacked planes and crashed them into buildings, or they didn't. That story was bad enough, but any alternative, whatever it might be, had at the time of the attacks been unthinkable. Literally unthinkable.

I remembered that on September 11 I wondered what had happened to the FAA, which I knew should have had fighter planes in the air alongside the hijacked planes. I wondered why none of the eight pilots had punched in the four-digit code to alert air traffic control that a hijacking was in progress. I wondered how the terrorists got into the cockpits. I wondered how the towers could possibly have fallen down into their own footprints when the damage had occurred on only one side. I didn't have answers, and news broadcasts didn't provide any. Eventually I turned away from these questions, as work and family beckoned.

What was different now was the heightened degree of skepticism with which I approached official stories due to my recognition of the importance of Principality and from what I'd learned about Kennedy's assassination. It was with these two thoughts in mind that I turned, finally, to look into the events of September 11.

Russell had seemed to hint that the official story might not be correct, just as the official account of Lee Harvey Oswald as lone gunman wasn't. I soon came across, in fact, so much information contradicting the official story, from so many angles, that I was entirely overwhelmed by it all.

I found that soon after September 11, 2001, a 9/11 Truth Movement had arisen that I'd been entirely unaware of. Professionals in many fields had formed their own organizations to examine how findings in their areas of expertise showed that the events of that day could not have unfolded the way the official account stated. Among those organizations were:

Actors and Artists for 9/11 Truth
Air Traffic Controllers for 9/11 Truth
Architects and Engineers for 9/11 Truth
Firefighters for 9/11 Truth
Intelligence Officers for 9/11 Truth
Journalists for 9/11 Truth
Lawyers' Committee for 9/11 Inquiry

Lawyers for 9/11 Truth
Medical Professionals for 9/11 Truth
Military Officers for 9/11 Truth
Muslim-Jewish-Christian Alliance for 9/11 Truth
Pilots for 9/11 Truth
Political Leaders for 9/11 Truth
Religious Leaders for 9/11 Truth
Scholars for 9/11 Truth
Scientists for 9/11 Truth
Veterans for 9/11 Truth

Adding to my confusion, findings in the various organizations sometimes conflicted with findings in others, and sometimes professionals in the same organization disagreed with each other.

To try to make sense of it all, I decided to follow the lead of C. S. Lewis. In *Mere Christianity* he'd laid out what all Christians believe. Setting aside the differences in beliefs of individual churches, he sought to identify which beliefs were common to all Christians, whether Catholics, Anglicans, Lutherans, Presbyterians, Methodists or Baptists. I now sought to do something similar with the beliefs of those active in the 9/11 Truth movement.

In organizing my thoughts, I turned first to what the researchers and scholars of the Truth movement had to say about the most visually spectacular event of that day, the destruction of the two World Trade Center towers in New York City. With the evidence they had uncovered and presented, and with my mind now open to considering it, it didn't take long to realize that the official story of the collapse of the towers was definitely wrong. The buildings hadn't simply collapsed because of damage caused by the impacts of the planes and the resulting fires. It seemed much more likely that the towers had been blown apart by multiple powerful explosions occurring within them.

The evidence and reasoning I found most persuasive included the following points:

✦ The buildings fell straight down into their own footprints, something that would have been physically impossible for buildings with asymmetrical damage; that is, with damage on only one part caused by the impact of the plane and the resulting fire.

✦ The tops of the buildings fell at freefall speed, that is, at the speed they would have fallen if there had been nothing beneath them but air, a physical impossibility given the resistance to their descent that would have been caused by the 80 or more stories beneath the points of the planes' impacts.

✦ The towers fell in roughly 10 seconds. But the pancaking theory, the idea that each floor fell because it was hit by the great weight of the floors above it crashing onto it, requires at least 97 seconds because each floor must start the fall over again. It can't begin to fall at the speed the higher floor had reached upon impact with it.

✦ Huge explosions occurred in the basements of the two towers 14 and 17 seconds before the planes hit.[142]

✦ At the moment of collapse, the massive explosions that occurred near the floors where the planes had hit created the appearance that the collapses and "pancaking" had begun, yet those explosions occurred several floors below where the impacts had occurred and where the fires had been the worst.[143]

✦ The top block of the south tower—the 25 or so floors above where the plane had hit, fell sideways at an angle of 23 degrees, not straight down, making the "pancaking" theory for that tower impossible. That block should have continued tipping in the same direction, landing on the street or a neighboring building. That didn't happen. [Editor: see photo on back cover.]

✦ Huge girders weighing hundreds of tons each had been ejected outward horizontally up to 400 feet at great speed. That could not have occurred if the buildings had simply collapsed.

The manner in which the towers collapsed was characteristic of controlled demolitions; that is, of buildings brought down in a controlled and deliberate manner by explosives planted inside them. Newscasters, CBS's anchor Dan Rather among them, commented during their live broadcasts that the collapses appeared to resemble controlled demolitions.

9/11 Truth scholars, I learned, had uncovered many other reasons for concluding that the buildings had been brought down by explosives. Here are some of them:

✦ The fires resulting from the plane impacts could not have caused the destruction of the buildings. The melting point of steel is 1,538 degrees Celsius (2,800 degreed Fahrenheit). The maximum temperature that can be achieved with jet fuel is 825 degrees C. (1,517 degrees F.), and in the conditions in existence in those buildings would not have exceeded 360 C. Furthermore, steel is an effective transmitter of heat; heat applied at any point on a steel beam would have dissipated as it spread throughout the beam.

✦ Hundreds of people reported hearing, seeing, or feeling explosions within the buildings. Fox 5 News, a New York channel, had broadcast a video showing "a large white cloud billowing out near the base of the South Tower" with the reporter's comment that 'There is an explosion at the base of the building . . . white smoke from the bottom . . . something has happened at the base of the building. . . . then, another explosion.'"[144]

✦ Videos captured squibs, forceful outward blasts that are characteristic of controlled demolitions occurring on floors well below the level of the planes' impacts and level of collapse.

✦ The massive steel supports that survived the destruction of the towers show evidence of having been cut, and cut at a diagonal, which would facilitate the buildings' collapses.

✦ The molten steel on the ends of some beams was still there, still molten, several months after September 11.

✦ Nano thermite, a high-powered military grade explosive capable of cutting through thick steel beams, was found at the site and in the dust cloud.

I also came across these follow-ups indicating controlled demolition:

✦ The massive steel supports had been cut during the "collapse" in just the right lengths to be most easily hauled away in trucks.

✦ The steel beans had been taken away and sold for scrap in Asia before they could be examined by investigators.

✦ Never before or since have modern steel-structured high-rise buildings collapsed, not even those hit by planes or those that had fires far more extensive and long-lasting than those on September 11.

✦ No change has been made to building codes to reflect the new knowledge that modern high-rise buildings could collapse because of fire.

Taken *en masse*, this evidence rose to the level of proof that the towers had not been destroyed by the impacts of planes and fires. Given that the hijackers could not have planted explosives in the buildings, the official story must be wrong about both the manner in which the buildings had been destroyed and who did it.

While absorbing all this information, I came across a photo of the "collapse" of the north tower—the tower that had been hit first but was the second to fall. Seeing it removed any remaining doubts I had. I was now convinced that the buildings had been brought down by explosives that had been pre-positioned within the buildings. [Editor's note: That photo, which had been stuck inside the MS., is reproduced on the cover of this book.]

I was amazed at how easily the official story had fallen apart now that I was looking at it dispassionately, separated by 18 years from the initial visceral impact that TV news reports had had on me. Suddenly I was angry—at myself for having allowed myself to be duped, then at the dupers for having duped me. Then I was angry at the perpetrators for what they'd done to the psych of the American people. And then for the murders they'd committed and the harm they'd inflicted on so many people who had survived.

Then I was angry at them for the harmful actions taken after that day justified by the official story: by the wars that have killed more than two million people and turned tens of millions more into refugees., and by the stream of legislation undermining the civil liberties of all Americans.

I hadn't yet examined other aspects of the events of that day, including the attack on the Pentagon or matters related to the planes and the hijackers. Before doing that, I was eager to share what I'd learned with others. I wrote up a short summary of what I'd found, and emailed it, along with the photo of the north tower being blown apart from inside, to family and friends scattered around the country. I asked them to look at the photo before reading my summary, and to immediately state out loud what they saw in front of their eyes, without taking time to consciously recognize the picture and recall what they'd been told it is of.

I also sent the summary and photo to selected former Foreign Service colleagues, most of whom were still on active diplomatic duty. I most urgently wanted to discuss what I'd found with Russell Fletcher, but he was out of town, returning only several days later. We agreed to meet for lunch the day after his return.

28

By the following morning, nearly 24 hours after I'd sent out the messages, I'd received only a few responses. None from anyone in my family, and none from former colleagues who were still on active duty, who had probably written me off as a crazy retiree with too much time on his hands. From other retirees I got a few responses, most stating that it was the tower collapsing. Only two (out of twelve) agreed that the tower was exploding from within, something they had already concluded.

So, this attempt at long distance messaging had opened no eyes. No one so far had been willing to consider the evidence in the photograph and my summary. Perhaps they believed they already knew what the photo showed, so saw no point in looking at my summary or considering the evidence in it.

Maybe I'd get a different response if I showed the photo to others in person. The trouble was that after having lived abroad for so many years I didn't know many people living in the Raleigh area. I didn't want to show it to the book club. We had a good dynamic in our discussions that I didn't want upset. Same with the Filipino community that I was now known to. I printed out a few copies, though, to be prepared if I should meet appropriate people to show them to.

Considering all this gave me a new angle from which to view Principality. I already knew that it wasn't enough to be the decision maker, that I had to make informed decisions. The new angle was that becoming informed meant not only seeking out information and context for the decisions to be made, but also rethinking what I already knew. It required believing the testimony of my own eyes over existing theories, expectations and beliefs. It meant re-evaluating them. That's at least as important as gathering new information.

29

Needing a break, I went out for a haircut at a new salon near my house, Deeza's Hair Care. My cutter was Deeza Jackson, not only owner of the salon but also possessor of one of the most dynamic personalities I'd met in years. While cutting my hair she explained that she'd worked for chain salons for two decades, but now, with three hungry cubs at home, she needed an income higher than a mere salary. To me, cubs usually refers to bear cubs, and I laughed as I pointed out to her that "bear" rhymes with "hair" and "care."

"You got that right, Hon. You're the first person to notice that. I nearly named the place Bear's Hair Care because Bear is a nickname of mine."

"Isn't opening your own place risky?" I asked. I'd touched a nerve, and she stepped back a step and looked at me. "Honey, I think about that all day long. I had to use all my savings to get the place open. My ex helped some, but not much. The previous salon in this location had hired unskilled cutters, and as a result got a bad reputation and went out of business. I hire only those I have trained or worked with in the past, so know they can do a good job. One challenge has been alerting people to the new ownership."

She nodded in the direction of the large banner on the window inviting those shopping at stores nearby to give her new salon a try.

"How old are your bear cubs?" I asked.

She again took a step back and looked at me before answering. I could see that this haircut was going to take quite a while, because Deeza couldn't seem to cut hair and talk at the same time, and she sure liked to talk.

Eventually the cutting came to an end. She'd done a great job, and I planned to return. As I was paying, I got the idea of showing her the photo of the "collapse" of the north tower and asking her what she saw in it.

"That a building exploding. There must be bombs inside," she said after a quick glance. "But wait a minute." She picked up the photo and held it at arms' length as she examined it. Isn't that one of them towers in New York, the ones hit by planes on September 11? That's a photo of the collapse caused by the plane crash."

"Look again, Deeza," I said, "If you didn't know what building it was, would you say it was a collapse or an explosion?"

She returned to her first impression. "There's explosions occurring inside the buildings. You can see that parts of it are being blasted not just out, but up."

"You've made my day, Deeza. That exactly what I see, too."

As I left, I was relieved she hadn't called me a "conspiracy theorist." I was glad that she accepted the evidence of her own eyes. I wondered how many others I intended to show the photo to would do the same.

30

Back home, I recalled that a third World Trade Center building, WTC 7, had also collapsed on September 11. Though small in comparison with the towers, it was huge compared to most other buildings. At 47 stories, it would have been the largest building in most American cities. It was also one of the most important buildings in New York, housing important offices of the Export-Import Bank, the U.S. Secret Service, the

Securities and Exchange Commission, the IRS and the Department of Defense.

What was so unusual about WTC 7's collapse, I learned, was that it hadn't been struck by a plane and that it was located 355 feet from the closest of the two towers. The fires that had developed on a few floors were minor and apparently out long before the building collapsed. It was and still is the only modern steel-framed high-rise building in history to have collapsed solely because of fire.

When it collapsed, at 5:20 p.m., it fell straight down into its own footprint and it fell as freefall speed; that is, at the same speed a billiard ball dropped from the top of the building would fall if there was nothing under it to slow it down. Yet the top floor of the building had 46 floors below it, all of which suggests, nay, requires, controlled demolition to explain the collapse.

Other factors I came across supporting that idea as the cause of WTC 7's collapse were:

✦ The owner, Larry Silverstein, later recalled in an interview that he'd told others to "pull it," a term used in the field of controlled demolition to give final clearance to launch the demolition.

✦ Police cleared the area in advance and told people that the building would come down.

✦ People in the area heard a countdown on police radios that reached zero just before the collapse occurred.

✦ The collapse was announced on TV news programs before it actually occurred.

✦ The collapse began at the bottom, not at the point in the middle of the building where minor fires had developed.

✦ Explosions had occurred in the basement of the building in the morning of September 11, and then throughout the building just before the collapse.

"How likely is it that all supporting structures on a given floor will fail at exactly the same time?" physicist Judy Wood asked in her examination of WTC 7. "What is the likelihood that supporting structures on every floor would fail at exactly the same time and that these failures would progress through every floor with perfect symmetry?"[145]

Those are good questions, and the only possible answer, I saw, was that it's so unlikely as to be impossible without controlled demolition.

I'd learned that it would have taken months of careful study of the architectural plans to design the demolition of a building that large—to determine how much explosive would be needed, exactly where it should be placed and the exact order in which each explosive device should be denotated—so that it would collapse at freefall speed into its own footprint.

It would also have taken weeks to place the explosives in just the right spots. WTC 7 could not have been rigged for controlled demolition in only a few hours even if all the planning had been completed in advance. Ergo, the explosives had to have been planted in the building before September 11. At this point I learned that all three buildings that were destroyed—WTC 1, 2 and 7—had been evacuated for fire drills, with all power turned off, several times during the weeks before September 11, something that had never happened before.

The "collapse" of WTC 7—at freefall speed into its own footprint—was clear evidence that the official story was wrong. Even to the media, the "collapse" appeared to be the result of controlled demolition. As Dan Rather commented live on the air, "For the third time today, it's reminiscent of those pictures we've all seen too much on television before when a building was deliberately destroyed by well-placed dynamite to knock it down."[146]

The obvious controlled demolition of the building was not just evidence, but proof, to me, at least, that the events of September 11 were an inside job; that mass murder had been committed by people with access to the interiors of all three buildings. Evidence rising to the level of proof has been in plain sight for all to see for the last 18 years, yet very few had recognized it.

After a four-year study of the collapse of WTC 7, a research team at the University of Alaska's Department of Civil and Environmental Engineering concluded that "fire did not cause the collapse of WTC 7 on 9/11, con-trary to the conclusions of NIST and private engi-neering firms that studied the collapse."[147] The study's secondary conclu-sion was that "the collapse of WTC 7 was a global failure involving the near-simultaneous failure of every column in the building." The report didn't say so, but the only way to achieve the near-simultaneous failure of every column in the building is through con-trolled demolition.

The media, I noted, ignored the Report, just as it had mostly ignored the destruction of the building itself.

Image 9. The collapse of WTC 7 into its own footprint at nearly freefall speed at 5:20 p.m. on September 11.

31

It had been less than a week since I'd seen Gina, but it seemed like a long time, given all the ground covered in my September 11 research since then.

I headed over to WORDS, ostensibly to pick up any new financial docs, but really to try to gauge Gina's feelings about what I'd told her during our last conversation. I feared that she'd been upset when we parted.

When I knocked on the open door of her office at the rear left of the studio, she stood up immediately, gave a short cry and smiled. She came over to me quickly and said "I must thank you again for the computer, Jubal. I've never bought one in the United States before and felt nervous and excited at the same time. I researched the type of computer with specs appropriate for this business, and wanted to get it in pink, because that's the color of the feeling I have when I think about this present from you. A computer, even if used also in a business, is a very personal machine, so I want it to have that color."

A pink computer? That caught me by surprise, and I laughed. Then I remembered that my daughter's computer is also pink.

"Here it is," she said, motioning toward the pink rectangle on her desk. It took several days for me to get this model with this color. It's only just arrived. I am truly happy and grateful to get this as this is one of the best laptops in the market right now. It's not super pink but rose gold, and it really looks gorgeous. Some people buy expensive stuff through installments or credit cards, but I just don't do that, I always wait and save money until I can afford what I want. But you have saved me from the agony of waiting for so long and tightening my budget; if not for you it would have been a long time before I'd have been able to replace my laptop, so thank you again so much."

"I'm relieved that you understand my motives, and that the gift of the computer hasn't made you uneasy," I replied. "So rarely do I meet people who value books and literature and whose sensibilities appear similar to my own in important ways, that when I do I want to help them in any way I can, now that I'm in a position to do so."

Gina nodded, then said, "I am not the most articulate person, but I hope you feel my gratitude. I am confident that your gift comes from genuine kindness and nothing of another sort as most people might think. I didn't feel skeptical about receiving it because my guts tell me that the person who bought me the gift is a genuinely nice person. Thus, I have nothing to worry about.

"Though I know lots of people here in the United States, my walls are incredibly high, in part for reasons I have already told you about. My inner circle is extremely circumscribed as I am very selective of the kind of people I let into my life. Not because I have trust issues. In fact, I don't. I just know that not everyone deserves to see certain parts of ourselves. That's why it makes me happy and grateful meeting people like you who give me your genuine trust and share with me what they are doing that they are passionate about."

What she said next caught me by surprise. "It sounds like you live in your mind. Your passions are internal."

I suddenly realized that that was true. Many of my connections to the rest of the world were gone. My career had reached its natural end, and Diana had reached her end, too, whether natural or unnatural I didn't know. My kids didn't need me as they once had. Although I had joined Gina's book club and formed a friendship with her and renewed by friendship with Russell Fletcher, she was right. My passions are internal. I was mostly absorbed in my literary and scholarly projects, with ideas in my mind.

I considered further that I was doing exactly what I wanted to be doing at this point in my life. I needed down time to adjust to the ending of my career and Diana's death. I'd often heard it said by new retirees from demanding careers that it took a full year to adjust to the new, less pressure-filled, way of life. Perhaps my activities now were my way of making that adjustment.

"I do the same," Gina continued, without having waited for a response from me. "I am a compulsive writer, but I don't write fiction, I write poetry and prose poems. I always carry a tiny notebook and a pen even if I am just going to the supermarket or while doing my workout at the gym. Because of my synesthesia, my head runs like a red Maserati Ghibli all the time. I guess not only my head but my life as well, it's always upbeat and never boring. It moves so quickly with different branches, each with different leaves and colors that I need to write it down quickly while it flowers to avoid missing the momentum."

I laughed at that. "I have to laugh to myself whenever I see that you carrying that tiny notebook and pen to capture your flashes of inspiration," I said. "I've done the same thing since age eighteen! We are kindred spirits!"

"In fact," Gina said, again continuing to talk at full speed, hardly noticing that I'd said anything, "when I thought about the computer and about things you have said to me recently, when I was at home a John Mayer song called "Carry me away" played in my head. Perhaps because of the surreal sound of that song, or perhaps I am just a weird person. What you have shared also made me think about aging. I know it's something that is bound to come to me too, but it is still too far away from me to even understand what it means. I just hope that my existence won't cause you any inconvenience or further dilemmas while having this kind and cordial friendship."

I'd already learned that when Gina was on a roll it was best just to let her talk. Besides, I was learning a lot about her.

"About the dilemma of being a principal or agent," she continued, "I don't know much about life for sure, but I think even if we make decisions for other people, that will never make us a Principal over them. Their response to our decisions will still be theirs. Our actions will still be a reflection of us and not of them."

"Yes, that's true," I said quickly, when she paused to take a breath. "I've never heard of John Mayer before," I added, while pulling out of my shirt pocket a small note pad to jot down a reminder to find him on YouTube. I also jotted down "synesthesia," to remind myself to find out more about this condition that Gina said she had, apparently something about feeling colors or connecting colors to things not usually associated with them.

While I was writing Gina said, "I want to send money to The Philippines so that my family back home can have a prosperous visperas and Media Noche.

"What is Media Noche?" I asked. Today she had mentioned

many things I'd never heard of.

"The New Year's Eve feast in The Philippines."

I thought for a moment, then said, "I'd like to make a contribution to the feast, if you'd let me."

"Nooooo!" she said without hesitation. "You have already done so much by giving me the computer. I can't let you do any more. Besides, not having to buy a computer means that I have a bit of money left that I can send home to my family. So you are already contributing to it."

I accepted that and made another note to learn more about visperas and Media Noche.

Then, with no introduction or context, I slid the photo of the destruction of the north tower across the desk toward her, the same photo that I'd shown to Deeza and sent to family and friends. "What do you see in this photograph, Gina?" Given her age—she was not quite seven years old on September 11, 2001—and her nationality, born as she was nearly halfway around the globe—I expected that she'd be more able to view the photo without all the emotional baggage that an American would bring to it.

That was almost the case. She recognized right off that it was a photo of one of the towers in New York, but also said that the building was clearly being destroyed by explosives inside it. She went on to comment on what a terrible event that was, and on the effect that watching the TV on that day had had on her as a child.

We talked a bit more and then I edged out. I had suddenly become uneasy without being able to pinpoint any reason for feeling that way. I needed to go home, follow up on the notes I'd jotted down, and think about the things Gina had told me.

32

Returning home, I saw a delivery man leaving an amazon box on the porch. It contained Dr. Judy Wood's *Where Did the Towers Go? Evidence of Directed Free-Energy Technology on 9/11*, which I had seen many references to. Knowing that Dr. Wood held a Ph.D. in Materials Engineering Science, I was eager to see her take on what had happened on September 11.

Skimming through it, I was surprised to learn that in addition to WTC 1, 2 and 7, four additional buildings in New York had been totally destroyed or almost totally destroyed on September 11 even though they hadn't been struck by planes. I'd never heard of this before. They were WTC 3, 4, 5 and 6. In fact, every building with a prefix of WTC was destroyed on that day, and only buildings with a prefix of WTC were destroyed. Nearby buildings suffered surprisingly little collateral damage. That's quite odd, I thought, looking at a map and noting that several buildings without WTC addresses were closer to the twin towers than several buildings with WTC addresses.[148]

WTC 3, the Marriot Hotel, was completely gone, except for a few stories at the southern end. The main part of Building 4 was also nearly gone, with only the north wing still standing. Oddest of all were Buildings 5 and 6, which had multiple circular holes in them. Wood called these holes "mysterious," and noted that

Image 10. Ariel view of the WTC complex showing that although all seven WTC buildings were destroyed, the surrounding buildings suffered only minor damage. Note also the small amount of debris remaining in the footprint of the two 110-story towers.

"because of the verticality of these holes, they could not have been caused by conventional explosives. WTC 6, an eight-story building, lost about half of its volume and yet there was remarkably little debris left at the bottom of the building. No one has attempted to explain these mysterious holes."[149] On seeing the photos in her book, my first thought was that the holes had been caused by giant lasers from satellites high up in the atmosphere.

An explosion at WTC 6 had "hurled gas and debris 170 meters high,"[150] I learned. CNN had filmed smoke rising up from street level near the base of the building at 9:40 a.m., one minute after the plane had struck the south tower, yet WTC 6 was on the far side of the north tower, which was between the two. Even odder, the major explosion in the building, the one that destroyed the center, occurred at exactly the same moment that the south tower collapsed. So what had caused it? What could have destroyed the inner part of WTC 6 so completely while leaving the outer parts still standing? Search as I might, I couldn't find an explanation anywhere.

I was then surprised to learn from Wood that only a small

Image 11. Aerial view of the destruction of the inner part of WTC 6.

fraction of debris from WTC 1, 2 and 7 remained at the end of the day on September 11. What happened to the massive steel supports near the center of the towers? They should have remained standing even if the rest of the buildings had collapsed around them. What had happened to the rest of the building materials, including an estimated 43,600 windows, 600,000 square feet of glass, 200,000 tons of structural steel, 5,000,000 square feet of gypsum, 6 acres of marble one yard deep, and 425,000 cubic yards of concrete? These building materials from the two towers alone totaled more than 1,000,000 tons and should have resulted in rubble 1,200 feet high.[151]

And where were the 45,000 filing cabinets, 30,000 computers, and tens of thousands of desks, phones, printers, ceramic toilets and sinks and other office equipment and facilities? Of all that equipment only one filing cabinet had been found, and it was crumpled into a ball a fraction of its former size.[152] If the towers had merely collapsed, all of these items should have been found in the rubble.

So where did the buildings and office equipment go? Wood had the answer. They'd been turned into dust, a transformation she called dustification. "The World Trade Center (WTC) towers did not 'collapse' on 9/11/01," she explained. "They were already turned to dust before a gravity-driven collapse was a possibility."[153] "The WTC towers did not collapse from fire, nor did they collapse from 'bombs in the buildings' (or conventional controlled demolition)," she reiterated. "The majority of the building mass did not fall to the ground, as evidenced by the seismic data. Nearly all of each tower was turned to dust in mid-air and either floated to the ground or blew away. The majority of what remained of the towers was paper and dust. A gravity collapse (with or without bombs in the building) cannot turn a building into powder in mid-air."[154]

Many of those present at the site on September 11 made the same observation. "As soon as the air began to clear," one said, "we could see that very little of the material of the buildings had been left behind. News reporters began to ask, "Where did the towers go?" [155] ABC news anchors Peter Jennings and George

Image 12. Dust from WTC 1 rolls through lower Manhattan.

Stephanopoulos, Wood noted, both commented on the lack of debris and wondered where the towers had gone. ABC reporter Robert Krulwich "described the solid material of the building as having turned to dust." Yet such observations, like those comparing the towers' collapses to controlled demolition, vanished from the airwaves after that first day.

One of the most astonishing images from September 11 is of the one remaining steel core column from WTC 1, which was

Image 13. Steel core column from WTC 1 disintegrating into steel dust.

captured on film disintegrating into steel dust. [See image 13.]

Also puzzling was the motion of the top 22 or so floors of WTC 2, the south tower (the first hit but the second to fall), which toppled over as a block at a 23-degree angle. [Editor's note: See photo on back cover.] Per the law of momentum, the toppling block should have continued to topple in the same direction, eventually landing on top of neighboring buildings. Yet, as Wood documented, there was very little collateral damage to buildings surrounding the WTC site. The block, she showed, like much of the rest of the building soon after, somehow turned to dust before it hit the ground.[156]

The block appeared to dissolve "from the bottom up." The bulges of dust from the bottom of it and from the top of the other 80 floors of the tower, in Wood's description, "protrude and blossom," eventually coalescing "into one large bulge surrounding the building almost like a giant snowball. . . . At this point, it appears that the top two thirds of the building have turned into a huge ball of dust, but the lower third of the building is still intact."[157] Since the top two-thirds of the building had turned to dust, pancaking cannot be cited as the cause of the collapse of the lowest third of the south tower.

⚘ 33 ⚘

As if all that hadn't been enough to convince me that something strange had happened, Judy Wood identified several additional anomalies that the official story cannot explain, including:

✦ The seismic impact measured that day was far less than would have been expected had 1,000,000 tons of material crashed to earth in only 10 seconds.

✦ More than 1,400 cars, some of them parked up to 1.5 miles from WTC 1 and 2, were toasted in bizarre ways.[158] Although the cars burned, paper near them didn't. Some cars wilted as if subjected to high heat, yet their plastic trim remained unaffected. Others were burned and melted on the inside but were mostly untouched on the outside. Still others were reported to have burst into flames through no apparent cause, while others were only partially burned, with the rest undamaged. Plastic and rubber on the cars often did not burn or melt, and street signs and trees next to the cars didn't burn.[159] [Editor's note: Similar phenomenon was observed after the fire that destroyed the town of Lahaina on the island of Maui, Hawaii, on August 8, 2023.]

✦ The presence of so much paper amid the dust was puzzling. "How do we account for the presence of so much paper when nearly everything else was turned to dust?" Wood asked. "What can turn a 110-story building into powder in mid-air,"[160] yet leave paper untouched?

✦ Changes in the earth's magnetic field on September 11 were also unexplained. "The magnetometer readings from the six different research stations in northern Alaska reveal anomalous changes in the Earth's magnetic field at the exact moments that key events were taking place in New York City on 9/11," Wood noted. "Until about twenty minutes before the first two events—those being the creating of the holes in WTC 1 and 2—values hovered close to the average. And then they revealed changes."[161]

Image 14. An ambulance parked near the WTC complex that burned and melted inside but was hardly touched outside.

These and other factors convinced me that the buildings hadn't been destroyed by traditional controlled demolition techniques, which would have merely broken them into smaller pieces that would then have fallen to the ground, creating a pile of rubble 1,200 feet high. Yet there were no mountains of smaller pieces of rubble, just as there were no piles of pancaked floors. Instead, the buildings had been turned into dust by some unknown force that had also caused cars to spontaneously burst into flames and had disrupted the earth's magnetic field.

This multi-faceted evidence, Wood showed, pointed toward one conclusion. "All of these descriptions are similar to the types of effects one would be experiencing in an energy field, such as a microwave field." A large microwave field "would explain why so much paper was not catching fire in the close vicinity of other burning debris, for that debris is literally—like the chicken on the paper plate in your microwave oven—being cooked from the inside out. Perhaps the outer aluminum cladding on the towers might itself have acted as a kind of 'microwave oven grating' to keep whatever kind of energy it was *locked inside of it* and building up an energy field, a kind of standing wave, that could—literally—turn the buildings to powder."[162] Only a large energy field could have produced "the micron-sized dust particles that were created on 9/11. The sheer amount of dust and the unusual behavior of that dust attest to the fact that no model of controlled demolition, thermite, or burning airplane fuel was at work in the destruction of the WTC towers.[163]

With the use of directed free-energy weapons or microwave energy on such a large scale, Wood wrote, "we stand at the dawn of an entirely new age. By all the evidence, man has in his hands a method of disrupting the molecular basis for matter."[164] As intriguing as the evidence pointing to this idea is, Wood hadn't explained how such forces had been harnessed and channeled into the buildings. Where was the equipment capable of generating such power located? Within the towers themselves? In a satellite in space that directed the energy it produced to the buildings in the form of a laser? She hadn't provided answers. I hadn't ruled out the idea of directed energy or microwave technology as the force that turned the buildings into dust, but I hadn't accepted it, either.

34

It was at this point—after I'd already accepted that the towers and other buildings had been turned to dust rather than pancaking downward with each floor largely intact or falling to the ground in smaller pieces after having been blown apart in a controlled demolition—that I came across the single most convincing item I'd yet seen. The new piece of evidence was a video of the destruction of the north tower accompanied by commentary by David Chandler.[165] If a picture is worth a thousand words, a video—this video, at least—must be worth a million.

Chandler guided viewers' attention to the "rapid sequence of explosive ejections of material," to "explosions that are not isolated and few" but are "continuous and widespread" and that "move progressively down the faces of the building, keeping pace with the falling debris." Most important to note, he pointed out, is that the "pile driver" effect resulting from upper floors collapsing onto and crushing lower floors didn't take place. "There is nothing above the ring of explosions except for a fountain of debris. . . . It does not appear that the building is being crushed by anything. The waves of destruction and explosive ejections of material are occurring over a wide zone that continues all the way to the top of what remains of the building."

I watched this video many times, each time observing that the upper floors of the building simply vanished. They were turned into dust and debris. There was no pile driver effect at all visible in the video, no pancaking effect as upper floors fell onto those below them. The official explanation for the "collapse" of the building couldn't possibly be correct. My own eyes told me so.

This video, together with the information Judy Wood provided on the same point already noted, shows conclusively—proves—that the two towers in New York had not, in fact, been blown apart by explosives planted inside them. I had misinterpreted the photo that I'd shown to others and sent out by email. Although many others had seen in it evidence of the building collapsing and I'd seen in it evidence of the building being exploded from within, we were all wrong.

The collapse idea was completely wrong. The explosion idea was not entirely wrong, but incomplete. There were indeed explosions, the force of which did indeed expel girders at high speed, but that was only a side effect. The main effect of whatever force was used was to turn the buildings—the steel core columns, the steel girders, the cement, the ceramic sinks and all other materials except paper—into dust, resulting in minimal debris on the ground and the existence of the huge cloud of dust that Judy Wood documented.

It was beyond puzzling that the mainstream media, and the vast majority of the American people, remained uninterested in all these facts and factors. I needed to discuss them with Russell

Image 15. An image from David Chandler's video, "North Tower Exploding." Note the three horizontal white lines of smoke in the center of the image, indicating explosions on three floor well below the top of the building and below the cloud of dust and debris. The video, which shows them even more clearly, can be viewed on the main page of Architects & Engineers for 9/11 Truth, at www.ae911truth.org.

Fletcher and looked forward to meeting him for lunch the next day.

❦ 35 ❦

"I've again stopped work on my Huxley-Kennedy-Lewis project," I told Russell as soon as we were seated, "this time to focus on September 11."

"Once I started examining things with an open mind, it didn't take long to see that the idea that 19 Arab men with boxcutters caused all this mayhem was utterly preposterous. I've now read a dozen books and many articles, and watched half a dozen videos. Some are of talks given by David Ray Griffin. He's very impressive as he lays out what really happened and didn't happen. I've had to make many pages of notes to keep it all straight in my head."

"I see you've become infected with the 9/11 bug, Jubal," Russell said with a rueful smile the first time I paused to take a breath. "I'm almost sorry I brought up September 11 with you."

"But Russell," I began again, hardly hearing what he'd said, "although the Truth researchers all are in agreement that the towers didn't collapse because of the impact of the planes or the fires, they disagree among themselves as to how the towers could have been destroyed and who did it.

"I agree with them that the impacts of the planes and the minor internal fires that resulted weren't the causes of the destruction of the towers, but only the cover story. After all, the jet fuel largely burned off in that huge fireball outside the building in less than one minute. And gasoline in our cars burns far hotter than the kerosene used as fuel in planes, yet our cars' engines don't melt or soften. The steel in the towers, even if the concrete reinforcement had been broken off, wouldn't either. No modern high-rise tower has ever been brought down by fire, not even by massive fires that lasted for several days.

"I'm also convinced now that the towers weren't brought brought down in floor-size pancakes or in the small chunks that would have resulted from ordinary controlled demolition. They were largely turned into dust, which settled over the following days and weeks. But what power could have turned more than one million tons of construction materials, plus all the desks, computers, steel filing cabinets and so on, into dust? Judy Wood presented much evidence pointing toward free-energy technology or a microwave field but didn't provide details about the technology that could have produced it. I don't know what to make of it. What do you think?

Russell thought for a moment before saying, "No question it was a government-run inside operation. A second Pearl Harbor. That's beyond a reasonable doubt. The orthodox view of the 9/11 Truthers is that the controlled demolitions of WTC 1, 2, and 7 were carried out with thermite, or nano thermite. Only thermite or similar substances could cut through steel and produce the tiny iron droplets found in great quantity in the dust cloud. But that can't be the full story.

"As awful as it is to contemplate, the U.S. military demolished the towers with nano-micro nuclear fusion weapons in addition to thermite. Thermite could not have vaporized steel and cement or turned them into that large dust cloud. Alone it could not explain the minimal amount of debris that remained or the structural steel found bent and ripped apart. It could not have produced the radiation detected in the rubble or the fires of 2,000 degrees that burned until early December. Nor could any form of thermite explain the people on the sidewalks who were vaporized in a fireball, or the cars parked blocks away that were set burning or destroyed in a superheated dust cloud."

"I've seen photos of cars burned by weird fires," I said. "Some were parked quite a distance away from the towers, yet they caught fire and burned in strange ways. Some were burned or melted only inside, and paper near the cars didn't catch fire. Plants and flags, too, seem to have been unaffected by the blaze and heat."

"It wasn't just cars," Russell continued. "People were vaporized. One witness observed people engulfed in some sort of fireball and disintegrating. Another turned around for just a moment and saw people vaporized where they were standing. Paper and paper products were undamaged because neutrons go right through them. And uranium and thorium, sure signs of nuclear explosions, were detected in the dust.

"Fourth-generation neutron nano-micro nuclear weapons produce little or no radioactive fallout," he added. "And in any event, the whole area was under tight control, and Geiger Counters that might have measured the degree of radiation at the site were strictly banned. No one who wasn't cleared was allowed onto the site.

"If you've got the stomach for it, Jubal, review Jim Fetzer's *9/11: America Nuked*. Check out the photographs first. You will be shocked! Then, like me, you will probably feel compelled to read about how a 4th-generation deuterium-tritium nano-micro nuclear bomb the size of an orange works and did what it did at the World Trade Center, producing a tritium-deuterium fusion reaction on a nano/micro scale. This is what most likely demolished WTC 1, 2, and 7, not fires or thermite, which could not do the damage seen in Fetzer's photographs."

"Russell, did you ever share these ideas and this information with anyone when you were still an ambassador?"

He laughed, then said, "No. Like you, Jubal, I didn't begin to investigate the issue until after I retired. I had accepted the official story at the time. It was just seared into me. Since retiring twelve years ago, I have mentioned the inconsistencies in the official 9/11 story to other retirees. Most have had the same response—telling me that only conspiracy theorists would spout such nonsense. Only about one out of seven was willing to consider alternative ideas and undertake the sort of research into it that you have.

"The idea that nuclear weapons were used is so explosive that I have steered clear of it and not mentioned it to anyone else that I have discussed 9/11 with. I'll never mention it in the courses I teach at UNC.

"But, as per Rule 9 ("Tell the truth—or, at least, don't lie") in Jordan Peterson's book, *Twelve Rules for Life* that I mentioned to you before, if asked I can't lie. I cannot support the official government version of 9/11. It is a lie. Fires resulting from planes impacting them could not have caused WTC 1 and 2 to collapse. Fires in WTC 7 could not have caused it to collapse eight hours later. If pressed, I would have to say the truth of 9/11 is this: 9/11 was a false-flag, nuclear event, set up to be a second Pearl Harbor. Franklin Roosevelt knew what was coming at Pearl Harbor and withheld warning Admiral Kimmel, Commander in Chief of the Pacific Fleet, thereby sacrificing 3,000 Americans to get the United States into WWII. It was the same scenario on September 11, except that in this case the United States government itself orchestrated the event."

As we parted, Russell gave me a copy of an 84-page article, "Treason: Who Did 9/11 and Why Did They Do It," by Anonymous Patriots.[166]

As I pulled into the driveway back home, I saw several boxes with the amazon.com logo stacked on the porch. I sighed and brightened at the same time. I was already overwhelmed with things to read and ideas to consider, but when it rains, it pours.

Walking to the porch to get the boxes, I reviewed the options for the cause of the destruction of the towers.

There was the government story of planes and fires, which was physically impossible.

There was the nano-thermite explanation that was the consensus view at Architects and Engineers for 9/11 Truth, which I believed to be partially correct but incomplete. There was the directed free-energy or microwave field technology explanation proposed by Judy Wood. And there was the fourth-generation neutron nano-micro nuclear weapons explanation put forth by Jim Fetzer and others that Russell had mentioned.

I suspected that the nuclear explanation was correct, and my suspicion was strengthened later that day when I came across an article by Mark H. Gaffney. In it he cited German physicist Heinz Pommer to the effect that "only the vast energy of a nuke can explain the conversion of hundreds of thousands of tons of concrete and steel into dust. And only a nuke can account for the sudden disintegration of the upper portion of the South Tower (WTC-2) which had tipped at a weird angle and was falling as a unit. And only a nuke can explain the near total absence of ceramic sinks and toilets, filing cabinets, furniture, and human bodies in the wreckage. Almost everything in the towers was vaporized by gamma radiation."[167]

Pommer also showed that "the nuclear reaction progressed over at least an hour, and this would explain a number of anomalies. These include electromagnetic interference of radio and TV transmissions, spontaneous fires in surrounding buildings and in nearby vehicles, the pyroclastic cloud that enveloped lower Manhattan, conspicuous venting of steam from underground sewers, strange rainbow effects and silverfish flashes in video footage, and the like." Perhaps the most conclusive evidence Pommer brought to the table is that "doctors at Mt. Sinai Medical Center reported 'an increased incidence of thyroid cancer among 9/11 rescue workers, . . . the etiology of which remains unclear. . . . Thyroid cancer has been recognized as the tell-tale signature of exposure to nuclear radiation. . . . [The] thyroid cancers are the true smoking gun of 9/11, and a wake-up call."

I saw that proponents of these various explanations were united by two points of overarching importance: Events had not occurred as laid out in the official story, and events could not have happened as they did without orchestration by people high up in the Bush administration and the U.S. military. All else was of secondary importance.

Still, I wanted to understand the details as comprehensively as possible. I could see that the next few weeks if not months would be filled with examining the books, articles, videos and websites that I was sure contained the answers I sought. I'd be as diligent and determined as I had to be to ferret out the explanations I wanted.

Looking at the growing mountain of books and papers and videos I'd amassed, and considering the astonishing probability that the government of the United States had been taken over by terrorists willing to destroy the tallest buildings in the country and kill thousands of people, somehow the Huxley-Kennedy-Lewis project didn't seem so pertinent at the moment. I'd get back to it eventually, I knew, but not in a big way until I had a better grasp of what had happened during the largest terrorist attack in history.

❧ 36 ❧

I astounded myself today. It was a few days before Christmas and my kids were set to arrive tomorrow afternoon, coming in from the different parts of the country where they now lived. Maja Mindanao, the Filipina friend of Gina's who provides tutoring services at WORDS, WORDS, WORDS, made me an offer I couldn't refuse—and I refused it.

I was at a coffee shop near WORDS, between North Raleigh and Morrisville, when Maja appeared out of nowhere and sat down across from me. This was the first time I'd seen her without Gina nearby. She had many surprising things to say, things I got the impression she'd wanted to say for some time.

"You know Gina is a virgin, don't you?" she began. "And determined to remain so until marriage? Even her name announces that."

"*Gina* announces that?" I responded.

"Gina is only a nickname. Her real name is Verginia, which means *virgin* in Tagalog."

That is interesting, I thought, and it reinforces the promise she made to her father and the strictures of traditional Catholic and Filipino cultures.

Maja then let me know that she wasn't, and that she was available, no strings attached. "I want to enjoy my life before settling down," she said, "and I'm not ready to settle down yet. Before I do, I want to know what it's like to be with an older man. A man with experience, a man who knows how to treat a girl right. Not just 'Slam, bam, thank you Ma'am.'"

To my amazement I refused her offer. She's beautiful, I considered, with just the kind of healthful, youthful beauty that makes a man pay attention. Still, I didn't want the complications that would come from "hooking up" with her. She said no strings, but I knew there'd be complications, even if she wasn't Gina's friend. There always are. And I wanted to remain disconnected right now.

Was I being faithful to Gina, I wondered, even though we

were just friends? I couldn't say.

After letting me know she'd like to try an older man, etc., Maja told me something else quite interesting. "You remember that first time you saw us, in Subway?" she asked.

"Oh, you remember that? I wasn't sure you even remembered that encounter or that the man who spoke to Gina was me."

"Believe me, we remembered," she said. "We discussed you afterwards several times before you magically reappeared at the book club. But not at Subway, not that day. There, Gina and I had other matters of immediate importance to deal with."

Here's where she revealed the rather provocative information that "Gina had just been 'let go' by the tutoring company she worked for."

"Really?" I said. "I thought she had her own informal company by that time, that she was tutoring kids on her own."

"She was, sometimes, but her main income still came from her work with that company. It was only after she was let go that she got the idea of formally launching her own tutoring business."

Maja gave me a minute to ponder this information before interrupting my thoughts to say, with a wicked smile, "Don't you want to know why she was let go?"

She answered her own question without waiting for me to respond. "She was fired after she complained to the owner about men touching her in inappropriate ways. But here's the thing: she has a habit of saying the most provocative things to men, and then acting shocked and innocent when they expect things from her that her words had seemed to promise."

"On that occasion, she'd said things to a man, a fellow tutor, which led him to put his hands on her waist and try to kiss her. She went to complain to the owner, and things looked bad for him. But once he explained the way she had provoked him and seemed to invite his advances, all of which she acknowledged, they let her go. This wasn't the first time something like this had happened at that company.

"And," Maja continued, "something similar had happened at

another tutoring company she'd worked for a year earlier, before she graduated. She'd been let go there, too, after similar incidents.

"I know she's tried to provoke you, too," she continued. "But you didn't let her lead you into a trap."

She let that sink in for a moment, then asked. "Are you sure you won't go with me?"

I was sure. I wanted time to think about what all this meant.

It certainly explained some things about Gina that had puzzled me. One being how she handled her sexual impulses while waiting for the ideal suitor to come along.

I now saw that she was caught between her sexual desires and her determination to remain untouched until marriage. I saw that she used her physical attractiveness to try to get men high on her list of suitors to come through with a proposal. She understood, at least to the extent that a virgin could, that men could be manipulated through their sexual desires, that that was perhaps the most vulnerable of their weak points. She used those desires in all their intensity in her efforts to snare a spouse. Once she had identified someone who scored high on her list of criteria, she behaved in such a way as to increase his desire for her. Yet this had backfired, repeatedly. In this day and age, men as attractive as those she wanted don't need marriage for sex. They saw her as promising what others give without marriage, and were puzzled and even angry when she didn't deliver what she so openly promised. She was a tease, and there's nothing men hate more.

Yet I saw her not so much as a tease as being a woman intent on luring a suitor into marriage using all the tools available to her. The vision she had of the kind of fulfilling marriage her parents had had, and her own ardent nature, pushed her to find a spouse with whom she could create such a family of her own. It was such an enchanting goal that surely almost any means to secure it would be justified.

I also realized that if I had been a dozen years younger, I'd have been one of her prey. She'd have deliberately aroused my desires in an effort to provoke a proposal from me. In fact, I was to find out that she'd eventually do just that with me, too, after having "taken it easy on me," for so long, as she would later explain.

37

The next morning, I turned to what had happened at the Pentagon on the morning of September 11. Many of the two dozen or so books I'd already consulted cited the same facts showing that the official story—that American Airlines Flight 77 had crashed into the building—was physically impossible. I jotted down a few of them into my notes.

✦ The hole made in the side of the Pentagon, approximately 9-10 feet high and 13-14 feet wide, was too small for the fuselage, which was 13 feet in diameter.

✦ The tail extended nearly 30 feet above the top of the fuselage, yet the wall above the hole was undamaged until the segment collapsed 20-30 minutes later. [See Image 16.]

✦ The wingspan of AA 77 was 60 feet wider than the section of the wall that collapsed some time after impact, yet there is no sign of impact on either side. There are even unbroken windows to the left of the collapsed segment where the wing would have hit. [See Image 18.]

✦ The plane supposedly hit the Pentagon at near ground level, a physical impossibility. The large engines attached to the wings hang down nine feet below the bottom of the fuselage. If the plane had hit the building near the ground, the engines would have dug holes in the lawn, yet no holes were visible after the "crash." [See Images 17 and 18.]

✦ Unless forced down, fixed wing aircraft cannot travel at fast speeds close to the ground because of the downdraft beneath the wings. At 500 mph, a 757 with a wingspan of 120 feet cannot fly lower than 60 feet above the ground. If forced lower, the plane would have become destabilized and the downdraft would have been strong enough to rip tiles and shingles off roofs, yet the lawn was in pristine condition.

✦ Several lamp posts were knocked over, but several others

in the flight path weren't. Large spools of cable were also in the flight path, as was a chain link fence and a generator, making the official story physically impossible.

✦ No wreckage of a Boeing 757 was seen at the supposed site of impact—no fuselage, engines, landing gear, wings or tail, and no bodies, seats or luggage. Even if the fuselage had somehow shrunk enough to fit into the small hole, as claimed, the other parts of the plane couldn't have, yet there was no sign of them outside the building—or inside.

I also came across credible reports by eyewitnesses that explosives had gone off inside the Pentagon. Many employees in the Pentagon reported smelling the distinctive odor of Cordite, a powerful explosive. There were also reports that a cruise missile, not a commercial airliner had hit the Pentagon, and that the missile had been fired from a U.S. warship parked in the Atlantic Ocean."[168] Witnesses also reported that a plane flew over the Pentagon above what would have been the flight path of the

Image 16. Point of impact at the Pentagon before the wall segment collapsed. Windows, covered with fire retardant, are unbroken, even those above the hole that would have been hit by the plane's tail and those on the sides supposedly hit by the wings and engines.

missile.

The cover-up of the impossibilities began immediately after the impact of whatever hit the Pentagon.

✦ Within minutes, FBI agents began commandeering security videos from all 47 locations in the area with security cameras that might have captured either the flight path or the Pentagon. None of those videos have ever been released to the public.

✦ Soon after the moment of impact, a line of 20 or so men walked side by side across the lawn in front of the "crash site" picking up every scrap of debris from whatever it was, if anything, that hit the Pentagon. All pieces except one were small enough to be carried away by one person.

✦ Within days the lawn was dug up and the field covered with dirt and rock, thereby destroying the crime scene before it could be examined by investigators.

A bizarre "coincidence" added to my doubts about the accuracy of the official story. Secretary of Defense Donald

Image 17. The Pentagon lawn in pristine condition. The arrow points to the point of impact. No airplane parts are visible.

Rumsfeld held a press conference on September 10, one day before the attacks, at which he announced that the Department could not track $2.3 trillion in transactions. The office in which accountants were attempting to trace them was the office in the Pentagon struck on September 11. All records in it were destroyed, leaving no way to trace what had happened to the $2.3 trillion.

One of the oddities about the minimal debris that remained was that it showed no signs of having been involved in a violent crash or exposed to intense heat.[169] It was also unusual that no parts of the plane were ever presented to the public, including the engines, which would easily have survived impact. No evidence was ever presented that the remains of passengers had been found and identified. Also puzzling was that all 69 outward-facing security cameras and sensors at the Pentagon had been turned off that day.

Particularly odd were the three circular holes, presumably caused by the "plane" that hit the Pentagon, which appeared in the inner face of the C ring even though there are no holes in the

Image 18. The Pentagon after the damaged segment collapsed. Note the light poles directly in the "plane's" flight path and the grass in pristine condition.

D ring, [See Image 19.] Since whatever hit the Pentagon hit the outer face of the E ring, it couldn't have impacted the C ring without passing through the D ring. This leads to the suspicion that the holes in the C ring were created by explosives planted in the building. Why three holes? Perhaps those who planted the explosives did so in the wrong location twice before getting it right.

If bombs had created the holes in the C ring, then perhaps explosives were planted in the E ring, too, as attested to by many witnesses. Perhaps in the D ring, also, but those failed to go off. All this led me to wonder whether the "plane" or whatever hit the Pentagon was just for show, to create an explosion that the damage created by bombs planted inside could be attributed to.

The Department of Defense presented little evidence to justify the claim that AA 77 had crashed into the Pentagon and made little effort to respond to those pointing out the physical impossibilities in the official story. The media simply repeated what it was told, with little attention given to the impossibilities or destruction of evidence.

One of the few persons who had worked for the U.S.

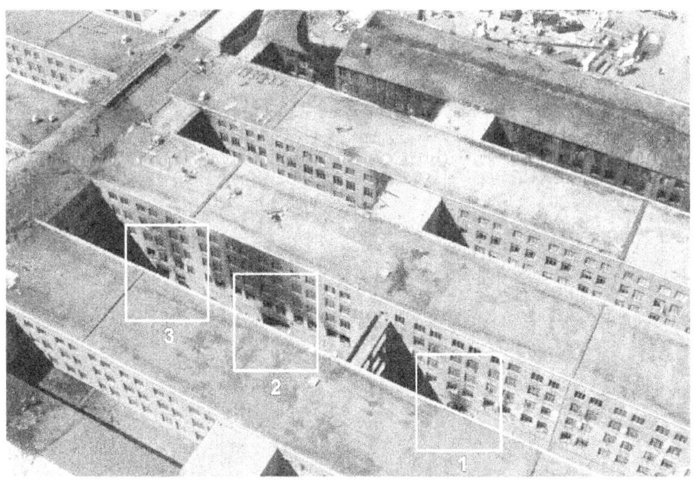

Image 19. The Pentagon with 3 circular holes in the C ring, but no holes in the D ring.

government to challenge the official story was Major General Albert Stubblebine, who before retiring had been the U.S. Army's top expert examiner of photographic evidence. Stubblebine recounted in a video how he had initially dismissed rumors that the attack on the Pentagon and the other events of September 11 had been false flag attacks orchestrated by the U.S. government at the highest levels. Impossible, he told himself. "Not my government!"

Painfully, haltingly, reluctantly and with growing horror as he examined the evidence, he came to see that the rumors were true. He found that the hole in the side of the Pentagon was too small to have been made by a commercial airliner, that no plane parts were found at the Pentagon, that in the hole was a turbine apparently from a missile, and that all security sensors and cameras at the Pentagon had been turned off that day, as had the air defense systems.

In the video, Stubblebine connected each of these and other "dots," repeatedly asking, "Don't you find that strange?"[170] He appeared almost physically ill after being forced into the conclusion that the government he had served so faithfully throughout his life could have murdered nearly 3,000 of its own citizens and wounded the spirits of everyone else in the country. His heartfelt comments in the final part show how troubled he was that the government—his government—could have betrayed the country—his country—on September 11. His sentiments matched mine exactly, and I have prepared a partial transcript of the video. [See textbox.]

Questions flooded into my head as I absorbed Stubblebine's outrage and sense of betrayal. How far could a government go in doing what it thought best for the country? How much harm could it impose on Americans today in order to bring about better conditions for future generations?

I needed to think more about this.

Excerpts from the statement by Major General Albert Stubblebine

"You have all of these dots. They're just bits of information. But, that's exactly how the intelligence world works. You get a bit of information here. A bit here, and a bit here. And, pretty soon you've got a picture. To me, what does the picture say? The picture says that what we heard and were told in the newspapers, the media, was not the real story. There's enough doubt in the official story where the story is absolutely not consistent with what happened. They paint a different picture than the one that was given to the media."

"How easy is it for you to shift your belief system from 'I totally believe in my government to 'Oh My God! What's going on?' That's exactly where I went in all of this. Because my belief system was so strong, from age five when I could remember standing on a parade ground at attention with not anybody telling me to do that–at West Point. I did it because I wanted to do it–because I believed! And then going to the military academy and serving, defending. . . ."

"The real story to me is: who was the real enemy? Who participated in this? Who planned this attack? Why was it planned? Were the real terrorists the people in Arab clothing? Or were the real people that planned this the people sitting in the authority in the White House?"

38

Both kids came to visit for nearly a week centered around Christmas. We helped each other cook the full Christmas turkey meal that we'd helped Diana prepare every year until now, and brought each other up to date on our current activities. I'll skip over further details of their visits, which were *restorative*, because they weren't related to the theme of this memoir, which is *transformative*. For that reason, too, I didn't introduce them to any of the people I'd gotten to know over the past few months. I was content, and believe they were, too, to bask in the family atmosphere and in memories of our lives together when they still lived at home and our family was still whole.

I'll mention one thing, though. I showed them the

photograph of the collapse of the tower that I'd sent them earlier by email. They had similar reactions. They accepted my explanation that the towers had exploded from within and turned into dust rather than merely collapsing into their own foundations. But, and this is the puzzling part, accepting the new cause of the towers' destruction didn't lead them to consider the obvious implication that people other than the 19 supposed hijackers had been responsible for the destruction. It was as though they, along with just about everybody else, were unwilling or unable to accept the full implications of the change in manner of destruction.

It was all very puzzling.

39

All too soon, Christmas was over and the kids had departed from what used to be their home but was now mine alone, to return to their current homes and the lives they were building for themselves.

After they'd gone, I returned to the questions I'd posed after viewing General Stubblebine's video about the extent to which government officials could impose costs on the country now to enhance its long-term interests. My brain had clearly been churning away on these questions while I'd been distracted from them by my kids' visits. It now presented two ideas for my conscious mind to consider.

One was that the U.S. Constitution and other legal constraints limit the government's actions. The president and Congress cannot not take any and every step they believe to be in the best interest of the country. In a democratic republic, each branch of the federal government is assigned specific duties. Each can legitimately carry out only those duties. It was true, I realized, that the range of duties being carried out by the president and Congress today is far wider than those assigned in the Constitution. Even so, limits remain, and the destruction of several large buildings and the murder of nearly 3,000 people were clearly beyond those limits.

That was the simpler of the two ideas. The other concerned

what was right and wrong morally. Does a natural law exist that makes a moral claim on our conduct, one that supersedes whatever written law states and current practice allows in any given country at any given time? Is there a standard of conduct to which all should adhere, one that claims that laws that differ from it are illegitimate and can therefore be disregarded?

I recalled that in *Mere Christianity* C. S. Lewis had introduced the idea of Natural Law as a sense of right and wrong, as a sense that there exists a moral code beyond what is merely legal or illegal and that is beyond the circumstances of our individual lives. This sense guides us, or should, Lewis believed, toward making good choices.

This sense of decent behavior is recognized in every society around the world and is the source of the various moral teachings that exist in them, Lewis stated, before making two key points about it. "First, that human beings, all over the earth, have this curious idea that they ought to behave in a certain way, and cannot really get rid of it. Secondly, that they do not in fact behave in that way. They know the Law of Nature; they break it. These two facts are the foundation of all clear thinking about ourselves and the universe we live in."[171]

Lewis used those ideas as the starting point in his discussion of Christianity in *Mere Christianity*, and developed them further in *The Abolition of Man*, which I'd read decades ago. Glancing through the book now, I saw that it had its origin as a series of lectures he'd given at the University of Durham in northern England during the Second World War to reassure his audiences that objective moral values did indeed exist even though it was easy to believe otherwise amidst the chaos and hardships so prevalent in the world during those years.

I learned from the first few pages that Lewis had written the book to push back against Logical Positivism, against the belief that only what can be measured scientifically is objective knowledge, that all other statements are merely subjective private opinions. Lewis believed that view to be incorrect, that objective knowledge also exists in areas of human life that cannot be scientifically measured. In defense of this view, he cited agreement on ethical principles between the great philosophical and religious traditions that have existed in societies around the world throughout all of recorded human history.

Emotional and intellectual responses to things outside us—works of art, people, situations—could also be objective knowledge, he argued. If our responses are appropriate to the qualities of the things being responded to, they are objective knowledge. If not, they are only internal subjective feelings. He especially wanted to, and believed that he had, re-established that objective statements could be made about truth, beauty and goodness.

Truth. Descriptive statements are objective knowledge to the degree they accurately describe the objects or events concerned.

Beauty. Statements about the beauty of an object are objective knowledge if they accurately reflect the degree to which the object really is beautiful.

Goodness. Statements about the goodness of an action are objective knowledge if they accurately reflect the degree to which the action really is good for human beings.

I knew my understanding was only superficial at this point, and that I'd need to re-read and in fact study carefully all of *The Abolition of Man* to absorb more deeply what Lewis had to say about objective knowledge and the specific moral strictures inherent in Natural Law. I suspected that I'd find that it provided no justification whatsoever for the illegal murder of 3,000 people on September 11.

January 2020

♣ 40 ♣

This month Timeless Classics discussed E. M. Forster's *A Passage to India*, a book in which the principal characters attempt to determine exactly what had happened at a critical moment in the recent past. Not a murder mystery exactly, but a book in which a murder occurred and an investigation took place.

After the discussion ended Gina and I went out for dinner, as had become our usual routine. Although the opening of her studio was only a week or two away, she wanted to talk about writers and their books.

As we sat down at our table in a Vietnamese restaurant, she laughed about the suggestion from one of the members that we read and discuss *The Secret Garden*, the children's book by Frances Hodgson Burnett.

I didn't find the suggestion so amusing. "I refuse to discuss that book and was glad to see it so soundly voted down," I said. "I want to read the world's greatest literature—books with the deepest insights into human beings and the world they live in. Perhaps we should consider reading *Hamlet*.

"Of course, I read *The Secret Garden* when I was young, and read it to my children when they were small," I continued in a softer voice, "but the book club's members are adults, ¿verdad?"

Gina responded quickly and in a rather excited way to my mention of *Hamlet*, not even noticing my use of a Spanish word I'd learned recently.

"I've been meaning to mention," she began, "that I recently read a book claiming that Shakespeare didn't write Shakespeare, or rather that the man from Stratford—whose name really was Shakspere, not Shakespeare—didn't write the plays and poems attributed to him. The author was very persuasive. After reading that book, I'll never see Shakespeare's works the same way again."

A few months ago, I would have scoffed at that idea, but now, after learning that the official stories about the Kennedy assassination and the events of September 11 were false—deliberately false—I was primed to doubt just about everything I'd ever believed.

Gina continued, saying, "The author made the case that Shakespeare's plays were almost autobiographical even if many of them were set in countries outside England. He claimed that since the characters and events in the plays didn't in any way match Shakspere and his life, he couldn't have been the author. I now see the Shakespeare hoax perpetrated way back then, as similar to the Global Warming hoax being perpetrated today."

That surprised me, too. I hadn't known that Gina felt that way about climate change. That was another subject with a well-established official story I'd have to revisit.

"I think more people will get angry if you say Shakespeare didn't write his own works than if you say God doesn't exist," I said.

Caught up in her own thoughts, Gina continued as though I hadn't spoken.

"In my observation," she said, "the greatest writers and scholars shed blood and brains to write about or investigate or attack an established idea or a belief for some significant reason. They breathe the core of the humanities; they found their voice then they put it out there. A good example is Jacques Derrida. He was brilliant but then he became a philosophical trickster promoting indoctrination of young people with his left-wing egalitarian agenda. His ideas are sold out tickets to the masses, especially in this day and age when it's not easy to sell conservatism, as most people want to reinvent the wheel while being reluctant to accept a sense of responsibility. I read that he came up with his ideas attacking the entire scope of western philosophy from Plato to Nietzsche to Heidegger, because of the severe bigotry he experienced in French Algeria."

I was learning things about Gina and her beliefs and observations that I'd never suspected of her.

"When I read the works of literary scholars," she continued, "though they are not telling a story in their books, I always feel like their works are multi-layered, and if given the chance, I would like to ask each scholar or writer I have read why they do what they do. I'd like to ask the author of the book on Shakespeare what made him write the book. Shakespearean literature is a well-established field in the study of language. There are tons of institutions built around it to protect it. I wonder what made him launch an attack, albeit well-founded, on such a well-defended cultural icon."

"Those would be interesting conversations for me to overhear, Gina," I said. "I've long believed that writers draw on their own personal experiences in writing their works, no matter how far afield the fictional settings seem to be from their own lives. I remember that one scholar, Doris Alexander, observed that writers 'are compelled to write particular works by the urgent life problems they face,' as they seek to 'resolve the[m] through the resolution[s] they found for the problems of their characters in their stor[ies].'

"How did you become so smart, so able to see through the cant of Chomsky and Derrida and so many others? How did you ever come to be one of the tiny percentage of people who recognize that Derrida is 'a philosophical trickster promoting indoctrination of young people with his left-wing egalitarian agenda'? I wish my kids could see as deeply as you do. They're super-smart in many ways but tend to accept the views of others around them regarding Chomsky and his ilk. Neither reads books beyond those needed for their work. For years I tried to get them to read Freud (*Civilization and Its Discontents*), Hayek (*The Road to Serfdom*), von Mises (*Human Action*), or anything by Russell Kirk, Thomas Sowell, Roger Scruton and on and on and on, but without success.

"I've spent so much time recently studying the works of investigators and scholars who have uncovered the real story of JFK's assassination and September 11," I continued, "that I'm thinking of writing a book about what I've learned. And about the process through which I learned it, which would require that I draw on my own experiences in writing it. But whether I write the book or not, personal motivations do play heavily into why I have dedicated so much time to my studies."

She nodded, and said, "I've been wondering why you're putting such effort into them."

"Principality plays into it, too," I continued, "because understanding what it true or real or correct is a core part of Principality. We can't be an effective Principal if we don't have a good grasp of the realities of a situation. We can't live the best possible life unless and until we know what is true.

"Understanding what is true/correct/right has always been important to me, ever since I was a boy. One of the reasons I love literature is that it can present the complexities of situations and of people in ways that non-fiction simply cannot. Have you read George Eliot's/Mary Ann Evans's *Middlemarch*? I've heard for decades that it presents the complexities of the characters' thoughts, feelings, dispositions, desires, attitudes and frustrations more deeply than any other novel. I'm just about to begin reading it and will let you know if it does what praise of it promises. Too bad it's too long for the book club to read and discuss."

"Yes," Gina interjected while I took a breath. I read *Middlemarch* last year, and it's one of the best books I have ever read."

"Another factor is that I like constructing things," I continued, "taking the pieces of information I have gathered and am gathering, and sorting them out, trying different ways of combining and structuring them so that an article or a book results. It's very satisfying.

"But perhaps most important, and most personal, is that my literary work helps me to block out aspects of the world that are upsetting and that I can't do anything about. Being absorbed in literary activities is a way of mentally withdrawing from those things so that I don't have to think about them too much. It keeps me sane. That may be more than you wanted to know, Gina, but that's why I'm so intensely involved in my investigations. At least that's what my conscious mind tells me."

I then turned to something she'd told me.

"You said recently that you have many colleagues but few deep friends, that you are very selective about the people you let into your life. I'm the same way. I'd love to have more friends who share my interests in literature and books by the authors I mentioned, but such people are hard to find."

I was relieved at the direction this conversation had gone in. I think we both recognized the need to draw back from the ultra-personal nature of our recent conversations into the merely personal. That they'd bordered on being too revealing, too intense, too dangerous. That it's best to let things cool off a bit so that neither of us gets hurt. So that we could think clearly and not make a mistake.

As we parted, Gina handed me a book, *Summer Storm: A Novel of Ideas*, and said, "It's by someone you might like to meet. He lives locally. In this one book he lays out the case for alternative views of both Shakespearean authorship and human-caused climate change."

As I walked to my car, I noticed that the author was James A. Warren. I'd known someone with that name in high school and wondered if it was the same person.

❧ 41 ❧

Reading about the events of September 11 and watching videos about them filled my days now. What I was learning from them reinforced my earlier conclusion that the official account of what happened couldn't possibly be true. If even one piece of evidence challenging it is correct—and I'd seen dozens—then it couldn't be true. All pieces of evidence must support it or it is false.

I was still confused, though, about the planes that hit the towers in New York. Did planes, in fact, hit the towers? I had found information supporting several distinct answers.

Answer 1: Yes. The commercial airliners—AA 11 and UA 175—hit the towers in New York as stated in the official story. No parts of the airliners were ever presented to the public because they were destroyed beyond recognition on impact. I found this answer impossible to believe.

Answer 2: Yes, but the planes were not commercial airliners. The plane that hit the second tower was too dark and didn't have windows. It appeared to be a military plane and appeared to have two objects not found on commercial airliners attached to the bottom. One was long, running the length of the plane; the other was bulkier and located on the right side only, just back from the wing. [See Image 20.]

The bulkier item was identified by an airline captain as a remote-control pod "manufactured by Martin Marietta Corporation in Los Angeles, [which has] been used extensively by the USAF for outfitting drone aircraft for over 22 years."[172] Another report, from an AWACS flight controller, stated that, "the two airplanes which were flown into WTC 1 and 2 were actually large 'drones' that were remotely controlled by U.S. military personnel. There were no passengers on board those two drones as they were not the same flights referred to in the official 9/11 Commission report."[173] They would have to have been drones, I reasoned, if the buildings had been brought down by explosives

Image 20. Bottom of plane with unusual items attached. Note also that the head of the plane is missing and that the plane doesn't cast a shadow on the building.

planted in them, so that the planes would hit at exactly the right spot.

Answer 3: No. Planes did not hit the towers. There are no realistic videos of planes impacting the towers. The videos we have show the impossible feat of a plane—a hollow aluminum tube—cutting through solid concrete and steel. In those videos the plane disappeared into the solid parts between floors as easily as into the office spaces. The thin wings cut through steel just as easily as the heavy engines and landing gear. All this was physically impossible.

In real life, the planes would have broken up on impact. Large parts of the planes—the fuselage, engines, landing gear, tail—would have fallen to the ground and been discovered later. No realistic evidence that parts of commercial airliners were found has ever been presented to the public.

Furthermore, the planes in the videos moved too smoothly, I thought. Large airliners cannot travel at high speeds at low altitudes because of the density of the atmosphere; that's why they travel above 30,000 feet, where the atmosphere is thinner. If they try to travel at high speeds lower down, they become unsteady, rocking and vibrating and shaking, eventually breaking apart. Yet the videos show the planes gliding smoothly as they approached the tower, as though they were images pasted in and moved along from frame to frame to give the appearance of forward motion.

All of the half dozen or so videos I'm aware of showing planes hitting the tower look like poorly done fakes. In stills taken from one video, the left wing seems to disappear before impact, and the building is completely undamaged between the fuselage and the left engine.[174] [See Image 21.]

The idea that images of a plane had been added to the photos was reinforced when I compared the sizes of the planes in various videos. In one comparison [see Image 22], the planes are very different in size even though the width of the towers is the same and the planes are shown only one second before impact. In the first, the plane looks too big; in the second, too small.

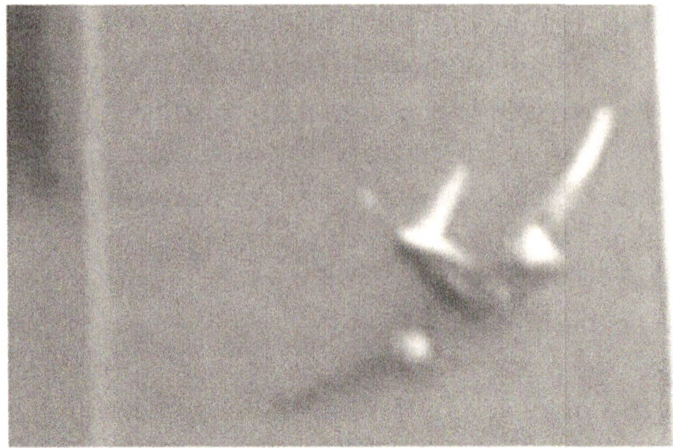

Image 21. Plane melting into solid steel and concrete with no visible damage to either the plane or the building.

Image 22. Comparison of the sizes of the planes in two videos one second before the moment of impact. The first looks too big, the second too small.

Again, I asked myself, if a plane hit the second tower, why is there no realistic video of its approach and impact?

If planes didn't hit the towers, then what did?

One possibility is that missiles hit them. If so, then the images of the planes could have been added to the videos to cover up the missiles. The missile idea would explain the thin nose of a "missile" coming out the opposite side of the second tower. [See Image 23.] The plastic nose of a thin hollow aluminum tube would not have survived impact with steel and concrete; the nose of a bunker-busting missile would have. That this image of the head of a "missile" exiting the building was blacked out on all TV news broadcasts after the first live showing further suggests that it was indeed missiles that hit the towers.

I'd nearly finished writing this memoir when I came across Wolfgang Staehle's photographs of the object that hit the first tower. [See Image 24.] These little-known photographs resulted from his time lapse photography of the skyline of New York City beginning on September 10, 2001. In them the object

Image 23. Head of a "missile" exiting WTC 2.

Image 24. One of Wolfgang Staehle's photographs showing what appears to be a missile streaking toward WTC 1.

streaking toward the north tower, the first tower hit, looks like a missile, not a plane. I don't see a tail or wings. The object appears to be a side view of the object that Dan Rather, looking at it head-on, described as a ball, as I'll explain later. [See Scene 46.]

Answer 4: The fourth possibility is that nothing hit the towers. Only a few witnesses on the morning of September 11 claimed to have seen a plane. Many more stated they heard explosions. The cries of shock and anguish that so many people on the ground uttered were in response to the huge fireball. Not having seen a plane, they attributed it to an explosion or explosions within the towers. The few who claimed to have seen planes hit the towers could have been assuming that the fireball was caused by the impact of a plane and then "remembered" that they'd seen it hit.

Several sites on the Internet show videos of the point of impact of the second tower, comparing the site with and without a plane approaching and impacting the tower. The explosion is the same in both. Here's one example comparing two stills from the videos [see Image 25]. The first shows the beginnings of the explosion with the tail of the plane still visible; the second shows the same beginnings of the explosion with no tail visible because no plane had hit the tower. The difference between the plane and no plane options is clearer in the videos than in these stills taken from them.

Answers 3 and 4 leave one important question unexplained. If someone was going to create a fake video of a plane hitting the second tower, he wouldn't use an image of a non-commercial plane with a pod attached to it, would he? He'd use an image of a commercial plane. So how to explain those fakes?

At this point I was left with a mystery I couldn't explain. Two weeks later I'd find images in the archives of the major TV news networks that would help clarify the situation.

I was also uncertain about what had happened to the people on board the planes, assuming that those commercial flights had actually taken off on September 11. The Millennium Report

Image 25. Two images of the beginning of the explosion from inside the second tower, the first with the image of a plane inserted, the second without it. The video can be seen at www.rumble.com/vm1ruy-the-planes-of-911-were-crude-cgi-graphics.html?e9s=src_v1_ucp.

suggests some interesting possibilities, one being that potential whistleblowers might have been on the flights. "Fourteen of the people on Flight 77 including the captain were potential whistleblowers for [the use of] an emergency command system for taking over control of hijacked aircraft. . . . They may or may not have been on board the actual flights. [If not,] they were killed, their bodies disposed [of], and their names added to the manifests (if they weren't there already) before being released to the public (and their personal histories changed to reflect them being on board, etc.)."[175]

The report also noted "identities on the manifest which, if researched extensively, do not appear to have been real people." Elsewhere, Vincent Sammartino documented that "of the passengers and crew of Flights 11, 77, 175 & 93, only 22%, 22%, 28% and 13%, respectively, are in the SSDI [Social Security Death Index]."[176] Citing a CNN news report, he also showed that "of the 266 people that we were told died on those jets, only 11 relatives applied for compensation. . . . Not a single relative from Flight 93 applied for compensation."[177]

I'm including here a few of the many other pieces of evidence that led me to doubt the accuracy of the official story.

✦ Air Force fighter planes failed to intercept three, and possibly all four of the supposed hijacked commercial airliners, even though fighter jets had scrambled and intercepted at least 67 planes in the ten months between September 2000 and June 2001. The "no planes" answer explains why fighters didn't intercept any of the planes: there were no planes to intercept.

✦ No parts of the supposed commercial airliners were observed by any witnesses on September 11, 2001, at any of the three crash sites—not in New York, not at the Pentagon and not at the field in Pennsylvania. Nor were any parts presented to the public later by the FBI or the FAA. This supports the "no planes" answer and the "no commercial airliners" answer.

✦ Thousands of parts on each commercial airliner are replaced on a regular basis; each part has a unique serial number, and these numbers are meticulously recorded. Yet no evidence was presented that parts with any of those serial numbers were found at any of the supposed crash sites. This is again explained by the "no planes" and the "no commercial airliners" answers.

✦ The FBI later claimed that it had recovered most of the plane that supposedly crashed in Pennsylvania—the plane that had supposedly hit the ground so hard that it was completely buried in the soft soil—yet it provided no evidence to support its claim: no pieces, no parts with serial numbers, no bodies.

✦ The same is true for the plane that supposedly hit the Pentagon. The FBI claimed that it had recovered most of the plane that had supposedly disappeared into the small hole in the side of the building, but never provided any evidence: no pieces, no parts with serial number, no bodies.

✦ A crushed Prat Whitney engine was found near the site of the twin towers in New York. But United used only GE engines, and the PW engine that was "found" had been buried in a land fill site a year earlier. There's no video evidence of an airliner engine being hurled out of the building at the time of impact. It could not have been thrust out later because it was found far enough away that it had to have been thrust out near the height of the supposed impact. Further, the photo of the engine shows it resting on an unbroken sidewalk. An object that heavy after having fallen several hundred feet would surely have destroyed the sidewalk and dug a deep hole in the ground.

✦ None of the eight pilots punched the four-digit code into their flight control's transponder to alert ground crews or the FAA to the hijackings that were supposedly in progress.

✦ The original passenger manifests for all four flights "included no names of any of the 19 alleged hijackers and, in fact, no Middle Eastern names whatsoever."[178] American Airlines confirmed that "These lists were published in many major periodicals and are now considered public record."[179] During the trial of Zacarias Moussaoui, the supposed 20th hijacker, the FBI claimed that Arab names had appeared on the passenger manifest for the flight Zacarias was supposed to have boarded, but it did not produce the manifest in court.

✦ The one video that exists showing two of the supposed hijackers going through airport security was taken at an airport in Maine, not Boston as claimed. Unlike usual security footage, it's dark and hard to make out, and does not have the date and time that all security cameras automatically stamp onto all security videos.

✦ The phone calls presented as having been made from the planes could not have been made. In 2001 cell phones did not work above altitudes of even a few thousand feet, and all planes were above 30,000 feet at the time the calls were supposedly made. None of the planes had phones available for passenger use.

✦ The calls had several other suspicious features. They have none of the background noise that would normally be heard on a phone being used on a plane, and many callers sounded preternaturally calm, as though they were reading a script in a drill rather than participating in a live hijacking.[180]

✦ Seismic evidence indicated large explosions beneath the towers;[181] however, "the Richter scale readings occur before the radar-based impact times of the planes and are too low in frequency to correspond to plane impacts.[182]

✦ AA 11 and UA 175, the two flights that supposedly crashed into the towers in New York, both flew over Stewart Air Force Base at exactly the same time, at approximately 8:36 a.m., nearly colliding with each other,[183] yet they arrived at the towers in New York 17 minutes apart.

There is also the unsettling possibility that Flight 93 was shot down by the U.S. Air Force, not because control of the plane had been taken over by hijackers, but because, by most accounts, "the passengers had, by about 9:56 a.m., wrested control of the aircraft away from the hijackers."[184] Michael Ruppert thought so. "Compelling evidence suggests that some aircraft were indeed scrambled, probably in time to shoot down Flight 93 over Pennsylvania when passengers aboard had apparently successfully regained control of it and might have landed the airliner, exposing a plot which had been orchestrated within the highest levels of the military and intelligence command structure."[185]

That story aside, I haven't found any substantive evidence that any planes were hijacked on September 11 or that any planes crashed at any of the supposed crash sites. What I've seen is four missing planes, planes that vanished into thin air, just like the World Trade Center towers vanished into dust.

42

I was finding it difficult to absorb the fact that senior officials in the U.S. government and military had committed treason against the United States by orchestrating the events of September 11. Intellectually I was convinced that's what happened, but emotionally I still hadn't been quite able to accept it.

At just this moment, I became aware of something particularly saddening about that day because it was personal. At one point in my career, I had worked on a team whose members had included Ted Olson, who later served as U.S. Solicitor General under President George W. Bush. I'd come away from that experience with tremendous respect for Olson's intelligence and dedication to the country for which we both worked. I admired him beyond measure and from time to time used him as a model for the type of officer I'd like to become.

My heart went out to him in 2001 after learning that his wife, Barbara Olson, had been on AA 77, the plane that supposedly crashed into the Pentagon. My respect for him increased even more after reading the transcript of a speech he gave to the Federalist Society two weeks after September 11. I thought it was one of the finest things I had read about that terrible day, in part because Olson so eloquently stated the Americanism beliefs that I so fervently held at that time. I have included a few excerpts. [See text box.]

Olson had received three phone calls from his wife before her flight crashed. One of them was of the greatest importance because it was the only source for our knowledge of the boxcutters that the hijackers had with them.

Yet now, I've learned, the FBI has acknowledged that none of the supposed phone conversations between Ted Olson and his wife actually occurred. That was unsettling. Also unsettling is that boxcutters are still highlighted in the official story even though the sole source for them has been discredited.

More unsettling still is that a year or two after September 11, Ted Olson married a woman who looked suspiciously like what his deceased wife, Barbara, would look if she had aged a bit and had had plastic surgery. His new wife seemed to have appeared out of nowhere. She had no work history, and the university from which it was claimed she had graduated said it had never heard of her.

It hit me hard to realize that Olson, someone for whom I had such great respect, was a participant in the charade that was enacted on September 11. Given the admiration I'd felt for him and my appreciation of the sentiments in his speech, I felt personally betrayed. That betrayal and the hundred other aspects of that day now shown to have been fabricated have made it very difficult to write this part of this memoir. I've been able to work on it for only short periods of time separated by lengthy breaks to allow my spirit to recover from the shock of the betrayals by so many high-level officials in the government—in my government.

My despondency deepened when I learned that the White House had resisted calls for an independent investigation into the events of September 11 for more than a year. And that once a Commission was finally set up, it was headed by a Bush insider. And further, that when George W. Bush agreed to testify before the Commission, he agreed to do so only in the Oval Office, not under oath, accompanied by Dick Cheney, and with no tape recorders or transcript or note-taking allowed.

As an antidote, I thought often of Gina. Even though I didn't see her more than a few times each month, recalling her intellectually challenging manner, her slim beauty, and her ambitious plans for her business brought my mood back to its usual spirited level.

Theodore Olson, U.S. Solicitor General
Speech to the Federalist Society, November 16, 2001

Americans "had been brutally murdered for the simple reason that they were Americans. . . . who believed in the values that their country stands for: liberty, democracy, freedom and equality. Their lives were cruelly extinguished because they were the living embodiment of the aspirations of most of the world's peoples. The people who killed them, and who planned their death, hate America and Americans for that very reason. They despise America and the beacon that America holds out to people who are impoverished, enslaved, persecuted and subjugated everywhere in the world.

"The men who planned the savage acts of Sept. 11 cannot prevail . . . as long as American ideals continue to inspire the very people they hope to tyrannize and enslave. Hence they have declared war, in fact they have declared hatred, on the U.S. and the values it holds dearest. . . . These terrorists can enslave the people they wish to subjugate only by keeping them poor and destitute, so they must undermine and discredit the one place in all the world that stands the most for the rule of law and individual liberty, and that allows its people and the people who flock to the U.S. daily by the thousands the opportunity to rise above those conditions. . . .

"It has, I suppose, always caused some resentment that the United States believes so passionately and so unquestioningly that freedom, equality, liberty, democracy and the rule of law are concepts and rights that should belong to all people. But how can that be seen as arrogance, as some have called it? I simply cannot accept that. What can possibly be wrong with the aspiration that moved the nation's founders to believe that people are entitled to self-determination, the right to chose their system of government, the right to freedom within an orderly and secure society and the maximum liberty to pursue happiness and fulfillment? . . .

"Americans will prevail for the very reason that they were attacked. . . . because of the values that made the nation free and strong; because of the principles that made it prosperous, creative, resourceful, innovative, determined and fiercely protective of freedom, liberty and the right to be individuals. Those values and those characteristics will lift the nation and defeat the black forces who have assaulted America's ideals, the country and its people. . . . These dreadful, despicable people have hurt the U.S., but they can never conquer it."

43

The most startling new information presented during the past decade has come from retired flight attendant Rebekah Roth. She chose to present her findings in five novels whose main characters investigate what really happened on September 11 because, she explained, a fictional format made it easier for people to overcome their aversion to revisiting the events of that painful day. Focusing on the main character's reluctant awakening in spite of wanting to avert her eyes from evidence damning the highest levels of the U.S. government—and a wide range of intelligence organizations and companies in the United States and other countries—made for a tense, engaging series of books.

One of Roth's most startling findings explained what happened to the planes that were supposedly hijacked. Knowing that none of the phone calls from the planes could have been made from high altitude, Roth reasoned that the planes must have landed before the calls were made. She then calculated how far each of the four flights could have travelled before the first of the calls on them took place. Drawing concentric circles at those distances around the three airports of origin, she found that they intersected at one point: Westover Air Force Base in Western Massachusetts. She later found witnesses who had observed planes travelling at high speed and low altitude that landed at that airport at the approximate times the four supposedly hijacked aircraft would have landed.

In addition to her five books, Roth established a website, www.behindthegallerycurtain.com, on which she posted nearly 200 hours of webcasts she's given on the events of September 11 and related subjects. I found them fascinating. She was a true insider in the small world of flight crews, who share a unique lifestyle regardless of which airline they worked for. Her experiences had given her insights into what really happened that no outsider could possibly have deduced. She feels betrayed, she stated, by people in that small, tightknit, family of colleagues who she believes were active, knowing participants in the events of September 11. All that added to the emotional intensity of her novels.

In the first book, *Methodical Deception*, Roth hadn't yet figured out what happened to the crew or passengers after the planes had landed, except that some of them made phone calls from the ground. She documented, though, that the procedures followed by the flight crews on that day violated in many ways the flight protocols for hijackings that are drilled into every member of the crew through mandatory annual training. The crews simply would not have acted in the ways that the official story has them acting.

Investigating further, Roth found persuasive evidence that there were no normal crew and probably no normal passengers on the planes; that is, they were all or almost all participants in the plot. She documented that last minute changes were made to most of the crew and passengers on the flights: all pilots and 20 of 25 cabin crew were last minute replacements. On one of the flights, seven of nine crew members were changed, with all changes made in ways that violated normal assignment procedures. The passengers, too, she stated in one of her broadcasts, were scheduled only the day before the flights.

Roth provided indications that six flights, not four, were supposed to have been involved on September 11.[186] One of them should have hit World Trade Center Building 7 (explosions in the lobby of the building went off before 10 a.m. but the plane never arrived), and another flight was supposed to hit Camp David. United 93, which crashed in Pennsylvania, was supposed to have hit the Sears Tower in Chicago, which was owned by the same person who owned the three principal buildings destroyed in New York (WTC 1, 2, 7): Larry Silverstein.

She also named four witnesses or investigators into September 11 who she believed were murdered to stop them from talking about what they knew.

In one of her later books, Roth described her discovery—made while examining FAA records released in response to a Freedom of Information Act (FOIA) request—that some of the calls hijackers supposedly made while the hijackings were in progress had been uploaded into FAA computers more than an hour before any of the flights had left the ground. Those recordings had also been copyrighted, which would block any rebroadcast of them without authorization. It's this piece of information—this smoking gun—that gave Roth a fear for her life. Following publication of that information, her websites were attacked and YouTube took down all of her videos and closed her channel. I have never seen even a single reference to Roth or her books on any 9/11 Truther website or in any Truther publication. Not one. Are her findings so radioactive that no one has the courage even to refer to them?

44

I stopped in again at WORDS to see how Gina was doing as she prepared for its grand opening scheduled for next week. Things must have been going well, because she wanted to talk instead about a problem she'd had for some time in another area of her life. I mention it here for what both of us revealed about ourselves in our discussion of it.

She'd been helping financially a family she knows that had fallen on hard times. The problem for the family was that the parents were unemployed and sat around doing little to help themselves beyond asking Gina and others for money. The husband played video games all day long and the mother lounged around, leaving the kids uncared for. That's what tugged at Gina's heartstrings.

"I try to talk to the mother about caring for her children," she explained. "I know well that my words may not be taken seriously. I mean, what does a 20-ish girl like me know about raising children? But I think being a good wife and mother requires a certain degree of intelligence—knowing how to think long-term, and being smart in handling finances, for example; otherwise, the children will suffer. I remember my dad used to say that the mother is the 'transmitter' of habits and values, so that if a person doesn't know how to groom himself then it's likely because his mom doesn't know either.

"I am from a culture where people are easy to talk to and excellent at having honest and difficult conversations. I am not used to talking, let alone explaining, anything to someone who is not on the same wavelength I am, so I find this difficult. I am very savvy when it comes to dealing with people and I never let anyone stress me out; I deal with people I can't deal with by not dealing with them, so this is the first time for me. I want to do this for her children. Sometimes I feel like I am being too dumb for being concerned with this family. They haven't done anything for me really, but I guess I just appreciate how this friend is so nice to me. She's not a bad person, in fact, she is a good person, it's just that I cannot reach her mentally, I guess. Still, she's one of the few friends I've made here outside of school and tutoring."

"What a nightmare, Gina," I said. "These people are not your friends. They might be friendly, but they are not your friends. You could give every dollar you have to try to help them, and it wouldn't make any difference. They could win $10 million in the lottery, but a few years from now they would be back in the same situation.

"The reason is that people are who they are. It's a hard truth of the world that people are who they are and rarely change to any significant degree.

"You cannot help people who are not already doing all they can do help themselves. You could talk to the woman again and again, but she won't be able to hear you. Your words will go right over her head. The children's situation is tragic, but that is the way of the world. Their situation is not something you can do anything about. You must simply accept their parents for who they are."

Gina nodded.

"Try to find people who are worthy of your help. People who have already demonstrated that they are worthy of help by doing all they can to help themselves. Put your money where you can make a difference, like helping your sisters.

"It's so rare to find people worthy of help, but when you do, help them all you can. That's why I was so taken with you the first time I saw you, in that simple yellow summer dress. I could see instinctively that you were someone worth helping, worth having as a friend, worth being a friend of, and, if circumstances allowed, becoming much more than a friend.

"I have the opposite reaction to that couple: I am instinctively repelled by them.

"So again, these people are not your friends. They can destroy your life if you let them into it too deeply. Turn away from them is my advice. Cut them out of your life. They are a cancer that will spread if you let them in."

"Yes," Gina said, "she is already hitting up my friends for money. I shouldn't have introduced any of them to her."

She followed that with a moment of silence before saying, "'They might be friendly, but they are not my friends.' That is the saddest thing anyone ever said to me. It's really sad because I thought that I had met at least one American outside of school that I could call a 'friend.' I refer to people I care about as 'friends,' for the lack of a better term, but yeah, in reality, this 'friend' isn't someone I spend time with frequently or someone I talk to about anything personal, deep, or profound; in fact, we don't really talk unless it's about me giving something to her and her children. It's only here that I've had a 'friendship' of this nature, so I don't know what's the term for that."

"Here's my definition of a friend," I said. "If someone is truly happy for you when something good happens in your life, or truly sad for you when something bad happens, they are a true friend. Friends want the best for each other. We cannot make someone into a friend. We can only sort out the people we meet into those who are friends and those who aren't, with perhaps some in the middle who could go either way. Time hasn't yet spoken about them."

Gina sighed. "I have never been in a situation where I have to accept something (or someone) as they are. It's only whether I like it or not. If not, then I am out. When I heard how many times you used the word 'accept,' it felt like I was hearing a word that never existed in my reality. I don't fix or change people, and never will in this case. I don't want to 'accept' and be okay with this because I don't like what my 'friend' and her husband are doing to their kids. I also realize that no matter how her kids get helped, no outsider can influence them because the drive to be better and break free of toxic upbringing always comes from within.

"Cutting them off will be painful, but we should never be around people that might slow us down. I appreciate your wisdom and for wanting the best for me, Jubal. I will just include them in my prayers, God always listens anyway."

"I'm glad you got the main point of what I was trying to say, Gina, the point that the effort to change must 'come from within.' That's true for people—nothing we do can help others who aren't trying to help themselves—and its true for countries—no amount of foreign aid will help a country that's ruled by a dictator who steals it. And anyway, much of what is called 'foreign aid' is really intended as bribes to get the recipient country to do what the United States government wants it to do.

"I think you also understood that by 'accept' I don't mean like or approve. I mean only that people, as well as things must be regarded, in a sense, as part of the world outside us, as entities that, like gravity, must be accepted as a reality that our actions cannot change. Of course that is not always true, but it is a baseline that can be relied on; exceptions are few and far between. I could give you many examples of experiences in my life, of many painful experiences over many years, that led me to that hard won knowledge."

In fact, I thought to myself, I have traveled quite a mental distance from the home I grew up in. My parents believed the best about everyone, believed that everyone had the best motives for everything they did, that everyone was loving and kind just as they were, that everyone could be helped; that if anyone did anything harmful, it must be because of an accident, a misunderstanding, a confusion. They would never, or could never, accept that anyone ever had underhanded motives for what he did. That naïve mindset left them vulnerable to individual predators and ill equipped to understand or deal with the psychopaths who seek to acquire political power and use it to dominate entire societies, including, I now see, our own.

While I was thinking those thoughts, Gina looked at me expectantly, waiting for me to tell her about one of the experiences I'd referred to.

"As one example," I said to her, "one day when I was already in the Foreign Service, I was eating lunch with my parents at a restaurant. Looking out the window I watched a man and woman, somewhat elderly, but still strong and healthy, walking toward a car parked in a handicap parking spot. The car had the blue tag hanging from the rear-view mirror, so they had parked there legally.

"Yet they had no trouble walking; they walked as well as I or anyone else with no mobility problems walk. I pointed them out to my dad and commented that they were abusing the system. His response was that they must be handicapped, or they wouldn't have the blue tag hanging from the license plate. Even when I pointed out how well they walked, he wouldn't budge from thinking only good thoughts about them. Not just in this instance, but in many others, when there was a conflict between what he saw and what he believed, he just couldn't bring himself to accept the testimony of his own eyes.

"And my mom wouldn't acknowledge savage realities, either." I recited the story of the six parakeets that Diana and I had had when our kids were young. One day one of the birds got out of the cage while we were feeding them, so we had only five. Two days later we caught it. It had been easy to catch; apparently it wanted to return to its home. We put it back into the cage.

"The next morning, we had quite a surprise. We again had only five birds. On the floor of the cage were what looked like a beak, feet and some feathers from the sixth bird. Apparently the other five now regarded the one we'd put back into the cage as an intruder and killed it. Not just killed it, but eaten it, leaving behind only the parts that couldn't be digested.

"Our kids ran inside to tell this news to their grandma. But she wouldn't hear it. She wouldn't let them tell the story more than once. She didn't put her hands over her ears, but she refused to believe what they told her, that the five birds had killed and eaten the sixth. She simply couldn't accept the reality of the situation, that such cute little birds who chattered away so happily among themselves could, in certain circumstances, as when they saw their home invaded by an outsider, become killers.

"Having absorbed such wishful thinking growing up left me ill prepared to enter adult life," I continued. "It was only after much painful disillusioning that I've come to the beliefs I hold today. Which isn't to say that they are right, only that they come from experiences I have had and observations I have made of the world around me, supplemented by much reading of literature and history to gain a sense of what human life has been like in other times and places."

Gina nodded, and after a pause, said, "I'm trying to recall which vintage dress I wore that day that left such an impression because I have several of them in yellow and they are all simple. But that aside, I can't remember how I talked or behaved that day, so I didn't expect that even way back then you already perceived me as someone who's worth knowing or helping. I am humbled beyond words, and please know that I deeply appreciate everything you do for me, Jubal."

As she was speaking, I thought of asking her to model all of her yellow dresses for me so that I could identify the right one. Out loud I said, "I don't remember the exact details of that 'summer dress,' only the stunning impression it, or rather you in it, made on me. And I remember commenting to myself that it looked like the type of summer dress my mother might have worn in the mid-1960s when I was still a very young child. I also remember that it was only with the greatest effort at self control that I stopped myself from looking at you for far longer than was appropriate or polite.

"Anyway, I don't mean to dissuade you from any kindnesses you might want to show the children, but only to caution you against expecting too much to come from them."

As we parted Gina gave me a picture of herself. "Now you can look at me for as long as you want," she said with a smile that indicated a playful side to her nature. The photo showed her in a provocative pose. Very intriguing, almost mysterious—disturbingly provocative. I put it in my pocket.

45

Nearly all Americans fell for the official story, the one stating that 19 Arabs armed with boxcutters had hijacked four planes and used them to kill nearly 3,000 people. They didn't seem to notice the obvious indications that that story couldn't possibly be true. I wanted to understand why they had allowed themselves to be fooled, conned, hoaxed and misled for so many years—and why I myself had been among them until very recently.

We might have been able to see the holes in the official story soon after September 11 if members of the government not involved in the scheme had voiced doubts or suspicions, but none had. Not a single official of the Bush administration or even one member of Congress publicly expressed doubt about the official story or pointed to any of the many holes in what was one of the most shocking and bizarre events in all of American history. On the contrary, Congress rushed to pass legislation that would profoundly undermine the civil liberties of all Americans and to provide massive funding for the War on Terror, both actions predicated on the supposed reality of the official story. They did so, so quickly that they couldn't possibly have read or digested the contents of the legislation they voted for. In fact, Michael C. Ruppert reported, "Congress was not allowed even to read the Patriot Act or the Homeland Security bills before being compelled to vote on them."[187]

Turning to the question of why the entire Bush administration and Congress remained silent even though few of them had been actively involved in the events of September 11 or the cover-up, I considered first that those folks aren't stupid. Senior government officials and members of Congress wouldn't be in those positions if they were. Surely the large majority of them suspected or even figured out what had happened and knew who was behind it. Yet they kept silent. In doing so, as I saw it, they became accessories after the fact. So why did they remain silent?

Senior officials and members of Congress, as insiders, want to remain in good standing with other insiders, and with their colleagues and social acquaintances. There's nothing wrong with that in itself. Yet given the enormity of the crimes that had been committed, how could it be that all of them, without exception, had and have remained silent about what they knew or suspected?

Enter the fear factor. They knew, as everyone did, what had happened to 3,000 people on September 11. They saw that only a week after that date Senate leaders Tom Daschle and Patrick Leahy, who had the power to delay or block a vote on the USA Patriot Act and other legislation and who wanted discussion before voting took place, were sent a particularly deadly strain of anthrax, which, though not killing them, did kill five others and infect 17 more.

The danger from the anthrax attacks were even greater than was known at the time. Some months later Michael Ruppert showed "that the Ames strain of anthrax, which was identified as the strain sent to Congress, was solely and exclusively the product of a CIA weapons research program involving the U.S. Army Medical Research Institute of Infectious Diseases and others. . . . All of the anthrax sent post-9/11 had come from within the United States and had originated in CIA-run covert research programs."[188] So it wasn't merely the anthrax itself that generated fear, but suspicion, later confirmed, about who had produced and sent it.

Such potentially deadly tactics were effective. The Patriot Act was passed without debate on October 24, 2001. As Ruppert observed, "Politically and physically frightened, a chamber full of pragmatists adapted to the new world by trading the Bill of Rights for their own political and physical security. In other words, Congress had gotten the message. The few opposition voices that remained, having been rendered ineffective, could be left in place as symbols to show that debate still existed."[189]

Congress would also learn of the unnatural death, some say assassination, of Senator Paul Wellstone in 2002, when he refused to support the war in Iraq. In Ruppert's account, "Senator Paul Wellstone was murdered just before the November 2002 elections . . . as the coup de grace in this final destruction of Constitutional government. Following the Patriot Act's statutory removal of constitutional protections, there will soon be few lower court judges in place to question the emperor's decisions, and few brave members remaining in Congress to ask the necessary questions."[190]

Senior officials and members of Congress with longer memories would have also recalled what happened to President John F. Kennedy and Senator Robert F. Kennedy when they opposed the CIA and the military 38 and 33 years earlier. They knew that their positions as senior members of the Bush administration or as members of Congress would not protect them from those who had already demonstrated their willingness to kill 3,000 people in one day and target a sitting president and at least two sitting senators.

They saw also that the Bush administration was successful in suppressing challenges to the official story. They saw that it resisted all calls to investigate September 11 for more than 400 days, before finally establishing a 9/11 Commission headed by someone closely connected with the White House. Surely they didn't take seriously the idea that the administration would investigate itself. It wouldn't, and it didn't. The Commission accepted the official story as fact and proceeded to hear mostly testimony that supported it and to ignore that which didn't. Although it did not conduct a legitimate investigation, its Report gave the administration and Congress the cover they needed to keep silent. They had an official Report they could point to if challenged, just as those formerly in their positions could point to the Report issued by the Warren Commission.

46

I turned next to the media. Americans might have been better able to see the holes if the media had actively investigated and reported on them, or if it had reviewed the many important books in which independent scholars and researchers laid out the evidence and reasoning showing that the official story couldn't possibly be correct. Or if it had accurately reported on the existence, activities and publications of the 9/11 Truth movement. But it didn't do any of these things. Instead, it actively supported the official story then and continues to do so to this very day.

The same fear that influenced the administration and Congress must also have pervaded the souls of writers, editors and publishers. How else to explain their one-sided promotion of the official story of that day, their silence about the physical impossibilities, their lack of investigation into the details of the legislation passed soon after September 11, and their distorted coverage of the Truth movement's investigations into what really happened. Yet even understanding the media's fear, I was appalled by its intellectual dishonesty.

Thinking further, I recalled that on September 11 some networks had covered in their live broadcasts developments or interviews that contradicted what would soon become the official story. That my recollection was accurate was confirmed by Gary G. Kohls in an article I'd just come across. Kohls documented that "truths expressed during the live coverage on September 11, 2001, were censored out by the mainstream media by 9/12/01. . . . What most television viewers saw and heard live from New York on 9/11/01 was soon to be heavily censored the very next day."[191]

As examples, Kohls cited the destruction of WTC 7, which several major news networks hadn't covered at all on September 11, and which wasn't rebroadcast on any major network after that date. The supposed crash site of UA 93 in Pennsylvania, too, wasn't shown on live TV. However, Kohls noted, from interviews conducted at the site viewers could see that it lacked any of the items usually found at the scene of plane crashes—no smoking fuselage, no luggage, passenger seats, or bodies. "Eyewitnesses to the Shanksville 'crash site' related their observations about the absence of debris, but when they contradicted the official narrative of 9/11, they were not given any more media exposure. The fix was in."

The Pentagon site was likewise poorly covered. The building was initially shown only from the opposite side from where a plane had supposedly crashed. Smoke seen rising above the building was the only indication that anything had occurred there. Once the side supposedly impacted was shown, after the wall segment had collapsed, it was shown only from a great distance, as though the zoom feature on every camera had stopped working. Jamie McIntyre, CNN's senior correspondent for military affairs, stated live on the air that there was no sign of a plane crash at the Pentagon. "From my close-up inspection," he reported, "there is no evidence of a plane having crashed anywhere near the Pentagon. . . . The only pieces left that you can see are small enough that you can pick them up in your hand. There are no large tail section, wing sections, fuselage, nothing like that anywhere around which would indicate that the entire plane crashed into the side of the Pentagon."[192]

On September 11 many of those interviewed in New York mentioned explosions and controlled demolition. CBS anchor Dan Rather commented about WTC 7, "Amazing, incredible, pick your word. For the third time today, it's reminiscent of those pictures we've all seen too much on television before, where a building was deliberately destroyed by well-placed dynamite to knock it down."[193]

Yet Rather's comment, like McIntyre's, was nowhere to be found in broadcasts on September 12. Instead, and in fact beginning by the evening of September 11, Kohls observed, "We began hearing the well-rehearsed opinions, . . . [as reporters and anchors] obediently mouth[ed] the official White House version about 'whodunit' and why. We were being inundated by the propaganda from the 'experts' who kept repeating the official conspiracy theories while simultaneously shouting down, ignoring or de-emphasizing the testimonial and video evidence that proved the controlled demolitions."

I then recalled something that I'd seen on September 11 as it occurred and wanted to see again. Dan Rather commented live on what appeared to be a round ball approaching the second tower through the air. At no point did it look like a plane, and Rather, puzzled, commented on it several times as it grew nearer. Although it looked round, like a ball, it could have been a missile viewed head on.

Wanting to see the image again, I pulled off the shelf the book and DVD collection titled *What We S*aw, published by CBS News, with an introduction by Rather. I was disappointed to see that the book and DVD gave only a very selective and incomplete account of what had been broadcast on September 11. They made no mention in the book and provided no video on the DVD of the ball approaching the tower or of Rather's comments about it. Nor did they reproduce his comments that the collapse of the buildings looked like controlled demolitions. I concluded that readers were being misled—lied to by omission, purposefully and deliberately—by CBS and by Dan Rather.

Determined to pursue this omission further, I searched for, and found, in the CBS archives, videos that were purported to be the original live news broadcasts from September 11. In them, though, there was no mention of the ball, explosions, or controlled demolition. They'd been edited out.

So, not only had coverage changed overnight, from September 11th to the 12th to align with the official narrative, the historical record of the live coverage in the archives had also been cleansed.

Even worse, I couldn't find in the archives of any of the five major news networks—ABC, CBS, NBC, CNN, and Fox—any images of the second plane approaching the second tower for more than a few seconds before impact. Surely it's approach would have been visible for at least several minutes. Even more astonishing, all channels except one showed the same coverage of those few seconds of the approaching plane from the same angle, as though all had been fed a short video clip from the same source. In that short clip the plane is too dark—it was in the direct sunlight and should have been as lit up as the tower in the center of the video. Even stranger, the tower shown is the one already hit; the one that the approaching plane will hit is completely hidden by the one shown. Live coverage of the moment of impact was thus hidden from viewers of all major networks. [See Image 26.]

The only news program I found in the archives that showed a different image of the approaching plane, CBS 9, in Washington,

Image 26. As shown on 4 of the 5 networks, the second plane was visible for only a few seconds before impacting the far side of WTC 2. Immediately before showing this clip, some networks had shown a wider view showing no plane approaching from either side of the towers. A big mistake!

D.C., showed the approach of the plane for only the second or two that it could be seen in the gap between a tall building and the towers. [See Image 27.] The buildings and the plane are shown at such a distance that the small dark smudge between them cannot be clearly identified as a plane. It's so small relative to the tower that even if it's a plane it's hard to imagine how it could have caused any significant damage to it. In this photo, too, the moment of impact is on the far side of the building and not visible to those watching the news broadcast.

Before the approach of the "plane" that supposedly hit the second tower, all news programs that I viewed in the archives showed the first tower, the one already hit, from multiple sides and angles, so it's clear that the networks had their own cameras or access to video feeds already in place before the approach of the second plane. They were set up to show its approach from the moment it appeared on the horizon until the moment of impact from the angle that would have provided the best coverage of both had they wanted to. Instead, all chose to provide coverage that hid both the approach of the plane except for the final few seconds and the moment of impact.

Further, in all of the live videos in the archives, all news announcers were surprised by the sudden appearance of the plane, as though neither they nor their colleagues had been monitoring input from their own cameras or the live feed provided by others, which would have shown the approaching plane.

But some of the broadcasters made a mistake: they showed a wide view of the sky, revealing no plane or any other object approaching the tower, before cutting to the closeup of a plane approaching and hitting the far side of the second tower [as shown in Image 26]. The plane, according to their own broadcast, had appeared out of nowhere. It was a fake video.[194]

It was only later in the day that several videos of the second plane impacting the second tower were shown—and they, as

Image 27. The second plane visible for only a few seconds between two tall buildings before impacting the far side of WTC 2.

already noted, gave every appearance of being photoshopped fakes because they showed the physically impossible image of a thin hollow aluminum tube (the plane's fuselage) slicing through solid concrete and steel as easily as a hot knife through butter. More ridiculous still was the thin holes supposedly cut into the towers by the wings at both edges of the point of impact. Wings, as any airline passenger who has viewed them from a window inside the plane can verify, are so fragile that "do not walk" is stenciled on them. Yet they cut through solid steel and cement.

Those clips of the moment of impact, if faked, couldn't have been assembled until after the exact spot of the "plane's" impact was known, which is why, I suspect, the moment of impact couldn't be shown live. In support of the idea that all are fakes—all the videos of a few seconds of a plane approaching the second tower shown live and the videos shown later in the day of the impact—is that the tens of thousands of September 11 photos released into the public domain by NIST don't include even one photo showing a plane in the sky. And, of the thousands of September 11 photos in the public domain available through Wikimedia Commons, only one shows a plane. I find that very strange, given how comprehensive those collections are for all other aspects of the events of that day.

47

At this point I came across an analysis by Ted Walter and Graeme MacQueen laying out how the bin Laden cover story was ultimately implanted in viewers' minds even though the idea that explosions had brought down the twin towers had been "the dominant hypothesis"[195] on the morning of September 11. It is "important to look into how the triumph of the Official Narrative was accomplished," they explained, because "if we are able to discover this, we will greatly advance our understanding of the psychological operation conducted on September 11, 2001—and, thus, our understanding of how other psychological operations are perpetrated on the public."[196]

Their analysis of how this audacious feat of psychological manipulation was accomplished was so well-done that I must pause to describe both the manipulation and their analysis of it.

Walter and MacQueen reviewed 70 hours of live coverage on 11 different television networks, cable news channels and local network affiliates, which included those of all the big-name anchors, before preparing their two-part analysis. In the first part, they established that "among individuals who witnessed the event firsthand, the more prevalent hypothesis was that the Twin Towers had been brought down by massive explosions." When members of the New York Fire Department, for instance, were interviewed in the weeks after September 11, "118 of them described witnessing what they interpreted that day to be explosions, . . . [while] only 10 FDNY members were found describing the destruction in ways supportive of the fire-induced collapse hypothesis."[197] Of reporters "who directly witnessed the destruction of the Twin Towers, . . . 21 of the 25, . . . or 84%, either perceived an explosion or explosions or they perceived the Twin Towers as exploding, blowing up, blowing apart, or erupting."

The purpose of their second article "was to determine how, despite its prevalence, the explosion hypothesis was supplanted by the hypothesis of fire-induced collapse."[198] They found that two strategies were employed to accomplish the triumph of "the Official Narrative." As part of both, news anchors moved from broadcasting reports from reporters present at the scene . . . who continued to view the destruction of the towers as an explosion-based attack subsequent to the airplane strikes . . . to interviewing guests who were tasked "with discovering and making sense of what was happening."

This strategy was used with anchors who were sincerely dedicated to discovering the facts of the situation. It "involved directly confronting the news anchor of the relevant network with an 'expert' who would explain that the destruction of the Twin Towers was caused by structural failure induced by the airplane impact and the ensuing fires. This would allay concerns about reports of explosions in the towers and would domesticate the new anchor so that he or she would stop raising problematic questions. Of course, as we can see clearly today, these experts could not possibly have known what they so confidently proclaimed. In fact, we can now see that their explanations were simply wrong. But their interviews seem to have accomplished their goals on 9/11."

"Was it chance that led a series of 'experts' to disarm these independent-minded news anchors with one false hypothesis after another?" Walter and MacQueen asked, before concluding, "not likely." "Consider that many building professionals and technical experts are known to have immediately suspected that explosives were responsible for the Twin Towers' destruction. . . . So, how is it that every 'expert' who appeared on national television that day advocated the fire-induced collapse hypothesis when there were so many who favored the explosion hypothesis? Although it cannot be proven, we suspect that intentionality, coordination, and deception are on display in these interviews."

The second strategy, used on all networks with all anchors, "involved developing two related narratives—two engaging, emotionally charged stories—that appeared to explain the day's horrors and offered viewers a set of active responses. They were not scientific hypotheses and were not directly related to the destruction of the Twin Towers, but indirectly they appeared to favor the fire-induced collapse hypothesis more than the explosion hypothesis."

The first of these two stories, which Walter and MacQueen call the War on Terror narrative, "explained how the righteous, the civilized, the United States had been subjected to an act of war from the evil, the uncivilized, the terrorists supported by nations in the Middle East and Central Asia; and how American leaders must respond to this aggression with an initiative that was warlike on many levels." The second was "the bin Laden narrative, which nested within the wider War on Terror narrative and was used to transform myth into plausible history. According to this narrative, an evil Saudi national based in Afghanistan had masterminded the attacks."

This psychological sleight of hand worked brilliantly. By presenting a stream of experts making "unfounded assertions about the inability of the buildings to withstand the airplane impacts and fires," and by distracting the viewers' attention away from the bombings and toward the emotionally charged terror and bin Laden narratives, "by the end of the day, they had silenced the explosion hypothesis." To the extent that these narratives were convincingly conveyed to viewers, no further argument against the explosion hypothesis was necessary. The foreign evildoers had crashed airplanes into the buildings and the buildings had come down, and that was all one needed to know."

In summing up the major propaganda elements at play on September 11, Walter and MacQueen showed how effectively "television was used to evoke shock and confusion in U.S. citizens, and in citizens around the world, by transmitting the horrific images of the day. No words, no analysis, can compete with the images of the airplane strikes, the disintegrating towers, and the shocked reactions of people on the street. Such shock ensures that critical thinking will be at a low ebb, while old loyalties and a desire to pull together in the face of violence will be very powerful."

They went on to identify nine major propaganda elements used on September 11. Because these elements had been so persuasive in convincing the large majority of people around the world of the validity of a narrative I have come to believe is false, and because these elements appear to have been used in coverage of other events before and after September 11, I am listing them here for easy reference. [See nearby textbox.]

Major Propaganda Elements at Play on September 11 Identified by Ted Walter & Graeme MacQueen

1. Identify the chosen perpetrator quickly.

2. Repeat this suspect's name very frequently, not allowing any other possibility to compete. (Fox News carried at least 56 important mentions of bin Laden and CNN carried at least 69 in the hours of news coverage we studied. [4 per hour on Fox, 8.6 per hour on CNN]

3. Make a variety of claims and suggestions about the perpetrator that make his/her guilt appear likely—no actual evidence necessary—and intimate that intelligence sources are, somewhere behind the curtain, building a strong case that we will eventually see.

4. Make strategic use of selected "experts." If news anchors are toying with heretical hypotheses about the destruction of the Twin Towers, bring building professionals in to set them straight—as before, no actual evidence is necessary.

5. Normalize the abnormal. Make it seen as if it is natural that this massive and complex operation could have been carried out by bin Laden's crew, and do not mention the state organizations far more suited to the task.

6. Do not hesitate to make use of flawed logic where it is helpful—we have given post hoc ergo propter hoc as the example that supports the fire-induced collapse hypothesis.

7. Tell gripping stories and repeat them throughout the day. Link these specific stories to Grand Narratives fundamental to the nation, such as those of aggression and savagery.

8. Push aside actual courtroom-worthy evidence (such as eyewitness evidence) explicitly when necessary, as through the use of select "experts;" otherwise erase such evidence indirectly through dramatic story-telling that appears to support the official hypothesis being constructed.

9. Make profligate use of state authorities. Citizens reduced to a state of fear will be open to hearing from a former Secretary of Defense, even if what he has to offer is thin gruel.

❦ 48 ❦

As time went on, though, why didn't the American people wake up? How could they not see through the absurdities of the official story? Why did they not rise up against those who had really been behind the atrocities of September 11? The unanimous silence of government officials and the persuasiveness of the propaganda consistently repeated in the media couldn't be the full answer. American adults were, after all, adults living in a seemingly free society where information was readily available even if one had to look for it.

Even if the report of the 9/11 Commission was in stock at Barnes and Noble, David Ray Griffin's *The 9/11 Commission Report: Omissions and Distortions* was readily available at amazon.com. The *Popular Mechanics* piece debunking the findings of scholars active in the 9/11 Truth movement was available at amazon, but so was Griffin's *Debunking 9/11 Debunking*. Other books presenting the official story were readily available, but so was Griffin's *9/11 Contradictions: An Open Letter to Congress and the Press*. Dozens of websites put up by individuals and organizations active in the 9/11 Truth movement were easily accessible. So why is it that, as English professor Eric Larsen phrased it, "the conspiracy of silence and secrecy and cover-up and distortion and disinformation"[199] continues to be effective?

Like many other scholars seeking to explain why recent events in the United States occurred as they did, Larsen regarded 1947 as a key date in American history. Unlike others, who cite only the creation of the CIA, the National Security Agency and related institutions that year, Larsen also cited a second factor: 1947 was the approximate year in which television began to reach a large portion of the American public. In his view, television was largely responsible for turning Americans into passive recipients of information, with the security agencies increasingly creating the content of that information.

"Since 1947," Larsen explained, "Americans have been steadily and purposively taught, encouraged, and indoctrinated to be more passive than active, more consumer than doer, and to see life and 'reality' not as they actually are but as the mass media have already pre-defined and pre-packaged them. So expert and so all-encompassing is this system of mass media that not only has it created what Americans see and perceive as 'real,' but it has also trained and conditioned (or 'cultivated') Americans to accept this prefabricated reality as something that they have both the right and the highly honorable duty to embrace and defend."[200]

I found Larsen's assessment of the passivity of American citizens who still adhere to the official story—an assessment in two sentences, one long and one short—so apt that I'm including it in this memoir. [See nearby textbox.]

Two sentences, one long and one short, by Eric Larsen

"So much scholarship has been done on 9/11, so much has been written, demonstrated, revealed, and shown about it, about the crucial and relevant events preceding it, about the tactical and strategic origins of the plot, about the precise manner of its execution, about the long and causative *political* history preceding it, and about the deliberate and intentional means by which the truth about the events of that day has been and remains suppressed and covered up—so much evidence has been accumulated and so much scholarship has been completed and written, including breath-takingly perceptive, thorough, and irrefutable *scientific* scholarship, that any American citizen with the least iota of political conscience, with the least sense of civic responsibility, with the least possession of independence, free agency, and intellectual curiosity, and with the least desire to bequeath to their children and to their children's children's a place and a way to live other than under torture, other than in chains, and other than in hunger—any such American citizens who still adheres to the government's seven-year-long chain of continuous and contemptible lies about what really happened on 9/11 is either a fool, a complete non-entity socio-politically, *or* a party to the cover-up and thus to treachery. *Or* is unbelieving and scared to death."

From Eric Larsen, *The Skull of Yorick*, pp. 155-56.

Larsen's account about the negative influence of television jelled with what I'd observed around me. It also served as a counterpoint to the concept of Principality. I'd seen people so reliant on electronic screens for information that, when wanting to know what the weather was like, reach for their phones rather than look out the window. Relying on pre-packaged information in TV news broadcasts, without getting a second opinion, was similar to the mistake I'd made in relying on the opinion of only one doctor before agreeing to the risky surgery than resulted in Diana's death. Blindly accepting as objective reality broadcasts studded with images and spoken commentary carefully calculated for their emotional impact almost guaranteed that viewers were sacrificing Principality.

Many Americans I know continue to regard themselves as informed because they watch TV news broadcasts. They apparently continue to believe that today's news programs have the same objectivity as the McNeil/Lehrer NewsHour, which ran from 1975 until 2009. But TV news isn't like that anymore. The few programs I've watched since returning to the United States five months ago all appeared to be propaganda. They'd been designed not to inform but to stir emotions up against or for selected people or subjects. The effect of repeated watching of such programs would be, in Larsen's characterization, a population that would "choose to see false reality as true or real reality, but . . . actually prefer, extol, and defend the false over the real." Americans, in his view, "have degenerated to a rank among the least perceptive, informed, intelligent, or thoughtful people in the entire world."[201] All that leads to the conclusion that "The thing that is destroying our nation and putting the entire world at risk—is *the disease of blindness that believes itself to be sightedness*."[202]

When so many Americans see a picture of the towers in New York being pulverized by explosions from within yet claim to see the towers collapsing—when they profess belief in their pre-existing beliefs over the testimony of their own eyes—what word is more appropriate than blindness? When they see a small hole in the wall of the Pentagon with no plane wreckage in front of it, or see a field in Pennsylvania with no plane wreckage littering the landscape, yet claim in both cases to see the sites of plane crashes, what phrase is more apt than self-deceived?

What am I to think of people who refuse to look, who refuse to see for themselves what actually happened during the most important event in their country in living memory? I must account myself as having been one of them until two months ago. I too hadn't taken the time to learn from the dedicated and determined scholars and researchers who have uncovered what really happened.

I now believe that as citizens of a republic, Americans have a duty to understand the events of that day. The heavy lifting has already been done for us by David Ray Griffin, Judy Wood, Richard Gage, Jim Fetzer, Jim Marrs, Webster Tarpley, Michael C. Ruppert, Peter Dale Scott and so many other scholars and investigators. Their work is readily available to anyone who wants to see it.

Sure these days, we have to scroll past top results giving the official story, but here's a shortcut: search for September 11 conspiracy theories, then read the sources critiqued. Don't simply accept characterizations of them; read the sources themselves. It's easy. It's simple. It's what every citizen of the United States should do to become informed about one of the most important events in the recent history of his country. It's what every person should do to become or remain a Principal.

I regret not having done that from day one, when first seeing images of the towers being destroyed and of the supposed crash sites at the Pentagon and in Pennsylvania. I regret that I was able to say to myself that yes, those buildings do appear to be falling as the result of controlled demolition, and yes, it would have been impossible for the Arab hijackers to have planted explosives in the buildings, and yet a moment later put all that out of my mind and continue watching the stunning images and absorbing the official narrative.

I'm beyond embarrassed, I'm ashamed that I allowed myself to be so blind for so many years. But I'm not, now, and I want to help others gain the clearer sight that I believe I now have.

If we as a nation can't find a way out of this blindness, we are, as Eric Larson concluded, "doomed to tyranny in place of freedom, chains in place of liberty, and, above all, to a cruel, demeaning, hollow, unforgiving, and empty imprisonment intellectually, emotionally, spiritually, and personally." To avoid all that we must "find a means to heal ourselves of and then inoculate ourselves to the crippling, enervating, disempowering disease of the blindness that believes itself to be sightedness."[203]

49

Although WORDS, WORDS, WORDS had been up and running for several weeks, the Grand Opening didn't take place until near the end of the month.

It was a simple affair, held in the entryway of the studio. Decorations had been strung up on all sides, and a ribbon had been hung in front of the aisle leading to the cubicles and offices. Food and drink had been catered from the Mexican restaurant at the end of the row of shops. About 40 people attended, including friends from the Filipino community and from Gina's school days. Half a dozen students she was tutoring were there, too, and several of them had brought their parents.

Gina wore a dress with vertical stripes of a light brown color on a white background, with a thin sash around the middle that tied in a small bow on her right side, which emphasized her slim figure while still presenting her as a professional educator. She looked stunning.

She made a short speech to thank all her supporters, and at the right moment Maja handed her a pair of scissors. The ribbon was soon cut and WORDS, WORDS, WORDS was officially open. It was a happy moment, and I was proud of Gina for having brought it off with such style.

50

At the party at Maja's place after the Grand Opening, I had a chance to see Gina in action, attempting to use her sexual attractiveness to provoke a suitor into proposing. About 20 people, a mix of Filipinos and Westerners, men and women, had gathered at Maja's apartment, and the living room was quite crowded. Across the room I saw Gina, now dressed in another of her vintage outfits, looking alluring in something a farmer's daughter might have worn in some man's wild fantasy. She was in a corner of the living room, talking to a man about 40 years old, telling him a story about a man who wanted to get married and wanted to be sure his bride was a virgin. "'But where can I find a virgin in today's world?' he asked his friend. 'In a convent,' was his reply. So he went to an abbey near their town and spoke with the Abbess. 'I'm concerned that the convent is located adjacent to a monastery, with monks living there,' he told her. 'Yes, it is,' she replied, 'but the wall between the abbey and the monastery is very thick. We have no communication with the monks.'

"So he picked a girl who was already scheduled to leave the convent, and was assured that she was a virgin," Gina continued. "On their wedding night, he had trouble entering her. She was so small and tight, and he looked around for some cream to make things easier.

"'Oh, just use spit,' his bride said. 'That what the monks always did.'"

Think how arousing this story would be when told to a man still in the full vigor of youth by an attractive young woman dressed in a sexy vintage outfit as a milkmaid or farmer's daughter. He might find the story so arousing that he'd try to hold her, kiss her, drag her off to a bedroom. In fact, that's exactly what the suitor tried to do. But when he tried, Gina went immediately into her all-innocent act, as though she'd done nothing to trigger the situation, nothing to arouse him.

Watching this example of twisted sexuality, this playing with that man's desires and affections, pissed me off, an ugly phrase I don't often use but that seemed applicable here. That a girl I respected and admired, one who was so intelligent and so accomplished in so many ways, would act in this manner was unsettling, so unsettling that once the party broke up I stayed behind and did with and to Maja what she'd offered before and what that suitor had wanted to do with and to Gina.

Later, during a midnight snack, Maja told me how confused Gina was. "She's of two minds, Jubal. There's nothing sexier to her than a man who is pursuing what he wants, a man who has a passion that he's absorbed in. She mentioned your obsession with your Kennedy and September 11 research. She was thrilled that you'd mentioned possibly writing a book about your experience of investigating those subjects, and wonders if there might be a way she could help you with it."

"But she's also puzzled because although often it seems that you want to get to know her better, at other times you tell her that any relationship would be impossible, not just because of the age difference, but because of your age in itself. She doesn't accept that reasoning, or at least doesn't want to accept it.

"And she's confused because although, she's said, 'he puts all my other suitors to shame,' and she wants to get to know you better, too, she recognizes how difficult it would be for both of you to start up with someone of a completely different culture. She sees the challenge as being more difficult for you, much easier for her because she is already in your country and is so much younger. And she sees how busy you are with your own projects, and wonders if you would have time for a new young wife and then for babies crawling around your house while you're trying to work. She says that 'Even though he's rare, I've decided, at least in my head, to let him go.' But she doesn't mean it. You're far and away at the top of her list of suitors."

"I'm not a suitor," I said to Maja, but at the same time I was thinking hard about what I'd just heard and about what I should do about Gina. Did I want to be a suitor, or not? I really should make a decision and let her know definitively either way. But hadn't I already done those things?

Driving home, I had two thoughts. One was that Gina, in trying to manipulate men by telling sexually arousing stories, hadn't a clue as to the power of the desires she was playing with. Like the sorcerer's apprentice, she was messing with powers far more powerful—she was triggering desires far more intense and insistent—than she could ever imagine given the limited range of her experiences.

I also recalled what I'd told Gina after I'd bought a computer for her: that through her I'd come to realize the hard truth that although I am mentally and physically ready, willing and able to begin again with someone new, to go through the joyous times of courtship and marriage and raising a family, I also knew that I was too old to do so. I'd be 77 years old when a child born to me a few years from now would graduate from high school. Some of my happiest memories were of raising my family when my kids were small; I'd love to do it all again, but suspect I'd be too old to do it well. It would be wonderful to try, though, but it wouldn't be fair to them, or their mother.

51

"Look at this, Russell!" I said, waving a sheet of paper as I approached him outside the Thai restaurant in Chapel Hill where we were meeting for lunch. Here's a statement, just released, signed by G. Robert Blakey, who had been Chief Counsel for the House Assassinations Committee, by Dr. Robert McClelland, one of the surgeons who tried to save Kennedy's life at Dallas's Parkland Memorial Hospital, and by other JFK experts. It expresses their beliefs about what really happened."

I read part of it to him as we huddled outside the restaurant. "'The conspiracy to assassinate President Kennedy was organized at high levels of the U.S. power structure, and was implemented by top elements of the U.S. national security apparatus using, among others, figures in the criminal underworld to help carry out the crime and cover-up.'"[204]

"This could change everything!" I said. Then, realizing that my initial enthusiasm might be overdone, added, "Though I'm not especially optimistic. My opinion of the media in this country is so low that I expect it will ignore the statement, just as it ignores so much solid evidence about what happened in Dallas in 1963 and in New York and Washington in 2001."

"I expect you're right," Russell said. "We'll need a much bigger jolt than this to shake the country out of its stupor. But it's a crack in the wall, a sign that things might finally be starting to shake loose. Let's keep our eyes on this to see what develops."

As we were waiting to be seated, he gave me an article he'd printed out—"How Lyndon Johnson Expropriated Control Over the Pentagon and CIA Soon After the Inauguration of the Kennedy-Johnson Administration," by Phillip F. Nelson—and said, "Here's an important new article. It reveals that Robert Caro, in his volumes on Lyndon Johnson, is apparently burying Johnson's involvement in the assassination planning and cover-up, and is burying his connections to Mac Wallace, Billie Sol Estes, Bobby Baker and others who carried out his most evil deeds. The article even quotes someone involved with protecting Johnson as saying 'We are not worried about Caro. He is on board.'"[205]

"Well that's disappointing," I said. "I had thoroughly enjoyed Caro's earlier volumes, beginning with his accounts showing how difficult life was in the Texas hill country in the days of Johnson's youth."

Once we were seated at a table inside, in a booth near a window, I expressed how increasingly disgusted I was becoming by the media's continued adherence to the official assassination and September 11 stories and its refusal to cover either the findings or the existence of the 9/11 Truth movement, except to mock and ridicule it. And by media I included the entire mainstream publishing industry, including publishers of books like Caro's.

"The same false stories are endless repeated in the media," I said, "even though new information has been uncovered. It's been known for years that at least five and perhaps as many as 11 of the 19 supposed Arab hijackers are still alive, yet the media and textbooks continue to present the original story with the original 19 names and photos. In fact, the director of the FBI had acknowledged on September 20, 2001, that the identity of several of the hijackers was in doubt. But there's no mention of this problem in the 9/11 Commission Report.[206]

"The FBI has also acknowledged that none of the supposed phone conversations between Ted Olson and his wife, who was supposedly on hijacked AA 77, actually occurred. One of those supposed calls was the only source for the boxcutters supposedly used by the hijackers. But if the calls hadn't taken place, then there is no source for the boxcutters angle. Yet the official story remains unchanged, with boxcutters prominently mentioned in the media and in textbooks. What will it take for any change at all to be made to the official story? All this reminds me of the 'no updates allowed' policy applied to the Kennedy assassination."

I realized that I was gushing, talking too much without giving Russell a chance to speak, yet wasn't able to stop myself.

"It's ridiculous that the wings of the plane that supposedly hit the Pentagon simply vanished, along with the engines attached to them, without causing any damage to the wall, while the wings that supposedly hit the towers in New York managed to cut right through solid concrete and steel. Both situations were absurd—to leave no mark and debris, and to cut through. Yet Americans didn't challenge either absurd story. Just like they didn't challenge the Magic Bullet theory used to justify the Oswald-as-lone-assassin story. How are we to explain this?"

At last, I forced myself to stop talking.

"I see you've been busy, Jubal," Russell said with a smile. "It was always impossible to reconcile these facts with the official story. In fact, the chairman and vice-chairman of the 9/11 Commission wrote books in which they partially disassociated themselves from their own Report. They stated that the Commission was set up to fail, that information was withheld from them, and that almost all witnesses who appeared before them had been selected because they'd support the government's account. They also stated that officials from the Pentagon and the FAA lied to them to such a degree that they'd considered referring them to the Department of Justice on obstruction of justice charges.

"I started to make a list of videos about September 11 for you," Russell continued, "videos from which I learned a lot over the dozen years since I began investigating the issue after retiring in 2008. But in checking the URLs, I found that most of them are no longer available on YouTube. Even sites available only a few years ago are gone. And when I type '9/11 Truth' into

YouTube, the first dozen entries to appear all have 'conspiracy theory' in the title. Anyone trying to investigate the issue now would have a much harder time than even three or four years ago."

He passed two lists to me as he spoke, explaining that he'd prepared a list of important websites available today and another of videos no longer available at YouTube. "Perhaps you can find them," he said as he pointed to one of the items. "You've probably already discovered that the Pentagon was hit by a cruise missile. One report says it was fired from a U.S. naval vessel. An incredible film of the launching of the missile, which had to have been filmed from a helicopter above the ship, used to be available on video.com, but it's not there now.

"And then there's Donald Trump's interview on the afternoon of September 11. He did at least two interviews, and one is still available on YouTube, but in the one I'm thinking of, the one that has vanished, he tells the interviewer, in a live report shortly after the towers had fallen, that he's an expert on construction of buildings such as those, and that in his expert opinion the buildings were brought down by explosives planted inside the buildings. That's a very important assessment by an expert in construction, but it's gone with the wind. It's very disappointing that Trump hasn't revealed what he knows or suspects even though he's now president.

"Anyway, here's a transcript of the Trump interview that I made when it was still available," Russell said as he passed another sheet of paper across the table. "It's still quite an important statement, in which Trump says that bombs must have been used to destroy the towers."

After giving me a minute to read it, he continued.

"Pilots for 9/11 Truth has completely vanished from the web. I learned much from its website a decade ago, but now there's hardly any trace that the organization ever existed. One by one, the videos that most clearly contradict the official story are vanishing."

After a pause to let Russell's information sink in, I said, "That's really distressing. It's like Orwell's "Memory Hole" in

Donald Trump Interview on September 11, 2001 on what destroyed the WTC towers

PARTIAL TRANSCRIPT

"Well, it was not an architectural defect. The World Trade Center was always known as a very, very strong building. . . . The reason the World Trade Center has such narrow windows, is that in between all the windows you had this steel on the outside of the building. That's why, when I first looked at it, I couldn't believe it because there was a hole in the steel. And this is steel that was, you remember the width of the windows of the World Trade Center, folks. I said, how could a plane, even a 767 or 747 or whatever it might have been how could it possibly go through the steel? . . . I happen to think that they had not only a plane, but they had bombs that exploded almost simultaneously because I just can't imagine anything being able to go through that wall. Most buildings are built with the steel on the inside around the elevator shaft. This one was built from the outside, which is the strongest structure you can have. And it was almost just like a can of soup."

"Donald Trump Thought Bombs Exploded Simultaneously on 9/11," NakedEmperor.substack.com, Sept. 11, 2023. Includes link to Trump's interview with WWOR/UPN 9 News, FOX 5. His comments are at 5:30.

1984. Information inconvenient to those in power simply vanishes.

"You know, Russell, there are things I remember seeing on TV news broadcasts on September 11, things I watched several times, as they were re-broadcast. I've wanted to see them again, but now those reports are no longer available, not even in the archives of the major studios. They've all been edited, yet still claim to be the full coverage from that day."

I mentioned to him the oddities of the videos of the plane approaching the second tower that I've already described in this memoir.

"I've also looked for videos of the towers after they'd supposedly been struck by planes, showing swarms of birds flying around the burnt-out holes in the towers that I clearly remember watching on September 11. It was weird that flocks of birds would fly in from somewhere unknown, fly around the burnt-out holes, then fly away to somewhere unknown. I suspect that those "birds" were really drones filming close up the damaged sites. Yet those broadcasts have now vanished, too. And isn't it strange that network TV never attempted to film those holes or those flocks of birds up close? Just like we were never shown any shots of the Pentagon or the crash site in Pennsylvania up close.

"It's hard, Russell, to see so much intellectual crime committed by the media, and to see how its dishonest coverage is blindly accepted by the American people. I don't know what's worse, the deliberate lying by the media or the stupidity of the American people. It's all so demoralizing that I can't work for more than short periods of time. I have to take frequent breaks to refresh my spirit. Half the time I'm ready to abandon my September 11 research altogether and return to my Huxley-Kennedy-Lewis project."

Russell nodded, and we both considered our own thoughts silently for a few minutes.

I then launched into something else on my mind. "Did you know that 46 exercises and drills related to the events of September 11 took place? Some took place in the weeks leading up to that day, most on that day, and some soon after. And get this: There was a drill for every key component of September 11!

"One investigator, Webster Griffin Tarpley, showed that the attacks were 'largely camouflaged' by the drills, which show that 'a privately controlled network or faction inside the U.S. government directly caused and created 9/11.'[207]

"This sure appears to me to be cover for a coup," I continued. Anyone noticing anything unusual would assume or be told that it was part of a drill, until the drill changed to an attack for real, at which point it would be too late to do anything to stop it."

"You've certainly been busy," Russell again commented briefly, observing that I still had more to say.

"And get this, Russell. Tarpley speculated that the plotters had to rely on outside contractors from the private sector for some aspects of September 11—contractors whose confidentiality would be less secure than military or government officials sworn to secrecy. He noted that an emergency drill for computer specialists and consultants was held in the WTC South Tower, on the 97th floor offices, on 9/11, and speculated that the plotters used the attacks to eliminate the risk that those in the training would later talk about their role, wittingly or unwitting, in organizing the events of that day.[208]

"And get this: remember John O'Neil, the FBI counter-terrorism expert who resigned before September 11 because of Bureau and White House obstruction of his investigations into bin Laden and terrorism?[209] He had discovered that 'something big' was going to happen but couldn't get anyone to listen to him. He was hired as chief of security for the towers shortly before September 11 and was in one of them when it collapsed. Another loose end taken care of, from the perpetrators' point of view."

We were both quiet again.

After coffee was served, I commented that "The scheme that was enacted on September 11 was so complex, so convoluted, with plane crashes, collapses of buildings, war games and so many other incidents all having to be timed just right, that the effort that had to go into designing and carrying it out is almost overwhelming in its scope and complexity. How could so many pieces ever have been conceived, managed and carried out without anybody involved coming forward since then to reveal their part in it?"

"They got away with it because of the complicity of the media," Russell responded. "A media controlled by the intelligence agencies that had a big role in those events. Here's an interesting angle from which to view the media's involvement, though I don't know if it's one that will lighten your spirit.

"Everyone knows that he shouldn't yell 'Fire!' in a crowded theater when there's no fire. But what if you are in a theater and see a fire but keep silent? If people die, are you criminally negligent?

"And what if you're the Fire Office or usher with the duty of keeping the place safe and clean, and you see the fire yet keep silent?

"What if you're the owner, see all, yet keep silent?

"And what if you're a journalist in the theater, and see the owner and the usher watching the fire and keeping quiet, yet don't write about it, don't let people know what happened? That's the situation we're in today. By remaining silent, the media has failed in its duty to report the news; and because criminal activity is involved, the media is an accessory after the fact because it had information about what and who yet kept silent.

"The only hope left, and it's a thin one, is if the American people awake from the stupor they're in and demand that the government and the media respond to holes and contradictions in the official story. If that doesn't happen soon, it will be too late to save the theater—the country."

I then mentioned something that had puzzled me. "I've been looking through *Skeptic Magazine* and the other one with a similar name, Russell. I'd expected them, magazines professing a skeptical attitude, to be among the leaders of the 9/11 Truth movement. Instead, they solidly support the official story and ridicule those who have examined the evidence and reached a different conclusion. My respect for Michael Shermer, publisher of *Skeptic Magazine*, has gone through the floor."

Russell supplied the answer. "Professional skeptics are skeptical about alternative theories; they are believers in mainstream explanations. So they aren't really born doubters after all. I've seen those magazines too, seen that they repeatedly use the terms 'conspiracy theory' and 'conspiracy theorist' to refer to investigators who bring to light evidence that conflicts with the official story."

He reached into his bag, pulled out an article and passed it to me, saying, "David Cogswell got it just right with his description of those labels."

He gave me a moment to read the article, which stated in part, "The official explanation of events of that day is unequivocally a theory of conspiracy. It's the ultimate conspiracy theory for the world's most spectacular crime, but it's not called a conspiracy theory. That term is reserved for any ideas that contradict the official story. This is a very important point. Conspiracy theories are not about conspiracies, they are about forbidden thought. The label 'conspiracy theory' is a stop sign on the avenues of rational thought and inquiry. It says, 'Stop here. Entrance forbidden.'"[210]

"Well, Americans as a people and as a country will have to get over those phrases and examine the evidence for themselves," I said in response. "They'll have to regain trust in the testimony of their own eyes that they lost when they accepted the Magic Bullet theory on that day in Dallas 56 years ago.

"But it's all so distressing, Russell," I continued. "I had throughout my life, and throughout my career, viewed the United States as the good guy in the world, leading it toward greater peace, security, prosperity and democracy. I was proud to be part of that effort. But now I'm aware of a thousand and one reasons to think otherwise.

"Realizing the truth about who assassinated Kennedy, I was able to put that behind me. It was one event, and it was long ago. But now with September 11 we have a second event, one much more recent and much more destructive to the country and the rest of the world. Both were committed by the same organizations within the U.S. government. The Warren Commission and the 9/11 Commission both disgraced themselves and their country by their mendacious reports that covered up what really happened and who was really behind it all.

"I no longer believe that the country remains sound and secure, that the democratic and economic systems I'd spent much of my career explaining to people in other countries are functioning well at all. I'd been duped and then proceeded to dupe others. I'd gone to work for the bad guys, Russell. I've been a tool used by the malign forces that have taken control of the government and the country I'd represented abroad."

I then remembered something that enabled me to end our lunch on a positive note. "Hey Russell," I said as we walked outside. "I just learned that William Hurt, one of my favorite actors, was aware of what really happened on September 11. He believed so strongly in what he'd learned that he wrote an article stating that the towers in New York were brought down by controlled demolition. It's on the website of Architects and Engineers for 9/11 Truth. In it he mentioned two new documentaries about that day, one that he produced. So progress is being made in spite of the odds so heavily stacked against it."

February 2020

❧ 52 ❧

At the appointed time for the book club's discussion of Graham Greene's *The Quiet American*, Gina breezed in wearing a mauve lace sleeveless dress extending down just far enough to cover her knees, which emphasized her slim figure. It was modest and revealing at the same time, and what it revealed was that there wasn't an ounce of fat anywhere on her body. Adding to the distinctiveness of the dress were gentle ruffles in the lowest six or so inches, suggesting a fashion popular in the '50s, the time in which Greene's novel was set.

Several aspects of the book gave it great relevance for my life at this time. One was the efforts made by Fowler, an older worldly British journalist based in Saigon, to determine the real status and activities of Pyle, a young seemingly naïve recently arrived American businessman. Fowler's suspicion grows that the American's presence in Saigon was connected to wider and more official concerns than mere business. Is Pyle naïve or cunning, straightforward or duplicitous? Fowler wants to know, and much of the novel details his efforts to uncover the American's real nature and activities when facts lend themselves to multiple interpretations. Kind of like my investigations into September 11 now, I thought.

The other main story line concerns Fowler's relationship with Phuong, a Vietnamese girl 30 years his junior, a situation with some relevance to my own life.

At dinner with Gina after the discussion, I began our conversation by noting the distinction between the unconscious brain and the conscious mind. "The unconscious brain is smarter than the conscious mind," I said. "The brain is hundreds of thousands of years old; the mind is only as old as we are, in my case 56 years. If experience is necessary for wisdom, which would you say is wiser?"

Without waiting for an answer, I explained that "I do my

most creative work of the day first thing in the morning. That work consists of listening to whatever thoughts my unconscious brain puts into my mind. Whatever the subjects I'm interested in, my brain has deliberated about them while I slept and in the morning, soon after I awake, if I let it speak, it presents to my mind the most interesting of its deliberations and insights. I make a point of being at the computer soon after awakening, to record what it tells me without my conscious mind getting in the way. I then spend the rest of the day using my mind to develop and add to the insights my brain has given me.

"We could start a new book club, Gina," I continued. "One that discusses these and related matters. Books to be discussed could be either fiction or non-fiction. Perhaps inspired by the title of Endo's *Silence* that we'll discuss in May, I made a list of books addressing one approach to the brain-mind distinction that the new club could consider. I passed a list of titles to her:

The Power of Silence: Against the Dictatorship of Noise, Robert Cardinal Sarah
In Pursuit of Silence: Listening for Meaning in a World of Noise, George Prochnik
Quiet: The Power of Introverts in a World That Can't Stop Talking, Susan Cain
Solitude: In Pursuit of a Singular Life in a Crowded World, Michael Harris
The Invention of Solitude, Paul Auster
Solitude: A Return to the Self, Anthony Storr
The Art of Solitude, Stephen Batchelor
The End of Solitude: Selected Essays on Culture and Society, William Deresiewicz
Noise: A Flaw in Human Judgment, Daniel Kahneman

Gina laughed as she glanced at it. "It's cute that at the end you included a book with a title contrary to all the others, Daniel Kahneman's *Noise*. Not silence or solitude in the title, but noise!"

"Oh, I have half a dozen of Kahneman's books," I said. Perhaps I should add another of his to the list, *Thinking Fast and Slow*. The brain thinks fast, the mind, slow. I hadn't thought of it earlier because the title is a bit different from the others.

"I got started thinking about all this because it's become distressing clear that many people don't seem to think at all. They can't think, what with so much noise pouring in on them all the time, whether from TV at home or from canned music in public, and everywhere they're staring at their phones, their eyes never leaving the screen, never giving themselves a chance to hear the quiet voice of the smarter half of their mental machinery.

I then went on to describe the latest things I'd learned about the events of September 11—the impossibility of the government's explanation for the destruction of the towers, the absence of plane parts at the supposed crash sites, the impossibility of phone calls being made from planes at high altitude and speed, and so on. I had half feared that she'd be bored by it all, but she seemed truly interested.

"I can see your great passion for your work," Gina said. "I am genuinely pleased to listen to people whose lives are being fulfilled by their intellectual work, as most people I know don't see things that way. Some even have the audacity to say that reading is a waste of time and energy as it doesn't produce real money. I wish that they would understand that reading isn't to kill boredom, that being able to read helps us understand ourselves, other people and the world way better. At least that's the reason why I read. I remember one of my professors, who said that 'People who read and write are deadly. People who read and write understand life way better than most people.'"

At this I lamented that no one in my family read books—not my siblings, not Diana, and not my kids, in spite of all my efforts to read books to them when they were young and my having in the house books suitable for kids of their ages as they progressed through childhood. "It was all kind of disappointing," I concluded.

"I understand what you are feeling," Gina responded. "I understand how important it is that people in our lives appreciate the things we value. It's not only about having the same level of intelligence; it's more about sharing a deep understanding of the things that make us happy and the cords that make us up as a person.

"No one in my family reads, either. In fact, nobody went to a university since my great grandparents. My genuine friends here and back home—none of them reads, either. But that's okay with me; what matters is what's going on inside of me and the genuine relationship I have with them. When I am interacting with them and when making new friends, it's my heart that I use anyway.

"Thank you, too, for sharing Adler's article with me," she said next, referring to an article I'd given her some months back, "Reading," by Mortimer J. Adler, that I'd especially liked. "I agree with him that being a person of culture is a lifestyle, which includes serious appreciation of beauty, value and excellence, usually through the works of the greatest minds. It reminded me of my college life," she continued. "My life at uni wasn't easy but it was so much fun because I enjoyed what I was studying."

"I also agree with the sentiments of the article regarding students not knowing how to read and write. The educational system back home focused on supplying competent corporate workers for foreign companies in and outside The Philippines. This meant that the study of the liberal arts was not given much importance. In the article, it says, 'to pass the examinations, you study the idiosyncrasies of your teachers.' This was so true in my schools. More students got their degrees and honors by catering to the whims of their professors, not because of their intelligence or love of learning.

"Though vocational skills can't be disvalued completely because competence requires hard work, I still think that competence alone isn't all that admirable," she continued. "For me, it's unwise to honor or recognize people who have achieved mere technical competence, because such people are only trained, not educated. Doing so devalues real education. Most people go to the university with no real intention of becoming educated. Some students enroll in top universities not for the education but for the name of the school. You can't blame them for that, though, as the name of the uni helps a lot in employment. Still, it's difficult to explain the value of the liberal arts to such people."

"I couldn't have said it better myself, Gina," I said, smiling at her like a proud teacher might gaze on an exceptionally brilliant student, though I didn't agree with everything she'd said.

"I also liked the part at the end where the author mentioned that Robert Maynard Hutchins was accused of being a fascist for telling people to read books. A similar thing is going on in the U.S. today. Jordan Peterson is being dubbed by the creator of the comics "Captain America" as a fascist and a Nazi just because he is always telling young people to read and clean their room."

Gina's mention of Jordan Peterson caught me by surprise. I recalled that Russell Fletcher had also mentioned him and his book *12 Rules for Life: An Antidote to Chaos* as an antidote to any distress I might be feeling due to the horrendous realities I was becoming aware of. I recalled that I'd made a mental note to get a copy, and this time made a written note.

She then moved on to yet another article I'd given her a copy of, "Winged Words: Reading & Discussing Great Books," by Peter Kalkavage. I'd thought it was one of the most inspiring pieces I'd ever read on the subject, and hoped she might appreciate it, too.

"Thanks for sharing it with me, Jubal. Everything in it is on point, a lot of people these days are only able to grasp the postmodern ideologies, with very little understanding of the perils those ideas can cause, thinking that old books are no longer relevant and valuable. Political correctness makes it even worse; classical culture is indeed at stake.

"I love the term 'winged words,' indeed, words from the pages or speech or conversation really do have wings. I would say, eternal wings.

"The article also reminded me of several instances in which teaching was looked down on by my western peers. For them, being an engineer, a corporate employee—being a boss or any job that pays more and needs more hustle—are more interesting and worth pursuing. Although I have high respect for people of high-caliber professions, I deem emotional well-being for females as more important. My humble profession allows me to do the things that I love, things that make me happy, like spending time with my books and cooking my meals, while still making ends meet."

Having finished her thought, she was silent, but only for a second.

"Oh, I haven't told you yet!" she continued in an even more animated manner, "Thanks to these articles, I'm now putting together a new course to introduce high school seniors to the humanities and arts. Unbelievable but true, most of them have never heard of the greatest names in the Western literary and intellectual traditions and have only the most cursory familiarity with the music of Beethoven and Mozart, or the painting of Cezanne or Manet. I was more familiar with these things a dozen years ago, in junior high school in The Philippines, than most of them are in high school today in the United States. I hope to teach group classes, both in the conference room at the studio, and in the homes of one student in each neighborhood where there are several families that home school their kids and might be interested."

I was beginning to feel outclassed, as though this young woman, thirty years my junior and from a less developed country, was more highly educated, more articulate, and more aware of contemporary intellectual life in the United States than was I, an American born and raised. But of course it was the quality of her education that had first attracted me to her. That and her in her vintage yellow dress.

Gina was silent while I was thinking those thoughts, and when she spoke again it was on a completely different topic, and in a softer and more reflective manner, as though she was thinking to herself rather than speaking aloud to me. "I know mine is a difficult route and extremely old fashioned given the harsh climate of modern dating, but, even if it may sound very naïve, I believe that anything that is great is always worth the wait; this is so proven in the other areas of my life, so I am sure that, whoever he is, my man will find me."

After she spoke, I still wasn't sure whether she knew she had spoken aloud. Even as I looked directly into her soft brown eyes I couldn't tell. As she stood up to leave, her words echoed in my mind. Driving home I knew I really had to decide whether I was a suitor or not.

53

As I considered September 11 further, I realized that the events of that day enabled two things to happen. Those two things were mutually supportive, and neither would have happened without the other. Together they altered the trajectories of American life and American history in fundamental ways.

The first was that the United States invaded Afghanistan and Iraq. The second was that Congress passed several pieces of legislation that greatly undermined the civil liberties of all American citizens. Both happened only because the American people had been so shocked and so scared by the attacks that they were willing to support any measures the Bush administration claimed were necessary to protect them and their country. Eric Larsen summed it up best: The perpetrators' goal was "to scare and intimidate the American people so badly that they would permit their 'leaders' to use any methods they wished in order to 'protect' the republic and its people from the enemy that 'attacked' them on 9/11."[211]

Regarding the so-called War on Terror, I saw that the perpetrators of September 11 had practically announced in advance what they'd hoped to achieve. The Project for a New American Century (PNAC), whose members included Dick Cheney, Donald Rumsfeld and other future officials in the George W. Bush administration likely to have been involved in orchestrating September 11, declared in *Rebuilding America's Defenses* issued in the fall of 2000, that "the process of transformation [of the United States to a degree of military capability suitable for their aims], even if it brings revolutionary change, is likely to be a long one, absent some catastrophic and catalyzing event—like a new Pearl Harbor."[212]

The events of September 11 were indeed seen as a new Pearl Harbor and were used as justification for the overnight transformation of the country's military capabilities called for a year earlier. David Ray Griffin found the phrase so telling that he used it for the title of his first book exposing the truth of what had really happened on September 11: *The New Pearl Harbor: Disturbing Questions about the Bush Administration and 9/11*.

President Bush declared a state of Emergency on September 11, Public Law 107-40, which "authorized the use of United States Armed Forces against those responsible for the recent attacks launched against the United States." It's still in effect today, 18 years later. The first legislation to the same effect, Authorization for the Use of Military Force, was passed by Congress one week later. It gave the president the power "to use all necessary and appropriate force against those nations, organizations, or persons he determines planned, authorized, committed, or aided the terrorist attacks that occurred on September 11, 2001, or harbored such organizations or persons, in order to prevent any further acts of international terrorism against the United States by such nations, organizations, or persons."

The legislation was not a declaration of war against any specific countries like all previous declarations had been. It named no specific enemies and defined no end point. It authorized the president to determine which countries, organizations or individuals would be targeted by U.S. military forces. Even though no significant evidence was provided tying Afghanistan and Iraq to the events of September 11, the president was permitted to launch wars against both countries.

The wars drained away trillions of dollars of the national wealth—$6 trillion by 2013 according to one estimate. They also resulted in the deaths or permanent injuries of tens of thousands of the young Americans who fought in them. Casualties, estimated to be in the millions, were far higher in the countries where the wars were fought. It's hard to see what benefits the United States gained by those wars, which are continuing to this day.

Two months after September 11, Secretary of Defense Donald Rumsfeld created the Office of Force Transformation, which would, in Thierry Meyssan's interpretation, "change the very function of the Armed Forces. . . . The United States will no longer try to win wars, but on the contrary to make them last as long as possible; this is what President Bush's expression 'endless war' means. Their aim will be to destroy local state structures so that natural wealth can be exploited without having to endure political control."[213] To wage these wars, Meyssan charged, drawing on internal U.S. military reports revealed by Julian Assange, "the Pentagon secretly created clandestine Special Forces: 60,000 soldiers without uniforms. They are capable of assassinating anyone in any country without leaving any trace."[214]

The Authorization for the Use of Military Force has been used to justify detaining American citizens without charges and holding them without access to counsel. It also legalized torture, swept aside habeas corpus and created concentration camps inside the United States. In a memo dated two weeks after September 11, Deputy Attorney General John C. Yoo stated, "In both the War Powers Resolution and the Joint Resolution, Congress has recognized the president's authority to use force in circumstances such as those created by the September 11 incidents. Neither statute, however, can place any limits on the president's determinations as to any terrorist threat, the amount of military force to be used in response, or the method, timing, and nature of the response. These decisions, under our Constitution, are for the president alone to make."[215]

In line with this determination, American citizen Yaser Esam Hamdi, who had been captured in Afghanistan, was declared an "illegal enemy combatant" and held for almost three years without charge. When a federal judge ordered that he be given evidence justifying Hamdi's treatment, the Justice Department "insisted that the judge must simply accept its declaration and cannot interfere with the president's absolute authority in 'a time of war.'" In May 2002 an American citizen, Jose Padilla, was arrested and then, "by a Bush executive order, removed from court jurisdiction to be held indefinitely in a U.S. Navy brig, without access to his lawyer."[216]

⸙ 54 ⸙

In addition to legislation giving the president broad authority to determine the nations, organizations or persons against which he would launch U.S. military actions, Congress also passed several pieces of legislation undermining Americans' civil liberties, the rule of law, and the Constitutional protections in place since the founding of the Republic in 1789. The purpose of that stream of legislation, which largely suspended the Bill of Rights in cases of "terrorism," was, I concluded, to give the government the powers it needed to suppress any challenges to the Wars on Terror.

The most harmful pieces of legislation were:

✦ The USA Patriot Act, HR 3162. Formally titled "Uniting and Strengthening America by Providing Appropriate Tools Required to Intercept and Obstruct Terrorism" (2001), the statute, like the wars themselves, had, according to several accounts, been largely prepared in advance of September 11, in part by the Federalist Society. Members of the Society who became important officials in the Bush administration included Theodore Olson, who became U.S. Solicitor General, and John Ashcroft, who became Attorney General.

This massive Act, Eric Larsen observed, was "voted for overwhelmingly by a stunned, shocked, and awed Congress who hadn't read it. . . . The pervasive atmosphere of fear at the time was in no way conducive to clear thought, extensive study, or the making of fine distinctions—all necessary in order for legislation to be passed responsibly, fairly, and meaningfully."[217] Michael C. Ruppert reported that members of Congress hadn't read the Act because they weren't allowed to: "The bill had not even been printed and members of the House could not read it before they were compelled to vote on it. . . . 'Meanwhile, efforts to obtain copies of the new bill were stonewalled even by the committee that wrote it.'"[218]

Once the Act was available after having been passed, Congress could see that many of its provisions had little to do with fighting terrorism and much to do with monitoring and tracking the movements and communications of American citizens. The ways in which this "so-called anti-terrorist measure undermined traditional American legal and civic practices were so extensive and so unprecedented that I have included Michael C. Ruppert's summation of many of them. [See nearby textbox.]

The Act also redefined "terrorism" so that many political activities such as protest marches and demonstrations could be considered terrorist acts. The logic behind that change and the increase in domestic surveillance, John and Nisha Whitehead explained, was "that if government agents knew more about each American, they could distinguish the terrorists from law-abiding citizens. . . . [This rationale] provided the government with the perfect excuse for conducting far-reaching surveillance and collecting mountains of information on even the most law-abiding citizen."[219]

✦ The Department of Homeland Security, created to implement the USA Patriot Act, brought together various existing agencies. The *Washington Post* reported in 2011 that the DHS at that time consisted of "835,000 civil servants, 112,000 of whom are secretly employed."[220]

The creation of that $40 billion Department was "the largest reorganization of the federal government in 50 years," Ruppert reported, before asking why it was needed. "Since we now know that the U.S. government and its intelligence agencies were in possession of enough intelligence to have prevented the attacks of September 11—and this truth has even been admitted, if obliquely, by the findings of at least one Congressional committee—then what is the justification for the Patriot Act [and the creation of the DHS]? The claim that these travesties are needed to gather enough knowledge to prevent future terrorist attacks is clearly absurd. The system wasn't broken. So why fix it? Just who or what is the enemy?"[221]

The answer became apparent in August 2002 when Attorney General John Ashcroft announced his intention to create camps for U.S. citizens deemed to be "enemy combatants." His plan, as characterized by one reporter cited by Peter Dale Scott, would result in "the indefinite incarceration of U.S. citizens and summarily strip them of their constitutional rights and

Michael C. Ruppert
Summation of some of the provisions in The USA Patriot Act, HR 3162 (2001)

• Any federal law enforcement agency may enter your home or business when you are not there, collect evidence, not tell you about it, and then use that evidence to convict you of a crime. (This nullifies the Fourth Amendment to the Constitution). . . .

• Any federal law enforcement agency may, if they suspect that you are committing a crime, monitor all of your Internet traffic and read your emails. They may also intercept all of your cell phone calls as well. No warrant is required. (This violates the Fourth and Fifth Amendments to the Constitution.) . . .

• The FBI or any other federal law enforcement agency may come to your business and seize any of your business records—if they claim it is connected with a terrorist investigation—and they can arrest you if you tell anyone that they were there. (This violates the First and the Fourth Amendments to the Constitution.) . . .

• The CIA can now operate inside the U.S. and spy on American citizens. And, as directed by Attorney General Ashcroft on November 13, it is also permitted to share its intelligence files with local law enforcement agencies (and vice versa). The CIA has spied on Americans for decades, but the fruits of that spying have never been admissible in court. Now law enforcement will have the ability to rewrite the intelligence as a probable cause statement, conduct an investigation, and introduce it as evidence. This, from material that was collected outside the rules of search and seizure. (There goes the Exclusionary Rule of the Fourth Amendment.)

From:
Michael C. Ruppert, *Crossing the Rubicon*
(2004; 8th printing, 2015), p. 484.

access to the courts by declaring them enemy combatants."[222] Ashcroft's announcement was in line with "an ambitions ten-year Homeland Security strategic plan, code-named Endgame, authorized in 2003, [which would] 'remove all removable aliens,' including 'illegal economic migrants, aliens who have committed criminal acts, asylum-seekers . . . or potential terrorists.'"[223]

After protests from legal scholars, Scott continued, "the plan for military detention camps was not discussed publicly further. It seems clear, however, that the camps exist and that in the case of martial law the authority already exists for them to be used."[224] That the plan was indeed being implemented became clear in January 2006, when "KBR, the engineering and construction subsidiary of Halliburton, announced it had been awarded a contract from the Department of Homeland Security for $385 million, to provide 'temporary detention and processing capabilities.'"[225]

✦ Total Information Awareness (TI), created by the Defense Advanced Research Projects Agency (DARPA) allows the government to monitor almost all activities of all Americans, ranging, Ruppert explained, "from bank deposits, to shopping, to web surfing, to academic grades, to divorce records, to spending, to phone calls, to utility usage, to travel. . . . It not only plans to track everything you do, it also plans to employ face recognition software that can be used to prevent you from making a withdrawal at your bank or from boarding a plane. It plans to identify you by your voice, and to recognize you by your unique body odor. It even plans, through the use of non-invasive neuro-electric sensors,' to read your mind." "There was a time, before the Patriot Act was passed," he noted, "that a search warrant—a process requiring a judge to review a request to ascertain whether your rights were being violated—would have been required for almost all of this. Those rights don't exist anymore."[226]

✦ The renewal and expansion of the Foreign Intelligence Surveillance Act (FISA) in April 2004 authorized warrantless surveillance of foreign citizens AND of any American who communicates with a non-U.S. citizen who is a target of surveillance AND any American who communicates with the American who communicates with the targeted non-American. I could see that this Act could be used to eavesdrop on the conversations, phone calls, text messages, emails and other communications of just about all American citizens.

✦ In September 2005, "NORTHCOM conducted a highly classified Granite Shadow exercise in Washington. As military affairs analyst William Arkin reported, . . . 'Granite Shadow . . . allows for emergency military operations in the United States without civilian supervision or control.' . . . Endgame's multimillion-dollar program for detention facilities will greatly increase NORTHCOM's ability to respond to any domestic disorders."[227] I'd soon learn much more about NORTHCOM.

✦ The Military Commissions Act (2006), under which, as Eric Larsen explained, "The United States is now legally entitled to declare anyone it wants an 'enemy combatant,' . . . [and] to throw those it so declares into cells, treating and torturing them in any way it chooses. . . . The writ of habeas corpus will be 'stripped' from them so that they will have no right to challenge their detentions in court. . . .[It's] the first time since 9/11 that a major law stripping away traditional . . . human rights and freedoms has been passed by Congress not peremptorily, as with the so-called 'Patriot Act,' but after full debate."[228]

✦ The 2007 Defense Authorization Bill, passed by Congress in September 2006, made it easier for the president to declare martial law, and to federalize the National Guard, even over the objections of the nation's governors. Section 1076 of the new law changed Section 333 of the 'Insurrection Act,' increasing the president's ability to deploy troops within the United States during a natural disaster, epidemic, serious public health emergency, terrorist attack, or 'other condition.' As Senator Patrick Leahy pointed out in February 2007, while moving to repeal the amendment, the change was merely slipped in at the administration's request as rider to a bill that was hundreds of pages long."[229]

✦ The Protect America Act (2007), which allows continued secret collection of Americans' phone calls and emails with no oversight.

As I considered these pieces of legislation, several other types of harm inflicted on Americans came to mind.

One was the immediate harm resulting from the events of September 11: the loss of loved ones, family and friends; the tens of billions of dollars worth of property destroyed and perhaps hundreds of billions more as stock markets crashed. There was also the shock to the sensibilities of just about everyone in the country as they watched the horrific events unfold on TV. The feelings of fear and confusion they generated lasted, for many people, for many weeks and months and years.

As a personal example of the fear that pervaded the country, a few days after September 11—I was in the Washington, D.C. area at the time—I went to Arby's for lunch. A man in line two persons ahead of me looked a lot like Mohammad Atta, the man the FBI claimed had piloted one of the planes. As I walked toward the line, I noticed that he was wearing one of those sweatshirts that has a pocket in the front that goes all the way through so that hands inserted on each side meet in the middle. His hands were in the pocket, which seemed rather bulky; that, combined with his scowling face, had me mostly convinced that he had a gun in his pocket and was on the verge of pulling it out and shooting everyone in the place. I was just about to leave when he pulled his hands out of the pocket, showing that he didn't have a gun after all.

Harmful also was Americans' loss of confidence in themselves. The pressure to forego the testimony of our own eyes and the judgments of our own minds in favor of the Magic Bullet theory was reinforced by pressure to accept that a building exploded from inside and pulverized into dust was really a building collapsing into its own footprint. The pressure to admit as true things that are physically impossible has destroyed the spirit and corroded the soul of the American people. It has undermined the Principality that should, I believe, guide us as we make our way through life.

⚘ 55 ⚘

As I considered all these cascading effects the events of September 11 had inflicted on Americans and their country, it became clearer to me how much my country had changed during the decades I'd been away. I'd lost touch with the nature of my own society. Overseas, my focus had been on the countries I'd been posted to. Beyond merely noting the formal institutions and organizations within them, I'd become quite adept, I thought, at ferreting out the informal chains of influence through which powerful individuals made their power and influence felt. All that had been necessary to be effective in my efforts to influence opinion makers in whatever country I was posted to, who in turn could influence government officials, university professors, think tanks, the media and the general public.

I could see that I'd need to apply to my own country the tradecraft I'd mastered and applied to other countries during my years as a Foreign Service officer. I began to do that by asking just how many persons were behind all this harm to the United States and the American people. I divided all Americans into several categories according to the degree of their involvement in the events of September 11 and the cover-up that is still on-going. Eric Larsen also proposed a way of dividing up the population; my categories overlap somewhat with his.[230]

Only a tiny number of persons were aware of the full range of events to be carried out on September 11, perhaps not more than a few dozen. Among them were those in high command positions in the government, military services and intelligence agencies, including Dick Cheney, Donald Rumsfeld, General Richard Meyers, Condoleezza Rice and, possibly, George W. Bush. Others were directly involved in either planning or carrying out various events of that day but without being aware of the full range of events being planned. These perpetrators totaled probably not more than several thousand, say 6,000, persons, which would amount to 2/1,000 of one percent of the U.S. population, which in 2001 totaled 300 million.

Those complicit in the coverup would include a wider array of politicians and members of the administration, Congress and local governments; and many in the so-called intellectual classes, including owners of corporate media, and many working in the media and academia. In short, people who learned or suspected the truth because of positions they held or hold, and who could have revealed what they knew or suspected but chose not to, to protect themselves and their careers, thereby tacitly or actively participating in the cover-up. Let's estimate these folks at roughly 144,000 people. Combined with the 6,000 perpetrators, that totals 150,000 people—exactly 1/20th of one percent of the U.S. population at that time—who actively or passively participated in the events and the cover-up.

That leaves 99.95 percent not involved. Let's call them ordinary citizens. They can be divided into two groups; I've borrowed Larsen's categories, but not his percentages:

✦ Thinking and observing Americans, who at some point have come to doubt the official story; and,

✦ Blind Americans, who continue to accept the official story told in the media.

Based on responses of those to whom I showed the photo of the tower in the process of being destroyed, I'd say that 15 percent of the population is either already aware of the real events or would quickly become convinced of them if shown the evidence.

That leaves 85 percent unaware of and resistant to learning more about the events of that day and the cover-up.

	Percent of pop.
Participants in the events of September 11	.002%
Complicit in coverup, either actively or passively	nearly .05%
Ordinary citizens I: thinking and observing	nearly 15%
Ordinary citizens II: blindly accepting official story	85%
Total	100%

With this effort to analyze my own country underway, I needed a break and left the house for several appointments outside.

56

I arrived early for my haircut appointment with Deeza. She wasn't there, so I had to wait, giving me a chance to read more of Rebekah Roth's fifth and final volume.

While reading, my attention was distracted by a woman talking in a loud angry voice. She turned out to be one of the hair cutters, who was carrying out an angry conversation with herself while cutting a customer's hair.

"He'd better not hit me again," she said, as the scissors in her right hand snipped the hair held upright between her left thumb and forefinger.

"I'll show him a thing or two," she said as the scissors chopped at the next bunch of hair.

"Just let him try it." She slashed with the scissors.

"He'll find out how tough I am." Another slash.

The man whose hair was being attacked sat bolt upright, his eyes bulging out, not daring to move a muscle.

At some point during this slaughter, Deeza returned to the shop. She sized up the situation quickly, and said, "Sherrie, calm down. This man's hair isn't your ex."

Sherrie started and seemed to see her surroundings for the first time. The man whose hair was being "cut" stood up, took off the apron, and left the shop without saying a word.

"Why don't you take a break, Sherrie," Deeza said, and Sherrie, too, left without saying anything.

Deeza sighed as I sat down in the chair next to the one where that guy's hair had been butchered, and said, "It's so hard to find good help. I tried hiring people from other salons, but most of them hadn't been adequately trained and now, regarding themselves as experienced, don't want to learn anything new. I've had better luck with newbies who have never cut hair before. I can train them from the get-go."

She didn't begin cutting my hair until she'd stopped talking, following her usual practice of not being able to talk and cut hair at the same time. But only a moment later she stopped cutting, took a step back and looked at me.

"And then we come to the second problem," she said, "that of the mental stability of the people who apply to work here."

"Every time I see a situation like this one," I responded, "I'm so glad I'm retired, and that I'll never again have to deal with difficult people. By the time I retired I'd concluded that there are no normal people. Everyone's crazy in a different way."

Deeza stepped back again and looked at me. "Ain't that the truth!" she said. "Everybody's crazy 'cept you and me. And lately I've been wonderin' about you!" Her big laugh boomed out of her after she uttered these words, and I joined her with my somewhat quieter laugh.

"So, how's business, Deeza?" I asked.

"You were here just after we opened," she recalled. "It was tough at first, but now we have many regular customers, and we're making a profit. I'm making about as much as I did before, working in someone else's salon. But I have high hopes for the future. We're getting new customers all the time."

Considering Deeza's experiences, I wondered how hard it had been for Gina to find suitable tutors to work at WORDS once it had opened.

Both Deeza and I were lost in our own thoughts for the rest of the haircut.

☙ 57 ☙

Initially I'd seen the assassination in 1963 and the attacks in 2001 as two separate, unrelated events occurring 38 years apart. But the more I learned about the 2001 attacks the more similarities I noticed between them.

Similarities in what happened:

In both events there was near instant identification of the supposed culprits. The Dallas police put out a description of the supposed killer within 15 minutes of the assassination. Yet the description was incorrect; it matched exactly the incorrect information in Lee Harvey Oswald's FBI and CIA files, not his actual measurements. This might indicate, Peter Dale Scott suggested, "that someone with access to those files had already determined Oswald to be the designated culprit, before there was any evidence to connect him to the crime."[231]

Something similar happened on September 11. Although the original flight manifests showed no passengers with Arabic or Islamic names on any of the flights, "The FBI already had a list of the 19 alleged hijackers by 9:59 a.m. on September 11, when the south tower collapsed," and well before then, at 9:03 a.m., "counterterrorism coordinator Richard Clarke had stated 'It's an al Qaeda attack.'"[232] "As with the identification of Oswald," Scott observed, "with respect to the FBI's list of hijackers on 9/11, there were, even within the bureaucracy, suspicions that the FBI was drawing on pre-9/11 files for its identifications."

In both events the concept of innocent until proved guilty was tossed out the window. Lee Harvey Oswald and Osama bin Laden had been declared guilty within minutes of the events without evidence provided to back up the charges; events in their past that would have made them persons of interest were cited as proof of their guilt. In Oswald's case that was his supposed defection to the Soviet Union in 1959; in bin Laden's, it was his having twice declared a fatwa against the United States. The charges against them were widely and repeatedly broadcast in the media as though they had already been convicted. Oswald and bin Laden both declared their innocence; neither would have the chance to defend himself in court.

In bin Laden's case, Afghanistan stated it would turn him over if the United States provided evidence of his guilt. The U.S. declined to do so, and never did charge him with the crimes of September 11. "After 9/11 Washington was put under considerable pressure by its allies in the war on terrorism, particularly by Pakistan, to produce evidence showing the involvement of al-Qaeda in 9/11," Peter Dale Scott observed. At the time Secretary of State Powell promised to provide evidence, but never did.[233]

The following year, on April 19, 2002, FBI Director Robert Mueller stated that "The hijackers also left no paper trail. In our investigation, we have not uncovered a single piece of paper—either here in the U.S. or in the treasure trove of information that has turned up in Afghanistan and elsewhere—that mentioned any aspect of the September 11th plot."[234] Mueller had been trying to convey just how clever and secretive the hijackers had been, but his words could also indicate there'd been no connection whatsoever between them and the events on September 11. He'd made no mention of Osama bin Laden's repeated denials that he'd had any involvement with September 11, one such statement being: "I have already said that I am not involved in the 11 September attacks in the United States. As a Muslim, I try my best to avoid telling a lie. I had no knowledge of these attacks."[235]

With bin Laden's usefulness as the patsy over by the end of 2001, he could be discarded. And, with no substantive evidence in support of his involvement having come to light, it was best to remove him from the picture. Hence, President George W. Bush's change from stating on September 13, 2001 that "The most important thing for us is to find Osama bin Laden; it's our number one priority, and we will not rest until we find him," to, on March 13, 2002, "I don't know where he is. I have no idea, and I really don't care. It's not that important. It's not our priority."[236]

In both events the testimony of witnesses that didn't fit into the official story was ignored by the FBI. After the assassination, 152 witnesses stated that gunshots came from the grassy knoll to the front right of the president's limousine. On September 11, several hundred persons, including 118 firefighters, reported hearing explosions coming from within WTC 1, 2 and 7. In both, witnesses were pressured to change their recollections, and in both cases only those whose testimony would support the official story were called to testify by the Commissions.

In both events faked or planted evidence implicating the patsies turned up at just the right moment to squelch public doubts. "In the JFK case, one can cite the forged bus manifest supplied by the Mexican secret police with Oswald's name on it, to show how he returned to the United States," Scott reported. But, "later, on the basis of a mint bus ticket, the Warren

Commission determined that Oswald had returned from Mexico on a different bus. The ticket was allegedly 'discovered' by Marina Oswald in August 1964."[237]

Both official stories relied on actions that were physically impossible. With the assassination, the Magic Bullet, which changed direction in mid air twice, caused five injuries in two men (Kennedy and Connally) before being found a day later in pristine condition, could be compared with the towers that supposedly fell at freefall speed into their own footprints without the use of explosives. The altered and faked portions of the Zapruder film and the faked autopsy photos could also be compared with the faked videos of the impact of a plane with the second tower in New York.

Further, with JFK, the bus ticket just noted could be compared with the passport of Satam al Suqami, one of the supposed hijackers, that was discovered a few blocks from the World Trade Center. It was in perfect condition, with not on a mark on it from the plane crash, explosion or dust cloud that blanketed lower Manhattan,[238] just as Oswald's supposed bus ticket was in mint condition even though he'd have had it with him during the 24-hour bus ride from Mexico City to New Orleans in the days before buses were airconditioned.

In both events, the Commissions set up to investigate the crimes were not independent and neither conducted an investigation. The Warren Commission, controlled by Allen Dulles who had a burning hatred of Kennedy, heard only from witnesses carefully selected by the FBI. It did not hear from Dr. George Burkley, the president's personal physician and the only doctor to examine Kennedy's wounds in both the hospital in Dallas and during the autopsy in Washington, D.C. The 9/11 Commission was under the control of Philip Zelikow, a Bush confidant. That Commission began with the assumption that the official story was correct and heard mostly from witnesses who supported it. The scholars whose books and articles showing the impossibility of the official story, published before the Commission met, were ignored. Zelikow reportedly had already drafted the final report before the first witness had been called.

In both, the media adhered religiously to the official story. Individuals who pointed out physical impossibilities with them were tarred with the "conspiracy theorist" label. In both, many witnesses died unnatural deaths, while others were fired from their jobs or otherwise pressured to remain silent.

In both events, later findings that contradicted the official story weren't reported on in the media or in textbooks. The House Committee on Assassination's findings in the 1970s that shots had been fired from two different directions in Dealey Plaza were ignored, as were discoveries that at least five, and perhaps as many as 11, of the 19 so-called terrorists on September 11 were still alive.

In both, government officials in other countries with decades of high-level experience in public life expressed doubts about the official stories, but their statements were ignored by the American media. Recall Fidel Castro, Charles de Gaulle and others who spoke out on the assassination of Kennedy. After September 11, German former Technology Minister and Deputy Defense Minister Andres von Bulow stated in early January 2002, that "Planning the attacks was a masterwork in technical and organizational terms. To hijack four big airliners within a few minutes and fly them into targets within a single hour and to do so on complicated flight routes. That is unthinkable, without backing from the secret apparatus of state and industry."[239] In December 2001 Helmut Schmidt, former Chancellor and Defense Minister of Germany stated that "proof had to be delivered that the Sept. 11 terror attacks came from abroad. That proof has still not been provided."[240] Former Italian president and prime minister Francesco Cossiga stated that, "It could not be accomplished without infiltrations in the radar and flight security personnel. . . . It is not thinkable that [bin Laden] did everything by himself."[241]

Similarities in why they occurred:

Both incidents were followed by major wars that had been planned in advance. Peter Dale Scott showed "1) that the death of JFK opened the doors to a major U.S. escalation, already planned, in Vietnam, and 2) that four decades later the attacks on 9/11 opened the doors to major U.S. wars, already planned, in Afghanistan and Iraq."[242]

President Johnson's Memo (NSAM) 273 authorizing planning for attacks on North Vietnam reversed Kennedy's NSAM 263 dated only five weeks earlier, as I've already noted. Regarding 2001, "it is clear that "there were pre-9/11 plans for the invasion of Afghanistan," Peter Dale Scott stated, citing a former Pakistani diplomat who told the BBC, right after September 11, "that senior American officials had told him in mid-July 2001 that military action against Afghanistan was likely to go ahead 'before the snows started falling in Afghanistan, by the middle of October at the latest.'"[243] Scott also stated that "According to the Taliban Foreign Minister, . . . the U.S. delivered threats to the Taliban before 9/11, in support of Unocal's desire to build oil and gas pipelines through the country from Turkmenistan to Pakistan." It was the events of September 11 that provided the cover justification for the U.S. attack.

<u>Similarities in psychological sophistication</u>:

I was especially intrigued by the sophistication of the psychological manipulation used to get key members of the government not involved in the plots to go along with the cover-ups.

Re JFK, the plotters had used fear of nuclear war with the Soviet Union to squash investigation into the idea of multiple gunmen, which might have revealed what had really happened. With Oswald's history of having supposedly defected to the Soviet Union four years earlier, and with his having supposedly travelled to Mexico City to meet with the official at the Soviet embassy there suspected of being the Soviet's top assassin in the Americas, the perpetrators had created the appearance that the Soviets were behind Kennedy's assassination. Confronting them could risk nuclear war, Johnson told Chief Justice Earl Warren as he attempted to strongarm him into serving as head of the Commission. Far better to shut down investigation into the idea of multiple gunmen by pinning the assassination on Oswald as lone nut. Better not to look too closely into Oswald's background, either.

With September 11, Webster Tarpley suggested that President Bush was "most probably not familiar in advance with the detailed outline of the 9/11 plot. . . . Bush's crime was not the crime of knowing everything in advance; it was rather the crime of not knowing what he should have known."[244]

The plotters found an ingenious way to convince Bush both to avoid returning from Florida to Washington, where his meddling might mess things up, and to agree to support the cover story of hijackings by 19 Arab men guided by a man living in a cave halfway around the world.

They convinced him by telling him two things. The first, while he was still in Florida, was that a threat had been made against Air Force One. The threat, which had supposedly come in over secure channels, had been that "Angel is next"—Angel being the code name for Air Force One, a code name changed daily—thus demonstrating two things to Bush. One was that the threat had come from someone highly placed within the U.S. military or intelligence bureaucracy, and that, therefore, the threat against his life had to be taken seriously. "The call," Tarpley explained, "was evidently an ultimatum to Bush from the coup faction to announce the war of civilizations by blaming the attacks on bin Laden and al Qaeda, or else be liquidated."[245]

The second, Tarpley speculated, was the idea that whoever had made the threat was so highly placed that he might also have the codes needed to launch nuclear missiles. It was essential, therefore, Bush was told, that he go to the headquarters of the Strategic Air Command in Nebraska, where he could countermand, "by the immediate physical presence of the commander in chief, any and all illegal attack orders."[246] He agreed to go to the there, via a stop at another base to refuel, and was thereby kept out of Washington until after eight p.m.

In Tarpley's judgment, "This surrender, carried out sometime in the afternoon or evening of September 11, constitutes Bush's great betrayal of the Constitution and his great crime against humanity. Everything Bush has done since . . . has been determined by the moment in which he declined to fight the rogue network, but rather preferred to follow its orders, in violation of his oath of office. Never before had the United States surrendered to an enemy in this way."[247]

Bush's surrender to the plotters on September 11 stands in stark contrast to Kennedy's refusal to give in to pressure from the Joint Chiefs of Staff to approve Operation Northwoods or to authorize a pre-emptive nuclear first-strike on the Soviet Union.

I realized that if Bush had been equally adamant about returning directly to Washington or had been equally resistant to "turning the U.S. government and polity in the direction demanded by the terror plotters,"[248] Air Force One could have been shot down, raising Dick Cheney to the presidency. The Kennedy assassination and the success of the cover-up had made it all the easier for future presidents to capitulate when faced with threats to their lives that, without the Kennedy precedent, would have seemed far less credible.

These similarities between the assassination and the events of September 11 in what happened, in the direction of the policy changes that resulted from them and in the psychological sophistication of the effort to convince key officials to support the official story, suggested to me that both events were committed by the same forces. Not the same individuals, obviously, in two events occurring 38 years apart, but the same forces and the same institutions.

Incidentally, I'd just learned of a bizarre coincidence that probably wasn't a coincidence at all. On September 11, the heads of many of the largest companies in America were also at the headquarters of the Strategic Air Command in Nebraska to which President Bush had been flown.

For many years Warren Buffet, at one time the world's richest man, organized an annual conference attended by leaders of the largest companies in the United States. The event was traditionally held at a hotel in Omaha, Nebraska. The annual dinner in 2001, held on September 10, however, was, for the first time, held on a military base—the headquarters of the Strategic Air Command to where Bush would be flown the following day until he, apparently, agreed to go along with the official story, as I've already noted.

Many of the guests were CEOs of companies whose headquarters were on the upper floors of the World Trade Center towers in New York. "The invited company bosses," who remained on the base overnight according to Thierry Meyssan, "had given their New York employees the [following] day off, which explains the relatively low death toll in the collapse of the Twin Towers."[249]

Perhaps my imagination has been over-active, but doesn't the presence of so many of America's top CEOs on a secure military base on September 10 and 11 suggest either their complicity in the events of September 11 or their being held against their will until they agreed, like President Bush apparently would, not to challenge the official story of what happened?

I recalled also the bizarre "coincidence" I'd noted back in October: that most members of President Kennedy's cabinet were on a plane over the Pacific Ocean, on their way to Japan, at the time of the assassination.

58

I stopped by Maja's place in the evening, and she welcomed me as she had several other times in the past month, with an ice-cold beer and a smile. This time with a story, too, about a mouse, an elephant and a monkey. "The mouse is male, the elephant is female, and he's in love with her," she told me. "The monkey is up in a tree throwing coconuts at the elephant, trying to hit her in the head. The mouse wants to have sex with the elephant and climbs up her tail to the right spot. Just as he thrusts himself into her, a coconut hit the elephant on the head, and she sank to her knees. 'Yeah, suffer bitch!' the mouse cried out."

As Maja led me into the bedroom, she said, "After I deliberately arouse a man, I give him what I know he wants."

Afterwards, I asked her if she was a Christian.

"Of course. We all are," she said, referring to her group of Filipinos that I'd gotten to know somewhat.

"But what I mean is, are you all as devout as Gina?"

"Oh, no. Most of us go to Mass on Sunday, but that's about it.

None of that morning and evening Mass during the week for us. We think she's a bit cracked.

"Gina is very intense," she continued, sitting up halfway, resting on her elbow as she faced me. "God help anyone who gets in her way or tries to deny her when she decides she wants something—or someone. And she's set her sights on you, Mr. J.

"She is wowed by you. At first she had doubts that you'd seriously be interested in her. And even if so, whether you, being a diplomat, are more like a dream than a reality. Still, you are at the top of her list of suitors."

"Well, I was a diplomat, but now I'm not. I'm retired," I said, interrupting her. "Gina shouldn't let herself be hyptotized by that word into thinking that a life with me would be filled with evenings in fancy dress at diplomatic receptions. I'm not the person I was then and my life is very different now. It's filled with quieter, more personal projects. And I'm too old for her."

"The age thing doesn't bother her," Maja continued. "She only dates guys who are at least 15 years older than she is anyway. She wants a guy who is more experienced than she is. 'Love conquers all,' she always says."

"Really?" That was startling news, but it fit in with her thinking in terms of suitors and courtship, a more formalized approach to relationships than I was used to but found appealing.

"Recently she told me she'd met someone who is all that she wants in a guy—matured, kind, responsible, smart, sensible, diligent, very romantic, a real gentleman—she went on and on. It was a bit odd, though. In the past she always used your name when discussing you. This time she didn't tell me the name of the man, but I knew it was you."

"It couldn't be," I responded to Maja, "I've told Gina several times there's no way that a relationship could develop between us. Marriage is out of the question, I told her, because I'm just too old to start a new family. And a shorter-term sexual relationship wouldn't be possible either, as you know."

"Nevertheless," Maja said, "no matter what she might say to you, in her mind you are a suitor, and your name is at the top of her list."

✿ 59 ✿

I went to see Russell at his home a few days later.

"Russell, I feel like I'm entering a whole new world. I see things I've never seen before, even though they've been right in front of me all the while. First the Kennedy assassination, and now September 11. It's unnerving. My whole world has been transformed by what I've learned. Robert Kennedy must have felt something similar after the murder of his brother. In 1968, not long before his own murder, he said, "I found out something I never knew. I found out that my world was not the real world."

"Insects live in a world very different from ours, too, because they can see things that we can see only under ultraviolet light. And dogs live in a world very different from ours, a world of smells that we can't detect at all. Their realities are very different from ours, yet to a casual observer we all live in the same place.

"It's like I now live in a different world, like I've acquired a new set of sensibilities or abilities to see things that are as different from the old ones as an insect's or a dog's are from a human's. I see things that I hadn't had a clue about only five months ago.

"I've reached the point where I doubt the truthfulness of everything I've ever been told, and not just about the JFK assassination or the events of September 11. Someone mentioned to me recently that human activity has no effect whatsoever on the climate and that Shakespeare didn't write the works attributed to him—ideas that I'd have rejected out of hand before but am now ready to examine with an open mind."

I thought to myself that here was a new facet of Principality. Until now I'd applied the concept only to events and decisions in my own personal life. Now I saw that as a citizen I needed to apply it to public events as well. I had to become fully informed about major developments in our society and the world. I couldn't take anything on faith, couldn't blindly accept anything I'd been told or had read.

"I've seen the same awakening in some of my students," Russell said, "as I've explained to them both the standard U.S. diplomatic history and the realities that lie behind it. Most students are more interested in the standard version, the version that will help them in their future careers. And even among those who seem interested in the realities behind the usual stories, most seem, oddly, to accept the new reality without the discomfort, let alone outrage, that I felt when first learning about them and that I'd expect anyone who admires the United States for its promotion of democracy and world order to feel when discovering that it's become the fox who is guarding the coop, and perhaps has been for a long time. As you feel now. There's a disconnect in them between knowledge and sensibility that puzzles me.

"You've given me a new idea, Russell," I said in response. "Your comments about differences in individual students leads me to see one path forward in my own investigations. I need to identify the specific individuals involved in the events of September 11. Not just those in the leadership positions who initiated and planned the events, but also those involved in carrying them out: Who were the American and United pilots and why did none of them send the signal for a hijacking? Who pushed the button that launched the missile that hit the Pentagon, if that's what happened? Who placed the explosives in the three WTC buildings, and in others surrounding them? Who created the fake scaring of the field in Pennsylvania, and when?

And which specific individuals were involved in the cover-up? Who were the heads of the professional organizations that issued the reports supporting the false stories? In short, who, inside and outside the U.S. government organized, carried out and covered up the events of September 11—and what level of knowledge did each have as they were doing it?

As usual, Russell was way ahead of me. "Here's a book that might help you on that path, Jubal," he said as he handed me Kevin Robert Ryan's *Another Nineteen: Investigating Legitimate 9/11 Suspects*. Even at a glance I could see that this book would help me prepare my list of the most powerful persons involved.

From there I could seek out those farther down, those involved in carrying out the specific tasks needed to make the events happen in just the right way.

I then changed the topic slightly. "You know, Russell, I've read that when the workers loading the debris from the towers onto trucks got down to the level of the basement, they found something interesting. The doors of the large safes down there, which had stored billions of dollars of gold, were open and the gold gone. Someone who knew about the impending attacks had taken the gold before they occurred. Someone got very rich that day.

"What I'm really fascinated about, but haven't been able to find much information on, is the works of art in the towers. So many large companies and wealthy individuals had offices in the towers, especially on the higher floors. I've seen scattered references to the works of art by famous artists in those offices, paintings worth many millions of dollars each. Do you know where I can get a complete inventory of those paintings? If any of them show up in the art market, that would indicate that their owners had advance warning of the attacks and had removed them in advance."

"That's a fascinating idea, Jubal, but, sorry, I don't know of any book or article on the artwork in the towers. But even if you do find painting still existing that would have been destroyed in the attacks if their owners hadn't known about them in advance, it's likely that no investigation or charges will be brought against them. You know about the huge purchases of put options on the two airlines whose planes were supposedly hijacked on September 11, don't you? And on companies located on the upper floors? Someone or some group made hundreds of millions of dollars in profits from that advance information. The SEC investigated and identified someone who had purchased large amounts of those put options. Then, rather than prosecuting him or investigating further, the SEC destroyed all records of its investigation. Word seeped out, though, that that buyer held a very senior position in the CIA, yet no charges were ever brought against him."[250]

I nodded, then thought for a minute. "In spite of all the books I've read and videos I've watched on September 11, several dozen so far, I still have only scattered pieces of the puzzle. I still have the feeling that there's something big that I'm missing that would pull all the pieces into a logical scenario.

Russell nodded, and I could tell that he was about to give me information that would tie things together.

"The reality, Jubal, is that we have two governments. There's the government we see, the three branches we're taught about in school: the Executive, the Legislative and the Judicial branches. But this is only the visible government. There exists another government, the Shadow Government, or the Deep State—call it what you will—that exists behind the curtain.

"You remember, I'm sure, that in the Soviet Union, the Party was the main source of power. Everyone knew that. Every party official had a number, and the lower his number the higher his rank. I remember once, at a public concert, the front row of seats was reserved for Party officials as it always was and several Party officials were seated in the center of that row. When an official with a lower number came in, the officials already seated immediately stood up and moved over in both directions to give the middle seats, those with the best view, to the lower-numbered—that is, more powerful—official and his wife. That incident always stuck in my mind as an example of how thoroughly Party membership and Party number dominated the country.

"In the Soviet Union, Party domination of the government was openly recognized. Everyone knew that the government was only the functional arm of the Party, that all important decisions were made by the Party and then implemented by the government.

"What people in the United States don't recognize is that it's the same here. The Party controls the government, all three branches. Americans see only the government they've been taught exists, and don't see the Shadow Government or Deep State or National Security State pulling the strings. Here, the Party, or its logical equivalent, is hidden.

"The key book to read to understand this reality is Michael J. Glennon's *National Security and Double Government*," he concluded.

"This is shocking, Russell," I responded. "I'd never thought of things this way before. Do you explain all this to your students at UNC?"

"Sure. In one class I even have them read Glennon's book."

After thinking for a moment, I said, "But Russell, you say that the Shadow Government or National Security State is hidden. But the institutions that comprise it—the CIA, the Pentagon, the FBI, the DHS, the NSA and so on are all easy to see. Everyone can see them. The CIA's and Pentagon's involvement in the assassination of Kennedy and in the events of September 11 might not be universally recognized yet, but the institutions themselves are right out in the open. Everyone knows they exist."

"That's true, Jubal," Russell said. "Those institutions have a dual role. Officially they are part of the visible government, just like the three formal branches. But there are parts of them that are secret, not known to outsiders. Those part of their operations form the Shadow government. Those agencies exist in both worlds, just like some Party members also had positions in the government in the Soviet Union."

I stood up to walk around Russell's study. I needed time to process this new information.

At just that moment Mary Fletcher, Russell's wife, returned home and stopped in to say hello. I hadn't seen her since I'd worked for Russell more than 20 years earlier. She was as charming now as then, and I was glad to see her. I'd always considered her the perfect Foreign Service spouse, the ideal wife for an ambassador. She was every bit Russell's equal. With her intelligence and charm, she could have been a Foreign Service officer herself, and if so, would have far outclassed ordinary officers such as me. But she chose to concentrate on raising their kids, on overseeing the management of the ambassador's residence and on being a visible but unofficial representative of the embassy to the elite social worlds of the countries to which they'd been posted.

I invited her to join us in our discussions, but she declined. Modest as always, she said that we knew far more about these things than she did—something I doubted was true—and didn't want to disrupt our conversation.

After she'd left, I turned to Russell. "It was good to see Mary again, Russell. She's as charming as ever. Seeing her brings back memories of the old days, 25 years ago, when I was a rather new officer, and you weren't yet an ambassador."

"Those were enjoyable but intense days indeed," he said. "I was Deputy Chief of Mission (DCM) at the embassy, and back in Washington I was in the mix, along with so many others, for consideration for appointment as ambassador. There were always crises arising and situations requiring deft handling. Any missteps could result in my name being scratched off the list. It was exhilarating and stressful at the same time, with so many pairs of eyes on me 24/7—in Washington, within the embassy and in the Foreign Ministry.

"I'm glad I had those experiences," he concluded. "And I'm glad they're over. I prefer a less stressful mode of living these days."

I felt exactly the same way.

"Since we're looking backward, there's something that has always puzzled me," I said. "You remember Bush Derangement Syndrome in the mid 2000s, when the Democrats and the media and even other Republicans criticized—no, condemned—the president for every crime and misdemeanor and gaffe under the sun—the war in Iraq, the state of the economy, Abu Ghraib, the use of torture, the price of gas, and on and on—and often in the most hysterical manner? I found it bizarre and was never able to explain it to myself.

"And now that I'm aware of the real events of September 11, another mystery has arisen. I now see that those hysterical diatribes had been directed against Bush for every crime imaginable except September 11! That crime far outweighed all the other things, real and imagined, for which he was criticized, yet it was never mentioned!"

Russell laughed. "It was a bizarre moment in American

politics. Here's how I see it. Bush's critics, many of them at least, understood what had really happened on September 11. But they couldn't accuse him of complicity in that crime. So, rage against him and the other perpetrators built up inside them. It had to come out one way or another and came out disguised as criticism for all those other things you just mentioned. It came out with an intensity and rage that would have been appropriate for September 11, but which was way over the top for those smaller crimes, real and imagined.

"The Republicans couldn't accuse Bush of the crimes of September 11 without destroying his administration and perhaps even the Republican Party," he continued. "The Democrats didn't accuse him because they're the party of big government, and September 11 and the legislation passed soon after greatly increased the power and funding for the federal government. The media couldn't accuse him of the crimes committed on September 11 because they were controlled by the CIA. So Bush and the other perpetrators walked away Scott free from those crimes, while being savaged in the most bizarre manner for smaller offenses."

Shaking my head, I concluded that "If that's not conclusive evidence that our government is a mere puppet of the Shadow Government, I don't know what would be."

Russell seemed to have answers for any question I might raise, so I tried one more on him.

"When I was a kid, and throughout my student years, investigative journalism was held up as the highest form of journalism. That attitude, I believe, arose during Watergate. Bob Woodward and Carl Bernstein were regarded as heroes for their investigate reporting that revealed the Watergate scandal, and the *Washington Post*, and Ben Bradlee, its managing editor, too. Their story, based on Woodward and Bernstein's book, was even made into a move, *All the President's Men*, staring several of the biggest Hollywood stars. Dustin Hoffman played Bernstein and Robert Redford, Woodward. Jason Robards played Bradlee.

"But then, 27 years later, in 2001, investigative journalism was thrown out the window. It's discouraged, not encouraged, at least on the subject of September 11. Reporters who on their own initiative investigated and wrote stories on what really happened found their pieces rejected by their editors. And on the rare occasions when editors tried to publish them, the owners of the papers or TV stations squelched the reports. The world of journalism had been turned upside down."

"That's right," Russell agreed. "Not only had the three branches of government—executive, legislative and judicial—all failed the country at that most critical moment in the nation's history, so did the so-called fourth branch, the media. Anger about this betrayal of its traditional mission to report on the most important developments of the day in an objective manner, and to provide context necessary for readers to understand their significance, has grown exponentially among those who figured out what really happened."

Russell picked up a paper lying on the table and read part of it. "The media's lies, by commission and omission, constitute, in Eric Larsen's view, 'treachery against the republic, against the Constitution, against the people, against the human race. . . . We are in a state of emergency, such as our own republic has never before been in, and we are being lied to about it, massively and absolutely, by the entirety of that very element of socio-political society that at one time in history was the *indispensable* freedom-preserving element—namely, the "Fourth Estate.'[251]

"Politicians will be politicians, so the thinking goes," Russell continued. "But the media, like university professors, the clergy and a few other groups, are supposed to be above all that. They're supposed to establish standards of correct behavior and point out when others violate them. They are supposed to be the moral conscience of society. Their failure to do that at that moment of such great peril for the country generated much anger. The rot, the corruption in American society goes far beyond the political sphere. It reaches into the very heart of the conscience of the nation."

I didn't know quite what to say to such a somber assessment of the nature of my country, so stood up to leave. I had much to think about once I got back home.

60

At this point I almost made a big mistake but was guided away from it just in time by C. S. Lewis.

After retirement and the loss of Diana, I'd set out to build a new life. Recalling Aristotle's "An unexamined life isn't worth living," I'd decided to cultivate friendships only with those persons who were living examined lives. Having no need for colleagues, I'd build a new life of meaning with people I respect as friends. Not colleagues, but friends. I realized that the number of acquaintances would drop as former colleagues dropped away, but that was fine. I wanted to focus on things that really mattered, not those that mattered for building a career.

In line with that way of thinking I'd developed much valued friendships with Gina de Larrocha and Russell Fletcher over the past six months, as I've recounted. I now got the idea that it would be good to bring the two of them together, to have them meet. Both were remarkable people; if I enjoyed meeting each of them separately, meeting them together would be even more pleasurable, right?

I was just about to arrange a lunch for the three of us when I began reading C. S. Lewis's *The Four Loves*. It's a short book, and I expected to toss it off in an hour or two. Instead, struck by the relevance of what he had to say about two of the loves—Friendship and Eros—to my own situation, to my friendships with Gina and Russell, I studied what he had to say very carefully. I now realized what a disaster bringing Gina and Russell together might have been. A lunch for the three of us might have been as awful as mixing ice cream and Malbec, two other things I enjoy.

Friendships, Lewis explained, arise "when two or more companions discover that they have in common some insight or interest or even taste which the others do not share and which, till that moment, each believed to be his own unique treasure (or burden). The typical expression of opening Friendship would be something like, 'What? You too? I thought I was the only one.' . . . It is then that Friendship is born."[252]

That certainly described how my friendship with Russell Fletcher had begun, how he in my mind had risen above all the other colleagues from my Foreign Service days who I was still in touch with. Our friendship was based on a common interest in understanding the real nature of American society, as shown by what really happened during the most dramatic events in its recent history, the assassination of President Kennedy and the events of September 11. I'd have welcomed others into our discussions, and think Russell would have, too, but neither of us knew anyone else who lived nearby who shared our interest in this subject and was open to re-examining what they thought they knew about those and other events in our country's history.

Lewis's insight also described my friendship with Gina de Larrocha and how it came about. We shared a common interest in literature, as did other members of the book club. Yet our approach to the subject—Gina's and mine—was so distinctly different from the others that a friendship arose between the two of us based on our shared common approach.

I saw now that bringing together these two friends, when my friendship with each was based on a shared interest in a specific subject, an interest not shared by the other, would have been a disaster. The lunch might have been pleasant enough, but the presence of Gina would have interfered with my discussions with Russell about JFK and September 11 and what they revealed about the real nature of our government and society. And Russell's presence would have hampered any real discussion about literature with Gina. Conversation would have descended into trivialities and the lunch would have been a frustrating waste of time. It might have also affected the bond I had with each of them, bonds that had at all costs to be protected.

There was another reason, too, why bringing them together wasn't a good idea.

My relationship with Gina was more complex than my friendship with Russell, a complication that arose from how attractive I found her and from her interest in me as a suitor. Those factors were distinctly different from a friendship based on a shared interest in literature. They formed the basis for another type of relationship discussed by Lewis, one based on another of his four loves, Eros, a love distinctly different from

Friendship.

"We can have erotic love and friendship for the same person yet in some ways nothing is less like a Friendship than a love-affair," Lewis had written. "Lovers are always talking to one another about their love; Friends hardly ever about their Friendship. Lovers are normally face to face, absorbed in each other; Friends, side by side, absorbed in some common interest."[253]

Lewis's explanation of the differences in the two types of love, or the relationships that grow out of them, hit home. He'd phrased it just right: Friends like me and Russell were indeed side by side, facing a common interest, even when we sat opposite each other at a table in a restaurant. Gina and I were always face to face, focused on each other as least as intently as on literature. That explained why our conversations so often veered from literature to more personal subjects.

Was that what Gina and I shared: Eros, rather than Friendship? Or did we have both? With Russell I could speak freely on the subject of our common interest. With Gina it was different. Sometimes I could speak freely, when the topic of our conversation was literature. But all too often we veered into talking about each other and ourselves. Then I was much more guarded. I didn't want romantic feelings to develop for someone with whom a romantic relationship was impossible. And as Gina's presence had brought home to me months earlier, a romantic relationship with anyone was ruled out because of my age.

Yet I couldn't deny that romantic feelings were growing and had in fact been present from the first moment I'd seen that attractive girl at Subway six month ago.

Gina, on the other hand, had no reservations about entering into a romantic relationship. She actively sought what she called suitors, a word that always intrigued me because it was representative of a mindset far outside the usual American approach to things. It wasn't amusing to her, though. She was intent on building a certain kind of life, one that required a husband for herself and a father for her children-to-be. She wanted a family.

And so we ventured on, each in our own way circling the other, the difference in our ultimate goals becoming more apparent all the time. For her, I now recognized, my status as suitor was the primary strand; literary discussions merely embellishment, though perhaps it hadn't been that way initially. For me it was the opposite. Literary discussions had been the primary strand; romantic possibilities, though impossible, added zest to our conversations.

But was that how things still stood with me? I didn't know. I knew for sure only that I enjoyed being with her. It seemed impossible to draw a line separating the pleasure I got from literary discussions with her from that arising from just being with her. I knew for certain that, in contrast with my Friendship with Russell, in which I'd welcome more true friends into our conversations, I didn't want anyone else intruding into the time I spent with Gina.

61

Gina was bubbling over with good spirits when we met for dinner. Her business was past the break-even point and she had high hopes for the future.

"I now have three tutors working for me every day during the week, for several hours each day. One or two students are in each session. As you know, I can handle up to six sessions at one time in the studio, and there's still the large conference room where I can tutor or where larger groups can meet. So there's plenty of room for growth before incurring any more fixed costs. And I'm still tutoring group classes for home schooled students several days a week, in their homes."

We didn't usually have alcohol during our meals, but this time each of us had a glass of wine to celebrate the success of her business.

After we ordered, I wanted to ask her about the importance of Catholicism in her life. I began by explaining what I've already recounted in this memoir about my journey from regarding Christianity as the source of wars and brutality in European history, to holding a more benign view as I began to see human nature itself as the source of the problem, and then on to holding a favorable opinion as I recognized how the Christian belief that all people are equal in the eyes of God had led eventually to the practice of equal civil and legal rights for all in the American republic.

I then asked her if she had always been a Catholic.

"Oh yes," she said. "Everyone in my larger family is Catholic, going back as many generations as I know of. At least three. And so is pretty much everybody I knew growing up and even at uni. For most people in my country the Church is an essential part of our lives—not just going to mass to sustain and deepen our religious beliefs, but also participating in Catholic holidays and fiestas; for many of us they're the most important part of their social lives.

"Growing up, All Saints Day—November 1—was always my favorite. My family would put up a big tent in the cemetery where our ancestors are buried, and every member of our extended family would spend the day there, sometimes more than a hundred people. It was one of the few times during the year when we all met together. Everybody dressed up, colorfully, and we played games with our cousins and had lots of food.

"Later, as we got older, the girls would gather together on one side of the cemetery and the young men on the other, each dressed in their colorful finery, with both groups pretending that they didn't know the other was there as they seemingly inadvertently moved closer to each other. There was lots of eye contact between the young men and us girls, and occasional short conversations, as we learned how to present ourselves by copying what the older girls did, and how to assess the merits of this, that and another young man. It was all such fun! Such innocent fun. There's nothing like it that I can see in American life."

Gina was then silent for a moment before speaking in a more restrained way.

"Of course, since nearly everyone was Catholic, the question of marrying someone who wasn't rarely arose. When it did, the outside potential spouse had to become Catholic."

She glanced quickly at me as she said that, and I sensed she was trying to gauge the effect of her words on me.

"You know, Gina," I said, "I am not Catholic, or even a Christian. Until recently my interest had been in the historical aspects of Christianity, in how it has influenced the development of Western civilization. But over the last year, as I've read works by C. S. Lewis and others, I've become more interested in the theological aspects of the religion. Lewis's *Mere Christianity*, and especially his *Surprised by Joy*, describe the process through which his belief in Christianity developed and the sudden transformation through which he became a Christian, an Anglican, at age 33.

"More recently, I've wanted to know how Lewis's experiences compared to those of others who converted to Christianity. Quite a number of writers not born Christian converted as adults," I said, and I listed off those I remembered: "Mortimer J. Adler, at age 82; Hilaire Belloc, G. K. Chesterton, T. S. Eliot, Graham Greene, Walker Percy and Roger Scruton."

Gina nodded as I recited this list, still watching me attentively. When after a moment of silence she still didn't say anything, I jumped in with the following.

"John F. Kennedy was raised Catholic, and I've wanted to learn more about how his religious beliefs affected his political thought, particularly his Peace Speech given in June 1963, and his other efforts to defuse international tensions that year. It was those efforts that led the security agencies and military in his own government to regard him as such a threat to national security that they felt they had no choice but to remove him from his position in the most permanent way possible."

A second later she nodded in a definitive way, as though she'd made up her mind about something. When she spoke again it was about her high hopes for the future of her studio.

A few minutes later we left the restaurant. After we parted to walk to our cars parked several rows apart, we looked over at each other more than once. I felt as if there was some unfinished business between us but didn't at that moment know what it was.

A minute later, driving home, I knew that if I had walked Gina all the way to her car, I, assuredly not a suitor, would have tried to put my arms around her and kiss her.

62

Reading Glennon's *National Security and Double Government*, I saw that he set out to explain the puzzle of why the approach of the Obama administration to multiple national security issues had been essentially the same as that of the Bush administration. "Why does national security policy remain constant even when one president [Bush] is replaced by another [Obama], who as a candidate repeatedly, forcefully, and eloquently promised fundamental changes in that policy?"[254] he asked.

What Glennon found challenged what he called "the myth that U.S. security policy is still forged by the president, Congress and the courts" [255]—by what he referred to as the Constitutional Government as established by James Madison and the other founders of the United States. He found that even the president now exercises little substantive control over the overall direction of U.S. national security policy, which is instead made by "several hundred executive officials who manage the military, intelligence, diplomatic, and law enforcement agencies responsible for protecting the nation's security."[256] This system of double government, he concluded, poses a "mortal threat . . . to accountability, democracy, and personal freedom."[257]

"Enough examples exist to persuade the public that the network is subject to judicial, legislative, and executive constraints," Glennon wrote. "This appearance is important to its operation, for the network derives legitimacy from the ostensible authority of the public, constitutional branches of the government." But, he continued, "The appearance of accountability is . . . largely an illusion. The courts, Congress, and even the president in reality impose little constraint. Judicial review is negligible, congressional oversight dysfunctional, and presidential control nominal."[258]

This dual system described by Glennon was largely consistent with Russell's observation that the U.S. government serves as the functional arm of a partially hidden power that operates mostly behind the scenes, in the same way that the government in the old Soviet Union served as the functional arm of the Communist Party. One principal difference between the two systems, I noted again, was that although in the old Soviet system it was universally recognized that the Party was the principal source of official power in the country, in the American system today the "party" is hidden and its existence not widely recognized.

Given this system of "double government," I saw that two questions needed to be asked about September 11. The smaller one concerned the identities of those who orchestrated the events of that day and managed them from some central control center as they unfolded. I set that question aside for now and turned to the larger question of the organization to whom the orchestrators of the September 11 events reported.

Some scholars and investigators into September 11, David Ray Griffin among them, have identified the key suspects as senior officials within the U.S. government, including the White House, the Pentagon and the intelligence agencies. Others, such as Webster Tarpley, have pointed to a wider organization inside and outside of government. "It is hardly likely that the command center of 9/11 could have been in the upper reaches of government," he concluded; "far more likely that it was outside of government altogether," just as that wider organization "most likely keeps its center of gravity and command center somewhere in the privatized public sector."[259]

"The September criminals," he continued, "were financiers, top-level bureaucrats, flag-rank military officers, top intelligence officials, and technical specialists; the prime focus of their operations was in all probability a series of private-sector locations, where confidentiality could be best assured by excluding elements loyal to the Constitution. It is therefore probably misleading to think of people like Cheney as the hands-on field commanders of the terrorist forces of 9/11, although

Cheney appears to have been complicit in other ways."[260]

The U.S. intelligence community had "been largely privatized under [Reagan's] Executive Order 12333," Tarpley noted, which meant that "the really crucial capabilities for an operation like 9/11 are no longer to be sought in the . . . CIA, but rather in a myriad of private military firms, technology companies, think tanks, law firms, public relations firms, and front companies of all types. It is here, rather than in a secret government office, that the planning and command center for 9/11 would normally be sought."[261]

Yet the CIA, I thought, remained a key member of that array of organizations, as well as a tool used by them. I accepted Barrie Zwicker's conclusion that "the CIA is at the heart," because it "long ago infiltrated the media at all levels," which enabled it to inject "information and disinformation directly into the arteries of media organizations, [manage] propaganda campaigns and . . . sidelin[e] or obliterat[e] important truths about the ruling elites."[262]

It had also established "a network of moles"[263] throughout the government" Tarpley believed, who use their positions to further the goals of that wider organization, rather than the goals of the various departments for which they ostensibly work. Terrorism of the 9/11 type "is generally conducted, not so much by identifiable institutions acting as a totality, but rather by a network or faction of like-minded plotters which cuts across the institutions transversally. It is not the visible, elected government which plots terrorism, but rather the parallel, invisible, or secret government, and that secret government is hidden inside the public and elected one. . . . The essence of this phenomenon is a private network which has ensconced its operatives in decisive, influential positions, from which entire bureaucracies can be controlled, manipulated, or paralyzed."[264]

These arrangements in 2001 were similar to those in place in 1963, Tarpley continued. "This U.S. network represents the current form of the Dulles Brothers-Lemnitzer-Landsdale network of the early 1960s, of the Bay of Pigs-Kennedy assassination-Gulf of Tonkin networks, and of the invisible government/secret government/parallel government/shadow government that was widely understood to have been the prime mover of the Iran-Contra affair."[265] Elsewhere he attributed to this same "secret, private network at the higher levels of the U.S. government which was behind 9/11"[266] such events as the U-2 crisis, the Martin Luther King and Robert Kennedy assassinations and parts of Watergate.

At this point I realized I needed one term to refer to all these entities mentioned by Glennon, Tarpley, Griffin and Zwicker that had in some significant way influenced if not directed government actions on September 11. It couldn't be "Party," as in the Soviet Union, because the word implied too formal a body. Nor should it have the word "government" in it, because what existed appeared to be a power behind the throne that had control over, or at least substantial influence on, the U.S. government. That ruled out such terms as Shadow Government, Double Government, Parallel Government and Invisible Government. Deep State wasn't quite right either, because it referred to the permanent bureaucracy that remains as elected officials come and go.

I considered many other terms—Confederation, Cabal, Gang, Coterie, Conglomerate, Syndicate, Combine, Alliance—but none seemed quite right. Complex had its attractions, as in Eisenhower's Military-Industrial Complex. But that term was too restrictive, and a more expansive term, Military-Industrial-Congressional-Financial-Intelligence Complex was too unwieldy. It's also inaccurate by implying that the entities mentioned are whole units, when it's really only parts of them, or key individuals within them, that are active in the behind-the-scenes way I'm examining here.

I nearly selected Coalition, given the word's definition of "a temporary alliance of distinct parties for joint action." "Temporary" was correct in that the parties came together for specific projects, such as September 11, while remaining separate entities, each with their own individual interests. But I needed a term that also said something about the nature of the parties who came together. I nearly settled on Network, given its definition of an informal, open-ended inter-connected group or association of persons or institutions that engages in fluid, open-ended interactions, but it had the same drawback.

I also considered milieu, a term Peter Dale Scott used to describe the social level from which members of the entity were drawn, but that had the opposite flaw: it didn't say anything about the temporary alliance for which the players came together. Same for coterie, an intimate and often exclusive group of persons with a unifying common interest or purpose, and clique, a narrow exclusive circle of group of persons, one held together by common interests, views or purposes.

I wanted a term that suggested something about the nature of the players and the types of projects for which they came together. I realized I needed more information about how a double government, to use Glennon's term, had come about before I could come up with a term or phrase by which to refer to the players *en masse*. I needed to understand how it had become so powerful that it could use parts of the U.S. government as tools in its pursuit of its own interests.

63

Looking into a number of books to refresh my memory of American history, I found that entities outside the U.S. government powerful enough to influence the president's decisions and Congress's legislation existed since the founding of the country. That wasn't surprising in the early years, when the newly established government was weak and still finding its legs. But it was apparently still the situation at the end of the 19th century. Webster Tarpley found that "the United States presidency tends to be dominated from above and behind the Oval Office by a group of financiers and officials in London and New York." "The current form of this arrangement," he explained, "goes back to about 1895, when President Grover Cleveland capitulated to the demand of J. P. 'Jupiter' Morgan, London's official agent, that the banking faction assume control of the public debt of the United States. . . . The Federal Reserve System soon followed, institutionalizing the Morgan-led financier domination of the U.S. government."[267]

I'd come across several comments by American presidents and a British prime minister at that time on just how powerful that outside influence was and included them in this memoir. [See nearby text box.]

A few decades later, General Smedley Butler, the retired Commandant of the Marine Corps and at that time the most decorated U.S. soldier in American history, commented on how his career in the military had been spent supporting American commercial interests. After retirement—after having fought in the Philippine-American War, the Boxer Rebellion, the Mexican Revolution and World War I—he began to suspect that he and the Marine Corps had been directed to fight more to defend the interests of large commercial enterprises than those of the United States and the American people.

Looking back over his career of 33 years and four months in active military service, he concluded that he had "spent most of my time as a high-class muscle man for Big Business, for Wall Street and the bankers. In short, I was a racketeer for capitalism. . . . I helped make Mexico, especially Tampico, safe for American oil interests in 1914. I helped make Haiti and Cuba a decent place for the National City Bank boys to collect revenues in. I helped in the raping of half a dozen Central American republics for the benefit of Wall Street. The record of racketeering is long. I helped purify Nicaragua for the international banking house of Brown Brothers in 1909-1912. I brought light to the Dominican Republic for American sugar interests in 1916. I helped make Honduras 'right' for American fruit companies in 1903. In China in 1927 I helped to see to it that Standard Oil went its way unmolested."[268]

Insider Testimony on Outside Influences on the Government

"Behind the ostensible government sits enthroned an invisible government owing no allegiance and acknowledging no responsibility to the people. To destroy this invisible government, to befoul the unholy alliance between corrupt business and corrupt politics is the first task of the statesmanship of the day."

Theodore Roosevelt,
26th president, 1901-1909

"There's a power so organized, so subtle, so watchful, so pervasive, so interlocked, that you'd better not speak above your breath when you mention it, in condemnation of it."

Woodrow Wilson
28th president, 1913-1921

After authorizing creation of the Federal Reserve: "I am a most unhappy man. I have unwittingly ruined my country. A great industrial nation is controlled by its system of credit. Our system of credit is concentrated. The growth of this nation, therefore, and all our activities are in the hands of a few men. We have come to be one of the worst ruled, one of the most completely controlled and dominated governments in the civilized world – no longer a government by free opinion, no longer a government by conviction and the vote of the majority, but a government by the opinion and duress of a small group of dominant men."

Woodrow Wilson
28th president, 1913-1921

"The world is governed by very different personages from what is imagined by those who are not behind the scenes."

Benjamin Disraeli
British prime minister,
1874-1880

"The real truth of the matter is, as you and I know, that a financial element in the larger centers has owned the Government ever since the days of Andrew Jackson."

Franklin D. Roosevelt
32nd president, 1933-1945

Incidentally, Butler had revised if not transformed his thinking only after retiring from the Marine Corp, just like I'm now in the process of revising if not transforming my thinking after retiring from the Foreign Service. He explained that "I suspected I was just part of a racket at the time. Now I am sure of it. Like all members of the profession, I never had an original thought until I left the service. My mental faculties remained in suspended animation while I obeyed the orders of the higher-ups. This is typical of everyone in the military service." And, I might add, the Foreign Service.

This use of the powers of the American government on behalf of private interests continued during the 1930s and 1940s, I now saw. Two of the men most successful in doing so were John Foster Dulles and his younger brother Allen Dulles. "From their earliest days on Wall Street," David Talbot explained, "where they ran Sullivan and Cromwell, the most powerful corporate law firm in the nation, their overriding commitment was always to the circle of accomplished, privileged men whom they saw as the true seat of power in America."[269] Even after entering government service during the Second World War, their loyalties were to their clients, who included many large companies in Nazi Germany, rather than to the government they supposedly served. Their activities were sometimes in such opposition to the interests of the United States that, Talbot concluded, if Franklin Roosevelt had outlived the war, "the Dulles brothers would likely have faced serious criminal charges for their wartime activities."[270] Supreme Court Justice Arthur Goldberg had the same view, declaring that "both Dulleses were guilty of treason."

The Dulles brothers' divided loyalties continued even after they reached the pinnacles of power in the U.S. government, with John Foster Dulles in the position of Secretary of State and Allen Dulles head of the Central Intelligence Agency throughout the Eisenhower administration. As one observer, Paul Craig Roberts, concluded, "The interests of the two men's law firm became in effect the agenda of the government of the United States." Both men, he stated, continued to "use their power in the service of their powerful law firm, Sullivan & Cromwell. Both are examples of the privatization of government to serve private interests. Foreign governments that got in the way of their firm's clients' interests, they plotted to overthrow."[271]

Once in those powerful positions in 1953, they turned first to overthrowing Mohammad Mossadegh, the first democratically elected leader of Iran and *TIME Magazine*'s "Man of the Year" in 1951, who had nationalized Iranian oil, thereby disrupting Sullivan & Cromwell's client, the J. Henry Schroder Banking Corp., "the financial agent for the Anglo-Iranian Oil Company on whose board Allen sat," and "Foster's activities on behalf of Chase Manhattan Bank."

"To justify their use of the U.S. government in service to the clients of their law firm," Roberts explained, "the brothers invented the 'communist threat of world subversion' and inaugurated the Cold War." To generate support for Mossadegh's overthrow, "a narrative was created and opinion manipulated. . . . Foster Dulles created a propaganda campaign against Mossadegh presenting him as a weak leader about to be overthrown by Soviet agents. The story fed to President Eisenhower, Congress, and media was that Iran was in danger of being lost to expansionist communism. It worked." In sum, Roberts noted, "What began as the removal of obstacles to their law firm's clients ended in an anti-communist crusade in which the brothers became believers of their own propaganda."

This was quite a different take on the origins of the Cold War than I'd ever heard before.

Having succeeded in manipulating the U.S. government, President Eisenhower and the American public regarding Mossadegh, the Dulles brothers turned to overthrowing Guatemala's first elected government to protect the interests of another Sullivan & Cromwell's client, United Fruit Company. Similar projects followed in the Congo, the Dominican Republic and other countries whose governments placed the interests of their country and people ahead of those of American companies operating in them.

These and other actions through the 1950s and into the

1960s show, Roberts explained, that "that long, expensive Cold War . . . was the creation of two holders of powerful U.S. government offices [who] used [them] in defense of their law firm's clients."

The capabilities of the Dulles brothers and others with similar loyalties to entities outside the U.S. government were greatly enhanced by passage of the National Security Act of 1947. This Act unified the military under a new secretary of defense, created the modern Joint Chiefs of Staff, set up the CIA and established the National Security Council. President Truman soon after set up the National Security Agency and created the position of National Security Advisor.

Many scholars and historians cite this Act as a turning point in American history and highlight Truman's role in its passage. Michael J. Glennon, for instance, observed that Truman's role was decisive in establishing the "network of several hundred high-level military, intelligence, diplomatic, and law enforcement officials within the executive branch who are responsible for national security policymaking."[272]

Establishing these new security agencies created vast new bureaucracies in which moles loyal to outside powers could be embedded. "The CIA routinely places its deep cover agents in every branch of the U.S. government," Michael Ruppert reported, based on the work of Peter Dale Scott and Philip Agee, "especially within the FBI, the DEA, and federal law enforcement agencies. They even do it with municipal police departments such as LAPD, NYPD, or the Chicago PD."[273] Because these intelligence and security agencies operate largely in secret, the moles could further the interests of the outside powers to which they had given their loyalty to a far greater extent than ever before, and do so continuously, not merely from time to time as in the past.

That is the situation that John F. Kennedy would inherit early in 1961.

64

I now felt I had a sure enough grasp of the history of the United States during those crucial years that I was nearly ready to return to the effort to find a term by which to refer to those outside powers. But first I wanted to read *The Power Elite*, sociologist C. Wright Mills's 1956 book that had been referred to in many books I'd read recently. I suspected it might help me to find the best term after learning that Mills had written it "to unmask illusion in order to define important features of social reality," and to "grind a lens through which we can perhaps see a little more clearly the world in which we live."[274]

And I was right. I realized soon after opening the book that Mills's phrase, "the power elite," was the phrase I sought. I will use it henceforth to refer collectively to the entities and the individuals, inside and outside of government, who were and are able to exert substantial influence if not control over various parts of the executive and legislative branches of the U.S. government.

More clearly than other terms I'd already considered—Network, Coalition, National Security State and Military-Industrial Complex—it emphasized the two qualities that all entities identified so far had in common: they were powerful in American society in the years just before Kennedy became president and still are today, and they were and are elites. They came from socially higher classes, were better educated and more accomplished than most persons, and by virtue of these accomplishments believed they deserved to hold and wield power.

In Mills's analysis, "within American society, major national power now resides in the economic, the political, and the military domains."[275] The Power Elites "rule the big corporations. They run the machinery of the state and claim its prerogatives. They direct the military establishment." Together "they occupy the strategic command posts of the social structure, in which are now centered the effective means of the power and the wealth and the celebrity which they enjoy."[276]

The power held by those at the pinnacles of each of these three domains had increased enormously over the decades leading up to the time of Mills' analysis—for two sets of reasons. One is that each domain had grown larger and more centralized within itself and become more integrated with the other two. "There is no longer," Mills observed, "on the one hand, an economy, and, on the other hand, a political order containing a military establishment unimportant to politics and to money-making. There is [now] a political economy linked, in a thousand ways, with military institutions and decisions. . . . There is an ever-increasing interlocking of economic, military, and political structures. . . . In the structural sense, this triangle of power is the source of the interlocking directorate that is most important for the historical structure of the present."[277]

The second reason for the increase in the power held by those at the pinnacles of each of the three domains is that they, "as individuals . . . have become more integrated with each other." "The leading men in each of the three domains of power—the warlords, the corporation chieftains, the political directorate—tend to come together, to form the power elite of America."[278] They increasingly "assume positions in one another's domains. . . . By their very careers and activities, they lace the three types of milieux together."[279]

The Power Elite as a distinct force in American society, then, rests upon the "coincidence of interests among economic, political, and military organizations . . . [and] upon the similarity of origin and outlook, and the social and personal intermingling of the top circles from each of these dominant hierarchies. This conjunction of institutional and psychological forces, in turn, is revealed by the heavy personnel traffic within and between the big three institutional orders. . . . The interchange occurs most frequently at the points of their coinciding interest, as between regulatory agency and the regulated industry; contracting agency and contractor."[280]

Secrecy necessitated by the Cold War and the nuclear threat from the Soviet Union contributed to the creation of the Power Elite as a distinct force in American society. "With the wide secrecy covering their operations and decisions, the power elite can mask their intentions, operations, and further consolidation. Any secrecy that is imposed upon those in positions to observe high decision-makers clearly works for and not against the operations of the power elite."[281]

With the Power Elite overseeing three large domains, acting largely in secrecy and making decisions affecting the entire country, the Congress and much of the executive branch of the government is reduced to players of only secondary importance. That's the key point. "Great decisions are made without benefit of public or even Congressional debate," as I'd seen with passage of the Patriot Act. The movement of "corporation executives into the political directorate has accelerated the long-term relegation of the professional politicians in the Congress to the middle levels of power."[282] The government—especially the Executive and Legislative branches—is bypassed, becoming, as Russell had noted, the functional arm of the Power Elite, just as the government had served the Party in the old Soviet Union.

None benefitted from this new structure of governance more than the military and security agencies. "The warlords have gained decisive political relevance, and the military structure of America is now in considerable part a political structure." American capitalism had become "in considerable part a military capitalism, and the most important relation of the big corporation to the state rests on the coincidence of interests between military and corporate needs, as defined by warlords and corporate rich. . . . Not politicians, but corporate executives, sit with the military and plan the organization of war effort."[283]

Here, then, was the source of what President Eisenhower would call the Military-Industrial Complex.

Standing armies have historically been dangerous because they potentially could escape control by the civilian government. That's the situation we now face: the military and the security and intelligence agencies, allied with large commercial interests, have escaped direction by the president and oversight by the Congress.

In his analysis of the Power Elite, Mills inadvertently provided an example of just how powerful the CIA had become. When discussing the power held by certain legal, financial and investment firms, he mentioned several of them by name and named powerful individuals within them. He mentioned Chase

Manhattan Bank, for instance, and named its chairman, John McCloy. But when he mentioned the law firm of Sullivan and Cromwell, he named no current leader of the firm and made no mention of either John Foster Dulles or Allen Dulles. When he discussed the power held by various departments or agencies in the government, he made no mention of the CIA and only one passing reference to the National Security Council. Even though the Dulles brothers held positions of the greatest power, Mills made only one passing reference to each.

Given the significant role the Dulles' brothers played in launching the Cold War and sustaining the tensions it generated—and the power the CIA held, as shown by the coups it engineered to replace governments in countries around the world—how are we to account for the near invisibility of the brothers and the complete invisibility of the CIA and related intelligence and security agencies in Mills's book? It is unlikely that an analyst as astute as Mills would have been unaware of them and the power they held. I suspect, therefore, that the brothers did not want to be noted personally and they did not want the CIA and related agencies to be mentioned. Mills, fearing the consequences of not bowing to their wishes, complied.

At this point I noted an aspect of the Power Elite that seemed paradoxical or counter intuitive. Mills observed that "No matter how great their actual power, [the Power Elites] tend to be less acutely aware of it than of the resistances of others to its use."[284] To those of us outside the milieu of the Power Elite, what is most noticeable is just how powerful they are. For those inside, it's the limits of or resistance to their power that strikes them most profoundly; it's that psychological perception from inside the milieu that accounts for the Power Elite's paranoia, for its obsessive desire for absolute control and the pursuit of it well beyond the point of diminishing returns.

Not knowing in February how profoundly that obsession would affect American society in the coming months, my desire then was to understand how this puzzling psychological orientation could arise. Then I had it, or at least an analogy that made sense to me. The analogy involved bowling. For ordinary folks like me, getting a strike is a cause for celebration because we don't get all that many of them. For professional bowlers, however, getting strikes is the usual result of their tossing the ball down the lane. It's the frames without strikes that are unusual; they're a cause of distress. For me, the greater the number of strikes in a game, the greater the cause for celebration; for them, the greater the number of frames without strikes, the greater the distress. I count upward starting at zero; they count downward from 300, the score in a perfect game. It all depends on your point of view.

And so it is within the milieu of the Power Elites. It's not that their massive power—their strikes—is a cause for celebration, but that the limits on their power—their frames without strikes—are causes of distress. That's what is foremost in their minds; that what gets their attention and causes them concern. And so, as they focus more and more intensely on eliminating the causes of that distress, it's ordinary folks like us who get crushed.

A final oddity I noted was that even though the Power Elites, as higher members of the military, corporate and political orders, live in a milieu in which they share with others similar "interests as well as the intricate, psychological facts of their origins and their education, their careers and their associations [that] make possible the psychological affinities that prevail among them,"[285] they often act counter to each other's interests. There is continual jostling as they compete against each other within and between the three orders. "Despite their social similarity and psychological affinities, the members of the power elite do not constitute a club having a permanent membership with fixed and formal boundaries," Mills observed. "It is of the nature of the power elite that within it there is a good deal of shifting about, and that it thus does not consist of one small set of the same men in the same positions in the same hierarchies."[286]

But—and this is the point that struck me—at certain key times or in certain key circumstances the interests of a critical number of the most powerful of the Power Elites align. "The power elite is . . . frequently in some tension; it comes together only on certain coinciding points and only on certain occasions of 'crisis,'"[287] Mills explained. At such moments the players can join together to undertake actions or projects not normally possible. It's those extraordinary moments—among which I expected to find the assassination of John F. Kennedy and the events of September 11—that I now wanted to consider more closely.

65

One day near the end of the month two surprising things happened.

The first was that I came across an article written by "Manuel Garcia, Jr.," who claimed to have been involved in the events of September 11. His article was written in the form of a confession by someone who had been part of a team that planted explosives in World Trade Center buildings 1, 2 and 7 during the previous Labor Day weekend, and who was now confessing his role because he had been diagnosed with terminal cancer.

Garcia described how he came to be "recruited into the most complex U.S. false flag operation in history: the secret controlled demolition of the World Trade Center: a cover for launching the Global War on Terror," which he called "the War for Complete National Control and World Domination."[288] He laid out in some detail how he and others calculated "what arrays and minimum doses of charges could collapse tall buildings instantly," and said he was "selected as the Physics Lead for Emplacement Team 6."

"My small platoon comprised of 20 people," he explained, included "a mix of demolition emplacement techs, electronics and circuitry interruption specialists and security troopers. . . . This was exciting adrenaline-pumping work." "In less than two weeks, staged as HVAC, plumbing, elevator, and electrical conduit repairmen working through the Labor Day weekend of 2001, all our teams got the WTC Twin Towers and Building 7 wired for demolition." "So that's my story," he concluded. "You can believe it or not as you like, I don't care. I'm at peace for having told it."

Garcia's article was so specific and detailed that it appeared to have been written by someone who knew what he was talking about. He convinced me that he had been an actual participant—at first. On second reading, however, I saw that his article appeared to be a spoof. He seemed to be taunting the 9/11 Truth movement, saying in effect, "Here's what happened. Now prove it. But you can't! Ha, ha, ha!"

I then came across a similar piece by Gary G. Kohls. Inspired by Garcia's article, Kohls created a monologue that he put into the mouth of a fictional former U.S. military intel officer, Greg Ziegler, who made statements that Kohls imaged someone like Dick Cheney or Donald Rumsfeld uttering. Among them were:

"You 9/11 conspiracy theorists have no real power, so go suck it. You are in a minority and you don't have the obedient mass media telling and endlessly re-telling the Big Lie day after day. 24/7 media blitzes like the press so willingly broadcast starting on 9/12/01 can't be overcome."[289] And, "You unpatriotic '9/11 Truthers' can even have annual conventions on 9/11, with a host of expert scientists who have figured out the conspiracy and know who were the conspirators. To use a Russian expression, the dogs may bark as the train roars along. You are the dogs, and we are the train. Keep whining. We will keep on declaring ourselves unconvinced. We still own the media, we still own the military and we still own the politicians. So you can chatter on the internet all you want as you fade into ineffectual obscurity."

Reading those pieces was demoralizing and infuriating, and I began to wonder whether the 9/11 Truth movement would ever be successful in alerting the American people to what had really happened.

It was now nearly noon, so I took a break to prepare lunch. The second surprising thing that happened that day happened as I was putting the making of my roast beef sandwich out on the counter.

I answered a knock at the door to find standing there a man about my own age who looked somewhat familiar but whose name escaped me.

"Jubal!" he said joyfully, but on the quiet side. "Remember me, your old buddy, Brian Boskow?" Brian and I had been friends in high school, but I hadn't seen him since a year or two after we'd graduated. I knew he'd gone off to study engineering, and a few years later I entered the diplomatic corps and left the country. We'd lost touch in those pre-email days. It was quite a surprise to see him standing on my porch.

"Can I come in?" he asked, then walked in quickly before I had a chance to respond. He looked carefully up and down the street before closing the door.

"Brian, are you being followed?" I'd asked the question only half seriously, but his answer was all serious.

"I don't think so. I think I lost them." He laughed quietly as he said it. Brian was someone who, once you'd met him, you don't forget him. He had an irrepressible personality and a friendly directness in his manner, combined with a laugh that infected everyone who heard it; all that won him many friends and made him a pleasure to be around.

Now, though, his laugh was more muted and his manner seemed dampened. He wasn't afraid, but he was cautious as he looked around the living room and glanced down the hallway visible from where he stood.

"It's great to see you again, Brian, but what brings you here?" I asked. "How did you know I live here?"

"Oh, word reached me that you've been passing around pictures of the towers in New York and asking people what they see in them, as though they're Rorschach inkblots."

I laughed at that, and he did too, with something of the exuberance in his laugh that I remembered.

He looked at me with one eye cocked, and I knew he wanted to know what I was up to. So I explained briefly my research into the findings of the 9/11 Truth movement. I didn't offer what I thought of what I'd found.

He waited silently for me to continue. So I explained that the photos I'd been passing around looked to me like a building being exploded from within and turned into dust, not a building collapsing directly into its own footprint after having been struck on one corner by a plane; and that the conflict between what my eyes told me and what the official explanation stated had led me to investigate the events of that day in more detail.

As I spoke, we walked into the kitchen. The bread and roast beef and lettuce and tomato were still out on the counter.

"Help yourself, Brian," I said as I finished making my sandwich. Brian made one for himself.

We then walked into the dining room. "Here's where I've been working," I said, motioning to direct his attention to the two dozen books and stacks of papers on September 11 spread out over the large dining table. The bookcase nearby was filled with several dozen more books on the same subject.

As we walked toward the far end of the table, the one area not covered with books and papers, Brian saw the article by Garcia that I'd just finished reading, the one claiming that he'd played a role in planting explosives in one of the World Trade Center buildings.

As we sat down, Brian's laugh now came out in full joyful exuberance, just as I remembered it from so long ago.

Now it was my turn to look at him with a cocked eye to encourage him to explain.

"Although Garcia's piece gives the impression of being a fictional presentation," he began, "it's quite accurate, though incomplete, about the activities his team was engaged in."

"You know Garcia?" I asked.

"I might have met him during sessions when various teams were brought together for briefings," he said. "We didn't know each other's full names. We were specialists brought together to work on this one project before disbanding and returning to our home units. I knew the identities of only a few of the others on my team because we'd worked together before. The others I knew only on a first name basis. The mission was classified, and we knew we'd never be able to discuss it with anyone even after it was over—ever."

Brian went on to lay out how his team had worked to design the plan to cut the core steel columns near the center of the buildings—the types of explosives needed, the placement of them, the order in which they'd need to be detonated, and so on. Many other teams worked on related projects in the same building and in others nearby.

"All we knew at first was that our mission was to bring down a tall modern skyscraper," he said. "We did several test runs with tall steel-structured buildings in other locations, not all of them in the United States. Then, several weeks before the day of the demolition, we began planting the explosives in the locations we'd selected. We knew which explosives to plant on each floor and which columns to attach them to, and on which face. So we were able to work quickly.

"We were like players on a football team, each with a different role to play that had to be performed well for the entire effort to succeed. Other teams were at work on other aspects of the demolition. We were never told the location of the building, but of course after seeing the architectural drawings and after entering the buildings themselves we figured it out. But not until the day of the event did we grasp the full magnitude of what we were part of. We were nearly as shocked as everyone else as we watched the events unfold on TV."

"So you were actually part of the destruction of the towers? If so, why are you telling me this. Wasn't your work classified?"

There was no more laughing as Brian became deadly serious.

"I'm going to come clean," he said. "My primary loyalty must be to my country, not to my unit. As a citizen of the United States, I have a duty to make known to others what I know about the events of that day. I have documented my experiences in as much detail as I can recall. I describe very specifically the work my team did, what skills the other team members brought to the task, and what the other teams were doing. I've put on paper everything I know, observed, or guessed."

"Why are you doing this now, Brian, nearly 20 years after that terrible day?"

Brian's grimace and his somber manner underlay what he said next. "Because all other members of my team are dead. I'm the only one left alive. I know they're coming for me, too.

"You remember hearing about the death of bin Laden, about the special SEAL team that went in to get him? Did you know that

that team had been comprised of SEALS from other units, brought together just for that one mission? Did you know that a month later that team was reassembled and all were murdered, so that none of them could ever reveal what really happened that day?"

"Something similar has happened to the teams involved in September 11. Something went wrong with the removal of my team though. Three of us were accidentally left out when the team reunited and its helicopter was shot down in Afghanistan. Since then, the other two have been murdered. I'm the only one left alive to reveal our role in 9/11."

Brian handed me a large envelope. "Here's my testimony as to everything I know about that day," he said. Three copies, all signed and notarized."

"Why are you giving this to me," I asked as I accepted the envelope.

"I want someone besides myself to have my testimony." His manner was dampened again, now even fearful.

"But why me? Why not send this information directly to others who can make it known. Why not the media?"

"Because as unrealistic as it sounds, I hope to live many more years. But just in case I don't I want someone else to have my testimony, someone who might have some sympathy with the effort to make the truth known, someone who won't just throw the envelope away. I want you to make my testimony widely known if and when I die."

"Why not just include it as part of your will, with instructions to a lawyer to disseminate it after your death?" I asked.

"Because lawyers could easily be bought off. They are only agents, with no skin in the game. You, I think, have an interest in knowing what the truth is and in making it known."

I'd been wavering about accepting Brian's envelope until his comment about lawyers being only agents, which I interpreted to mean the opposite of Principals. As I've mentioned, I am, or am trying to become, a Principal. Brian was right to intuit that my interest was not a mere passing fancy or a hobby, but a substantive commitment to understanding and making known the truth, and his explanation was decisive. He'd somehow known just what to say to convince me to accept the envelope and promise to make his testimony known after his death.

We then turned to eating our sandwiches and catching each other up on the decades of our lives since we'd last met. Like me, Brian had retired recently and had two children, both younger than mine. Unlike me, his wife was still living. He had a lot to live for, and was planning to take his family far away, to somewhere where no one knew any of them. He still wanted his pension, though, and planned to have funds from his bank account transferred abroad, to an account that couldn't be traced.

After Brian left—he went out the back door and hopped over the fence—I realized that his reappearance had altered my life. Before seeing him, I wanted to know the facts of September 11 and make them widely known. Yet now, after receiving a notarized statement that could trigger greater awareness of the events of that day, I had to ask myself whether I really did want to make the truth widely known. It hadn't occurred to me before to ask what costs, financial and otherwise, the United States would have to pay if its government's role became known. Surely the country would face condemnation by the rest of the world. Did I really want that to happen? I'd need to carefully calculate both sides of the scale—the benefits and harm that would accrue to the country I still loved—before I could decide whether or not to disseminate Brian's testimony. I could see that gathering the information needed to make that determination, and then pondering what to do, could take some time, and that the decision would be difficult.

PART III

March 2020

66

The book club's discussion of Mark Twain's *Adventures of Huckleberry Finn* was especially enjoyable for me because of the similarities between Huck's dilemma and my own. I almost laughed out loud during the discussion when it dawned on me that Huck's torment about whether to turn Jim in was similar to mine about whether to reveal Brian's testimony, thereby possibly bringing down the United States government. What was the right thing to do?

Huck faced the decision of whether or not to return Jim, the slave who'd run off, to his owners. Due to his upbringing and social pressure, he'd always believed that runaway slaves must be captured and returned. Yet he ended up helping Jim escape after he'd been captured by others. His thinking about what the right thing to do was had been transformed through his experiences and adventures with Jim. He'd come to see him, although a slave, as a true friend and fellow man. I was especially moved by how Jim's fooling Huck about the death of Huck's father mirrored the tricks Huck had played on Jim, and the subtle way that Twain, through those tricks, had showed their similar nature as human beings.

Huck had progressed from childhood, from blindly accepting the values of the society he'd grown up in, to become a Principal, an informed decision maker able to withstand social pressure against what he had come to see was the right thing to do. He'd been shocked to learn that his childhood buddy, Tom Sawyer, had become a member of respectable society, accepting and enforcing the social code that Huck now saw as flawed, even morally wrong.

Over dinner after the discussion ended, I explained to Gina as best I could at that point—my thinking was to become clearer over the next two months—my own dilemma about what to do with Brian's testimony. "Should I reveal it to others, thereby possibly harming my country or at least its government, or should I sweep it under the rug to protect the reputation of the country I still love in spite of all its flaws?"

"I'm curious," Gina said. "I remember my question to you some time ago about why you are so passionate about your investigations into the Kennedy assassination and the September 11 attacks, and I felt like there's more to it than what you shared that time, as passion towards such things that require conviction must come from something personal."

I paused to sort out my thoughts before responding.

"I hadn't expected to get so absorbed in these events. I'd intended to investigate the lives and writings of Huxley, Kennedy and Lewis, and still want to get back to them. But the more I learned about the reasons for Kennedy's assassination, the more personal it became to me. I might not have mentioned before that it was being inspired by Kennedy's June 10, 1963, Peace speech that led me to a career in diplomacy."

"During my student years—high school and college—I read a lot of literature and listened to a lot of classical music. Russian writers and composers were among my favorites. Dostoevsky, Tolstoy, Turgenev, Chekov and others among the writers; Tchaikovsky, Prokofiev, Shostakovich, Mussorgsky and many others among the composers. During those years I was always careful to distinguish between Russia, Russians and Russian culture on one hand, and, on the other, the Soviet Union and the terror it inflicted on Russia and other countries in Eastern and Central Europe.

"When the Soviet Union fell apart at the end of 1991, soon after I began my career as a Foreign Service officer, I was ecstatic.

Here was the demise of the biggest geo-political threat to world peace and prosperity, and the most powerful opponent of the United States, gone. Most important to me personally was that Russia itself was finally free from Soviet terror. I rejoiced, as did so many others, not only for the geo-political advantages that would accrue to the United States, but also for the Russian people who had regained their freedom from the cabal that had dominated them for more than 70 years."

This was the first time I had put these thoughts into words, and it was all so new that I felt like I was explaining it to myself as well as to Gina.

"I expected Europe to invite Russia to join the European Union and that the split in Europe that had existed since the Second World War ended in 1945, more than 45 years earlier, would finally be healed. Both Russia and Europe would finally become normal again. I expected my government to work to make the transition as easy and as quick as possible.

"When the Warsaw Pact, the military organization composed of countries in Eastern and Central Europe dominated by the Soviet Union, declared itself out of existence, I fully expected that European countries and the United States would abolish its Western counterpart, NATO. With the Soviet Union gone and the Warsaw Pact of Communist countries dissolved, the principal reason for NATO's existence—to counter aggression from the east—no longer existed.

"In addition, Russia itself had lost its hold on conquered eastern and central European countries. Eastern Europe, which had largely been incorporated into the U.S.S.R.—now because independent countries. Germany at the end of the Second World War lost 48 percent of its pre-war territory and would have been much less of a threat to its neighbors even if it hadn't been split into two countries. Something similar happened to Russia in the early 1990s. The new country of Russia was far smaller than the Soviet Union had been. It was perhaps only 52 percent of the territory of the Soviet Union, and therefore, like Germany after the War, for that reason alone much less of a threat to other countries.

"So, still inspired by Kennedy's Peace speech 30 years earlier, I looked forward to doing all I could to bring his vision of peace between the United States and Russia to fruition. It was a heady moment to be in the Foreign Service.

Gina nodded encouragingly, and I was grateful that she appeared to be genuinely interested in what I was saying.

"But it was not to be. The U.S. government, with Europe following its lead, continued to keep Russia at arms length. NATO remained in existence even though its chief enemy—indeed its only enemy—no longer existed.

"Step by step, almost without realizing it, I became involved in implementing policies that kept Russia out of Europe and NATO in existence. It is only now that I am beginning to see just how complicit I had become in actions that violated some of my most heartfelt ideals. I'd actually helped implement the policies that I now realize were so misguided and destructive. I have blood on my hands. Not at lot, to be sure; I was too low-level an officer for that. But blood just the same.

Gina was quiet. She looked thoughtful.

"But it gets worse, I continued. "I allowed myself to be convinced that keeping Russia out of Europe and NATO in existence were the right policies for the United States and Europe to follow. Eager to be accepted by my peers and more senior officers in those first years in my career, I allowed myself to become blinded. It is, in fact, only now, after my career has ended, that I have the disconcerting realization that I betrayed my own youthful ideals inspired by Kennedy's Peace speech. Ideals I still think are valid. I'm beyond embarrassed; I'm ashamed.

"In my training class, two retired Foreign Service officers who spoke to us newly hired officers emphasized the importance of having a clean conscience at the end of our careers. As I retired 28 years later, I recalled their words and thought I had lived up to them. I congratulated myself for having avoided actions that were shady or underhanded. It isn't until almost this very moment, after learning about the JFK assassination and September 11 nightmares, that I see clearly that I had betrayed my ideals and my love of Russian literature and music and people. I had buried that knowledge so deeply in my unconscious that I didn't even realize it until now.

"I bought into the false assassination story as much as anyone. And I bought into the false September 11 story, too, perpetrated by the same military and security organizations that had murdered the president 38 years earlier. I'd been duped, but I shouldn't have been. I was as blind and passive as most others, but I shouldn't have been. And so, I'm seeking all the information I can find about who killed Kennedy and why, and who has participated in the cover-up over the past 56 and 1/3 years, a cover-up that began the day I was born.

"That's why my investigations are so intense, Gina. Because they are so personal. All this plays into Principality. As a Principal I must make every effort to become fully informed about issues requiring decisions or judgments by me, such as the decision about whether or not to release Brian's testimony."

I suddenly realized that I had done nearly all the talking since we'd sat down and was silent.

Gina, who had listened silently, with interest, then said, "That's quite a string of experiences, Jubal. I knew there had to be some deeply personal reason why you were so intensely investigating those events. Thank you for sharing them with me."

I sighed, and said, "I'm so glad I retired when I did rather than waiting until the mandatory age of stepping down. When I said soon after we met that I wanted to become a different person, I meant in part escaping being an agent of the U.S. government even though at that time I didn't realize just how severely I had betrayed my younger self. Now I want to atone for that betrayal. I want to live a more normal life, a more private life, now that I have ceased being a representative of a large octopus whose tentacles are spread over the entire globe."

"I don't know much about European history," Gina said in response, "just the basics that everyone is familiar with. I'm much more familiar with the ways that Europe has affected Asian countries—has colonized them, and, yes, abused them and their peoples. The United States did this, too, most directly to my country and people."

I was tired of talking about such topics, though, and was glad when Gina changed the subject. She wanted to talk about her three sisters in The Philippines, who ranged from three to eleven years younger than herself. The oldest had married just before Gina left the Philippines three years ago; the youngest was still in high school. I hadn't thought I would, but I enjoyed hearing about their adventures and concerns, and about how much Gina missed them.

This distraction from my own concerns was just what I needed for my mind to relax. Having talked so much earlier, I was content to let Gina prattle on. And, having talked so much earlier, my plate was still full while hers was nearly empty. I now had a chance to catch up.

Then it was time to go our separate ways. Before we split up, I gave Gina an article I'd finished reading recently, one I thought might provide her with content for some of the courses she was designing for her home-schooled students, "The Case for the Liberal Arts: Stronger than Ever?" by Wilfred McClay.

67

Back home I realized that there was one subject boring in on my mind and spirit even more insistently than JFK and September 11: Gina. Thoughts of her were always there in the background, even when I was intensely focused on my research.

As I'd told myself repeatedly, and explained to her more than once, I'm too old to start a new family. Trying to do so with her wouldn't be fair to her, even if she couldn't see that right now. It would rob her of the normal family life that I know she wanted, the kind of relationship she witnessed between her mother and father, one of loving and tender care for each other—one similar to that of my own parents from the beginning of their marriage until their deaths more than half a century later. It was clear that Gina envisioned herself in a similarly warm and loving marriage, that she expected her husband to hurry home to her at the end of the workday in the same way that her father had hurried home to her mother. And Gina, being such a strong-willed person, would settle for nothing less than that.

Yet it was just that that I couldn't give her, at least not for long, for the simple reason that, being 30 years older, I'd die 30 years sooner. That realization simplified things for me. If I couldn't give her what she wanted, and what she deserved to have, the only options were non-sexual friendship or nothing. There were no other options. I'd long understood that a short-term sexual relationship, such as I was enjoying with Maja, wouldn't be possible with Gina for reasons already noted. I wouldn't even think of interfering with her determination to convey her virginity to her future husband.

Would I want marriage with Gina if it were possible, if I were ten or twenty years younger? Absolutely. Her beauty, liveliness, and intelligence, and her active approach to building a life for herself—all were immensely appealing. Having Gina in my bed night after night for the rest of my life, helping her as a junior partner in building her business, working on my own intellectual projects, and, without doubt, raising a new family of little Ginas and Jubals—I couldn't imagine a better way to spend the rest of my life.

One thing that impressed me no end about her was that she had an internal theater in her brain, in which ideas generated in one part of it could be shared with others. Most women I'd known didn't. Diana, for instance, without such an internal sharing mechanism, had to say a thought out loud to get it from one part of her brain to others. "Change lanes," or "Turn left here," she'd say while driving, or "Add 1¼ cups flour," she'd say when baking. She couldn't just do it without saying it out loud first.

Gina, though, could act without announcing her actions in advance. She would think through what she wanted to say to others before saying it. Her thought processes, though, registered on her face as her brain went through its gyrations, giving subtle change to her mouth or eyes as her thoughts developed. It made her endlessly fascinating to observe.

Perhaps this internal theater, which I believed I also had, was an essential piece of mental equipment for appreciating literature, perhaps also history, philosophy, art, art music also known as classical music—for any aspect of a life of the mind.

I'd also seen her speaking more spontaneously with friends her own age than she spoke to me in our conversations. That was a revelation. So active, bubbling over, speaking so quickly, without thinking, but still with intelligence and feeling behind her words. And her laughter when speaking with friends was something to hear. A memory to treasure.

It would be like that too, for both of us, if circumstances were a bit different. But they are what they are. If we could both recognize the impossibility of marriage, tension could lessen. We could interact normally, interlaced with occasional flirting without danger because we'd both know in advance that it couldn't go anywhere.

But neither of us could accept that it wouldn't/couldn't go anywhere. That was clearer to me than to her, though. Even though intellectually she understood the situation, the fact that I met her criteria for a suitor in so many ways continually pushed her to regard me as just that, a suitor. And when I flirted with her, she took the words at face value. I was giving her hopes that couldn't be fulfilled.

There were other differences between us, too, that led me to consider whether Gina was in fact someone I would want to link up my life with. She's religious, and I know that's a big part of her. I'm not, yet I'm curious about that part of her, and about what C. S. Lewis had written about Christianity.

Then there's her brilliance. She's smarter than I am, and it's only because I have decades of experience in many situations that I'm able to keep up with her. She's smart to seek suitors who are at least 15 years older than herself. But since men die on average seven years before women, she's setting herself up for 22 years of widowhood. That's the situation her mother is in now. Only 48 years old, and yet a widow already for ten years. Since Gina, the oldest child, was 16 when her father died, her mother probably married at 18 or so. Her father might have been in his early 30s.

Then there were Gina's rigidities. She had certain unusual

categories and concepts in her mind—courtship, suitor, and so on. Stepping up to play that game would be like stepping back in time half a century or more. It might be fun, but it also could be unnerving; it's been decades since I've had to present myself to a woman to be judged and possibly rejected. There was also the rigidity in her concept of the ideal husband and father for her children and their family life. All good things, but could any man live up to them?

That brought up the question of children. I'd loved being a father and raising a family. I suspect that she'd find me more than adequate there. But I'm not now the youngish man I was then. Did I still have the energy to raise children? Their needs can't be denied. Meeting them can be so exhausting.

I remembered something my marketing professor had told his class. As a new professor 25 years earlier, he'd thoroughly enjoyed being the faculty advisor for the student Marketing Club, in which capacity he'd hosted meetings at his home every month. As his career neared its end he again volunteered to serve as advisor. After the first meeting of the Club, which he again hosted at his house, he resigned, shocking everybody, including himself. He explained to us that circumstances weren't the same now as they had been nearly three decades earlier. Perhaps it was him; perhaps he valued his time and privacy now too much to have his living room and backyard filled with chattering students. Or perhaps students were different today. In either case, it was not a good fit, and he'd resigned. Would I find the same thing if I started a new family—that as much as I'd loved being a father the first time around, would I find it the same fulfilling experience now? I didn't know.

Then there was the time and independence thing. Gina would, rightfully, want much of my time and energy. But I liked being disconnected right now, free to engage in my Huxley-Kennedy-Lewis project, or rather my Kennedy-September 11 research.

And there was the fact that we were in different phases of our lives. It wasn't just the matter of age, but of experience. She was 26 years old and a virgin who, as she'd said, had never been kissed. She had so much to learn that could only be learned by experience. Did I have the patience to go through all that? And, I wondered, is there a critical period in which first close physical relationships most easily develop, like there is a critical period for language-learning? If so, has that period ended by the time a woman is 26 years old? Would she be able to move from a life of abstinence and preservation of chastity to a life of nightly love making? And, conversely, would she, at 26 want to make love more times each night that I, at 56, was capable of? There were so many factors to consider.

And what's with her sexually provocative stories? Do they result from the frustration that any normal hot-blooded woman without a legitimate way of engaging in physical closeness with a man would feel while waiting for her husband to come along? Or are they a cover for frigidity?

And is the INS closing in on her? She'd recently let slip that she'd entered the United States on a student visa but was no longer a student. She was "out of status," as they say. The simplest way for her to adjust status would be to marry an American citizen. Perhaps the fear of deportation led to the aggressiveness with which she's used the sex talk to try to provoke her suitors into proposing.

What did I really want?

68

Having adopted C. Wright Mills's phrase "Power Elite" to refer to the entities capable of authorizing such extraordinary events as the assassination of President Kennedy and September 11, I now wanted to understand just who had carried them out on its behalf. I found the answers I was looking for in L. Fletcher Prouty's book *The Secret Team: The CIA and Its Allies in Control of the United States and the World*.

Before retiring from the Air Force, Colonel Prouty had run "the global system designed to provide military support for the clandestine activities of the CIA from 1955 to 1964."[290] Drawing on this high-level first-hand experience, he identified what he called the Secret Team as those parts of the CIA and its allies who design and carry out clandestine special projects on behalf of the Power Elite. In doing so he cast light on the question of "Who, in fact, is in control of the United States and the world?"[291]

The Secret Team, Prouty stated, "is the functional element of the dominant power;" that is, of the Power Elite. "It is the point of the spear and is neither military nor police. It is covert: and the best (or worst) of both. It gets the job done where it has political authorization and direction, or not. In this capacity, it acts independently. It is lawless. It operates everywhere with the best of all supporting facilities from special weaponry and advanced communications, with the assurance that its members will never be prosecuted. It is subservient to the Power Elite and protected by them."[292]

The Secret Team is led by top executives of the CIA, the National Security Council and the National Security Advisor to the president. Its effectiveness comes from the large number of officials placed in other organizations, sometimes without those organizations knowing that their employees' primary loyalty is to the CIA. "It is often quite difficult to tell exactly who many of these men really are, because some may wear a uniform and the rank of general [yet] really be with the CIA, [while] others may be inconspicuous as the executive assistant to some Cabinet officer's chief deputy."[293]

The CIA had even "infiltrated the Department of Defense, just like it had the Departments of State, Treasury, [and] Commerce," Prouty revealed. Although without question those serving in the DoD "all were military men, they all also had assignments of various types that made them effective CIA operators. By the very nature of their work, they worked with, for, and in support of the CIA. It was their first allegiance."[294]

Out beyond this ring, Prouty continued, "is an extensive and intricate network of government officials with responsibility for, or expertise in, some specific field that touches on national security or foreign affairs."[295] "The power of the Team derives from its vast intragovernmental undercover infrastructure and its direct relationship with great private industries, mutual funds and investment houses, universities, and the news media, including foreign and domestic publishing houses."[296] "All true members of the Team remain in the power center whether in office with the incumbent administration or out of office. . . . They simply rotate to and from official jobs and the business world or the pleasant haven of academe."[297]

When the Secret Team is tasked with a specific project, assassinating the president of the United States, for instance, it assembles a team whose members have the skills needed for that particular job from among those already on its payroll, either overtly or covertly. These teams are "a bewildering collection of semi-permanent or temporarily assembled action committees and networks that respond pretty much *ad hoc* to specific troubles and to flash-intelligence data inputs from various parts of the world."[298] At no time, Prouty stated, "did the powerful and deft hand of the Secret Team evidence more catalytic influence than in the events of those final ninety days of 1963."[299]

Although the CIA's original assignment had been to serve as a clearing house for intelligence gained by the U.S. government, its mission was formally changed in March 1954. NSC Directive #5412 "for the first time in the history of the United States defined covert operations and assigned that role to the Central Intelligence Agency. . . . At the same time, the Armed Forces were directed to 'provide the military support of the clandestine operations of the CIA' as an official function."

I noticed that this change was made one year after the CIA had orchestrated the overthrow of the democratically elected leader of Iran. Perhaps, I speculated, the "success" of that possibly unauthorized covert operation demonstrated the usefulness of having an organization authorized to undertake similar operations in the future; hence, NSC Directive #5412.

Several of Prouty's revelations about Secret Team operations immediately caught my eye. One was his admission that the CIA's most important "cover story" is that it is an "Intelligence" agency. "Of course the CIA does make use of 'intelligence' and 'intelligence gathering,'" he explained, "but that is largely a front for its primary interest, 'Fun and Games.' The CIA is the center of a vast mechanism that specializes in Covert

Operations." He went on to describe the CIA as "the willing tool" of the Power Elite, as well as a member of it.[300]

Another startling revelation was Prouty's admission that the Cold War itself was a Secret Team operation. "The power structure that kept the Cold War at that level of intensity has been driven by the Secret Team and its multinational covert operations, to wit: This is the fundamental game of the Secret Team."[301] This revelation dovetailed with the Dulles brothers' role in the creation and maintenance of the Cold War I'd already noted.

One tactic used to keep the Cold War at a high level of intensity—"the fundamental game of the Secret Team"—involved manipulating "parts of the U.S. government, usually the Defense Department," by convincing it that the Communist enemy "is about to strike or has begun a subversive insurgency campaign in a third country."[302] It did this by "launching a very minor and very secret provocative attack of a kind that is bound to bring open reprisal. These secret attacks . . . will undoubtedly create [a] reaction which in turn is observed in the United States. . . . The next step is to declare the enemy's act one of 'aggression' or 'subversive insurgency.'" The CIA would then bring the situation to the NSC and on up the chain of command, "as high and as mighty as the situation and authorities will allow."[303]

Contributing to the success of this strategy was the CIA's infiltration of the Department of Defense. "What most people in Defense were totally unaware of was that in the very office that was supposed to serve the military departments and shield them from promiscuous requests, there were concealed and harbored some of the most effective agents the CIA has ever had. Their approval of CIA requests was assured. The amazing fact was that their cover was so good that they could then turn right around and write orders directing the service concerned to comply with the request."[304]

Another factor was the practice of briefing the president piecemeal, informing him of isolated facts in separate briefings without presenting the whole picture to him at once. Without that context he couldn't interpret correctly the significance of the separate pieces of information presented to him. "Technically, he'd been informed of many of the key parts of a plan, but never the plan itself,"[305] Prouty explained about briefings given to Eisenhower.

The most astonishing example of the Secret Team in action I learned of was the steps it took to derail President Eisenhower's most important foreign policy initiative because its success would have harmed Special Team and Power Elite interests. After Stalin's death in 1953, Eisenhower launched a Crusade for Peace with the aim of reducing tensions with the Soviet Union. That effort was to be capped by a summit conference between Eisenhower and Soviet Premier Nikita Khrushchev in May 1960, less than a year before the end of Eisenhower's second term.

Khrushchev also sought to make the event a success. He'd pledged not to renew nuclear testing unless the United States did and announced the demobilization of 1.2 million men from the Soviet armed forces. The stars appeared aligned for the two leaders to transform international politics and perhaps end the Cold War.

"Everything was in readiness," as the day approached. "It was hard to discover anyone in government not vitally concerned with preparations for this most magnificent meeting," Prouty observed. "This was to be the crowning achievement of a long life devoted to outstanding public service. Seven years of work [had been] dedicated to this goal,"[306] and the moment and goal was nearly in hand. "The aging men who had led the world through World War II and then through the bitterness of the Cold War were preparing to culminate their long efforts in a great summit conference and then . . . [pass] the mantle of government to a new generation who would reap the benefits of peace—hopefully true and lasting peace."[307]

Yet it was not to be. On May 1, an American U-2 spy plane, piloted by Francis Gary Powers, crash-landed at Sverdlovsk, nearly a thousand miles deep into Soviet territory. The Administrator of the National Aeronautics and Space Administration (NASA) announced that one of its civilian high altitude weather research aircraft had inadvertently strayed over Russian territory. When Khrushchev produced the wreckage of the spy plane and the pilot, alive, who had been captured with several military identification cards on him, the NASA cover story was shown to be a lie.

Khrushchev stated that "'I am prepared to grant that the president had no knowledge of a plane being dispatched to the Soviet Union and failing to return." "He stopped short," Prouty explained, "of accusing Eisenhower of knowing that the flight had been ordered over the Soviet Union." The Russian premier had in effect said, Prouty explained, "'We are so close to the summit and to peace. I am ready to accept that this was a cruel and terrible provocation made by others without the knowledge of the American president.'" Let the president stand up and say that he had no knowledge of this flight, and then back up his statement by firing "the men who had organized the flight, and the Summit could go forward."[308]

It is entirely possible, Prouty concluded, "in fact it is most probably the whole truth, that Eisenhower did not know that the U-2 had been dispatched on that fateful flight." "In preparation for the summit and its theme of worldwide peace and harmony, the White House had directed all aerial surveillance activity . . . of Communist territory to cease until further notice and had ordered that no U.S. military personnel were to become involved in any combat activities, covert or otherwise, during that period."[309] "Every top official in the government knew how important the summit conference was to the president," Prouty explained. "And only high-level officials—or knowledgeable ST members—could have launched that flight. All of the regular launch authorities certainly knew they were under strictest orders to do nothing that would jeopardize the success of the conference."[310]

"This was not the normal U-2 flight," Prouty continued, and documented half a dozen significant ways that the flight violated normal procedures in addition to the president's express command that no such flights take place. He showed that the problem that developed with the plane's engine was not a normal flame-out, and concluded that the plane had been deliberately engineered to crash deep in Soviet territory by the CIA—Deputy Director of Plans Richard Bissell was in charge of the U-2 program—to skuttle the summit, thereby blocking Eisenhower's effort to ease tensions with the Soviets, a development counter to the interests of the Power Elite and the Secret Team.

"The president had to choose. He could either discredit Allen Dulles and the CIA for operating that clandestine flight . . . without his knowledge," thereby admitting that he was not in control of his own government, but enabling the summit to go forward, "or he could . . . take the blame himself on the basis that he knew of and had ordered the flights and was in complete control of everything done in the foreign arena by his government,"[311] thereby dooming the summit.

When "Eisenhower accepted the blame, Khrushchev concluded that Eisenhower had deliberately wrecked what had been planned as the 'ultimate summit conference' in Paris. This incident served to reverse the trend toward détente that had been carefully orchestrated by"[312] the two of them. Eisenhower "had come within two weeks of achieving not only the goal of an aging president who had given his entire adult life to his country; but of realizing the hope of the entire country for a lasting and hopeful peace."[313]

Had Eisenhower at that key moment reigned in the CIA, John F. Kennedy would never have been assassinated. Of course, the whole history of the world would have been different, with Kennedy possibly not even nominated or elected. He was nominated and elected, though, and was therefore in a position for the CIA to deceive him in the lead up to the Bay of Pigs invasion, just as it had deceived Eisenhower.

But, Prouty asked, "Did Eisenhower really have a choice? Could he just fire Allen Dulles and a few of his top lieutenants and clean house that simply? He knew that he could not. Those other men who had seen to it that all the little things fell into place and that the U-2 had gone aloft on that precise day were men of the ST, and wiping out Dulles and his staff would not touch them."[314] Removing the CIA's leadership would not be more than a pinprick on the hide of the much larger Power Elite. It would have changed nothing. Perhaps Eisenhower had in mind Woodrow Wilson's cautionary words I'd noted earlier: "There's a power so organized, so subtle, so watchful, so pervasive, so interlocked, that you'd better not speak above your breath when you mention it, in condemnation of it."

And so, "The president may have realized that he was not really in charge of events," and so "did the only thing he could. He announced to the world that he had known about the flight and that it had been his sole responsibility as Commander in Chief of the United States."[315] "With that, Khrushchev had no choice but to face the same facts, his way. How could he hope to reach a peaceful settlement and meaningful agreements with a president who was admitting to the world that at the very time he had been speaking peace he had been plotting overflights and the invasion of the territorial integrity of . . . the Soviet Union. . . . Khrushchev had no alternative either. All hope for a successful summit conference had gone."[316]

Eisenhower was sobered by the range and power of the Secret Team and its willingness to use its power to protect itself first and foremost, whatever the cost to the United States or to him as president. Cold War tensions had to remain high to justify high levels of funding for the CIA, the other intelligence agencies, the military and the large commercial firms that benefited from their activities. Any movement by the president or anyone else toward a lessening of that tension had to be blocked by whatever means were necessary.

69

I'd learned from C. Wright Mills and L. Fletcher Prouty that a new class of powerful individuals and institutions had arisen: not just new powerful players, but a new class of such players. I'd learned that through the creation of the CIA and the security and intelligence agencies this new class was able to influence policies continuously, not just from time to time as powerful elites had earlier. And I'd learned that when the interests of powerful players within the Power Elite aligned, it was able, through its use of the Secret Team, to carry out such extraordinary actions as the scuttling of Eisenhower's Crusade for Peace summit with Khrushchev, the assassination of President Kennedy and the events of September 11.

I now wanted to revisit the presidency of JFK with this new information in mind.

Upon becoming president, John F. Kennedy may have recognized the scope of the Power Elite's power, but I suspect he didn't yet fully appreciate just how powerful and dangerous the Secret Team was. Its clandestine activities to overthrow governments around the world were, by their very nature, secret. Even if Kennedy knew of its activities in other countries, and as a senator he probably did, it's less likely he'd have understood that the Power Elite would purposefully sabotage even the president's most important policies if it believed its interests were threatened by them. Eisenhower had learned the hard way just how determined the hard men of the Power Elite were to protect their interests. It was that sobering lesson, I think, more than any other development that led him to issue his warning about the Military-Industrial Complex in the final days of his presidency. His awakening had come too late for him to do anything more than convey a warning in his speech to those who would listen.

I was surprised to learn that the CIA, perhaps pleased at how effectively its U-2 stunt had destroyed President Eisenhower's summit with Khrushchev, apparently tried the same stunt with President Kennedy. At the height of the Cuban Missile Crisis in October 1962—two and a half years after the Gary Powers U-2 flight—it sent up a U-2 spy plane whose pilot supposedly "had become disoriented and inadvertently flown his plane into Soviet airspace."[317] Jeffrey D. Sachs, who told this story and who was less suspicious of what lay behind that flight than I now am, nevertheless recognized how catastrophic the results could have been: "Soviet fighter jets scrambled to intercept the U-2, while due to the high alert status prompted by the crisis, the U.S. planes sent to escort it back to base were armed with nuclear warheads and had the authority to fire. By dumb luck the world survived."

But it wasn't dumb luck. Kennedy, unlike Eisenhower, wrote to Khrushchev to say that he regretted the incident and would take every step to see that such flights wouldn't happen again. As a result of Kennedy's deft handling of the Cuban Missile Crisis—in the face of fierce opposition from his own military leadership—he won the respect of Nikita Khrushchev, who later stated that "he held 'deep respect' for Kennedy. 'He didn't allow himself to become frightened, nor did he become reckless. . . . He showed real wisdom and statesmanship when he turned his back on right-wing forces in the United States who were trying to goad him into taking military action against Cuba.'"[318]

Khrushchev followed up that praise of Kennedy's statesmanship with praise of his June 1963 Peace speech. "The entire speech was published and broadcast in the Soviet press. Khrushchev . . . told Averill Harriman that it was 'the greatest speech by an American president since Roosevelt.'"[319]

Kennedy's comment about that U-2 flight, "There's always some son-of-a-bitch who doesn't get the word," showed that he hadn't considered the possibility that the pilot had, under orders, deliberately flown into Soviet airspace at that very tense moment in order to spark a war between the two countries. Not considering that possibility, he probably hadn't considered the possibility that Gary Powers U-2 flight had also been a deliberate act undertaken to sabotage the Eisenhower-Khrushchev summit. Kennedy, who lived in more naïve pre-Kennedy assassination times, hadn't yet plumbed the depths of Secret Team duplicity.

Another surprise concerned the Bay of Pigs invasion of Cuba. My understanding had been that Allen Dulles had told Kennedy that the invasion by Cuban forces would succeed even without cover by the U.S. Air Force even though he believed that such cover would be necessary. It is "clear that the CIA's Bay of Pigs expedition was not simply doomed to fail, it was *meant* to fail," David Talbot concluded. "Its failure was designed to trigger the real action—an all-out, U.S. military invasion of the island."[320]

Kennedy had repeatedly told Dulles that under no circumstances would he authorize the use of U.S. forces, yet Dulles was confident that if or when the invasion began to falter, Kennedy would "cave in to pressure from the Washington war machine, just as other presidents had bent to the spymaster's will."

As duplicitous and manipulative as all that was, what actually happened was even more so. My new understanding is that "the final tactical plan for the invasion that was approved by President Kennedy . . . could well have succeeded"[321] if it had been followed. The plan failed because it wasn't followed; it "was sabotaged from inside," by Kennedy's special assistant for national security affairs, McGeorge Bundy, who intervened to block the second essential wave of air strikes by the American-supported Cuban brigade. In Prouty's judgment, "McGeorge Bundy's telephone call to General Cabell that cancelled the president's air strike order was the primary reason for the failure on the beach and the surrender of the Cuban Exile Brigade."[322]

This was shocking new information. When it appeared possible that the plan could succeed in spite of having been "meant to fail," the Secret Team stepped it to ensure that it did indeed fail, thereby, it thought, trapping Kennedy into authorizing cover by the U.S. Air Force, which would have set the stage for a full-scale invasion of Cuba by the U.S. military. I suspect that Kennedy did not know about Bundy's phone call cancelling the second wave of air strikes; it's hard to believe that if he had he'd have kept Bundy on his staff after he had fired Dulles and two other CIA officials.

After revealing that information, Prouty cited similarities between "that sabotaged plan, which damaged Kennedy so drastically," and "the sabotaged flight of Gary Powers's U-2 spy plane over the Soviet Union on May 1, 1960, which destroyed Eisenhower's Crusade for Peace." Neither defeat, Prouty stated, "had been the result of a normal or expected turn of events." And, he noted, "Some of the same men, in high places, were in key positions in both projects."[323] He might also have mentioned the third attempt at sabotage that I noted earlier, the one that didn't succeed: the U-2 flight that entered Soviet air space at the height of the Cuban Missile Crisis.

The Bay of Pigs episode "seared" Kennedy," Supreme Court Justice William O. Douglas recalled. "He had experienced the extreme power that these groups had, these various insidious influences of the CIA and the Pentagon on civilian policy, and I think it raised in his own mind the specter: Can Jack Kennedy, President of the United States, ever be strong enough to really rule these two powerful agencies? I think it had a profound effect. . . . It shook him up!"[324]

"Certainly we did not control the Joint Chiefs of Staff," Arthur Schlesinger, Special Assistant to President Kennedy later recalled.[325] "The National Security State's 'secret government,' which had controlled foreign policy in the previous two administrations of Truman and Eisenhower, 'was not prepared to cede power to the new Kennedy government. This was soon made clear to the president's team by the top military commanders.' . . . Even Defense Secretary Robert McNamara was struggling to control the generals under his command."[326] Over at the CIA, Allen Dulles explicitly said he would not follow Kennedy's lead. Recalling his brother John Foster Dulles's policies as Secretary of State under Eisenhower, he stated, "That's a much better policy. I've chosen to follow that one."[327]

Kennedy had learned early in his presidency the same hard lesson Eisenhower had learned near the end of his. Unlike his predecessor, though, he had time to take action to restore presidential control over the wayward military and CIA leadership. He knew that the stakes were high, stating in a speech before Congress on May 25, 1961, less than two months after the Bay of Pigs fiasco, "Before my term has ended, we shall have to test anew whether a nation organized and governed such as ours can endure. The outcome is by no means certain."[328]

70

The outcome was by no means certain, I repeated to myself as I continued my research the next morning.

In June 1961, only two months after the Bay of Pigs fiasco,

Kennedy took a major step toward reigning in those powerful yet wayward parts of the U.S. government that nominally reported to him by issuing two National Security Action Memoranda, NSAM 55 and NSAM 57, designed to straighten out the lines of authority and to clarify which projects would be carried out by the CIA and which by the military.

NSAM 55 "was a brief memorandum of greatest significance," Prouty explained, because it ended nearly all military support for CIA covert operations. "That memo meant there would be no more clandestine military operations in peacetime and that such things as . . . the Bay of Pigs were a thing of the past."[329] NSAM 57 "recognized that there might be requirements for clandestine activity from time to time," and said that "any small and truly covert type of operation 'may be assigned' to the CIA and that any which were larger would be the subject of special study and planning and then 'may be assigned' to the military, that part of the military which would be sufficient only to carry out that one operation on a one time basis. It directed that large covert operations would not be assigned to the CIA."[330]

This distinction between which activities would be assigned to the CIA and which to the military would be of the greatest importance as U.S. military involvement in Vietnam escalated after Kennedy's death. I'd always thought that the Vietnam War had been a military operation, a war. (The Vietnamese, I knew, called it the American war, to distinguish it from the earlier war with the French and later wars with Cambodia and China.)

U.S. involvement in Vietnam, I now learned, had begun as a clandestine CIA counter-insurgency operation. The CIA itself provided whatever paramilitary support was needed, and directed the activities of U.S. military personnel who served as civilian advisors in Vietnam. "It was the CIA that created and directed the tens of thousands of paramilitary forces of all kinds in South Vietnam during those difficult years of the Diem regime,"[331] Prouty explained. That never changed. "From start to finish the U.S. military in Vietnam operated under the direction of civilians. . . . [They] were under the control of the U.S.

ambassador to South Vietnam to whom the CIA station chief in Vietnam also reported."[332]

By 1963 Kennedy sensed that the American counterinsurgency operations were out of control. Sixteen thousand American military were there, in the role of advisors under the direction of the CIA, a situation that clearly violated his orders in NSAM 57 that CIA activities be limited to "small and truly covert operations," and those in NSAM 55 that U.S. military forces report to the Joint Chiefs, not the CIA. However, even a decade later, after the number of U.S. military personnel in Vietnam had grown to 550,000, they remained under the direction of the U.S. ambassador and the CIA station chief.[333]

"If anyone ever wanted an example of how the Secret Team can turn things around, this is one of the best," Prouty stated. "In June 1961 the president stated one thing categorically; by 1962 the Army's spokesman (actually in Army uniform, but a CIA/Secret Team spokesman) had totally turned this around. . . . The Secret Team retained control of most of the Vietnam war from its earliest birth pangs to the peak of escalation. Even to this day [Prouty was writing in 1972] the combat phase of the Vietnamese war . . . is totally under the direction and control of the CIA."[334]

In October 1963, a "growing feud" between Ambassador Henry Cabot Lodge and Saigon CIA station Chief John Richardson about how the "war" should be conducted erupted into public view. "Richard Starnes, a Saigon correspondent for the Scripps-Howard Newspapers, filed a remarkable report on the rift, quoting 'a high U.S. official here' who charged the CIA with insubordination. The official called the agency a 'malignancy' and said he 'was not sure even the White House could control [it] any longer.' [Starner] then added this eyebrow-raising observation: 'If the United States ever experiences a [coup attempt] it will come from the CIA and not the Pentagon. . . . [The Agency] represents a tremendous power and total unaccountability to anyone.'"[335]

Starnes's report received widespread notice after it was quoted by *New York Times'* columnist Arthur Krock on October

3. In the same column Krock commented, "This is disorderly government. And the longer the president tolerates it, the greater it will grow.'"[336]

The problem, Prouty explained, was that even though the CIA's counter-insurgency operations grew and grew, "there never was a time when the 'war' transitioned from the clandestine operations to the military operators." With no declaration of war from Congress, the ambassador "remained as a sort of minor commander in chief, one step down from the Commander-in-chief role of the president. And this has been done so that he could serve as a referee between the CIA and the military, the end result being that neither one of them has been really in complete control since 1964, when the first Marines arrived in Vietnam."[337]

The Army "never did take over full responsibility for what was called a 'war,'" Prouty saw, because "there never was a real honest to God military objective of this war. There never has been in Vietnam that objective, which when achieved by military force, would have spelled victory. There never has been that battle which, if won, would assure victory." I'd see later that the so-called War on Terror suffered from the same limitations.

The Vietnam War, as we call it, had little downside for the Power Elite and the Secret Team. Our longest war up to that time, it generated a steady stream of benefits for them—benefits paid for by the American people. The war, in Prouty's estimate, consumed more than $200 billion of the country's wealth by 1972 (more than $2 trillion in 2020 dollars). More than 58,000 young Americans lost their lives, and they and the hundreds of thousands more who suffered severe permanent disabilities came largely from families outside the milieu of the Power Elite and the Secret Team. In return for these extraordinary costs, in Prouty's opinion, the United States found itself "demoralized and precariously degraded in the eyes of much of the world, including our friends."[338]

Kennedy had issued NSAM 55 and NSAM 57 so that this very situation would not arise. Yet it did. To understand why, I had to return to the very beginning of the Kennedy administration.

Born in 1917, and replacing the older generation of Roosevelt, Truman and Eisenhower—all born in the years from 1882 to 1890—Kennedy had announced in his inaugural speech that "the torch has been passed to a new generation of Americans born in this century." Replacing the aging leaders who had led the country through the difficult years of the Depression, the Second World War and the onset of the Cold War, he had new priorities matched to the new world coming into its own after the end of the Second World War. He sought to develop a constructive relationship with the former colonial countries wanting to address their own concerns free from the constraints of the Cold War. He wanted to restore the pre-eminence of the civilian government over the military and the intelligence agencies. He resisted their bizarre schemes to invade Cuba and launch first-strike nuclear attacks on the Soviet Union. He introduced the concept of peaceful coexistence and called for the protection of civil liberties for all Americans.

His principal error, I now saw, had occurred in the appointments he'd made to key positions at the time his presidency began. He had erred in retaining Allen Dulles as head of the CIA and General Lyman Lemnitzer as head of the Joint Chiefs of Staff. He had erred in appointing General Curtis LeMay to the position of Chief of Staff of the United States Air Force, given his responsibility for the massive firebombing of many Japanese cities, which had resulted in the deaths of more than 500,000 civilians. These men approached world affairs very differently than Kennedy intended to. They should not have been appointed.

Kennedy had had several opportunities to correct his staffing mistakes but hadn't done so. When at a National Security Council meeting in July, 1961 Dulles and Lemnitzer, on behalf of all the Joint Chiefs, urged Kennedy to authorize a surprise nuclear attack on the Soviet Union, he would have been justified in immediately relieving all of them from active duty on the grounds that they were morally unfit for command. Instead, he merely walked out of the meeting. He had another opportunity in 1962 when the Joint Chiefs presented him with Operation

Northwoods, which called for attacks on American cities and American citizens that would be blamed on Castro and used as pretexts for an invasion of Cuba. Again, he didn't act. After the Cuban Missile crisis, when General LeMay called the blockade tactic "almost as bad as the appeasement at Munich"[339] and had denounced the agreements that ended the crisis as "the greatest defeat in our history,"[340] Kennedy had the opportunity to remove him for insubordination, but didn't.

When Kennedy had acted, in late 1961 by firing Allen Dulles and two other top CIA officials who had sandbagged him during the Bay of Pigs invasion, and in 1962 by removing General Lemnitzer from head of the Joint Chiefs of Staff and sending him off to Europe to become Supreme Commander of NATO, it was too little too late.

"When you change a policy, you must change the men, too"—change more than just the men at the very top, was the advice that General George Marshall once gave a colleague, who repeated it to one of Kennedy's senior advisors well into his presidency. "[The] CIA has the same men—on the desk and in the field—who were responsible for the disasters of the past and naturally they do things to prove they were right. Every big thing the CIA has tried in the Far East has been catastrophic, and the men responsible for these catastrophes are still there.' Kennedy's purge of the CIA, Harriman made clear, had not been sweeping enough."[341]

In removing only four individuals, Kennedy had left the overall structure in place. Even relieving from command every member of the Joint Chiefs would not have been sufficient. In seeking to veer away from the Cold War mindset that would have extended tensions and barely suppressed hostilities between the United States and the Soviet Union indefinitely, Kennedy would have had to change all key personnel. But because those with the Cold War mindset filled the ranks of government and non-government institutions, he would have needed to replace so many individuals that his government would have been crippled.

"It's not just that the CIA and the DoD are involved," Prouty observed. "It is also the FBI, the AEC, the DIA, elements of State and of the Executive Office Building, NSA and the hidden pulse of secret power coursing through almost every area of the body politic. It extends beyond into governmental business, the academic world, and certain very influential sectors of the press, radio, TV, papers, magazines, and the publishing business. Before any president can rule this covert automatic control system, he must find out it is there—he must be aware of the fact it exists—and he must devise some means to discover its concealed activity."[342]

By trying to introduce such radically new policies as peaceful coexistence with the Soviets, the Nuclear Test Ban Treaty and the withdrawal of all U.S. military and intelligence personnel from Vietnam, without also making deep changes in personnel, Kennedy enabled the Power Elite and Secret Team to strike back. "These groups," Prouty saw, "realized that Kennedy was gaining real knowledge, experience, and political power and that he had to be removed from office before winning the inevitable mandate from the U.S. public, which was certain to be his in 1964."[343]

Even "in the first decade of the American Empire," at the time the U-2 shootdown had doomed Eisenhower's summit with Khrushchev, Andrew G. Marshall observed, the power of the Power Elite and the Secret Team was already "so vast that it threatened to take over the government and subvert democracy itself."[344]

I now realized just how consistent Power Elite influence on American presidents had been from the 1950s to the present. When President Eisenhower sought to lessen Cold War tensions through a Summit with Khrushchev, the Power Elite, through the clandestine activities of the Secret Team, sabotaged him. When President Kennedy sought to lessen Cold War tensions and move to a state of peaceful coexistence, it killed him. When President Nixon sought to lesson Cold War tensions through rapprochements with the Soviet Union and China, the Secret Team destroyed his presidency by orchestrating the Watergate break-in and subsequent cover-up. By some accounts that seem to have a degree of veracity, the Secret Team attempted to promote former head of the CIA, Vice President George Bush, to the presidency in 1981 through the assassination attempt on President Ronald Reagan, who had pledged to end the Cold War by winning it. Currently, President Trump, having declared his intention to lessen tensions with Russia, finds himself portrayed as a Russian agent.

The United States is not the country I had long thought it was.

71

The other matter on my mind at the moment, apart from Gina, was what to do about Brian's statement—his notarized testimony detailing his involvement in the events of September 11 and whatever else he knew or suspected about that day. In the event of his death, do I release it, thereby possibly triggering an avalanche of harm on my country, or keep it under lock and key?

Since Brian had hopped over the back fence, I'd been working on a list of the benefits for the United States of releasing the document on one side of a page, and on the other the harm that the country would suffer if the Bush administration's active role in orchestrating the events of September 11 became widely known.

On the "release" side, I saw that widespread awareness of what really happened could lead to the perpetrators being held responsible for their crimes. It could lead to Americans cleaning out of the government the moles whole primary loyalty was to the Power Elite rather than to the governmental departments they worked for and to the Constitution that underlay the government's operations.

It could lead to ending the War in Afghanistan, after a cost exceeding $2 trillion, and of the War in Iraq and all other overseas activities undertaken on the basis of the lies told about the attacks on September 11.

It could lead to a large reduction in outlays for the military and the intelligence agencies, now officially at nearly a trillion dollars a year but by some accounts actually far higher.

It could lead to cancelling or substantially revising

legislation passed by a confused and unnerved Congress since September 11 that undermined traditional American liberties and privacy. Perhaps the Department of Homeland Security could be abolished.

Americans angry at having been deceived and betrayed by those they'd trusted could demand investigations into other questionable activities, perhaps even a real investigation into what happened on that day in Dallas and a rejection of the absurd Magic Bullet theory.

Exposing the truth about September 11 could be the single most effective way to restore Americans' confidence in the testimony of their own eyes. Gaining the confidence to state that photos and videos showed the towers being blown apart and turned into dust rather than merely collapsing into their own footprints could lead them to view other videos and images with fresh eyes. None would be more important than recognizing the alterations to the Zapruder film and the fraudulent nature of the JFK autopsy photos.

Recognizing the reality of what happened on those two days, and having the confidence to say so publicly, would give a sense of release and relief to nearly everyone in the country. The schism in the American soul could then begin to heal.

On the other side of the page I noted the immediate harm to the country I still loved. The financial costs alone could reach into the trillions of dollars as the U.S. sought, for example, to reimburse the insurance companies who paid out for losses incurred on September 11. The financial impact of compensating those harmed by the U.S. invasions of Afghanistan and Iraq and elsewhere would be incalculable.

The hit to America's reputation would be deep. The damage might even extend to the American ideals of democracy, liberty and the rule of law. The dishonor could tarnish America's name for generations to come. Perhaps forever.

How would we deal with the hatred directed toward us by those living in the Middle East, particularly Muslims, for having been slandered and demonized for nearly 20 years?

The assassination of John F. Kennedy had generated

immense and deeply felt sympathy for the United States around the world. Revealing the truth about September 11 could result in sentiments as intensely heartfelt but in the opposite direction.

How could the United States ever expect forgiveness for crimes so numerous and so horrendous?

I could see that the government would never, ever, admit the truth of what had happened unless forced to. Having already killed 3,000 people on that day, it had demonstrated its willingness to do whatever was necessary to hide its crimes. It wouldn't—it hadn't—hesitated to kill again to keep its actions hidden. Brian's dead team, of which he was the sole survivor, is all the evidence that's needed. It was all so reminiscent of the hundreds of witnesses to various aspects of the Kennedy assassination who died from unnatural causes.

The harm and benefit to the United States seemed equally balanced. I didn't know whether it would be better to publicize Brian's statement or keep it hidden. Would it be better to put that event behind us, to sweep it under the rug, and instead work to improve the country as it stands now, as best we could? Or was a new start impossible until the truth of the past was widely known? I didn't know.

I began to see the need to distinguish between protecting the government and protecting the country. Perhaps harm to the government, to the criminals in the government, was necessary to protect the country. To identify who within the government had perpetrated September 11, to identify who in the White House and Pentagon and the security organizations had been knowingly involved, and to distinguish them from those who had been used unwittingly on that day and in the cover-up that followed, wouldn't be easy. It might not even be possible to determine who was who and what was what.

Could worldwide recognition of the reality of September 11 as a false flag attack increase the chances for world peace that John F. Kennedy had envisioned? Or, conversely, would it lead to violence spiraling out of control? How would the perpetrators respond if it looked like exposure of their deeds was imminent? There was no guarantee that the Power Elite and the Secret Team wouldn't bring out and use the big guns, thereby making their control over the U.S. government as obvious as the Communist Party's control over the government of the Soviet Union had been.

So again, the scales seemed evenly balanced, and I was relieved that I didn't have to make a decision now.

I realized that all presidents since Bush had considered similar factors, and I set out to determine briefly what additional factors each president might have taken into account, just as Russell and I had reviewed the thinking behind each president's decision to remain silent about what they knew lay behind Kennedy's assassination.

The factors I considered regarding September 11 overlapped with those already considered for the earlier assassination but had much more immediacy because that day was much more recent. Many of the orchestrators were still alive, as were many of those who suffered from the attacks and the wars launched in response to them.

The Republicans couldn't lift a finger against Bush without destroying their own party and probably their own careers, I saw. As the party that supported the military and security organizations, they wouldn't want those institutions harmed. The Democrats, as the party of big government, couldn't have been unhappy about the huge increases in governmental funding and power resulting from the legislation passed in the wake of September 11. Both parties, then, had incentives to remain quiet.

I wouldn't have expected George W. Bush to reveal his role in the events, nor his father, the elder George Bush (1924-2018), who was 77 on that day, and who after all had served as head of the CIA before becoming vice president and then president.

I turned first to the other former presidents still living on September 11, 2001. Gerald Ford (1913-2006), 88 on that day, would live another five years. As the "FBI's man" on the Warren Commission and as the president who brought Donald Rumsfeld and Dick Cheney into high positions in his administration, I wouldn't expect him to reveal what he may have known or deduced.

Jimmy Carter (1924-still living), was 76 on that day. The only statement I could find by him about September 11 had been the one issued on September 9, 2002, in which he'd noted the "strength and resilience of our nation in the face of the unconscionable acts of last September." He'd called for "the United States [to] lead the fight to secure human rights for all peoples," but hadn't attributed those "unconscionable acts" to any specific persons or organizations. Nor had he openly indicated any doubts about the official story.

Ronald Reagan (1911-2004), 90 on that day, lived another three years, but in 2001 he'd already suffered from Alzheimer's disease for eight years.

Bill Clinton (1946-still living), was 55 on that day. I haven't found any statement that Clinton made in response to the events of September 11 in the years just after they occurred. Coincidentally, though, just hours before the planes supposedly hit the towers, he raised the subject of bin Laden during a speech he gave in Australia, saying, "I nearly got him. And I could have killed him, but I would have had to destroy a little town called Kandahar in Afghanistan and kill 300 innocent women and children, and then I would have been no better than him. So, I didn't do it."[345] Given that Clinton was speaking to business leaders in Australia on a subject having nothing to do with bin Laden or terrorism in the Middle East, it might occur to those with suspicious minds might he had known in advance about the upcoming events and that bin Laden would be blamed for them. He may have been attempting to defend in advance charges that he could have, but failed to, remove bin Laden during his presidency.

Only two presidents had been elected after the second Bush presidency ended, Obama and Trump.

Barack Obama (1961-still living), was 40 on September 11 and 48 when he became president. If it's correct to say that Obama was a product of "the left wing of the U.S. intelligence community, . . . a world composed of the Ford Foundation and other foundations specializ[ing] in social engineering, social manipulation, social control, and political counterinsurgency against possible challenges to the system of oligarchical financier domination of national affairs,"[346] then it shouldn't be surprising that he took several steps as president that furthered the aims of the real orchestrators of the events of September 11.

One was that a high official in his administration actively sought to destroy the 9/11 Truth movement. One of the several reports I saw, one by David A. Hughes, cited Cass Sunstein, Obama's head of the Office of Information and Regulatory Affairs, as advocating "the use of anonymous government agents to engage in 'cognitive infiltration of extremist groups, designed to introduce informational diversity into such groups and to expose indefensible conspiracy theories as such.'"[347] 9/11 Truth was the primary target, Hughes reported. "Government agents (and their allies) might enter chat rooms, online social networks, or even real-space groups and attempt to undermine percolating conspiracy theories by raising doubts about their factual premises, casual logic, or implications for action, political or otherwise." "It is clear," Hughes concluded, "that there has been massive infiltration of the 9/11 Truth movement by agents seeking to subvert it. . . . The fracturing of the 9/11 Truth movement is not accidental but, rather, the result of deliberate attempts to undermine it."

There's also Obama's firing of White House aide Van Jones after he signed a petition asking for a reinvestigation of the 9/11 attacks that suggested that the Bush administration may have been involved in them.[348]

And, instead of reestablishing respect for civil liberties undermined by the Bush/Cheney administration, Obama and his administration, Paul Craig Roberts observed, "went further . . . and asserted the unconstitutional power not only to hold American citizens indefinitely in prison without bringing charges, but also to take their lives without convicting them in a court of law. Obama asserts that the U.S. Constitution notwithstanding, he has the authority to assassinate U.S. citizens, who he deems to be a 'threat,' without due process of law."[349]

Donald Trump (1946-still living), 55 on that day, was 70

when he became president. I've noted already the radio and TV interviews on September 11 in which he stated that in his expert opinion the towers had been brought down by explosives planted in them. He'd remained silent since then, apparently considering it best for his country to have that ugly episode buried. "Make America Great Again" apparently meant forgetting what he knew about September 11.

I'd mentioned to Gina months ago that as a teenager I'd begun to realize that every book I read separated me more and more from almost everybody else around me, who didn't read books. I was starting to feel that way again as I considered all that I had learned about the real nature of my country and its government over the last six months, things that few others were aware of. September 11 had become a touchstone, a dividing line. On one side were those few persons, including myself today, who had examined the evidence and reached conclusions based on it.

On the other side were the large majority of persons who shunned any examination of the events of September 11, who unthinkingly accepted the official story. I'd been among this group for nearly two decades; now, firmly on the other side of the line, I felt almost estranged from those who remained blind to the truth of what had really happened on the most important event in American history in living memory.

Once I'd examined the evidence for the JFK assassination and the events of September 11, there was no going back. I'd become convinced that the official stories were wrong, deliberately wrong. My world had irrevocably changed. I hadn't just changed my opinion on a subject of importance; I had become a different person, one with less in common with others still on the far side of the line. We lived in different worlds.

I now judged people by their beliefs about the events of that day in 2001. I judged their intellectual and moral qualities by whether they'd made an effort to examine the evidence or whether they turned their eyes away, unwilling for whatever reason to seek to know what the truth was.

I had begun to form my own opinions, to reach my own

conclusions, rather than accept the usual stories that I'd heard from others about many subjects, not just the JFK assassination and September 11. I'd began to distinguish between those subjects I'd examined and those that I hadn't. I was a Principal on the first, still blind on the others. I was even willing to examine and make up my own mind about the two bizarre ideas that Gina had mentioned to me—that human activity had little effect on the earth's climate and that Shakespeare hadn't written the works attributed to him. I realized that until now I had merely accepted the official explanations without ever examining them for myself. I'd need to find time to look through the book that Gina had given me, the one by Jim Warren. I wondered again, briefly, if the author was the same Jim Warren I'd known in high school.

And, I saw, others judged me, too. When I tried to point out facts that undermined the official stories of JFK and September 11, most people looked at me like I'd lost my mind. They'd accepted the usual beliefs that anyone who held such ideas was a "conspiracy theorist," a freak. They no longer recognized me as the person they'd known, just as the birds in the cage no longer recognized the one that had escaped for a few days and then been put back inside. Like that bird, I was now an outsider, someone who didn't belong.

I needed to think more about this sobering idea that I was now separated from nearly everyone around me by my willingness to seek to understand what had really happened on September 11 and their unwillingness to do so.

My thoughts on the assassination and September 11 were soon to be swept aside by a third extraordinary event in American society, only to return more fully developed by what that new event revealed to me.

☙ 72 ☙

Suddenly, seemingly out of nowhere, a new virus, Covid-19, was everywhere I looked, or at least media reports on it were.

How dangerous was it? Was it dangerous at all? No one seemed to know.

What was obvious was the weird language. Social distancing. Flatten the curve. Lockdowns. It was all so reminiscent of other unnatural, awkward, non-American phrasings such as Homeland Security, Significant Other, Native American and Differently Abled that had been forced on us.

Also obvious was the ubiquity of the propaganda campaign about the virus. It was everywhere. I'd never seen anything like it.

And what's with the face masks? People didn't wear masks during previous viral outbreaks, not even during the height of the Spanish Influenza outbreak in 1918-1919, the worst viral infection ever to hit the United States.

It all seemed too weird to take seriously, yet the propaganda was everywhere and could hardly be ignored.

73

I stopped by WORDS, WORDS, WORDS to pick up the latest financial docs. As soon as she saw me, Gina ran over to me, took my arm and led me into her office. The physical contact was unusual, showing just how upset she was. I guessed she was upset about the effect the Covid lockdowns were having and would have on her studio, which turned out to be correct.

"What am I going to do, Jubal? The government is forcing me to close my studio. This is a disaster. My mind is not in a very good condition at this point. I've been sick with worry about what will happen with the business, and about my future if it goes bankrupt.

"I came here with such high hopes. The moment I felt the plane was slowly going up, leaving and seeing The Philippines from above, was the most exhilarating experience I ever had. I know that for most people, flying is just a mundane thing, but for me, it was like touching a miracle. And that first flight was leading me to start a new life in America.

"To be honest, I never dreamed or wanted to live anywhere in the United States. Houses are meters away from each other, the residents are doing their own thing, and in winter the sky looks like a giant white plate with melted vanilla ice cream. The trees on the street look like skeletons with giant dry leaves stuck on the ground and people come out of their house looking dull with their three layers of wrinkly clothes.

"I imagined that my arriving in the United States would be like dropping an atomic bomb. People might think I am a crazy person because of how I dress and my demeanor. Or I might get arrested for giggling or being too annoying."

"But here you are," I said.

"Yes, here I am still, three years later, but I've missed home so much," she continued. "I have never been able to visit since I came here. Life is difficult there, but it's been always a place full of joy and love. I always get asked here when will I go home. At first, I didn't know how to answer that question, but later on I figured that I would be going home, at least for a visit, once I had finally chosen the best new surname.

"I only stayed here after graduating to earn money to help my family. To help my sisters. But now I can't even do that with my studio closed. And then there's my visa problem. I may have mentioned that because I entered the United States on a student visa, I was supposed to leave after graduating. So I'm now out of status and could be deported if anyone notices."

"Let's see how things develop, Gina. The health authorities might have second thoughts and end the closures. After all, there's never been a closure like this before, not even during pandemics far worse than this one."

Her lips were still pressed tightly together, so I knew she was still fraught with anxiety. Then I thought of something to say to lighten her mood.

"Hey, Gina!" I said brightly. "In what way is Covid like a smile?"

She shook her head and shrugged.

"You can share both and still have them!" We both laughed at that. It felt good to know that I was with someone who could appreciate a joke, even at a time when so many others were terrified and she was so stressed out.

She laughed again as she told me about one couple, fully masked, that she passed on a hiking trail near her apartment. "As

I approached them," she said, "they stood well off the trail until I had passed. It was ridiculous."

"I've even seen people wearing two masks, outdoors," I said. As I was speaking Gina got up and closed the door to her office. After she sat down again at her desk, she looked directly at me. I wondered what was up.

I've indicated that I'd asked myself several times what I really wanted from Gina, and that I was uncertain of the answer. She had been asking herself the same question because my intentions were unclear to her, too. She now wanted clarification.

"You've said several times that the age difference makes any relationship between us impossible," she began. "But then you come on with such sweet words that I'd expect to hear only from the most serious suitor. It's confusing. So I'm giving you the chance to tell me what you really want and let myself hear your heart speak. We have been talking for months now, so I am comfortable with you opening up to me. What do you really want, Jubal? Do you want me to be your girl? Do you want to date me? Is that what our dinners and lunches are? Are they dates or mere conversations? I am asking because I care about you. You are an important person in my life."

"Gina," I said, leaning forward and resting my arms on her desk. I'd have put my hands on hers, but she had pulled back and was sunk deep in her chair, her eyes watching mine intently.

"Every time I see you, I have to stop myself from telling you how I feel about you because it's crazy to have feelings this strong for someone I know it's impossible to have a long-term intimate relationship with. I suspect that you view me as a suitor, and I always have to be careful not to harm you because any greater intimacy in our conversations or actions could distract you from seeking someone else who could be a real suitor, something I can't be. I can't become a life partner for you because so much of my life has already passed, and because, being 30 years younger than me, so much of your life will be lived after the natural end of mine.

"Still, that doesn't stop me from fantasizing about you, from thinking about being with you during the decades our lives overlap, about you introducing me to your family and having you meet my children. But none of that can happen. So don't be confused. Expressions of feelings for you that slip out, no matter how heart-felt, cannot be more than words—words that would surely lead to something further if circumstances were different. But they aren't different; knowing that circumstances are what they are does not stop the feelings, but does help me to reign them in somewhat, and does stop me, regretfully, from acting on them.

"It's the logic of the situation, Gina. The logic being that a lifelong relationship between us being impossible for reasons beyond my control and yours, there is no point in going down the usual path that a man and a woman would travel in getting to know each other intimately. Trying to do so when the normal end of such a process is impossible would be painful for both of us and harmful for you."

I could see she was still unsatisfied even before she said, "You still didn't really answer my question."

"Perhaps I didn't," I said. "You asked me what I want, and I responded with what I want within the parameters of what is possible. Not quite the same thing, I know. I've said before that if circumstances were different—if I was even a decade younger—I'd court you to the moon and back.

"But desires and circumstances must go together. There is little point in talking about the first without the second. But if I was to do that, I'd tell you that every cell in my body wants me to pursue you, court you, make every effort to establish a life-long bond with you for as long as my life lasts. But at the same time, if I was to do that, I'd be doing it against my better judgment about what would ultimately be best for you. I would be giving in to desires too strong to resist even though I could see the difficulties inherent in an age difference of almost 30 years. We are simply in different phases of our lives. Still, I'm always almost ready to sweep all that aside and be the fool who rushes in where angels fear to tread.

"So I must reign in my feelings and desires, and I think I have found a way to do that. I now have the idea of trying to think of you as I would think of a niece, if I had any—I have only nephews—like someone I care about but who is untouchable no matter how charming and willing she may be.

"So, I'm continuing to try to establish a pattern of interactions commensurate with the realities that exist. I will probably fail to do that consistently, but that is my aim."

Gina remained silent after I'd finished speaking, before saying, icily, "Thank you for clarifying things for me, Jubal. I'm not confused anymore. I think I fully understand that your romantic words are just words, and not tangible realities."

And, she added, " I am sooo happy that you see me as your niece."

The way she said it didn't indicate happiness at all, though, and the way she stood up indicated that it was time for me to leave.

⸙ 74 ⸙

Conversation with Russell was just what I needed. Too many ideas were bouncing around in my head and I needed to share them with someone who would understand them. I regretted that I knew only one person living nearby with whom I could share ideas about the most important events in recent American history.

Russell was beyond surprised when I told him about Brian's testimony and his authorization upon his death for me to use it in any way that might help increase public awareness of what had really happened.

I explained the factors that weighed on both sides of the scale, and we fleshed them out more without adding anything weighty enough to tip the balance one way or the other. In the end, I was right where I'd started, glad that I didn't need to make a decision now.

"You know, Russell, Kennedy, from beyond the grave, is helping me in this difficult decision. I recall that he once said he never made a decision until he absolutely had to,[350] because he needed to weigh all the factors, including those that he wasn't aware of at the moment but that he might become aware of later, before the moment the decision had to be made. That puts my mind somewhat at ease about not knowing now how I'll decide later. The title of his book, *Profiles in Courage*, also gives me an ideal to live up to. I am confident I'll have the courage to make the best possible decision when the time comes.

I then went through with him what I'd already told Gina about the shame I felt about my betrayal of Kennedy's vision of peace by the support I'd given to the U.S. effort to keep Russia out of Europe and to keep NATO in existence after the Soviet Union and the Warsaw Pact had vanished into history.

His response confirmed that my interpretation of events was accurate, as far as it went. "The American policy of blocking Russia from full membership in the EEC—the European Economic Community, which was later renamed the EU—and in keeping NATO in existence were at that time the worst foreign policy blunders since the war in Vietnam," he said.

"Yet we've managed to do even worse—by expanding NATO," he continued. "Later Russian leaders would feel that they'd been betrayed by the United States and Europe, saying, 'After 1991, when Russia expected that it would be welcomed into the brotherly family of "civilized nations," nothing like that happened. You tricked us. . . . The promise was that NATO would not expand eastward, but it happened five times, there were five waves of expansion. We tolerated all that, we were trying to persuade them, we were saying, 'Please don't, we are as bourgeois now as you are, we are a market economy, and there is no Communist Party power. Let's negotiate.'[351] But we didn't and we don't. We steamrolled right over Russia."

"George Kennan called the enlargement of NATO a 'strategic blunder of potentially epic proportions' and 'the most fateful error of American policy in the entire post-Cold-War era.' Doing so would, he explained, 'inflame the nationalistic, anti-Western and militaristic tendencies in Russian opinion; have an adverse effect on the development of Russian democracy; restore the atmosphere of the Cold War to East-West relations, and impel Russian foreign policy in directions decidedly not to our liking.'[352] So your instincts and ideals were right, Jubal. But don't blame yourself for the support you gave to the exclusion of Russia. You were such a junior officer at the time that your involvement in the process had no effect on U.S. policies."

I smiled at that as Russell continued.

"In the early 1990s, the U.S. had several options. One was to admit all of the countries of Europe, including Russia, into the EEC. It got that part almost right, inviting nearly all countries in Europe to join. There are now 27 members. Only Russia has been excluded.

"At the time, I, too, supported admitting countries such as Hungary and the Czech Republic, and the Baltics—Latvia, Estonia and Lithuania—into NATO, to lock in the gains resulting from the demise of the Soviet Union. I also supported admitting Russia, so that Europe would, for the first time ever, be a coherent unity, just like the United States is a coherent unity of 50 states.

"Soon after, though, I concluded that NATO should be abolished. As you noted, there was no longer a need for the organization."

I was about to speak, but saw that Russell was on a roll, so only nodded.

"Consider this, Jubal: The Warsaw Pact was one of the chief ways that the Soviet Union dominated 11 Communist countries in Eastern and Central Europe. The Soviets never seriously believed the Pact's stated purpose, to protect the Communist countries from invasion by the West. No, it was a military organization created to threaten the West and to dominate the Communist countries that were members of it.

"Today, NATO has the same purpose that the Warsaw Pact had. It is one of the principal organizations through which the United States dominates Europe, just as the Soviets used the Warsaw Pact to dominate its communist neighbors. That has been true since the early 1990s, and it is certainly still true today."

I was aghast. "I'd never thought of NATO as being designed or used by the United States to dominate Europe, Russell. That's an entirely new way of looking at things.

"And," I added a moment later, "one right in line with the thinking that the Power Elite organized the false flag attack on our country on September 11."

I felt the need to say something humorous to lighten the mood but couldn't think of anything suitable. So I launched into another story from my early Foreign Service days that had been on my mind.

"Here's another part of my FS story that I haven't mentioned yet, Russell, one difficult to talk about. Very early in my career, when I was still an untenured officer—before I worked for you—when discussions were ablaze across the Department about how to deal with Russia after the collapse of the Soviet Union, I spoke up forcefully on several occasions in support of full admittance for Russia into the EU—and for the dismantling of NATO. I had been unwise to do so. I spoke coherently, I thought; my reasonings made sense in the historical context. But those running the meetings had different views. They didn't appreciate a very junior officer speaking up forcefully and marked me as someone whose views were out of line with their own. And, we were all to learn, out of line with what eventually became U.S. policy.

"At the time, I didn't even realize the danger of speaking up. I was used to bull sessions in college in which anyone who wanted to speak, on any aspect of the subject under discussion, could express his ideas or opinions. But by doing so in those meetings I nearly wrecked my career before it had really begun.

"After one of the meetings, one of the senior officers present called me aside and explained the way things work. 'It may appear to you that we are in the process of trying to decide U.S. policy,' he said, 'but that's not the case at all. Policy has already hardened for the positions you are arguing against. The discussions at which you have spoken up are a mere charade. Your positions make sense, but you must be careful to whom you express them. The Foreign Service is structured on the Military Service model. That is, it is hierarchical. Officers more senior that you—which is just about everybody at this point in your career—expect you to listen and to carry out their orders, not speak.'

"This was a revelation to me. I didn't say so, but I immediately thought of the 'Let a Hundred Flowers Bloom' era in China in 1956. Mao had encouraged Party members to express their thoughts, seemingly so that he'd have a wider range of options to consider, but his goal really had been to identify those who opposed his policies and eliminate them.

"That senior officer, who will remain unnamed and who put in a good word with my boss to counter what he might have heard from others opposed to the ideas I had expressed, had probably saved my career. I later learned that he had supported my advancement behind the scenes at other key moments in my career.

"Here's what's most traumatic for me now, Russell: that officer, for whom I had the greatest respect and to whom I owed the sincerest gratitude, was later, in 2001, one of the principal aides to Vice President Dick Cheney. I suspect that he was one of the planners of the September 11 attacks, one of those who directed those carrying out critical events on that terrible day. Learning this, or at least suspecting it, has demoralized me beyond words. I felt and still feel personally betrayed. It will take some time to get over this shock."

Russell listened thoughtfully and nodded but didn't say anything. So I continued.

"You know, Russell, sometimes I feel like an amoeba. With amoebas and other single-celled creatures that reproduce asexually, their bodies continue forever. Whatever damage to body or spirit that occurs along the way is divided among the two daughter amoebas when it reproduces. With human beings and other species that reproduce sexually, however, the body with its inevitable damage acquired over the years does not pass into the new generation. Each generation gets a brand-new body. Sometimes I feel like the amoeba, carrying within me all the damage suffered over a lifetime. Thinking about the past is sometimes wearying."

I thought of reviewing with Russell the men who had been president since Bush to examine why they hadn't revealed what they knew about September 11, about how they'd faced a decision similar to mine regarding Brian's testimony. But I wasn't up to talking more on such serious subjects.

So instead I said, "Hey Russell! In what way is Covid like a smile?" I waited only a second before giving him the answer, "You can share both and still have them!"

We both laughed at that, and went on to talk of more pleasant subjects: our children and how they were making their way in this crazy world we all live in.

75

By the end of the month, I was becoming more and more certain that Covid was not nearly as dangerous as the headlines in the newspapers and on TV news broadcasts continually suggested and claimed. By some accounts, it was in fact less harmful than the flu that affects many people each winter. As I interpreted the data, its effect was, in fact, similar to that of a new strain of the flu. It differed from current strains by attacking the most vulnerable people, whereas the strains we were familiar with are more likely to attack people of all ages. I saw that most people who'd died from Covid were quite old and were living in nursing homes; that is, they were folks already on the verge of death. The average age of those who died from Covid was over eighty. Healthy people of working age, those under 65, were hardly affected. The few in that age range who died from Covid already suffered from severe life-threatening illnesses. Children were the least affected of all.

Yet government spokespersons and the media presented the virus as exceedingly dangerous for everybody of all age groups. Never before had I seen such a massive government-sponsored propaganda campaign. Every business and store I'd been to had signs up about Covid, every website, too, even weather channels, which have nothing to do with the virus or medical issues.

The propaganda campaign resulted in widespread fear among Americans and blind obedience to whatever measures governments proposed and required. I was aware of very few people making an effort to determine for themselves whether the information presented in the news was accurate on this, the most important issue of the day. For those who did make an effort, numbers of cases and deaths were easy to find—at first. By the end of March, however, they were hard to find. After wasting many hours trying to find that information on the websites of the Centers for Disease Control (CDC) and other government agencies, I gave up and turned to international websites to get information about the United States.

What I found was that government agencies and news reports were able to paint such a scary story about Covid only because they had changed several key definitions.

A new definition of pandemic had been introduced, one that cited the spread of a disease across international boundaries, but which didn't include any measure of the degree of harm it caused. By that definition, the common cold and yearly influenza outbreaks were also pandemics. But I'd yet to see that pointed out.

A new definition of "case." Until now, a case of a disease such as influenza always meant that the person affected was sick; he had symptoms. Now it meant only that someone had tested positive—on a test that was known to be flawed. By some accounts 97 percent of positive results were false positives. Even the creator of the test stated that it wasn't accurate for viruses that were forms of the corona virus, as were Covid and the common cold, because it couldn't distinguish between them. The test also gave a positive result when it detected even small strands of dead virus, which are inactive and harmless. This new definition resulted in the previously unknown condition of "asymptomatic Covid." I'd never before heard of any disease or virus being asymptomatic. You either had it or you didn't.

A new definition of "cause of death." Never before had the cause of death listed on a death certificate meant that someone had died within 30 days of having tested positive for a virus (the number of days varied by state). Before Covid, cause of death had always meant that someone had died because of harm caused by the disease or injury stated on the certificate. With the new definition, even people who died by drowning or gunshot wounds or having been struck by lightning were deemed to have died from Covid if they'd tested positive on that flawed test within 30 days of their deaths. In truth, such people had actually died with Covid (supposedly), not from it.

Yet the CDC and other government agencies and the news reports did not make clear that new definitions were being used, leaving people to assume that a "case" meant what it had always meant, and that a "death from Covid" meant that the deceased person had been killed by the virus.

The numbers of cases and deaths were being manipulated in other ways, too, I saw. Never before had hospitals been reimbursed a far larger amount than usual if the cause of death stated on Death Certificates was one particular disease, in this case, Covid. These inordinately large payments gave hospitals incentive to list Covid as the cause of death even if it was only a minor contributory cause for someone who already had major life-threatening illnesses. They were, in effect, being bribed.

Never before had hospitals been reimbursed three times that already high rate if a patient diagnosed as having Covid died after being placed on a respirator; I'd learn more than a year later that it took the medical industry a full year to acknowledge that respirators were not an appropriate treatment for Covid, and that many of those on respirators had been killed by the machine, not the virus.

In short, it appeared to me that Covid was a manufactured crisis, a hoax. There never was an emergency, so there never was justification for declaring a State of Emergency.

I was particularly distressed to see that articles in newspapers I'd always had confidence in failed to provide the context that readers needed to judge the severity of Covid for themselves—by, for instance, providing numbers of cases and deaths from other viral infections such as the flu or pneumonia in an average year. Numbers by themselves, such as cases and deaths, are meaningless without a context or baseline to compare them to. Journalists used to understand that.

I tried repeatedly to alert family and friends to the real

situation, to the fact that they and everybody else were being fed blatant propaganda. But I never received a response from anyone I'd sent this information to. Two weeks ago, when I was still trying to find out what the real situation was and had sent out requests for information, saying that I didn't have much confidence that the numbers of cases and deaths listed in the media were accurate, I got back several angry messages. Apparently, it wasn't acceptable to express doubts and to try to find more accurate information. One friend even furiously accused me of wanting his mother-in-law to die, for merely questioning the information I had seen and trying to verify it.

That Covid actually posed limited harm was already known before any lockdowns were declared, before any stay-at-home orders were issued and before President Trump declared a National Emergency on March 13. The evidence from the number of Covid cases and deaths on board the Diamond Princess cruise ship couldn't have been clearer. After a case of Covid was detected on board in February, no one was allowed to leave the ship. The story made headlines around the world.

Yet of the 3,711 people on board (2,666 passengers and 1,045 crew), only 696 persons (19 percent) tested positive for Covid and 410 of them (59 percent) were asymptomatic. Only 286 (8 percent) became ill, with the large majority having only mild symptoms.[353] As of March 10—after a full month of quarantine and before the national State of Emergency was declared—only seven passengers had died (0.26 percent), all over seventy years old, for a survival rate of more than 99.7 percent even in a population heavily skewed toward the elderly.

The evidence couldn't have been clearer, I thought, yet it was ignored. If public health officials and politicians had paid attention to the evidence clearly before their eyes, they would have seen that customary methods for responding to the outbreak of a virus would have been sufficient; that is, provide special protection for the most vulnerable while everybody else goes about their normal lives. They wouldn't even have considered the extreme measures of quarantining those without symptoms, imposing lockdowns, or requiring masks.

It appeared to me that the world had gone mad over a virus far less harmful, by all traditional definitions and standards, than the half-dozen or so far more deadly outbreaks of influenza over the past century. For those under age 80 not already suffering from a life-threatening illness, Covid was, clearly, less harmful than the flu in a typical year.

Never had H. L. Mencken's pithy aphorism—"The whole aim of politics is to keep the populace alarmed (and hence clamorous to be led to safety) by menacing it with an endless series of hobgoblins, most of them imaginary[354]—seemed more relevant.

April 2020

❦ 76 ❦

"I'm sorry to hear that the book club discussion is cancelled," I said to Gina. "I'd be happy to host the next discussion in my house, if the bookstore and restaurants are still not operating as normal. But I won't allow anyone in my house who has a mask covering his face."

We were sitting outdoors at one of the few coffee shops still open, though for drive through service only. The outdoor seating area had been roped off, but we sat there anyway.

"I'd especially wanted to discuss Thornton Wilder's *The Bridge of St. Luis Rey* because it's of such great relevance for events unfolding all around us," I continued, wanting to raise a neutral subject after the tense conversation we'd had the last time we'd met, when I'd stopped by WORDS a few days earlier.

To myself, I recalled that in Wilder's book, an investigator tries to determine the facts of a recent incident. The situation was that an old rope bridge over a deep chasm that separates two small towns somewhere in South America was so old and rickety that the townspeople wouldn't cross over on it. As a result, the two towns, which had once been two halves of the same town, had grown apart, with little contact between them.

A group of peddlers from out of town attempted to cross the bridge, and the weight of themselves and their carts caused the bridge to collapse. All fell into the ravine and died. Before going on the bridge, the peddlers had asked the local priest if the bridge was safe, and he'd assured them that it was. If he'd known that it wasn't, he could be charged with murder. If he hadn't known, but should have known—it was, after all, common knowledge in the town—he could be charged with manslaughter.

In trying to determine the facts of the case, the investigator has a difficult time. At first no one would talk to him because he's from the capital city, far away. Once they start to open up, the stories they tell him are contradictory. It appeared that friends of the priest were trying to protect him, while his enemies were trying to smear him. The investigator had to weigh the motives of each townsperson as he tried to make sense of what he's told.

"The investigator's difficulties are just like those I face in my investigations about JFK and September 11," I told Gina. "And, about Covid. We're hearing different stories. Is it really dangerous, or merely a new strain of the flu? Are lockdowns really an effective way to deal with it? Is it really necessary to disrupt society so extensively?"

In fact, I noted as I continued my internal conversation, all of the books we'd read and discussed were about the main character's efforts to discover the truth of a situation. Or were they? Was I reading that into the books, making it a larger part of them than it really was, because I'd become so obsessed with discovering the truth of certain real-life events?

The search for truth was certainly one of the themes in Aldous Huxley's *The Devils of Loudun*, which I'd read recently. In it, different teams of investigators reach different conclusions about the same events, in part because witnesses with ulterior motives lie to them.

I didn't say any of that out loud, however, because I could see that Gina was sunk deep in thought. I suspected that she was thinking about her business. What would happen to it and to her if it failed because state and local governments forced it to remain closed? I wasn't sure what I could say to reassure her that all would be well in the end.

Finally she spoke.

"Wearing two masks is funny alright," she said, picking up on part of our last conversation.

I wondered whether she'd heard anything I'd said to her. I knew she hadn't heard the parts I'd only said mentally to myself.

"I'd noticed that, too, when I go out," she continued. "So many do it, as if another layer of thin cloth would make any difference. Two times zero is still zero. One hundred times zero is still zero. I read somewhere that if the virus was one inch high, the holes between the fibers in masks typically worn around here would be the size of eight-story buildings. So, useless. There's madness all around us."

"Yes," I agreed. "Masks provide protection against particles suspended in the air, like pollen or smoke. But the virus isn't a particle suspended in the air; it's so small that it's part of the air itself.

"One international medical website I saw last month recommended masks only in unusual situations, such as being in a small, enclosed space with little or no ventilation, like an elevator with a broken fan, with someone who has active symptoms, for at least fifteen minutes. It takes at least that long for the concentration of the virus in the air to become high enough to overpower our immune systems. None of those conditions exist outdoors, and they don't exist indoors either in most situations.

"But when I went back to look at that guidance recently, it was gone. It had been replaced by a strong recommendation that everyone wear masks whenever they're outside their home. Scientific knowledge has been thrown out the window."

Gina shook her head. "I'm so embarrassed by what I see, and so fearful that people's madness will destroy my business, that it makes me want to hide under my dining table. Then there maybe I will pray hard, hoping it will make some difference."

"Prayer always reminds me of wish lists that children submit to Santa Claus," I unwisely ventured to say.

Gina's face flushed a dark red. "You so misunderstand things," she said after calming down somewhat. "We don't pray for material things, or even for other things we want, like a promotion at work. Christians pray to God for strength to resist temptation, for strength to persevere in difficult times, for guidance on how to understand and deal with complex situations. We pray for divine assistance in becoming better people. And for greater understanding of God's will, to bring our hearts in line with His divine will."

"I'm sorry," I said. "Of course you are right. I shouldn't have spoken so flippantly at such a serious moment. I have never had prayer explained to me like this before, as best I can remember. I must rethink some things."

I made a mental note to see how this new understanding of prayer fit into the spiritual journey I'd been on, mostly unconsciously, over the past year or more.

"Are you able to tutor any students now?" I asked, wanting to change the subject.

I was surprised when she said she was. "The studio is forcibly closed, of course. But some parents still want us to come to tutor their kids in their homes. In fact, with the schools closed, there's a greater demand for in-home tutoring than ever before. And the group classes have grown larger.

"Another bright spot is that parents who home school their kids are more independent in their thinking, on average, than parents whose kids attend public schools. That means they're less likely to wear masks or insist that their kids' tutors do. It's such a relief to see people's faces in their homes, because I sure don't see any elsewhere. Tutors can tutor so much more effectively when they can see their students' faces and gauge their level of understanding, and when their students can see theirs.

"I'm also so relieved that at least some money is continuing to come in, enough to pay the rent for my apartment and for food. But I can't cover the rent for the studio at all. I'm going to talk to the landlord tomorrow. I expect he's having a hard time, too, but I hope to convince him to waive half the rent, since the studio is forcibly closed. I'm worried about how I'm going to repay my uncle.

"But enough of that," she said. "I've been thinking about the last time we met. Since you are determined to see me as a niece, at least I can be happy that you see a stranger like me as a relative. If you think another man would be better for me than you, then there's nothing I can do about it. Since you are letting me go, one day I will be marrying someone else. Still, your affections will always be dear to me."

"You are a very complex person, Gina. Intelligent, educated, fascinating—and complex," I said in response.

"I am not monochromatic," she agreed. "I am made of

multiple layers and hues—people say I am unpredictable, complicated, difficult to be understood, too risky to get to know. I don't fit in any mould; I always shock people no matter how hard I try to be 'ordinary.' I always cause emotional roller coaster rides to all the guys I get involved with, and so many other weirdnesses about me cause some people to think I'm not normal—things that I have learned to embrace about myself."

I jumped in when she paused to take a breath. "You're not only complex, Gina, you know it. You revel in it. Every time we meet, I see more clearly that the man you choose to marry will be the most fortunate man in the world." Then I added, "Of course he must also be a bit crazy, to appreciate your craziness."

"Thank you for the compliment, Jubal. I bet I'll be just as lucky to have the guy that I will marry because it means he is the strongest of all the guys that I have met, someone who is not afraid of all the danger that comes along by having me. It may not be a perfect marriage but surely a marriage full of fun and freedom; we'll be free to be crazy around each other.

"I forgot to tell you that I enjoyed Nina Farewell's book, *The Unfair Sex*, that you gave me on Valentine's Day. It's the kind of book that my dad or my uncles would have given me. Were you already thinking of me as a niece back then? But never mind. I am learning a lot from you—you are building me up for that man who is about to enter my roller-coaster-like world—the man who will see my different sides and edges, meet my family; the man who will handle my naughtiness and who I will do crazy and fun things with—you are preparing me to have that beautiful and exciting marriage with that man."

I saw that Gina was in a mood to talk, so I kept quiet, only nodding.

"We see things from different angles," she continued. "For you the issue is your age. Can I tell you something? The guy I am going to marry, whoever he is, will be surely decades older than me. That is set in stone. So if it's not you, it will be somebody else, who probably is around your age or just a bit younger. He might have been divorced, have kids, who cares. If we only spend a few decades together then so be it; a few years full of joy is better than decades of misery. After all I am not aiming for a perfect marriage and if I want certain things, I know that I have to compromise.

"Holly Golightly said that a man's magic number is age 42."

Holly Golightly, I knew, was a character in *Breakfast at Tiffany's*, Truman Capote's novel that was later made into a movie in which Holly was portrayed by Audrey Hepburn.

"All the guys I dated are at least 20 years older than me and I've been through several long-term relationships. I was wondering if I have to reiterate to you that your age never bothered me at all. If I'd met you as a 36-year-old guy, I would have discarded you right off the bat. Guys of my age and guys in their 30s are not emotionally mature. That's why a lot of those guys who get married in their 20s or 30s get divorced in midlife. Their tastes upgrade when they get older. A lot of people think that their younger selves are better than their present selves, but I don't think that's true. If you had met me when you were younger, I don't think I would have liked you the way I like you now.

"You don't have the air of a typical Western man," she continued. "You smell like a different breed to me. Sometimes I think you are way too sophisticated for an American. You're not Asian, either. Anyway, I have tried to be easy on you and haven't gone as hard on you as I would have if you hadn't lost your wife in the past year."

I assumed she was referring to telling me the provocative stories that she hoped would trigger a proposal. I decided to say something provocative myself.

"Gina, I've never been intimate with a Catholic girl before. I had an American girlfriend years ago who was a strong Christian, but not a Catholic. So I have questions about what restrictions Catholicism places on intimate interactions between a man and a woman after the wedding ceremony. I've heard that the Church permits sex only for the purpose of procreation, that actions taken purely for pleasure are discouraged if not forbidden.

"For instance, would it be permissible for me to put the tip of my right index finger on the tip of the nipple of your left breast? Would it be permissible to do that while the tip of my tongue touches the tip of the nipple of your right breast?"

I hadn't intended to ask questions so personal, so intrusive; they'd just come out before I'd known I was asking them. Perhaps I'd been influenced by her talk about her and her future spouse being free to be crazy around each other.

"Yes, it would be permissible for a husband to do both of those things with his wife. Very few things are not allowed to a married couple. But, Jubal, we aren't married, and we aren't going to be, so there's no point in talking about this."

I was again amazed that a girl with such limited or non-existent sexual experience would be able to speak so matter-of-factly about such personal matters. But she was, which added to the mystery of her.

Although she didn't appear fazed or flustered by my questions, it did appear that she considered them in bad taste and that it was time for our conversation to come to an end.

That was fine with me. That she seemed to be ending something with me—not just writing me off as a suitor but maybe also suggesting an end to our friendship—wasn't fine. I needed to think more carefully about whether I had interpreted what she'd said correctly.

77

Having already determined that there was no medical crisis caused by Covid, no emergency and so no justification for the States of Emergency that had been declared, I now turned to examining the edicts that governments had issued in response to this non-existent emergency. Even after noting the propaganda campaign and the widespread fear it generated, I still didn't get it; I saw only that government actions in response to the virus were bizarre and unprecedented. It wasn't until the end of April, several weeks in the future, that I would understand that the Covid lockdowns were the third tragic dislocation in American life during my lifetime, the first being the assassination of John F. Kennedy and the second being the events of September 11.

The most astonishing government action during any of the

three disruptive events was the lockdowns and stay at home orders issued by state and local officials in accordance with guidance released by national health organizations. These measures had little effect on the spread of the virus, a virus that I already knew was no more harmful than the flu in a typical year for nearly everyone under the age of 80.

Yet millions of businesses and other organizations were forced to close their doors. By one estimate, 3.3 million small businesses were forcibly shuttered. Gina's was one of them. Yet it was only small businesses that were closed; large chain stores such as Target and Walmart selling the same products were allowed to remain open. Owners and employees of these small businesses lost their livelihoods. Owners such as Gina not only lost income, but were in danger of losing their businesses completely. Having to continue to pay rent and related expenses even though no revenue was coming in, they were in danger of bankruptcy. They faced the prospect of seeing their investments made in those businesses, in many cases over years or decades, wiped out. These unnecessary tragedies and near tragedies in the lives of the owners of those 3.3 million businesses and their families were, even a few short weeks ago, beyond imagining.

These small businesses, owned by individuals or families, included barber shops and salons, movie theaters, gyms, restaurants, Hallmark greeting card stores, Ghirardelli chocolate stores, and franchises of all kinds, some of which I visited regularly. Yet the closures were not comprehensive even among small businesses. Certain favored businesses and organizations were allowed to remain open. Bars were closed but not shops selling marijuana, which had been illegal only a few years earlier. Churches were ordered closed, yet casinos were allowed to continue their operations. I even saw reports that police surveilled church parking lots, recording license plate numbers and issuing warnings even to those attending outdoor services satisfying all state requirements.

Every business that was still open had signs posted telling customers to wear masks and to maintain a distance of six feet from everyone else. Arrows on the floor told customers where to walk, where to stand, and which direction to walk in. Some grocery stores had locked some of their doors so that customers could enter at only one set of doors and exit only at another. I couldn't understand why stores suddenly decided it was their business to boss their customers around. The old business model—the one that had been in existence during the first 56 years of my life—had been to provide good quality products and services at reasonable prices to attract customers away from competitors. Yet they now thought it wise to abandon that successful model.

Nearly everybody followed the mask requirements and arrows, some going beyond the requirements to wear two and even three masks, even while outdoors or while driving alone. It was all quite bizarre.

Nearly all businesses that remained open had installed plastic barriers between customers and cashiers. Some even stopped accepting cash. Restaurants, those that remained open, required customers to wear masks while walking from the entry way to their table, but not while seated at the table. Don't these people realize, I repeatedly asked myself, that a virus is an airborne disease, that it travels in the air? That the air circulates over, under and around those ridiculous plastic barriers? That it exists at the tables just as much as in the entryway and walkways?

And the hand wringing! Dispensers with sterilizing liquid had been set up everywhere I looked. So many people, after getting a squirt of the liquid, walked around rubbing their hands like Lady Macbeth trying to wash the blood off hers while sleepwalking, after she'd murdered Duncan. That might be the most bizarre image of all.

Especially harmful and disheartening was the forced closure of all institutions involving the life of the mind. Schools and libraries and museums and art galleries were closed. Hardest hit were the performing arts. Symphony orchestras and ballet and opera companies, and theater companies, all cancelled the rest of their seasons. Musicians, dancers, and actors were all thrown out of work and denied the performances they needed to remain at the top of their form. The same was true for athletes.

I recalled what C. S. Lewis had said about education in wartime in a piece I'd read back in September: that the war, in this case Covid, "creates no absolutely new situation; it simply aggravates the permanent human situation. . . . If men had postponed the search for knowledge and beauty until they were secure the search would never have begun."[355]

I recalled, also, my thoughts in response to his piece: that we should sacrifice those things that make life worth living only to the extent that we must. It seemed to me that we had abandoned them sooner than we were forced to in the absence of any real, demonstrated, threat.

Nothing was making sense. Long-standing medical practices and principles were seemingly abandoned with little or no thought or justification. We'd been told forever that sunshine, fresh air and exercise promote good health, yet we were now ordered to remain indoors. There's a reason that the flu season occurs in the winter in the northern and southern latitudes and in the summer in the tropics, I knew. It's because that's when people spend more time indoors, breathing the same recirculated air—in the north and south, because it's warmer inside during the cold winters, and in the tropics because it's cooler inside than outdoors in the tropical summer heat. So we were ordered to do the opposite of the activities we'd formerly known promote good health.

Remaining at home was less restrictive for people with large homes and backyards, who could still get fresh air and exercise, and perhaps even work in a garden. But what about people who live in apartments? They're confined like inmates during prison lockdowns.

Beaches and public parks were closed. Playgrounds at schools and in parks were roped off by police tape. Some schools even removed basketball hoops so that kids couldn't play basketball. In some cities, police patrolled the streets, challenging people who they determined had no valid reason for being outside their homes. I saw a photograph of a father being

Image 28. A playground in Milliken Park closed during the Covid pandemic.

Image 29. A father being arrested for playing catch with his daughter in a public park.

handcuffed and hauled away by police in front of his six-year-old daughter for tossing a softball back and forth with her in a public park. Another media report showed a photo of a man being fined $1,000 for daring to surf alone on a beach in California.

Several aspects of the governmental response to the virus deserve special note.

One was the fear campaign generated by unrelenting propaganda, as already noted. Before the virus hit, getting second opinions on serious medical matters was not unusual, something I'd failed to do with Diana, to my everlasting regret. Yet now we were expected—forced—to accept the dictates of national organizations staffed not by doctors but by bureaucrats. No second or contrary opinions were allowed.

Medicines that had long been approved and used to ward off a variety of illnesses and that were effective against Covid were blocked from being prescribed for those who really had Covid and needed treatment. The antiparasitic medication Ivermectin, I learned, had a very high degree of effectiveness and was shown to be extremely safe. Hydroxychloroquine was not as effective but was generally safe."[356] Dr. Blaylock documented that countries in Africa, where Ivermectin has been used for decades to treat river blindness, had the lowest incidence of Covid and the lowest death rates. He noted that this information "was not just ignored, it was doggedly contested by governments, pharmacies, and hospitals, some of which refused to allow doctors to prescribe those medications even when requested by the family. Some pharmacies also refused to fill legitimate prescriptions written by doctors. These were unprecedented measures. Never in the history of medicine had such things been done."[357]

Discussions of Covid that challenged the government fear campaign or the accuracy of data about cases and deaths due to Covid were removed from social media sites or hidden to make them hard to find. Never before had opportunities to discuss serious medical issues facing the nation been so restricted.

Beyond the continuous propaganda to which Americans were being subjected, other bizarre situations arose, designed purposely, it seemed, to enhance fear and discomfort. A national toilet paper shortage suddenly arose in the United States. Grocery store shelves that until now had stocked toilet paper, tissue paper, paper towels, baby wipes and other similar products were suddenly empty. That this was a brilliant PsyOp designed to unsettle and scare Americans was confirmed, to me at least, by the fact that the shortage existed only in the United States. Foreign Service officers I knew still working in U.S. embassies around the world confirmed that there were no shortages of these products in the countries where they were working.

The destruction of relationships between people was one of the most horrific effects of the governmental edicts that I witnessed. The constant barrage of propaganda seemed designed to increase fear not only of the virus, but also of other people, who might carry it. The masks and six-foot distancing kept people from interacting face to face, as people had interacted since the beginning of time. Social events and cultural events were cancelled. Funeral homes were closed, denying relatives the opportunity to hold memorial services for loved ones who had died. Cafeterias for those in community living, such as assisted living centers for older folks, were closed. Seniors living there were forbidden from entering the common areas; food was hung on their doorknobs twice a day, severing their relationships with their fellow boarders. People on their death beds in hospitals were denied visits by their children and grandchildren. People were even encouraged to inform on their neighbors who violated these ridiculous procedures. Life in American society had become an anti-human nightmare.

78

The most dangerous aspect of all this, it seemed to me, was that these emergency edicts issued by federal, state and local governments had no basis in law. As far as I could see, no legislatures, state or national—the bodies with the authority to issue laws—had done so, nor had they challenged the edicts issued by the executive branches, whose legitimate authority was limited to carrying out the laws enacted by the legislative bodies. Common sense suggested that emergency orders should remain valid only until legislatures had a chance to meet, at which time they would be either validated or ended. That didn't happen.

The courts also failed to do their duty. I wasn't aware of any decisions issued by courts that challenged the illegitimate edicts issued by governors, mayors and other officials.

It appeared to me that the legal system in the United States had collapsed. We'd never seen anything like it since the days of Woodrow Wilson's widespread violations of civil liberties during World War One and Abraham's Lincoln's during the Civil War. Even in those two periods it was only those who challenged the government's line who were affected. Everyone else was able to continue their normal activities undisturbed.

With Covid, everyone's lives were disrupted over a virus with a 99.5 percent survival rate. As I've already noted, kids were pulled out of school. Weddings and funerals were cancelled. Routine medical and diagnostic appointments were cancelled. Even non-emergency surgeries were cancelled. The aged and hospitalized were isolated. Those terminally ill died without being able to see and hold and touch and talk with their children and grandchildren a final time. Nothing like this perversity and cruelty had ever existed in American life.

Even during the Asian flu in 1957, which caused five times as many deaths as the average flu season, schools weren't closed, travel wasn't restricted, borders weren't closed, masks weren't required, no lockdowns were declared. Yet Covid, a rather ordinary virus, had been inflated into a catastrophe by politicians and so-called experts.

Even more shocking to me than the bizarre edicts was the passivity of the American people. Never before had governments quarantined healthy people, yet now those who tested positive on a flawed test but had no symptoms were kept isolated as though they had the Black Plague. Almost everybody accepted being confined to their homes, except for brief excursions out for food or other essentials. What was going on? How could these bizarre and destructive and unprecedented steps be so quickly and easily accepted by almost all Americans?

Just yesterday, when at the grocery store, I saw a family of six people drive up, all masked in their car. They got out and walked, with even the littlest children masked, to the ice cream parlor a few shops down from Gina's studio. They then waited outside, masked, because the shop wouldn't let more than a few customers inside at a time even though they were all one family. The degree to which Americans had become indoctrinated was beyond belief; seeing all that was saddening beyond words.

Americans, the people I had thought were the most independent minded in the world, went meekly along with the illegitimate edicts. What had happened to the country of rugged individualists such as Daniel Boone, the pioneers, and the 49ers? Where were the independent and enterprising people described by de Tocqueville in the 1820s? They would never have fallen for this scam. Their descendants, though, apparently so terrified of a disease no more harmful than the flu for nearly everyone, voluntarily gave up their rights to assemble, to meet, to talk, to discuss, to investigate. They seemingly refused to see the danger in allowing governments to restrict movements, close businesses, limit individual liberty, and lock down nearly the entire country in response to a supposed danger that we were discouraged if not prohibited from seeking more information about.

If Americans looked around, they could see for themselves that very few of them knew anyone who had died recently, certainly not in numbers greater than in a typical year. They could see that the large majority of those who tested positive for Covid had no symptoms. Many could see that loved ones who had Covid listed as the cause of death on their Death Certificates had died from other causes. They could see all that, yet they refused to believe the testimony of their own eyes.

I continued to try to alert my family and certain friends to this disconnect between what they could see with their own eyes and what they were being told. Yet I could sense that no one was listening. Certainly no one responded to my messages, except those who told me to stop sending them information on the subject.

I even tried to coach them on how to examine the information, on how to respond if they disagreed with the points I'd made. I explained Mortimer J. Adler's guidance on how to conduct an intellectual discussion with someone who had made statements with which they disagreed. The proper response, Adler had explained, was to show where the speaker had misstated the facts, or misinterpreted them, or where his logic or reasoning was flawed. Those were the only grounds on which intellectual discussions could be conducted. Yet not one of those to whom I shared my take on the developments occurring all around us responded.

It was all quite bizarre. The lockdowns caused far more harm to the American people than had September 11, yet there were no protests as far as I could see. The nonstop barrage of propaganda had done its work.

Americans might have been more likely to take the propaganda with a grain of salt and push back against the lockdowns and other measures that were destroying their lives if they had seen important segments of American society doing just that. But all, or nearly all, failed.

The medical industry failed. I've already noted the changed definitions and the grossly inaccurate Covid test through which the hoax was perpetrated. Apparently the Hippocratic Oath had been tossed out the window, along with second opinions and sunshine and exercise. I wondered if I'd ever regain confidence in any medical practitioner, as nearly all of them appeared to support this horribly destructive hoax perpetrated on the American people, and in fact on nearly everyone in the world.

The government failed. I've already noted ways that governments in all branches and at the federal, state and local levels failed to respond in a reasoned and effective way. All three branches allowed themselves to be sidelined so that one person acting on a whim—a governor, a mayor, a county supervisor—was able to overthrow Constitutional guarantees of civil liberties and even bypass the legal system.

Much of the disruption and harm caused to the lives of so many people in the United States could have been avoided if only senior officials had kept in mind a statement made by the U.S. Supreme Court back in 1866: "The Constitution of the United States is a law for rulers and people equally in war and in peace, and covers with the shield of its protection all classes of men, at all times, and under all circumstances. No doctrine, involving more pernicious consequences, was ever invented by the wit of man than that any of its provisions can be suspended during any of the great exigencies of government.'"[358]

Both political parties failed. The Republicans abandoned their traditional stands for limited government, free enterprise and the rule of law; the Democrats abandoned their traditional stands for equality, free speech and civil liberties. Both were mute as their traditional principles were violated in ways never before imagined.

The media failed. As already noted, it served as cheerleader for the unprecedented lockdowns, provided wildly inflated numbers of cases and deaths while ignoring the changed definitions of both terms, and failed to provide contexts and baselines that would have enabled readers to understand the real significance of the data reported.

Social media and big tech failed. Instead of promoting discussion, they censored discussion of the facts, and demonized and deplatformed those with curious minds who sought to find accurate data and publish it. It was the same on YouTube. Only one view of Covid and the measures enacted by edict in response to it was allowed.

Businesses failed. Large stores of course were allowed to remain open; why would they protest the closure of their competitors? But they gave in to the hysteria and furthered it by posting Covid restrictions on their websites and windows. It was only notices about Covid they posted; I didn't see a single sign about other crimes such as murder or rape. Stores could have distinguished themselves by alerting shoppers to the efforts they'd made to keep the air in their stores clean and fresh, but I didn't see even one store that did that. Instead, they installed those ridiculous plastic barriers and drew lines and arrows on floors. In my state, North Carolina, the government deputized stores, threatening them with huge fines if they didn't strictly enforce the state's Covid edicts, contrary to the usual practice of having police enforce the laws. I wasn't aware of even one store that pushed back against this bizarre duty forced on it.

The airlines failed. Instead of defending their success in providing on their planes air that tests repeatedly showed was cleaner and fresher than air in office buildings and malls, they strictly enforced the ridiculous mask requirements imposed by the FAA. Airline staff, too, had become law enforcement officers.

Schools and universities failed. Having failed to instill in teachers and students the ability to think for themselves and ensure that they understood the intellectual process through which information and data could be found and examined, the schools simply closed. Students, the segment of society least likely to be affected by Covid, were deprived of their education and robbed of their social lives. Universities, supposed bastions of higher thought and independent judgment, instead enforced lockdowns by sending their students—their paying customers—home.

Most disheartening of all, the intellectuals failed. The pundits, the editorial writers, the commentators—almost all of them in almost all of the mainstream media—failed to do their duty to report and comment objectively on developments of importance in our society. Flawed medical pronouncements, illegitimate government lockdowns, unwarranted school closures—all were left unchallenged, and often supported. My confidence in their independence of thought and astuteness of judgment was shown to be misguided. Nearly every so-called intellectual discredited himself.

Seeing all this, I had to ask, "How does one respond to seeing one's lifelong friends and family so willing to accept the Covid hoax, so willing to go along with the lockdowns?"

I'd mentioned earlier the idea of using September 11 as a benchmark by which to judge other people's sanity, ability to reason and think, and the degree to which they were a true

Principal; now Covid beliefs served as a similar indicator. But what to do when nearly everyone I knew failed the test? What to do when loved ones failed? We couldn't stop loving them. Could we stop respecting them yet still love them?

It was only at this point, as I began to notice similarities between the lockdowns and the legislation passed in the wake of September 11 that I began to understand just how firmly those two events and the JFK assassination were connected. I began to see substantial indicators that all were perpetrated by the same Power Elite. I needed to think further about this—later. My brain was tired now.

79

Considering the lockdowns further after lunch, I recalled the questions I'd started to consider at the end of December addressing the extent to which it is legitimate for governments to impose costs on us now in exchange for hypothetical benefits in the future. Of course, tradeoffs occur all the time; the question here is whether governments can go beyond ordinary and customary actions—go beyond legal actions—to do what they think is best for their country, state or city. Can they engage in illegal activities to further the interests of their citizens? Is there a natural law that would justify disregarding whatever laws exist in a given time and place?

In considering these questions I assumed that a government's leaders sincerely do have their country's best interests at heart and aren't merely using such claims as cover for actions really designed to benefit themselves and their political allies. I also assumed that the actions taken beyond what a country's laws would authorize would be harmful now in return for expected benefits later—actions such as assassinating a president, or destroying several large buildings and killing 3,000 people, then falsely blaming others for those actions, or locking people down inside their homes, forcibly shuttering millions of small businesses, thereby pushing their owners into or near bankruptcy, while allowing large businesses selling the same products to remain open, and closing schools, thereby robbing tens of millions of students of their education and social lives.

Does a moral law or Natural Law exist that justifies such actions? Does the existence of Natural Law mean that a country's laws themselves are illegitimate if they deviate from it?

I'd now finished reading *The Abolition of Man*, the book in which C. S. Lewis concluded that Natural law does indeed exist and that we should all be guided by it in our private and public lives. I'd also recently read Aldous Huxley's *The Perennial Philosophy*, which in part explored similar ethical territory. I was surprised that two such very different men had focused their attention on similar subjects, and at the same time, and had reached similar conclusions about them.

Before considering the specific ethical beliefs that they found inherent in Natural Law, I glanced briefly at biographies of them to try to understand how they had arrived at such similar positions.

I saw that Lewis and Huxley had been born only three years apart, in 1894 and 1897, but in very different circumstances. Huxley was born into a family of intellectual giants, Lewis into a family with no noteworthy intellectual accomplishments. Both, however, experienced bouts of adversity early in their lives. Both lost their mothers at an early age. Lewis, also, he later wrote, lost his father at the same time, because his father, after the loss of his wife, had never been able to regain his mental balance. Huxley became blind as a teenager; only after a year of blindness did he regain partial sight in one eye. Both overcame these hardships and went on to lead somewhat similar lives as writers before focusing their attention on the subject of the ethics of Natural Law.

Lewis had given the lectures that became *The Abolition of Man* in the spring of 1943, and the book was published at the end of that year. Huxley's much longer *The Perennial Philosophy* was well underway by the spring of 1944 and nearly finished by early 1945. It was published that summer.

In his book, Lewis referred to Natural Law by the term TAO. "This thing which I have called for convenience the TAO, and which others may call Natural Law or Traditional Morality or the First Principles of Practical Reason or the First Platitudes, is not one among a series of possible systems of value," Lewis explained. "It is the sole source of all value judgements. If it is rejected, all value is rejected. If any value is retained, it is retained. The effort to refute it and raise a new system of value in its place is self-contradictory. There never has been, and never will be, a radically new judgement of value in the history of the world."[359]

The moral precepts of the TAO, Lewis showed, had been recognized around the world, as the sampling of them nearby shows. [See nearby text boxes.]

That none of these precepts is surprising should not be surprising, given that they encapsule the common wisdom of human beings over more than two millennia and because many of them are found in the Ten Commandments.

There is nothing in what Lewis found in the TAO—the Natural Law, the common moral inheritance of mankind—from what I can see, that justifies a government's murder of 3,000 people. What about Huxley?

Whereas Lewis argued that an objective moral standard, the TAO, exists and should be used as a benchmark to determine when our thoughts and desires lead us astray in everyday life, Huxley investigated the lives of mystics in Christian, Indian, Chinese and Hindu cultures who sought revelations about human life and the nature of the world not apparent in everyday life. These revelations were available only to those who had freed themselves from superficial pleasures and distractions; those whose minds had been awakened, through unusual physical practices or narcotics, from the dogmatic slumber that daily life can induce.

By achieving states of consciousness that transcend everyday experience, mystics could, Huxley found, "establish communication between the soul and the integrating principle of the universe." The nature of the spiritual reality that underlies the phenomenal world of everyday perception "cannot be directly and immediately apprehended except by those who have chosen to fulfill certain conditions, making themselves pure in heart, and poor in spirit."[360]

Because these states of mind cannot be experienced by those whose minds are not yet awakened, nor communicated to them, the nature of reality cannot be reduced to the simple maxims that form the TAO. The closest Huxley came to doing so was stating in his book *Ends and Means* that only good means can bring good ends, that good ends cannot justify bad means.

Moral precepts expressed in Lewis's Tao

"Do not murder." (Ancient Jewish, Exodus)

"Slander not." (Babylonian, Hymn to Samas)

"Never do to others what you would not like them to do to you." (Ancient Chinese, Analects of Confucius)

"Speak kindness . . . show good will." {Babylonian, Hymn to Samas)

"Love thy wife studiously. Gladden her heart all their life long." (Ancient Egyptian)

"Nothing can ever change the claims of kinship for a right thinking man." (Anglo-Saxon, Beowulf)

"Honor thy Father and thy Mother" (Ancient Jewish, Exodus)

"To care for parents." (Greek, list of duties in Epictetus)

"Children, old men, the poor, and the sick, should be considered as the lords of the atmosphere." (Hindu, Janet)

"To marry and to beget children." (Greek, List of duties in Epictetus)

"Nature produces a special love of offspring." Roman, Cicero, De Off.)

"Thou shalt not commit adultery." (Ancient Jewish, Exodus)

"I have not stolen. I have not spoken falsehood." (Ancient Egyptian, Confession of the Righteous Soul)

"Choose loss rather than shameful gains." (Greek, Chilon Fr.)

"Whoso takes no bribe . . . well pleasing is this to Samas." (Babylonian)

"I sought no trickery, nor swore false oaths." (Anglo-Saxon, Beowulf)

"Hateful to me as are the gates of Hades is the man who says one thing, and hides another in his heart." (Greek, Homer, Iliad)

continued . . .

Sentiments expressed in the Lewis's TAO, continued

"Whoso makes intercession for the weak, well pleasing is this to Samas." (Babylonian)

"I have given bread to the hungry, water to the thirsty, clothes to the naked, a ferry boat to the boatless." (Ancient Egyptian)

"One should never strike a woman; not even with a flower." (Hindu)

"There are two kinds of injustice: the first is found in those who do an injury, the second in those who fail to protect another from injury when they can." (Roman, Cicero, De Off.)

"To take no notice of a violent attack is to strengthen the heart of the enemy. Vigor is valiant, but cowardice is vile." (Ancient Egyptian, The Pharaoh Sensusert III)

"Courage has got to be harder, heart the stouter, spirit the sterner, as our strength weakens." (Anglo-Saxon, Maldon)

"The Master said, Love learning and if attacked be ready to die for the Good Way." (Ancient Chinese, Analects)

"Death is better for every man than life with shame." (Anglo-Saxon, Beowulf)

"We must . . . strain every nerve to live according to that best part of us, which, being small in bulk, yet much more in its power and honor surpasses all else." (Ancient Greek, Aristotle, Ethics)

"The soul then ought to conduct the body, and the spirit of our minds the soul. This is therefore the first Law, whereby the highest power of the mind requireth obedience at the hands of all the rest." (English, Hooker)

C. S. Lewis, *The Abolition of Man*, pp. 84-104.

Neither Lewis in the ethical maxims of the TAO nor Huxley in the transcendental experiences of the mystics found any justification for extra-legal killing. Both writers, in fact, doubted that political leaders could be trusted to make decisions with the best interests of their populations in mind. Lewis argued that "The real reason for democracy is that . . . mankind is so fallen that no man can be trusted with unchecked power over his fellows."[361] Elsewhere he stated that "Of all tyrannies, a tyranny sincerely exercised for the good of its victims maybe the most oppressive. It would be better to live under robber barons than under omnipotent moral busybodies. The robber baron's cruelty may sometimes sleep, his cupidity may at some point be satiated; but those who torment us for our own good will torment us without end for they do so with the approval of their own conscience."[362]

Huxley repeatedly expressed skepticism about the motives of political leaders, as in this statement from *Brave New World Revisited*: "Democratic institutions are now being undermined from within by the politicians and their propagandists."[363]

In sum, nowhere in the TAO or the writings of the mystics can any justification be found for the murder of the president on November 22, for the mass murder of nearly 3,000 people on September 11, or for the extra-legal lockdown edicts blocking the normal human interactions of more than 300 million people.

80

One thought filled my head when I awoke the next morning: no, not Gina as was often the case, but the idea of connections or similarities between Kennedy's assassination, the events of September 11 and the Covid disruption beyond the mere fact that all three extraordinary events had been orchestrated and carried out by elements within federal, state and local governments.

I noted that the three events had disrupted American life in progressively harmful ways. The first, the assassination of President Kennedy, had been a coup by the Power Elite against the president of the United States, with little immediate effect on the lives of ordinary Americans other than the shock of the event itself; the effect of changing the policy toward Vietnam wouldn't become apparent until several years later.

The second, September 11, had been a coup by the top of the U.S. government acting on behalf of the Power Elite against the rest of the government and against the American people. Unlike the earlier event, wars began almost immediately, first in Afghanistan, with others to follow—wars that continue to this day. The change most immediately felt at home was increased security at airports. The effects of the Patriot Act and other legislation that undermines civil liberties haven't yet been fully felt, not even with the lockdowns in place now.

The third, the Covid lockdowns, are a coup against the American people perpetrated by governments at various levels on behalf of the Power Elite. Beyond the shock of the lockdowns and propaganda campaign themselves, the lives of nearly all Americans have been severely disrupted. Thirty million Americans have been thrown out of work, more than three million small businesses forcibly shuttered, schools closed, performing arts and sporting events cancelled. More personal measures, such as forced masking and "social distancing" have resulted in breaks in personal ties, social connections and friendships. All of these extraordinary measures, enacted by edict rather than legislation, have caused, I concluded, far more harm and disruption than Covid itself, a virus no more harmful for society as a whole than the flu in a typical year.

I'd begun to notice how aspects of the first two extraordinary events facilitated the third.

The increase in the CIA's influence over the media after the Kennedy assassination had facilitated the propaganda campaign in support of the official story of September 11. The success of that effort served as a model for the even more extraordinary propaganda blanketing the country now during the Covid disruptions.

The pressure to accept the absurd Magic Bullet theory, which contributed to Americans' doubting the testimony of their own eyes and the reasoning of their own minds, had contributed to the ease with which the official September 11 story had been accepted. And both had blinkered the eyes and prepared the minds of most Americans to unthinkingly accept the false claims made in the ongoing Covid propaganda campaign.

All three extraordinary events were signaled in advance. The generals had openly condemned Kennedy as a failure and a traitor for more than two years. September 11 had been signaled in advance by various publications, most notably *Rebuilding America's Defenses*, put out by the Project for a New American

Century in 2000. The Covid lockdowns and other measures were similarly signaled in advance by Event 201, the pandemic planning session in October 2019 that called for lockdowns, censorship, tracking of those exposed to Covid and suppression of those skeptical of these measures. Like Hitler in *Mein Kampf*, the perpetrators clearly and publicly signaled what they intended to do.

I'd just learned that Kevin Ryan had noted and developed a number of parallels between the events of September 11 and the Covid "emergency." Richard Gage, one of the founders of Architects & Engineers for 9/11 Truth, had developed them further and organized them into a presentation titled, "The Astonishing Parallels of 9/11 & Covid."[364] Having already touched on some of these, I'll simply refer readers of this memoir to Gage's presentation for side-by-side comparisons of the others.[365] [See nearby textbox.]

One similarity not yet noted was the destruction and hiding

Parallels from Richard Gage's "The Astonishing Parallels of 9/11 & Covid"

Foreknowledge: Insider trading.

Foreknowledge: Drills that 'Go live" – anticipating the actual event.

Foreknowledge: Predictive Programming – telegraphing of things to come.

Abuse of science – Abandoning the scientific method.

Creating a climate of great fear in order to manipulate people.

A solution provided that is far worse than the original problem.

False accounts by government officials and the media.

Extreme control of the narrative by government and intelligence agencies.

No real investigation – or fraudulent investigations.

An elusive powerful enemy.

Media censorship of, and attack on, critical questioning.

Implementation of draconian policies and surveillance.

From: www.richardgage911.org/parallels-9-11-covid-the-video-you-want-to-watch.

of official records. The Secret Service had destroyed its records for the trip to Dallas. Apparently, there were so many incriminating documents that couldn't be removed from the files without creating gaps that would arouse suspicion that it was decided just to destroy all records, in violation of the law. The same illegal actions took place with September 11. The massive files related to some of the exercises that took place on that day—exercises that in some cases exactly mirrored the real-life events that occurred—were apparently destroyed. The SEC reportedly destroyed the files of its investigation into insider trading of stocks of companies that would be impacted by the attacks. These were all criminal offenses, yet no one was charged with the crimes.

For Covid, I've already noted how difficult it had become to find accurate information on the numbers of Covid cases and deaths in the United States. Information had been readily available on the CDC website and other government sites early in the "crisis," so the later difficulty or impossibility of finding the information on official sites from the end of March onwards appears to have been the result of deliberate steps to hide it.

For the Kennedy assassination, it's possible to go to library archives and read printed copies of newspapers reporting on the assassination. They contain details and statements from witnesses later airbrushed out of the official version of what happened.

On September 11, the media initially covered the events in real time, openly broadcasting what their reporters found. I've already noted Dan Rather's live observation of a ball (rather than a plane) approaching the second tower and his comments that WTC 1, 2 and 7 appeared to have been brought down by dynamite. Word had apparently come down by the night of September 11 as to what the official story would be, and the major networks then cleaned up their broadcasts so that from then on they conformed to the official story. Unlike the printed newspapers from the Kennedy era, the networks' original broadcasts are not available to the public; as noted, the archives for five major networks that I found and accessed had been cleansed and contain only reports supportive of the Bush administration's version of what happened.

With the Covid crisis, the message has been much more tightly controlled almost from the minute that President Trump announced a State of Emergency on March 13. The extent and repetitive nature of the propaganda supporting the official story has been unprecedented in my lifetime.

The events of September 11 created a wave of fear that the media sustained. The danger, though, was only that some unknown persons might set off bombs at some unknown point in the future at some unknown location. With Covid, government officials and the media *created* the wave of fear before working to sustain it. The message this time was that everyone is potentially dangerous, everywhere, and at all times. This time it wasn't, "If you see something, say something," but "Stay away from each other. Don't get within six feet. Hide your face. Stay in your home." The propaganda coming from multiple sources was continuous and relentless.

"The 'covid experiment,'" Jim Quinn observed, "was a masterclass in the use of authority to coerce, intimidate, and compel the ignorant masses into conforming to made up rules and regulations regarding lockdowns, masks, social distancing, [and] the use of safe and effective medicines like Ivermectin and Hydroxychloroquine."[366] It is this contrived "emergency," and the fear campaign based on it, along with the destructive lockdowns and related measures, that have made "Covid" surpass the immediate harm caused by the previous two extraordinary disruptions in American life during my lifetime.

Not only has "Covid" done more harm to the lives of most Americans than the previous two events, it has also set the stage for future such events by establishing the precedent of governments waving aside the Constitution, replacing it with rule by edict. These illegal usurpations of power by the executive branches of governments, if they remain unchallenged by the legislative and judicial branches—and so far no challenges have arisen—will become established as legitimate responses any time a president, governor or mayor decides to declare a state of emergency.

That possibility scares me far more than any possible viral outbreak or terrorist attack. I don't know why it doesn't scare others. Very few have noticed, as Jim Quinn has, that the governmental response this time is "setting the stage for their next planned existential threat exercise to abscond with more of our wealth, while increasing their power and control over our lives. Continued submission to their demands will result in continued loss of our liberties, freedoms, and civil rights."[367]

81

I was stressed out by all this thinking about September 11 and the Covid scare propaganda. I needed a break. Maja had become engaged—so visiting her one-on-one was out—and she and her intended—Mike Ramos—were holding an engagement party at her place. She and Gina had both invited me. I hadn't planned to go, but at the last minute realized that the party was just what I needed to distract me from the distressing aspects of the research I was immersed in.

Maja welcomed me at the door and gave me the kind of impersonal hug that she gave to all other guests. I could sense the difference in her manner from her previous greetings. However our previous get-togethers might have been characterized, it was clear that they now belonged to her past. She was sparkling in her new role as fiancée. She had become again the virgin that Gina had always been.

A few persons had arrived with masks on, but on seeing that others didn't wear them, had taken them off. They kept them hung on strings around their necks, though, as if they were about to again cover their faces and set out to rob a stagecoach or a bank.

I milled around with a beer in one hand, talking with the mostly Filipino crowd there, all of them apparently much younger than me. I felt out of place and was thinking about leaving when I saw a group of them on one side of the living room watching a video and laughing loudly. Whatever they were watching had their full and pleasurable attention. As I walked closer, I saw on the screen a Filipino stand-up comedian, Jo Koy, talking about how embarrassing it was when as a small boy in the United States his Filipino mom sometimes packed his lunch in a Cool Whip container instead of the Tupperware box that all the other kids had. He was really funny, and I started laughing as he described his embarrassment, because I'd felt the same way when something similar had happened to me in elementary school.

When his routine ended, someone switched to videos featuring an Annoying Orange, which I'd never heard of before. In them an orange with a human mouth and eyes says annoying things in an annoying way to other fruits that also have human mouths and eyes. It was all so stupid that it was funny, even if, yes, annoying. Soon I was laughing as loudly as everyone else. Laughter and comradery over something so ridiculous were just what I needed to take my mind off the distressing events of September 11 and now the Covid nonsense. I was glad that the two girls had invited me.

I was standing at the back of the group, watching the screen and laughing with everyone else, when suddenly there was Gina beside me. A second later she'd linked her arm around mine and held on to it. Her closeness and grasp felt so warm and natural that it was a long moment before I understood that everyone in the room would interpret her action as an announcement that she and I were together. That we were a couple. That I was her primary suitor.

I didn't quite know what to do about that, but in the moment, in that moment of closer physical contact with her than I'd ever experienced before, it didn't seem to matter too much what anyone else thought. Yet I knew that if I followed my inclination to turn and kiss her, even briefly, even on her forehead rather than her lips, there was the chance she'd go into her innocent act. So I just enjoyed the moment while it lasted.

As always, I needed time alone to figure out what my thoughts were about this new development.

82

To escape further from Covid I finally delved into several books by Peter Dale Scott that I'd bought over the past several months. Their combined effect was to yet again revolutionize my understanding of the Power Elite and the political forces behind the first two extraordinary events. The information Scott presented was so extensive and so fundamental that I again felt like a naif, as though all my previous research had merely scratched the surface of those events and the real nature of the American system of governance.

I'd already understood that the Power Elite consisted of players in the corporate, financial, academic and media worlds in addition to various departments and agencies within the federal government. I knew that moles loyal to the Power Elite worked in many governmental departments. And I'd understood that extraordinary events such as the assassinations and September 11 occurred when the interests of key players in the Power Elite aligned in support of them.

What I learned now from Scott was that the Power Elite also included players who were heavily involved in illegal as well as legal activities, among them organized crime, narcotics trafficking and money laundering. I learned that elements of the U.S. government were involved in these activities, too, perhaps none more intensely than the CIA. I now understood that legitimate political and economic activities were inextricably linked with those that crossed the line into illegality, and that both had seeped deep into the very core of the American political system.

"One of the most disturbing findings" in his research, Scott stated, "has been the extent to which agencies of the U.S. government, including the Justice Department, have been involved in actively protecting international drug traffickers, and indeed in the traffic itself."[368] When examined closely, drug trafficking "will be seen to consist of overlapping networks, relating official to private power through collusion and corruption."[369] And again, "The postwar international alliance between intelligence and drug traffickers is perhaps the best-documented instance of such a connection. . . . It is not the only such connection, and indeed merges with others, notably unassailable networks responsible for gambling and prostitution in the United States."[370] Learning all this, I recognized that I not only felt like a naif, I deserved to.

By "deep politics," Peter Dale Scott referred to analysis that looks "beneath public formulations of policy issues to the bureaucratic, economic, and ultimately covert and criminal activities which underlie them."[371] Here was analysis that tied together and deepened everything I'd learned so far about Glennon's Dual Government, Mills's Power Elite and Prouty's Secret Team.

I now saw that events such as the assassination of John F. Kennedy, the murder of 3,000 people on September 11 and the lockdowns now in place weren't outside events that impacted the system of governance in the country; they were adjustments within the larger system of governance. These seemingly extraordinary events had resulted not from a "'a few bad people,' but [from] the institutional and parapolitical arrangements which constitute the way we are systematically governed. The conspiracies . . . are part of our political structure, not exceptions to it."[372] I had mistakenly thought they were extraordinary outside events because my understanding of the system had been too narrow.

Six months ago, I'd mistakenly thought that the system of governance in the United States was the Constitutional system designed by James Madison and enshrined in the Constitution—the executive, legislative and judicial branches—with the military and security agencies off to the side. That government, I knew, was influenced from time to time by powerful financial and corporate entities.

Two months ago I'd moved to a new understanding, to a system of governance in which the Madisonian system served as the functional arm of the Power Elite, which effects its will through the Secret Team and a network of moles strategically placed throughout the government. The Power Elite's influence, if not control, wasn't merely from time to time as in the past, but continuous. With this understanding in mind, "it would . . . be helpful to ask ourselves," Scott proposed, "how far our officeholders, including our president, have been reduced to the status of clients, dispensable when that more enduring patronage is withdrawn. To what extent has our visible political establishment become one regulated by forces operating outside the constitutional process, rather than through it?[373]

I'd now moved to a still deeper level of understanding of the American system of governance, one that in Scott's description, "involves more than just institutions. What is really operating here is a widely disseminated willingness, not to be blamed on any single individual or agency, private or public, to resort to fraud, violence, and even murder. Organized crime in this sense could also be called tolerated crime: it is the milieu which private and government interests have turned to when there was fraud, violence, or murder to be done."[374] We've reached the point, Scott concluded, where "this symbiosis has gone on so long that no president or Congress can now easily change it. It is engrained in our way of life, and perhaps increasingly threatens it."

In passing through these sequential transformations in my understanding, I thought I knew how Carlos Castaneda felt as he'd passed through repeated transformations in his perception of reality through his studies with the Yaqui mystic Don Juan in Mexico, as recounted in several books beginning with *The Teachings of Don Juan: A Yaqui Way of Knowledge* (1968), and *Separate Reality: Further Conversations with Don Juan* (1971).

In later books, such as *Journey to Ixtlan: The Lessons of Don Juan* (1972), and *The Power of Silence: Further Lessons of Don Juan* (1987), Castaneda says things like "Oh, no, no, no. I have misunderstood everything I said previously!" before describing his new, deeper understanding of reality. But then, in his next book, he presents an even deeper level of awareness.

Recalling his experiences, I suspected that additional transformations of my understanding of the nature of American governance and society awaited me.

With all this in mind, I wanted to return to the three big events to view them from my latest perspective.

I turned first to the the Kennedy assassination and the objection that some believers in the Oswald-as-lone-gunman idea sometimes make: that if the assassination took place as I've described it in this memoir, "someone would have talked." To make that claim, they must set aside the hundreds of witnesses who provided evidence that contradicted the official story, including the 152 persons present in Dealey Plaza that day who stated that at least one shot came from the grassy knoll in front of the president, and the medical team at Parkland Hospital in Dallas who saw the gaping hole in the back of the president's head.

But even if those believers were referring only to participants in the assassination and those actively involved in the cover-up, their objection would still be flawed. It would have more value if the traditional government of three branches was the power that ran the country. But it isn't. The country is not the open society they imagine it to be. "Beneath the open surface of our society," Scott had shown, "lie connections and relationships of long standing, virtually immune to disclosure, and capable of great crimes, including serial murder. To the stock objection that it would be virtually impossible to assemble a murder conspiracy without leakage, the response is that an existing conspiratorial network or system of networks, already in place and capable of murder, would have much less difficulty in maintaining the discipline of secrecy."[375]

I saw now, too, that the involvement of the U.S. government in drug trafficking was an important factor in Kennedy's assassination. "A key reason to suspect drug involvement in the assassination is the sustained effort of administration and congressional officials, in 1964 and again in 1978, to conceal the extent of Jack Ruby's involvement with both drug traffickers and law enforcement."[376]

The Warren Commission, Scott showed, "suppressed Ruby's links to organized crime and the political establishment. The House Committee [on Assassinations] rectified the first half of this suppression, but not the second."[377] It chose to ignore that "Ruby was part of this symbiosis of crime and enforcement at a federal level, not just a local one, [and that the] flood of drugs into this country since World War II was one of the major 'unspeakable' secrets leading to the ongoing cover-up of the Kennedy assassination."[378] "The overriding collective purpose" of the Warren Commission and the House Committee "was not so much the truth as damage control. . . . What was being protected, it appeared, involved politicians as well as mobsters. . . . What remained unmistakable . . . was prima facie evidence of a political cover-up protecting organized-crime figures and their allies in politics—a cover-up apparently conducted by those who should in theory have been committed to the exposure of organized crime. . . . Our justice establishment was by no means at arm's length from the criminals it was supposed to prosecute."[379]

Attorney General Robert Kennedy's determined efforts to suppress organized crime and to cut the linkages between legitimate authorities and criminal forces gave powerful players on both sides of those linkages reasons to want to see the Kennedys gone. "By November 1963," Scott showed, "the Kennedys had put together a formidable coalition to purge the Democratic party of mob alliances,"[380] and on the other side, "Hoover and the FBI were . . . in 'revolt' against their nominal superior, Attorney General Robert Kennedy."[381]

The Mafia wanted to be rid of Bobby as much as John, Scott showed.[382] Marrs agreed, writing: "So the decision was made at the highest level of the American business-banking-politics-military-crime power structure that should anything happen to Kennedy, it would be viewed as a blessing for the nation, and certainly for them."[383]

It's interesting to note that the Dulles brothers who ruled the roost in the 1950s had been replaced by another set of brothers, the Kennedys, who appeared likely to remain the dominant political force indefinitely. "Two more Kennedys—Robert and Edward—were waiting in the wings for their turn at the presidency. A Kennedy 'dynasty' was in place. . . . Simply voting him out of office wouldn't suffice. After all, what was to stop someone [else] from carrying on his policies."[384] "Therefore, the decision was made to eliminate John F. Kennedy by means of a public execution for the same reason criminals are publicly executed—to serve as a deterrent to anyone considering following in his footsteps."

The flaw in the thinking of those adhering to the official lone-gunman story, then, "is to look for an external conspiracy violating a systemic political order from without."[385] From the "enlarged and deeper perspective of power as a symbiosis of public government, organized crime, and private wealth with deep connections to both government and crime" that Scott described, "the forces behind the assassination no longer appear as extraneous, but as deeply systemic; and the violation to the enlarged power system can be seen as coming from the Kennedys, with their policies of détente abroad and an attack on a CIA-sanctioned Hoffa-crime connection at home. From this perspective, the assassination was not a corrupt attack from outside an honest system. The assassination was a desperate, extraordinary defense, or adjustment, of a system that was itself corrupt."[386]

Chief Justice Earl Warren, in a statement defending the conclusions of the Commission he'd headed, stated "Practically all the cabinet members of President Kennedy's administration, along with Director J. Edgar Hoover of the FBI and James Rowley of the Secret Service, . . . testified that to their knowledge there was no sign of any conspiracy. To say now that these people, as well as the Commission, suppressed, neglected to unearth, or overlooked evidence of conspiracy would be an indictment of the entire government of the United States."[387]

Well, yes, that is exactly the point. Many persons in the upper levels of the government and many powerful players in the Power Elite outside of government were in on the hit. Even those who didn't actively participate in it or in the cover-up but who learned of them later were guilty of being accessories after the fact by their silent approval.

The events of September 11, too, need to be re-examined in light of my new understanding that core components of the U.S. system of governance, both inside government and outside, include entities operating on the far side of the legal-illegal line. I'll provide only the briefest of glances here.

The use of U.S. intelligence and military assets on behalf of the production and trafficking of illegal narcotics was exposed by the events of September 11. "One of the biggest secrets of 9/11," Michael Ruppert stated, "is the connection between drug money and Wall Street."[388] The stage for this connection had been set decades earlier. "The CIA is Wall Street. Wall Street is the CIA," Peter Dale Scott had noted, "with the first seven deputy directors of the CIA [coming] from New York legal and financial circles.[389]

Prima facia evidence of the CIA's trafficking in illegal narcotics is the increase in opium production in Afghanistan after the United States invaded the country in the fall of 2001. "When the harvest of June 2002 came," Ruppert reported, "Afghanistan had again become the world's largest producer of the opium poppy and the world's largest heroin supplier. From a paltry 180 tons under the Taliban in 2001, according to the UN, the estimated 2002 harvest, under CIA protection, was close to 3,700 tons."[390]

This active participation in narcotics production and trafficking wasn't something new in 2001. It had continued for decades, Scott showed, citing, the "CIA habit of turning to drug-supported, off-the-books assets for fighting wars—in Indochina and the South China Sea in the 1950s, 1960s, and 1970s; in Afghanistan and Central America in the 1980s; in Columbia in the 1990s; and again in Afghanistan in 2001."[391] "Nearly all these wars" funded by drug trafficking, Scott showed, "were in defense of the overseas interests or aspirations of major U.S. oil companies."[392]

83

The response to Covid, too, must be re-examined from this same new understanding. In doing so I learned two things, both disturbing, one small and one big.

The small one was that a pandemic training exercise, Event 201, had taken place in October 2019. Organized by the World

Economic Forum and Johns Hopkins University, it was held to identify where "public-private partnership will be necessary during the response to a severe pandemic in order to diminish large-scale economic and societal consequences." Participants included the World Economic Forum and the Bill and Melinda Gates Foundation—all full-fledged players in the Power Elite.

Event 201 published its findings and recommendations in November 2019. One month later China recorded its first case of Covid. How ironic that the exercise designed to identify responses "to diminish large-scale economic and societal consequences" resulted in economic and societal consequences far larger than any responses to any previous pandemic in all of recorded history. What was most disturbing was that the full range of measures for dealing with a pandemic of the utmost deadliness—a propaganda campaign, masking, lockdowns, stamping out of data and information, whether true or not, that interfered with these measures—was implemented for a virus less harmful than the flu for those under the age of 80 not already suffering from life-threatening illnesses. And that this minimal level of harm was known in advance from real-life indicators such as the Princess cruise ship quarantine already noted.

The mindless bureaucratic implementation of procedures designed for the most serious pandemics should terrify everyone wanting commonsensical, balanced approaches to public health concerns. Rather than scale back the measures discussed at Event 201 to match the mild nature of the Covid virus, definitions were changed and propaganda unleashed to create a level of fear suitable for the deadliest of viruses. Rather than match remediation efforts to the level of harm, the level of harm was made to appear horrific enough to justify the most extreme measures. In doing so medical and political authorities destroyed their credibility.

The second thing I learned was even more disturbing. Whereas the process just described could possibly be attributed in part to bureaucracy run amok, this second involved a deliberate, purposeful breach of trust, a purposefully underhanded effort to dominate every aspect of American society.

Having watched several Covid press events in which President Trump was accompanied by the director of the Department of Health and Human Services (HHS) and the directors of several organizations within the HHS family, including the Centers for Disease Control (CDC), the National Institutes of Health (NIH) and the National Institute of Allergy and Infectious Diseases (NIAID), I had assumed—as had everybody else—that these organizations were responsible for establishing and carrying out the national response to Covid.

But it wasn't so. As of March 13, it was the National Security Council (NSC) that was officially in charge of the U.S. government's Covid policy. Then, beginning on March 18, the Federal Emergency Management Agency (FEMA)—which operates under the Department of Homeland Security (DHS), which in turn operates under guidance from the National Security Council—was placed officially in charge of the government's Covid response.[393] This meant that "the doctors on the White House Task Force who headed HHS departments . . . had no authority over determining or implementing Covid policy and were following the lead of the NSC and the DHS." That national security organizations rather than public health agencies were in charge was unsettling. And that the federal government had repeatedly gone through the charade or pretense that government health agencies were in charge was beyond disturbing.

In explaining how this deception came about, Debbie Lerman noted that although the NSC provides advice on foreign and national security policies, it "does not include as regular attendees [in its meetings] any representatives from public health-related agencies." Further, FEMA, empowered to respond to natural disasters such as hurricanes, floods, earthquakes and volcanic eruptions, had never before led a national response to a pandemic. Yet, Lerman documented, "HHS—the agency designated by statute and experience to handle public health crisis—was removed, and FEMA—the agency designed by statute and experience to 'help people before, during and after disasters' like earthquakes and fires—was put in charge."

So why was FEMA suddenly and unexpectedly given this lead role? Lerman's explanation drew on two key factors. One is that the NSC Advisor operates, according to an official document she quoted "with minimal input from cabinet-level departments such as State or Defense" and that "there is little statutory or legal constraint (beyond budgetary limits) in how the role of the NSC Advisor is defined or how the NSC staff is organized and operates." In other words, Lerman explained, "if the NSC is in charge of the Covid response, it can pretty much decide and impose anything it wants without any constraints or oversight, as long as the president agrees, or at least lets them take the lead."[394]

And second, the existing Covid plan at the time FEMA replaced the NIH as the Lead Federal Agency (LFA) was not updated to "address the changes that ensued when FEMA was designated the LFA. Furthermore, FEMA (and HHS) did not update the [plan] or issue interim guidance addressing the changes in critical roles and responsibilities for each agency."

What all this means, Lerman concluded, is that "the NSC wanted to ensure that no policy or response initiative emanating from the public health departments would play any role in the Covid response. Since FEMA had no planning documents or policies regarding disease or pandemic outbreaks, there would be nothing in the way of whatever the NSC wanted to do."

So again, why was this unexpected and unprecedented change made? The clue Lehman found is that at the time the NSC became officially in charge of the government's Covid response, the existing pandemic response plan was "adapted"—that is, changed—to give the NSC the authority "to implement broader community and healthcare-based mitigation measures." What that meant is not spelled out.

She then turned to the PanCAP-A Plan, which had been announced on March 13. It stated that it "'layers in the COVID-19 Containment and Mitigation Strategy developed by the NSC.' The words "Containment," "Mitigation" and "Strategy" are capitalized, suggesting they may be the title of an actual document. But such a document, if it exists, is nowhere to be found."[395] Again, no specific information or plans are available to the public.

"The fact that we know nearly nothing about what the National Security Council—the group in charge of U.S. Covid-19 response policy—was planning," Lerman continued, "suggests that they did not want to reveal what their actual objectives and strategy were. Could this be because they were responding to a potential bioweapon—a genetically engineered virus that they themselves might have been involved in developing? Did their strategy involve military-style draconian lockdowns which they never announced, and which they had to terrify the population into accepting—two weeks at a time?"[396]

Had the national security authorities taken "control of the Covid pandemic response not just in the U.S. but in many of our allied countries (the UK, Australia, Germany, Israel and others) because they knew SARS-Cov-2 was an engineered virus that leaked from a lab researching potential bioweapons? Whether or not the 'novel coronavirus' was in fact a highly lethal pathogen, it was a military threat because it was a potential bioweapon, and therefore it required a military-style response, [including] strict lockdowns. . . . Once the national security authorities were in charge, the entire biodefense-industrial complex—consisting of national security and intelligence operatives, propaganda/psy-op (psychological operations) departments, pharmaceutical companies and affiliated government officials and NGOs—assumed leadership roles."[397]

It all sounded to me like the government was preparing the legal authority needed to declare a nationwide lockdown and other society-wide measures mandated by the National Security Council if the states hadn't implemented them first. The more I learned about it, the scarier the whole episode seemed. Whatever the plans were, it appeared that FEMA would have a leading role in designing and implementing them.

What I was soon to learn about FEMA was even scarier than anything I had seen so far.

84

A few days later I learned from the books of Peter Dale Scott that there was indeed a sense in which "shadow government" was an accurate term, and that FEMA was in the thick of it.

At 10 a.m. on September 11, 2001, the official government of the United States ceased to function. At that moment, Thierry Meyssan explained, Richard Clarke, National Coordinator for Security, Infrastructure Protection, and Counterterrorism, "triggered the 'Continuity of Government Plan.' At that very moment, President Bush and Congress were suspended from office and placed under military protection. President Bush was taken to an air base in Nebraska where the CEOs of the upper floors of the Twin Towers had been since the previous evening; and Congress to the Greenbrier megabunker. Power fell into the hands of the 'Continuity Government' . . . [and] was not returned to the civilians until the end of the day."[398]

A FEMA press release issued on September 11, 2001, titled "FEMA Fully Activated in Response to Apparent Terrorist Events," stated that "In response to the apparent terrorist events, FEMA's Washington-based Emergency Response Team (EST) has [been] fully activated and on 24-hour operations. All 10 of the FEMA regions – headquartered in Boston, New York City, Philadelphia, Atlanta, Chicago, Denton, TX, Denver, San Francisco and Bothell, Wash. – are also fully activated."[399]

That transfer of power had bizarre consequences. One, noted by Meyssan, was that Vladimir Putin, president of the Russian Federation, "informed by his staff that a Russian satellite had just observed a missile being fired from a Navy ship off the coast of Washington at the Pentagon, . . . tried to contact his U.S. counterpart. He was unable to do so. Not because the telephone networks had broken down, but because George W. Bush was temporarily no longer president."[400]

How had this bizarre situation come about? How was it that Clarke had the authority to make that declaration in the first place? Who were the members of the "Continuity Government?" What did they do during the hours when they were running things? We have only sketchy answers.

The idea of establishing a "Continuity government" arose during the 1950s, when it seemed conceivable that a major nuclear attack on the United States by the Soviet Union could wipe out many senior members of the government. Tracing the development of the idea, Scott found that in the 1970s Marine Colonel Oliver North "and his allies," believing that the war in Vietnam "was not lost on the battlefield, . . . [but] in the streets of America, quietly and secretly . . . began to make arrangements, through Continuity of Government planning, to ensure that in any future military engagement, American dissent at home would not be allowed to endanger the outcome."[401] The original purpose of the project had, therefore, expanded to include steps against American citizens to ensure their passivity during any future conflicts.

Planning for the COG continued under President Gerald Ford, involved Donald Rumsfeld served as Secretary of Defense and Dick Cheney as Ford's Chief of Staff—positions, Scott noted, that were "roughly the same positions of dominance in the Pentagon and White House that they would come to occupy in the George W. Bush administration after 2001."[402] The two men remained key players in the continuing development of the COG idea during the 1980s, during the Reagan administration, when Cheney was a congressman and Rumsfeld worked outside of government, thereby serving as continuity in the development of the idea during the 25 years leading up to September 11, 2001, when it was first activated.

During the Reagan years, planning was conducted by the Federal Emergency Management Agency (FEMA), operating under the National Program Office (NPO). Vice President George H. W. Bush, had overall responsibility, "with Lt. Col. Oliver North . . . as the National Security Council action officer."[403] The NPO plans gave FEMA sweeping new powers, including the power, "in the event of a national emergency . . . for imposing censorship [and] preventive detention of civilian 'security risks,' who would be placed in military 'camps.' These plans continued to be developed throughout the 1980s, with the secret participation of Dick Cheney and Donald Rumsfeld, as part of the super-secret continuity of government planning."[404]

The plans "eventually called for the suspension of the Constitution, not just 'after a nuclear war,' but for any 'national security emergency,'" Peter Dale Scott reported. "This was defined in Executive Order 12656 of 1988 as 'any occurrence, including natural disaster, military attack, technological emergency, or other emergency, that seriously degrades or seriously threatens the national security of the United States.'"[405]

"What is most astonishing about this 1980s planning is that Congress was . . . bypassed," Scott observed. "Private power . . . was imposing policies and structures by secret procedures that radically redirected the course of the public state. It was doing so at a constitutional level. COG—more properly characterized as *change* of government rather than *continuity* of government—was not seeking to influence or assist constitutional authority, but to control it, and if necessary, to override it."[406]

In fact, as I learned from Ruppert's *Crossing the Rubicon*, "In a declared major emergency . . . FEMA's authority divides the U.S. into ten regions under FEMA control, which then operate semi-autonomously with the full cooperation of the military."[407] Under the powers granted to FEMA it can even seize private vehicles, force civilian labor on government projects and appropriate food and fresh water supplies. It can take total control of highways, seaports, airports, and all electrical power and the national media. All that and much more, laid out by Ruppert, sounds suspiciously like military rule. And it's all legal under the American system of government, just waiting to be implemented should the president declare a Code Red alert.[408]

With the collapse at the end of 1991 of the Soviet Union, the only enemy capable of decapitating the American leadership, planning for COG appeared to lapse. Yet FEMA's COG planning continued throughout the 1990s, under the Clinton Administration, with Cheney and Rumsfeld still active as key players. In fact, Scott reported, only part of the COG program had been terminated. He cited a Pentagon official's description of continued planning for a "'secret government-in-waiting' (which still included both Cheney and Rumsfeld) [as] very close to the standard definition of a cabal, as a group of persons secretly united to bring about a change or overthrow of government. . . . In light of how COG was actually implemented in 2001, one can legitimately suspect that, however interested this group had been in continuity of government under Reagan, under Clinton the focus of Cheney's and Rumsfeld's COG planning was now a change of government."[409]

On May 8, 2001, four months into his presidency, George W. Bush appointed Vice President Cheney to oversee a task force that would develop a coordinated national effort against terrorists' use of weapons of mass destruction in the United States. He also created a new office within FEMA, the Office of National Preparedness (ONP), which in effect, authorized "a resumption of the kind of planning that Cheney[, Rumsfeld] and FEMA had conducted under the heading of COG"[410] in the 1980s and 1990s. These steps were, in Scott's judgment, "extreme, controversial, and highly secretive plans 'to establish a new American 'president' and his staff, outside and beyond the specifications of the U.S. Constitution.'"[411] Scott further cited a report by Alfonso Chardy of the *Miami Herald*, who described the plan as calling for "suspension of the Constitution, turning control of the government over to FEMA, emergency appointment of military commanders to run state and local governments and declaration of martial law during a national crisis."[412] The plan "gave the Federal Emergency Management Agency, which had been involved in drafting it, sweeping new powers, including internment."[413]

In June, final planning for September 11 apparently intensified. Cheney is said to have spent the entire month of August at his home in Teton Pines, Wyoming. That news item, Scott stated, "is less innocuous when we recall that Cheney, as part of his secret COG planning, had 'regularly gone off to undisclosed locations in the 1980s.' On either August 4 or August 6, the president also left Washington 'for his Crawford ranch for nearly a month-long vacation. . . . Why at this point did the president and vice president both stay out of town?"[414]

Their absences from Washington reminded me that Vice-

President Lyndon Johnson had been absent from Washington and at his ranch in Texas for nearly the entire week leading up to November 22, 1963.

On September 11, Scott observed, "COG plans were officially implemented for the first time, by Vice-President Cheney and Defense Secretary Rumsfeld, the two men who had planned them for so many years."[415] With President Bush kept out of Washington as I'd noted back in February, and with cabinet members and key Congressional leaders transported to secure sites outside Washington—and with the heads of many of the country's largest companies isolated at the same air base as the president—the situation resembled the moment of Kennedy's assassination, when nearly every cabinet member was on a plane over the Pacific Ocean, a 14-hour journey from Washington.

Both Cheney and Rumsfeld remained in Washington, however. This meant, Scott explained, "that for a time there were two parallel governments in place."[416] "The National Command Authority effectively devolved in [Bush's] absence to Vice President Cheney, acting in conjunction with Secretary of Defense Rumsfeld, and the acting chairman of the Joint Chiefs, Air Force general Richard Myers."[417] Despite the prominence of these men, Scott reported, "the movements of all three on that morning are surrounded by mystery and controversy."

Scott pinpointed an exact time on September 11 when the locations of none of the three can be verified: 9:45 a.m. "At a moment when the nation was under attack, Cheney and Rumsfeld both simultaneously absented themselves for a period from their associates and their appointed posts, to hold a significant conversation about which (a) they have since been deceptive, (b) the report is silent or misleading, and (c) the facts are unknown." "The two of them were almost certainly not acting on their own," Scott stated. "More probably they were the key figures in a highly classified operation that must have involved others."[418] The question is whether Cheney and Rumsfeld "were acting in concert with other aspects of the deep state. That is a key question for 9/11. And it is a question made even more urgent by Cheney's and Rumsfeld's activities with respect to COG."[419]

After September 11, Cheney was absent from Washington for much of the next five months.[420] At those times he was working from a COG base—"Site R," the so-called Underground Pentagon at Raven Rock Mountain near Blue Ridge Summit in Pennsylvania.

Knowing now of this COG planning and FEMA's central role in it, FEMA's being assigned as the lead agency to respond to Covid began to make more sense. FEMA clearly had been poised to impose lockdowns at the national level had states not done so.

Is it a stretch to consider that certain high-level officials considered the Covid virus so potentially dangerous as to constitute an emergency justifying invoking the measures FEMA was authorized to use in response to a crisis? After President Trump's Declaration of a State of Emergency on March 13, I'd read of proposals for using camps to isolate those with the virus, and even those only suspected as having been exposed to the virus by being near someone who'd contracted it. This was actually happening in Australia. I suspected that this was on the verge of happening in the United States, too.

☙ 85 ☙

I now turned to Naomi Wolf to take me from the aftermath of September 11 to the existing lockdowns and other measures taken in response to Covid. Wolf had documented in 2007 just how far along the path to tyranny the United States had already travelled in the years after September 11. Concerned about legislation recently passed by Congress that violated traditional American civil liberties, she undertook, in *The End of America: Letter of Warning to a Young Patriot*, a study of countries that had moved from democratic to tyrannical systems of government over the past century.

She found that countries that go through that transition "always take the same ten steps,"[421] and that those steps were being implemented in the United States as she wrote. [See nearby text box.] "Our country," she feared, "is in the process of being altered forever. History has a great deal to teach us about what is happening right now. . . . But fewer and fewer of us have read much about the history of the mid-twentieth century—or about the ways the Founders set up our freedoms to save us from the kinds of tyranny they knew could emerge in the future, . . . so it is hard for [us] to know how urgent the situation is, let alone what [we] need to do."[422]

After the Covid lockdowns hit, Wolf reissued the book with a new Introduction. Observing the events unfolding in the United States since March, 2020, she concluded that the country had, "I am so sad to say, arrived at and begun to inhabit Step Ten of the ten steps to fascism. . . . Today, a much-hyped medical crisis has taken on the role of being used as a pretext to strip us all of our freedoms, that fears of terrorism did not, in spite of twenty years of effort, ultimately achieve."[423]

In the immediate wake of the announcement of a Covid pandemic in March 2020, she observed, "most of the elements of a locked-in, 360-degree totalitarianism have been put into place. . . . It all happened very quickly and comprehensively." She documented that the emergency measures in many states suspended due process of law, closed schools, forced closure of businesses, placed restrictions on assembly, suppressed free

The Ten Steps identified by Naomi Wolf that would-be tyrants always take as they move their countries from democracies to tyrannies

(from *The End of America*)

- Invoke an external and internal threat
- Establish secret prisons
- Develop a paramilitary force
- Surveil ordinary citizens
- Infiltrate citizens' groups
- Arbitrarily detain and release citizens
- Target key individuals
- Restrict the press
- Cast criticism as "espionage' and dissent as "treason"
- Subvert the rule of law

speech, hijacked science and weakened bonds between human beings and family members. This was, she concluded, "a war against human beings and the qualities that make us human."[424]

If the post-September 11 legislation had been designed to make the American people more controllable by monitoring their movements and communications and undermining their civil rights—and hence increase the government's ability to suppress opposition to its imperial policies abroad—the Covid measures had the same effect by restricting in-person interactions between people. "Masks break human beings' ability to bond face to face," Wolf placed first on her list of the indignities forced on us. It was followed by "Forbidding assembly keeps us from forming human alliances against these monstrous interests; . . . [and] forcing kids to distance at school and wear masks, ensures a generation of Americans who don't know *how* to form human alliances, and who don't trust their own human instincts." These steps "seem designed to ensure that humans will have no . . . way to feel comfortable simply gathering in a room, touching one another as friends or allies, or joining together," she continued. "Driving all human interaction onto Zoom . . . is not only a way to harvest all of our tech, business secrets and IP—it is a way to ensure that intimacy and connection in the future will be done online and that human face-to-face contact will be killed off."[425]

Wolf, who for decades had been a celebrity intellectual within the cultural milieu of the elites in the United States and Europe, but who would find herself deplatformed and shunned by most of those in her former milieu, observed that "The United States has stood for the rule of law in the past: We set a standard for other leaders and set a point of aspiration for other citizens," and then asked the all-important question, "If we lose that, what force on Earth will stem any barbarism that any despot wishes to impose on his people?"[426]

Perhaps the most severe danger could come from the United States itself: "If a democratic America, with working checks and balances, often exempts itself from international agreements when its strategic interests don't coincide with international goals, would a United States led by a dictatorial regime be likely to subdue in itself any level of aggression internationally or restrain itself from any plunder of resources that it seeks, simply because it was upsetting the rest of the world?"[427]

"If we keep going down this road," she warned, "the 'end of America' could come. . . . Or else we can stop going down this road: We can stand our ground, and fight for our nation, and take up the banner the Founders asked us to carry."

♣ 86 ♣

"You know, Russell, it almost seems that the Covid lockdowns are a coup," I said as we were seated at a hamburger joint near UNC, the university in Chapel Hill where he was scheduled to teach a class on international relations later in the afternoon. "A non-violent coup so far. During the Kennedy coup, only three people died initially: Kennedy, Officer Tippet and Lee Harvey Oswald. In the September 11 coup, nearly 3,000 people were killed initially. But with the Covid coup, very few have died at the onset. Given the 1,000 times increase between the first two coups, I'd have expected the number of deaths in the third to be 1,000 times higher than in the second, or three million. But in this case, it's not actual deaths but fear of death that is off the scale.

"The nature of the coup differed in each case, too. In the first, the coup was against one man, Kennedy, with the goal of changing government policies, mostly in foreign policy. One of Johnson's first acts was reversal of Kennedy's decision to withdraw all U.S. advisors from Vietnam by the end of 1965, as you know.

"In the second, September 11, the coup was against the American people. It was designed to create such a high level of fear and shock that they'd support changes in government policies—wars to strengthen American predominance abroad, and at home, through legislation to dampen and preempt opposition to those wars.

"And in the third, Covid, the coup is again against the

American people. It again seems designed to create a high level of fear so that we'll acquiesce not in changes in specific government policies, but in the overthrow of the American system of governance itself. The legislative process has been dispensed with altogether, replaced by rule by edict. It's like George III has returned, 244 years after we rebelled against his dictatorial treatment of the American colonies."

Russell nodded as he responded. "Yes, it's quite strange that Americans are so spun up about Covid, given that it affects mostly only the very elderly, whereas the flu is more likely to affect people of all ages.

"It's clear that most of the deaths have been among people above the age of 80, and most were living in nursing homes. Typical nursing home residents survive only three to four months in those facilities. They're already at the very end of their lives anyway, so dying a month or two earlier from Covid isn't that big a deal. Not at all comparable with a child or young adult, with many decades of life in front of them, dying from influenza. In that sense, Covid is far less harmful than the flu."

"Two things still puzzle me, Russell," I said. One is that the adage 'Follow the money' doesn't seem applicable here. With JFK, the change in Vietnam policy resulted in huge flows of money into the Military-Industrial Complex. September 11 had the same result, what with the wars in Afghanistan, Iraq and elsewhere. But with Covid, I haven't seen any big changes in flows of government money into its patronage systems."

"Actually, 'Follow the money' is still valid, Jubal. Financial flows have changed in two ways. Forcibly shuttering small businesses even as large companies selling the same products remain open allows the big companies to clean up. Companies that sell through the internet are going to skyrocket, too, if the lockdowns continue. Amazon.com is already up 30 percent in the last month, even as small businesses are being driven into bankruptcy. And borrowing by the federal government is off the charts, enabling it to get its hands on additional funds without any immediate negative effect on the American people. It's their future that's being looted, but in a way not apparent to them.

"And," he added, "I suspect there are factors not yet visible behind all this."

"OK. So it's still 'Follow the money,'" I said. "The second puzzle is why the American people are so scared. As you note, Covid has less effect on children and working age adults than the flu, yet everybody is so spun up about it that they're willing to engage in all sorts of ridiculousness like wearing masks and following arrows on the floors of stores. What is most astonishing is the ease and quickness with which so many people have accepted all this nonsense.

"Why?" I said in a voice that surely conveyed my disbelief and frustration. "Surely they can see that the medical guidance overturns long-standing health practices. We've known forever that being outdoors, sunlight and exercise promote good health, yet we're now ordered to remain at home, indoors. How could so much hard-won medical and health knowledge have been tossed out the window so quickly? Not disproved or shown to be false, but simply ignored?

"Surely people haven't forgotten that it's common practice to get a second opinion on medical matters, yet we're now supposed to blindly follow one opinion—an opinion by government bureaucrats who aren't even physicians. Surely no one seriously believes that those plastic dividers around cashiers are effective. Don't they know that Covid is an airborne virus, and that the air circulates under, over and around those ridiculous plastic dividers?

"Same thing for the absurdity of the 'stand here' signs and the one-way arrows telling us where to walk in supermarkets, and the strictures to stay at least six feet away from all other people. Don't they see the absurdity of churches being forcibly closed while marijuana stores remain open? Don't they realize the importance of human contact, of interaction with friends and family, for good mental health?

"Has the American public lost its mind?

"And worst of all, they don't even raise a fuss when illegitimate edits have replaced legitimate legislation. The entire American political system and rule of law have been upended with hardly a whimper from anyone."

Russell had nodded occasionally during my jeremiad. Perhaps he'd concluded it was best just to let me roll on rather than try to interrupt. It occurred to me that's what I'd often done with Gina.

I then thought of something I'd observed showing how much the American character had changed during the decades I'd lived abroad.

"Two years ago, when Diana and I visited the United States, we attended a baseball game—the local AAA baseball team, the Durham Bulls, playing against a team from Tennessee. We sat just behind first base, so had an excellent view of the infield. I couldn't believe what I saw. What sissies the players had become! When a batter was walked, he couldn't just run to first base as in the old days. He had to stop to take off his ankle protector, his knee protector, his elbow protector, and if he had one, his mouthpiece and hand them to the bat boy. Then, once at first base, he had to take off his batting gloves and hand them to the first base coach and put on his running/sliding gloves. He kept his batting helmet on all the time he was on base. All players on both teams did this, so it must be MLB policy. I remember shaking my head and asking myself "What would Ty Cobb or Lou Gehrig or Mickie Mantle or Ted Williams or Joe DiMaggio say if they saw these wimps?"

"What has happened to the land of Lincoln, the land of the Pilgrims and the Pioneers, the land of people who endured great hardships to accomplish great things? We've apparently become so soft that when we're hit by a virus only slightly different from the flu, people are already primed to be terrified. They're sitting ducks for propaganda and fear campaigns."

Russell finally raised his hand to stop my flow of words.

"One explanation is that many people have entered a psychological state sometimes called the Stockholm Syndrome, Jubal. You probably recall hearing about the case in which some bank employees taken hostage in Stockholm fifty years ago, over the six days they were held, became more and more sympathetic to the views of their captors, more and more attached to them, even devoted to them, to the point that they'd begun to fear their rescuers. There were several other well-publicized cases of this happening, one involving Patti Hearst.

"In times of uncertainty and fear, people tend to turn for protection to whatever authority figures they see, even if those figures are the kidnappers who created the problem in the first place. Because of the fear generated by the ever-present Covid propaganda, we're perhaps seeing this same psychological condition arise on a mass scale. People instinctively turn to the government for guidance and solutions, even though it was the government that had created the fear."

"Well, that may be one way of responding to fear and confusion," I said, "but it's a way that leads ultimately to, well, the opposite of Principality, whatever that may be."

I paused to consider what the opposite was and came up with serfdom. "Mental serfdom, that's what it is, Russell. Blind deference to whatever authority presents itself, and to whatever beliefs it pushes on us, is mental serfdom."

"Whatever you call it," Russell continued, "the force of the propaganda arises from the three-step process Aristotle described in his *Rhetoric*.

"An effective speech," he explained, "has three parts. In the first part, the speaker presents himself in such a way as to gain the confidence of his audience. He then presents information designed to spark concern or fear or some other unpleasant emotion that leaves the audience uneasy. And finally, he presents a course of action that, if taken, will resolve the problem or lessen the fear or relieve the tension.

"The classic example of this is Antony's speech at Caesar's funeral in Shakespeare's *Julius Caesar*. This method is very effective because of the way the human brain works. With Covid, the ever-present propaganda you referred to is directed not at a small audience, but toward everyone in the country at once."

After a moment of thought, I responded with, "I'm almost ready to conclude that human beings are dumber than animals. We've congratulated ourselves on our wisdom—*sapiens*, as in *homo sapiens*, meaning wise—yet I've never seen animals using whatever intelligence they may have do things against their own self-interest, with the lemmings as a possible exception."

"No," Russell interjected. "The popular image of lemmings committing suicide *en masse* by jumping off a cliff is false. It arose in part after this behavior was staged in a Disney documentary, *White Wilderness*, in 1958."

I nodded, then said, "I've even begun to model my own behavior after that of animals, to try to absorb some of their wisdom. For instance, after seeing in a documentary about the savannah in Africa that a herd of zebras will run a considerable distance out of its way to get into the shade and out of the direct sun, I now do the same thing even when only walking!

"My goal, at all costs, is to avoid becoming like Elsa the lion in *Born Fre*e, the movie about lions raised in captivity who had become domesticated and could no longer survive in the jungle or on the savannah. The world is still, in large part, a jungle where sharp instincts are better guides than pampered so-called sophistication. Educated, we're smarter than animals with their instincts as guides. But miseducated, we're dumber. And propaganda, related to Covid or any other subject, is miseducation. It's psychological manipulation.

"It's hard enough to free myself from it. I don't yet see how to help others free themselves."

And with that we'd opened up a whole new subject. Russell had to leave for his class, but I hoped we'd discuss it next time we met.

❧ 87 ❧

I'd been feeling unsettled ever since my last conversation with Gina, and even more so since Maja's engagement party. Finally, a week after we'd last talked, I overcame my uneasiness and stopped by the studio to see how she was faring.

She seemed glad to see me, which was a relief. I thought I detected a bit of uneasiness, though, which matched my own.

She opened the conversation by talking about her business. Although the lockdowns had already lasted longer than the 15 days originally announced and there was no end in sight, she didn't appear overly concerned. Given the school closures, she had more requests for tutoring in students' homes than she could handle personally and had already sent two of her tutors on such assignments. She had her head above water but was only just barely able to cover the half-rent that the studio landlord had agreed to for the duration of the lockdowns. If she was careful, she'd be able to begin sending small monthly payments to her uncle.

Her concern at the moment was finding a Catholic church that would be open for mass on Easter. Most churches, Catholic and every other denomination, were closed now and would remain closed on Easter. I understood the maxim "Give to Caesar what is Caesar's, and give to God what is God's," but as Gina explained it, nearly all churches seemingly believed themselves to be agents of government power, enforcing illegitimate edicts to the strictest possible degree. However, she'd finally found a church that understood that its primary duty was to God and to the souls of its parishioners and would hold morning and evening Mass on Easter. Whatever the government might do about that was its own business, not the church's.

So Gina, I saw, was developing a network of like-minded people among those few still able to use common sense, who understood the harm that was being inflicted on American society and who were determined to resist it to the greatest extent they could.

"As bad as things are here, they're far worse in my country," I heard her say. "President Duterte has imposed a strict lockdown in Manila and the surrounding areas. People are forced to stay in their homes. No work means no food. People are starting to protest in the streets, and the president has ordered the police and military to shoot anyone making trouble. Anyone violating curfew will be arrested."

That sounded bad, I thought, but I was only half listening. I'd been thinking about her visa problem and considered that with most international flights cancelled she couldn't be deported even if the INS did nab her. That brightened my outlook.

At the same time, it occurred to me that there were two aspects of Gina's make up—Christianity and being Filipino—that were largely a mystery to me. And she was a woman. Three important aspects of her being that I could only view from the outside. I'd never be an insider in any of them.

I heard her begin to talk in a stronger voice and turned to face her and to focus on what she was saying.

"We touched on intimacy in our last conversation, Jubal. I want to clarify what I mean by the term. When I talk about intimacy, I am not referring to physical intimacy. For me, intimacy involves every cell of the body, nerve endings, strands of hair, weirdness and quirkiness and what not. That's why people take off their clothes while having sex. We get to let other people see the most private and dirtiest parts of our body, and this kind of intimacy starts through the mind–baring our soul naked to another soul. Without that level of deep connection, sex is a mere physical act."

I was startled by the frankness with which this inexperienced virgin spoke, but merely nodded.

"I mean the intimacy that is the most important, the kind of intimacy that will penetrate your brain cells and every vein in your heart," she continued. "If I am your girl, you might not be able to work on your investigations, or on a book based on them, because I am naughty and a magnet of danger. Unfortunately, nothing normal happens when I am around, which may not be good for you."

My hair stood on end at hearing all that, and I made quick mental notes to think later about her apparently continuing to regard me as a suitor, about the intensity of the intimacy of the life she envisioned, which would wipe out the time I needed for the types of investigations I'd been involved in over the last eight months.

She continued with hardly a pause for breath.

"I learned, early on when I started dating, how extremely important it is that the guy I will choose be superior to me in all aspects, especially intellectually. That's the only way I can achieve what Jane Austen deems a happy marriage. The types of men I dated and entertained is based on that knowledge, and awareness that if I want a man like that, I have to go outside my age group."

This was somewhat reassuring, but also frightening in a different way. "Superior to her in all aspects, especially intellectually?" My God! Her intellect and knowledge in many subjects, and the strength of her personality and the vividness of how she expresses herself—what will she think once she realizes that she outclasses me in all of these ways? Love is blind, sure, but blindness sometimes wears off. Where would I be then?

But perhaps I'd be saved by a contradiction in things she'd said. She wanted a man superior to her intellectually, but at the same time warned that I might not have time for the intellectual work she admired.

Hold on a minute! Here I was thinking as though I wasn't just a suitor, but already a husband, when I was neither. How had she done that? She'd apparently set aside everything I'd said a week ago, and somehow got me to do that, too. She wasn't talking like a niece, nor was I thinking like an uncle. She was a wizardess, and I, I didn't know what I was.

Gina had been eating while I'd been thinking those thoughts.

We looked directly at each other before she spoke again.

"As you can see," she said, "I am always yearning for greater intimacy in our talks, even though you, concerned with the age thing, are holding yourself back from the normal course of events. We will never be able to achieve full intimacy—and I'm talking about the non-physical intimacy I just described—only by sitting here talking. As you might have gathered from things I've told you about myself recently, you'll never get the full Gina experience from mere conversations. I am from a culture where people value laughter, real communication and not taking ourselves too seriously. Conversations, even those as stimulating as ours have been, are only a part of life.

"We are different in many ways," she continued. "I even think we are different in millions of ways. Some of those differences might even annoy you at some point. But poof! In our situation that's not gonna happen. The thing we have will only stay in our conversations and never manifest itself in reality, right? We have our own separate and different lives."

I was startled to hear Gina imply that perhaps I wasn't the right person for her. Wait a minute! Wasn't it supposed to be me that had doubts? Wasn't she the aggressor? Suddenly seeing that she had doubts, too, that she might really toss me aside, cross me off the list of suitors, left me dumbfounded. That's not how this was supposed to work.

It suddenly became clear to me, again, how much I'd come to enjoy her company, how much our relationship, as limited as it had been, meant to me, and how much more fulfilling a wider relationship could be. But if she dropped me off her list of suitors, she might drop our friendship altogether. I couldn't let that happen, could I?

I wanted to respond by saying that I was thrilled by the crazy way she'd described intimacy. I also wanted to say that the intense intimacy she'd described couldn't be achieved apart from sexual intimacy. All types had to be bound together or be incomplete. I wanted to tell her that I envisioned long leisurely intimate sharings of souls and bodies with her, stretched out and intertwined in the privacy of a bedroom, something that would be possible with her only after a wedding ceremony. With physical intimacy between us not possible before such a ceremony, marriage, always a leap into the unknown, would be with her a more daunting leap than it otherwise would be. But I didn't say any of this.

The thinking I had already done this evening while listening to her had made my brain tired, yet I felt the need to go home and think further about what she'd said tonight and over the past several weeks.

I rose, said my goodbyes, and as I walked toward my car wondered what she thought of my abrupt departure.

88

The next morning, I woke up with the following vision in my head:

The three events—the three coups or partial coups—did not just share similar events or *modus operandi* or have similar results; they were, I now saw in my dream, linked by being sequential steps in the transformation of the United States from a republic into an empire, and from an empire into a colony. I doubted that this progression was the goal back in 1947 or even in 1963, but it had been the result, nonetheless. I suspected that the initial steps on this path were taken to deal with events of the day, but with each step taken it became more likely that additional steps would be taken in the same direction, to take advantage of opportunities that the previous steps had made possible.

Prior to 1947, the United States had been a republic whose government was intermittently influenced by powerful financial interests. In 1947, the first big steps toward establishing an American empire abroad were taken with passage of the National Security Act, which established the CIA, the NSA and the positions of Secretary of Defense and the Joint Chiefs of Staff. The following year Truman created the National Security Council by executive order. These steps also served to greatly increase the influence of the Power Elite over the activities of the government by creating within the government positions that could be filled by moles whose primary loyalty was to the Power Elite.

In 1963, the first big event, the assassination of John F. Kennedy, was undertaken to prevent him from blocking a key part of the Power Elite's plan, already drawn up, for military engagement with Communism in southeast Asia. The most important areas designated for engagement were Vietnam and resource-rich Indonesia. (The patsy in the first event was Lee Harvey Oswald.)

In 2001, the second big event, September 11, was undertaken to spark public support for the Power Elite's plans to expand the empire into new areas. Of primary importance was the war in Afghanistan needed to instill a government supportive of American extraction of resources and the safety of the pipelines the U.S. intended to run through that country from Turkmenistan to Pakistan. Like the war in Afghanistan, the war in Iraq to gain control over its oil was planned in advance of September 11. (The patsy in the second event was Osama bin Laden.)

The post-September 11 legislation served two goals. From one perspective it gave the government tools to suppress domestic opposition to its empire building activities in Afghanistan, Iraq and elsewhere. From another, those same tools could be used to change the relationship between the government and the people of the country, preparing the way for the conversion of the United States from the head of the empire (which it really ran on behalf of the Power Elite) to becoming simply another part of the empire.

It was at this point that my vision moved from the past to the future.

In 2020, the third big event, the suspension of civil liberties and implementation of rule by decree, would have, if permanent, brought under the Power Elite's control not only the government of the United States but the country itself. The United States would have become a colony of the Power Elite, with the U.S. government becoming in effect the colonial administration that oversaw the American colony on behalf of the Power Elite. (The patsy in the third event was Covid.)

At some unknown date, I saw in my vision, a fourth big event would occur. The Power Elite had been forced to pull back from the 2020 suspension of civil liberties and rule by decree, so a future event or events would be needed to complete the process of transforming the United States into full and permanent colonial status. (Patsy or patsies not yet known.)

89

Once fully awake, I realized that my vision of my country over the course of my lifetime hadn't come entirely out of nowhere, that certain things I'd learned about the recent history of the United States had come together in the form of the vision. But was it more fantastical than real? Were the three extraordinary events really coups? Had the United States really become an empire, and was it now becoming a colony? Would the future events I foresaw in my vision really happen to complete the transformation?

I set about organizing some pieces of what I'd learned recently to try to determine how things stood. I'll record here only some of the more relevant indicators of a move from a republic to an empire, and then from an empire to a colony, a full examination of these subjects being beyond the scope of this memoir.

I knew that the U.S. military operates more than 800 military bases in more than 70 countries and territories around the world.[428] And I knew that the U.S. Navy operates seven fleets. The 7th Fleet, for instance, based in Yokosuka, Japan, is the largest of the forward-deployed U.S. fleets. Were the 800 bases also operated under the authority of seven unified military commands, just as the fleets were? Either way, U.S. military forces appeared capable of projecting military force nearly anywhere on the planet at a moment's notice.

Common sense told me that no country achieves this capability by accident. It is acquired only through the most determined effort. I now learned that the U.S. Department of Defense had aimed at exactly that result. It's blueprint for the future, *Joint Vision 2020*, issued in 2000, called for "Full-spectrum dominance" by 2020. "The ultimate goal of our military force is to accomplish the objectives directed by the National Command Authorities. For the joint force of the future, this goal will be achieved through full-spectrum dominance—the ability of U.S. forces, operating unilaterally or in combination with multinational and interagency partners, to defeat any adversary and control any situation across the full range of military operations."[429]

In other words, the Department of Defense is no longer primarily concerned with defense of the United States; its primary goal is military dominance over the entire globe.

The Project for a New American Century (PNAC) appeared to regard the United States as already an empire, one whose reach it sought to expand. The original language in its 2000 publication, *Rebuilding America's Defenses*, since altered, declared that "the process of transformation [to a degree of military preparedness suitable for its new aims], even if it brings revolutionary change, is likely to be a long one, absent some catastrophic and catalyzing event—like a new Pearl Harbor."[430] Here was clearly a statement of intent to create an empire even more extensive than the one already existing, to the degree that circumstances allowed.

The PNAC was and is dominated by Republicans, but its goals were shared by Democrats, too. In 1997, three years earlier, Zbigniew Brezinski, National Security Advisor under President Carter, had written that "America is too democratic at home to be autocratic abroad. . . . Never before has a populist democracy attained international supremacy. . . . Democracy is inimical to imperial mobilization. . . . A truly massive and widely perceived direct external threat"[431] would be needed to gain public support for it. In other words, prominent members of both political parties called for "revolutionary change" toward "imperial mobilization"—that is, toward creating military forces capable of running an empire—the same goal called for in the Department of Defense planning document. Both recognized that some catastrophic event would be necessary to convince the American people to go along with it.

Only a year after the Republican document and only four years after the Democratic document, such a catastrophic event occurred on September 11, 2001. All this was in line with two conclusions I'd already been led to by Peter Dale Scott: 1) seemingly extraordinary events occur when the interests of powerful players in the Power Elite align in support of them; and 2) those events are not, in fact, extraordinary; they arise from within the Power Elite system; they're not external events forced on it.

That high officials in the George W. Bush administration after September 11 saw the United States as an empire was explicitly confirmed when a senior military aide stated as much to journalist Ron Suskind, who wrote about their conversation in the *New York Times Magazine*. "The aide said that guys like me were 'in what we call the reality-based community,' which he defined as people who 'believe that solutions emerge from your judicious study of discernible reality. . . . That's not the way the world really works anymore,' he continued. 'We're an empire now, and when we act, we create our own reality. And while you're studying that reality—judiciously, as you will—we'll act again, creating other new realities, which you can study too, and that's how things will sort out. We're history's actors . . . and you, all of you, will be left to just study what we do.'"[432]

I also recalled General Smedley Butler's statement to the effect that he had spent his career in the military fighting battles on behalf of U.S. Fruit and other American companies. That seemed similar in his day, during the first several decades of the 20th century, to the U.S. military fighting in Afghanistan to establish a safety corridor for a pipeline and for access to the minerals in which that country is rich, in the early decades of the 21st. I'd already noted that the big American military bases in Afghanistan are located along the projected path of the oil pipeline.[433]

Of course, none of these items are enough to conclude that the United States has become an empire, but they do suggest that possibility and intention.

If the United States had indeed become an empire, it had done so by moving away from the republican ideals that had guided the country in its engagement with the rest of the world in its first decades. Those ideals had rarely been stated better than in John Quincy Adams's Independence Day speech in 1821, only 32 years after the founding of the republic, and almost exactly 200 years before today. "Wherever the standard of freedom and independence has been or shall be unfurled, there will America's heart, her benedictions and her prayers be. But she goes not abroad, in search of monsters to destroy. She is the well-wisher to the freedom and independence of all. She is the champion and vindicator only of her own. She will commend the general cause by the countenance of her voice, and the benignant sympathy of her example. She well knows that by once enlisting under other banners than her own, were they even the banners of foreign independence, she would involve herself beyond the power of extrication, in all the wars of interest and intrigue, of individual avarice, envy, and ambition, which assume the colors and usurp the standard of freedom.'"

These are the principles that guided the United States until well into the 20th century. The country had moved away from them twice, to enter the two world wars, but both times returned to its traditional stance. Yes, even after the Second World War, there had been a brief period before the U.S. changed direction.

The establishment of the intelligence agencies in 1947 was a key moment in the evolution of U.S. policies away from Adams's guiding principals. The war in Korea in 1950 was another. That was the moment when the United States began to substantially increase its military forces, reversing the drawdown that had followed the end of the Second World War five years earlier. David Stockman cited 1950 as the year when "the foolish, destructive, unnecessary and fiscally calamitous Forever Wars" began. In his view, "Nearly without exception they were waged against alleged foreign monsters of the very kind which John Quincy Adams urged his countrymen not to pursue. . . . Yet without exception not one of these assorted authoritarians, dictators, tyrants, thugs and revolutionists, along with the nations they ruled, posed a direct threat to the American homeland."[434]

David Neal identified the "coup d'état" in 1963 as the key event that "set the U.S. on the course we've been on since, namely hegemony and military dominance on the world stage, driven by the needs of a thriving war machine. First the war in Vietnam, a ten-year debacle started by Lyndon Johnson in 1964, but planned years before, made a lot of money for those who promoted it, and devastated thousands of families in America and millions of people in Southeast Asia. . . . This nauseatingly tragic story could easily have been avoided had the violent coup d'état not murdered John Kennedy, and later Robert Kennedy. Every president after JFK understood, either viscerally or subliminally, this reality and was circumspect because of it. None could ignore the significance of the Zapruder film."[435]

It was in the context of that war in Vietnam that "Martin

Luther King, Jr., called the United States "the greatest purveyor of violence in the world today." Seeing his statement again brought me back to the string of 800 U.S. military bases around the world, of which Jacob Hornberger has written, "Its empire of foreign military bases plays an important role in the death and destruction wreaked by America's federal killing machine."[436] According to Brown University's Costs of War Project, those American wars have killed an estimated 4.5 million people, injured tens of millions, and displaced at least 38 million more.

I now saw that planning for this move to an empire had begun soon after the dismantling of the Soviet Union in the early 1990s, about the time I joined the Foreign Service. The so-called Wolfowitz Doctrine, given to the ideas presented in a paper prepared for the Department of Defense in 1992, declared that it was the intent of the United States to remain the world's sole superpower, that it would not permit challenges to that status, and that it would act unilaterally if and when necessary to protect its interests. Focused on diplomacy rather than the military in my career, I'd been only vaguely aware of all that at the time, and even later in my career, for that matter. It was only now, after retirement, that I was learning about the imperial ambitions of the government I had served.

It wasn't that planning for the invasion of Afghanistan and Iraq had taken place before September 11 that struck me hardest—or that the Patriot Act and other legislation had been drafted in large part before that date; it was that planning for the major shift to empire had begun during the Clinton administration, long before the election that brought the second Bush into the presidency.

"The plans for an invasion of Afghanistan in a so-called 'military option' had been . . . initiated during the Clinton administration," Ruppert reported. "It is also known that India, Russia, Pakistan, Uzbekistan, and Tajikistan had been part of the preparations for what was reportedly a joint U.S.-Russian military action against Afghanistan scheduled for October 2001. . . . Even the *Washington Post* reported that a quiet U.S. military buildup was taking place in Kazakhstan, Kyrgyzstan, and

Uzbekistan for months before the Presidential election. . . . The military option was clearly initiated under Clinton."[437]

It even appeared that the CIA's strategy of creating enemies so as to have someone to fight, as Prouty had revealed, was still being followed and had been used with the Taliban and al Qaeda. The Proactive Preemptive Operating Group (P2OG), the interface between the CIA and the Pentagon's Joint Special Operations Command, Ruppert showed, would launch covert attacks to generate responses that could then be cited as justifying overt action by the U.S. forces.[438]

Still, the United States needed a good cover story for the larger operations to take place in Afghanistan. September 11 provided that, with bin Laden the designated patsy. "Fortunately for the plotters," Ruppert noted, parts of the Clinton administration "had been protecting, grooming, and nurturing the Taliban and al Qaeda to make sure that a needed enemy would be in place for several years. . . . This need to keep al Qaeda and bin Laden in play would also explain why the Clinton administration overlooked so many opportunities to capture or neutralize bin Laden between 1998 and 2001. Osama bin Laden was going to be needed for a long time."[439]

Absorbing all this new information, I jotted down the following timeline.

Timeline: U.S. Transition to Empire

1991	Collapse of the Soviet Union.
1990s	bin Laden and al Qaeda cultivated as possible future enemies.
1997	Brezinski's book, *The Grand Chessboard.*
2000, Sept.	Project for a New American Century's report, *Rebuilding America's Defenses.*
2001, Jan-April	Bush step 1: Cheney placed in charge of newly established National Energy Policy Development Group.
2001, May-Sept.	Bush step 2: Cheney placed in charge of

	Task Force to coordinate national plan for response to terror attacks.
2001, Sept. 11	The Big Event.
2001, October	U.S. invasion of Afghanistan.
2001, fall	Passage of the USA Patriot Act and other legislation; establishment of the Department of Homeland Security.
2003	U.S. invasion of Iraq.

In the first few months of George W. Bush's presidency, I now saw, two sets of steps were taken that facilitated the events of September 11. In the first, taken in January 2001, Bush created a National Energy Task Force headed by Vice President Dick Cheney. The group's stated objective was to develop a national policy to ensure dependable supplies of energy for the country. By May, Peter Dale Scott reported, the Task Force "had already set out, urgently and in some detail, plans for taking control over Iraqi oil, . . . [giving the] impression of preparation for 9/11 and its consequent war[s]."[440]

The second step was Bush's appointment on May 8 of Cheney to oversee the development of a task force to develop a coordinated national effort against terrorism, something that I'd already noted when looking into Continuity of Government planning. If the first step had formulated the rationale for securing oil from sources in the Middle East and elsewhere, the second had created the authority, offices, procedures and other governmental infrastructure that made September 11 possible.

The Project for a New American Century, in its study, *Rebuilding America's Defenses*, had foreseen the need for transforming America's military forces and for more aggressive use of them abroad. It had also foreseen that political realities would not support such developments "absent some catastrophic and catalyzing event—like a new Pearl Harbor."

The question now, Scott asked, "is [whether] Cheney, Rumsfeld, or any others whose projects depended on 'a new Pearl Harbor' were participants in helping to create one."[441] Or, alternately, were those plans, reports and Task Forces noted in the Timeline—all aligned in support of events that occurred on September 11 and those subsequently made possible by them—merely a string of coincidences?

I'd say that with its invasion of Afghanistan soon after September 11, the United States had become a colonial power. In Jay Bookman's view, the U.S. didn't achieve that status until it attacked Iraq in 2003. Writing in 2002, a few months in advance of that attack, he wrote, "This war, should it come, is intended to mark the official emergence of the United States as a full-fledged global empire, seizing the sole responsibility and authority as a planetary policeman."[442] The U.S. entry into Iraq, he concluded, was "the culmination of a plan 10 years or more in the making, carried out by those who believe the United States must seize the opportunity for global domination, even if it means becoming the 'American imperialists' that our enemies have always claimed we were.'"

Either way, the American republic had become an empire.

90

With the American invasion of Afghanistan, the United States had demonstrated its ability and willingness to subdue and rule other countries as though they were American colonies. It had demonstrated its capacity to move massive amounts of military equipment and personnel to a land-locked country nearly halfway around the world quickly, with the implication that it could do the same anywhere else it chose to. That it targeted Afghanistan even though the country had had nothing to do with the attacks in the United States on September 11 showed how hollow its stated rationale for the invasion really was. And by refusing to provide evidence of bin Laden's guilt even though Afghanistan stated it would turn him over to the U.S. if it did so, it showed its disdain for world opinion. The United States was behaving like a true colonial power.

The British historian Arnold Toynbee had stated as long ago as 1971 that "To most Europeans, I guess, America now looks like the most dangerous country in the world. Since America is unquestionably the most powerful country, the transformation of America's image within the last thirty years is very frightening for Europeans. It is probably still more frightening for the great majority of the human race who are neither Europeans nor North Americans, but are Latin Americans, Asians, and Africans. They, I imagine, feel even more insecure than we feel. They feel that, at any moment, America may intervene in their internal affairs, with the same appalling consequences as have followed from the American intervention in Southeast Asia."[443]

"For the world as a whole," Toynbee continued, "the CIA has now become the bogey that communism has been for America. Wherever there is trouble, violence, suffering, tragedy, the rest of us are now quick to suspect the CIA had a hand in it. Our phobia about the CIA is, no doubt, as fantastically excessive as America's phobia about world communism; but in this case, too, there is just enough convincing guidance to make the phobia genuine. In fact, the roles of America and Russia have been reversed in the world's eyes. Today America has become the nightmare."

If that was how people in other countries saw the United States nearly 60 years ago, how must they see it today, after it has invaded Afghanistan and Iraq and intervened elsewhere?

Even if it's true that the entire world outside the United States held the views laid out by Toynbee, it's still true that most Americans have no idea that their country is viewed in that way. Some, like me, are starting to wake up. Since retirement from the Foreign Service, I've become much more in agreement with Caitlin Johnstone's judgment that "The U.S.-centralized empire is the most tyrannical power structure on this planet. And make no mistake, it is an empire. Washington serves as the hub of an undeclared empire comprised of alliances, partnerships, assets, public deals and secret agreements which knit a large number of nations together into what functions as a single power structure with regard to international affairs."[444]

If Americans had a fuller understanding of the extraordinary military capabilities the United States has established around the world through its string of 800 far-flung bases and seven fleets—and greater familiarity with the Wolfowitz Doctrine and the concept of Full-Spectrum

Dominance—they might become inclined to ask, "What it is all for? Are there serious dangers out there that require the United States to spend more on 'defense' than all other nations combined? Or are these 'defensive measures' the results of steps taken by paranoid madmen who have seized the reigns of power in the United States in order to create defenses against enemies that exist only in their perverted fantasies?"

David Stockman's perspective, one that I had dismissed during the course of my career but that I now agree with, is that "The whole intellectual foundation of the enterprise is false. The planet is not crawling with all-powerful would-be aggressors and empire-builders who must be stopped cold at their own borders, lest they devour the freedom of all their neighbors near and far. Nor is the DNA of nations infected with incipient butchers and tyrants like Hitler and Stalin. They were one-time accidents of history and fully distinguishable from the standard run of everyday tinpots which actually do arise periodically. But the latter mainly disturb the equipoise of their immediate neighborhoods, not the peace of the planet."[445] So," he concluded, "America's homeland security does not depend upon a far-flung array of alliances, treaties, military bases and foreign influence operations. In today's world there are no Hitlers, actual or latent, to stop."

I've come to believe that the United States could return to the foreign policy ideals laid out by John Quincy Adams, thereby reducing its intelligence-security-military budget from close to $1.5 trillion a year to a small fraction of that, with little risk of harm. A sensible country would make that reduction; an empire won't.

91

I accepted that with the wars in Afghanistan and Iraq, and the 800 military bases around the world, the United States had become an empire in all but name. But was it true, as I'd seen in my vision, that the United States itself had become a colony ruled by the the Power Elite? Was the United States government a mere colonial administrator administering the American colony in the same manner that the British Raj had administered the British colony of India in the old days, or in the same manner that the American Civilian Governor had administered The Philippines on behalf of the United States?

Absurd, I thought as I set about examining the situation from this new perspective. I realized, of course, that setting down pieces of information that were in line with the conversion of the United States into a colony was not by itself sufficient to prove that such a conversion had really taken place. But I wasn't trying to prove anything; I wanted only to know whether the idea was ridiculous and could be rejected, or whether enough credible information pointed in that direction to justify further investigation.

The first piece of information I jotted down was that the U.S. military now operates more than 800 bases *within* the borders of the United States, in addition to a similar number overseas. What possible need could there be for those bases, I wondered. The country was protected by oceans stretching 3,000 to the east and 5,000 miles to the west. Neither Canada nor Mexico was going to invade the United States, nor was it conceivable that armies from other countries would invade through them.

I recognized the benefits for the military of having bases in every state in the union; they gave every Senator and hundreds of Congressmen reasons to vote for the military's budget each year. Bases, after all, employ citizens in their states and districts and bring in other resources. A clever strategy on the military's part! But 800? Wouldn't 500 be sufficient for that purpose? Or even 200?

I also noted that the United States has a standing military force of 1.3 million active-duty personnel and another 850,000 reserve personnel. The Army, the largest of the eight uniformed services, has 1.1 million uniformed personnel; the Air Force, 496,000; the Navy, 280,000; and the Marines, 181,000.

The American colonies, I recalled, had rebelled against England in part because of its practice of basing a standing army in their territory. In enumerating the colonies' grievances against King George III in the Declaration of Independence in

1776, the founders had stated, "he has kept among us, in times of peace, Standing Armies without the Consent of our legislatures" and "has affected to render the Military independent of and superior to the Civil power."

The newly freed colonies, in 1783, had no permanent military forces. Thomas Jefferson, writing in 1789 at the time of the establishment of the United States, recognized that "There are instruments so dangerous to the rights of the nation and which place them so totally at the mercy of their governors. . . . Such an instrument is a standing army." Later, as president, he declared that "Standing armies [are] inconsistent with a people's freedom and subversive of their quest."[446] James Madison weighed in, too, observing that "A standing military force, with an overgrown executive will not be safe companions to liberty. The means of defence against foreign danger have been always the instruments of tyranny at home."

With its 800 domestic bases and more than 1.3 million active-duty soldiers, sailors and airmen, the United States had veered away from its founding principles in military matters as stated by Thomas Jefferson, just as surely as it had from its founding principles in foreign affairs as stated by John Quincy Adams.

The danger from the existence of the bases and standing army, I saw, was that once they existed the temptation to use them not just could, but would, arise. The very existence of the bases in every state in the union meant that the military could be swiftly ready for combat anywhere within the country on short notice. If there's no need to use the bases and soldiers to fight off foreign invaders, another use for them would have to be found to justify the expense of maintaining them. The only other folks around to be fought and dominated are American citizens.

I already knew that the U.S. military had been used against American citizens—well, one citizen—on November 22, 1963, during the assassination and faked autopsy of John F. Kennedy, and again against nearly 3,000 others on September 11, 2001. The likelihood that American bases and combat troops would again be used against Americans increased significantly during the Obama administration, when he issued an executive order moving the government's focus from the threat of foreign terrorism to that of domestic terrorism.

Recalling that the U.S. Navy had divided the rest of the world into seven areas, each patrolled by a U.S. fleet, it occurred to me that perhaps the U.S. military regarded the continental United States as Area 8, as territory to be militarily controlled just like the other seven areas outside our borders. Doing so would be right in line with a transition from the United States as the seat of the American empire to that of a colony under the administration of the U.S. government on behalf of the Power Elite.

In support of the idea that the U.S. military regards the United States as Area 8 and contemplates military action against American citizens, consider this: In April, 2002, the U.S. military created a new U.S. Northern Command (CINC-NORTHCOM) to implement U.S. military operations in the continental United States, Mexico and Canada, a step that Defense Secretary Donald Rumsfeld called the "the most sweeping set of changes since the unified command system was set up in 1946."[447] The NORTHCOM commander, it was announced, "will command U.S. forces that operate within the United States in support of civil authorities. The command will provide civil support not only in response to attacks, but for natural disasters." The NORTHCOM commander at the time commented that "the United States itself is now for the first time since the War of 1812 a theater of war. That means that we should apply, in my view, the same kind of command structure in the United States that we apply in other theaters of war."

This was shocking. I'd never heard anything like this before. I wondered if any other Americans not directly involved in implementing the U.S. Northern Command knew anything about it.

The U.S. military's freedom to act within the borders of the United States was greatly expanded in 2006, when the Military Commissions Act of 2006 lifted many of the restraints that had been placed on the military's actions within the country by the

Posse Comitatus Act of 1878. In 2008 the 3rd Infantry Division's 1st Brigade Combat Team was assigned to the U.S. Northern Command; it is now on call to respond to natural or manmade emergencies and disasters within the United States. Presumably President Trump's declaration of a State of Emergency last month, on March 13, was all the authorization needed for the U.S. military to become active within the borders of the United States. We appear to have entered a whole new world.

Turning to the political aspects of a transition from empire to colony, I noted that a government's relations with its own citizens is mirrored by its relations with other countries. A republic respects the rights of its citizens and deals with them through a trustworthy legal system that protects and implements the rule of law. It respects the rights of other countries and deals with them through established diplomatic procedures.

An empire, however, does not deal with other countries as equals; it regards them as subservient to itself. Can it respect the rights of its citizens if it doesn't respect the rights of other countries? Not if domestic and foreign relations are mirror images of each other.

So, what happens when a republic becomes an empire? The manner in which it deals with other counties changes, of course. That's obvious. But what hadn't been apparent to me until now was that when the government of a republic becomes an empire, its relations with its own citizens must change, too. It changes from a republic to something else.

Even recalling Zbigniew Brezinski's statement noted earlier that "America is too democratic at home to be autocratic abroad. . . . Never before has a populist democracy attained international supremacy. . . .Democracy is inimical to imperial mobilization,"[448] I was still startled to read something Hannah Arendt stated in *The Origins of Totalitarianism*: "Although tyranny, because it needs no consent, may successfully rule over foreign peoples, it can stay in power only if it destroys first of all the national institutions of its own people."[449]

If Arendt's observation is correct, and if the United States has indeed become an empire, then it would follow that the system of governance in place would change from a republic into something very different than we've ever known before. Isn't that what the legislation passed in the wake of September 11 was designed to do when it authorized unprecedented warrantless tracking and monitoring of communications of everyone in the country and the cancelling of habeas corpus? Isn't that what happened with the creation of the Department of Homeland Security? Isn't that what happened with the creation of the new U.S. Northern Command authorized to engage in military action within the United States? Isn't that what is happening all around us now, with the suspension of the Constitution and its replacement by rule by edict during the so-called Covid "emergency"?

I was startled again by Arendt's use of the word tyranny to describe the system of governance that a republic would descend to if it became an empire; and then again by how appropriate that term seemed for what our government, or our governments at all levels, have become in just the last month or two. In a republic the executive branch administers; in an empire, it rules by edicts, and what it rules is colonies. Ergo, if the country is being ruled by edicts, it must now be a colony.

Confirmation that this interpretation of recent events isn't outlandish came from Peter Dale Scott, who observed that, "We should not be surprised that [the] CIA's special powers, having done so much to impose brutes, criminals, and terrorists on other parts of the world, have weakened the cause of decency and democracy at home as well. The erosions of American civil liberties since 9/11 cannot be just blamed on the Bush administration. They are the outcome of a tension between the public state and covert notions of security, that has been deforming U.S. politics since the special powers assumed at the outset of the Cold War."[450]

"The proponents of the deep state who agreed with Oliver North that the Vietnam War was lost in Washington were waiting all along to neutralize those reforms [enacted in the post-Vietnam War years]," Scott continued. "9/11 was a victorious moment for the proponents of the deep state. And prominent in this camp, for at least two decades, have been Dick Cheney and Donald Rumsfeld."[451]

Additional confirmation that the United States had become a colony came from Michael Ruppert, who concluded that, "The entire continuum of public and private life in the United States has been transformed by 9/11, the lengthy preparations for it, the ensuing cover-up, and the massive consolidation of authoritarian policies and institutions achieved in its wake. In short, I maintain that unless this phenomenon is exposed at its roots, the fundamental changes it has wrought will become permanent. That would constitute the death of the American republic. . . . It's not just private, elite control over the legal system, nor private evasion of the rule of law. It's a crisis-induced transition from a society with a deeply compromised legal system to a society where force and surveillance completely supplant that system."[452]

At this point I came across Francis Christian's analysis of American governance, which seemed outrageous at first, but the longer I thought about it the more accurate it seemed. It suggested that the United States has become the new U.S.S.R., that the United States government oversees the country as a colony in the same manner that the government of the Soviet Union oversaw Russia as a colony. Sure Moscow, the capital of the Russian Republic/colony was located in Russia; but it also served as the capital city of the Soviet Union, which oversaw 13 internal colonies, of which Russia was one. In the same way, Washington D.C. is the capital city of the country/colony of the United States and the capital city of the Power Elite that runs a worldwide empire.

It's to hide that analogy, Christian explained, that Soviet tyranny is being airbrushed from history. The closer the United States comes to resembling the Soviet Union, the more the distinction between Russia and the U.S.S.R. is buried. "A remarkable disappearing act has taken place in the last thirty odd years since the demise of the Soviet Union in 1991," he observed. "Through a coordinated propaganda campaign by think tanks, legacy media, the internet and governments, the mass genocides, murders, terrors, tortures, incarcerations, disappearances, show trials, famines and multiplied miseries of Communism have been all but completely hidden from the masses. . . . [There has been] a desire by the ruling classes to induce a sense of mass amnesia about the horrors of Communism. Why is this?"[453]

"The answer is quite simple," Christian continued. "The ideological descendants of the same people behind the murderous Bolshevik Communist regime that brought unspeakable suffering to millions of Russians and Eastern Europeans . . . *are in charge of our Western Governments and institutions today*. The same players, the same playbook, the same international goals. They don't want you to know of the connection of course—because if you do, the similarities are so stark that you will take notice and be enraged. The Bolsheviks/Communists of today are just as determined, just as ruthless, just as efficient and likely much more powerful than their Soviet ancestors. We ignore them at our peril."

Russell Fletcher's comparison of the Soviet system, in which the government was the mere functional arm of the Party, with the American system in which the government is the mere functional arm of the Power Elite, is an even more fruitful analogy than I'd realized.

So, there it is: The republic once known as the United States of America has become an empire abroad and at home a colony—a colony administered by the U.S. government on behalf of the Power Elite.

I now saw that my original take on the Patriot Act was wrong. I had seen it as an attempt to create the legal infrastructure needed to silence critics of the wars that the United States launched in the wake of September 11. Now I saw that Act and other related legislation as part of the application of "full-spectrum dominance" to the United States itself. Full-spectrum dominance, I now saw, meant "the ability of U.S. forces, operating unilaterally or in combination with multinational and interagency partners, to defeat any adversary and control any situation across the full range of military operations"[454] within as well as outside the territory of the United States.

92

Every well-run colonial administration expects the colony it administers to pay the costs of that administration and to produce additional revenue that it will forward to the owners of the colony. That was true of the British Raj in India, and it's true of the American colony administered by the U.S. government on behalf of the Power Elite today.

I'd already noted General Smedley Butler's observation that the armed forces had been used to further the interests of large American commercial firms, important players within the Power Elite *outside* the government. "War is a Racket," Butler wrote in a speech, later published as a book with the same title. "It always has been. It is possibly the oldest, easily the most profitable, surely the most vicious. It is the only one international in scope. It is the only one in which the profits are reckoned in dollars and the losses in lives. . . . Though war is indeed profitable for the financiers and industrialists who champion it, it is invariably a disaster for a free citizenry."[455]

More recently I'd noted that wars were now being fought for the benefit of important Power Elite players *inside* the government. "The series of so-called wars since 1945 were never fought to achieve victory," Prouty observed. "They were waged for dollars, without a true military objective, under the control of civilian leaders, with the generals in a supernumerary role."[456] He calculated that the war in Vietnam generated six trillion dollars, in 2011 dollars, for its beneficiaries. The much smaller war in Afghanistan launched in 2001 and still ongoing has already generated more than two trillion dollars. In both cases the funds have flowed largely to the same players within the Power Elite—those within the Military-Industrial Complex.

Peter Dale Scott wrote an entire book, *The War Conspiracy*, to show that in his analysis America's involvement in two disastrous wars, in Vietnam and Iraq, "was not an outcome of the people's will, but rather in large part of deep events that were used to manipulate that will:"[457] the assassination of John F. Kennedy, which created the conditions leading directly to the war in Vietnam, and the events of September 11, which created the conditions for the wars in Afghanistan and Iraq.

James Madison had warned about the dangers that wars pose for a republic. "Of all the evils to public liberty, war is perhaps the most to be dreaded, because it comprises and develops every other. War is the patent of armies; from these proceed debts and taxes. And armies, and debts, and taxes, are the known instruments for bringing the many under the dominion of the few. In war, too, the discretionary power of the executive is extended; its influence in dealing out offices, honors, and emoluments is multiplied; and all the means of seducing the minds are added to those of subduing the force of the people! No nation could preserve its freedom in the midst of continual warfare.'"[458]

Most Americans, it appears, don't yet recognize that, in Caitlin Johnstone's words, "the U.S. empire is not a national government which happens to run nonstop military operations; it's a nonstop military operation that happens to run a national government."[459] Until recently I'd have dismissed this view. But now I fully believe, with her, that these wars are "not waged to benefit the American people or their security, but to benefit the . . . U.S. empire, which has very little in common with the U.S. as an individual nation. . . . Until you understand this, nothing the U.S. government or the U.S. war machine does will make sense."

Jeffrey Sachs reached a similar conclusion. "The $1.5 trillion in military outlays is the scam that keeps on giving—to the Military-Industrial Complex and the Washington insiders—even as it impoverishes and endangers America and the world. To understand the foreign-policy scam, think of today's federal government as a multi-division racket: . . . The Wall Street division is run out of the Treasury. The Health Industry division is run out of the Department of Health and Human Services. The Big Oil and Coal division is run out of the Departments of Energy and Interior. And the Foreign Policy division is run out of the White House, Pentagon and CIA."[460]

So how does the Power Elite get away with it? "The first such measure is unrelenting propaganda. . . . The second is to hide the costs of the foreign policy operations." It did this by making "military service a job for hire" and recruiting soldiers from lower economic strata and by shifting "the military budget to deficit spending which protects it from popular opposition that would be triggered if it were tax-funded." It succeeded in this effort because "this system is underpinned by the complete subordination of the U.S. Congress to the war business, to avoid any questioning of the over-the-top Pentagon budgets and the wars instigated by the Executive Branch."

"It is the urgent task of the American people," Sachs concluded. "to overhaul a foreign policy that is so broken, corrupted, and deceitful that it is burying the government in debt while pushing the world closer to nuclear Armageddon."

Warnings are coming fast and furious from respected public figures. But is anyone listening? I am, now.

93

I hadn't seen Gina for nearly a week when I stopped by Words to pick up more financial documents and to see how she and the studio were faring. Mike told me that Gina had gone home in the morning, sick, and had cancelled all her tutoring sessions that would be held there, surreptitiously, and in student's homes for the rest of the day, and that he would be filling in for her on some of them. I was immediately alarmed. Gina wouldn't have cancelled sessions and lost tutoring income unless she was severely unwell. I wondered if she had Covid; if so, she'd be the first person I knew who had severe Covid symptoms, as opposed to merely testing positive on a flawed test, among everyone I was in contact with—family, long-time friends and former Foreign Service colleagues.

Mike had another hour free before his next tutoring session, so I asked him to go with me to Gina's apartment. I knew where it was but had never been inside, just like she'd never been in my house, following her rule never to be alone with a suitor in a private place.

"My fever and headaches are getting more intense," she said when she saw me. We were talking in the living room while Mike, our chaperone, waited at some distance, in the entryway. "I've had them for a full week, and today was the most intense yet. The cold medicine hasn't helped at all. It doesn't relieve the pain and only makes me sleepy."

"Have you seen a doctor?" I asked, remaining focused on Gina while at the same time glancing at the bookcases filled with books against the far wall.

"No," she said, with some frustration. "I called a Filipina nurse I know last night to check up on me. She wanted me to go to the hospital, but I can't. I must not miss any more work, but I'm not ready to pay any hospital bills. This is a time when I badly need work. I'm so stressed and scared. What will happen to me and my studio?"

She closed her eyes and sank back on the sofa, wrapping her robe more tightly around her. She seemed to have the symptoms I associate with the flu, but her case appeared to be exceptionally severe. I wondered again if she'd contracted the dreaded Covid virus, which I'd gathered produced symptoms similar to those produced by the flu.

"Get dressed, Gina," I told her. "You're going to see a doctor." She started to protest that she couldn't afford to do so, but I waved that away. "Let's worry about that later. The important thing is to find out what's wrong and get you back on your feet."

We dropped Mike off at WORDS and then Gina and I headed into what was to be quite a bizarre experience at the medical clinic.

Gina was not allowed to enter the clinic until she'd had a Covid test while in the car. The technician giving the test wore a face mask and a plastic face shield, and a hazardous materials suit that covered all of his clothes except his hands, over which he wore surgical gloves. He administered the test while standing at full arm's length from her, as though she might have the Black Plague. Then, after the results were known and she'd tested positive, she wasn't allowed to enter the clinic.

The doctor, without examining her in person, and on the

basis solely of a short phone conversation with her and the positive result on the test—a test known to produce many false positives for every real case of Covid, as I've noted—concluded that she had Covid. She then prescribed no treatment or medicine other than those available over the counter.

Now I was angry. Gina had Covid, supposedly, but the doctor and the clinic weren't prescribing any medicine? I'd already lost a wife by not challenging a diagnosis by a doctor. I wasn't going to make that mistake again.

"Come on, Gina," I said. "We're going into the clinic." I walked around to her side of the car and helped her get out and walk to the door.

Gina stopped to take a mask from her bag, and then we entered. Immediately the staff was on alert and almost panicky, first, because I wasn't wearing a mask, and then because Gina had tested positive for Covid. The receptionist told me that I had to put a mask on immediately and motioned toward two boxes of them on the counter.

"I'm not sick. I don't have Covid, so I don't need a mask," I said, to which they again told me I had to leave immediately if I didn't put one on. "I'll leave if a doctor agrees to examine my friend in person," I said. "A phone conversation and reliance on a test known to be grossly flawed is not an acceptable way to diagnose her illness."

After a nurse escorted Gina to an examination room, I turned to leave. But then I turned back, determined to say what was on my mind.

"What's with this clinic?" I asked. "Is Covid so dangerous that my friend can't enter it and be examined in person by a doctor? So dangerous that the technician has to dress up in that ridiculous costume and act in that ridiculous way? But if it's so dangerous, then why is no medicine or treatment prescribed? There's a contradiction here."

Shaking my head at the ridiculousness of it all, I said, "You're all trained medical professionals, aren't you? So why is this clinic engaging in these ridiculous medical theatrics over a virus no more deadly than the flu?"

Turning to leave as the staff continued to try to shoo me out, I glanced at the boxes of masks on the counter.

"Will you look at that!" I said with a harsh laugh. "That box says, 'intended for general, non-medical use,' yet its masks are being distributed in a medical clinic! And the other one says, 'effective protection against pollen, mold, bacteria.' Neither box says anything about protection against viruses, yet you all insist that I wear one of them? Unbelievable!"

Twenty minutes later Gina came out. After an in-person examination, the doctor had diagnosed her with borderline pneumonia and prescribed a strong medicine appropriate for it. I was relieved. We stopped at a pharmacy to pick up the medicine, and then I took Gina home. I said goodbye at the door, not wanting to trespass on her sensibilities.

Two days later I stopped by WORDS. Gina was there, sitting quietly in her office. Her tutoring classes hadn't yet begun. When she saw me, she jumped up and came to the door to guide me to the chair in front of her desk. In doing so, she held my arm, just

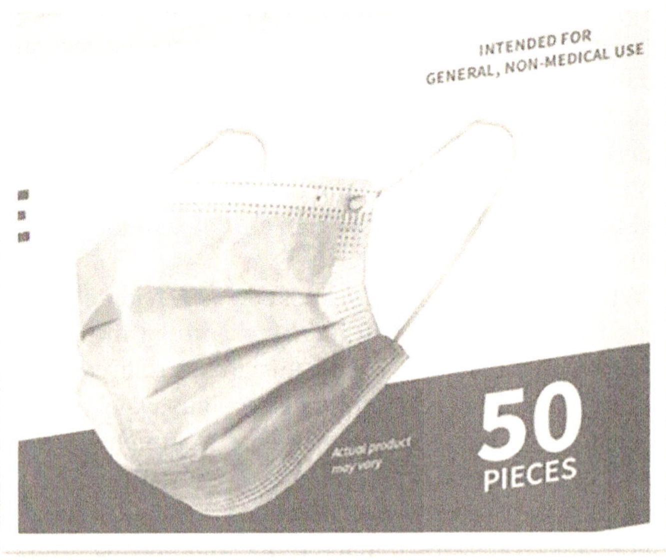

Image 30. Box of masks in the medical office stating "INTENDED FOR GENERAL, NON-MEDICAL USE."

as she had at Maja's engagement party. I could see that although she wasn't fully back to normal, most of her usual vitality had returned.

"I don't know how to thank you enough for caring for me, Jubal," she said. "I suspect it was your concern, your taking the time to take me to see a doctor, as much as the medicine she prescribed, that was responsible for my quick recovery. I'd been so overwhelmed by my worries and burdens. Right now, I can't express it properly, but please know that you make me feel safe and happy."

"I'm just glad and relieved to see you nearly back to normal, Gina," I said.

Before I could say more, she continued, laughing as she spoke. "The doctor and I could hear every word you said to the receptionist and nurses!" But then she became serious. "She explained that as an employee of the clinic, she has to follow the protocols set by the clinic, even when they conflict with her own best medical judgment. She's quite distressed about that but doesn't know quite what to do about it. Her hands are tied."

"Well, I expect that that's a more common situation than those of us outside the medical community realize," I said. "People are afraid to speak out. I'm just glad that she agreed to examine you and to change the diagnosis to something that would allow her to prescribe medicine that helped you."

I saw Gina glance at the clock and realized that it was almost time for her next tutoring session. As she walked out to the door with me, again grasping my arm as we walked, she said. "And thank you so much for paying for the doctor and the medicine, Jubal. I don't know what I would have done without you."

94

Thinking further about how this transformation of the American system of governance came about, I came up with the concept of Third-Party Interventions.

In the American republic, the president, elected by the citizens of the country as a whole and assisted by his appointed staff, carries out the laws and policies enacted by a Congress whose members were elected by citizens in various electoral districts. American citizens had some control over their president and representatives because if they didn't pay enough attention to their constituents' wants and needs, they could be replaced by others who would. The system worked well until something went awry.

What went awry, I saw, was that third parties intervened. Special interests stepped in between citizens and elected officials with campaign contributions in amounts far larger than most constituent donors could match. Those contributions from special interests, so critical to winning elections, came with strings attached. Candidates for office, and office holders, turned to courting the donors rather than the voters. This situation worsened beyond measure after the U.S. Supreme Court, in its Citizens United ruling in 2010, declared that corporations have the same right to provide campaign contributions as citizens. Large corporations could provide vastly more funding to candidates than individual voters; that's especially the case when national corporations intervene in state and local elections. The constituents in those districts have effectively lost their say because of interventions by outsiders.

I saw other forms of intervention at work, too. In the old days, regulatory agencies had been forbidden from accepting outside funding. Today they're allowed to accept funding from the very companies they're supposed to regulate. Seventy-five percent of one large agency's budget comes from such funds. This intervention weakens if not cuts the connection between those agencies and the president they supposedly serve and the Congress that provides their basic funding. Their loyalty has been corrupted.

The Constitution as originally enacted gave states the power to appoint senators, enabling the states to play a role in the legislation passed by the federal government. The 17th Amendment, enacted in 1913, changed all that. Senators are now elected directly by voters, making possible the intervention by special interest donors that I've already noted.

The power of the states to check abuses by the federal

government has been weakened by yet another form of intervention. Federal grants to states come with mandates, providing the means through which the federal government intervenes between the citizens in each state and their state government. Federal funds distributed to the states for highway construction, for instance, at one time came with a requirement that recipient states enforce a speed limit of 55 miles per hour regardless of what the people of the state wanted or what speeds safety engineers determined were safe on each particular road. With interventions of these types far more common than half a century ago, state governments are in danger of becoming merely local branches of the federal government, thereby destroying the distinctive feature of the American system of governance known as Federalism.

The Power Elite's placement of moles in government agencies is another form of intervention, as is the corruption of other officials through bribery and blackmail. The use of blackmail should not be underestimated. Tucker Carlson recently observed that "Members of Congress are terrified of the intel agencies. . . . They've told me that, including people who run the Intel Committee." "Whenever you have unelected people who are not accountable to anyone making the biggest decisions," Carlson continued, "you don't have a democracy. You have something else, another system. I would call it a tyranny. . . . If you look at the committee chairmen who allow this sh*t [warrantless spying] to happen, year after year after year, they're all—people say they're [all]—being compromised or blackmailed."[461]

Interventions by security agencies also block whistle-blowers from passing information about corrupt or immoral governmental actions on to the public. Michael C. Ruppert cited one former CIA agent who explained to him how the process worked. "The ideal 'solution' for the dark forces is the gratuitous possibility that the target of discreditation, if subjected to the most personally embarrassing and social reprehensible kind of (false) allegation, might self-destruct—thus reinforcing the concocted aura of suspicion and negating the necessity for further character assassination. This is standard MO [*modus operandi*] for the Agency's counter-intelligence operations and has become a blueprint for other federal entities as a means of quieting the most threatening whistle-blowers. Lo be it if you have any kind of vulnerability (or skeleton in the closet!) This is particularly the case in matters of sex or moral turpitude. How many have been taken out by suicide, devastated mentally or emotionally and institutionalized, or sought some escape in drugs and alcohol? Lives destroyed in one way or another in the pursuit of truth—by false accusation."[462]

Criminal law has also become corrupted by governments' intervention between victims and those who have perpetrated crimes against them. Citizens in a republic have renounced the practice of revenge or vigilante justice in return for the state's prosecuting perpetrators on their behalf. But often the state's intervention makes redress for victims impossible. If a court fines the perpetrators, the fine goes to the court, not the victim. Those who can't pay the fine go to jail. It's pretty hard to recover damages by filing a civil case once a criminal case has either drained the perpetrator of his assets or jailed him.

With these examples of how interventionism has transformed the American system of governance in mind—only a few of the many I might have cited—I've come to believe that Hannah Arendt was right on the money when she'd observed that tyrannical governments that manage empires, stay "in power only by destroying first of all the national institutions of their own people."[463]

The United States continues to have the appearance of a republic, allowing casual observers to believe they still live in a country with such a system of governance, just as Wily E. Coyote still believed there was solid ground beneath his feet even after he'd run off a cliff in pursuit of the Roadrunner. The system has been hollowed out over the course of my lifetime. The oppressive post-September 11 legislation and the current lockdowns and rule by edict are only the most visible and most dramatic shifts among the many steps that, taken together, constitute the transformation from a republic to a colony—a colony ruled by a colonial administrator known as the U.S. government on behalf of the Power Elite. Or so it seemed in my vision.

95

The same destructive practice of third-party intervention now exists in many aspects of American life outside of politics and governance. In theory, patients have some control over their doctors just like voters in theory have over their elected officials. Doctors who are attentive to their patients prosper; those who aren't, will see patients drift away to other doctors. At least that's how it used to be. But now third parties have intervened. Big drug companies often pay commissions—bribes, I'd call them—to doctors to prescribe their drugs. Some doctors these days receive more in bribes than in fees from patients. You can guess to whom they give their primary loyalty.

In the old days, patients were billed directly by doctors and suppliers of medical equipment such as wheelchairs and glasses; there was a direct flow of money from patients to doctors. Those who had medical insurance would then request reimbursement from their insurance companies. But now, with insurance companies paying doctors and providers of medical equipment directly, those third parties have intervened between patients and doctors. Doctors tend to give their primary loyalty to the insurance companies who pay them, rather than patients, who often come to be seen as necessary nuisances they must endure to get the payments from the insurance companies.

Intervention of another sort is forcing doctors, who have traditionally run private practices, to close them and become employees of large corporations. Medicare reimburses doctors with independent practices at a rate far below those who work as employees at large hospitals. For the average doctor in private practice, this underpayment totals $114,000 per year.[464]

Once doctors have become employees, their employers intervene between them and their patients. As employees, they must follow the directives of their employers rather than rely on their own experienced medical judgment in diagnosing and treating their patients. As employees, they become mere technicians applying treatments and prescribing drugs according to inflexible protocols.

I'd already seen that Gina's doctor, bound by the clinic's protocols, had been prohibited from even examining in person patients who had tested positive for Covid. By taking the legitimate steps of examining Gina in person and reaching a diagnosis other than Covid, Gina's doctor had apparently put at risk her job and possibly even her medical license. I've already noted the trouble doctors who prescribed Ivermectin and Hydroxychloroquine can get into, even though much evidence shows these drugs to be effective against Covid.

From the Covid lockdowns I'd become aware of other instances of third-party interventions in the economic and commercial areas. Governments had intervened between store owners and customers, with small businesses forced to close even though large stores selling the same products were allowed to remain open. Many of them faced bankruptcy as they still had rent and other overhead costs to cover, and trained employees to keep on staff so that they'd be available to work once the lockdowns ended. Gina, I knew, was only one of millions of people suffering in this situation.

Even though millions of owners of small businesses found their livelihoods destroyed, I'd seen that not a single government employee had lost even a nickel of income during the lockdowns. Although government offices were closed, employees were told to work from home as best they could, at full salary. The same practice applies to employees at many large companies whose offices were closed. It's small companies, those owned by families and individuals, that are suffering the most.

Landlords, too, are seeing their lives destroyed by orders to the effect that tenants are freed from having to pay rent during the Covid "emergency." Yet landlords must still cover property taxes, mortgages and maintenance costs, all without rental revenue coming in. Never before had I seen contracts between private individuals declared invalid. How many landlords are watching their hard-earned equity in their property, built up slowly for years or decades, being wiped out? How many are facing bankruptcy and the loss of their property? The numbers must be huge, and I would have been one of them if I hadn't retired and moved back into my house, which had been rented out while Diana and I were overseas.

Thomas Jefferson had believed that an independent source of income was essential to the health of the republic that he'd helped found. Yet now it's small businesses, which generate incomes independent from the government and large corporations, that are being driven out of business. Was destroying these independent sources of income the goal all along? It sure seemed that way. Those folks will have little choice but to go to work for large corporations or governments at one level or another, thereby losing the independence they'd enjoyed as business owners.

I suddenly realized that this effort to destroy independent sources of income was not new or unprecedented at all. It fit right in line with government efforts over the past several decades to the same effect. I recalled reading that in some states franchises would henceforth be regarded as local branches of the franchise company, in violation of all past practice and in destruction of private contracts. In those states, the owners of local businesses that had purchased franchise rights—from companies such as McDonalds, Burger King, or Baskin Robbins—were turned into mere employees of those large corporations.

Other lines of independent sources of income are also being squashed, I saw. Independent contractors and freelancers are finding it much harder to remain in that status. Uber and Lyft were forced to treat the independent contractors who drive for them as employees, not contractors. These new laws greatly increase the cost of their services, forcing the companies to raise their prices to a level comparable with taxis, thereby depriving customers of cheap sources of transportation and contractors of their independence. People who rent rooms in their homes for short-term periods, too, face onerous rules and regulations making it more difficult and more expensive to conduct this type of independent business.

Now comes a report showing that "The Labor Department recently imposed 300 pages of new regulations "to reclassify many individual contractors as payroll employees." Beyond the loss of contractors' independence and flexibility, "what followed was what usually happens when politicians pass bad laws. Politically connected people pay lawyers and lobbyists to exempt them. Truck drivers got an exemption from California's new law. So did writers, photojournalists, graphic designers, illustrators, musicians and more than a hundred other professions. Uber and Lyft got exemptions, too."[465] With so many categories of contractors receiving exemptions, the whole process smacks of being a shake-down operation by the state government. The only winners in this operation are politicians who've been bought off and larger companies who are freed from competition from smaller, more aggressive competitors.

I recalled reading that in some states a six-month course at a beauty school is required simply to braid a neighbors' hair for pay. I even read of one state that made it illegal to comb a horse's hair for pay without holding a veterinarian's license. Examples of governmental interventions between private persons to suppress independent incomes appear to be uncountable.

"Even worse," Jacob Hornberger observed, is "the psychological mindset of dependency on the federal dole that the federal government has produced and nurtured within the American people."[466] The federal welfare state, Social Security, Medicare—all come between people and their own Principality by placing them "in a politically narcotized state in which they become convinced that they would never survive without their dole. In that way, they are less equipped, psychologically, to oppose the actions of the federal government, especially those of the national-security establishment (the Pentagon, CIA, and NSA)." How right Jefferson had been in recognizing the importance of independent sources of income.

As these examples show, the United States has been transformed from a country in which all economic activity was permitted unless it violated other laws, such as contracting for murder does, to a society in which many ordinary activities have become illegal without first obtaining a license or permit. This top-down overregulation of the American economy has steadily increased over the course of my lifetime. Colonials have little recourse against arbitrary regulations imposed by colonial administrators. That's as true here as in other colonies.

96

Most distressing of all was not the political colonialization or economic colonialization I observed, but the mental colonialization. Mental serfdom. Call it what you will, it all came down to being unable or unwilling to trust the testimony of one's own eyes, of waiting to be told what to think, what to believe or what to do. It was the opposite of Principality.

I still remember a sentence in Thomas Wolfe's novel *Look Homeward Angel* that I memorized when I was 18 years old. "He was the last of the giants, the last of the men to whom we give the faith of our youth, believing like children that the riddle of our lives might be solved by their quiet judgments."

The narrator is expressing sentiments characteristic of a young man on the cusp of full manhood, who refers to someone he admires as "the *last* of the giants to whom we give the faith of our *youth*," implying that his youth is already coming to an end and that he is on the verge of becoming able and willing to form his own judgments about how best to make his way in the world. I'd say he's on the verge of becoming a Principal.

Wolfe's book was published in 1929. Eighty-five years later, in 2014, William Deresiewicz published a book titled *Excellent Sheep: The Miseducation of the American Elite and the Way to a Meaningful Life*. In it he reported that his students at Yale, though smart, had learned only how to be good students, not how to use their minds independently. "Most of them," he wrote, "seemed content to color within the lines that their education had marked out for them. Very few were passionate about ideas. Very few saw college as part of a larger project of intellectual discovery and development, one that they directed by themselves and for themselves."[467]

Reading this, I recalled again Eric Larsen's observation that since television was introduced into American life in the 1940s, "Americans have been steadily and purposively taught, encouraged, and indoctrinated to be more passive than active, more consumer than doer, and to see life and 'reality' not as they actually are but as the mass media have already pre-defined and pre-packaged them."[468]

That subservient mindset or disposition or attitude is, again, the opposite of Principality, of actively seeking the information needed to make informed decisions, of examining previously held beliefs to determine whether they're still valid, and of acting on the basis of our own judgments even in the face of pressure not to.

That many people distrust the testimony of their own eyes in favor of unexamined ideas absorbed from the media is obvious. How else to explain those who unthinkingly accept the Magic Bullet theory in which a bullet changed direction twice in mid air while causing five severe wounds to two men before ending up in pristine condition? How else to explain those who have accepted the idea that minor fires caused three modern high-rise buildings in New York City to collapse into their own footprints at nearly freefall speed even though videos show clear evidence that they were exploded from within and turned to dust?

How else to explain those who accept that a virus less harmful than the flu for anyone below the age of 80 not already suffering from life threatening illnesses is so dangerous that its existence justifies lockdowns that throw 30 million people out of work and shutter three million small businesses even though large businesses are allowed to remain open? And that justify the suspension of the political and legal systems of the country in favor of rule by decree or edict?

Unthinking acceptance of these false narratives is what I'd expect from people living in colonial status or in the third world dictatorships that I lived in for so many years.

Perhaps I shouldn't be surprised, though. Students today have significantly weaker reading and math skills than those a few decades ago, a decline shown by testing results over the course of my adult lifetime. They also have less knowledge of the history and government of their own country. The titles and subtitles of reports by the American Council of Trustees and Alumni say it all: *No U.S. History? How College History Departments Leave the United States Out of the Major* (2016) and *Losing America's Memory: Historical Illiteracy in the 21st Century* (2000). Reports issued by the Intercollegiate Studies Institute tell a similar story: *The Coming Crisis in Citizenship: Higher Education's Failure to Teach America's History and Institutions* (2006).

This gap in this crucial area of knowledge is just what I'd expect to find in an educational system overseen by a colonial government subservient to the Power Elite. Writing after the September 11 coup but before the Covid coup, Professor Eric Larsen expressed a similar idea: "Americans *must* be kept blind every minute of every day of every month of every year to the fundamental truth that their country is run and ruled by criminal plutocrats whose greatest and most despised and feared natural enemy is—yes, a conscious, informed, knowledgeable, *thinking* population."[469]

Censorship is the norm in third world countries and becoming the norm in the United States. Yet censorship has been misunderstood. The point of it is not to prevent people from *speaking* or *writing*, but to block all of us from *receiving* information or ideas contrary to the official story. Information, along with willpower and determination, is essential for Principality. Hence the relevance of Thomas Jefferson's well-known observation, "If a nation expects to be ignorant and free in a state of civilization, it expects what never was and never will be."

The intellectual corruption that flows from the failure to acknowledge the reality of the three coups and to recognize the country's decline into colonial status has seeped deep into the intellectual and artistic life of the country. The arts "are so fundamentally, radically, profoundly important," Eric Larsen explained, because "their chief task—a task that, in any healthy culture, constitutes the highest of callings—is to tell, show, manifest, or reveal the truth. . . . Any 'arts,' that fail to be constituted in this way or fail to exist for the purpose of being, showing, manifesting, consisting of, or revealing truth . . . are, in a word, phony."[470]

Writing of September 11, Larsen observed that "The creation of a true, real, or significant literature is impossible when a people lives or is forced to live in ignorance of the whole truth of their own lives, of their nation's life, and of all the lives of those they live among. For so long as America remains a nation straitened, encumbered, and diminished by its idiotically determined dedication to a cheap lie . . . neither it nor its people can or will be productive in the arts in any way except in that same way as they live. Cheaply and falsely."[471]

Cultural and intellectual activities are at this moment beyond corrupted; they have been cancelled outright by the edicts that have locked down much of the country. I've already noted that musicians and actors of all kinds are out of work. Opera and ballet companies, symphony orchestras, the theater, schools and universities, libraries, art galleries and museums—anything related to the higher reaches of the human mind—have been forcibly shuttered. Churches and institutions dedicated to the higher reaches of the human spirit have been likewise closed.

I'd already accepted the idea that it isn't necessary during wartime and other difficult circumstances "to exclude entirely from our lives those interests and pursuits which, in peace time, make life worth living."[472] To curtail these worthy activities before we're absolutely forced to is to spiritually impoverish ourselves. In sacrificing the intellectual and artistic parts of our lives unnecessarily, we have acted in a servile and cowardly manner. We have acted as one might expect a colonized people to act.

It's the betrayal by academia that rankles most. Even with the tenure that protects their positions, very few professors have dared to examine the events of September 11 with much honesty. David A. Hughes reported that "International Relations (IR) scholars uncritically accept the official narrative regarding the events of 9/11 and refuse to examine the massive body of evidence generated by the 9/11 truth movement."[473] "A near-total silence has descended over academia when it comes to questioning the official 9/11 narrative," he observed. "This is especially worrying given the largely voluntary nature of that silence. There is no enforced consensus as there was, say, in Nazi Germany. . . . Instead, academics are choosing to self-censor, voluntarily conforming to an official 9/11 narrative. . . . If 9/11 was a false flag event, then academics have been complicit in maintaining the pretense that it was not. By extension, they are complicit in the horrific consequences that have flowed from 9/11, because they have failed to challenge the Great Lie on which everything was based."[474]

Failing to come to terms with the reality of what has happened corrupts the soul of America. "The death of conscience, the death of wholeness, the death of perceptiveness, and, corollary to all these, the death of art, truth, intellectual dignity, of the self, politics, freedom, liberty, of the republic; of America; and, if things continue unchecked in the direction they're now going, perhaps far more than only these."[475] Prescient words, these, written by Eric Larsen in 2009, 11 years ago, about the collapse of American culture that is happening all around us, before our very eyes.

What we need in America, Jacob Hornberger concluded, "is not a citizenry that buries its head in the sand and pretends that everything is okay with our country. What we need is a critical mass of people with the courage and intestinal fortitude to acknowledge and confront the evil that came with the national-security state governmental structure that was foisted upon our nation, including its dark-side power of assassination, and who have the courage and will to restore our nation's founding governmental system of a limited-government republic. That's how we get our nation on the road toward liberty, peace, prosperity, and harmony."[476]

"Insouciant Americans"—that's the most telling and succinct phrase I've heard yet describing why today's dismal situation exists. Paul Craig Roberts has used the phrase repeatedly in his commentaries on American domestic and foreign policies over the last several decades. Examples include:

✦ "Having watched the insouciant American public for a lifetime, I have been convinced by them that they are incapable of defending their liberty and incapable of recognizing the challenges to their liberty. They forever fall for the 'foreign enemy' pitch of the ruling establishment. Insouciance is inconsistent with liberty."[477]

✦ "Then we had the orchestrated 'Covid Pandemic' that used propaganda and fear to accustom Western people to the removal of their freedoms and Constitutional civil liberty protections in order 'to be safe.' And again the insouciant Western peoples fell for it, and again diminished their liberties."[478]

✦ "And what happens? Nothing. The American people continue to be insouciant dumbshits who are unconcerned that their liberties are being erased as they sit using social media, watching CNN, ABC, CBS, listening to NPR, reading the *NYTimes*, *Washington Post*. Instead of defending their liberties, they submit to brainwashing and indoctrination by the forces of tyranny and support those who deceive them with their patronage. A country with a population this stupid has no future."[479]

✦ "Time and time and time again, insouciant Americans allow the prestitutes to brainwash, indoctrinate, and deceive them. Afterwards they, or some of them, eventually catch on. But despite lessons learned, another precedent that erodes truth and liberty has been established. And despite lessons learned they will sit in front of their TV screens for their next brainwashing and indoctrination by the presstitutes who serve the ruling oligarchy by deceiving Americans."[480]

✦ "How did a people intended by their founders to be the most free in human history end up subservient to official narratives that destroy their freedom, their health, their independence? Why is the American population content with its impotence and loyal to a government that is unaccountable to the people? The only answer is that the insouciant American population has zero awareness of their situation. When people don't understand that they are threatened, how can they resist a threat of which they are unaware? . . . America has been overthrown by the insouciance of the population."[481]

I was only saddened but not surprised, given this situation, to learn that at least the first eight books casting doubt on the official but false September 11th narrative were written not by Americans revealing the truth about the recent history of their own country, but by persons who were not American and who lived outside the United States:

In 2002:* (see note below)

In England, Nafeez M. Ahmed's *The War on Freedom: How and Why America Was Attacked, September 11, 2001.*

In England, David Icke *Alice in Wonderland and the World Trade Center Disaster: Why the Official Story of 9/11 is a Monumental Lie.*

In France, Thierry Meyssan's *9/11: The Big Lie* (*Effroyable Imposture: 11 Septembre 2001*) (*The Appalling Imposture*).

In France, Thierry Meyssan's *Pentagate.*

In Germany, Mathias Bröckers's *Verschwörungen, Verschwörungstheorien, und die Geheimnisse des 11.9* (*Conspiracies, Conspiracy Theories, and the Secrets of 9/11*).

In 2003:

In Italy, Urbano Pilar's *Jefe Atta (El Secreto de la Casa Blanca).*

In Germany, Andrew von Bülow's *Die CIA und der 11. September: Internationaler Terror und die Rolle der Geheimdienste.*

In Germany, Gerhard Wisnewski's *Operation 9/11: Angriff auf den Globus.*

The first book by an American challenging the official narrative of September 11 to be published in the United States was David Ray Griffin's *The New Pearl Harbor*, released early in 2004. Michael C. Ruppert's *Crossing the Rubicon: The Decline of the American Empire at the End of the Age of Oil* followed soon after. In it, Ruppert laid out his findings as effectively as any first-rate prosecutor, identifying who had the motive, means, and opportunity to commit the crimes of September 11. In doing so he tied those events so tightly to America's imperial activities around the globe both before and after that day, and to the American government's ongoing effort to undermine civil liberties at home, that his book remains essential reading even today, 16 years after it was published. (Also published in 2004 were Paul Thompson's *The Terror Timeline* and Jim Hoffman and Don Paul's, *Waking Up from Our Nightmare*.)

Ruppert's 146-minute film, *The Truth and Lies of 9/11*, released in 2002, only a year after that terrible day, was the earliest video I know of to expose the 9/11 myths. Based on a public lecture given on November 28, 2001 that tied September 11 to fears about the consequences of the world running out of oil, it showed the persuasiveness of Rupert's "strategy of using only government documents, official statements or verifiable press reports as the basis for his work." That approach struck me as similar to Vincent Salandria's, whose work exposed internal contradictions within the Warren Report.

Michael Ruppert committed suicide on April 13, 2014, apparently after being overwhelmed by despair at how little he had achieved through so many years of intense and frustrating effort to alert his fellow American to the dangers they and their country faced.[482] Surely every scholar and researcher who has attempted to bring to light the truth of what happened to John F. Kennedy, of what happened on September 11 and of the absurdity of governments' responses to Covid has been frustrated by the insouciance of the American people, who have allowed these things to happen.

This, then, is how I interpreted or fleshed out the political, economic and psychic/intellectual implications of the vision I'd had of the American colony overseen by the U.S. government on behalf of its colonial masters.

*It was only in the final weeks of writing this memoir that I discovered that the list of first books about what really happened on September 11 is incomplete. The first book published by an American, which might have been the very first book of all, was Eric Hufschmid's *Painful Questions: An Analysis of the September 11th Attack*, published in 2002. Even at that early date, Hufschmid built solid cases for most of the most important factors cited by later 9/11 Truth scholars and researchers to show the falsity of the official story about September 11. Backed up by nearly 200 photos and diagrams, this book is one of the most important ever published on what really happened.

Hufschmid followed up his book with *Painful Deceptions: An Analysis of the September 11th Attack*, a two-hour documentary analyzing the truth behind the cover stories of WTC 7, the Pentagon attack and the World Trade Center towers that remains one of the most important and persuasive documentaries ever produced on September 11.

I became aware of Eric Hufschmid and his work only at the tail end of my extensive and dedicated research into September 11 in part because the most important later researchers inexplicably failed to mention him or it. David Ray Griffin, Michael C. Ruppert, Webster Tarpley, Peter Dale Scott—none of them mention Hufschmid. That his important work remains largely unknown even within the 9/11 Truth movement, let alone by the population at large, reinforces the ideas about mental colonialization or mental serfdom stated above.

97

I had long wanted to re-read Aldous Huxley's novel, *Brave New World*, and to read for the first time a book he wrote 26 years later, *Brave New World Revisited*, published in 1958. I did so now and hadn't read much before realizing just how insightfully these books, published 88 and 62 years ago, portray and analyze important aspects of American society today.

In *Brave New World*, Huxley portrayed a society in the distant future in which an Institute had been set up to increase happiness and contentment by "conditioning"—altering—people so that they "like their unescapable social destiny."[483] If many more people are needed for mind-numbing repetitive tasks than would be born naturally, then "conditioning," before and after birth, must be used to produce them. "Nothing [succeeds] like oxygen-shortage for keeping an embryo below par" the Director of the Institute explains. "The lower the caste, the shorter the oxygen."[484]

Conditioning continues after birth by implanting messages in the minds of all persons. Children hear messages thousands of times, including while sleeping, which condition them to like certain things and to hate others. The messaging differs for each caste, and continues, the Director explains, "till at last the child's mind *is* these suggestions, and the sum of the suggestions *is* the child's mind. And not the child's mind only. The adult's too—all his life long. The mind that judges and desires and decides—made up of these suggestions. But all these suggestions are *our* suggestions!"[485]

Conditioning is supplemented by providing all persons with recreational drugs and pleasant entertainment to keep their minds sedated when not at work. The large majority, having been sterilized, become, in effect, drones who engage mindlessly and promiscuously in the initial reproductive act without later parts of the reproductive process—pregnancy and birth, for instance—ever occurring. They never become mothers or fathers. No one has a family; embryos are produced in the Institute, which raises and educates children until they reach working age.

I was startled by the degree to which the American society I've lived in since returning home nine months ago resembles Huxley's fictional dystopian society. I've been struck by the large number of people I've seen in public who appear to live in an eternal uninformed present. With their eyes glued to their phones and the trivia portrayed on those tiny screens, and with ear buds stuck in their ears, they appear to be almost completely disconnected from the society around them.

Even groups of friends sit silently together, not talking among themselves but instead texting with others not present. Apparently much of their texts consists of emojis, which channel the complex range of human thought and emotion into a few simplistic cartoonish symbols. Communicating by pictures—a modern form of hieroglyphs—rather than words, contributes to a growing number of people seemingly no longer capable of reflection, subtlety or nuance. Now, with face masks and social distancing the norm, their disconnect from the people around them is almost complete. They'd fit easily into Huxley's Institute-controlled society.

Before the lockdowns I'd sometimes see families eating together in restaurants without much communication taking place. Often every member of the family was off in his or her own world, all staring at small screens, either sending or receiving texts from persons not present, or playing games, with their eyes rarely leaving their screens. Add to that the number of broken families headed by only one parent—apparently the United States leads the world in this category—and I'm beginning to wonder if there's really much difference between our society and Huxley's society of the future in which families don't exist at all.

The most disturbing aspect of all this was realizing that this mindless pleasure-seeking existence had arisen in American society without the extensive and intrusive "conditioning" instilled by the Institute in Huxley's novel. Here there is no harmful natal chemical poisoning to produce large numbers of people with stunted brains suited only for repetitive mind-numbing tasks. No sleep messaging occurs. Children aren't raised by an Institute that controls or directs every hour of their days. Narcotics and trivia aren't pushed on people by a coordinated government plan to deaden their sensibilities.

Yet these self-isolating behaviors that I'd witnessed so frequently had arisen anyway. Sure, I'd seen these things in the countries where I'd worked. When I had, I told myself, that's why they're called less developed countries. They were less developed because the minds and sensibilities of most people in them were less developed. I contrasted them with the people in developed societies such as my own.

Seeing these same behaviors here I realized two things. One was that my country had changed significantly while I'd been away. And, I've begun to realize, in Huxley's imaginary society these behaviors hadn't been instilled entirely by the Institute; the germ for them already existed in human nature. All the Institute had done was develop one aspect of human nature over others. It had brought to the fore the lowest rather than the highest aspects of our nature.

With that thought in mind, I recalled again the religious journey I'd undergone over the course of my life, the move from regarding religion as the source of wars and barbarity to realizing that it had been only the proximate cause of those things in human history, that the ultimate cause had been the nature of human nature itself; that I'd come to see religion, particularly Christianity, as capable of leading people upward, toward the higher reaches of their nature.

That thought led me to the further realization that even in American society such persons as Gina and Russell were rare, that individuals who had broken out of society's smothering embrace were hard to find, and that my friendships with them were so precious that I'd be devastated if they vanished from my life.

Writing *Brave New World* in 1931, Huxley had expected that a society like the one he depicted—"the completely organized society, the scientific caste system, the abolition of free will by methodological conditioning, the servitude made acceptable by regular doses of chemically induced happiness, the orthodoxies drummed in by nightly courses of sleep-teaching"[486]—would arise only in the distant future. Yet only 26 years later, writing *Brave New World Revisited* in 1957, he saw it as imminent. "Not just freedom," he wrote, but "even the desire for this freedom seems to be on the wane.... The nightmare of total organization, which I had situated in the seventh century after [the present], has emerged from the safe, remote future and is now awaiting us, just around the next corner."[487]

Yet not everyone in Huxley's novel is entirely satisfied with this state of affairs. Two young men make some effort to create space in their lives to think their own thoughts and to decide for themselves what to with their free time each day. Neither, though, is able to make much progress in freeing himself from social pressure; it's just too strong and their conditioning had been too extensive.

Into the mix comes John, who, as a "barbarian" born and raised outside "civilization," had never been subjected to the Institute's conditioning. He doesn't fit into the mindless activities that others fill their days and lives with, and he doesn't want to. Able to cast off the social pressure applied on him since arriving, he lives as an individual able to think for himself. He wants a world with the full range of human emotions and interactions, not the uniformity pervasive in a society with engineered, bottle-grown babies and hypnotic persuasion of adults. Life for him has meaning beyond the play of the senses and immediate gratification of all desires. He makes the effort to think about what aspects of life are most important and seeks to structure his life around them.

Raised outside "civilization" with the works of Shakespeare and the Bible the only printed materials to help him learn English, he'd grown up guided by the sentiments expressed in them, and often quotes an apt phrase from one or the other as he seeks to determine how best to respond to unusual situations in the strange society he's now in. He finds few people in "civilization" who have read any of Shakespeare's works or the Bible, another aspect of Huxley's imaginary society that resembles American society today.

When John asks the Controller why the Institute pushes mindless entertainment on people—"Why don't you let them see *Othello* instead?"—he's told that mindless entertainment is what people want, and that plays like *Othello*, which require thought and present tragic situations, would cause instability. "The world's stable now," he says with pride. "People are happy; they get what they want, and they never want what they can't get. They're well off; they're safe; they're never ill; they're not afraid of death; they're blissfully ignorant of passion and old age; they're plagued with no mothers or fathers; they've got no wives, or children, or lovers to feel strongly about; they're so conditioned that they practically can't help behaving as they ought to behave."[488]

Limiting them to light entertainment is "the price we have to pay for stability," the Controller continues. "You've got to choose between happiness and what people used to call high art. We've sacrificed the high art. We have the feelies [movies] . . . instead. They don't mean anything [in] themselves, [but they provide] a lot of agreeable sensations to the audience."

"Civilization has absolutely no need of nobility or heroism," the Controller continues. In our society, there are "no wars, no instability, no divided allegiances, no temptations to be resisted, no objects of love to be fought for or defended. So no need for nobility and heroism. . . . And if ever, by some unlucky chance, anything unpleasant should somehow happen, why, there's always soma [narcotics] to give you a holiday from the facts. There's always soma to calm your anger, to reconcile you to your enemies, to make you patient and long-suffering. In the past you could only accomplish these things by making a great effort and after years of hard moral training."[489]

In that society, I saw, everything personal that might upset stability had been eliminated. Personal relationships of any but the most superficial kind were discouraged because intense feelings could be disruptive. There was no need for great effort or great accomplishment because there was nothing great to strive for or accomplish. Bureaucratic norms governed the society, so there was little need for privacy or personal thoughts. People had become infantilized. In such a society human sheep or human cows would have been ideal if only they could perform the mindless tasks needed to keep society functioning.

Is that society really so different from our own, with its emphasis on efficiency, stability and bureaucratic routines that enforce some aspects of a good rather than the whole good? Here, too, it is difficult to be alone with one's own thoughts in public or in private. In public there's music playing everywhere; worst of all are those restaurants that play short snippets of music interspersed between lengthy spans of advertising. And everywhere, in public and in private, so many people inflict their cell phones on themselves, sacrificing whatever time they might have spent in thought or reflection for the stimuli that comes from trivial entertainment.

The people in Huxley's fictional society are so thoroughly conditioned and their more meaningful human qualities so completely suppressed, that it's a shock to them when John, born and raised outside "civilization" enters their world. At first fascinated by this "barbarian," they quickly become disenchanted with his strange ways that conflict with their own rules and practices, which result in the dreaded "instability" they've been taught to fear.

John, too, rejects their society, telling the Director, "But I don't want comfort. I want God, I want poetry, I want real danger, I want freedom, I want goodness, I want sin. . . . I'm claiming the right to be unhappy."[490] He escapes from that society, with its endless pursuit of mindless pleasures, preferring to live by himself outside "civilization."

98

There was another aspect of *Brave New World*—the novel, not Huxley's later reassessment of it—that hit home with me. John the "barbarian" desires Lenina, a young woman he meets in the "civilized" society he's entered. He does more than merely desire her; he loves her. Lenina also loves him, but he doesn't understand that. Seeing that men and women in that perverse society engage in frequent promiscuous sex, he assumes that Lenina's desire for him is merely her desire for mindless sex with a new male. It isn't though; Lenina, having for the first time met a man capable of the full range of human feelings, falls in love, for the first time, with him.

John, still believing Lenina to be capable only of mindless pleasurable sex, not love, believes that sex with such a person would degrade himself. Misunderstanding her, he seeks to convince himself that he doesn't love her—that he couldn't possibly love a woman capable only of mindless copulation—and that he only lusts her. Believing that giving in to lust by accepting her offer of sex would lower himself to the animal level he mistakenly believes characterizes her desire, he flees from her, flees to the countryside where he beats himself to try to drive the lust for her out of his body.

So how does all this relate to me? I had reached a point where every story of love, romance, charm, courtship, attraction, desire and so on—even a story as bizarre as Huxley's—led me to thoughts of Gina. My problem was different than John's, though. It wasn't that I refused to act on my desire for Gina because I thought that she was below me—if anything she was above me—but that acting on my desire in the only way that I knew Gina would accept me wouldn't, ultimately, be good for her.

All this led to thoughts about the ways that literature could present the complexities of human life more fully and more deeply than any work of non-fiction. Literature's glorying in its three-dimensional portrayals of human beings and human life is in sharp contrast to the flattened human beings that the Institute tried to create in its illusive quest for perfect stability. It's entirely fitting that John the "barbarian" often turned to Shakespeare, quoting passages to himself, to guide him in the unusual situations he faced.

This idea of literature's being able to capture the complexity of human life struck home again, when, near the end of *Brave New World*, the Controller digresses on why it is that "the religious sentiment tends to develop as we grow older." He explains that as the passions grow calm as the fancy and sensibilities are less excited and less excitable, . . . God emerges as from behind a cloud."[491]

Was that what was behind my turn toward C. S. Lewis and his books on Christianity, books that I was eager to return to as soon as I'd wrapped up my investigations into the three coups? It was certainly true that my "fancy and sensibilities are less excited and less excitable" now than even a decade ago. I'd moved from fancying many women to desiring only one, Gina. Did her intense religious nature increase my desire for her? Or was it that my desire for her strengthened my religious sensibilities? God only knows!

Returning to thoughts of the novel, I saw that it wasn't just personal desires that might conflict with stability that the Institute suppressed; it was also also any concepts outside the personal—Beauty, Truth, and Goodness, for instance—that might become lodestars providing meaning other than stability. The pursuit of them could be disruptive, and so awareness of them had to be suppressed.

The Director of the Institute acknowledges that in the old days, before the Institute was founded, "knowledge was the highest good, truth the supreme value; all the rest was secondary and subordinate." But now, through the work of the Institute, the emphasis had shifted "from truth and beauty to comfort and happiness. Mass production demanded the shift. Universal happiness keeps the wheels steadily turning; truth and beauty can't. And, of course, whenever the masses seized political power, then it was happiness rather than truth and beauty that mattered."

The shift "hasn't been very good for truth, of course," he admits. "But it's been very good for happiness. One can't have something for nothing. Happiness has got to be paid for."[492]

Replace "happiness" with "safety," and isn't that what we're seeing right now all around us? The distortions and changed definitions of pandemic, case, death, and so on, all are geared to provide increased safety. Of course, there is little to be protected from, but that's a truth that must be hidden to secure the tiny gain in safety that the lockdowns provide—at a nearly incalculable cost.

Truth and the pursuit of it is dangerous, the Director explains. "Every discovery in pure science is potentially subversive; even science must sometimes be treated as a possible enemy. Yes, even science. . . . That's another item in the cost of stability. It isn't only art that's incompatible with happiness; it's also science. Science is dangerous; we have to keep it most carefully chained and muzzled."[493]

Stability, not truth, was the value of greatest importance in the Institute's society. "Great is the truth," the Director admits, "but still greater, from a practical point of view is silence about truth." Yet even silence isn't enough, he tells John. Active propaganda against ideas the Institute believes are dangerous must be used to sway the masses. Huxley returned to this idea in

Revisited, explaining, "By simply not mentioning certain subjects, by lowering what Mr. Churchill calls an 'iron curtain' between the masses and such facts or arguments as the local political bosses regard as undesirable, totalitarian propagandists have influenced opinion much more effectively than could have been done by the most eloquent denunciations, the most compelling of logical rebuttals. But silence is not enough. If persecution, liquidation and other symptoms of social friction are to be avoided, the positive sides of propaganda must be made as effective as the negative."[494]

The few individuals in *Brave New World* who insist on thinking or acting independently—those who value art and science and literature—were able to do so only in very limited ways. They were like the early adventurers heading out into the western wilderness filled with many dangers. Of course they didn't get far. Yet they got far enough to concern the Controller, who plucked them out of society and sent them off to live on remote islands among other independent thinkers, AKA misfits.

Helmholtz Watson, one of those misfits, is about to be sent to one of those islands. "That's to say," the Controller tells him, you're "being sent to a place where [you'll] meet the most interesting set of men and women to be found anywhere in the world. All the people who, for one reason or another, have got too self-consciously individual to fit into community life. All the people who aren't satisfied with orthodoxy, who've got independent ideas of their own. Everyone, in a word, who's anyone. I almost envy you, Mr. Watson."[495]

The Controller himself had once been inclined to independent thought, science, art and silence—to all the things that contribute to disruption, to humanness. But in the end, he chose to remain in society and block others from these higher things in order to instill stability as the highest value.

"Because, finally, I preferred this," he explains, "I was given the choice; to be sent to an island, where I could have got on with my pure science, or to be taken on to the Controllers' council with the prospect of succeeding in due course to an actual Controllership. I chose this and let the science go.'"[496]

Once exiled to the island, the misfits, the independent thinkers, will be free to engage in science, art, literature—in any and all serious endeavors for which there was no place in a society dedicated to stability. If and when they produce inventions or works of art or literature that the Controller thinks would contribute to greater stability in society, they will, at his discretion and pace, be introduced. For the Controller, this was the best of all possible worlds.

Is American society today significantly different from the society in Huxley's novel? When Huxley re-examined the fictional world he'd created, in *Brave New World Revisited*, he wrote about aspects of American society as he saw it then, from his vantage point as a novelist and screenwriter living near Los Angeles. Much of his analysis of American society as it was then, it seemed to me, is still relevant for the society I was now living in. If independent thinkers allow themselves to be marginalized within their own society, it will become increasingly characterized by the features that Huxley described so presciently more than 60 years ago. Among them would be:

✦ The impossibility of liberty in a country at war, as the United States has been since September 11: "But liberty, as we all know, cannot flourish in a country that is permanently on a war footing, or even a near-war footing. Permanent crisis justifies permanent control of everybody and everything by the agencies of the central government."[497]

✦ That a democratic system of government is incompatible with running an empire: that once an empire exists the domestic system of government must be changed: "A democratic constitution is a device for preventing the local rulers from yielding to those particularly dangerous temptations that arise when too much power is concentrated in too few hands. . . . Where the republican or limited monarchical tradition is weak, the best of constitutions will not prevent ambitious politicians from succumbing with glee and gusto to the temptations of power."[498]

✦ The unreal nature of society today, with people locking themselves in their homes and wearing face masks while driving alone: "At the time the book was written this idea, that human beings are given free will in order to choose between insanity on the one hand and lunacy on the other, was one that I found amusing and regarded as quite possibly true.. . . . Today I feel no wish to demonstrate that sanity is impossible. . . . though I remain no less sadly certain than in the past that sanity is a rather rare phenomenon, I am convinced that it can be achieved and would like to see more of it."[499]

✦ The growing totalitarian nature of society: Huxley expected that American society would become more like the Institute's society, with its search for absolute certainty, absolute safety, absolute stability. "To deal with confusion, power has been centralized and government control increased. It is probable that all the world's governments will be more or less completely totalitarian even before the harnessing of atomic energy; that they will be totalitarian during and after the harnessing seems almost certain."[500]

✦ The advent of the colonial mindset: People would become conditioned not only to love their work, but to love their servitude. Is there any better description of our society today than this? "A really efficient totalitarian state would be one in which the all-powerful executive of political bosses and their army of managers control a population of slaves who do not have to be coerced, because they love their servitude. . . . . To make them love it is the task assigned, in present-day totalitarian states, to ministries of propaganda, newspaper editors and schoolteachers."[501]

I now understood enough about the present condition of my country to turn to thinking about how to right the ship.

May 2020

☙ 99 ☙

The book club's discussion of *Silence*, Shusaku Endo's novel about the travails of Christian missionaries in Japan in the 1600s, was cancelled, so Gina and I met for dinner earlier than usual. We managed to find a restaurant still open, but for take out only, and picked up food to eat outdoors, on a park bench out of sight of the road and passing patrolmen. Gina's protocols of course prohibited her from being alone with a man indoors.

I saw when we met that she hadn't taken my abrupt departure last time amiss. I knew she had looked forward to discussing *Silence*, so opened our conversation by mentioning it. "There is much meat in this book. We should reschedule it once the group can meet in person. Maybe in June. *Emma* can be pushed back a month."

"I'm pleased to hear you say that," she replied. "You're right, that book is deep and multi-layered, one of the best novels I have ever read. But I guess what made me love it is the fact that I am from an Asian country where faith, a very western concept, successfully blossomed. *Silence* depicts perfectly how different it was when the Cross was planted in the Asian soil."

"What was most important for me," I replied, "was that priests in Japan weren't put to death, but instead subjected to the most gruesome tortures to force them to publicly renounce their faith in Christianity. That pressure and how determined they were not to give in to it are subjects of great importance today. It's quite a timely book."

In fact, thanks to *Silence* and the ongoing lockdowns, I now saw that Principality has four aspects: not just being a decision maker and not just making informed decisions; and not just accepting the testimony of my own eyes over existing theories, expectations and beliefs, as I already knew, but also acting on the basis of my informed decisions even in the face of extraordinary social and governmental pressure to follow the thinking and actions of the herd.

"*Silence* is now one of my most favorite books ever, . . ." Gina said.

I wouldn't have gone that far, but I sensed this was her religious side talking, a side I could intellectually understand but didn't feel.

". . . not only because it's written by a Catholic," she continued, "but because it's so complex, has lots of layers in it and is so deep. Endo has accomplished something difficult that a lot of other writers haven't and will never. It raises so many important and interesting questions that I find difficult to answer, as there are so many concepts, terminologies and names of people sprinkled all over the book that only people with real exposure to Asian Christianity or someone who has deep understanding and vast knowledge of the history of Christianity and its role in certain parts of Aisa and of the Scriptures will understand. The characters in that book were real historical figures and the events in it are recorded in history.

"The first time I learned about it I was 15, in my second year of high school. I have never forgotten it since then. I cried when I watched the movie adaptation by Martin Scorsese in 2016. The film was so beautiful."

I made a mental note to watch the movie the next day, though I usually don't like to watch movies made from books I'd already read. Adaptations tend to present those aspects of a book that lend themselves to cinematic portrayal, rather than those aspects most important to the author or those best expressed in print. Sometimes producers don't even make a pretense of presenting a film based on the book; they merely grab the title and names of characters while substantially reworking the plot and characterizations. Even if the movie is faithful to the book, I prefer to imagine for myself what the people and settings I'm reading about look like, guided only by what the author has written and my own sensibilities.

I also made a note to return to a study of the history of Christianity. I still didn't know much about its history in Asia, though I'd begun filling in gaps in my knowledge of it elsewhere.

I'd known for decades of the bloody Thirty Years' War between Europe's Catholics and protestants between 1618 and 1648, in which somewhere between five and eight million people were killed, and had been astounded by that number when learning of it. But recently I'd learned that "the number of people killed in the Mongol invasions of Europe and China in the 13th century alone was between 40 and 60 million," and that 100 million Hindus had been killed by Muslims during their thousand-year rule in India.[502] Comparing the 5,000 people killed in the Inquisition with those huge numbers slaughtered elsewhere increased my appreciation of the history and unique core beliefs of Christianity.

Gina was quiet while I was thinking those thoughts. When she spoke again it was in a softer voice and on a different topic. "I thought of you last night, Jubal. I hadn't slept yet since I came home from the studio. I'd just finished taking a shower and hadn't yet gotten dressed for bed. . . ."

Instantly I was on full alert. "My God, Gina!" I said, interrupting her. "I can see how it is that you've had difficulties from time to time with men losing control of themselves around you. Whether from naiveté or design, telling a man that you just got out of the shower but haven't gotten dressed for bed yet—that you're either naked or have only a towel wrapped around you—is a sure-fire way to spark his desire. Something you don't need to do in my case; you know I am always having to restrain myself whenever I am near you or thinking about you."

"Well maybe that's the problem," she said, suddenly appearing as angry as I felt. "You talk on and on about the importance of Principality, but then you refuse to treat me as a Principal, as someone fully capable of making an informed decision. You think you must decide for me what is best in my life. Whether it would be better for me to be with no one than to be with a man who loves me and who I love, for only two decades instead of the forty or fifty years I could expect with a younger man—a theoretical man younger than yourself who would love me as I think you do, but who I have never encountered despite many years of dedicated search for him.

"You say you can't fully relax when you are with me. I don't see why not. Other suitors are fully relaxed when they are with me, and they desire me as much as you apparently do.

"And another thing. I could never consider myself your niece. I would never want to call 'uncle' the kind of manly guy that I would love to have grab me by my waist."

"I can see that you have all the right instincts, Gina," I said. "You want a real man. No real woman wants a gentleman in her bed."

She appeared taken aback by that, and said, "I was trying to flirt with you, but I guess I am just horrible at it. Now that I am feeling better my naughty self is back. Forgive me for being annoying."

"Your flirting comes through loud and clear, Gina, and it's all the more relished because it comes with a scent of danger from the forbidden developments that could follow from it. But that makes it all the harder to be around you. I can't fully relax around you when you flirt, when you give any appearance at all of inviting advances that I know you'd reject. Your flirting leads me to want to take the next steps of kissing you, of grabbing you by your waist, as you've said. But I know that if I did that you'd pull back, like a turtle pulling its head, legs and tail into its shell. I'm fully aware you intend to bring an untouched body to your future husband, and I respect that. But in that regard, you are so different from all other women I've encountered and desired that it's difficult for me to reign in my feelings and desires. Perhaps we should restrict our conversations to more impersonal subjects such as literature.

"It's difficult for me, too, Jubal," Gina said. "It's confusing when you say such wonderful things to me about how you'd court me to the moon and back. But then you pull back and say it's all a nice dream, but that you couldn't court me in real life because of your age. Yes and no, advancement and retreat, again and again. It's still confusing and distressing, as we talked about before. So yes, let's reign in our conversations to literature and other non-personal subjects."

We were silent for several minutes, eating and thinking our

own thoughts. Then she spoke, in a softer, more intimate voice.

"Sometimes I imagine bringing my future husband to my hometown. It will be a breath of fresh air to him; my grandparents, my mom, my uncles and aunts will throw a hero's welcome for him. My grandpa said that he will kill two pigs and will cook food enough to feed the entire town for whoever I will marry, because that's how Filipinos welcome a new man into the family. Most likely my family will love him more than they love me!"

"I have had the same fantasy!" I said, excitedly. "I've had visions of your triumphant return home with your new husband at your side, of you introducing me to your family, to others in your home neighborhood, of meeting your mother and sisters and other relatives."

Suddenly we both laughed.

"We can't do it, can we?" I said. "We can't restrict our conversations to merely non-personal subjects. We did before, but we can't seem to do it for very long now."

She nodded. "I just said that you can relax, but I see that when you do, you speak words almost romantic, words that I'd expect to hear from a suitor in love with me, which you say you are not. And as for me, I don't do superficial or fake conversations, so its hard not to be girly or flirtatious with you, though, to be honest, I do my best to go easy on you because you've said that a relationship is impossible. I don't want to cause uneasiness to you. So perhaps we must try harder to keep our conversations limited to my studio, your research and literature."

As we stood up to go our separate ways, it occurred to me that neither of us had suggested not meeting at all.

100

"I see it all now, Russell. The U.S. has been taken over by a cabal, just as Russia had been. But whereas Russia had been taken over in 1917, in one blow easily seen by the rest of the world, the United States has been conquered in a rolling coup, or a series of partial coups. First in 1963, then in 2001 and now in

2020 with the Covid lockdowns taking place before our very eyes. Because each coup has been only partial, or only partially visible, the reality hasn't been recognized by the rest of the world or even by most Americans themselves.

"Do you know the Japanese insult, 'He doesn't know where he is,' which is said of someone acting inappropriately, someone who is behaving in a manner not suitable for the situation and setting he's in? For Americans today a more relevant comment might be, 'He doesn't know what time it is.'

"Most Americans appear to think it's still 2019, that we're still living in relatively normal times. They can't see the madness swirling around them because they are part of it.

"Others are even worse. They still think they're living in 2000, before government leaders demonstrated their ability and willingness to launch attacks on their own country, and before the Patriot Act was passed and the Department of Homeland Security was created, giving the USG authorization to spy on us all the time, to track our locations, to monitor our communications, and before the unending series of wars launched by the United States ended the decade of relative peace following the self-immolation of the Soviet Union at the end of 1991.

"Still others think they're living in 1962, before the CIA and military murdered our president, and the media and the American people allowed them to get away with it."

I knew I was once again hogging the conversation, but I felt such a strong need to express my thoughts that I continued regardless, though in a softer voice.

"For them, apparently, Americanism remains fully intact. Their belief in the goodness of American society and of the American government, and in the American mission, has weathered all the storms over the last fifty-six years. I shudder to recall that until only recently I was one of them. How could I have allowed myself to remain so blind for so long?

"Why didn't you tell me about all this earlier, Russell?" I said as I waved my hand over all the books and papers spread out on the table and shelved on the bookcases surrounding us. We were once again meeting at his house, in his office.

"Because we must all find things out for ourselves," he said. "We must absorb things at our own pace. If I tried to push too much information on you too quickly, you'd push it away. Think how many years it took before the circumstances were right for you to see the evidence about Kennedy's assassination."

I knew he was right. Just as we can't help someone who isn't doing all he can to help himself, so too, I now saw, we can't push someone to re-examine existing beliefs or consider new evidence when they aren't ready to consider doing so on their own. All we can do is help along the way those who are already making the effort.

"So, I feed information to my students in bite size chunks," Russell continued. "And I see you doing the same thing with family and friends. You didn't go in full bore with the full September 11 story in great detail; you presented a photograph and asked folks what they saw. I'd say that's the best approach. Those who are interested and ready to hear more will ask for more information; those that aren't, show they aren't by their silence."

"But I feel the need to push, Russell. I want everyone to see Brian's testimony, for instance. I want everyone to wake up and recognize the reality of the country they live in, just as I have."

Russell smiled sympathetically before speaking. "Yup. What we want rarely coincides with what's possible. But with constant effort to identify people who are interested in learning more, and in helping them by suggesting sources of information, we can make progress."

"Just like you've done with me!" I responded.

"Yup!"

We were silent for a moment, each thinking his own thoughts, before I spoke again.

"Over the past nine months I've gone from believing, as William J. Bennett did when he titled his three-volume history of the United States *America: The Last Best Hope*, to concluding that Martin Luther King, Jr., had it right when he called the U.S. government 'the greatest purveyor of violence in the world.' We have a lot of work to do to make America great again."

"That might be a more arduous task than you think, Jubal," Russell said. "Before we can make America great again, we must first make America good again."

He let that sink in for a moment before continuing. "Right now, there's a sickness in America's soul that must be excised.

"There is something mentally disturbed about a society that makes movies like those I've seen advertised in previews, so full of violence," he continued. "Culturally, this change can be seen by comparing two suspense movies, *North by Northwest* from 1959, with the three *John Wick* movies, from 2014 to 2019. In the older film, staring Cary Grant, a film of sophisticated interactions between adults, few people are murdered, and those who are, die mostly off screen. In the John Wick movies, staring Keanu Reeves, who I like, scores of people are murdered on screen and in the most gruesome ways. The films lack any charm or grace.

"I think it likely that the unresolved issues of the Kennedy assassination and the events of September 11 have cracked the American mind, have damaged the American soul. We've never had closure on these and so many other tragic events in our lifetimes."

"And now," I added to what Russell had just said, "with the lockdowns and replacement of the American political system with rule by government edict, and with the American people's acquiescence in all this, we appear to have reached the worst of all possible worlds. It can't possibly get any worse."

Russell smiled his wry smile again. "It can always get worse, Jubal. Shakespeare said it best, in *King Lear*: 'The worst is not / So long as we can say 'This is the worst.'"

I nodded, then said, "I've always shied away from the later works of Graham Greene and John le Carré because the two men expressed increasingly intense anti-Americanism in them. Or so I've heard. But now, myself experiencing great distress over what has become of my country, perhaps I should read some of their later works. Perhaps they weren't anti-American at all, at least not in the sense of blind hatred of the country. Perhaps Greene and le Carré had realistically portrayed the country as it is today and offered valid critiques of it, critiques that I would now agree with."

I made a mental note to order copies of their later works as soon as I got home.

Russell had refilled our glasses, and we were now sitting on the sofa. I was in a more reflective mood than before as I said, "Nine months ago I lost Diana and my career came to its natural end. Now it seems I am losing my lifelong faith in my country and its government."

"Disentangle the two, Jubal," Russell said. "Country and government are not identical. The shadow government at this moment is a cancer growing on the country, one that needs to be excised. Cutting it out is the most important task facing the country. Just how the ship might be righted isn't clear to anyone at the moment."

I aped one of Russell's wry smiles. "With the government, the visible government, firmly controlled by the Power Elite—and with the media and so many other institutions under its control, it's hard to see how it can be cut out or overthrown. Maybe the rot is too deep to be fixed. Sometimes it's best to abandon a house rotten down to its foundation and start over somewhere else.

Russell smiled another of his wry smiles, perhaps in sympathy with mine. "In the old days they lit out for the Territories, like Samuel Langhorne Clemens. But today there is nowhere else, Jubal. It was the United States that stepped in to rescue Europe from its own horrendous mistakes in 1917, and again in 1941 when we entered the Second World War. We again protected Western Europe from the Soviet Union during the long decades of the Cold War. I don't think Europe today is in any condition to save us. And no one else will, either. We must, somehow, find the strength and the will to save ourselves."

On that note we said our goodbyes.

Later, while driving home, I thought of more to say to Russell.

"It's not just that my understanding of my country has changed so radically over the past nine months, it's that my opinion of other people has been transformed. What happened on September 11 is so fundamental to what our country is, or has become, that I can't help using that day, like Barrie Zwicker does, as 'my touchstone, my compass, the litmus test by which I measure all individuals, organizations and institutions.'[503] How can it be that anyone who refuses to recognize the reality of what has happened has anything of value to offer me or our country?

"I have fewer years left to me than I have behind me. I'm reaching the point at which I don't have any time for those who are so blind that they can't see what is right in front of them after it's pointed out to them. I have no space in my life for people unwilling to trust the testimony of their own eyes even after I point things out to them."

I pictured Russell giving me another of his wry smiles as he responded with words of caution. "No, Jubal, think hard before you go down that road. Life will be awfully lonely if you cut out of your life everyone who isn't as open to new ideas as you have proven to be. Remember how caught up in your life you were for decades, how little time and energy was left over to consider such things as September 11 beyond its immediate effect on your life at that time."

Nodding as though Russell were in the car with me, I realized I needed to think this over carefully. I wondered how I would have responded ten years ago if someone had pushed in front of me the image of the tower and the explanation of its being exploded from within. I hope I would have responded with the willingness to believe the testimony of my own eyes that I've shown recently.

While turning into the driveway, Russell's final thought before I'd left reminded me of something Flannery O'Connor once wrote, "You must push back as hard as the age pushes against you."[504] That idea surely is part of Principality, I said to myself. So Principality as I now understood it included making decisions, making informed decisions, making an effort not just to get relevant information but also to revisit beliefs relevant to the decisions to be made, acting on the basis of decisions made even when doing so is difficult, and, finally, seeking to make the world outside ourselves more supportive of Principality.

Perhaps that final aspect, that of working to improve the society and country in which I now live, should be my principal task in the next phase of my life.

⸙ 101 ⸙

Back home, I realized that there was more I could learn from Lewis's *The Abolition of Man*. So far, I'd examined his thoughts on the TAO to see whether they'd provided any justification for assassinating a president, for murdering nearly 3,000 people and launching wars that killed millions more, or for disrupting the lives of nearly every American through forced lockdowns.

They hadn't.

I now wanted to see how Lewis's thoughts on the TAO could help me directly in my own life by providing a standard by which I could judge the appropriateness of my own desires, emotions, thoughts and actions. "Certain emotional reactions on our part could be either congruous or incongruous," Lewis had written, "Objects did not merely receive, but could *merit*, our approval or disapproval, our reverence or our contempt."[505] That made sense to me: Specific objects *merited* certain responses and judgments; our visceral responses and cerebral judgments could be appropriate or not; comparing them to the TAO was how we could sort them out.

Then, once I understood how my emotional responses and cerebral judgments stood in relation to the TAO, I could work to moderate those that were wayward, to bring them more and more in line with it. I could work to integrate the rational and the sensual parts of my nature. In Lewis's analogy, cerebral judgments are produced by the head and emotional or visceral reactions by the belly. Mature sentiments are produced by the chest. Our goal, Lewis explained, is to become Men of Chests, men whose judgments and emotional responses result from stable sentiments in line with the TAO.

This was good stuff. I could see that developing stable sentiments would make me a more effective Principal. I'd be able to make better judgments and decisions more quickly. Only with stable sentiments that unite emotions and judgments with the

TAO would I be a full Principal.

I could also see that I had much work to do to become a Man with a Chest. I was still ruled too often by wayward emotions and desires and sterile judgments. Much thought and effort would be required to understand and master the process through which the two could become united in stable sentiments.

This need for learning was to be expected in children. Aristotle, Lewis noted, "says that the aim of education is to make the pupil like and dislike what he ought."[506] Plato thought likewise: "The little human animal will not at first have the right responses. It must be trained to feel pleasure, liking, disgust, and hatred at those things which really are pleasant, likeable, disgusting and hateful."[507]

Yet here I was 56 years old and still needing to work on these same aspects of myself. My undeveloped state was clearly evident in my dealings with Gina. My desires pushed me toward a union with her. Of course, sexual in nature, but also incorporating friendship and companionship. I desired her in many ways. There was nothing incongruous about these desires in themselves, but they conflicted with my cerebral judgment that I was too old for her and too old anyway to begin a new family.

So which was correct, my desires or my judgments? Were my judgments simply sterile and incongruous, or were they valid? What did the TAO say? I didn't know; I wasn't yet a Man of Chests with stable sentiments uniting desires and judgments with the TAO.

I needed this quality in myself now. I had the feeling that a decision had to be made about Gina very soon. It could no longer be put off.

⁂ 102 ⁂

This morning, I learned to my great distress that Brian Boskow was dead. Someone had placed a newspaper account of his death from a car accident in my mailbox overnight. The report cited witnesses who had seen a Toyota Venza speed up and crash head on into the driver's side of the car when Brian was stopped at a red light. The driver and a passenger ran off and hadn't been caught. The car had been stolen earlier in the day, and the police ruled the death accidental, caused by teenage joyriders with little experience driving.

I didn't believe for a minute that it was an accident by unskilled drivers. I knew Brian had been murdered, just like all the other members of his team. This news threw me for a loop. I wondered for a moment if his assassins knew about his testimony and that he'd given copies to me. Would I be next?

But I calmed down when I looked at the back of the newspaper report. A handwritten message read, "Brian told me to let you know if anything happened to him. Please destroy this note. For the safety of both of us, please do not try to contact me." It was signed, "Jeanette," who I knew was Brian's wife. I could see that Brian had likely told her about his part in the events of September 11 and that he'd given copies of his testimony to me. And that she wanted the story to have an end now that Brian was dead.

As I absorbed this tragic development, I returned to the question of whether or not to release Brian's testimony to others. A month ago, I had determined that the short-term harm to the country if the truth of the September 11 events became known was roughly balanced by the long-term benefits. Since then, I'd been undecided, pondering about and even anguishing over which course of action was best for the country.

But I was now aware of several new factors that had to be taken into account. Before, I'd considered only events in the past and the effect of making them known. Now I believed that JFK's death and September 11 weren't isolated incidents. They were connected to each other, and more importantly were connected to the Covid lockdowns. That connected the harm they'd produced to the present, to the lockdowns that were continuing at this very moment. I realized that more extraordinary events would hit us in the future, perpetrated by the same Power Elite that had done first two and the one ongoing. The cost of those future events, too, had to be weighed.

It was the shock of the Covid lockdowns that alerted me to

the need to consider future events. They showed me that massively disruptive false flag events weren't just in the past, that they could occur in the future, too. That's what my vision had been trying to tell me.

I realized that future events on the scale of September 11 and the Covid lockdowns were not only possible but inevitable, for several reasons. One, as I'd seen in my vision, was that the Power Elite had overreached with the lockdowns and rule by decree or edict. It had had to withdraw. But it wouldn't withdraw permanently. Having established the precedent that rule by decree could, in fact, take place, albeit temporarily in this instance, it would return to finish the job. It would engineer another big event to use as justification for declaring rule by edict again, this time making it stick permanently. At that point the United States would descend into full and permanent colonial status. I drew all this, as I've explained, from a vision of the future. But, writing this memoir now in 2023, I know that the temporary nature of the 2020 lockdowns in the vision was entirely on the mark, leading me to suspect that the future parts of the vision would be equally accurate.

Another reason why I was sure that future massively disruptive events would occur is that the Power Elite understood it had to keep the people in the dark about the true events of September 11 and the JFK assassination and now about the Covid hoax—and about its control over the government and the country's near-colonial status. The appearance that the government was continuing to function normally, that the country was still a republic, had to be maintained.

If it looked like the truth of these events and conditions was about to come out, or if it looked like serious investigations were about to begin, the Power Elite would have no choice but to launch a new disruptive event to keep the populace fearful and distracted. This very situation has already happened, twice, when Robert F. Kennedy was assassinated to prevent him from becoming president and opening an investigation into his brother's death, and again when John F. Kennedy, Jr., was killed for the same reason. This reasoning leads to an endless chain of horrific events, each more destructive than the last, to maintain the shock value. The logic of the situation practically guaranteed future crises. Like Russian Roulette or a chain letter or a pyramid scheme, this series of events couldn't continue indefinitely, but it would continue as long as it could.

And so, I now knew that I had to release Brian's testimony. The country had to be woken up to avoid destructive events like these happening again and again—or even once more. And that required a shock to the system to wake people up. It didn't matter so much what the shock was as long as it would get large numbers of people seeing things with fresh eyes, and this time believing the testimony of their own eyes.

I also realized that the Power Elite had far more to lose than I'd suspected several weeks ago. It could be blamed for three, not two events—three connected events—and for its control of the U.S. government—not mere influence, but control. Because the Power Elite has far more to lose than I'd realized, its reaction to likely exposure could be even more extreme than I'd considered.

In its reaction to likely exposure, it would be aided by those parts of American society that had hitched their wagons to the new post-September 11 order of things. For that reason, exposure soon after September 11 would have been far easier than now, nearly twenty years later. Both political parties had long since bought into the official story. The media, of course, supports it. Academia, the defense industry, military contractors—all the sectors that have benefited from the official story will be allies of the Power Elite if and when the substantive challenge already mounted by the 9/11 Truth movement begins to gain traction with the public.

Perhaps the harm from that extreme reaction by the Power Elite and its allies would be balanced by the additional benefits that I now saw could come from releasing Brian's statement? Had the balance been maintained? Was I back where I'd started?

No. I now saw that the benefits from avoiding the great harm that would come from a stream of future events far outweighed the short-term harm that would flow from widespread recognition of the government's and Power Elite's responsibility for all three events.

There were many strands of yarn to pull on to start the great unravelling. The strand available to me was Brian's document. If releasing it could be the tug that unraveled the whole ball of yarn, then that's what I had to do. If that would launch a movement to rid the country of the cancer growing on its government, then that's what had to be done. The long-term benefits from surgery would outweigh the short-term costs and inconveniences.

For the first time I knew what to do. I must release Brian's testimony.

But do I dare do it? Brian's death still reverberated.

103

"A republic, if you can keep it," was running through my head repeatedly when I woke up from a nap.

That, I knew was Ben Franklin's reply when asked what he and others had created at the Constitutional Convention in Philadelphia in September 1787.

I usually emphasized "if" and "keep" when I said the phrase aloud, underscoring the need to defend James Madison's carefully balanced governmental structure during its early, fragile years, until its value had proved itself and the processes it outlined strengthened through precedent and custom.

But this time I emphasized "you," as in "if YOU can keep it." "You" I understood to refer to all of us, to the American people as a whole. It's up to us, in every generation, to defend this document, which had laid the basis for the unprecedented prosperity, security and freedom that Americans have enjoyed over the past 230 years.

We'd messed up, I knew. The country had become a colony of the Power Elite, with the Constitution all but suspended. State and local governments were ruling largely by decree while legislatures and courts sat silently by.

We needed saving, but there was no cavalry on the horizon riding to our rescue. The Power Elite wasn't going to miraculously disappear; it wasn't going to abandon its empire and pull its moles from the government. The president, elected representatives and courts, all seemingly blackmailed or bribed, had largely been in the Power Elite's pockets for years.

Large businesses were clearly part of it, being allowed to remain open while their smaller competitors were forcibly closed. Big tech, same story. It was profiting immensely from the lockdowns and leading the way in censuring and deplatforming critics of the government's Covid measures.

In James Madison's design, the American political system rested on two foundations. One was the division of power that he'd built into the system by dividing governmental power at the federal level into three competing branches, and by splitting it further between the federal and state governments. The other foundation was a citizenry that was educated and virtuous; only such a people could elect officials committed to advancing the interests of the country. The two foundations would support each other; they'd protect each other and the precious freedoms that, after brief flowerings, had been lost in all previous political systems known to him.

I'd already concluded that the American government had been captured by the ultimate special interest, the Power Elite, which used it as a tool to pursue its own interests. The division of power between three branches was meaningless if all branches were controlled by the Power Elite. The same for the division of power between federal and state governments if both were under its control.

That left only the citizenry.

To Madison's original design the media might usefully be added to the second foundation, so that the citizenry would be both informed and virtuous. With this modification, there existed two sources of outside power effective in exposing wrongdoing in government and in society, and in pushing for needed reforms.

Having introduced the media as part of the second foundation supporting the health of the American republic, I now had to withdraw it. The media, like the federal government, had been increasingly influenced and finally controlled by the Power Elite, as shown by its biased coverage of each of the three coups. The number of corporate giants that owns the majority of the media in the United States has shrunk from 50 in 1983 to only five today,[508] making the Power Elite's control even easier and more complete.

We'd reached the point where the media, with hardly an exception, acted as cheerleader for whatever lunacy the government came up with. Lockdown society? Sure! Push three million small businesses to the verge of bankruptcy and maybe beyond? Yes! No price is too high for others to pay to stop the Covid menace. Prohibit those on their deathbeds from seeing their children and grandchildren a final time? If that's what it takes! Arrest a father for tossing a softball back and for with his six-year-old daughter in a public park? Sure! We can't let them get away with disobeying our edicts!

So that left only one source of power remaining: public opinion. If the American republic was to be saved, we'd have to do it ourselves.

Yet, as Glennon alerted us, public opinion is vulnerable to the same pressures as the media. Both "are manipulable, and their vitality depends heavily upon the vigor of constitutionally established institutions, which would not have withered had those external constraints had real force."[509] Ample indications suggest that "educated" and "virtuous" aren't the first two adjectives that spring to mind when characterizing the American citizenry today.

So what to do?

Sherlock Holmes once stated that "When you have eliminated all which is impossible, then whatever remains, however improbable, must be the truth."[510]

In this situation, with rescue by any other force being impossible, the American populace, however improbable it may seem, must be the savior, if there is to be one. The other option, that there would be no savior, that the United States had sunk into permanent colonial status, seemed more likely, but I wasn't willing to make that bet quite yet.

Why not, you may ask? After all, the rule of law had been weakened and the protection of civil liberties undermined by legislation passed in the wake of September 11, and then suspended in large part and replaced by rule by edict; and the economic basis of independent thought and action had been undermined by the ongoing destruction of small businesses and by turning so many Americans into mere wage slaves of large corporations and governments after so many other options once open to them had been eliminated.

I was further aware that:

✦ Michael J. Glennon had observed that the American people "themselves are not troubled about new linkages forged among the newly created components of military, intelligence, homeland security, and law enforcement agencies—linkages that together threaten civil liberties and personal freedom in ways never before seen in the United States."[511]

✦ Jacob G. Hornberger had seen that "acknowledging the very real evil at the center of the federal government is simply too frightening for these people. And so they bend over backwards to do everything they can to avoid acknowledging and confronting the overwhelming evidence that establishes that the national-security establishment engaged in autopsy fraud and film fraud as part of its cover-up of its assassination of President Kennedy." They simply do not want to recognize "the evil that came to our nation when our governmental structure was changed from a limited-government republic to a national-security state."[512]

✦ Eric Larsen had showed that Americans "don't know that the entirety of the fraudulent, illegal, and criminal 'war on terror' is itself a lie made up of other lies, an immense fraud made possible only by the earlier great lie of 9/11. They don't know that 'Islamic terrorism' . . . insofar as it exists at all, was created by Americans for America's own purposes, something that has been stirred up and kept most carefully in 'existence' ever since 9/11 for the simple purpose of giving the impression that America really does face a dangerous and ruthless foreign enemy when in truth, fact, and actuality it faces no such thing—except from within."[513]

✦ Larsen, again, had asked "Just *how deeply* corrupted . . . have the United States and its people been made since 9/11? The answer is: Widely, profoundly, and devastatingly. The republic may be lost already, having been reduced to a condition so stupefied and enfeebled as to allow it no longer means of becoming able to recover from the forms of tyranny that have, even now, eaten away great pieces of its most vital elements and are poised in readiness to devour the entirety, digest it, then pass it on, pass it through, and pass it out again in the form of a perfected police state."[514]

✦ John le Carré, the novelist, had concluded that, "America has entered one of its periods of historical madness, but this is the worst I can remember: worse than McCarthyism, worse than the Bay of Pigs and in the long term potentially more disastrous than the Vietnam War."[515]

✦ le Carré, again, had reached the pessimistic conclusion that although "the U.S. still has a strong civil society that could, at least in theory, overcome the entrenched interests of the armed forces and the Military-Industrial Complex," he feared that "the U.S. has indeed crossed the Rubicon and that there is no way to restore Constitutional government short of a revolutionary rehabilitation of American democracy."[516]

✦ Chalmers Johnson had concluded that, "American imperialism and militarism are so far advanced and obstacles to its further growth have been so completely neutralized that the decline of the U.S. has already begun. The country is following the path already taken by its erstwhile adversary in the Cold War, the former Soviet Union. The U.S.'s refusal to dismantle its own empire of military bases when the menace of the Soviet Union disappeared, combined with its inappropriate response to the blowback of September 11, 2001, makes this decline virtually inevitable."[517]

✦ Johnson, again, had concluded that, "Our political system may no longer be capable of saving the United States as we know it, since it is hard to imagine any president or Congress standing up to the powerful vested interests of the Pentagon, the secret intelligence agencies, and the Military-Industrial Complex. Given that 40 percent of the defense budget is now secret as is every intelligence agency budget, it is impossible for Congress to provide effective oversight even if its members wanted to."[518]

In the face of all this testimony to the passive sensibilities of the American people, to their blindness and lack of Principality in the face of grave threats to their country—not to mention Paul Craig Robert's testimony to their insouciance—what grounds did I have for believing that they would come through and rescue themselves and their country?

I didn't have any.

I had only the same confidence in the American people that Winston Churchill had when he observed that "Americans will always do the right thing, after they have exhausted all the alternatives."

I had only the hope that in spite of the odds against them Americans would decide as Whittaker Chambers had when he abandoned Communism and turned to supporting the American republic in the 1930s even though, as he told his wife, "we are leaving the winning world for the losing world."[519] "In the revolutionary conflict of the 20th century," he'd explained, "I knowingly chose the side of probable defeat. Almost nothing that I have observed or that has happened to me since, has made me think that I was wrong about that forecast. But nothing has changed my determination to act as if I were wrong—if only because, in the last instance, men must act on what they believe right, not on what they believe probable."[520]

Dipping into a book I'd bought because I liked its title, *Last Stands: Why Men Fight When All is Lost* by Michael Walsh, I read of a dozen other occasions when men had been determined to "embrace (often, at first, reluctant[ly]) . . . a great cause, one that allows, or propels, the individual into the service of his people. Concomitant with this commitment is the hero's acceptance that he may have to give his life in this endeavor, that there are some things, big things, worth dying for so that others might live, or live freely."[521]

Some things are indeed worth defending regardless of the cost. The preservation of what was left of the American republic was, for me, one of them. Still, I hoped the price I'd have to pay for sending out Brian's testimony wouldn't be the ultimate one.

I held tightly to what remained of my faith in Americanism; my confidence in the ultimate goodness of the American enterprise remained undiminished. I still believed "that liberty, equality, and democracy were ordained by God for all mankind, and that America is a new promised land richly blessed and deeply indebted to God."[522] I still believed in the nation that, in Abraham Lincoln's words at Gettysburg, had been "conceived in liberty and dedicated to the proposition that all men are created equal." I still had hope that the American people would throw off their blinders and rise up, so that "this nation, under God, shall have a new birth of freedom—and that government of the people, by the people, for the people, shall not perish from the earth."

Americanism remained for me the "the last [gift] of the giants," the last of the ideas to whom I'd "given the faith of my youth." Perhaps in my youth I'd accepted Americanism unthinkingly, but decades of experience living in countries around the world and much time and effort devoted over the years to learning about societies distant from our own in time and space had, I believed, replaced that early faith by hard won substantive knowledge of just how extraordinary the American enterprise had been and still was. I wasn't going to let go of it easily.

The way forward, I knew, was widespread acceptance by the American people of what had really happened on November 22, 1963, and September 11, 2001, as well as the reality behind the ongoing Covid lockdowns. Yet the large majority of my fellow Americans instinctively turned away from examining these things. They hadn't shown—and weren't now showing—much interest in understanding the real dangers their country faced.

So what to do? Releasing Brian's testimony would be a first step. Beyond that, I just didn't know.

⚘ 104 ⚘

But I couldn't let it go at that. I had to make one final effort to determine the best way forward.

I could see that two distinct steps would be needed. The first would consist of steps to awaken the American people to the real nature of their country; the second would be steps they could take once awakened. John Adams had made this distinction clear in correspondence with Thomas Jefferson long after they'd both retired from government service: "What do we mean by the revolution? The War? That was no part of the revolution; it was only an effect and consequence of it. The revolution was in the minds of the people, and this was effected from 1760 to 1775, in the course of fifteen years, before a drop of blood was shed at Lexington.'"[523]

I knew that if the American people were to wake up, something had to happen to wake them up. Once awake, public pressure could reverse the flow of influence, from

Power Elite → government → media → American People

to

American People → media → government → Power Elite.

That reversal would put the American people in charge and the Power Elite, for once, on the defensive.

But what could wake them up? I began by reviewing what I already knew about how public attitudes are set.

I knew something that the Power Elite also knew: that people's minds are more easily changed in times of crisis and upheaval and uncertainty, when levels of fear are high. That's why it had orchestrated September 11 the way it had, for its shock value. It's at such emotionally hot times that new ideas and new sentiments become baked in, making them difficult to change later, after the crisis has passed and emotions cooled, just like ingredients in a cake can't be separated back out after it's been baked.

I also realized that it's late in the game. Two coups had already been perpetrated and the third was unfolding all around me. Many additional steps were being bandied about beyond the current lockdowns. A forthcoming vaccine against Covid was mentioned from time to time in the media, along with the idea of vaccination passports that would be needed for entry into all public venues. Knowing that pharmaceutical companies had tried for decades to produce a vaccine for the flu, but failed, I dismissed all speculation about a Covid vaccine and the unprecedented medical passports based on it. Efforts to produce a flu vaccine failed, I knew, because they were impossible. The flu virus, like the Corona virus whose variants include the common cold and Covid, mutates too fast. Vaccinations provide permanent protection against a disease, ergo, Covid vaccines were impossible, and so I dismissed the idea of medical passports based on a vaccine that I was sure wouldn't exist.

(Finishing this memoir in 2023, I now see that I hadn't considered the possibility that the definition of "vaccine," like those of "pandemic," "case," and "cause of death," would also be changed so that a "Covid injection" that wasn't a vaccine in the spring of 2020 would satisfy the criteria for a vaccine by the end of that year, becoming yet another way in which the American people would be hoodwinked.)

Far more dangerous was the precedent that legislation and civil liberties could be suspended on the mere say so of the senior elected official in a particular district: the president for the country as a whole, governors for states, mayors for cities, and so on. All that was needed was a declaration of a State of Emergency, such declarations being in the hands of those same officials. A month ago I'd seen that those dictatorial powers were part of the emergency powers granted to FEMA and the National Security Agency. I now realized that the overthrow of the American political was built into that very system.

It was urgent, then, that the American people take action soon, before the precedent of overthrowing legislation on the mere say so of the chief executive officer became fully established. Becoming aware of any of the coups could generate the public outrage needed to stop the Power Elite in its tracks. It almost didn't matter which of them the public became aware of first. Most people were too immediately fearful of Covid to make that coup the easiest entry point, and the Kennedy assassination was too distant in the past. That left September 11.

The Power Elite's weakest point was the official story of that day, which could easily be seen to be physically impossible in a dozen different ways, if only people would take the time to look into it. Realizing that they'd been lied to about September 11 could provide the shock needed to get things started. Learning of the reality of September 11 could trigger a tsunami of outrage that would flow backwards in time to reconsideration of the Kennedy assassination and forward to reassessment of the Covid propaganda that had flooded over the country in the past two months.

I realized most people were not willing under current circumstances to look into the events of September 11 on their own. A shock was needed to get them to do that. But what event could shock people who had already endured the murder of their president, the destruction of the tallest buildings in the country and the killing of 3,000 people on one day, as well as the ongoing lockdown of their society, with its massive violations of civil procedures, its robbing their children of their education and social lives, and its forced closures of small businesses? If they had endured all this shock and awe with hardly a whimper to disrupt public life, could anything spur them to action?

What would it take to wake people up from the stupor that the concerns of daily life can cause, from the distractions of trivia and mindless entertainment on their phones, and from the propaganda continually washing over them?

A public admission by a senior government official of what had really happened might do it. It didn't need to be a confession by Dick Cheney or Donald Rumsfeld or George W. Bush, though that would be ideal. All were still living, nearly 20 years after the murderous deeds of that terrible day. Might one of them have a change of heart, feel remorse, and confess? Not likely. Far more likely they themselves would be murdered to stop such a confession if they had any such sentiments and expressed them to anyone else.

Was there another high official who had inside knowledge of the events of that day? Yes. President Donald Trump, who, I recalled, on September 11, 2001, long before he'd become president, had stated in a live broadcast that in his expert opinion the World Trade Center towers were immensely strong and could have been brought down only by explosives planted inside them.

But how to get President Trump to make such a statement? Perhaps it could be arranged for a reporter at a press conference to ask him a question about what he really thought brought down the WTC towers. The shock of such a direct question asked unexpectedly in public in a provocative manner might jolt him into revealing his true thoughts. It remained now only to find and motivate a reporter to ask such a question.

Aside from that possibility, I was heartened to see that some prominent Americans were waking up, in a manner similar to my own. I'd been led into reassessing my beliefs by examining the Zapruder film of the Kennedy assassination, as recounted in this memoir. Jeffrey Sachs, professor at Columbia University, had been led to reconsidering his own beliefs about the Covid virus after being named Chairman of the *Lancet*'s Covid Commission. In that position, Ron Unz explained, Sachs "gradually became aware that the facts surrounding the origin of the disease that has killed so many millions around the world were being concealed, with attempts to bring them to light being blocked by the concerted efforts of government and media."[524] Sachs "has also now apparently become far more suspicious of numerous historical matters he had previously accepted on faith, notably including the circumstances of the Kennedy assassination. In a remarkable recent podcast interview, he voiced sentiments strikingly similar to some of [Unz's] own, saying that he had discovered that on many different issues of great importance, we are all living in 'a sea of lies.'"

Ron Unz himself had gone through an awakening similar to Jeffrey Sachs' and my own. His entry point had been his being "disturbed by the ease with which so much of the country was soon persuaded that Saddam Hussein's Iraq had somehow been responsible [for September 11] and stampeded into a disastrous war as a consequence. The extremely suspicious aspects of the anthrax attacks had also led me to begin questioning the reported version of events presented in our mainstream media."[525]

"After a major crack in one's wall of skeptical disbelief occurs," he'd continued, "it is natural to carefully re-examine much of the past. . . . The realization that the world is often quite different from what is presented in our leading newspapers and magazines is not an easy conclusion for most educated Americans to accept, or at least that was true in my own case. . . . Certainly the events of the past dozen years have forced me to completely recalibrate my own reality-detection apparatus, . . . resulting in . . . the production of my American Pravda series, now approaching a half-million words and extending into the controversies of the 1990s that I had so casually dismissed at the time."[526]

Unz had eventually been led from the Kennedy assassination to question the Covid virus and responses to it. "Once we recognize that for nearly six decades our government and our media had successfully concealed the reality of JFK's assassination, we must necessarily turn a skeptical eye to more recent events. If the president of the United States—the most powerful man in the world—could be struck down in public by a conspiracy involving rogue elements of his own government, and that truth then kept hidden from the American people for generations, other important matters may have been treated in a similar manner."[527]

Roger Simon, too, has questioned whether "American Democracy [Has] Been a Hallucination for Nearly 60 Years." "If indeed the CIA was in any way involved in the assassination of JFK on Nov. 22, 1963, then anything that has happened in the public sphere in our country since that day has basically been a hallucination created by an intelligence agency far deeper than most of us—certainly me—ever imagined."[528] His entry point had been the killing of Lee Harvey Oswald. "I cannot remember seeing anything more inexplicable in my life," he'd stated. "How could this have been allowed to happen only hours after the assassination? In retrospect, it becomes even more incredible. In a certain sense, I now feel that in most of my adult life, what I have thought was real, has been erased. . . . If all this is true, the question becomes how do we get out of this hallucination? . . . To begin with, we need the full information, every document, and we need it now. Without the public being able to review the last three percent we can go no further. We should be calling for that—loudly."

Tucker Carlson, also, Ron Unz reported, had changed his mind about Kennedy's assassination. "For almost sixty years, nearly the entirety of the American mainstream media engaged in a conspiracy of silence to avoid discussing the obvious facts surrounding the death of President John F. Kennedy, an information embargo finally broken a few days ago by Tucker Carlson. So perhaps our country will finally begin to understand why that one man had died, a death that occurred before the overwhelming majority of today's Americans were even born. But I think it is even more necessary that we break the same conspiracy of silence regarding the Covid deaths of well over a million Americans, deaths that were probably caused by the extremely reckless and illegal actions taken by elements of our own government."[529]

Perhaps all these examples of prominent Americans waking up and re-examining recent events in American history are preparing the ground for President Trump to publicly state what he really believes about September 11. Or perhaps, as Jacob G. Hornberger has concluded, "Trump has been Hoovered"? "Why didn't Trump order the release of those long-secret records of the CIA? Why did he . . . participate in the CIA's assassination cover-up by authorizing the CIA to continue keeping its half-century-old records secret? Indeed, why doesn't Trump . . . go public right now with what he saw in those records? One possibility is that the CIA 'Hoovered' Trump into continuing to keep the CIA's decades-old assassination-related records secret. By 'Hoovered' I am referring to J. Edgar Hoover, who was a serial blackmailer when he was serving as FBI director. Hoover would acquire personal information about people with the aim of blackmailing them into bending them to his will. . . . My hunch is that that is what happened with Trump."[530]

ᴥ 105 ᴥ

After lunch I turned to thinking about Gina, to the tense moments in our last conversation. I was struck again by how devastated I'd be if I lost her. Yet the age thing still held me back.

Then it occurred to me that although 30 years was a big age difference, Gina was determined to marry someone at least 20 years older than herself anyway. I'm only five to ten years beyond the range she'd already been looking in. Perhaps I wasn't too old after all. Her mother was widowed at 38, so Gina already had that model in mind.

And she was right about another thing. It was up to her to make the decision; I should not decide for her. I must treat her as a full Principal. She had, in fact, considered all relevant factors about her suitors more thoroughly than anyone I'd ever met.

Then it hit me! Many other men had married women much younger than themselves, including men I knew of and respected. I did a bit of research and made a list of some of them, with details of how it worked out for all concerned:

Mortimer J. Adler, Chairman of the Board of *Encyclopedia Brittanica*. At age 63 he'd married a woman 26 years old, a difference of 37 years. By all accounts, their marriage was satisfying for both of them. And he, dying at age 99, had outlived his young bride by more than a decade.

Senator J. William Fulbright, who had founded the U.S. government's Fulbright Scholarship Program, among many other significant accomplishments. His second wife was 28 years younger than himself. They married when he was 85 and she was 57.

Socrates. At the time of his trial and death at age 71, in 399 B.C., his youngest child was still small enough to be held in his mother's arms. So he was perhaps 68 when his son had been conceived. His wife was of childbearing age then, so their age difference was perhaps 40 years.

Many actors I admired had married younger women. Robert Duvall married his fourth wife when he was 73; she was 41 years younger than himself. Alec Baldwin married a woman 26 years younger. And Jeff Goldblum, when 63, married a woman 32 years younger than himself.

Celeste Holm, the actress who played the violinist in the Frank Sinatra-Debbie Reynolds movie *The Tender Trap*, later married a man 46 years younger than herself. She was 87 and he was 41. And Emmanuel Macron, the current president of France, is married to a woman 24 years older than himself.

So wide age differences, while not common, are not unheard of. The 30 years that separates my age from Gina's wouldn't even be close to a record.

And then another concern fell away. Many men are fathers of a special type: grandfathers. Even if I couldn't be as active playing sports with my kids, I could certainly be as active as many grandfathers are. Yes, that just might work. Perhaps I wasn't too old to be a father after all. Sure, I might value quiet and privacy more than I had 30 years earlier, which would make some aspects of raising children more unsettling now than then. But—and here's the interesting part—as a retiree with a pension and not needing to work to put food on the table, I could still claim the work hours for my own time. Gina's father, like most other fathers, went off to work every day, returning home at dinnertime. I could do the same, even if my work was done in an office at home. So that wouldn't be much different from the family life we'd have if I was younger and still working for a living. In fact, that would be less demanding than trying to build a career and raise a family at the same time, the mere thought of which made me tired now.

And as for the inevitable decline in energy that I might face in the future after the kids were born, well, many grandparents raise their grandchildren. If they could do it, so could I.

The more clearly I saw that it might be possible to establish a long-term relationship with Gina, i.e., marriage, the stronger my desire for her grew. I'd been a fool not to have seen all this before. Of course I needed to think it all through again, but at this moment I didn't see any obstacles at all to marrying the one and only woman that I now saw I couldn't bear to lose.

⚘ 106 ⚘

If a major public figure such as President Trump revealed the truth of what had happened on September 11, would the American people demand an official accounting? Would they demand that a real investigation take place, in public, conducted by a body authorized to compel testimony under oath?

And if such an accounting took place, would people rise up to demand changes in the political system to restore the republican form of government that the country had had during its first 150 years? Could the American people, once aroused from their slumber, make a difference?

It had happened before. In 1776, they'd rebelled against violations of their rights as Englishmen when all reasoned approaches to the King and Parliament had been rebuffed. Violations of the rights of Americans are far more severe now than when the Declaration of Independence was drafted and signed by the 13 colonies.

Half a century ago, Americans had awakened to the injustice of the violations of civil rights of black Americans, resulting in the Civil Rights Movement. They had risen up again in opposition to their country's involvement in the civil war in Vietnam, forcing the withdrawal of the 550,000 American troops stationed there.

I recalled also the example of Solidarity, the Polish trade union, whose pressure on the Communist Party beginning in the early 1980s, backed by widespread public support, eventually resulted, in 1989, in the first pluralistic election in Poland since 1947. Going back farther, it was public opinion that led first England, then countries throughout the west, to outlaw slavery and to suppress the slave trade.

Another example was the People Power revolution in The Philippines that, beginning in 1983, had swept Ferdinand Marcos from power in 1986. I wanted to look most carefully at this revolution because The Philippines had been a colony of the United States and because it was Gina's home country.

I knew that even after The Philippines had gained independence in 1946 it remained subject to extensive American influence. On the positive side, "America had endowed the Filipinos with universal education, a common language, public hygiene, roads, bridges, and, above all, republican institutions. Americans and Filipinos had fought and died side by side at Bataan and Corregidor and perished together on the ghastly Death March."[531]

I also knew that the United States had supported President Ferdinand Marcos after he declared martial law in 1971, and agreed with Stanley Karnow that "by backing Marcos, even as an expedient, the United States [government] had betrayed its proteges and its own principles."[532]

Now I wanted to know how the largely Americanized Filipinos had wrested power away from the American-backed dictator. Perhaps understanding how that process played out would reveal strategies or tactics useful for Americans today in wresting power away from the American government that administers their country as a colony on behalf of the Power Elite.

Before considering the relevance of the Filipinos' People Power revolution against Marcos for our situation today, I jotted down some of the similarities between The Philippines' semi-colonial status under the United States then and America's semi-colonial statues under the Power Elite today.

Similarities abound. During the U.S.-backed Marcos regime, The Philippines hosted the two largest American bases outside the United States: Clark Air Force Base and Subic Bay Naval Base. The U.S. also controlled another 21 bases in the country, similar to the U.S. military operating 800 bases within the United States today. Given the wide seas surrounding the archipelago and the absence of historic or traditional enemies, Luis Francia explained, "the only credible threat to the stability of the country and the government of The Philippines "would be from within, from its own population, and it was in the domestic arena where U.S. military assistance could be and was often utilized."[533] The United States, surrounded by two large oceans, was in a similar position, and its government increasingly considers using military force to control the American people. Perhaps that hasn't happened directly yet, but that's what much of the post-September 11 legislation and the militarization of police departments since then have been designed to make possible, not to mention the establishment of the U.S. Northern Command I'd already noted.

Marcos declared martial law after a spate of bombings secretly perpetrated by his own government set the stage for it. "A series of provocative incidents," Francia recounted, were "stage-managed so the government could blame violent anti-government factions, and thus justify declaring a state of emergency. . . . Martial law wasn't necessary to achieve these goals, but . . . Marcos needed a legitimate reason to stay on in power—the constitution limited a president to two terms."[534] Are Marcos's actions significantly different from those of the Power Elite's in the United States, which included blowing up several large buildings and killing nearly 3,000 people, then blaming Muslim terrorists for its crimes?

Even after the independence of The Philippines, "the U.S. was still very much a dominant player in both its internal and external affairs."[535] Likewise, today the Power Elite, in part through the Military-Industrial Complex, is a dominant player in the internal and external affairs of the United States.

The United States supported Marcos throughout his 14 year stint of martial law, during which he stole an estimated $15 billion dollars from the country and left it more than $50 billion in debt (equivalent to $150 billion today). In the United States on September 10, 2001, Secretary of Defense Donald Rumsfeld announced that the Pentagon could not account for $2.6 trillion in expenditures. All records related to those expenditures were destroyed in the attack on the Pentagon the next day. There were apparently no backup files. The U.S. government's debt since 2001 has increased by more than $20 trillion. Is all that significantly different from Marcos's looting of The Philippines?

During the weeks after his declaration of martial law, "Marcos closed down newspapers and radio and television stations, [and] imposed censorship on those that remained in operation."[536] Is that significantly different from the Power Elite's near complete control over the mainstream media even before the Covid lockdowns?

"With the army buttressing him, Marcos wielded complete authority, imposing his will through decree."[537] Is that significantly different from the United States today, in which most states are ruled by governors who have complete authority and who rule through decree? How is all that significantly different from the legislation passed after September 11, legislation that members of Congress were not allowed to read, let alone debate, before voting on it?

In The Philippines, "Americans were to be treated the same as Filipinos in economic investment" even though, as President Garcia declared in 1960, "the control of the economy by aliens 'makes a mockery of our independence and robs it of substance and meaning." In fact, "Filipinos were prohibited from selling any products that might 'come into substantial competition' with articles made in the United States—meaning no manufactured goods could be produced. So the archipelago, its industrial potential stunted, was to be preserved as an agricultural land dependent on America."[538]

How is that significantly different from the United States today, in which large companies are granted special permission to remain open even though small stores selling the same products are forcibly shuttered, which likewise makes a mockery of our independence and robs it of substance and meaning? In both instances preferential treatment was and is given to the politically well-connected.

Garcia explained that ending the special rights given to Americans would be "simply an honest-to-goodness effort of the Filipino people to be masters in their own economic household for exactly the same reason that Americans would be masters of the U.S. national economy."[539] Such reasoning, if applied to the United States today, would require the immediate and permanent reopening of small businesses and the abolishing of restrictions enacted against independent contractors.

In these and innumerable other ways, Filipinos then were, and Americans today are, treated as colonials with little say in the government or administration of their own country. I just couldn't avoid the conclusions that the U.S. government today is acting as the colonial administrator of the American quasi-colony on behalf of the Power Elite, just as the Marcos regime acted as colonial administrator of The Philippines quasi colony on behalf of the U.S. government.

Turning to foreign policy, "Marcos's dictatorial rule exposed the darkness at the heart of U.S. foreign policy," Francia stated. "In spite of the rhetoric, democracy was hardly the most important issue for the U.S. government when it came to its client states. Paramount were its economic and security interests. . . . If martial law meant taking liberties with the people's own liberties, so be it."[540] What better phrase describes the post-September 11 legislation than "taking liberties with the people's own liberties"? What better phrase describes the post-September 11 wars in Afghanistan and Iraq and elsewhere than the Power Elite's looking after "its economic and security interests" at the expense of the people in those countries?

"Even as economic conditions and the state of human rights deteriorated over the course of twenty years of Ferdinand and Imelda Marcos's rule," Francia observed, "five successive U.S. presidents supported the Marcoses with little to no restraint exercised: Johnson, Nixon, Ford, Carter, and Reagan." The situation reached an absurd peak in 1981 when Vice President George Herbert Walker Bush, at a dinner hosted in his honor by Marcos at Malacanang, the presidential palace, praised Marcos in his toast by saying, "We love your adherence to democratic principles and to the democratic process."[541] At that time I was closely following events in The Philippines, and detested Bush for those remarks that must have seemed insulting to the sensibilities of all Filipinos other than the Marcoses and their cronies. That was several years before I joined the Foreign Service and President George H. W. Bush submitted my name, along with others, to the Senate for confirmation.

Equally insulting was his son's, George W. Bush's, statement on October 6, 2005, that "the world has seen the swiftest advance of democratic institutions in history. And Americans are proud to have played our role in this great story."[542] How bitter those words must have seemed to the people of Afghanistan and Iraq, whose countries had seen more than a million people killed since American military forces had entered them in the years after September 11, 2001.

So how did the Filipinos manage to overthrow the corrupt, brutal and kleptomaniacal Marcos regime, backed as it was by the strongest nation in the world?

The overthrow proceeded in two phases, the first gradual, the second quick. Both were triggered by actions taken by the Marcos regime itself. First, his dictatorial and corrupt rule generated intermittent and sporadic protests throughout the country that increased in size and frequency over a period of several years. During one large demonstration, 30,000 people were arrested for peacefully expressing their democratic right of dissent, and independent media were shut down. "The crackdown on civil liberties and media, the roundup of student activists, organizers, and left-leaning urban professionals, the use of torture, and the senseless savagings," Francia recorded, resulted in the creation of a "radicalized, educated, sophisticated

Image 31. People Power in The Philippines, 1986.

middle-class segment, with networks all over the country, . . . hastening its emergence as a nationwide movement."[543]

The second phase of the overthrow was triggered by the assassination of opposition leader Benino (Ninoy) Aquino on August 21, 1983. Larger and more frequent demonstrations followed, culminating in a period of four days, from February 22 to 25, 1986, when at least a million people gathered in Manila to protect the leaders of their movement. People Power, it came to be called.[544]

Soon after Corazon Aquino, widow of the revered politician Benino Aquino who had been murdered by Marcos's men, became president of The Philippines, she addressed a joint session of the U.S. Congress. In stirring remarks, she called on the United States to rise to its highest self by supporting a country that was itself trying to implement the highest American ideals in its new post-Marcos restructuring. "Has there been a greater test of national commitment to the ideals you hold dear than what my people have gone through?" Corazon asked. "You have spent many lives and much treasure to bring freedom to many lands that were reluctant to receive it. And here you have a people who won it by themselves and need only help to preserve it."[545]

Although at the last minute the United States had partially redeemed itself by easing Marcos's departure from the country, thereby avoiding great bloodshed, it provided only moderate aid to The Philippines and did little to help it recover the $15 billion that Marcos had looted from the country.

So far, Americans appear to be stuck in the first phase, in which groups protesting against Marcos's corruption and brutality arose spontaneously, with networks growing between them. The rise of the 9/11 Truth movement in the United States has been similar, with a score or more organizations being formed and networks growing between them, but which have not yet succeeded in generating widespread re-examination of the events of September 11.

No event similar to the assassination of Ninoy Aquino has occurred to trigger the onset of a wider movement. No crisis has arisen that could open large numbers of people's minds and compel them to examine the three coups and other related events. The crisis that has occurred, the Covid lockdowns, has done the opposite: it's made people so fearful that they have become even more blind than before.

We haven't had a leader of the stature of Corazon Aquino to draw large numbers of people into re-examining recent events in American history and demanding an accounting for them. Or, to draw on an American example, we haven't had rise to the occasion a leader of the stature of Dr. Martin Luther King, Jr., who, during the Civil Rights Movement called on the United States to rise to the highest ideals of its own founding and traditions. A leader who, as King did in his "Letter from a Birmingham Jail," would call for Americans to "stand up for what is best in the American dream and for the most sacred values in our Judeo-Christian heritage, thereby bringing our nation back to those great wells of democracy which were dug deep by the founding fathers in their formulation of the Constitution and the Declaration of Independence."

107

What to do while waiting for the right moment and the right inspirational leader to arrive, I wondered.

It could be that there's little direct action those who recognize the reality of the three coups can do to trigger a crisis of the magnitude needed to awaken the large majority of their fellow colonials or to conjure up a charismatic leader out of thin air. If so, we might be guided by the old adage, "Trust in God and keep your pants and your powder dry" until conditions are right. In doing so we'd be following the advice of economist Milton Friedman, who explained that "Only a crisis—actual or perceived—produces real change. When that crisis occurs, the actions that are taken depend on the ideas that are lying around. That, I believe, is our basic function: to develop alternatives to existing policies, to keep them alive and available until the politically impossible become the politically inevitable."[546]

Friedman's advice to keep ourselves primed for the moment

when change becomes possible is right on target. We can do that in three ways. One is by taking his advice in its most literal meaning: preserve and extend the evidence of what really happened during the three extraordinary events—the three coups—and related events of important but lesser impact. Included in this is preserving the books, articles, videos and websites that already document what really happened.

Two others relate to Principality. One is internal: strengthen our own individual Principality so that we're ready to go when moments of decision, judgment and action arrive. The other is external: strengthen institutional support for Principality in American society to increase the likelihood that things will break our way when the moment of crisis and the charismatic leader arrive.

In considering how to do these latter two things I found guidance and inspiration in the writings and lives of John F. Kennedy, Aldous Huxley and C. S. Lewis. And from Christianity.

Kennedy pointed the way forward in a speech he gave on July 4, 1946, early in his political career: "Our government was founded on the essential religious idea of integrity of the individual."[547] The integrity of the individual—what is this but Principality, the duty we owe to ourselves to arrive at informed decisions, judgments and actions.

This idea, Kennedy explained in the same speech, is rooted in the history of the West: "Conceived in Grecian thought, strengthened by Christian morality, and stamped indelibly into American political philosophy, the right of the individual against the State is the keystone of our Constitution. Each man is free. He is free in thought. He is free in expression. He is free in worship."[548]

Elsewhere Kennedy emphasized the importance of knowing what is true in deciding and acting well, for both the individual and the country. "I am not so much concerned with the right of everyone to say everything he pleases as I am about our need as a self-governing people to hear everything relevant. . . . If our people are to choose . . . then we need to know all the available facts, . . . hear all the alternatives and listen to all the criticisms. . . . We need to keep our minds open to criticism and to new ideas—to dissent and alternatives—to reconsideration and reflection. Only in this way can we as a self-governing people choose wisely and thoughtfully in our task of self government."[549]

"Let us not be afraid of debate or dissent," he continued. "Let us encourage it. For if we should ever abandon these basic American traditions in the name of fighting Communism [or terrorism or viruses], what would it profit us to win the whole world when we would have lost our own soul?"[550]

Kennedy closed his July 4, 1946, speech with an echo of Thomas Jefferson that is still relevant today: "Eternal vigilance is the price of liberty. It was the price yesterday. It is the price today, and it will ever be the price."[551]

Aldous Huxley, too, kept his focus on individuals by distinguishing between crowds of persons who retained their individuality even when amidst large numbers of other persons, and masses of men who had submerged their individuality in the rampages of impersonal mobs. It is individuals who act, he'd said. "The individual can never be explained away. . . . Everything that is done within a society is done by individuals."[552]

He recognized that "individuals are, of course, profoundly influenced by the local culture, the taboos and moralities, the information and misinformation handed down from the past and preserved in a body of spoken traditions or written literature." But he also showed that individuals might respond to that influence in two distinctly different ways. There's the man who, whatever he takes from society, actively uses it "in his own unique way—with *his* special senses, *his* bio-chemical make-up, *his* physique and temperament, and nobody's else's." Then there's the man who passively follows what is fashionable, who mindlessly goes with the flow. The first is a Principal; the second, a serf.

In Huxley's imaginary society in *Brave New World*, the Institute began its pursuit of ultimate uniformity by producing as many human clones as possible from a single embryo. Doing so made it easier to impose "social and cultural uniformity upon adults and their children."[553]

In their efforts to impose uniformity in real life, Huxley saw, conditioners "will (unless prevented) make use of all the mind-manipulation techniques at their disposal and will not hesitate to reinforce these methods of non-rational persuasion by economic coercion and threats of physical violence."[554] They have been quite successful. "This doctrine [of uniformity] has been incorporated into the prevailing mode of thought of many who have had to do with shaping educational and governmental policies and is often accepted unquestioningly by those who do little critical thinking of their own."

As Principals, we must push back against mindless indoctrination and mindless uniformity. "If this kind of tyranny is to be avoided, we must begin without delay to educate ourselves and our children for freedom and self-government. Such an education for freedom should be . . . an education first of all in facts and in values—the facts of individual diversity and genetic uniqueness and the values of freedom, tolerance and mutual charity which are the ethical core."[555] We must create an environment, a society, in which using the mind to become informed, to make informed decisions and judgments and to choose wisely between alternative courses of action, is the norm, the baseline. In such a society the majority of persons would be more likely to re-examine the three coups, the events surrounding them and the consequences that have flowed from them.

Thinking these thoughts, I recalled the title of a book I'd read decades ago, Robert Maynard Hutchins's *Education for Freedom* and jotted down a note to take another look at it. I'd never forgotten that, when writing it in the midst of the Second World War, he'd said something like "Over most of Europe the books and monuments have been destroyed and bombed. To destroy European civilization in America you do not need to burn its records in a single fire. Leave those records unread for a few generations and the effect will be the same."[556] That book was one of many I'd thought of recently that I'd read in earlier years of intellectual awakening, before the hectic years of building a career and raising a family submerged all that. Since retiring, I'd found myself more and more recalling those years and resurrecting the life I'd lived in those earlier days. It felt good to recall them, not nostalgically, but as though I was now returning home to them and to the manner of living that suited me best.

"Always be thinking about how to make yourself a better person and your society a better place," I'd often urged my kids. I now saw that those two tasks were in essence the same as those I was now proposing for myself and others: make ourselves stronger Principals so we're ready to act when the moment arrives, and create and strengthen institutions that support Principality to prepare the ground for its arrival.

C. S. Lewis had a name for the sorry state of mass uniformity that Huxley had portrayed: the abolition of man, which he'd used for the title of his book. Man's conquest of man will come through eugenics, he divined, through a process in which "the ultimate springs of human action" will be altered. "They know how to produce conscience and [will] decide what kind of conscience they will produce,"[557] he wrote. Change will follow change until, ultimately, "Man's conquest of Nature turns out, in the moment of its consummation, to be Nature's conquest of Man."[558]

How this abolition of human nature, this replacement of individual human beings by a uniform unhuman nature, might come about is portrayed in Lewis's novel, *That Hideous Strength*. Though written in 1945, I found it disturbing to read because of how closely harmful aspects of that fictional society match conditions in the United States in the post-September 11 and continuing Covid eras.

In both the book and real life, a severe crisis (or crises) had been deliberately engineered by those who wanted to gain control over society. "Emergency regulations" is the key, Mark is told in the novel. "We'll never get the power we want until the Government declares that a state of emergency exists."[559] In the book, the government triggers a large-scale riot to justify a state of emergency. In the United States, the government declared a state of emergency in response to September 11 (still in effect today), and governments at various levels declared states of emergency in response to Covid.

In both, a large and powerful Department is set up to wield the emergency powers on a permanent basis: in the novel, it's the National Institute of Co-operation in Economics, N.I.C.E.; in the United States, it's the Department of Homeland Security. In both the goal is the suppression of individuality; in both an effort is made to convince people to support the measures that will result in their own enslavement.

"Sweep away all idea of co-operation!" a director of N.I.C.E. tells Mark. "Does clay *cooperate* with the potter? . . . These people will be used. I shall be used too. . . . You have no choice whether you will be used or not. There is no turning back."[560] In the novel those steps were "the beginning of what is really [the creation of] a new species. . . . They will call it the next step in evolution. And henceforward, all the creatures that you and I call human are mere candidates for admission to the new species or else its slaves—perhaps its food."[561]

Like *Huxley's Brave New World*, Lewis's *That Hideous Strength* packs an emotional punch unique to literature. Through these novels I'd felt the power of forces aligned against Principality more forcefully than I ever had by reading non-fiction books or articles about the three coups. Only the images and videos of September 11 came close to literature's visceral impact.

I've come to see human beings as open-ended: bound on one end by genetic inheritance, but open to influences and surprising revelations of what that genetic inheritance, or rather the mix of that genetic inheritance with environmental influences, might produce. We're not open-ended on both ends as the fantasists would have us believe, nor closed at both ends as behaviorists would like to believe. Each person is unique, full of possibilities and surprises from a nature that can never be fully known but that literature can go a long way toward revealing to us.

These novels portray "two fundamentally different ways of seeing the world—the static, literal, explicit, mechanical view and, by contrast, the dynamic, vivid, metaphorical, mysterious, implicit view,"[562] as Jonathan Gaisman stated the distinction between them in a different context. The former is the view of the dominant powers in the societies in both novels, as well as, apparently, the Department of Homeland Security that tarnishes the American landscape. In all three worlds the latter "dynamic" view is in the minority. This is the world of individuals and Principals, the world in which "Everyone must feel that he is the supreme arbiter of his own [destiny], that no power on earth shall rise over him, that he is and always shall be sovereign of himself and all relating to his individuality,"[563] as C. Bradley Thompson phrased it.

I wasn't surprised to learn that several of the most important early investigators to expose the real events of September 11 were religious scholars. David Ray Griffin, author of a dozen books on September 11 and the main speaker at a dozen public events about the events of that day, was professor of the philosophy of religion and theology at the Claremont School of Theology and at Claremont Graduate University. He was also co-director of its Center for Process Studies at the same university. Graeme MacQueen, long-time professor of religious studies at McMaster University in Ontario, Canada, was also Founding Director of the Center for Peace Studies. And Kevin Barrett, a devout Muslim, spearheaded the founding of MUJCA-NET, the Muslim-Jewish-Christian Alliance for 9/11 Truth. He was also the organizer of the first big event of the 9/11 Truth movement, the conference held on April 18, 2005, at the University of Wisconsin, Madison, which was filmed by C-SPAN.

All three were and are models for how to undertake the two critical tasks before us: strengthening ourselves as Principals and creating conditions in society supportive of Principality. All three had done the second by founding and directing institutes or organizations, and by organizing and participating in important public events to alert others to the real facts behind the official cover stories. All had been dedicated to discovering truth and to promoting the ethical principals and practices arising from Christianity, Judaism and Islam. Their research into the truth of September 11 had grown out of their long-time scholarly work in religion.

"The 9/11 truth movement poses a unique spiritual challenge," Barrett stated on behalf of himself and all others determined to uncover the truth of what had happened. "Are you going to go on living a comfortable lie? Or can you handle an uncomfortable truth? If so, what are you going to do about it? The great monotheistic wisdom traditions—Judaism, Christianity and Islam—offer a guide to the perplexed. Since the 9/11 attacks were designed to stir up hatred between these three great faiths, it is only fitting that we turn to them for advice in our dilemma."[564]

With all this in mind, it was inspirational to read of another model for resisting pressure to abandon truth and to resign ourselves to going with the flow: Jesus. In John and Nisha Whitehead's take, Jesus, "the religious figure worshipped by Christians for his death on the cross and subsequent resurrection, paid the ultimate price for speaking out against the police state of his day. A radical nonconformist who challenged authority at every turn, Jesus was a far cry from the watered-down, corporatized, simplified, gentrified, sissified vision of a meek creature holding a lamb that most modern churches peddle. In fact, he spent his adult life speaking truth to power, challenging the status quo of his day, and pushing back against the abuses of the Roman Empire."[565]

The Whiteheads went on to describe similarities between the harsh realities of the American Empire today and the Roman Empire of Jesus's day—"secrecy, surveillance, a widespread police presence, a citizenry treated like suspects with little recourse against the police state, perpetual wars, a military empire, martial law, and political retribution against those who dared to challenge the power of the state"[566]—before lamenting that "the radical Jesus, the political dissident who took aim at injustice and oppression, has been largely forgotten today, replaced by a congenial, smiling Jesus trotted out for religious holidays but otherwise rendered mute when it comes to matters of war, power and politics."

With the man who had been the embodiment of Christianity so misunderstood by most American churches today, it's no wonder, I thought, that they meekly closed their doors to their parishioners in response to governments' illegitimate Covid edicts. No wonder so many in our country unthinkingly accept the cover stories for the three coups when in doing so they're merely following the lead of those who are their spiritual and intellectual guides.

The Whiteheads went on to nail that point, too. "Yet for those who truly study the life and teachings of Jesus, the resounding theme is one of outright resistance to war, materialism and empire. What a marked contrast to the advice being given to Americans by church leaders to 'submit to your leaders and those in authority,' which in the American police state translates to complying, conforming, submitting, obeying orders, deferring to authority and generally doing whatever a government official tells you to do."[567]

"Telling Americans to blindly obey the government or put their faith in politics and vote for a political savior flies in the face of everything for which Jesus lived and died," they continued. "Will we follow the path of least resistance—turning a blind eye to the evils of our age and marching in lockstep with the police state—or will we be transformed nonconformists 'dedicated to justice, peace, and brotherhood'? As Martin Luther King, Jr., reminds us in a powerful sermon delivered 70 years ago, 'This command not to conform comes . . . [from] Jesus Christ, the world's most dedicated nonconformist, whose ethical nonconformity still challenges the conscience of mankind."[568]

Their mention of Martin Luther King, Jr., brought back to me the need for a non-violent movement in the United States to restore the constitutional republic that I had been born into. Such movements, I recalled, had resulted in England's abolishing the slave trade, and could have resulted in a nonviolent ending of slavery in the United States, too, if only we'd followed the British model of compensating slave owners for their losses when their slaves were freed.

Such movements, Peter Dale Scott observed, teach us "that

tyrannical oppression from above, no matter how invincible it may outwardly appear, is vulnerable to organized nonviolent resistance when it is grounded in a sufficiently broad social base."[569] As Principals dedicated to truth, we must seek to broaden that social base. But that's the same old sticking point. "The question is whether the American nation can develop resistance, sedated as it is by material comforts and insecurity."

I took heart from people who have converted to Christianity later in life, having already noted that Mortimer J. Adler, Walker Percy and Roger Scruton had done so. That's a much bigger transformation in beliefs and sensibilities than merely opening one's eyes to the realities of the world we live in. They had convinced themselves or perhaps allowed a divine spirit to infuse their souls. Something similar needs to happen now among large numbers of persons for any individual transformation to make a difference.

But how to convince others of the value of things they don't value—things like independent thought and action? How does one convince them of the value of free speech and democratic practices when they've never thought much about these things, when their scope of awareness doesn't extend much beyond their own immediately pressing daily concerns? And for that matter, how does one interest persons with little intellectual capacity in the products of intellectual effort, in things such as literature, history, philosophy, science, art and classical music?

I wondered how Gina does it, how someone of her ardent, religious nature functions in the world rather than recusing herself in a convent. She'd largely freed herself from the nonsense in the world by her faith in a higher power, by letting herself be guided by it as she determined how best to go about her life. I could see that her educational activities were valuable in themselves and that she largely avoided activities of little importance. But how did she live her life among people so radically different from herself? One way, I saw, was by not trying to convert anyone to anything. She'd never made any effort to try to convert me to Christianity or Catholicism, nor had I seen her try to do so with others. There was much of interest about her that still puzzled me.

But I, today, wasn't like that. I didn't want to live and let live. I could see that the tyranny that was step by step descending on my country through coup after coup and legislation after legislation and edict after edict would continue to transform the lives of everyone in it unless it was stopped. I could see that it could be stopped only by the public actively pushing back against it—not by a few people resisting as individuals, but by a large minority of people actively pushing back as had happened in the People Power revolution in The Philippines. Yet most of my fellow Americans, their eyes firmly shut, remained oblivious to the approaching dangers. Being the large majority, their blindness and inactivity would drag even those aware of the dangers down with them.

How had it come to this, I wondered. How had we abandoned the society I'd been born into and grown up in, a world that C. Bradley Thompson described as "a social system that recognized, defined, and protected as sacrosanct the rights of individuals"?[570] "The greatest achievement of the American Revolution was to subordinate society and government to this fundamental moral law,"[571] he'd continued. "Human flourishing requires freedom—the freedom to think and act without interference, which means security from predatory threats against one's person or property. Freedom requires government, but only government of a particular sort—the sort that protects individuals from force and coercion and that defines a sphere of liberty in which individuals are free to pursue their own welfare and happiness. Within that protected sphere American revolutionaries and their nineteenth-century heirs created a new world unlike anything anywhere else."[572]

"What makes America a unique and extraordinary nation"—I'd change that to "had made"—is the philosophy that allows ordinary men and women to pursue their own selfish values—to be inventive, imaginative, and hard working—free of social control and government meddling. The United States of America has made"—again, I'd change that to "had made"—great progress precisely because its 'Don't Tread on Me' philosophy liberated ordinary people to achieve great things both individually and cooperatively."[573]

Yet it had slipped away within one lifetime—my lifetime. Had all the images I'd had of Americans being adventurous, independent-minded, and self-reliant turned out to mere illusions? Land of the free and home of the brave? Those appeared to be hollow phrases now, given that nearly everyone cowered behind face masks and stood at least six feet away from everyone else. Had I always misunderstood Americans so completely? Or had their nature changed so drastically while I'd been away?

Seeing all this after returning to the United States, I felt much as Ronald Reagan must have when he'd said, "I didn't leave the Democratic Party; the Democratic Party left me." I had left the United States only physically in working abroad for so many years. I hadn't left it intellectually or emotionally. I still had American sensibilities. But I'd returned home to find that while I'd been away the country had left me.

How did we get from the world of my childhood—years spent up at the schoolyard playing baseball or football with friends, or riding our bikes around the neighborhood dressed up like Superman or Batman, or engaging in mock battles in the ruins of what had been a military base during the Second World War, where we shot bows and arrows and caught lizards, or waded in the creek to catch frogs and tadpoles and minnows and from where we'd collected creek water and moss to look at under a microscope back home—to where we are today? We were always on the move. How did all that activity get replaced by kids, even ones very young, sitting motionless except for their thumbs, off by themselves, staring at their phones, saying not a word to those around them as they play video games. It's beyond odd, beyond queer. It's perverse.

It's beyond dismaying that those kids will grow into adults who don't know they are living in a colony even though the evidence is now right out in the open, just as they don't recognize the reality of September 11 even though the evidence, in photographs and videos, is right in front of their eyes.

All this reinforced my belief in the critical importance of Principality—in making informed decisions, in examining existing beliefs, in acting on the basis of informed decisions even in the face of pressure not to, and in creating institutions to support widespread Principality throughout the country. Principality, I now knew, was not just the answer to how to live my own life, but also the way out of the difficulties the United States is now enmeshed in.

It was almost time to leave to meet Gina for lunch, but I had one final thought I needed to get down on paper before leaving.

108

Perhaps one effective was to open people's eyes to the real story of the assassination of JFK, the real events of September 11 and that the real harm from Covid comes not from the virus itself but from the misguided governmental responses to it, would be to highlight the work of the extraordinary men and women who've been active in truth movements for all three events. It was, after all, independent individuals who have exposed the truth. Jim Marrs said it best: "When a final 'truth' concerning the assassination of President John F. Kennedy is generally accepted by the population of the United States, it will have to be acknowledged that this truth came not from the government, the legal profession, or the news media—rather, the truth will have come from the legion of individual citizens who have refused to accept official but superficial and unsupported explanations."[574]

The stories of those independent and courageous men and women have it all: underdogs striving to take down murderous, evil villains, friendships and betrayals among the underdogs, even romances between them for all I know.

I could tell the stories of the scholars' and researchers' (the underdogs') gradual or sudden awakening to the reality that all official investigations into these events have been cover-ups, that all have been designed to keep certain information hidden, even if that meant presenting a falsified story to the public.

That had certainly been the case with the Warren Commission and House Select Committee on Assassinations.

"The Warren Commission did not investigate what had happened," L. Fletcher Prouty had stated. "It merely took prepackaged, precooked data and published its prescribed report, as it had been ordered to do."[575] The 9/11 Commission's "investigation" and report was similar, Peter Dale Scott observed: Although "9/11 was the largest homicide by far in American history, . . . it has never been adequately investigated." "Key evidence requested by the Commission was initially withheld until subpoenas were issued, and some evidence was deliberately destroyed. Worse, there are systematic suppressions of evidence in the 9/11 Commission Report itself, along with unresolved contradictions in testimony and occasional misrepresentations of some crucial facts. . . . The 9/11 report is an example of concerted cover-up, partly by omissions and just as important by its cherry-picking of evidence and contrived misrepresentations."[576]

Perhaps all this skullduggery should have been expected; perhaps we should never have expected the government to investigate itself in the first place. "There's a good reason why no one has ever been reprimanded for his or her performance on 9/11," Michael Ruppert observed. "Any reprimand (or more severe sanction) opens the doors to hearings, administrative processes, exculpatory information, discovery, and the legal process that would put these monstrous inconsistencies directly under bright light where they would have to be resolved in order to sustain the punishment. That would be the very last thing the Commission would want."[577]

"The Empire insists upon the maintenance of its own decorous appearances and its customary credibility," Ruppert continued, "no matter how transparent those appearances, nor how empty that credibility becomes. . . . The American people should never have expected anything different from what we got. It was designed, planned, constructed, and functioned to achieve one and only one objective: damage control."

I now saw the need for a book recounting the determined efforts of those intrepid individuals working on shoe-string budgets who had uncovered the real events behind the assassination and September 11. Having put so much effort into learning what had happened and becoming somewhat familiar with the names of some of the most important scholars and researchers who brought to light the information I was absorbing, I wanted to tell their stories.

Perhaps alerting Americans not just to what had occurred on those terrible days, but to the extraordinary, even heroic efforts to uncover what had really happened—the stories of generations of courageous investigators and scholars who dedicated years of their lives to making the truth known—could be inspirational for Americans today.

I knew of Vincent Salandria's early work to expose contradictions between the evidence presented in the Warren Report and the conclusions stated by the Commission, and of Mark Lane's *Rush to Judgment: A Critique of the Warren Commission*. It had been the first book to create widespread awareness of the flaws of the Warren Report and of how the Commission had ignored, suppressed and altered evidence to reach its pre-determined conclusion that Oswald had acted alone. Lane's book was a tour de force, with more than 4,100 citations documenting every piece of information in its 330 pages. On its persuasiveness, Lord Bertrand Russell had stated, "Mark Lane's evidence comprises one of the most remarkable documents I have seen and is an unanswerable indictment of the United States government's attempt to suppress the truth and conceal the circumstances surrounding the death of the president."[578]

Rush to Judgment had become a *New York Times* #1 bestseller in 1966, so from that time onward Americans couldn't say they didn't know that solid grounds existed for doubting the accuracy of the Warren Commission's conclusions. By 1967 Lane and other investigators had apparently convinced two-thirds of Americans, but I didn't come across any evidence of a groundswell of popular opinion for a new investigation. That came later after Oliver Stone's film *JFK*, which generated enough public outrage to push Congress to form the House Select Committee on Assassinations in the mid 1970s. The Committee had been lied to and stonewalled, though, and its recommendations to the Department of Justice were dead on arrival.

All that would be an interesting story to tell, as would the story of how most members of the Warren Commission itself had come to doubt that its conclusions were valid. So would the story of Gerald Posner's *Case Closed: Lee Harvey Oswald and the Assassination of JFK*, which supported the official story—not so much the book itself but that Posner himself came to question whether key parts of that story really were right. In an essay in *Newsweek* in 2003, he stated that "The CIA's deception of Congress is not a performance that inspires public confidence.'"[579]

I hadn't gone far down this road of gathering information about the efforts by early researchers to bring the truth to light, and to describe the difficulties and opposition they faced from those determined to stamp out criticism of the official story, when I came across John Kelin's extraordinary book, *Praise from a Future Generation: The Assassination of John F. Kennedy and the First Generation Critics of the Warren Report*. Kelin presented the findings and experiences of those brave early researchers, who included, in addition to Salandria, Cook and Lane, Edward Jay Epstein, Harold Feldman, Mary Ferrell, Maggie Field, Gaeton Fonzi, Jim Garrison, Richard Groden, Penn Jones, Jr., Wesley Liebeler, David Lifton, Raymond Marcus, Shirley Martin, Sylvia Meagher, Leo Sauvage, Josiah Thompson, Cyril Wecht and Harold Weisberg.

A similar book was needed about early researchers and scholars looking into the real story of September 11. Already coming to mind were Richard Gage, who had founded Architects & Engineers for 9/11 Truth, the fearless scientists Steven Jones and Niels Harrit, the physicist David Chandler, Graeme MacQueen, who exposed the Anthrax deception, and David Ray Griffin, who had written book after book challenging the official story. Also Michael Ruppert, Michel Chossudovsky, Jim Fetzer, Peter Dale Scott, Webster Tarpley and so many others.

And Kevin Barrett, too. I had to laugh when I read his

challenge to readers of the 9/11 Commission Report: "Are you willing to live with a 571-page lie as the official record of the most important historic event of the 21st century? Are you willing to live with a 571-page lie that has served as the basis for two criminal wars of aggression, and many massive catastrophic rollbacks in Constitutional civil liberties, that were all ordered and implemented as policy—not just as contingency plans—before the event that allegedly made them necessary? . . . If your answer is yes, I submit that you are insane."[580]

Barrett had summed it all up so succinctly. There had been such optimism in the air in 2005, 2006 and 2007, and so many fascinating stories were now waiting to be told.

I set aside work on that book, though, until I could determine whether such a book had already been written. And of course it was too early to write such a book about Covid and the ongoing bizarre government-ordered lockdowns in response to it.

It then occurred to me that rather than—or perhaps in addition to—telling the stories of others I could tell my own story—the story of my own investigations, well not investigations exactly, but my research into what others had already discovered through their investigations. I could document my growing awareness of the real events of those terrible days and of the broader realities that lay behind them. I could record how distraught I felt on realizing that for decades of my adult life I had fallen for the propaganda and lies just like so many others; that I had spent decades working to promote what I'd thought were the interests of the United States but were really only the interests of the Power Elite that controlled the U.S. government. I could record how all this played into my growing interest in becoming a Principal, an informed decision maker and actor. These realizations were the genesis of this memoir.

Still, I thought, would such a book ever be possible? I still had so much to learn, I thought as I looked over at the 300 books I'd purchased on the three coups and other events in American history during my lifetime that were still unread. I thought, too, of the many important websites on the same subjects that I hadn't yet investigated, and the many videos I hadn't yet watched. Much work lay ahead.

I also wondered if there might be ways that Gina could help me with this project, just as I'd helped her by setting up an accounting system for WORDS and was now serving as her bookkeeper. In any event, it was now time to meet her for lunch.

109

Gina and I met outdoors, as planned. After our last encounter, we were both apprehensive, wondering if we'd be able to keep our conversations within the bounds we agreed on. We needed to find a way to settle our nerves, to relax, to again enjoy the freely flowing conversations we'd both enjoyed so much over the past nine months. And I wondered how best to convey my new understanding of my intentions toward her.

As soon as we sat down Gina burst out with her fears for WORDS, WORDS, WORDS if the lockdown continued much longer, and about her own future if her business failed. I could see that she was under a great deal of stress, the moment of optimism she'd expressed previously apparently having faded. And I recalled the visa problem she'd told me about. Marrying an American would be the simplest way to adjust her visa status, enabling her to remain in the United States legally. I wanted to help her with both problems and could think of only one way to do so—a way that would give me what I wanted, too. My only concern now was with finding the right words to convey to her how I felt and what I wanted, to find a way to ask a question that was burning inside me without using any clichéd phrases.

"When you say you're wary of me," she said, abruptly moving to an even more personal area of concern, "I'm always surprised because when I'm with you I don't think too far beyond just enjoying the conversation."

Alarm bells rang in my head as she spoke, because what she had said couldn't possibly be how she really felt. I'd never met anyone else who came close to her in regarding men as suitors and grading them on the criteria of how suitable they'd be as husbands and fathers. She was truly in a class by herself when it came to courtship and thinking long-term.

The alarm bells rang far louder when I heard what she said next.

"Last night I imagined what might happen once you become 'completely relaxed' around me. In my dream, since you know my address, you came to my apartment after midnight and entered through the sliding glass door to the patio, which I had forgotten to lock. Then you came to my fluffy bed like a conqueror, stripped away everything that covered me, and claimed me. You were so strong and powerful, and I was so weak, that I had no choice but to give in and let you do whatever you wanted to me. I was able to see the realest and most uninhibited version of you while you turned me from a girl into a woman. You were transformed, too, into a Greek God. You devoured me and satisfied your hunger."

She was giggling as she spoke.

I saw instantly that Gina was going for broke, throwing the Hail Mary pass that in her girlish, inexperienced way, with her garbled view of male sexuality, she hoped would get her across the finish line and win the game, that would incite me into a proposal of marriage, that would result in nights of love with a suitor, now a husband, worthy of her and worthy of being the father of her children.

I understood all that, but what I felt was anger. I suspected that she'd related this supposed dream story to other suitors before me, that she was attempting to manipulate me in the same underhanded way she'd tried to spark a proposal from them.

I stood up before replying, and she rose, too.

"My God, Gina, if there's one thing guys hate, it's a tease. A girl who gets them all excited and then says no, which is what I know you'd say if I responded to your sexual words with sexual actions. I think you need a man more than any woman I've ever met. I hope you find someone to marry soon. Or take a lover or two or three. Saving yourself for your future husband is not the way things work in the real world. Virginity is what economists call a 'wasting asset,' one that declines in value as it ages, like a mango."

All might still have been OK if we'd parted then. But we didn't, and in my anger, I spoke words that should never have been said. "I also had a dream last night. I dreamed I was with a girl, someone other than you but who I pretended was you. In my dream it was your mouth I kissed. Your body I touched. Your body I entered. It was you who moved under me. Your arms that held me tight. You who gasped as I pounded into you again and again and again. And then, only a short time later, it was your hands, your mouth, your tongue that made me hard again. It was your long skinny legs I spread wide apart, your pussy I entered. It was you I fucked for the second time in an hour."

She gasped before speaking. "I haven't ever had a guy talk like this to me. I am not angry, but I am just hurt. Very hurt. I never cried for a man, and it sucks that it's happening now."

She was indeed in tears.

"So, if you're mad, that's fine. It's my fault too, I pulled the trigger. If I teased you, I did that on purpose. I want to kill your feelings for me. Yes, I want you to be angry, and hate me even, but the most I expected was for you to totally pull away. I don't want to be an emotional torment to you. I don't want to be attached to a man I can never have. This is so difficult for me, more than you can ever imagine. Do you know how foolish it is for a girl in her twenties to be attracted to a guy who's way older? However, I didn't expect you could go that low to the point of insulting me, my choices and my womanhood. Somehow, I thought you were different, and I was so wrong."

I started to speak, but she cut me off.

"If you only knew how many guys I pushed away because I hold my values very close to me and I continue to push away any man that I don't see as fit, no matter how they try to sell me that same statement that you said about virginity as something that depreciates. I have been called prude, lunatic, an idiotic Catholic, a unicorn, and all sorts of names to harm my self esteem so I will end up sleeping with them. Some are like you; they make up stories about me being abnormal just because I haven't had sex with anyone. I have been dealing with all these men who pressure me into a relationship and try bribing me with comfortable lifestyles left and right.

"In fact, I'd rather be alone than be with a guy who looks down on me and doesn't appreciate my strength in making all these decisions. You don't know how much mental and emotional strength it takes to do this by choice in this day and age where promiscuity is normal. You don't know anything about me.

"And it hurts that you make assumptions that my problems at the tutoring companies were about me being sexual, as if my work problems are a laughing matter. Of course, you'll never understand.

"I have been going through tons of tough things right now, with my family, my studio, my finances, my personal life with guys pressuring me to give in, and here you are, adding to all of these.

"Never mind. I can't blame you, you don't know me, and I never bother explaining myself to anyone, especially to a guy who makes wild assumptions about me without properly talking his anger out. At least I now know what kind of person you are. Maybe I should return the computer to you. Even if I am struggling with so many problems right now, I'll just work harder. I don't want to know a man who see me as someone who has no dignity."

I watched as she strode angrily to her car, wondering if I had lost her forever.

110

Thinking things through at home, I saw that this was such a mess that there appeared no way out of it, no way to continue our friendship.

Gina'd gone for broke in the only way she knew how, no longer taking it easy on me because of my age and loss of my wife less than a year ago. She'd given me the full treatment that she'd given some of her other suitors and that had caused such problems for her in the past. I hadn't responded to her sexual words with sexual actions as some had; I knew that she'd pull back if I did. Nor had I withdrawn, as she'd expected. Instead, angered that she'd tried to manipulate me, to use my desires to trigger a proposal, I responded angrily, with such ugly words that I didn't see how to recover the friendship both of us had so enjoyed for the past nine months. She'd played with fire and we'd both been burned.

I suddenly saw her position in full clarity. She was caught by my attentions and by her own feelings for me, someone who had many of the qualities she sought in a husband. She couldn't help but regard me as a suitor, which blocked her from thinking of any other man in that way as long as I was around. We'd reached the point that if I wasn't going to come through with a proposal, she had to push me away. That was the logic of the situation.

But I had already reached the point where I didn't want to be pushed away. I had overcome my concerns about the age difference and my advanced age in itself, only to have this blowup occur. I'd reached the point where I wanted to propose, only to fumble the ball just short of the goal line in anger at her attempted manipulation—manipulation into doing what I already knew I wanted to do anyway. What a fool I was.

It seemed too late to propose to her now. A logjam existed and I needed my own Hail Mary pass to break through it. But what could I do? There didn't seem to be any way forward or backward. I was stuck and likely to lose Gina and her friendship and companionship forever.

111

Several times that night I woke up feeling disjointed, beyond uneasy, drenched in sweat. It had hit me again, while asleep, just how much I'd miss Gina if our friendship ended, as it appeared it already had. Was it too late? Had I lost her forever? There didn't seem to be any way back after what had been said. I needed to make a truly dramatic gesture, but my unconscious brain, like my conscious mind, couldn't see what it might be.

I pondered the situation all morning without coming up with any way to right things, so headed out for a drive. Sometimes I think better while walking or driving around than by sitting around at home.

I drove by Deeza's Hair Care and realized that I hadn't had a haircut for nearly two months. The few salons that had still been open a month ago had required masks, and I'd refused to demean myself by putting a diaper on my face in order to get my hair cut.

It was only after I'd parked and had begun walking toward the salon that I remembered that most small businesses had been forcibly shuttered. As I peered into the darkened salon, I thought I saw someone inside motioning me around the side of the store. I walked around the edge of the building—her salon was an end unit—and toward the back. After I turned the far corner, I saw Deeza and had to laugh. She was dressed for business, wearing her apron and hat, and had moved a chair outside, and a table with all her equipment on it. She was set up to give haircuts in the alley behind her salon. She had a mask around her neck, but her face was wide open. Here was someone who wasn't going to be intimated by government edicts that made no sense.

As I sat down, I wondered if there was a connection between those who were independent minded enough not to wear the face diaper and those independent mindedness enough to recognize the reality of September 11. If the same people lined up on the same sides of those two very different issues, and those who disagreed with them on one issue also disagreed with them on the other, perhaps a schism was developing within the country, a split that had begun that day in Dallas between those few willing to believe the testimony of their own eyes and the large majority who blindly accepted the government "Oswald-as-lone-gunman" line repeated endlessly in the media.

Deeza soon went into a lament similar to what I'd heard from Gina so many times about how the forced closure would push her into bankruptcy, causing her to lose her life savings invested in the business. Rent still had to be paid for the salon and for her apartment. Her cubs still had to eat. What was she to do? She stepped back and looked at me as she spoke, following her usual practice of not being able to cut hair and speak at the same time.

Once she went silent, I went into my own lament about how

distressed I was about Gina. I explained the whole situation, about her ideas of courtship, suitors and virginity. And about the dream she'd told me two days earlier, and my anguish ever since over my response to it.

"Honey," Deeza said, stepping back again and looking directly at me, "she done told you what she wants you to do. She practically invited you in."

"Really?" That hadn't occurred to me. "Was she trying to guide me and the other suitors she told the dream to, to spur us into undertaking an act from which there could be no retreat?"

"Hell, yeah," Deeza said. "I see it now. She done tried this with other suitors before you, but none were man enough to do it."

"Or perhaps they wanted her only for a time or two, not a lifetime," I responded. "Perhaps they were wise to avoid being manipulated by her."

Deeza pondered the situation, then said, "Well, none of them was transformed into a Greek god. None was willing to pay the price she demanded for devouring her and satisfying their hunger. Are you?"

112

I wrestled all that night with thoughts of what to do about Brian's September 11 testimony and about Gina, rarely sleeping, and not more than an hour at a time. Finally, I got to sleep just before dawn and didn't wake up until almost noon.

When I woke up, I knew what to do about Brian's document. I knew I had the courage to send it out. I printed out forty copies of his testimony and addressed large envelopes to forty of the most important media in the country—print, broadcast and online; and local, regional and national in scope. After I put the copies in the envelopes and sealed them, I drove to the post office. As I was mailing them—through the slot in the door, the building being closed to the public—it occurred to me that the envelopes were covered with my fingerprints. But I dismissed that as unimportant; after all, I wasn't committing any crime.

I was so relieved that the weeks of agonizing over what to

do about Brian's testimony were over. It was now up to the media, based on this new information, to open an examination and discussion of what had really happened on that day nearly 20 years earlier. Finally, I hoped, the country would know what had happened and would hold those guilty of murder responsible for their actions. Finally, the country, after a period of some difficulty, could reverse the worst aspects of the actions taken in response to September 11 by repealing the Patriot Act and abolishing the Department of Homeland Security, and by withdrawing from Afghanistan and Iraq. We'd all, country and citizens, be able to move forward again by returning to the state we'd been in at the end of the 1990s.

Perhaps this revelation about the events of September 11 would even trigger a reassessment of what had happened in Dallas. Perhaps it would trigger a deeper examination of American actions over the last century and finally clear the air for good. Perhaps we'd restore the American republic, the reputation of the American government and the mental robustness of the American people. Perhaps we'd finally be able to believe the testimony of our own eyes again.

Whether Brian's testimony triggered these things or not, mailing the envelopes was a great relief. I felt so relieved that I'd made a decision and carried it out, that such a great weight had been lifted from my shoulders, that I treated myself to a wonderful dinner at my favorite Italian restaurant. It was open but provided seating only at every other table. It also required masks when walking from the entrance to my table, though not at the table itself. I ignored that, of course, and no one said a word to me about my open face. I ordered my favorite pasta and half a bottle of a good Malbec. I sure wished Gina was sitting opposite me to help me celebrate having made a decision about Brian's document, but that was impossible. In any event, the glow from having made a decision eased the pain I felt over her.

As I drove home, I noticed the moon over my left shoulder, slightly larger than the thin crescent I'd seen yesterday. A new moon. It was the start of a new month in the lunar calendar, and perhaps a new life for myself. Maybe now I could finally get back to my Huxley-Kennedy-Lewis project.

Without intending to, I found myself parking my car in the parking lot of Gina's apartment complex. It was now shortly after midnight and there was no one else around. After walking through the courtyard, I paused just before my hand touched the handle of the sliding glass door leading into her bedroom. Then, clutching the handle, I pushed the door sideways. It slid smoothly and silently open.

* * * * *

END MATERIALS

Editor's note: Jubal Jepson appended to his manuscript lists of books, articles, videos and websites he'd consulted in his research. I tracked them down, ferreted out the places from which he drew specific pieces of information and prepared the End Notes below. I also reorganized and added to his lists to form the For More Information section. And, I identified the sources of the images he included and secured the rights to reprint those not in the public domain.

Contents of the End Materials

IMAGE CREDITS

Covers

Image 1. WTC 1 exploding. front cover
Public domain (from NIST 9/11 Release 37).
www.archive.org/details/NIST 9-11 Release 37/International Center for 911 Studies NIST FOIA/Release 37/Release%2037/42A0522%20-%20G38D1/ImagesfromWebsites/collapse%20of%20tower%20%232%20from%20wtc 919.nac 919.net 63 919.144 919.52 919.29 919.jpg.

Image 2. Aldous Huxley. front cover, viii
Public domain (from Wikipedia).
www.en.wikipedia.org/wiki/C. S. Lewis#/media/File:C.s.lewis3.JPG.

Image 3. John F. Kennedy. front cover, viii
Public domain (from Wikimedia Commons).
www.commons.wikimedia.org/w/index.php?search=aldous+huxley&title=Special:MediaSearch&go=Go&type=image.

Image 4. C. S. Lewis. front cover, viii
Public domain (from Wikimedia Commons).
www.commons.wikimedia.org/wiki/File:President John F. Kennedy with Robert F. Kennedy, Jr. (03).jpg.

Image 5. WTC 2 exploding, top block tilted 23 degrees. back cover
Public domain (from NIST 9/11 Release 37).
www.ia800301.us.archive.org/11/items/NIST 9-11 Release 37/International Center for 911 Studies NIST FOIA/Release 37/Release%2037/42A0522%20-%20G38D1/ImagesfromWebsites/ScottRossi/Tower%20%232%20breaking%20%20in%20folder%20scottrossi.com%20from%20misc imagesziggy.dreamland.nes wtc screencaps.jpeg.

Jubal Jepson's Manuscript

Image 6. The MS. as given to the editor on September 11, 2023. --
Photo by editor.

Kennedy Assassination (Scene 14)

Image 7. Twelve witnesses to the massive hole in the back of President Kennedy's head. 57

These images were in Robert J. Groden, *The Killing of a President* (1993), pp. 86-88. Arrangements of them have been reprinted in many books and on many websites. This one is from impiousdigest.com, which invites readers to share its content. www.i0.wp.com/impiousdigest.com/wp-content/uploads/2017/02/exitwounda.jpg?resize=1253%2C1006.

Image 8. Faked JFK Autopsy photo. 57
Public Domain (from Wikimedia Commons). www.commons.wikimedia.org/wiki/File:JFK_posterior_head_wound.jpg.

September 11 (Scene 30)

Image 9. The collapse of WTC 7. 127
Three still images captured from the video.
Public domain, (Wikimedia Commons). www.commons.wikimedia.org/wiki/File:WTC_Building_7_Collapse_001.gif.

September 11 (Scene 32)

Image 10. Aerial view of the WTC complex. 132
Public domain (through Wikimedia Commons, from NIST FOIA release 37). www.archive.org/details/NIST_9-11_Release_37/International_Center_for_911_Studies_NIST_FOIA/Release_37/Release%2037/42A0525%20-%20G38D4/WTCI-415-STB%20Andre%20Booker/Aerials/Aerial67.jpg.

Image 11. Aerial view of the destruction of WTC 6. 133
Public domain (Wikimedia Commons). www.commons.wikimedia.org/w/index.php?search=wtc+6&title=Special:MediaSearch&go=Go&type=image.

Image 12. Dust from WTC 1 rolls through lower Manhattan. 134
Public domain (from cdc.gov). www.search.brave.com/images?q=wtc%20dust%20cloud.

Image 13. Steel core column from WTC 1 disintegrating into dust. 135
www.yandex.com/images/search?from=tabbar&img_url=https%3A%2F%2F2.bp.blogspot.com%2F-ttMS2yP-c-U%2FVmQlXzgu1GI%2FAAAAAAAAEOA%2Ft3Zr0ebBGl0%2Fs1600%2Fwhere-did-the-towers-go-main.jpg&lr=109901&pos=1&rpt=simage&text=9%2F11%20steel%20column%20turns%20to%20dust.

Similar images are in Jim Fetzer & Mike Palecek (editors), *America Nuked on 9/11*, p. 135; and in Judy Wood, *Where Did the Towers Go?*, p. 109. Wood got the image from a site that can no longer be reached: www.img156.imageshack.us/img156/2044/p9111200 ms2.jpg. Related video are at www.youtube.com/watch?v=AG57LD7lkGw, www.youtube.com/watch?v=7ZMjVXtNUec, www.youtube.com/watch?v=goGGQhhTcDY&t=4s and www.youtube.com/watch?v=9Sv0My2zfFA&t=42s.

September 11 (Scene 33)

Image 14. An ambulance parked near the WTC complex. 137
From pininterest.com.
www.yandex.com/images/search?from=tabbar&img_ur l=https%3A%2F%2Fsun9-44.userapi.com %2Fvj48hkplXR1wmDVafWqDg9GYoJRQX5kVe5N3Ew %2FZLI6ANKdG94.jpg&lr=109901&pos=0&rpt=simage &source=related-duck&text=9%2F11%20Cars.

September 11 (Scene 34)

Image 15. Still image from David Chandler's video, "North Tower Exploding." 140
From the main page of www.ae911truth.org.

September 11 (Scene 37)

Image 16. Point of impact at the Pentagon before wall segment collapsed. 150
Public Domain. Photo taken by Corporal Jason Ingersoll.
www.nara.getarchive.net/media/the-pentagon-in-flames-moments-after-a-hijacked-jetliner-crashed-into-building-8b554c
Image is used in Thierry Meyssan, *Pentagate*, Plate VIII, and at www.serendipity.li/wot/crash_site.htm.

Image 17: Pentagon lawn in pristine condition. 151
Public Domain (from Wikimedia Commons).
Photo taken by Corporal Jason Ingersoll.
www.commons.wikimedia.org/wiki/File:Pentagon_pre collapse.jpg.
This particular image, with the arrow inserted pointing to the supposed point of impact, is from:
www.serendipity.li/wot/pentagon/spencer05.htm.

Image 18. The Pentagon after segment collapsed. 152
Public domain (through Wikimedia Commons, from NIST FOIA Release 37).
www.commons.wikimedia.org/wiki/File:US Navy 010 911-N-3783H-009 Pentagon damage, Sept. 11, 2001.jpg.

Image 19. Three circular holes in the Pentagon's C ring, but none in the D ring between it and the outer E ring. 153
From Leonard Spencer's "The Attack on the Pentagon," www.serendipity.li/wot/pentagon/spencer05.htm.

September 11 (Scene 41)

Image 20. Bottom of plane with unusual items attached. 164
This image is used in many books and on many websites. This one is from the Millennium Report, www.themillenniumreport.com/2014/08/911-video-evidence-proves-airplane-was-remotely-controlled-into-twin-tower/.

Image 21. Plane melting into solid steel and concrete. 166
This image is used in many books and on many websites. This one is from:
www.911planeshoax.com/2020/09/11/proof-that-no-real-planes-were-used-on-911/.

Image 22. Comparison of the size of the planes in two videos one second before the moment of impact. 166
From "No Plane on the Original Footage," at www.rumble.com/vlh9mj-no-plane-on-the-original-footage.html?e9s=src v1 ucp.

Image 23. Head of a "missile" exiting WTC 2. 167
From "September 11 Attacks," Dutch language documentary. www.youtube.com/watch?v=L2PMT3TdBxM.
Also shown at :40 and 6:00 and 6:39 in www.youtube.com/watch?v=814rcm4KC5w.

Image 24. One of Wolfgang Staehle's photographs showing what appears to be a missile streaking toward WTC 1. 168
From Rare Footage of First Plane Impact, www.youtube.com/watch?v=gKhfQDcDxUI.

Image 25. Two images of the beginning of the explosion 169
From within the second tower, the first with an airplane, the second without.
The video is clearer than the stills taken from it.
From "Shape of explosion from within is the same, with or without a plane," at: www.rumble.com/vm1ruy-the-

END NOTES

Scene 5

[1] C. S. Lewis, *Mere Christianity*, pp. 54, 55.
[2] Lewis, *Mere Christianity*, pp. 45, 46, 47.
[3] Kathleen Norris, "Foreword," in Lewis, *Mere Christianity*, p. xvii.

Scene 6

[4] E. Martin Schotz, "Letter to Vincent J. Salandria," April 5, 1995, in E. Martin Schotz, *History Will Not Absolve Us*, p. 10.
[5] Vincent J. Salandria, "The Warren Report Analysis of Shots, Trajectories, and Wounds: A Lawyer's Dissenting View," *The Legal Intelligencer*, Nov. 2, 1964. [Reprinted in Schotz, *History Will Not Absolve Us*, pp. 89-98.]
[6] In 1969, Dallas Police Chief Jesse Curry disclosed in his book *JFK Assassination File* that paraffin tests revealed no power residues on Oswald's cheek, indicating that had not fired a rifle on November 22, 1963.
[7] Salandria, "The Warren Report Analysis of Shots," quoted in Schotz, *History Will Not Absolve Us*, p. 98.
[8] Salandria, "The Warren Report Analysis of Shots," quoted in Schotz, *History Will Not Absolve Us*, p. 91.
[9] Vincent J. Salandria, "A Philadelphia Lawyer Analyzes the Shots, Trajectories, and Wounds," *Liberation*, vol. IX, no. 10 (Jan. 1965): 13-19. [Reprinted in Schotz, *History Will Not Absolve Us*, pp. 99-115.]
[10] Salandria, "The Warren Report?" quoted in Schotz, *History Will Not Absolve Us*, p. 154.
[11] Vincent J. Salandria, "The Warren Report?" *Liberation*, vol. X, no. 1 (March): 14-33. [Reprinted in Schotz, *History Will Not Absolve Us*, pp. 117-177 (140).]
[12] Salandria, "The Warren Report?" quoted in Schotz, *History Will Not Absolve Us*, p. 150.
[13] Schotz, *History Will Not Absolve Us*, pp. 209-10. [Commenting on Harold Feldman's article, "Oswald and the FBI," *The Nation*, Jan. 27, 1964.]
[14] David Talbot, *Brothers*, p. 258.
[15] Fred J. Cook, *Maverick*, quoted in Schotz, *History Will Not Absolve Us*, p. 224.

Scene 8

[16] Fidel Castro, "Concerning the Facts and Consequences of the Tragic

Death of President John F. Kennedy." [A speech given on November 23, 1963; reprinted in Schotz, *History Will Not Absolve Us*, pp. 53-86 (56, 59).]

[17] Castro, "Concerning the Facts," in Schotz pp. 56, 57.
[18] Castro, "Concerning the Facts," in Schotz, p. 59.
[19] Castro, "Concerning the Facts," in Schotz, pp. 61-62.
[20] Castro, "Concerning the Facts," in Schotz, p. 78.
[21] Castro, "Concerning the Facts," in Schotz, p. 84.
[22] Marina, "The Ultra-Reactionaries: Global Analysis of the Dallas Coup," Medium, November 22, 2022. www.medium.com.
[23] Peter Dale Scott, *Dallas '63*, p. 205.
[24] Charles De Gaulle, quoted in David Talbot, *Devil's Chessboard*, p. 567.

Scene 9

[25] Editor, "Comments by the Editor," *East Anglian Magazine*, vol. 4/11 (Oct. 1939): 610.
[26] C. S. Lewis, "Learning in Wartime," in *The Weight of Glory*, p. 49.
[27] Lewis, "Learning in Wartime," p. 49.
[28] Lewis, "Learning in Wartime," p. 50.
[29] Lewis, "Learning in Wartime," p. 52.
[30] Lewis, "Learning in Wartime," p. 54.
[31] Lewis, "Learning in Wartime," pp. 58-59.

Scene 11

[32] Peter Dale Scott, *The War Conspiracy*, p. 43.
[33] Scott, *Dallas '63*, p. 147.
[34] James Bamford's *Body of Secrets*, p. 82, quoted in Scott, *Dallas '63*, pp. 146-47.
[35] James W. Douglass, *JFK and the Unspeakable*, p. xxii.
[36] Douglass, *JFK and the Unspeakable*, p. xxvii.
[37] General Curtis LeMay, quoted in Scott, *Dallas '63*, pp. 207.
[38] Daniel Ellsberg, quoted in Talbot, *Brothers*, pp. 172-73. See also Scott, *Dallas '63*, p. 208.
[39] Scott, *Dallas '63*, p. 141; also in Scott, *The Road to 9/11*, p. 7.
[40] Scott, *Dallas '63*, p. 126.
[41] Scott, *Dallas '63*, p. 126.
[42] Scott, *Dallas '63*, p. 160.
[43] President Kennedy, Speech at the University of Maine, October 19, 1963, quoted in Schotz, *History Will Not Absolve Us*, pp. 207-08.
[44] Quoted in Schotz, *History Will Not Absolve Us*, p. 208.
[45] Scott, *The War Conspiracy*, p. 28.
[46] Scott, *The War Conspiracy*, p. 26.
[47] Scott, *The War Conspiracy*, pp. 27-28, quoting David Kaiser,

American Tragedy, p. 211.
[48] David Neal, "Why the Assassination of JFK Matters to Us Today," David Neal Observations, July 28, 2023. www.davidnealobx.blogspot.com.
[49] Neal, "Why the Assassination of JFK Matters to Us."

Scene 12
[50] These Ideas are drawn from Donald W. Miller, Jr., and Lew Rockwell, "Why Three Kennedys Were Assassinated," www.lewrockwell.com, Oct. 2, 2012.

Scene 14
[51] For Jacob Hornberger, see especially *An Encounter with Evil: The Abraham Zapruder Story* and his articles, books and videos available at the Future of Freedom Foundation, www.fff.org. For Douglas Horne, see especially the five volumes of *Inside the Assassination Records Review Board*, and his other articles, books and videos available at www.fff.org.
[52] In "Why Doesn't the CIA Just Destroy Its Secret JFK Records?" Future of Freedom Foundation, Nov. 17, 2021. www.fff.org. Hornberger lays out seven actions the Secret Service took prior to and immediately after the assassination that contributed to its success.
[53] Jacob G. Hornberger, "The Evidence that Convicts the CIA of the JFK Assassination, Part 1" Future of Freedom Foundation, Aug. 11, 2023. www.fff.org.
[54] Hornberger, "The Evidence that Convicts, Part 1" Aug. 11, 2023. www.fff.org.
[55] Hornberger, "The Evidence that Convicts, Part 1" Aug. 11, 2023. www.fff.org.
[56] Hornberger, "The Evidence that Convicts, Part 2" Aug. 14, 2023. www.fff.org.
[57] Hornberger, "The Evidence that Convicts, Part 5" Aug. 17, 2023. www.fff.org.
[58] Hornberger, "The Evidence that Convicts, Part 1" Aug. 11, 2023. www.fff.org.
[59] Jacob G. Hornberger, "The Mafia Did Not Orchestrate JFK's Assassination," Future of Freedom Foundation, June 27, 2023. www.fff.org.
[60] Hornberger, "The Mafia Did Not Orchestrate," Future of Freedom Foundation, June 27, 2023. www.fff.org.
[61] Jacob G. Hornberger, "Autopsy Fraud Convicts the Military in the JFK Assassination," Future of Freedom Foundation, Aug. 17, 2023. www.fff.org.
[62] The witnesses and their statements are listed in Robert J. Groden,

JFK: Absolute Proof, pp. 149-56.
[63] Noel Twyman, *Bloody Treason*, p. 94. Lengthy excerpts from the verbatim transcript are reprinted at various points in Twyman's book.
[64] Douglas P. Horne, "Photographic Evidence of Bullet Hole in JFK Limousine Windshield 'Hiding in Plain sight'," Future of Freedom Foundation, June 3, 2012. www.fff.org.
[65] Noel Twyman, *Bloody Treason*, p. 799.
[66] See especially Phillip F. Nelson, *LBJ: The Mastermind of the JFK Assassination.*
[67] Jacob G. Hornberger, "The Achilles' Heel of the JFK Assassination," Future of Freedom Foundation, July 14, 2023. www.fff.org.
[68] Lee Harvey Oswald, quoted in John Armstrong, *Harvey & Lee: How the CIA Framed Oswald*, p. 1.

Scene 15

[69] John Armstrong, *Harvey & Lee*, p. 909.
[70] Phillip F. Nelson, "The Strange Synchronicity of Seemingly Unrelated Enigmatic Events," LBJ: The Master of Deceit, July 3, 2020. www.lbjthemasterofdeceit.com.
[71] Richard Charnin, "Executive Action: JFK Witness Deaths and the *London Times* Actuary," April 19, 2023. www.lewrockwell.com.
[72] Peter Janney, *Mary's Mosaic*, p. 192.

Scene 16

[73] Joseph Pearce, "Walking with Chesterton and Lewis," www.theimaginatiesonservative.org.

Scene 17

[74] Scott, *Dallas '63*, p. 205.
[75] Robert Groden, *The Killing of a President*, p. 205. See also Talbot, *Brothers*, pp. 290-294, and 18:40 in disc 2, Director's Cut edition of Oliver Stone's movie, *JFK*.
[76] Philip F. Nelson, "Why JFK Went to Texas," LBJ: The Master of Deceit, March 31, 2020. www.lbjthemasterofdeceit.com.
[77] Schotz, *History Will Not Absolve Us*, p. 19.
[78] Schotz, *History Will Not Absolve Us*, p. 17.
[79] Schotz, *History Will Not Absolve Us*, p. 18.
[80] Schotz, *History Will Not Absolve Us*, p. 18.
[81] Schotz, *History Will Not Absolve Us*, p. 32.
[82] Schotz, *History Will Not Absolve Us*, p. 24.

Scene 18

[83] Jim Marrs, *Crossfire: The Plot that Killed Kennedy*, p. 94.
[84] Marrs, *Crossfire*, pp. 44, 542-43.
[85] Dick Russell, *The Man Who Knew Too Much*, p. 362.

[86] Marrs, *Crossfire*, pp. 542-43, 551.
[87] L. Fletcher Prouty, *JFK: The CIA, Vietnam, and the Plot to Assassinate John F. Kennedy*, pp. photo caption three pages before 253, 278, 281.
[88] Donald Jeffries & William Matson Law, *Pipe the Bimbo*, p. 86.
[89] Marrs, *Crossfire*, p. 306.
[90] Marrs, *Crossfire*, p. 306.
[91] James Fetzer, *The Great Zapruder Film Hoax*, p. 67.
[92] Peter Janney, *Mary's Mosaic: The CIA Conspiracy to Murder John F. Kennedy, Mary Pinchot Meyer, and Their Vision for World Peace*, p. 231.
[93] John Newman, *Oswald and the CIA*, p. 637.
[94] Jeffrey Hart, "Lionel Trilling in the Classroom," *New Criterion*, vol. 16/9 (May 1998): 75

Scene 20
[95] C. S. Lewis, *An Experiment in Criticism*, pp. 2-3.
[96] Lewis, *Experiment*, pp. 18-19.
[97] Lewis, *Experiment*, p. 24.

Scene 21
[98] David Gelernter, *Americanism: The Fourth Great Western Religion*, p. 1.
[99] Gelernter, *Americanism*, p. 20.
[100] David Gelernter, *1939: The Lost World of the Fair*, p. 49.
[101] Dana Sawyer, *Aldous Huxley: A Biography*, p. 1.

Scene 22
[102] Chesterton, from "Culture and the Coming Peril," quoted in Joseph Pearce, *Literary Converts* (1999), p. 254. The full article is reprinted in *The Chesterton Review*, vol. xviii, no. 3 (August 1992): 333-343.
[103] Luis H. Francia, *A History of the Philippines*, p. 160. Francia states that 20,000 Filipino soldiers died in direct conflict; estimates for civilian deaths range from 250,000 to a million.
[104] Francia, *A History of the Philippines*, p. 155.
[105] F. Sionil José, "Notes on the Writing of *Dusk*," in *Dusk*, p. xxi.

Scene 23
[106] Donald Jeffries, "My New Book 'Pipe the Bimbo in Red,'' I Protest by Donald Jeffries, Nov. 17, 2023. www.donaldjeffries.substack.com.
[107] Schotz, *History Will Not Absolve Us*, p. 34.
[108] Joseph Mercola, "All Wars are Bankers' Wars," Mercola: Take Control of Your Health, Oct. 20, 2023. www.mercola.com.
[109] Carl Bernstein, "The CIA and the Media," *Rolling Stone*, p. 2.
[110] Bernstein, "The CIA and the Media," p. 13.
[111] Bernstein, "The CIA and the Media," p. 15.
[112] Bernstein, "The CIA and the Media," p. 18.

[113] Schotz, *History Will Not Absolve Us*, p. 11.
[114] Schotz, *History Will Not Absolve Us*, pp. 11-12.
[115] Richard Charnin, "Executive Action: JFK Witness Deaths and the *London Times* Act," www.lewrockwell.com, April 19, 2023.
[116] Joseph Mercola, "How the Media Secretly Carries Out Assignments for the CIA," Mercola: Take Control of Your Health, July 5, 2022. www.mercola.com.
[117] Peter Dale Scott, *Deep Politics and the Death of JFK*, p. 280.
[118] Scott, *Deep Politics and the Death of JFK*, p. 281.
[119] Schotz, *History Will Not Absolve* Us," p. 18.
[120] Wiesak, *America's Last President*, pp. 235-36.
[121] Wiesak, *America's Last President*, p. 236.
[122] John F. Kennedy, Address before the American Newspaper Publishers Association, April 27, 1961, quoted in Wiesak, *America's Last President*, p. 236.
[123] Robert F. Kennedy, Landen Lecture, March 18, 1968, quoted in Wiesak, *America's Last President*, p. 236.
[124] Wiesak, *America's Last President*, pp. 236-37.
[125] Wiesak, *America's Last President*, p. 237.
[126] Wiesak, *America's Last President*, pp. 237, 238, 240.
[127] Wiesak, *America's Last President*, p. 247.
[128] Wiesak, *America's Last President*, p. 248.

Scene 24

[129] David Talbot, *Brothers*, p. 396.
[130] Scott, *The Road to 9/11*, p. 371, citing Kevin Anderson, "Revolutions and Gaps on Nixon Tapes," BBC News, March 1, 2002 (www.news.bbc.co.uk/2/hi/americas/14848157.stm).
[131] Scott, *Dallas '63*, p. 180.
[132] See the following, from Scott's *The Road to 9/11*, p. 294: "Not only did McCord needlessly tape or retape a number of doors inside the building, . . . he apparently affixed the tape horizontally in a way that made it easily visible when the door was shut. . . . Hard also to explain is the prompt arrival at the scene of Carl Shoffler, a junior police officer whose regular shift that night (for desk work) had already ended and who "had assisted the CIA in the past." . . . Finally, how can one explain the burglars' possession of easily traceable, sequentially numbered $100 bills, which led investigators within days to . . . the Finance Committee for the Re-election of the President.. . . . Like an oak tree in an acorn, the whole subsequent drama of Watergate was implanted in the unnecessary giveaway evidence of that day."
[133] *Dallas '63*, p. 209.
[134] Scott, *Dallas '63*, p. 210.

[135] Scott, *Dallas '63*, p. 209.
[136] Glenn Ellmers, "Federal Foes," *New Criterion*, vol. 41/5 (Jan. 2023): 16.
[137] Ellmers, "Federal Foes," p. 16.
[138] Ellmers, "Federal Foes," pp. 16-17.
[139] Schotz, *History Will Not Absolve Us*, p. 238.
[140] Eisenhower is quoted in Bamford, *Body of Secrets*, 82-83, which is quoted in Scott, *Dallas '63*, p. 147.
[141] Scott, *Dallas '63*, p. 125.

Scene 27

[142] James H. Fetzer, *The 9/11 Conspiracy: The Scamming of America*, p. xiii.
[143] David Ray Griffin, *Christian Faith and the Truth Behind 9/11*, pp. 26-27.
[144] Tarpley, *9/11 Synthetic Terror*, p. 222.

Scene 30

[145] Wood, *Where Did the Towers Go?*, pp. 20-21.
[146] Dan Rather, quoted in L. Reichard White, "9/11 & The Strangest Fires Ever Told," Sept. 12, 2023. www.lewrockwell.com.
[147] University of Alaska's Department of Civil and Environmental Engineering Study, quoted in Paul Craig Roberts, "The Official Story of the Collapse of WTC Building 7 Lies in Ruins," Sept. 4, 2021. www.paulcraigroberts.org.

Scene 32

[148] Wood, *Where Did the Towers Go?*, pp. 197-98.
[149] Wood, *Where Did the Towers Go?*, p. 198.
[150] Tarpley, *9/11 Synthetic Terror: Made in USA*, p. 226. See also Von Bülow, *Die CIA und der 11. September*, pp. 163-64.
[151] Wood, *Where Did the Towers Go?*, p. 298.
[152] Wood, *Where Did the Towers Go?*, p. 145.
[153] Wood, *Where Did the Towers Go?*, p. 131.
[154] Wood, *Where Did the Towers Go?*, pp. 171-72.
[155] Wood, *Where Did the Towers Go?*, p. 297.
[156] Wood, *Where Did the Towers Go?*, p. 168.
[157] Wood, *Where Did the Towers Go?*, p. 306.

Scene 33

[158] James H. Fetzer, *The 9/11 Conspiracy: The Scamming of America*, p. 289.
[159] Wood, *Where Did the Towers Go?*, p. 213. Image is from www.nyartlab.com/bombing/09-13/DSC07998.jpg.
[160] Wood, *Where Did the Towers Go?*, p. 298.

[161] Wood, *Where Did the Towers Go?*, p. 413. Data is from www.magnet.gi.alaska.edu/table index/2001 table.html.
[162] Wood, *Where Did the Towers Go?*, p. 262.
[163] Wood, *Where Did the Towers Go?*, p. 318.
[164] Wood, *Where Did the Towers Go?*, p. 485.

Scene 34
[165] David Chandler, "North Tower Exploding," www.ae911.truth.org.
[166] Anonymous Patriots, "Treason: Who Did 9/11 and Why Did They Do It," The Millennium Report, Oct. 14, 2016, www.themillenniumreport.com.
[167] Mark H. Gaffney, "The Demolition of the World Trade Center on September 11, 2001," Unz Review, Aug. 17, 2023. www.unz.com.

Scene 37
[168] Anonymous Patriots, "Treason: Who Did 9/11 and Why Did They Do It" The Millennium Report, Oct. 14, 2016. www.themillenniumreport.com.
[169] James H. Fetzer, *America Nuked on 9/11*, pp. 112, 113.
[170] General Albert Stubblebine, "I can prove that it was not an airplane" that hit the Pentagon—Major General Albert N. Stubblebine." Transcript prepared by the editor. www.themillenniumreport.com/2014/09/911-must-see-i-can-prove-that-it-was-not-an-airplane-that-hit-the-pentagon-major-general-albert-n-stubblebine/

Scene 39
[171] Lewis, *Mere Christianity*, p. 8.

Scene 41
[172] "9/11 Video Evidence Proves Airplane was Remotely Controlled into Twin Tower," Millennium Report, Aug. 29, 2014, www.themillenniumreport.com.
[173] Anonymous Patriots, "Treason: Who Did 9/11 and Why Did They Do It," Millennium Report, Oct. 14, 2016. www.themillenniumreport.com.
[174] See "Remembering the 9/11 Truth Movement, Unz Review, Sept. 11, 2023. www.unz.com.
[175] Quoted in "9/11 Video Evidence Proves Airplane was Remotely Controlled into Twin Tower," Millennium Report, Aug. 29, 2014. www.themillenniumreport.com.
[176] Vincent Sammartino, "The 9-11 Passenger List Oddities," in *Phantom Flight 93*, edited by Victor Thorn and Lisa Guiliani, p. 109.
[177] Vincent Sammartino, "The 9-11 Passenger List Oddities," in *Phantom Flight 93*, edited by Victor Thorn and Lisa Guiliani, pp. 109-10.

[178] David Ray Griffin, *The New Pearl Harbor Revisited*, p. 175.
[179] Griffin, *The New Pearl Harbor Revisited*, p. 313.
[180] David Ray Griffin, *9/11 Ten Years Later*, pp. 16-18.
[181] Consensus 911, www.Consensus911.org.
[182] David A. Hughes, "9/11 Truth and the Silence of the IR Discipline," *Alternatives*, vol. 45/2 (Feb. 27, 2020).
[183] "9/11 Video Evidence Proves Airplane was Remotely Controlled into Twin Tower," Millennium Report, Aug. 29, 2014, www.themillenniumreport.com.
[184] Scott, *The Road to 9/11: Wealth, Empire, and the Future of America*, p. 231.
[185] Michael C. Ruppert, *Crossing the Rubicon*, p. 310.

Scene 43

[186] Roth identified one of the other two as Delta Airlines Flight 1989, but Michael C. Ruppert identified them as American Airlines Flight 43, from Boston and United Airlines Flight 23 from New York. See his *Crossing the Rubicon*, p. 332.

Scene 45

[187] Ruppert, *Crossing the Rubicon*, p. 480.
[188] Ruppert, *Crossing the Rubicon*, p. 271.
[189] Ruppert, *Crossing the Rubicon*, p. 270.
[190] Ruppert, *Crossing the Rubicon*, p. 480.

Scene 46

[191] Gary G. Kohls, "Understanding the Guilty Culprits that Got America into Afghanistan—and Got Away with the Crime AND the Cover-up!" Sept. 7, 2021. www.lewrockwell.com.
[192] Jamie McIntyre, quoted in Kohls, "Understanding the Guilty Culprits."
[193] Dan Rather, quoted in Kohls, "Understanding the Guilty Culprits."

Scene 47

[194] For a systematic and thorough analysis of how this fakery was done, see Simon Shack's video *September Clues*, at www.archive.org/details/2008-Simon-Shack-September-Clues.
[195] Ted Walter & Graeme MacQueen, "How 36 Reporters Brought Us the Twin Towers' Explosive Demolition on 9/11," Architects & Engineers for 9/11 Truth, July 8, 2020. www.ae911truth.org.
[196] Ted Walter & Graeme MacQueen, "The Triumph of the Official Narrative: How the TV Networks Hid the Twin Towers' Explosive Demolition on 9/11," Architects & Engineers for 9/11 Truth, Sept. 8, 2022. www.ae911truth.org.
[197] Walter & MacQueen, "How 36 Reporters," www.ae911truth.org.

[198] Walter & MacQueen, "The Triumph," www.ae911truth.org.

Scene 48

[199] Eric Larsen, *The Skull of Yorick*, p. 133.
[200] Larsen, *Skull of Yorick*, p. xiv. See also Larsen's *A Nation Gone Blind: America in an Age of Simplification and Deceit.*
[201] Larsen, *Skull of Yorick*, p. xiv.
[202] Larsen, *Skull of Yorick*, p. xx.
[203] Larsen, *Skull of Yorick*, p. xxiii.

Scene 51

[204] David Talbot, "The JFK Assassination at 60: The Public Knows the Truth—Why Won't the Media Report It?" Kennedy Beacon, Nov. 21, 2023. www.thekennedybeacon.substack.com.
[205] Phillip F. Nelson, "How Lyndon Johnson Expropriated Control Over the Pentagon and CIA Soon After the Inauguration of the Kennedy-Johnson Administration," May 8, 2019. www.lewrockwwell.com.
[206] Scott, *The War Conspiracy*, pp. 353-54.
[207] Tarpley, *9/11 Synthetic Terror*, p. 288.
[208] Tarpley, *9/11 Synthetic Terror*, pp. 316-17.
[209] Ruppert, *Crossing the Rubicon*, pp. 97, 99, 388, 423-26,
[210] David Cogswell, "See No Evil," Online Journal, Feb. 27, 2008, www.onlinejournal.com, quoted in Larsen, *Skull of Yorick*. p. 178.

Scene 53

[211] Larsen, *Skull of Yorick*, p. 100.
[212] "Rebuilding America's Defenses," The Project for a New American Century, www.newamericancentury.org, quoted in Larsen, *The Skull of Yorick*, p. 122. See also Wikipedia.
[213] Thierry Meyssan, "Everything Points to Thierry Meyssan Being Right Today," Voltaire Network, Sept. 3, 2021. www.voltairenet.org.
[214] Meyssan, "Everything Points," Voltaire Network.
[215] John C. Yoo, "The President's Constitutional Authority to Conduct Military Operations Against Terrorists and Nations Supporting them," [memorandum to the president], Sept. 25, 2001. www.fas.org/irp/agency/doj/ok092501.html
[216] Scott, *The Road to 9/11*, p. 239.

Scene 54

[217] Larsen, *Skull of Yorick*, p. 17.
[218] Ruppert, *Crossing the Rubicon*, p. 484.
[219] John & Nisha Whitehead, "Betraying the Constitution: Who Will Protect Us from an Unpatriotic Patriot Act?" Rutherford Institute, Dec. 2, 2019. www.rutherford.org.
[220] Meyssan, "Everything Points," Voltaire Network.

[221] Ruppert, *Crossing the Rubicon*, p. 472.
[222] Scott, *Road to 9/11*, pp. 239-40.
[223] Scott, *Road to 9/11*, p. 240. See also Scott, "Homeland Security Contracts for Vast New Detention Camps," www.news.pacificnews.org, Feb. 8, 2006.
[224] Scott, *Road to 9/11*, pp. 239-40.
[225] Scott, *Road to 9/11*, p. 240.
[226] Ruppert, *Crossing the Rubicon*, p. 477.
[227] Scott, *Road to 9/11*, p. 242.
[228] Larsen, *Skull of Yorick*, p. 17.

Begin 55
[229] Scott, *Road to 9/11*, p. 242.
[230] Eric Larsen, *Skull of Yorick*, pp. 101-03.

Scene 57
[231] Scott, *War Conspiracy*, pp. 347-48.
[232] Scott, *War Conspiracy*, p. 348.
[233] Scott, *War Conspiracy*, p. 349.
[234] Scott, *War Conspiracy*, p. 351.
[235] Osama bin Laden, quoted in David Alden, *The North Tower*, p. 421.
[236] President George W. Bush, quoted in Ruppert, *Crossing the Rubicon*, p. 123.
[237] Scott, *War Conspiracy*, p. 352.
[238] Scott, *War Conspiracy*, pp. 352-3.
[239] Tarpley, *9/11 Synthetic Terror*, p. 60.
[240] Helmut Schmidt, quoted in Tarpley, *9/11 Synthetic Terror*, p. 59. [From N-TV, Dec. 10, 2001; EIR, Dec. 13, 2001.]
[241] Francesco Cossiga, quoted in Tarpley, *9/11 Synthetic Terror*, p. 59. [From *La Stampa*, Sept. 14, 2001 and EIR, Dec. 13, 2001.]
[242] Scott, *War Conspiracy*, p. 30.
[243] Scott, *War Conspiracy*, p. 375.
[244] Tarpley, *9/11 Synthetic Terror*, p. 339.
[245] Tarpley, *9/11 Synthetic Terror*, pp. 324-25.
[246] Tarpley, *9/11 Synthetic Terror*, pp. 371-72.
[247] Tarpley, *9/11 Synthetic Terror*, pp. 352-53.
[248] Tarpley, *9/11 Synthetic Terror*, p. 339.
[249] Thierry Meyssan, "Everything Points," Voltaire Network.

Scene 59
[250] Michael C. Ruppert reported that "Puts on UAL were 90 times the usual among between September 6 and 10, and 285 times higher than average on the Thursday before the attack. American Airlines put options 60 times higher than normal on September 10. Companies

located on the upper floors also were targeted. Morgan Stanley, 27 times normal purchase of put options on the two business days before September 11. Merrill-Lynch, 12 times normal in the days before the attacks. (*Crossing the Rubicon*, pp. 238-39.) By one estimate, profits by inside traders netted $15 billion in profits. (244)

After Ruppert broke this story of connections between the trades and the CIA on October 9, 2001, "the government never uttered another affirming public word about the insider trades as an avenue of post-9/11 investigation. And the major media, being unwilling to look at anything that pointed at the CIA, went dead silent." (247)

"Nine agencies—SEC, NYSE, CBOE, Department of Justice, FBI, Secret Service, CIA, Treasury, and the National Security Agency—opened investigations into insider trading immediately after 9/11 based upon initially admitted and obvious evidence that it had, in fact, taken place. Much of the major press immediately recognized the importance of the story and then shirked its obligation to follow up. Not one of the agencies involved has to this day divulged any information to the public." (253)

[251] Larsen, *Skull of Yorick*, p. 99.

Scene 60

[252] C. S. Lewis, *The Four Loves*, p. 83.
[253] Lewis, *The Four Loves*, p. 78.

Scene 62

[254] Michael Glennon, *National Security and Double Government*, p. 3.
[255] Glennon, p. back cover.
[256] Glennon, p. 113.
[257] Glennon, p. back cover.
[258] Glennon, *National Security and Double Government*, p. 114.
[259] Tarpley, *9/11 Synthetic Terror*, p. 127.
[260] Tarpley, *9/11 Synthetic Terror*, p. 31.
[261] Tarpley, *9/11 Synthetic Terror*, p. 124.
[262] Barrie Zwicker, *Towers of Deception*, pp. 250-51.
[263] Tarpley, *Synthetic Terror*, p. 127.
[264] Tarpley, *9/11 Synthetic Terror*, p. 124.
[265] Tarpley, *9/11 Synthetic Terror*, p. 31.
[266] Tarpley, *9/11 Synthetic Terror*, pp. 124-25.

Scene 63

[267] Tarpley, *9/11 Synthetic Terror*, p. 279.
[268] Smedley D. Butler, "America's Armed Forces: 2. In Time of Peace: The Army," *Common Sense*, vol. 4/11 (Nov. 1935).
[269] David Talbot, *The Devil's Chessboard*, pp. 3-4.

[270] Talbot, *Devil's Chessboard*, p. 29.
[271] Paul Craig Roberts, "Did the Dulles Brothers Seal Our Fate?" Institute for Political Economy, May 22, 2024. www.paulcraigroberts.org. In this article Roberts drew on Stephen Kinzer's *The Brothers: John Foster Dulles, Allen Dulles, and Their Secret World War*.
[272] Glennon, *Double Government*, pp. 12-13.
[273] Ruppert, *Crossing the Rubicon*, p. 219.

Scene 64
[274] C. Wright Mills, "Why I Wrote *The Power Elite*," quoted in www.currentaffairs.org/news/2023/02/who-are-the-power-elite.
[275] C. Wright Mills, *The Power Elite*, p. 6.
[276] Mills, *Power Elite*, p. 4.
[277] Mills, *Power Elite*, pp. 7-8.
[278] Mills, *Power Elite*, pp. 8-9.
[279] Mills, *Power Elite*, pp. 288-89.
[280] Mills, *Power Elite*, pp. 294, 288.
[281] Mills, *Power Elite*, p. 294.
[282] Mills, *Power Elite*, p. 275.
[283] Mills, *Power Elite*, p. 276.
[284] Mills, *Power Elite*, pp. 4-5.
[285] Mills, *Power Elite*, p. 283.
[286] Mills, *Power Elite*, p. 287.
[287] Mills, *Power Elite*, p. 276.

Scene 65
[288] Manuel Garcia, Jr., "Confessions of a Secret Controlled Demolitions Special Operative for 9/11," Counterpunch, Sept. 2, 2021. www.counterpunch.org.
[289] Kohls, "Understanding the Guilty Culprits," Sept. 7, 2021. www.lewrockwell.com.

Scene 68
[290] L. Fletcher Prouty, *The Secret Team*, back cover.
[291] Prouty, *Secret Team*, back cover.
[292] Prouty, *Secret Team*, pp. xxxviii-xxxix.
[293] Prouty, *Secret Team*, p. 4.
[294] Prouty, *Secret Team*, p. 22.
[295] Prouty, *Secret Team*, p. 4.
[296] Prouty, *Secret Team*, p. 3.
[297] Prouty, *Secret Team*, p. 4.
[298] Prouty, *Secret Team*, pp. 4-5.
[299] Prouty, *Secret Team*, p. 5.

[300] Prouty, *Secret Team*, p. xxxiv.
[301] Prouty, *Secret Team*, p. xxxv.
[302] Prouty, *Secret Team*, p. 41.
[303] Prouty, *Secret Team*, p. 42.
[304] Prouty, *Secret Team*, pp. 51-52.
[305] Prouty, *Secret Team*, p. 57.
[306] Prouty, *Secret Team*, p. 442.
[307] Prouty, *Secret Team*, pp. 446-47.
[308] Prouty, *Secret Team*, p. 453.
[309] Prouty, *JFK*, p. 124.
[310] Prouty, *Secret Team*, p. 449.
[311] Prouty, *Secret Team*, p. 35.
[312] Prouty, *JFK*, p. 136.
[313] Prouty, *Secret Team*, p. 453.
[314] Prouty, *Secret Team*, p. 453.
[315] Prouty, *Secret Team*, p. 455.
[316] Prouty, *Secret Team*, p. 456.

Scene 69

[317] Jeffrey D. Sachs, *To Move the World: JFK's Quest for Peace*, p. xi.
[318] Nikita Khrushchev, quoted in Monika Wiesak, *America's Last President*, p. 169.
[319]Wiesak, *America's Last President*, p. 182.
[320] Talbot, *Devil's Chessboard*, p. 400.
[321] Prouty, *JFK*, p. 129.
[322] Prouty, *JFK*, p. xxxii. See also pages 130-35.
[323] Prouty, *JFK*, p. 131.
[324] William O. Douglas, quoted in Prouty, *Secret Team*, p. 500.
[325] Arthur Schlesinger, quoted in Andrew Gavin Marshall, "The National Security State and the Assassination of JFK," Global Research, Nov. 23, 2010. www.globalresearch.ca.
[326] Marshall, "The National Security State," citing Talbot, *Brothers*, pp. 64-65.
[327] Talbot, *Brothers*, p. 43.
[328] John F. Kennedy, Speech before Congress about space, May 25, 1961.

Scene 70

[329] Prouty, *Secret Team*, p. 482.
[330] Prouty, *Secret Team*, p. 483.
[331] Prouty, *Secret Team*, p. 72.
[332] Prouty, *Secret Team*, pp. 463, 485.
[333] Prouty, *Secret Team*, pp. 483, 485.
[334] Prouty, *Secret Team*, p. 485.

[335] Talbot, *Brothers*, pp. 217-18.
[336] Talbot, *Brothers*, p. 218.
[337] Prouty, *Secret Team*, p. 480.
[338] Prouty, *Secret Team*, p. 43.
[339] LeMay, quoted in Scott, *Dallas '63*, p. 207.
[340] LeMay, quoted in Scott, *Dallas '63*, p. 125, and p. 207.
[341] Talbot, *Devil's Chessboard*, p. 442.
[342] Prouty, *Secret Team*, pp. 500-01.
[343] Prouty, *Secret Team*, p. 501.
[344] Amdrew Gavin Marshall, "The National Security State and the Assassination of JFK," Global Research, Nov. 23, 2010. www.globalresearch.ca.

Scene 71
[345] ABC News, "Bill Clinton, Hours Before 9/11 Attacks: 'I Could Have Killed' Osama bin Laden," August 1, 2014. www.abcnews.go.com/US/bill-clinton-hours-911-attacks-killed-osama-bin/story?id=24801422.
[346] Webster Tarpley, *Barack H. Obama: The Unauthorized Biography*, p. 17.
[347] David A. Hughes, "9/11 Truth and the Silence of the IR Discipline," *Alternatives*, vol. 45/2 (Feb. 27, 2020).
[348] David Alden, *The North Tower*, p. 329.
[349] Paul Craig Roberts, "The Day America Died," Institute for Political Economy, Sept. 3, 2011. www.paulcraigroberts.org.
[350] Theodore Sorensen, quoted in Talbot, *Brothers*, p. 217.

Scene 74
[351] Vladimir Putin, quoted in Llewelyn H. Rockwell, Jr., "What We Can Learn from Putin," Feb. 19, 2024. www.lewrockwell.com.
[352] Michael J. Glennon, *National Security and Double Government*, p. 144, quoting George F. Kennan's "A Fateful Error," *New York Times*, Feb. 5, 1997.

Scene 75
[353] David Stockman, "The Donald's Disastrous Fourth Year—But Don't Blame the Covid," David Stockman's Contra Corner, July 22, 2024. www.davidstockmanscontracorner.com.
[354] H. L. Mencken, *In Defense of Women* (1918).

Scene 77
[355] Lewis, "Learning in Wartime," p. 49.
[356] Russell L. Blaylock, "Medical Science Has Changed with Covid," *Blaylock Wellness Report*, vol. 21/7 (July 2024): 3.
[357] Blaylock, "Medical Science Has Changed with Covid," p. 3.

Scene 78

[358] U.S. Supreme Court, *Ex parte Milligan*, 71 US 2 (1866), quoted in Ruppert, *Crossing the Rubicon*, p. 488.

Scene 79

[359] Lewis, *Abolition of Man*, p. 43.
[360] Aldous Huxley, *The Perennial Philosophy*, pp. viii, x.
[361] C. S. Lewis, "Equality," in *Present Concerns*, p. 7.
[362] C. S. Lewis, "The Humanitarian Theory of Punishment," in *God in the Dock: Essays on Theology*.
[363] Aldous Huxley, *Brave New World Revisited*, p. 72.

Scene 80

[364] Richard Gage, "The Astonishing Parallels of 9/11 & Covid," Richard Gage 9/11. www.richardgage911.org/parallels-9-11-covid-the-video-you-want-to-watch.
[365] Gage, "The Astonishing Parallels of 9/11 & Covid." www.richardgage911.org.
[366] Jim Quinn, "'The Covid Experiment,'" The Burning Platform, March 13, 2024. www.theburningplatform.com. Also at www.lewrockwell.com.
[367] Quinn, "'The Covid Experiment,'" www.theburningplatform.com, www.lewrockwell.com.

Scene 82

[368] Scott, *Deep Politics and the Death of JFK*, p. 72.
[369] Scott, *Deep Politics*, p. 17.
[370] Scott, *Deep Politics*, p. 299.
[371] Scott, *Deep Politics*, p. 10.
[372] Scott, *Deep Politics*, p. 11.
[373] Scott, *Deep Politics*, p. 312.
[374] Scott, *Deep Politics*, pp. 311-12.
[375] Scott, *Deep Politics*, p. 17.
[376] Scott, *Deep Politics*, pp. 17-18.
[377] Scott, *Deep Politics*, p. 70.
[378] Scott, *Deep Politics*, p. 71.
[379] Scott, *Deep Politics*, pp. 58, 60-61.
[380] Scott, *Deep Politics*, p. 222.
[381] Scott, *Deep Politics*, p. 73. "Revolt" is Arthur M. Schlesinger's term.
[382] Scott, *Deep Politics*, pp. 69-74.
[383] Marrs, *Crossfire*, p. 549.
[384] Marrs, *Crossfire*, p. 549.
[385] Scott, *Deep Politics*, p. 74.
[386] Scott, *Deep Politics*, p. 74.

[387] Earl Warren, *The Memoirs of Earl Warren*, 1977, p. 367, quoted in Scott, *Deep Politics*, p. 295.
[388] Ruppert, *Crossing the Rubicon*, p. 50.
[389] Ruppert, *Crossing the Rubicon*, p. 57. See also Scott, *The Road to 9/11*, pp. 12-17.
[390] Ruppert, *Crossing the Rubicon*, p. 68.
[391] Scott, *Road to 9/11*, p. 15.
[392] Scott, *Road to 9/11*, p. 15.

Scene 83
[393] Debbie Lerman, "Government's National Security Arm Took Charge During the Covid Response," Brownstone Institute, Nov. 3, 2022. www.brownstone.org.
[394] Lerman, "Government's National Security Arm, www.brownstone.org.
[395] Debbie Lehman, "Was There a Covid Response Plan? If So, Where is It?" Brownstone Institute, Nov. 7, 2022. www.brownstone.org.
[396] Lehman, "Was There a Covid Response Plan?" www.brownstone.org.
[397] Lerman, "Government's National Security Arm," www.brownstone.org.

Scene 84
[398] Meyssan, "Everything Points," Voltaire Network.
[399] FEMA Press release, wwwfema.gov/nwz01/nwz01_92.htm, quoted in Ruppert, *Crossing the Rubicon*, p. 417.
[400] Meyssan, "Everything Points," Voltaire Network.
[401] Scott, *Road to 9/11*, p. 9.
[402] Scott, *Road to 9/11*, p. 54.
[403] Scott, *Road to 9/11*, p. 184.
[404] Scott, *Road to 9/11*, p. 47.
[405] Scott, *Road to 9/11*, p. 186.
[406] Scott, *Road to 9/11*, p. 23.
[407] Ruppert, *Crossing the Rubicon*, p. 415.
[408] Ruppert, *Crossing the Rubicon*, pp. 415-17.
[409] Scott, *Road to 9/11*, p. 187.
[410] Scott, *Road to 9/11*, p. 185.
[411] Scott, *Road to 9/11*, p. 210.
[412] Scott, *Road to 9/11*, p. 85, quoting Alfonso Chardy, "Some Secret Activities," *Miami Herald*, July 5, 1987.
[413] Scott, *Road to 9/11*, p. 185.
[414] Scott, *Road to 9/11*, pp. 210-11.
[415] Scott, *Dallas '63* (2015), p. 191.
[416] Scott, *Road to 9/11*, p. 237.

[417] Scott, *Road to 9/11*, p. 219.
[418] Scott, *Road to 9/11*, p. 234.
[419] Scott, *Road to 9/11*, p. 235.
[420] Scott, *Road to 9/11*, p. 237.

Scene 85
[421] Naomi Wolf, *The End of America: Letter of Warning to a Young Patriot*, p. xi.
[422] Wolf, *End of America*, p. 4.
[423] Wolf, *End of America*, pp. xi-xii.
[424] Wolf, *End of America*, p. xv.
[425] Wolf, *End of America*, pp. xv-xvi.
[426] Wolf, *End of America*, p. 151.
[427] Wolf, *End of America*, p. 152.

Scene 89
[428] Jacob G. Hornberger, "America's Military Empire," Future of Freedom Foundation, Jan. 25, 2024. www.fff.org. Cites David Vine, *Base Nation: How U.S. Military Bases Abroad Harm America and the World*.
[429] U.S. Department of Defense, *Joint Vision 2020*, quoted in Scott, *Road to 9/11*, p. 281. www.dtic.mil/jointvision/jv2020.doc.
[430] "Rebuilding America's Defenses," The Project for a New American Century. www.newamericancentury.org. Quoted in Larsen, *Skull of Yorick*, p. 122. See also Wikipedia.
[431] Zbigniew. Brezinski, *The Grand Chessboard*, pp. 35-36, 211.
[432] Ron Suskind, "Faith, Certainty and the Presidency of George W. Bush," *NY Times Magazine*, Oct. 17, 2004. Quoted in Larsen, *Skull of Yorick*, p. 39.
[433] Ruppert, *Crossing the Rubicon*, p. 100.
[434] David Stockman, "Wilson's Folly, the Washington Hegemon, and Why There is Still No Peace on Earth," David Stockman's Contra Corner, Dec. 2, 2023. www.davidstockmanscontracorner.com.
[435] David Neal, "Why the Assassination of JFK Matters to Us Today," David Neal Blog, July 27, 2023. www.davidnealobx.blogspot.com.
[436] Jacob G. Hornberger, "America's Military Empire," Future of Freedom Foundation, Jan. 25, 2024. www.fff.org.
[437] Ruppert, *Crossing the Rubicon*, p. 106.
[438] Ruppert, *Crossing the Rubicon*, p. 473, which draws on William Arkin, "The Secret War," *Los Angeles Times*, Oct. 27, 2002.
[439] Ruppert, *Crossing the Rubicon*, p. 576.
[440] Scott, *Road to 9/11*, p. 187.
[441] Scott, *Road to 9/11*, p. 193.
[442] Jay Bookman, *Atlanta Journal Constitution*, Sept. 29, 2002, quoted

in Ruppert, *Crossing the Rubicon*, p. 527.

Scene 90

[443] Arnold Toynbee, quoted in the *New York Times*, May 7, 1971, reprinted in Prouty, *JFK*, pp. 230-31.
[444] Caitlin Johnstone, "If You've Just Started Paying Attention to U.S. Foreign Policy," www.caitlinjohnstone.com. Also at www.lewrockwell.com, Jan. 16, 2024.
[445] David Stockman, "Why Washington D.C. is the War Capital of the World," David Stockman's Contra Corner, May 16, 2024. www.davidstockmanscontracorner.

Scene 91

[446] Donald Jeffries, "The Rise and Fall of the Second Amendment," I Protest by Donald Jeffries, Feb. 18, 2024. www.donaldjeffries.substack.com. See also Jacob G. Hornberger, "America's Military Empire," Future of Freedom Foundation, Jan. 24, 2024. www.fff.org.
[447] Scott, *Road to 9/11*, p. 241.
[448] Brezinski, *Grand Chessboard*, pp. 35-36, 211.
[449] Hannah Arendt, *The Origins of Totalitarianism*, p. 128.
[450] Scott, *Road to 9/11*, p. 136.
[451] Scott, *Road to 9/11*, p. 137.
[452] Michael C. Ruppert, *Crossing the Rubicon*, pp. 14-15.
[453] Francis Christian, "Know Your Enemy," Francis Christian's Essays, Feb. 17, 2024. www.francischristian.substack.com.
[454] U.S. Department of Defense, *Joint Vision 2020*, quoted in Peter Dale Scott, *Road to 9/11*, p. 281. www.dtic.mil/jointvision/jv2020.doc.

Scene 92

[455] Smedley D. Butler, *War is a Racket*, pp. 24.
[456] Prouty, *JFK*, p. xxv.
[457] Scott, *War Conspiracy*, p. 395.
[458] James Madison, quoted in John Leake, "U.S. Foreign Policy is a Scam Built on Corruption," Courageous Discourse, Jan. 6, 2024. www.petermcculloughmd.substack.com. Also at www.lewrockwell.com, Jan. 8, 2024.
[459] Caitlin Johnstone, "The U.S. Empire Isn't a Government that Runs Nonstop Wars, It's a Nonstop War that Runs a Government," Caitlin Johnstone: Daily Writings about the End of Illusions. www.caitlinjohnstone.com. Also at www.lewrockwell.com, June 3, 2024.
[460] Jeffrey D. Sachs, "US Foreign Policy Is a Scam Built on Corruption," Common Dreams, Dec. 26, 2023. www.commondreams.org.

Scene 94

[461] Tucker Carlson, quoted in Tim Hains, "Tucker Carlson: Members of Congress Are Terrified of the Intel Agencies, That's Not Democracy," Real Clear Politics, April 20, 2024. www.realclearpolitics.com.

[462] Former CIA Agent Bradley Earl Ayers, in a letter to Michael C. Ruppert, April 3, 2000. Quoted in Ruppert, *Crossing the Rubicon*, p. 175.

[463] Arendt, *Origins of Totalitarianism*, p. 128.

Scene 95

[464] Paul Craig Roberts, "In My Lifetime I Have Witnessed the Death of Independent Medicine and Fair Trials," Institute for Political Economy, Jan. 18, 2023. www.paulcraigroberts.org.

[465] John Stossel, "A Ban on Freelance Work," Townhall, April 10, 2024. www.townhall.com.

[466] Jacob G. Hornberger, "The Stronger the Government, the Weaker the Nation," Future of Freedom Foundation, Feb. 13, 2024. www.fff.org.

Scene 96

[467] William Deresiewicz, *Excellent Sheep: The Miseducation of the American Elite*, p. 13.

[468] Larsen, *Skull of Yorick*, p. xiv. See also Larsen's *A Nation Gone Blind*.

[469] Larsen, *Skull of Yorick*, pp. 139-40.

[470] Larsen, *Skull of Yorick*, p. 241.

[471] Larsen, *Skull of Yorick*, p. 229.

[472] Editor, "Comments by the Editor," *East Anglian Magazine*, vol. 4/11 (Oct. 1939): 610.

[473] David A. Hughes, "9/11 Truth and the Silence of the IR Discipline," *Alternatives*, vol. 45/2 (Feb. 27, 2020).

[474] Hughes, "9/11 Truth and the Silence," *Alternatives*.

[475] Larsen, *Skull of Yorick*, p. 243.

[476] Jacob G. Hornberger, "Autopsy Fraud Convicts the Military in the JFK Assassination" Future of Freedom Foundation, Aug. 17, 2023. www.fff.org.

[477] Paul Craig Roberts, "Insouciant Americans Have Doomed America to Tyranny," Institute for Political Economy, May 25, 2023. www.paulcraigroberts.org.

[478] Roberts, "Insouciant Americans," Institute for Political Economy, May 25, 2023. www.paulcraigroberts.org,.

[479] Paul Craig Roberts, "The American Population is Not Defending Our Liberty," Institute for Political Economy, May 8, 2023. www.paulcraigroberts.org.

[480] Roberts, "Insouciant Americans," Institute for Political Economy,

May 25, 2023. www.paulcraigroberts.org.
[481] Paul Craig Roberts, "Ivermectin Emerges as a Significant Aid in Cancer Treatment," Institute for Political Economy, April 9, 2024. www.paulcraigroberts.org.
[482] Michael Ruppert's story is told in Jenna Orkin's *Scout: A Memoir of Investigative Journalist Michael C. Ruppert.*

Scene 97
[483] Aldous Huxley, *Brave New World*, p. 12.
[484] Huxley, *Brave New World*, p. 11.
[485] Huxley, *Brave New World*, p. 23.
[486] Huxley, *Brave New World Revisited*, p. 3.
[487] Huxley, *Brave New World Revisited*, p. 4.
[488] Huxley, *Brave New World*, p. 194.
[489] Huxley, *Brave New World*, pp. 209-10.
[490] Huxley, *Brave New World*, pp. 211-12.

Scene 98
[491] Huxley, *Brave New World*, pp. 205-06.
[492] Huxley, *Brave New World*, p. 201.
[493] Huxley, *Brave New World*, p. 198.
[494] Huxley, *Brave New World*, p. xlviii.
[495] Huxley, *Brave New World*, pp. 199-200.
[496] Huxley, *Brave New World*, p. 200.
[497] Huxley, *Brave New World Revisited*, p. 15.
[498] Huxley, *Brave New World Revisited*, p. 13.
[499] Huxley, *Brave New World*, p. xlii.
[500] Huxley, *Brave New World*, p. xlvii.
[501] Huxley, *Brave New World*, p. xlvii.

Scene 99
[502] Dennis Prager, "Were More People Killed in the Name of God or in the Name of Equality?" Townhall, July 9, 2024. www.townhall.com.

Scene 100
[503] Barrie Zwicker, *Towers of Deception*, pp. 200-01.
[504] Flannery O'Connor, *The Habit of Being: The Letters of Flannery O'Connor*, edited by Sally Fitzgerald, p. 229.

Scene 101
[505] Lewis, *The Abolition of Man*, p. 15.
[506] Aristotle, *Ethics*, 1104b, quoted in Lewis, *Abolition of Man*, p. 16.
[507] Plato, *The Laws*, p. 653, quoted in Lewis, *Abolition of Man*, p. 16.

Scene 103
[508] Barrie Zwicker, *Towers of Deception*, p. 232.

[509] Glennon, *National Security and Double Government*, p. 114.
[510] Arthur Conan Doyle, *The Case-Book of Sherlock Holmes.*
[511] Glennon, *National Security and Double Government*, pp. 105-06.
[512] Jacob G. Hornberger, "Autopsy Fraud Convicts the Military in the JFK Assassination," Future of Freedom Foundation, Aug. 17, 2023. www.fff.org.
[513] Larsen, *Skull of Yorick*, p. 206.
[514] Larsen, *Skull of Yorick*, pp. 221-22.
[515] John le Carré, "The United States of America Has Gone Mad," *The Times* (London), Jan. 15, 2003. Quoted in Zwicker, *Towers of Deception*, p. 255.
[516] John le Carré, "The United States of America Has . . .," Jan. 15, 2003. Quoted in Zwicker, *Towers of Deception*, p. 255.
[517] Chalmers Johnson, "Sorrows of Empire," *Foreign Policy in Focus*, Nov. 2003. Quoted in Zwicker, *Towers of Deception*, p. 255.
[518] Chalmers Johnson, *Nemesis*, p. 9. Quoted in Scott, *The Road to 9/11*, p. 385.
[519] Whittaker Chambers, *Witness*, p. 25.
[520] Chambers, *Witness*, p. 25.
[521] Michael Walsh, *Last Stands*, pp. 21-22.
[522] David Gelernter, *Americanism*, p. 20.

Scene 104

[523] John Adams, quoted in Scott, *Road to 9/11*, p. 257.
[524] Ron Unz, "American Pravda: Major Mysteries of the 1990s," Unz Review, Dec. 12, 2022. www.unz.com.
[525] Unz, "American Pravda: Major Mysteries," Unz Review.
[526] Unz, "American Pravda: Major Mysteries," Unz Review.
[527] Unz, "The JFK Assassination and the Covid Cover-Up," Unz Review, Dec. 19, 2022. www.unz.com.
[528] Roger L. Simon, "Has American Democracy Been a Hallucination for Nearly 60 Years?" Epoch Times, Dec. 17, 2022. www.theepochtimes.com.
[529] Ron Unz, "The JFK Assassination and the Covid Cover-Up," Unz Review. www.unz.com.
[530] Jacob G. Hornberger, "Is Trump Tucker Carlson's JFK Assassination Source?" Future of Freedom Foundation, Dec. 27, 2022. www.fff.org.

Scene 106

[531] Stanley Karnow, *In Our Image*, pp. 3-4.
[532] Karnow, *In Our Image*, p. 4.
[533] Luis H. Francia, *A History of the Philippines*, pp. 199-200.
[534] Francia, *History of the Philippines*, p. 230.
[535] Francia, *History of the Philippines*, p. 197.

[536] Karnow, *In Our Image*, p. 359.
[537] Karnow, *In Our Image*, p. 366.
[538] Stanley Karnow, *In Our Image*, p. 334.
[539] Garcia, quoted in Francia, *History of the Philippines*, p. 215.
[540] Francia, *History of the Philippines*, p. 235.
[541] Francia, *History of the Philippines*, p. 236.
[542] George W. Bush, "President Discusses War on Terror at National Endowment for Democracy," October 6, 2005.
[543] Francia, *History of the Philippines*, p. 246.
[544] Francia, *History of the Philippines*, p. 260.
[545] Corazon Aquino, quoted in Karnow, *In Our Image*, p. 7.

Scene 107
[546] Milton Freidman, *Capitalism and Freedom*, p. xxviii.
[547] John F. Kennedy, Speech on July 4, 1946, quoted in Wiesak, *America's Last President*, p. 1.
[548] John F. Kennedy, Speech on July 4, 1946, quoted in Wiesak, *America's Last President*, p. 2.
[549] John F. Kennedy, *Strategy of Peace*, p. 162, quoted in Wiesak, *America's Last President*, p. 19.
[550] John F. Kennedy, *Strategy of Peace*, p. 163, quoted in Wiesak, *America's Last President*, p. 19.
[551] John F. Kennedy, Speech on July 4, 1946, quoted in Wiesak, *America's Last President*, p. 2.
[552] Huxley, *Brave New World Revisited*, p. 131.
[553] Huxley, *Brave New World Revisited*, p. 135.
[554] Huxley, *Brave New World Revisited*, p. 132.
[555] Huxley, *Brave New World Revisited*, p. 135.
[556] The President of Dalhousie University, quoted in Robert Maynard Hutchins, *Education for Freedom*," p. 17.
[557] Lewis, *Abolition of Man*, p. 61.
[558] Lewis, *Abolition of Man*, pp. 64, 68.
[559] C. S. Lewis, *That Hideous Strength*, p. 127.
[560] Lewis, *That Hideous Strength*, p. 78.
[561] Lewis, *That Hideous Strength*, p. 194.
[562] Jonathan Gaisman, "The Thing About Things," *New Criterion*, vol. 42, no. 2 (October 20 22): 63.
[563] C. Bradley Thompson, "What America Is," *New Criterion*, vol. 40/1 (Sept.): 45.
[564] Kevin Barrett, *Truth Jihad: My Epic Struggle Against the 9/11 Big Lie*, p. 103.
[565] John & Nisha Whitehead, "Rule by Criminals: When Dissidents Become Enemies of the State," Rutherford Institute, March 26, 2024.

www.rutherford.org.
[566] Whitehead, "Rule by Criminals," Rutherford Institute.
[567] Whitehead, "Rule by Criminals," Rutherford Institute.
[568] Whitehead, "Rule by Criminals," Rutherford Institute.
[569] Scott, *Road to 9/11*, p. 252.
[570] Thompson, "What America Is," p. 42.
[571] Thompson, "What America Is," p. 42.
[572] Thompson, "What America Is," pp. 42-43.
[573] Thompson, "What America Is," p. 49.

Scene 108
[574] Marrs, *Crossfire*, p. xiii.
[575] Prouty, *JFK*, p. 302.
[576] Scott, *Road to 9/11*, pp. 194-95.
[577] Ruppert, *Crossing the Rubicon*, p. 450.
[578] Bertrand Russell, quoted on the back cover of Mark Lane's *Rush to Judgment*.
[579] Gerald Posner, quoted in Talbot, *Brothers*, p. 396.
[580] Barrett, *Truth Jihad*, p. 15.

INDEX

THE THREE GUIDES

CHARACTERS

REAL-LIFE PERSONS, ORGANIZATIONS, PLACES AND EVENTS

FOR MORE INFORMATION

ALDOUS HUXLEY

1932 *Brave New World*. New York: Vintage, 1994.
1937 *Ends and Means: An Inquiry into the Nature of Ideals*. New York: Transaction Publishers, 2012.
1939 *After Many a Summer Dies the Swan*. Chicago: Ivan R. Dee, 1993.
1944 *Time Must Have a Stop*. Daikey Archive Press, 1998.
1945 *The Perennial Philosophy*. New York: Harper Perennial, 2009.
1952 *The Devils of Loudun*. New York: Harper Perennial, 2009.
1955 *The Genius and the Goddess*. New York: Vintage, 1988.
1958 *Brave New World Revisited*. New York: Vintage, 1994.

Bedford, Sybille
2002 *Aldous Huxley: A Biography*. Chicago: Ivan R. Dee. [1973]
Sawyer, Dana
2002 *Aldous Huxley: A Biography*. Maine: Trillium Press.

JOHN F. KENNEDY

1945 *Prelude to Leadership: The European Diary of John F. Kennedy, Summer 1945*. Introduction by Hugh Sidey. Washington, DC: Regnery Pub. [1995]
1946 "Some Elements of the American Character" [Independence Day Oration], July 4. www.jfklibrary.org/search?search=july+4%2C+1946.
1956 *Profiles in Courage*. New York: Harper, 2003.
1960 *Strategy of Peace: A New Approach on Foreign Policy*. New York: Harper. [Reprint of a speech delivered before the Senate on June 14, 1960.]
1961 Address before the American Newspaper Publishers Association, April 27. www.jfklibrary.org/archives/other-resources/john-f-kennedy-speeches/american-newspaper-publishers-association-19610427.
1961 Address to Joint Session of Congress, May 25. [The space program.]

www.jfklibrary.org/search?search=1961,%20may%2025,%20space&items_per_page=25&sort_by=search_api_relevance&sort_order=DESC.

1962 Remarks on the 20th Anniversary of the Voice of America, February 26. www.jfklibrary.org/asset-viewer/archives/jfkpof/037/jfkpof-037-020.

1963 Commencement Address, American University, June 10. ["Peace" speech.] www.jfklibrary.org/asset-viewer/archives/tnc-319-ex.

1963 Remarks at the University of Maine, October 19. www.jfklibrary.org/asset-viewer/archives/jfkpof-047-034#?image_identifier=JFKPOF-047-034-p0001.

1963 Remarks at Amherst College, October 26. www.jfklibrary.org/archives/other-resources/john-f-kennedy-speeches/amherst-college-19631026.

Kennedy, Jacqueline

2011 *Historic Conversations on Life with John F. Kennedy*. New York: Hyperion Books.

Kennedy, Robert

1968 Landen Lecture, March 18.

O'Donnell, Kenneth & David F. Powers (with Joe McCarthy)

1972 *"Johnny, We Hardly Knew Ye:" Memories of John Fitzgerald Kennedy*. Boston: Little, Brown.

Sachs, Jeffrey D.

2013 *To Move the World: JFK's Quest for Peace*. New York: Random House.

Schlesinger, Arthur

1965 *A Thousand Days: John F. Kennedy in the White House*. Boston: Houghton Mifflin Co.

Sorenson, Theodore

1966 *Kennedy*. New York: Harper & Row.

Wiesak, Monika

2022 *America's Last President: What the World Lost When It Lost John F. Kennedy*. Monika Wiesak.

C. S. LEWIS

1942 *The Screwtape Letters and Screwtape Proposes a Toast.* New York: HarperCollins, 2016.
1942 "Learning in Wartime," in *The Weight of Glory*, pp. 47-63.
1943 "Equality," in *Present Concerns*, pp. 7-12.
1944 *The Abolition of Man.* New York: HarperCollins, 2001.
1945 *That Hideous Strength.* New York: Scribner, 2003.
1946 *The Great Divorce.* HarperOne, 2001.
1949 *The Weight of Glory.* New York: HarperCollins, 2001.
1949 "The Humanitarian Theory of Punishment," in *God in the Dock: Essays on Theology.*
1952 *Mere Christianity.* New York: Harper, 2001.
1955 *Surprised by Joy.* New York: HarperOne, 2017.
1960 *The Four Loves.* New York: HarperOne, 2017.
1961 *An Experiment in Criticism.* Cambridge Univ. Press, 1992.
1970 *God in the Dock: Essays on Theology.* Edited by Walter Hooper. Grand Rapids: Eerdmans.
1986 *Present Concerns: Journalistic Essays.* Edited by Walter Hooper. New York: HarperCollins.

Green, Roger L. & Walter Hooper
2002 *C. S. Lewis: The Authorised and Revised Biography.* New York: Harper Collins. [1974]

Hooper, Walter
1996 *C. S. Lewis: A Complete Guide to His Life & Works.* New York: HarperCollins.

Kreeft, Peter
2008 *Between Heaven and Hell: A Dialog Somewhere Beyond Death with John F. Kennedy, C. S. Lewis & Aldous Huxley.* Downers Grove, IL: IVP Books. [1992]

Pearce, Joseph
1999 *Literary Converts.* San Francisco: Ignatius Press.
2021 "Walking with Chesterton and Lewis," www.theimaginativeconservative.org.

Sayer, George
1988 *Jack: A Life of C. S. Lewis.* Wheaton, IL: Crossway.

Ward, Michael
2021 *After Humanity: A Guide to C. S. Lewis's The Abolition of Man.* Park Ridge, IL: Word on Fire.

GENERAL BOOKS AND ARTICLES

Adler, Mortimer J.
2021 "Reading," *The Great Ideas Online*, no. 1015 (April). Center for the Study of the Great Ideas. www.thegreatideas.org.

American Council of Trustees and Alumni
2000 *Losing America's Memory: Historical Illiteracy in the 21st Century.*
2016 *No U.S. History? How College History Departments Leave the United States Out of the Major.*

Austen, Jane
2003 *Emma*. New York: Penguin. [1816] [Book club's June book.]

Castaneda, Carlos
1991 *A Separate Reality: Further Conversations with Don Juan.* New York: Washington Square Press. [1971]
1991 *Journey to Ixtlan: The Lessons of Don Juan*. New York: Washington Square Press. [1972]
1991 *The Power of Silence: Further Lessons of Don Juan*. New York: Washington Square Press. [1987]
1998 *The Teachings of Don Juan: A Yaqui Way of Knowledge.* New York: Washington Square Press. [1968]

Chambers, Whittaker
1980 *Witness*. Washington, DC: Regnery Publishing, Inc. [1952]

Chesterton, G. K.
1992 "Culture and the Coming Peril," *The Chesterton Review*, vol. xviii, no. 3 (August): 333-343. [Reprint of a talk given at London University on January 28, 1927.]
1993 *The Everlasting Man*. San Francisco: Ignatius Press.[1925]

Deresiewicz, William
2015 *Excellent Sheep: The Miseducation of the American Elite & the Way to a Meaningful Life*. New York: Free Press.

East Anglian Magazine
1939 "Comments by the Editor," vol. 4/11 (October): 610.

Endo, Shusaku
2003 *Silence*. London: Picador Classic. [1966] [Book club's May book.]

Farewell, Nina
1953 *The Unfair Sex: An Exposé of the Human Male for Young Women of Most Ages*. Illustrated by Roy Doty. New York: Simon and Schuster.

Fein, Ellen & Sherrie Schneider
1996 *The Rules: Time-Tested Secrets for Capturing the Heart of Mr. Right.* Grand Central Publishing.
Forster, E. M.
1992 *A Passage to India.* [1924] [Book club's January book.]
Francia, Luis H.
2021 *A History of the Philippines: From Indios Bravos to Filipinos.* New York: Abrams Press. [2014]
Friedman, Milton
2020 *Capitalism and Freedom.* Chicago: University of Chicago Press. [1962]
Gaisman, Jonathan
2022 "The Thing About Things," *New Criterion*, vol. 42, no. 3 (November): 62-67.
Gelernter, David
1995 *1939: The Lost World of the Fair.* New York: Avon Books.
2007 *Americanism: The Fourth Great Western Religion.*
Greene, Graham
2004 *The Quiet American.* New York: Penguin. [1955] [Book club's February book.]
Hart, Jeffrey
1998 "Lionel Trilling in the Classroom," *New Criterion*, vol. 16, no. 9 (May): 74-80.
Hutchins, Robert Maynard
1943 *Education for Freedom.* Louisiana State University Press.
Intercollegiate Studies Institute
2006 *The Coming Crisis in Citizenship: Higher Education's Failure to Teach America's History and Institutions.*
José, F. Sionil
1992 *Dusk* [*Po-on*], New York: Modern Library. [1984]
Kalkavage, Peter
2021 "Winged Words: Reading & Discussing Great Books," www.theimaginativeconservative.org.
Karnow, Stanley
1989 *In Our Image: America's Empire in the Philippines.* New York: Ballantine Books.
Knebel, Fletcher & Charles Bailey II
1962 *Seven Days in May.* New York: Harper & Row, Publishers.
Malvasi, Mark
2022 "On Teaching, Writing and Other Discontents," www.theimaginativeconservative, July 13.

McClay, Wilfred
2021 "The Case for the Liberal Arts: Stronger than Ever?" www.theimaginativeconservative.org.

National Commission on Excellence in Education
1983 *A Nation at Risk: The Imperative for Educational Reform*.

Nicholson, Eleanor Bourg
2021 "Jane Austen's Vision of a Happy Marriage," www.theimaginativeconservative.org.

O'Connor, Flannery
1979 *The Habit of Being: The Letters of Flannery O'Connor*. Edited by Sally Fitzgerald. New York: Farrar, Straus and Giroux.

Peterson, Jordan B.
2018 *12 Rules for Life: An Antidote to Chaos*. Random House Canada.

Rizal, José
2006 *Noli Me Tangere* (*Touch Me Not*). New York: Penguin. [1887] [Book club's October book.]

Soseki, Natsume
2010 *Kokoro*. New York: Penguin. [1914] [Book club's December book.]

Stevenson, Robert Louis
2003 *The Strange Case of Dr. Jekyll and Mr. Hyde.* New York: Penguin. [1886] [Book club's November book.]

Thompson, C. Bradley
2021 "What America Is," *New Criterion*, vol. 40, no. 1 (September): 41-49.

Twain, Mark
1985 *Adventures of Huckleberry Finn*. New York: Penguin. [1885][Book club's March book.]

Wilder, Thornton
2003 *The Bridge at St. Luis Rey*. [1927] [Book club's April book.]

Wolfe, Thomas
1929 *Look Homeward Angel*. New York, Scribner's.

COUP #1: THE ASSASSINATION OF JOHN F. KENNEDY (and the republic endangered)

BOOKS AND ARTICLES

Albarelli, H. P., Jr.

2013 *A Secret Order: Investigating the High Strangeness and Synchronicity in the JFK Assassination*. New York: Skyhorse Publishing.

2021 *Coup in Dallas: The Decisive Investigation into Who Killed Kennedy*. New York: Skyhorse Publishing.

Armstrong, John

2003 *Harvey and Lee: How the CIA Framed Oswald*. Arlington, TX: Texas Quasar Ltd. [Full text (1028 pages) in PDF format is available at www.krusch.com/books/kennedy/Harvey_And_Lee.pdf.]

Bartholomew, Richard

2018 *The Deep State in the Heart of Texas: The Texas Connections to the Kennedy Assassination*. Say Something Real Press, LLC.

Belzer, Richard

2016 *Hit List: An In-Depth Investigation into the Mysterious Deaths of Witnesses to the JFK Assassination.*

Bernstein, Carl

1977 "The CIA and the Media: How Americans Most Powerful News Media Worked Hand in Glove with the Central Intelligence Agency and Why the Church Committee Covered It Up," *Rolling Stone*, October 20, pp. 1-64.

Bolden, Abraham

2008 *Echo from Dealey Plaza*. New York: Crown.

Burris, Charles

2011 "The Bay of Pigs and JFK's Assassination," www.lewrockwell.com, April 17.

2013 "The Killing of President Kennedy," www.lewrockwell.com, July 19.

2013 "JFK's Embrace of Third World Nationalists," www.lewrockwell.com, November 27.

2015 "Dallas '63: A Brilliant Synthesis Regarding the November 22, 1963 Coup d'état," www.lewrockwell.com, December 28.

2016 "The Deep State and the November 22 Coup d'état," www.lewrockwell.com, March 16.
2016 "De Gaulle: The Deep State Murdered JFK," www.lewrockwell.com, April 2.
2017 "Neocon Lies about JFK," www.lewrockwell.com, June 27.
2019 "JFK Assassination Resources," www.lewrockwell.com, July 24.
2020 "The 'Legend' of Lee Harvey Oswald," www.lewrockwell.com, July 22.
2020 "General Curtis LeMay and His War Against the Kennedys," www.lewrockwell, August 25.
2020 "LBJ Versus the Kennedys: Means, Motive and Opportunity Leading to November 22, 1963," www.lewrockwell.com, August 25.
2022 "Remembering the November 22, 1963 Deep State Coup d'état," LRC Blog, www.lewrockwell.com, November 22.
2024 "Revisiting the 'Legend' of Lee Harvey Oswald," www.lewrockwell.com, July 18.

Canfield, Michael & Alan J. Weberman
1992 *Coup d'Etat in America: The CIA and the Assassination of John F. Kennedy*. New York: The Third Press. [1975]

Castro, Fidel
1963 "Concerning the Facts and Consequences of the Tragic Death of President John F. Kennedy." [A speech delivered on November 23, 1963.] Reprinted in Schotz, *History Will Not Absolve Us*, pp. 53-86.

Charnin, Richard
2023 "Executive Action: JFK Witness Deaths and the *London Times* Act," www.lewrockwell.com, April 19.

Cirignano, Douglas
2019 *American Conspiracies and Cover-Ups*. New York: Skyhorse Publishing.

Cook, Fred J.
1984 *Maverick: Fifty Years of Investigative Reporting*. New York: Putnam's Sons. [See especially the chapter titled "The Truth is Too Terrible" based on two pieces in the *Nation*, June 13 and 20, 1966.]

Crenshaw, Charles A.
1992 *JFK Has Been Shot*. New York: Kensington Publishing Corp. [Reprint of *J.F.K.: A Conspiracy of Silence*.]
2001 *Trauma Room One: The JFK Medical Coverup Exposed*. New York: ParaView Press.

Curry, Jesse
1969 *JFK Assassination File*. Dallas: American Poster and Printing Company.

Curtin, Edward J.
2020 *Seeking Truth in a Country of Lies: Critical & Lyrical Essays*. Atlanta: Clarity Press, Inc.
2021 "President John F. Kennedy: His Life and Public Assassination," *Garrison: The Journal of History and Deep Politics*, issue 8.
2022 "JFK Revisited: Through the Looking Glass," Edward Curtain: Behind the Curtain, January 16. www.edwardcurtain.com. Also at www.lewrockwell.com, Jan. 18, 2022.
2024 "The JFK Assassination Chokeholds that Inescapably Prove There Was a Conspiracy," Edward Curtain: Behind the Curtain, www.edwardcurtain.com, May 10. Also at www.lewrockwell.com, May 11, 2024.

DiEugenio, James
-- "Deconstructing JFK: A Coup d'Etat Over Foreign Policy?" www.citizentruth.org.
1997 "The Posthumous Assassination of John F. Kennedy," Kennedys and King, Dec. 15. www.kennedysandking.com.
2012 *Destiny Betrayed: JFK, Cuba and the Garrison Case*. Second edition. New York: Skyhorse Publishing. [1992]
2016 "How CBS News Aided the JFK Cover Up," Consortium News, April 22.
2018 *The JFK Assassination: The Evidence Today*. New York: Skyhorse Publishing.
2021 "The Ordeal of Malcolm Perry," Kennedys and King, May 24, www.kennedysandking.com.
2022 *JFK Revisited: Through the Looking Glass*. New York: Skyhorse Publishing.
2024 *JFK Assassination Chokeholds*. Camp Street Press.

DiEugenio, James & Lisa Pease (editors)
2003 *The Assassinations: Probe Magazine on JFK, MLK, RFK, and Malcolm X*.

Douglass, James W.
2008 *JFK and the Unspeakable: Why He Died and Why It Matters*. New York: Touchstone.
2023 "The Truth about JFK's Assassination," www.lewrockwell.com, November 27. [Douglass interviewed by Lew Rockwell.]

Eisenhower, Dwight D.
1961 Farewell Address, January 17. Transcript and video at: www.youtube.com/embed/OyBNmecVtdU.

Ellmers, Glenn
2023 "Federal Foes," *New Criterion*, vol. 41, no. 5 (January): 13-18.

Epstein, Edward J.
1966 *Inquest: The Warren Commission and the Establishment of Truth*. New York: Viking Press.

Ernest, Barry
2013 *The Girl on the Stairs*. Gretna, LA: Pelican.

Farrell, Joseph P.
2011 *LBJ and the Conspiracy to Kill Kennedy: A Coalescence of Interests.* Kempton, IL: Adventures Unlimited Press.

Feldman, Harold
1964 "Oswald and the FBI," *The Nation*, January 27.
1965 "Fifty-one Witnesses: The Grassy Knoll," *Minority of One*, March.

Fetzer, James
1998 *Assassination Science: Experts Speak Out on the Death of JFK*. Chicago: Catsfeet Press.
2000 *Murder in Dealey Plaza: What We Know Now That We Didn't Know Then About the Death of JFK*. Chicago: Catfeet Press.
2003 *The Great Zapruder Film Hoax: Deceit and Deception in the Death of JFK*. Chicago: Catsfeet Press.
2006 "Reasoning About Assassination: Critical Thinking in Political Contexts," *International Journal of the Humanities*.

Fetzer, James & Mike Palecek (editors)
2017 *JFK: Who, How and Why: Solving the World's Greatest Murder Mystery*. Crestview, IL: Moon Rock Books.

Fonzi, Gaeton
1993 *The Last Investigation*. New York: Thunder's Mouth Press.

Galanor, Stewart
1998 *Cover-Up*. New York: Kestrel Books.

Garrison, Jim
1988 *On the Trail of the Assassins: My Investigation and Prosecution of the Murder of President Kennedy*. New York: Skyhorse Publishing.

Good, Aaron
2023 "The Kennedy Assassination Scare and Its Haunting Resonance," Kennedy Beacon, September 29.

www.thekennedybeacon.substack.com. Also at www.lewrockwell.com, September 30.

2023 "How the CIA and Corporate Media Covered Up the JFK Assassination," Kennedy Beacon, October 5. www.thekennedybeacon.substack.com.

Groden, Robert J.

1993 *The Killing of a President: The Complete Photographic Record of the JFK Assassination, the Conspiracy, and the Cover-Up.* New York: Penguin Group.

1995 *The Search for Lee Harvey Oswald.* New York: Penguin Books USA.

2013 *JFK: Absolute Proof: The Killing of a President, vol. III.* Kansas City, MO: Conspiracy Publications, LLC.

Groden, Robert J. & Harrison E. Livingstone

1998 *High Treason: The Assassination of JFK & the Case for Conspiracy.* Carroll & Graff Publishers. [1980]

Guyénot, Laurent

2017 *JFK-9/11: 50 Years of the Deep State.* San Diego: Progressive Press.

Hancock, Larry

2006 *Someone Would Have Talked: The Assassination of John F. Kennedy and the Conspiracy to Mislead History.* Southlake, TX: Lancer Productions & Publications.

Hepburn, James (pseud.) [William Turner?]

2002 *Farewell America: The Plot to Kill JFK.* Roseville, CA: Penmarin Books.

Hinkle, Warren & William Turner

1992 *Deadly Secrets.* New York: Thunder Mouth.

Hornberger, Jacob G.

2013 "JFK and the Deferentials," Future of Freedom Foundation, June 4. www.fff.org.

2013 "No Military Coups for America? What about November 1963?" Future of Freedom Foundation, July 9. www.fff.org.

2014 *The Kennedy Autopsy 1.* Fairfax, VA: Future of Freedom Foundation.

2015 *Regime Change: The JFK Assassination.* Fairfax, VA: Future of Freedom Foundation.

2016 *The CIA, Terrorism, and the Cold War: The Evil of the National Security State.* Future of Freedom Foundation, www.fff.org.

2017 "The Mainstream Media's Deference to Authority in the JFK Assassination," Future of Freedom Foundation,

December 10. www.fff.org.

2019 *The Kennedy Autopsy 2: LBJ's Role in the Assassination.* Fairfax, VA: Future of Freedom Foundation.

2020 "Fear in the JFK Assassination, Part 1," Future of Freedom Foundation, June 22. www.fff.org.

2020 "Fear in the JFK Assassination, Part 2," Future of Freedom Foundation, June 23. www.fff.org.

2021 "Why the Mainstream Media Remains Silent on the JFK Records Deadline," Future of Freedom Foundation, October 17. www.fff.org.

2021 "Why Doesn't the CIA Just Destroy its Secret JFK Records?" Future of Freedom Foundation, November 17. www.fff.org.

2022 "Why They Hated Kennedy, and Why They Killed Him," Future of Freedom Foundation.com, February 22. www.fff.org.

2022 *An Encounter With Evil: The Abraham Zapruder Story.* Fairfax, VA: The Future of Freedom Foundation.

2022 "America's Last President," Future of Freedom Foundation, October 6. www.fff.org.

2022 "Is Trump Tucker Carlson's JFK Assassination Source?" Future of Freedom Foundation, December 27. www.fff.org.

2023 "JFK's Different Direction for America Got Him Killed," Future of Freedom Foundation, January 17. www.fff.org.

2023 "Lyndon Johnson's Role in the Kennedy Assassination," Future of Freedom Foundation, April 17. www.fff.org.

2023 "Why JFK Was Deemed a Threat to National Security," Future of Freedom Foundation, June 14. www.fff.org.

2023 "The Mafia Did Not Orchestrate JFK's Assassination," Future of Freedom Foundation, June 27. www.fff.org.

2023 "The Cancer of the National-Security State," Future of Freedom Foundation, June 29. www.fff.org.

2023 "The Achilles' Heel of the JFK Assassination," Future of Freedom Foundation, July 14. www.fff.org.

2023 "Lee Harvey Oswald: Dead Man Walking," Future of Freedom Foundation, August 2. www.fff.org.

2023 "The Evidence that Convicts the CIA of the JFK Assassination," Future of Freedom Foundation, August 11. www.fff.org.

2023 "The Evidence that Convicts the CIA of the JFK Assassination, Part 2," Future of Freedom

Foundation, August 14. www.fff.org.
2023 "The Evidence that Convicts the CIA of the JFK Assassination, Part 3," Future of Freedom Foundation, August 15. www.fff.org.
2023 "The Evidence that Convicts the CIA of the JFK Assassination, Part 4" Future of Freedom Foundation, August 16. www.fff.org.
2023 "Autopsy Fraud Convicts the Military in the JFK Assassination," Future of Freedom Foundation, August 17. www.fff.org.
2023 "JFK Plotters Could Never Have Been Convicted," Future of Freedom Foundation, September 5. www.fff.org.
2023 "The Darkly Brilliant and Ingenious Aspects of the Kennedy Assassination," Future of Freedom Foundation, November 22. www.fff.org.
2024 "America's Military Empire," Future of Freedom Foundation, January 25. www.fff.org.
2024 "CIA Secrecy on JFK Points to Criminal Culpability," Future of Freedom Foundation, March 2. www.fff.org.
2024 "Why the JFK Assassination Still Matters," Future of Freedom Foundation, April 10. www.fff.org.
2024 "Lyndon Johnson's Role in the JFK Assassination," Future of Freedom Foundation, April 29. www.fff.org.
2024 "JFK's Peace Speech Got Him Killed," Future of Freedom Foundation, June 11. www.fff.org.
2024 "The Kennedy Assassination: Fraudulent Photos, X-Rays, and Film," Future of Freedom Foundation, August 1. www.fff.org.
2024 "JFK's War Against the Military Industrial Complex," Future of Freedom Foundation, August 8. www.fff.org.

Horne, Douglas
2009 *Inside the Assassination Records Review Board: The U.S. Government's Final Attempt to Reconcile the Conflicting Medical Evidence in the Assassination of JFK.* 5 vol.
2012 "The Two NPIC Zapruder Film Events: Signposts Pointing to the Film's Alteration," Future of Freedom Foundation, May 18. www.fff.org.
2012 "Photographic Evidence of Bullet Hole in JFK Limousine Windshield 'Hiding in Plain Sight'," Future of Freedom Foundation, June 3. www.fff.org.

2013 "The AF1 Tapes and Subsequent Events at Andrews AFB on November 22, 1963," Future of Freedom Foundation, July 9. www.fff.org.

2014 *JFKs War with the National Security Establishment: Why Kennedy Was Assassinated*. Future of Freedom Foundation.

Hughes-Wilson, Col. John

2013 *JFK: An American Coup d'Etat: The Truth Behind the Kennedy Assassination*. London: John Blake Publishing.

Hurt, Henry

1985 *Reasonable Doubt: An Investigation into the Assassination of John F. Kennedy*. New York: Hold, Rinehart and Winston.

Janney, Peter

2016 *Mary's Mosaic: The CIA Conspiracy to Murder John F. Kennedy, Mary Pinchot Meyer, and Their Vision for World Peace*. Third Edition. New York: Skyhorse Publishing. [2013]

Jeffries, Donald

2016 *Hidden History: An Exposé of Modern Crimes, Conspiracies, and Cover-ups in American Politics*. New York: Skyhorse Publishing.

2016 *Crimes and Cover-Ups in American Politics, 1776-1963*. New York: Skyhorse Publishing.

2023 "My New Book 'Pipe the Bimbo in Red'," I Protest by Donald Jeffries, November 17. www.donaldjeffries.substack.com.

2024 *American Memory Hole: How the Court Historians Promote Disinformation*. New York: Skyhorse Publishing.

2024 "The Rise and Fall of the Second Amendment," I Protest by Donald Jeffries, February 18. www.donaldjeffries.substack.com.

Jeffries, Donald & William Matson Law

2023 *Pipe the Bimbo in Red: Dean Andrews, Jim Garrison, and the Conspiracy to Kill JFK*. Walterville, OR: TrineDay.com.

Kelin, John

2007 *Praise from a Future Generation: The Assassination of JFK and the First Generation Critics of the Warren Report*. San Antonio: Wings Press.

Khrushchev, Nikita
1971 *Khrushchev Remembers: The Last Testament*. Translated and edited by Strobe Talbott. New York: Little, Brown & Company.

Kinzer, Stephen
2013 *The Brothers: John Foster Dulles, Allen Dulles, and Their Secret World War*. New York: Henry Holt and Co.

Krock, Arthur
1963 "The Inter-Administration War in Vietnam," *New York Times*, October 3, p. 34.

Lane, Mark
1963 "Lane's Defense Brief for Oswald," *National Guardian*, December 19. [Reprinted in *Plausible Denial*, pp. 321-344.]
1975 *A Citizen's Dissent*. New York: Dell.
2011 *Last Word: My Indictment of the CIA in the Murder of JFK*. New York: Skyhorse Publishing.
2013 *Rush to Judgment: A Critique of the Warren Commission. Introduction by Hugh Trever-Roper.* [1966] Charlottesville, VA: The Lane Group, LLC. [See also documentary with the same title.]
2013 *Plausible Denial: Was the CIA Involved in the Assassination of John F. Kennedy?* Charlottesville, VA: The Lane Group, LLC. [1991]

Lifton, David
1988 *Best Evidence: Disguise and Deception in the Assassination of John F. Kennedy*. New York: Carroll & Graf [1980]

Livingstone, Harrison E.
1992 *High Treason 2: The Great Cover-Up: The Assassination of President John F. Kennedy*. Carroll & Graf Publishers.
1993 *Killing the Truth: Deceit and Deception in the JFK Case*. New York: Carroll & Graf.
2004 *The Radical Right and the Murder of John F. Kennedy: Stunning Evidence in the Assassination of the President*. Victoria, BC: Trafford Publishing.

Livingstone, Harrison E. & Robert J. Groden
1998 *High Treason: The Assassination of JFK & the Case for Conspiracy*. Carroll & Graff Publishers. [1980]

Manchester, William
1968 *The Death of a President: November 20-25, 1963*. New York: Popular Library. [1967]

Mantik, David W.
2023 *The JFK Assassination Decoded: Criminal Forgery in the*

Autopsy Photographs and X-Rays. David W. Mantik
2024 *Final Analysis: Assassination of President John F. Kennedy.* New York: Post Hill Press.

Marina
2022 "The Ultra-Reactionaries: Global Analysis of the Dallas Coup," www.medium.com, November 22.

Marrs, Jim
2013 *Crossfire: The Plot that Killed Kennedy. Revised and Updated.* New York: Carroll & Graf. [1989]

Marshall, Andrew Gavin
2010 "The National Security State and the Assassination of JFK," Global Research. November 23. www.globalresearch.ca.

McBride, Joseph
2013 *Into the Nightmare: My Search for the Killers of President John F. Kennedy and Officer J. D. Tippit.* Berkeley, CA: Hightower Press.

McClellan, Barr
2011 *Blood, Money & Power: How LBJ Killed JFK.* New York: Skyhorse Publishing.

McKnight, Gerald
2005 *Breach of Trust: How the Warren Commission Failed the Nation and Why.* University Press of Kansas.

Meagher, Sylvia
1967 *Accessories After the Fact: The Warren Commission, the Authorities & the Report.* New York: Bobbs-Merrill.

Mellen, Joan
2005 *A Farewell to Justice: Jim Garrison, JFK's Assassination, and the Case That Should Have Changed History.* Dulles, VA: Potomac Books.

Mercola, Joseph
2022 "How the Media Secretly Carries Out Assignments for the CIA," Mercola: Take Control of Your Health, July 5. www.mercola.com. Also at www.lewrockwell.com, July 7.
2023 "All Wars are Bankers' Wars," Mercola: Take Control of Your Health, October 20. www.mercola.com. Also at www.lewrockwell.com, October 23.

Miller, Donald W., Jr., MD
2012 "Pursuing Truth on the Kennedy Assassination," August 21. www.lewrockwell.com/1970/01/donald-w-miller-jr-md/pursuing-truth-on-the-kennedy-

assassinations/.
[Video available at:
www.youtube.com/watch?v=YNgKwS7qQD4&t=376s.]

2012 "Why Three Kennedys Were Assassinated," October 2. [Transcript of the Lew Rockwell Show episode 309.] www.lewrockwell.com/1970/01/donald-w-miller-jr-md/why-three-kennedys-were-assassinated-a-transcript-of-the-lew-rockwell-show-episode-309-with-donmiller/.

2013 "Reflections on the Assassination of President John F. Kennedy, 50 Years Later," November 16. www.lewrockwell.com/2013/11/donald-w-miller-jr-md/jfk-thought-control-and-thought-crimes/.

2019 "If Not Oswald, Who Killed President Kennedy and Why?" www.lewrockwell.com/2019/07/donald-w-miller-jr-md/if-not-oswald-who-killed-president-kennedy-and-why/, July 24.
[Video available at:
www.youtube.com/watch?v=kKZinCtkSgo&t=564s.]

Model, Peter (with Robert J. Groden)

1976 *JFK: The Case for Conspiracy*. New York: Manor Books.

Morley, Jefferson

2000 *Morley v. CIA: My Unfinished JFK Investigation*. Kindle.

2008 *Our Man in Mexico: Winston Scott and the Hidden History of the CIA*. Lawrence: University of Kansas.

2016 *CIA & JFK: The Secret Assassination Files*. Kindle.

Neal, David

2023 "Why the Assassination of JFK Matters to Us Today," David Neal Observations, July 27. www.davidnealobx.blogspot.com.

Nelson, Philip F.

2013 *LBJ: The Mastermind of the JFK Assassination*. New York: Skyhorse Publishing. [2011]

2014 *LBJ from Mastermind to "The Colossus."* New York: Skyhorse Publishing.

2018 *Who Really Killed Martin Luther King, Jr.: The Case Against Lyndon B. Johnson and J. Edgar Hoover*. New York: Skyhorse Publishing.

2019 "How Lyndon Johnson Expropriated Control Over the Pentagon and CIA Soon After the Inauguration of the Kennedy-Johnson Administration," LBJ: The Master of Deceit, May 7. And at www.lewrockwell.com, May

8.
2020 "Why JFK Went to Texas," LBJ: The Master of Deceit, www.lbjthemasterofdeceit.com, March 31. Also at www.lewrockwell.com, April 2.
2020 "The Strange Synchronicity of Seemingly Unrelated Enigmatic Events," LBJ: The Master of Deceit, www.lbjthemasterofdeceit.com, July 3. Also at www.lewrockwell.com, July 17.

Newcomb, Fred T.
2011 *Murder from Within: Lyndon Johnson's Plot Against President Kennedy*. Santa Barbara: Probe. [1974]

Newman, John M.
1992 *JFK and Vietnam: Deception, Intrigue, and the Struggle for Power*. New York: Warner.
2008 *Oswald and the CIA*. New York: Skyhorse Publishing. [1995, Carroll & Graf]
2017 *Countdown to Darkness: The Assassination of President Kennedy, vol. 2*. Create Space.
2017 *Where Angels Tread Lightly: The Assassination of President Kennedy, vol. 1*. Create Space.
2019 *Into the Storm: The Assassination of President Kennedy, vol. 3*. John Newman.
2022 *Uncovering Popov's Mole: The Assassination of President Kennedy, vol. 4*. John Newman.

North, Mark
1991 *Act of Treason: The Role of J. Edgar Hoover in the Assassination of JFK*. New York: Carroll & Graf.

Oglesby, Carl
1977 *The Yankee and Cowboy War*. New York: Medallion.

O'Toole, George
1975 *The Assassination Tapes: An Electronic Probe into the Murder of John F. Kennedy and the Dallas Coverup*. New York: Penthouse Press.

Palecek, Mike & James Fetzer (editors)
2017 *JFK: Who, How and Why: Solving the World's Greatest Murder Mystery*. Crestview, IL: Moon Rock Books.

Pease, Lisa
2018 *A Lie Too Big to Fail*. Port Townsend, WA: Feral House.

Piper, Michael Collins
1993 *Final Judgment: The Missing Link in the JFK Assassination Conspiracy*. Washington, D.C.: Wolfe Press.

Popkin, Richard H.
1966 *The Second Oswald*. New York: Avon Books.

Posner, Gerald.
1993 *Case Closed: Lee Harvey Oswald and the Assassination of JFK*. Garden City, NJ: Doubleday.
Poulgrain, Greg
2020 *JFK vs. Allen Dulles: Battleground Indonesia*. New York: Skyhorse.
President's Commission on the Assassination of President Kennedy
1964 *Report of the President's Commission on the Assassination of President Kennedy*. [The Warren Report, 26 vol.] Washington, D.C.: United States Printing Office.
Prouty, C. L. Fletcher
1975 "The Guns of Dallas," *Gallery*, October.
2011 *The Secret Team: The CIA and Its Allies in Control of the United States*. New York: Skyhorse. [1973, 2008]
2011 *JFK: The CIA, Vietnam, and the Plot to Assassinate John F. Kennedy*. New York: Skyhorse. [1992]
Rivera, Larry
2018 *The JFK Horsemen: Framing Lee, Altering the Altgens 6 and Resolving Other Mysteries*. Crestview, IL: Moon Rock Books.
Roberts, Craig
1994 *Kill Zone: A Sniper Looks at Dealey Plaza*. Typhoon Press.
Roberts, Craig & John Armstrong
1995 *JFK: The Dead Witnesses*. Consolidated Press Int'l.
Roberts, Paul Craig
2023 "President John F. Kennedy: His Life and Public Assassination by the CIA," Institute for Political Economy, November 22. www.paulcraigroberts.org.
2023 "Two Contrasting Commencement Addresses a Half Century Apart," Institute for Political Economy, June 2. www.paulcraigroberts.org.
Rockwell, Llewellyn H., Jr.
2012 "Why Three Kennedys Were Assassinated." [Transcript of the Lew Rockwell Show with guest Donald W. Miller, Jr., MD, episode 309.] www.lewrockwell.com, October 2.
2022 "Who Killed President Kennedy?" www.lewrockwell.com, December 26.
2023 "The Truth About JFK's Assassination." [Interview with James Douglass.] www.lewrockwell.com, November 27.
Rosenbaum, Ron & Phillip Nobile
1976 "The Curious Aftermath of JFK's Best and Brightest

Affairs," *New Times*, July 9.

Roth, Jack

2022 *Killing Kennedy: Exposing the Plot, the Cover-up and the Consequences*. New York: Skyhorse Publishing.

Royster, Vermont

1988 "A New Look at that Day in Dallas," *Wall Street Journal*, December 7, p. A14.

Russell, Bertrand

1964 "16 Questions on the Assassination," *The Minority of One*, September 6. [Reprinted in Fetzer (editor), *Murder in Dealey Plaza*, pp. 413-20; and in Paul Zarembka, *The Hidden History of 9-11*, pp. 349-52.]

Russell, Dick

1992 *The Man Who Knew Too Much: Hired to Kill Oswald and Prevent the Assassination of JFK*. New York: Carroll & Graf Publishers.

2008 *On the Trail of the JFK Assassins*. New York: Skyhorse Publications.

Salandria, Vincent J.

1964 "The Warren Report Analysis of Shots, Trajectories, and Wounds: A Lawyer's Dissenting View," *The Legal Intelligencer*, November 2. [Reprinted in Schotz, *History Will Not Absolve Us*.]

1965 "A Philadelphia Lawyer Analyzes the Shots, Trajectories, and Wounds," *Liberation*, vol. IX, no. 10 (January): 13-19. [Reprinted in Schotz, *History Will Not Absolve Us*.]

1965 "The Warren Report?" *Liberation*, vol. X, no. 1 (March): 14-33. [Reprinted in Schotz, *History Will Not Absolve Us*.]

2004 *False Mystery: Essays on the Assassination of JFK*. Louisville, CO: Square Deal Press. [Collection of 10 articles by Salandria, 1964-66, 1971, 1997-99.]

Schall, Lars

2013 "The JFK Assassination Marked the End of the American Republic." [Interview with Martin Broeckers.] www.lewrockwell.com, August 21.

Schotz, E. Martin

1995 "Letter to Vincent J. Salandria, April 5, 1995," reprinted in *History Will Not Absolve Us*, pp. 9-35.

1996 *History Will Not Absolve Us: Orwellian Control, Public Denial, and the Murder of President Kennedy*. Brookline, MA: Kurtz, Ulmer, & DeLucia Book

Publishers.

Scott, Peter Dale

1993 *Crime and Cover-Up: The CIA, the Mafia, and the Dallas-Watergate Connection.* Santa Barbara: Open Archive Press.

1993 *Deep Politics and the Death of JFK.* Berkeley: University of California Press.

1995 *Deep Politics II: Essays on Oswald, Mexico, and Cuba.* Stokie, IL: Green Archive Publications.

2013 *The War Conspiracy: JFK, 9/11, and the Deep Politics of War.* New York: Skyhorse Publishing. [1972]

2013 *Oswald, Mexico, and Deep Politics: Revelations from CIA Records.* New York: Skyhorse Publishing. [1994]

2014 "The Fates of American Presidents Who Challenged the Deep State (1963-1980), *Asia-Pacific Journal*, vol. 12, issue 43/4 (October 20). www.apjjf.org/2014/12/43/peter-dale-scott/4206.

2015 *Dallas '63: The First Deep State Revolt Against the White House.* New York: Open Road.

2017 *The American Deep State*, new edition. New York: Rowman & Littlefield.

Scott, Peter Dale & Paul L. Hoch & Russell Stetler

1976 *The Assassinations: Dallas and Beyond—A Guide to Cover-Ups and Assassinations.* New York: Random House.

Select Committee on Assassination of the United States House of Representatives, 95 Congress, 2nd Session.

1979 *Report of the Select Committee on Assassinations.* Washington, D.C.: United States Printing Office.

Shaw, J. Gary & Larry R. Harris

1992 *Cover-Up: The Governmental Conspiracy to Conceal the Facts about the Public Execution of John Kennedy.* Thomas Investigative Publications, Inc. [1976]

Shaw, Mark

2022 *Fighting for Justice: The Improbable Journey to Exposing Cover-Ups about the JFK Assassination and the Deaths of Marilyn Monroe and Dorothy Kilgallen.* New York: Post Hill Press.

Sloan, Bill (with Jean Hill)

2008 *The Last Dissenting Witness: Jean Hill.* New York: Pelican Publishing Company.

Stone, Oliver & Zachary Sklar

2000 *JFK: The Book of the Film.* Applause.

Stone, Roger
2013 *The Man Who Killed Kennedy: The Case for LBJ*. New York: Skyhorse Publishing.

Summers, Anthony
2013 *Not in Your Lifetime: The Defining Book on the JFK Assassination.* Headline. [Third edition of *Conspiracy* (1980) and *The Kennedy Conspiracy* (1998).]

Suskind, Ron
2004 "Faith, Certainty and the Presidency of George W. Bush," *New York Times Magazine*, October 17.

Swanson, Michael
2013 *The War State: The Cold War Origins of the Military-Industrial Complex and the Power Elite, 1945-1963.* Create Space.
2015 "JFK, McGeorge Bundy, and the Continuity of Government," Future of Freedom Foundation, July 30. www.fff.org.

Talbot, David
2004 "The Mother of All Cover-ups," *Salon*, September 15.
2007 *Brothers: The Hidden History of the Kennedy Years*. New York: Free Press.
2015 *The Devil's Chessboard: Allen Dulles, the CIA, and the Rise of America's Secret Government*. New York: Harper Perennial.
2023 "The JFK Assassination at 60: The Public Knows the Truth. Why Won't the Media Report It?" Kennedy Beacon, November 20. www.thekennedybeacon.substack.com.

Tannenbaum, Robert K.
1995 *Corruption of Blood*. New York: Penguin Group.

Tate, Tim & Brad Johnson
2018 *The Assassination of Robert F. Kennedy*. London: Thistle Publishing.

The Third Decade: A Journal of Research on the John F. Kennedy Assassination. Published by Jerry Rose.

Thompson, George C.
1964 *The Quest for Truth: A Quizzical Look at the Warren Report*. Glendale, CA: G. C. Thompson Engineering Co.

Thompson, Josiah
1967 *Six Seconds in Dallas: A Micro-Study of the Kennedy Assassination*. Bernard Geis Associates.
2021 *Last Second in Dallas*. University Press of Kansas.

Trask, Richard B.
1994 *Pictures of the Pain: Photography and the Assassination.* Danvers, MA: Yeoman Press.
2013 *That Day in Dallas: Three Photographers Capture on Film the Day President Kennedy Died.* Danvers, MA: Yeoman Press.

Truman, Harry
1950 Special Message to the Congress on the Internal Security of the United States.
1963 "Limit CIA Role to Intelligence," *Washington Post*, Dec. 22, p. A11. www.ia801202.us.archive.org.
1974 [Conversations with Merle Miller transcribed and published in] *Plain Speaking* by Merle Miller. London: Gollancz.

Turner, William
2001 *Rearview Mirror: Looking Back at the FBI, the CIA and Other Tails*. Granite Bay, CA: Penmartin Books.
2002 *Farewell America: The Plot to Kill JFK*. Roseville, CA: Penmarin Books. [By James Hepburn, suspected to be a pseudonym for William Turner.]

Turner, William & Jonn Christian
1978 *The Assassination of Robert F. Kennedy: The Conspiracy and Coverup*.

Turner, William & Warren Hinkle
1992 *Deadly Secrets*. New York: Thunder Mouth.

Twyman, Noel
1997 *Bloody Treason: On Solving History's Greatest Murder Mystery: The Assassination of John F. Kennedy*. Rancho Santa Fe, CA: Laurel Publishing.

Unz, Ron
-- The Unz Review: An Alternative Media Selection: A collection of interesting, important, and controversial perspectives largely excluded from the American mainstream media. www.unz.com.
2016 "American Pravda: How the CIA Invented 'Conspiracy Theories'," Unz Review, September 5. www.unz.com.
2018 "American Pravda: The JFK Assassination, Part I – What Happened?" Unz Review, June 18. www.unz.com.
2018 "American Pravda: The JFK Assassination, Part II – Who Did It?" Unz Review, June 25. www.unz.com.
2022 *Conspiracy Theories: From the JFK Assassination to the 9/11 Attacks*. Palo Alto: Unz Review Press.
2022 "Anne Frank, Sirhan Sirhan, and AIDS," Unz Review,

January 31. www.unz.com.
2022 "Major Mysteries of the 1990s," Unz Review, December 12. www.unz.com.
2022 "The JFK Assassination and the Covid Cover-Up," Unz Review, December 19. www.unz.com.
2022 "Collapsing Conspiracy Cover-Ups?" Unz Review, December 25. www.unz.com.
2023 "RFK Jr. vs. I.F. Stone on the Kennedy Assassinations," Unz Review, July 31. www.unz.com.
2024 "Prof. Jeffrey Sachs and the JFK Assassination," Unz Review, March 18. www.unz.com.
2024 "The Transformation of Prof. Jeffrey Sachs," Unz Review, April 1. www.unz.com.
2024 "JFK, LBJ, and Our Great National Shame," Unz Review, June 24. www.unz.com.

U.S. House of Representatives
1979 *Report of the Select Committee on Assassinations and Twelve Accompanying Volumes of Hearings and Appendices*. U.S. Government Printing Office.

U.S. Senate
1975 *Select Committee to Study Governmental Operations, with Respect to Intelligence Activities, Alleged Assassination Plots Involving Foreign Leaders,* Interim Report. U.S. Government Printing Office.

Vankin, Jonathan
1991 *Conspiracies, Cover-Ups, and Crimes: Political Manipulation and Mind Control in America*. New York: Paragon House.

Warner, Dale G.
1964 *Who Killed the President?* New York: American Press.

Weberman, Alan J. & Michael Canfield
1992 *Coup d'Etat in America*. San Francisco: Quick Trading Co. [1975]

Wecht, Cyril H. & Jeff Sewald
2020 *Life and Deaths of Cyril Wecht: Memoirs of America's Most Controversial Forensic Pathologist.* Jefferson, NC: Exposit.

Wecht, Cyril H. & Dawna Kaufmann
2022 *The JFK Assassination Dissected.* Jefferson, NC: Exposit.

Weisberg, Harold
1967 *Oswald in New Orleans: Case for Conspiracy with the CIA.* New York: Canyon Books.
1994 *Case Open: The Unanswered JFK Assassination Questions.*

New York: Carroll & Graf.
2007 *Never Again! The Government Conspiracy in the JFK Assassination*. New York: Skyhorse. [1995]
2013 *Post Mortem: The Classic Investigation of the JFK Assassination Medical and Ballistics Evidence and Cover-Up*. New York: Skyhorse Publishing. [1975]
2013 *Whitewash: The Report on the Warren Report*. New York: Skyhorse. [1965]
2013 *Whitewash II: The FBI-Secret Service Cover-up*. New York: Skyhorse. [1966]
2013 *Whitewash III: The Photographic Whitewash of the JFK Assassination*. New York: Skyhorse. [1967]
2013 *Whitewash IV: The Top Secret Warren Commission Transcript of the JFK Assassination*. New York: Skyhorse.[1974]
Unpub. *Inside the Assassination Industry*. Available online in the Weisberg Archives at Hood College.

White, Ricky, as told to J. Gary Shaw & Brian K. Edwards
2024 *Admitted Assassin: Roscoe White and the Murder of President Kennedy*. Peniel Unlimited.

Wicker, Tom
1966 "CIA: Maker of Policy or Tool?" *New York Times*, April 25, p. 20.

Zirbel, Craig I.
1991 *The Texas Connection: The Assassination of President John F. Kennedy*. Texas: Texas Connection.

WEBSITES AND VIDEOS

Even more than the list of books and articles, this list of websites and videos is a work in progress. Items on it are those I found helpful in understanding what happened, but it's far from comprehensive.

Films/Movies/Documentaries/Public Talks

Altered History: Exposing Deceit and Deception in the JFK Assassination Medical Evidence. Douglas P. Horne's five-part documentary. [All have same title except for number at the end.] Future of Freedom Foundation. www.fff.org/explore-freedom/article/altered-history-exposing-deciet-and-deception-in-the-jfk-assassination-medical-evidence-part-1/.

America: Untold Stories
Eric Hunley and Mork Groubert.
www.youtube.com/@AmericasUntoldStories.
Assassination Medical Evidence
by Douglas Horne. www.fff.org.
Best Evidence: The Research Video (1990)
Rhino Home Video.
"A Coup d'état in America" (2016)
Dr. Cyril Wecht on JFK's murder.
Video and transcript at:
www.whowhatwhy.org/video/dr-cyril-wecht-jfks-murder-coup-detat-america/.
Crisis: Behind a Presidential Commission (1963)
Directed by Robert Drew.
Crossfire: The Plot that Killed Kennedy (DVD)
Based on Jim Marrs's book.
A Current Affair: The JFK Assassination
Dark Legacy (2009) (103 min.)
www.youtube.com/watch?v+YYmombA4WwE
www.youtube.com/watch?v=d8njj6gaSnk&rco=1.
Executive Action (1973)
Four Days in November (1964, 120 min.)
Documentary directed by Mel Stuart.
How the JFK Autopsy Led to the Truth
By Jacob Hornberger. www.fff.org.
If Not Oswald, Who Killed President Kennedy and Why? (2019)
A presentation by Donald W. Miller, MD.
www.youtube.com/watch?v=kKZinCtkSgo&t=564s
Transcript:
www.lewrockwell.com/2019/07/donald-w-miller-jr-md/if-not-oswald-who-killed-president-kennedy-and-why/.
Image of an Assassination: A New Look at the Zapruder Film
The JFK Assassination: Sixty Years Later
www.fff.org.
The JFK Assassination
By Jacob Hornberger. www.fff.org.
JFK: The Case for Conspiracy
Produced by Robert J. Groden
The JFK Conspiracy (1992)
Hosted by James Earl Jones. All American Television Co., Inc.
JFK and its Depiction of History (1992)
Panel of seven debates the depiction of history in Oliver Stone's film *JFK*. American University. Panel includes Col. Fletcher

Prouty and John Judge.
Broadcast on C-SPAN as "Cinema as History"
www.c-span.org/video/?23934-1/jfk-depiction-history.

The JFK Assassination: Three Programs on "Best Evidence"
May 9, 14, 21, 1990. Los Angeles. David Lifton

The JFK Assassination
Jacob G. Hornberger 30 episode video presentation, Future of Freedom Foundation, www.fff.org.

JFK Lancer Assassination Research Conference

JFK: A President Betrayed (2014)
Narrated by Morgan Freeman.
www.tubitv.com/movies/314077/jfk-a-president-betrayed.

JFK Revisited: Through the Looking Glass (2021) (DVD)

JFK 3 Shots that Changed America (2009)
History Channel.

The Kennedy Assassinations: Coincidence or Conspiracy.
All American Communications. 90 minutes.

The Last Two Days
Documentary film by Thomas Atkins.

Lee Oswald's Life & Brother. Three Shows
Three talks by David Lifton.

Medical Experts and the Kennedy Assassination
Dr. Gary Aguilar presentation on C-SPAN
www.c-span.org/video/?321702-3/medical-experts-kennedy-assassination.

The Men Who Killed Kennedy
Produced by The History Channel, directed by Nigel Turner.
- Part 1: Coup D'Etat (1988)
  Covers the events in Dallas on the weekend of the shooting.
- Part 2: The Forces of Darkness (1988)
  Presents witnesses and commentators.
- Part 3: The Cover-up (1991)
  Presents witnesses and commentators.
- Part 4: The Patsy (1991)
  Focuses on Lee Harvey Oswald.
- Part 5: The Witnesses (1991)
  Focuses on James Hosty and Ruth Paine and others.
- Part 6: The Truth Shall Make You Free (1995)
  Interviews with Marina Oswald and others.
- Part 7: The Smoking Guns (2003)
  Secret Service complicity in the assassination, the integrity of the medical evidence, and the bullet hole in the windshield. Banned in the United States.

Part 8: The Love Affair (2003)
Judyth Baker talks of her relationship with Lee Harvey Oswald and their involvement with a covert CIA project. Banned in the United States.
Part 9: The Guilty Men (2003)
Indicts Lyndon Johnson of conspiring to kill Kennedy. Banned in the United States. Perhaps the best video ever made about the JFK assassination.
Murder of JFK, a Revisionist History (2006)
Directed by Matthew White.
The National Security State and the JFK Assassination (2021)
Online conference hosted by Jacob Hornblower, at least 29 episodes posted between March 3 and April 21. www.fff.org.
Jeffrey Sachs
"JFK's Quest for Peace"
Stephen Kinzer
"Regime change: Roots of the Imperial Temptation"
Michael Glennon
"Double Government and the 'Best Truth' about the Assassination"
Douglas Horne
"The National Security Establishment's Obsession with Invading Cuba"
Michale Swanson
"What is the Purpose of the National Security State?"
Peter Janney
"JFK & Mary Meyer: Relationship as Redemption"
Paul, Ron
"Enemies: Foreign and Domestic"
Jefferson Morley
"Angleton, Cuba, and Assassination"
James DiEugenio
"Vietnam Declassified: Kennedy, Johnson, Nixon"
Oliver Stone with James DiEugenio
"If JFK Were Alive Today"
Jacob G. Hornberger, Jacob G.
"The National Security State: The Biggest Mistake in U.S. History"
The Plot to Kill JFK: Rush to Judgment (1967)
By Mark Lane and Emile de Antonio.
Pursuing Truth on the Kennedy Assassination (2021)
A presentation by Donald W. Miller, MD

www.youtube.com/watch?v=YNgKwS7qQD4&t=376s.
Transcript:
www.lewrockwell.com/1970/01/donald-w-miller-jr-md/pursuing-truth-on-the-kennedy-assassinations/.

Reasonable Doubt: The Single-Bullet Theory (1995)
Directed by Chip Selby.

Rush to Judgment (1967)
Film based on Rush's book.
www.dailymotion.com/video/x8flmyo

The Searchers
Features prominent JFK assassination researchers Josiah Thompson, John Judge, Mark Lane, Cyril Wecht, Robert Groden, Jim Marrs, Lisa Pease, Gary Aguilar and others.

Seven Days in May (1964)
A movie based on the book by Fletcher Knebel and Charles W. Bailey II.

Who Shot President Kennedy? (1988)
Nova documentary.

Z
A film by David Lifton.

Zapruder Film
Excellent examination of alterations to the film. No longer available. www.youtube.com/watch?v=5Am4qdl9PTA.

The Zapruder Film Mystery [85 min.]
Douglas P. Horne
www.youtube.com/embed/J_QIuu6hsAc.

Websites

Assassination Science (Jim Fetzer)
www.assassinationscience.com.

CTKA: Citizens for Truth about the Kennedy Assassination
www.ctka.net.

History Matters
www.history-matters.com.

JFK Facts: Completing the Story of the Assassination
Jefferson Morley, editor.
www.jfkfacts.substack.com, www.jfkfacts.substack.org.

Kennedys and King
www.kennedysandking.com.

The Mary Ferrell Foundation: Preserving the Legacy
www.maryferrell.org.

Len Osanic interviews assassination researchers
www.blackopradio.com.

Shorter clips

www.jfkmurder.com

Robert Groden website. No longer exists.

www.youtube.com/watch?v=TF0kBdk0fQ.

At :24, in Moorman photo, shows material on back hood of limo not visible in the Zapruder film. Jean Hill's interesting account about how her photos were stolen from her by the FBI. No longer available.

60 Minutes

Episode on Judyth Baker and Lee Harvey Oswald. Never Broadcast.

JFK Assassination: The Truth Told by Secret Service Agent Clint Hill

At 28:20: Clint Hill says that there was brain matter and bone fragments all over the back of the limousine. But it's not visible in the Zapruder film. "From above I could see into the wound. All the brain matter was gone. Just completely gone." www.youtube.com/watch?v=vzYwCmDDSLA.

JFK Assassination Forum for photos and YouTube channel

Users must register to access photos and documents. www.jfkassassinationforum.com.

The Kennedy Detail: JFK's Secret Service Agents

At 24:40: Clint Hill says that a shot hit Kennedy's upper right head causing a gaping hole in the upper right rear part of the head about the size of his palm. Brain matter scattered over the entire car.

www.youtube.com/watch?v=lYpY8zI_wwA.

COUP #2: SEPTEMBER 11, 2001
(and the United States as head of an empire)

The books I found most helpful as I began to research this subject were:

- Anything and everything by David Ray Griffin; his *9/11 Ten Years Later* is a good place to start;
- Elias Davidsson's *Hijacking America's Mind on 9/11*;
- Jim Fetzer's *The 9/11 Conspiracy* & *America Nuked on 9/11*;
- James Gourley's *The 9/11 Toronto Report: International Hearings on the Events of September 11, 2001*;
- Ian Henshall's *9/11 Revealed: The New Evidence*;
- Eric Hufschmid's *Painful Questions: An Analysis of the September 11th Attack*;
- Eric Larsen's *The Skull of Yorick: The Emptiness of American Thinking at a Time of Grave Peril*;
- Jim Marrs's *The Terror Conspiracy*;
- Michael C. Ruppert's *Crossing the Rubicon*;
- Peter Dale Scott's *The Road to 9/11: Wealth, Empire and the Future of America*;
- Webster Tarpley's *9/11 Synthetic Terror Made in USA*;
- Judy Wood's *Where Did the Towers Go?*;
- Barrie Zwicker's *Towers of Deception*.

BOOKS AND ARTICLES

ABC News

2014 "Bill Clinton, Hours Before 9/11 Attacks: 'I Could Have Killed' Osama bin Laden," August 1. www.abcnews.go.com/US/bill-clinton-hours-911-attacks-killed-osama-bin/story?id=24801422.

Ahmed, Nafeez M.

2002 *The War on Freedom: How and Why America Was Attacked, September 11, 2001*. Joshua Tree, CA: Tree of Life Publications.

2005 *The War on Truth: 9/11, Disinformation, and the Anatomy of Terrorism*. Northampton, MA: Interlink.

Alden, David

2018 *The North Tower: Controlled Demolition and the Bush, Cheney, Giuliani Cover-up*. Chandler, AZ: Liberty Bell Books, Ltd.

Anonymous Patriots

2016 *Treason: Who Did 9/11 and Why Did They Do It?* Millennium Report, October 14. www.themillenniumreport.com/2016/10/treason-who-did-911-and-why-did-they-do-it/.

Architects and Engineers for 9/11 Truth

2015 *Beyond Misinformation—What Science Says About the Destruction of World Trade Center Buildings 1, 2 and 7.* www.beyondmisinformation.org.

Arendt, Hannah

1985 *The Origins of Totalitarianism. New edition with added prefaces.* Boston: Mariner Books. [1948]

Arkin, William M.

2002 "The Secret War," *Los Angeles Times*, October 27.

2013 *American Coup: How a Terrified Government is Destroying the Constitution.* New York: Little, Brown and Co.

Baker, Russ

2009 *Family of Secrets: The Bush Dynasty. America's Invisible Government, and the Hidden History of the Last Fifty Years.* New York: Bloomsbury Press.

Baldwin, Chuck

2018 "9/11: The Biggest Con Job Since JFK," Chuck Baldwin Live, September 13. www.chuckbaldwinlive.com, Also at www.lewrockwell.com, September 14.

Bamford, James

2002 *Body of Secrets: Anatomy of the Ultra-Secret National Security Agency.* New York: Anchor Books.

2004 *A Pretext for War: 9/11, Iran, and the Abuse of America's Intelligence Agencies.* New York: Doubleday.

Barrett, Kevin

2007 *Truth Jihad: My Epic Struggle Against the 9/11 Big Lie.* Joshua Tree, CA: Progressive Press.

2009 *Questioning the War on Terror: A Primer for Obama Voters.* Khadir Press.

2022 "9/11, 22 Years Later: Will We Ever Get the Truth?" Unz Review, September 2. www.unz.com.

Barrett, Kevin, John Cobb & Sandra Lubarsky (editors)

2006 *9/11 and the American Empire: Christians, Jews and Muslims Speak Out.* Northampton: Interlink.

Benjamin, Amy Baker

2017 "9/11 as False Flag: Why International Law must dare to care," *African Journal of International and Comparative Law*, vol. 25, no. 3: 371-392.

Benz, Mike
2024 "The End of Democracy: What I'm Describing is Military Rule," February 16. [Interview with Tucker Carlson.] www.x.com/TuckerCarlson/status/1758529993280205039. Transcript: www.happyscribe.com/public/the-tucker-carlson-podcast/mike-benz.

Berwick, Jeff & Charlie Robinson
2020 *The Controlled Demolition of the American Empire.* Independently published.

Bleier, Ronald
2019 *No Plane Crashes on 9/11: Exposing the Illusion.* Kindle Direct Publishing.

Bollyn, Christopher
2012 *Solving 9/11: The Deception that Changed the World.* Christopher Bollyn. Lightning Source, Inc.
2017 *The War on Terror: The Plot to Rule the Middle East.* Christopher Bollyn.

Bovard, James
2024 "The Never-Ending Federal Surveillance Spree," March 26. www.jimbovard.com.

Box, Woody
2007 "The Cleveland Airport Mystery," second edition, February. www.911woodybox.blogspot.com/2007/02/cleveland-airport-mystery.html.

Brezinski, Zbigniew
2016 *The Grand Chessboard: American Primacy and Its Geostrategic Imperatives.* Updated with a new epilogue. New York: Basic Books. [1997]

Bridge, Robert
2009 "911 Reasons Why 9/11 was (Probably) an Inside Job," *HomeUSA News*, September 9.

Burris, Charles
2022 "9/11: A Conspiracy Theory – Lew Rockwell," September 13. [Transcript of James Corbett's five and a half minute video.] www.lewrockwell.com.

Bush, George W.
2001 "Remarks by the President to United Nations General Assembly," White House Archives. www.georgewbush-whitehouse.archives.gov/news/releases/2001/11/20011110-3.html.

2005 "President Discusses War on Terror at National Endowment for Democracy," October 6.

Butler, Smedley D.

1935 "America's Armed Forces: 2. In Time of Peace: The Army," *Common Sense*, vol. 4, no. 11 (November): 8-12.

2003 *War is a Racket*. Port Townsend, WA: Feral House. [1935]

Carlson, Tucker

2024 "The End of Democracy: What I'm Describing is Military Rule," February 16. [interview with Mike Benz.] www.x.com/TuckerCarlson/status/1758529993280205039. [transcript: www.happyscribe.com/public/the-tucker-carlson-podcast/mike-benz.

CBS News

2002 *What We Saw: September 11: The Events of September 11, 2001—In Words, Pictures, and Video.* Introduction by Dan Rather. New York: Simon & Schuster.

Chossudovsky, Michel

2002 *War and Globalization: The Truth Behind September 11*. Shanty Bay, Ontario: Global Outlook.

2005 *America's "War on Terrorism."* (2nd ed.). Global Research.

2015 *The Globalization of War: America's "Long War" Against Humanity*. Global Research Publishers.

2023 "9/11 Analysis: From Reagan's Al Qaeda Sponsored War on Afghanistan to George W. Bush's 9/11," Michel Chossudovsky, September 11. www.michelchossudovsky.substack.com.

2023 "Was 9/11 a False Flag?" Michel Chossudovsky, December 27. www.michaelchossudovsky.substack.com. www.lewrockwell.com, December 30.

Christian, Francis

2024 "Know Your Enemy," Francis Christian's Essays, February 17. www.francischristian.substack.com.

Christison, William

2006 "Stop Belittling the Theories about September 11," Dissident Voice, August 14. www.dissidentvoice.org.

Cirignano, Douglas

2019 *American Conspiracies and Cover-Ups*. New York: Skyhorse Publishing.

Cogswell, David

2008 "See No Evil," www.onlinejournal.com, February 25. Also on www.davidcogswell.com/Essays/SeeNoEvil.html.

Cole, David
2003 *Enemy Aliens: Double Standards and Constitutional Freedoms in the War on Terrorism*. New York: New Press.

Crotty, William (editor)
2004 *The Politics of Terror: The U.S. Response to 9/11*. Boston: Northeastern University Press.

Curtin, Edward
2020 *Seeking Truth in a Country of Lies: Critical & Lyrical Essays*. Atlanta: Clarity Press, Inc.
2023 "'Peace, War, and 9/11': A Cinematic Portrait of Graeme MacQueen, a Warrior for Peace," Edward Curtin: Behind the Curtain, October 19. www.edwardcurtin.com.

Davidsson, Elias
2013 *Hijacking America's Mind on 9/11*. New York: Algora Publishing.
2018 "HuffPost's Attack on Academic Integrity, Truth and Justice," Global Research, December 6. www.globalresearch.ca.

Davidsson, Elias & Craig McKee
2018 "Ten Irrefutable, Devastating 9/11 Facts," Global Research, April 2. www.globalresearch.ca.

de Haven-Smith, Lance
2013 *Conspiracy Theory in America*. Austin: University of Texas Press.

DeMasi, Nicholas
2004 *Ground Zero: Behind the Scenes*. New York: TRAC Team.

DeMott, Benjamin
2004 "Whitewash as Public Service—How the 9/11 Commission Report Defrauds the Nation," *Harper's Magazine*, October.

Fetzer, James (editor)
2007 *The 9/11 Conspiracy: The Scamming of America*. Catfeet Press.

Fetzer, James & Don Trent Jacobs (editors)
2004 *American Assassination: The Strange Death of Senator Paul Wellstone*. VoxPop.

Fetzer, Jim & Mike Palecek (editors)
2016 *America Nuked on 9/11: Compliments of the CIA, the Neocons in the DoD & Mossad*. Crestview, FL: Moon Rock Books.

Gaffney, Mark H.
2015 *The 9/11 Mystery Plane and the Vanishing of America*. Walterville, OR: Trine Day, LLC.
2016 *Black 9/11: Money, Motive and Technology*. Updated second edition. Walterville, OR: Trine Day, LLC.
2021 "The Demolition of the World Trade Center on September 11, 2001," Unz Review, August 17. www.unz.com.
2023 "The Demolition of the World Trade Center," Unz Review, August 17. www.unz.com.

Ganser, Daniele
2020 *USA: The Ruthless Empire*. New York: Skyhorse Publishing.

Garcia, Jr., Manuel
2021 "Confessions of a Secret Controlled Demolitions Special Operative for 9/11," Counterpunch, September 13. www.counterpunch.org, September 2.

Glennon, Michael J.
2015 *National Security and Double Government*. Oxford: Oxford University Press.

Global Outlook: The Magazine of 9/11 Truth (Ian Woods, editor)
2002- www.globaloutlook.ca.

Gourley, James R. (editor)
2013 *The 9/11 Toronto Report: International Hearings on the Events of September 11, 2001*. Dallas: International Center for 9/11 Studies.

Griffin, David Ray
2005 *The New Pearl Harbor: Disturbing Questions About the Bush Administration and 9/11.* Northampton: Interlink. [2004, Olive Branch Press] [There is also a 2008 edition with a new section.]
2005 *The 9/11 Commission Report: Omissions and Distortions*. Northampton: Interlink Books. [2004: Olive Branch Press]
2005 "What if Everything You Know about 9/11 is Wrong?" *Hustler*, August. [Link at www.911truth.org.]
2006 *Christian Faith and the Truth Behind 9/11*. Louisville: Westminster John Knox Press.
2006 "The Destruction of the World Trade Center: A Christian Theologian Speaks Out," in Zarembka, *Hidden History*. [Also at www.911review.com.]
2006 "The Destruction of the World Trade Center: Why the Official Story Cannot Be True," in *Hidden History of 9-11-2001, Research in Political Economy*, vol. 23

(Spring). [Also link at www.911review.com.]
2006 "Flights of Fancy—Flights 11, 175, 77 and 93: The 9/11 Commission's Incredible Tales," Global Outlook, no. 11 (Fall-Winter). [Based on lecture given on December 4, 2005.] [Link at www.911truth.org.]
2008 *9/11 Contradictions: An Open Letter to Congress and the Press.* Northampton, MA: Olive Branch Press.
2008 "September 11, 2001: 21 Reasons to Question the Official Story about 9/11," Global Research, September 11. www.globalresearch.ca.
2009 *Osama bin Laden: Dead or Alive?* Northampton, MA: Olive Branch Press.
2010 *The Mysterious Collapse of World Trade Center 7: Why the Final Official Report about 9/11 is Unscientific and False.* Arris Books.
2011 *9/11 Ten Years Later: When State Crimes Against Democracy Succeed.* Northampton, MA: Olive Branch Press.
2011 *Cognitive Infiltration: An Obama Appointee's Plan to Undermine the 9/11 Conspiracy Theory.* Northampton, MA: Olive Branch Press.
2011 *The New Pearl Harbor Revisited: 9/11, the Cover-Up, and the Expose.* Northampton, MA: Olive Branch Press.
2017 *Bush and Cheney: How They Ruined America and the World.* Northampton, MA: Olive Branch Press.
2017 *Debunking 9/11 Debunking: An Answer to Popular Mechanics and Other Defenders of the Official Conspiracy Theory.* Revised & Updated Edition. Olive Branch Press. [2007]
2018 *The American Trajectory: Divine or Demonic.* Atlanta: Clarity Press, Inc.

Griffin, David Ray & John Cobb, Richard Falk, and Catherine Keller
2006 *The American Empire and the Commonwealth of God: A Political, Economic, Religious Statement.* Westminster John Know Press.

Griffin, David Ray & Peter Dale Scott (editors)
2006 *9/11 and the American Empire: Intellectuals Speak Out.* Northampton, MA: Interlink.

Griffin, David Ray & Elizabeth Woodworth
2018 *9/11 Unmasked: An International Review Panel Investigation.* Northampton, MA: Olive Branch Press.
2022 "The 'Best Evidence' Contradicting the Official Position on 9/11" [Excerpts from *9/11 Unmasked: An*

International Review Panel Investigation"], Global Research, November 29. www.globalresearch.ca.

Guyénot, Laurent

2017 *JFK-9/11: 50 Years of the Deep State*. San Diego: Progressive Press.

2022 "The 9/11 'Double-Cross' Conspiracy Theory," Unz Review, September 6. www.unz.com.

Hains, Tim

2024 "Tucker Carlson: Members of Congress are Terrified of the Intel Agencies, That's Not Democracy," Real Clear Politics, April 20. www.realclearpolitics.com.

2024 "Living with Perpetual Violence," Future of Freedom Foundation, July 18. www.fff.org.

Hanley, Dan

2022 "Were the 9/11 Aircraft Electronically Hijacked and Remotely Controlled?" www.lewrockwell.com, November 24.

Hartwell, Dean T.

2015 *Was 9/11 a Movie?* Dean T. Hartwell.

Henshall, Ian

2007 *9/11 Revealed: The New Evidence*. Completely revised and updated. New York: Carroll and Graf Publishers.

Hershberg, Eric & Kevin W. Moore

2002 *Critical Views of September 11: Analyses from Around the World*. New York: New Press.

Hicks, Sander

2005 *The Big Wedding: 9/11, the Whistle-Blowers, & the Cover-Up*. Vox Pop.

2012 *Slingshot to the Juggernaut*. New York: Soft Skull Press.

Hoffman, Jim & Don Paul

2003 *9/11: Great Crimes / A Greater Cover-Up*. San Francisco: Irresistible Revolutionary.

2004 *Waking Up From Our Nightmare: The 9/11/01 Crimes in New York City*. San Francisco: Carroll & Graf.

Holmgren, Gerard

2006 "Manufactured Terrorism—The Truth about Sept. 11." www.supremelaw.org/authors/holgren/911.Closeup.2.html.

Honegger, Barbara

2006 "Seven Hours in September: The Clock that Broke the Lie," in Jim Marrs, *The Terror Conspiracy*, pp. 439-465; and in Marrs, *The Terror Conspiracy Revisited* (2011), pp. 553-583. See also link at:

www.spingola.com/pentagon_attack_papers.html.

Hopsicker, Daniel

2004 *Welcome to Terrorland: Mohamed Atta and the 9/11 Coverup in Florida*. Eugene: MacCow Press.

Hornberger, Jacob G.

2024 "America's Military Empire," Future of Freedom Foundation, January 25. www.fff.org.

2024 "The Stronger the Government, the Weaker the Nation," Future of Freedom Foundation, February 13. www.fff.org.

Hufschmid, Eric

2002 *Painful Questions: An Analysis of the September 11th Attack*. Goleta, CA: Endpoint Software.

Hughes, David A.

2020 "9/11 Truth and the Silence of the IR [International Relations] Discipline," *Alternatives*, vol. 45, issue 2 (February 27): pp. 55-82. www.doi.org/10.1177/0304375419898334. Reprinted at www.paulcraigroberts.org on March 10.

2020 "Peer-Reviewed Journal Publishes Article on Academic Resistance to 9/11 Truth," March 12. www.lewrockwell.com.

Hurt, William

2021 "It Took Me a Long Time to Face What I Knew to be True About 9/11," Architects & Engineers for 9/11 Truth, November 10. www.ae911truth.org.

Icke, David

2002 *Alice in Wonderland and the World Trade Center Disaster: Why the Official Story of 9/11 is a Monumental Lie*. Isle of Wight: David Icke Books.

2019 *The Trigger: Exposing the Lie that Changed the World—Who Really Did It and Why*. Derby, UK: Ickonic Publishing.

Jeffries, Donald

2016 *Hidden History: An Exposé of Modern Crimes, Conspiracies, and Cover-Ups in American Politics*. New York: Skyhorse Publishing.

2024 *American Memory Hole: How the Court Historians Promote Disinformation*. New York: Skyhorse Publishing.

2024 "The Rise and Fall of the Second Amendment," I Protest by Donald Jeffries, February 18. www.donaldjeffries.substack.com.

Johnson, Andrew
2011 *9/11 Finding the Truth.* www.checktheevidfencve.co.co.uk.
2017 9/11 *Holding the Truth.* www.checktheevidence.com.ipage.com.

Johnson, Chalmers
2003 "Sorrows of Empire," *Foreign Policy in Focus*, November.
2006 *Nemesis: The Last Days of the American Republic*. New York: Metropolitan Books.

Johnstone, Caitlin
2024 "If You've Just Started Paying Attention to U.S. Foreign Policy," www.caitlinjohnstone.com. Also at www.lewrockwell.com, January 16.
2024 "The U.S. Empire Isn't a Government that Runs Nonstop Wars, It's a Nonstop War that Runs a Government," www.caitlinjohnstone.com. Also at www.lewrockwell.com, June 3.

Jones, Steven E.
2007 "Revisiting 9/11/2001 – Applying the Scientific Method," *Journal of 9/11 Studies*, May. www.journalof911studies.com/volume/200704/JonesWTC911SciMethod.pdf.

Keenan, John Leo
2023 "On Terrorism," www.lewrockwell.com, December 23.

Kennan, George F.
1997 "A Fateful Error," *New York Times*, February 5.

Kohls, Gary G.
2013 "Duty to Warn: 9/11 and Cognitive Dissonance," Global Research, September 3. www.globalresearch.ca.
2019 "9/11 Truth: Why Do Good People Become Silent About the Documented Facts that Disprove the Official 9/11 Narrative?" Global Research, September 4. www.globalresearch.ca.
2021 "Understanding the Guilty Culprits that Got America into Afghanistan—and Got Away with the Crime AND the Cover-Up!" www.lewrockwell.com, September 7.
2022 "The PNAC Perpetrators of 9/11/01 Speak Out," www.lewrockwell.com, September 12.

Lance, Peter
2004 *Cover Up: What the Government is Still Hiding about the War on Terror*. New York: Harper-Collins/Regan Books.

Larsen, Eric

2006 *A Nation Gone Blind: America in an Age of Simplification and Deceit*. Shoemaker & Hoard.

2011 *The Skull of Yorick: The Emptiness of American Thinking at a Time of Grave Peril*. New York: The Oliver Arts & Open Press.

le Carré, John

2003 "The United States of America has Gone Mad," *The Times*, January 15. www.timesonline.co.uk.

Leake, John

2023 "A Dictatorship Without Tears," Courageous Discourse, November 18. www.petermcculloughmd.substack.com.

2024 "U.S. Foreign Policy is a Scam Built on Corruption," Courageous Discourse, January 6. www.petermcculloughmd.substack.com. Also at www.lewrockwell.com, January 8.

Life Magazine

2001 *One Nation: September 11: America Remembers September 11, 2001*. Introduction by Mayor Rudolph W. Giuliani. New York: Little, Brown and Company.

Lindauer, Susan

2010 *Extreme Prejudice: The Terrifying Story of the Patriot Act and the Cover-Ups of 9/11 and Iraq*. Susan Lindauer.

Liverani, Petra

2018 "9/11 and the WTC Towers: Why Do Self-Styled 'Skeptics' Believe in Their Own Brand of Miracles?" Global Research, March 3. www.globalresearch.ca.

Lofgren, Mike

2016 *The Deep State: The Fall of the Constitution and the Rise of a Shadow Government*. New York: Penguin Books.

MacQueen, Graeme

2006 "118 Witnesses: The Firefighter's Testimony to Explosions in the Twin Towers," www.journalof911studies.com, August 21.

2014 *The 2001 Anthrax Deception: The Case for a Domestic Conspiracy*. Clarity Press, Inc.

2017 "9/11: The Pentagon's B-Movie," www.globalresearch.ca.

2023 *The Pentagon's B-Movie: Looking Closely at the September 2011 Attacks*. [A 626-page collection of 23 articles, available as PDF at www.ratical.org/PentagonsBMovie.]

MacQueen, Graeme & Ted Walter
2020 "How 36 Reporters Brought Us the Twin Towers' Explosive Demolition on 9/11," Architects & Engineers for 9/11 Truth, July 8. www.ae911truth.org. Also at www.lewrockwell.com, July 16.
2022 "The Triumph of the Official Narrative: How the TV Networks Hid the Twin Towers' Explosive Demolition on 9/11," Architects & Engineers for 9/11 Truth, September 8. www.ae911truth.org.

Magnum Photographers
2001 *New York September 11*. Introduction by David Halberstam. New York: Powerhouse Books.

Mann, James
2004 *Rise of the Vulcans: The History of Bush's War Cabinet*. New York: Viking Penguin.

Marrs, Jim
2011 *The Terror Conspiracy Revisited: What Really Happened on 9/11, and Why We're Still Paying the Price*. The Disinformation Co., Ltd. [2006]

Marshall, Phillip
2008 *False Flag 9/11: How Bush, Cheney and the Saudis Created the Post-9/11 World*. BookSurge Publishing.
2012 *The Big Bamboozle: 9/11 and the War on Terror*. Create Space.

Matlock, Jack
2014 "Who is the Bully? The U.S. Has Treated Russia Like a Loser Since the End of the Cold War," *Washington Post*, March 14.

McGinnis, Ray
2021 *Unanswered Questions: What the September Eleventh Families Asked and the 9/11 Commission Ignored*. Vancouver, Canada: NorthernStar Publications.
2022 "How the Sept. 11th Victims' Families Search for Answers was Met with Stonewalling, Lies and Political Theatre," www.lewrockwell.com, September 18.

McMahon, Dennis P.
2012 "Psychology Experts Speak Out: 'Why is the 9/11 Evidence Difficult for Some to Accept?'" Architects & Engineers for 9/11 Truth. www.ae911truth.org.

Mercola, Joseph
2023 "From 9/11 to Domestic Threat Actors—Control is the Goal," Mercola: Take Control of Your Health.

www.mercola.com. Also at www.lewrockwell.com, September 9.

2023 "What Really Happened on 9/11?" Mercola: Take Control of Your Health, www.mercola.com. www.lewrockwell.com, September 22.

Meyer, T. H.

2005 *Reality, Truth and Evil: Facts, Questions and Perspectives About September 11th, 2001*. London: Temple Lodge.

Meyssan, Thierry

2002 *9/11: The Big Lie*. London: Camot. [*Effroyable Imposture: 11 Septembre 2001* (*The Appalling Imposture*), Chatou: Camot]

2002 *Pentagate*. London: Carnot.

2018 "Open Letter to President Trump Concerning the Consequences of 11 September 11, 2001," Voltaire Network. www.voltairenet.org. Also at www.lewrockwell.com, August 31.

2019 *Before Our Very Eyes: Fake Wars and Big Lies: From 9/11 to Trump*. Progressive Press.

2021 "Everything Points to Thierry Meyssan Being Right Today," Voltaire Network, September 3. www.voltairenet.org.

Millennium Report, The

2014 "9/11 Video Evidence Proves Airplane Was Remotely Controlled Into Twin Tower," August 29, 2014 www.themillenniumreport.com/2014/08/911-video-evidence-proves-airplane-was-remotely-controlled-into-twin-tower/.

2014 "9/11 Fact: The Pentagon Was Hit By a Cruise Missile From the U.S. Military Arsenal," September 10. www.themillenniumreport.com/2014/09/911-fact-the-pentagon-was-hit-by-a-cruise-missile-from-the-us-military-arsenal/.

2016 Anonymous Patriots, "Treason: Who Did 9/11 and Why Did They Do It?" October 14. www.themillenniumreport.com/2016/10/treason-who-did-911-and-why-did-they-do-it/.

2019 "Conclusive Proof that 9/11 was an Inside 'Nuclear' Job," August 30. www.themillenniumreport.com/2019/08/conclusive-proof-that-9-11-was-an-inside-nuclear-job/.

2019 "New WTC 7 Controlled-Demolition Analysis Scientifically Proves 9/11 Terror Attacks were a U.S.

Govt.-Sponsored, False Flag Operation and Inside Job," September 7. www.themillenniumreport.com/2019/09/new-wtc7-controlled-demolition-analysis-scientifically-proves-9-11-terror-attacks-were-a-us-govt-sponsored-false-flag-operation-and-inside-job/.

2019 "Fake 9/11 Commission Report: The Most Absurd Conspiracy Theory of All Time," September 12. www.themillenniumreport.com/2019/09/fake-9-11-commission-report-the-most-absurd-conspiracy-theory-of-all-time/.

2019 Joseph A. "Olson, Hard Scientific Evidence Proves the 9/11 Controlled Demolitions were Nuclear Events," October 25. www.themillenniumreport.com/2019/10/hard-scientific-evidence-proves-the-9-11-controlled-demolitions-were-nuclear-events/.

Miller, John & Michael Stone with Chris Mitchell

2002 *The Cell: Inside the 9/11 Plot, and Why the FBI and CIA Failed to Stop It.* New York: Hyperion.

Miller, Merle

1974 *Plain Speaking: An Oral Biography of Harry S. Truman.* London: Gollancz.

Mills, C. Wright

2000 *The Power Elite.* Oxford: Oxford University Press [1956]

2023 "Why I Wrote *The Power Elite.*" Quoted in www.currentaffairs.org/news/2023/02/who-are-the-power-elite, February.

Monaghan, Aidan

2012 *Declassifying 9/11: A Between the Lines and Behind the Scenes Look at the September 11 Attacks.* iUniverse.

Morgan, Rowland & Ian Henshall

2005 *9/11 Revealed: The Unanswered Questions.* New York: Carroll & Graf Publishers.

2009 *Flight 93 Revealed: What Really Happened on the Heroic 9/11 'Let's Roll' Flight?* London: Constable & Robinson.

Naiman, Arthur & Gregg Roberts

2011 *9/11 The Simple Facts: Why the Official Story Can't Possibly Be True.* Soft Skull Press.

Naked Emperor

2023 "Donald Trump Thought Bombs Exploded Simultaneously on 9/11" September 11.

www.nakedemperor.substack.com.

National Commission on Terrorist Attacks Upon the United States
2004 *The 9/11 Commission Report*. New York: Norton.

Newhouse, John
2003 *Imperial America: The Bush Assault on the World Order*. New York: Knopf.

Olbermann, Keith
2007 *Truth and Consequences: Special Comments on the Bush Administration's War on American Values*. New York: Random House.

Olson, Theodore
2022 "Why America Will Win," *Asian Wall Street Journal*, September 11, 2002.

Orkin, Jenna
2014 *Scout: A Memoir of Investigative Journalist Michael C. Ruppert*. Create Space.

Pasin, Patrick
2019 *The FBI: Accomplice of 9/11*. Dublin: Talma Studios.

Paul, Don
2009 *The World is Turning: 9/11, the Movement for Justice, and Reclaiming America for the World*. www.wireOnFire.com.

Paul, Don & Jim Hoffman
2004 *Waking Up from Our Nightmare, the 9/11/01 Crimes in New York City*. San Francisco: Carroll & Graf.

Pijl, Kees van der
2019 "Academic Corruption, the Israel Lobby, and 9/11 or, Why I have resigned from my emeritus status at the University of Sussex." www.academia.edu/.

Pilar, Urbano
2003 *Jefe Atta (El Secreto de la Casa Blanca)*. Barcelona: Plaza Janés.

Polya, Gideon M.
2020 *U.S.-Imposed Post-9/11 Muslim Holocaust & Muslim Genocide*. Korsgaard Publishing.

Pommer, Heinz [and colleagues]
2020 *The Ground Zero Model*. Independently published.

Prager, Dennis
2024 "Were More People Killed in the Name of God or in the Name of Equality?" July 9. www.townhall.com.

Priest, Dana & William M. Arkin
2011 *Top Secret America: The Rise of the New American Security State*. New York: Little, Brown and Company.

Project for the New American Century
2000 *Rebuilding America's Defenses: Strategy, Forces and Resources for a New Century*. September. www.newamericancentury.org.

Raimondo, Justin
2003 *The Terror Enigma: 9/11 and the Israeli Connection*. Lincoln, NE: iuniverse.

Remner, James
2006 "Plan 9/11 from Cyberspace: The Body Snatchers of United 93 and Other Tales of Terror from Cleveland," *Cleveland Free Times*, vol. 14, issue 20. September 6. www.freetimes.com/story/681.

Reynolds, Morgan
2006 "We Have Some Holes in the Plane Stories," No More Games, March. www.nomoregames.net.
2023 "The 9/11 Airplane Magic Show," No More Games, March 10.www.nomoregames.net.

Roberts, Paul Craig
2008 "How Republicans Created Executive Branch Hegemony," March 5. www.onlinejournal.com.
2009 "Evidence that the U.S. is a Failed State is Piling Up Faster than I Can Record It," in "Are You Ready for the Next Crisis?" November 4. www.onlinejournal.com.
2011 "9/11 and the Orwellian Redefinition of 'Conspiracy Theory,'" Institute for Political Economy, June 20. www.paulcraigroberts.org.
2011 "The Day America Died," Institute for Political Economy, September 3. www.paulcraigroberts.org.
2011 "9/11 After a Decade: Have We Learned Anything?" Institute for Political Economy, September 11. www.paulcraigroberts.org.
2012 "The 11th Anniversary of 9/11," Institute for Political Economy, September 11. www.paulcraigroberts.org.
2014 *How America was Lost: From 9/11 to the Police/Warfare State*. Atlanta: Clarity Press, Inc.
2015 *The Neoconservative Threat to World Order: America's Perilous War for Hegemony*. Atlanta: Clarity Press, Inc.
2019 "The Official Story of the Collapse of TWC Building 7 Lies in Ruins," Institute for Political Economy, September 4. www.paulcraigroberts.org.
2019 "9/11 After 18 Years," Institute for Political Economy, September 9. www.paulcraigroberts.org.

2019 "When Americans Fell for the 9/11 Deception They Lost Their Country," Institute for Political Economy, September 11. www.paulcraigroberts.org.
2019 "How Controlled Explanations Are Achieved," Institute for Political Economy, December 28. www.paulcraigroberts.org.
2020 "Peer-Reviewed Journal Publishes Article on Academic Resistance to 9/11 Truth," Institute for Political Economy, March 10. www.paulcraigroberts.com.
2022 "9/11 After 21 Years," Institute for Political Economy, September 11. www.paulcraigroberts.org.
2023 "Was There a 'War on Terror' Or a War on the American People?" Institute for Political Economy, September 12. www.paulcraigroberts.org.
2024 "Did the Dulles Brothers Seal Our Fate?" Institute for Political Economy, May 22. www.paulcraigroberts.org.

Rockwell, Llewelyn H., Jr.
2024 "What We Can Learn from Putin," www.lewrockwell.com, February 19.

Rodriguez, William &Victor Thorn, et. al.
2005 *Debunking 9-11: Includes 100 Unanswered Questions about Sept. 11*. American Free Press.

Roth, Rebekah
2015 *Methodical Deception*. KTYS Media.
2015 *Methodical Illusion*. KTYS Media.
2016 *Methodical Conclusion*. KTYS Media.
2018 *Methodical Exposure*. KTYS Media.
2021 *Methodical Agenda*. KTYS Media.

Ruppert, Michael C.
2004 *Crossing the Rubicon: The Decline of the American Empire at the End of the Age of Oil.* Gabriola Island, BC, Canada: New Society Press.

Ryan, Kevin R.
2013 *Another Nineteen: Investigating Legitimate 9/11 Suspects*. Microbloom.
2008 "The Top Ten Connections between NIST and Nano-thermites," Journal of 9/11 Studies, July 2. www.journalof911studies.com.
2010 "Evidence for Informed Trading on the Attacks of September 11," *Foreign Policy Journal*, November 18. www.foreignpolicyjournal.com
2013 "Noam Chomsky and the Willful Ignorance of 9/11," Dig

Within, November 29. www.digwithin.net/2013/11/29/chomsky/.

Sabrosky, Alan
2021 "Out-Thought, Out-Bought, Out-Fought: Why the '9/11 Truth' Movement Failed," Unz Review, October 23. www.unz.com.

Sachs, Jeffrey D.
2023 "U.S. Foreign Policy Is a Scam Built on Corruption," Common Dreams, December 26. www.commondreams.org.

Sammartino, Vincent
2007 "The 9-11 Passenger List Oddities," in Victor Thorn & Lisa Guiliani, editors, *Phantom Flight 93*, pp. 105-111.

Scott, Peter Dale
2006 "Homeland Security Contracts for Vast New Detention Camps," Pacific News, February 8, p. 124. www.news.pacificnews.org.
2007 *The Road to 9/11: Wealth, Empire, and the Future of America*. Berkeley: University of California Press.
2013 *The War Conspiracy: JFK, 9/11, and the Deep Politics of War*. New York: Skyhorse Publishing.
2017 *The American Deep State: Wall Street, Big Oil, and the Attack on U.S. Democracy*, new edition. Lanham, MD: Rowman & Littlefield.

Shoestring911
2013 "Shanksville, Pennsylvania, on 9/11: The Mysterious Plane Crash Site Without a Plane," Shoestring 911, February 19. www.shoestring911.blogspot.com/2013/02/shanksville-pennsylvania-on-911.html?m=1.

Siegel, Jacob
2023 "A Guide to Understanding the Hoax of the Century," *Tablet*, March 28.

Spencer, Leonard
---- "The Attack on the Pentagon." www.serendipity.li/wot/pentagon/spencer05.htm
---- Flight 11 Revisited," www.serendipity.li/wot/spencer03.htm.
---- "The Incredible 9-11 Evidence We've All Been Overlooking," www.serendipity.li/wot/aa11.html.
---- "What Hit WTC 2? Another Look at the Second Plane," www.serendipity.li/wot/spencer06.htm.
---- "What Really Happened?: A Critical Analysis of Carol

Valentine's 'Flight of the Bumble Planes' Hypothesis," www.serendipity.li/wot/spencer02.htm.

Stockman, David

2023 "Wilson's Folly, the Washington Hegemon, and Why There is Still No Peace on Earth," David Stockman's Contra Corner, December 27. www.davidstockmanscontracorner.com.

2024 "The Donald's Disastrous Fourth Year—But Don't Blame the Covid," David Stockman's Contra Corner, July 22. www.davidstockmanscontracorner.com.

2024 "Why Washington, D. C. is the War Capital of the World," David Stockman's Contra Corner, May 16. www.davidstockmanscontracorner.com.

Stubblebine, Major General Albert N.

2014 "I can prove that it was not an airplane that hit the Pentagon." www.themillenniumreport.com/2014/09/911-must-see-i-can-prove-that-it-was-not-an-airplane-that-hit-the-pentagon-major-general-albert-n-stubblebine/.

Suskind, Ron

2004 *The Price of Loyalty. George W. Bush, the White House, and the Education of Paul O'Neill*. New York: Simon and Schuster.

2004 "Faith, Certainty and the Presidency of George W. Bush," *New York Times Magazine*, October 17.

Tarpley, Webster

2005 *9/11 Synthetic Terror Made in USA*. Joshua Tree, CA: Progressive Press.

2008 *Barack H. Obama: The Unauthorized Biography*. Joshua Tree, CA: Progressive Press.

Thompson, Paul

2004 *The Terror Timeline: Year by Year, Minute by Minute: A Comprehensive Chronicle of the Road to 9/11—and America's Response*. Regan Books.

Thorn, Victor

2005 *9-11 on Trial: The World Trade Center Collapse*. Sisyphus Press.

Thorn, Victor & Lisa Guiliani

2007 *Phantom Flight 93: And Other Astounding September 11 Mysteries Explained*. Washington. D.C.: American Free Press.

Time Magazine
2006 "Why the 9/11 Conspiracies Won't Go Away," September 3.
Toynbee, Arnold
2002 [Quoted in an article.], *New York Times*, May 7.
Trento, Joseph J.
2005 *Prelude to Terror: The Rogue CIA and the Legacy of America's Private Intelligence Network*. New York: Carroll & Graf.
Turley, Jonathan
2002 "Camps for Citizens: Ashcroft's Hellish Vision," *Los Angeles Times*, August 14.
Unger, Craig
2004 *House of Bush, House of Saud: The Secret Relationship Between the World's Two Most Powerful Dynasties*. New York: Scribner.
2004 *The Fall of the House of Bush: The Untold Story of How a Band of True Believers Seized the Executive Branch, Started the Iraq War, and Still Imperils America's Future.* New York: Scribner.
Unz, Ron
2021 "Seeking 9/11 Truth After Twenty Years: Who Attacked America in 2001 . . . and Why?" Unz Review, September 7. www.unz.com.
2022 *Conspiracy Theories: From the JFK Assassination to the 9/11 Attacks*. Palo Alto: Unz Review Press.
2022 "Alex Jones, Cass Sunstein, and 'Cognitive Infiltration,'" Unz Review, August 8. www.unz.com.
2022 "American Pravda: Major Mysteries of the 1990s," Unz Review, December 12. www.unz.com.
2023 "Remembering the 9/11 Truth Movement," Unz Review, September 11. www.unz.com.
Van Bergen, Jennifer
2002 "The USA Patriot Act was Planned Before 9/11," Truthout, May 20. www.truthout.org.
Veale, William W.
2020 *9/11: The Awful Truth: An Account of the Conspiracy Behind the 9/11 Attack*. William Veale.
Vine, David
2017 *Base Nation: How U.S. Military Bases Abroad Harm America and the World*. New York: Skyhorse Publishing.
2020 *The United States of War: A Global History of America's*

Endless Conflicts, from Columbus to the Islamic State. Oakland, CA: University of California Press.

Von Bülow, Andreas

2003 *Die CIA und der 11. September: Internationaler Terror und die Rolle der Geheimdienste*. München: Piper Verlag.

Walia, Arjun

2019 "FBI Sued for Failure to Report Known 9/11 Evidence to Congress," Collective Evolution. Reprinted at www.lewrockwell.com, April 24.

2019 "First Responders Urge Congress to Reopen 9/11 Investigation," Collective Evolution. Reprinted at www.lewrockwell.com, September 26.

Walter, Ted & Graeme MacQueen

2020 "How 36 Reporters Brought Us the Twin Towers' Explosive Demolition on 9/11," Architects & Engineers for 9/11 Truth, July 8. www.ae911truth.org. Also at www.lewrockwell.com, July 16.

2022 "The Triumph of the Official Narrative: How the TV Networks Hid the Twin Towers' Explosive Demolition on 9/11," Architects & Engineers for 9/11 Truth, September 8. www.ae911truth.org.

Webb, Whitney

2019 "More Americans Questioning Official 9/11 Story as New Evidence Contradicts Official Narrative," Unz Review, September 11, www.unz.com.

White, Reichard

2023 "9/11 & the Strangest Fires Ever Told," September 12. www.lewrockwell.com.

Whitehead, John & Nisha

2019 "Betraying the Constitution: Who Will Protect Us from an Unpatriotic Patriot Act?" Rutherford Institute, December 2. www.rutherford.org.

2024 "Rule by Criminals: When Dissidents Become Enemies of the State," Rutherford Institute, March 26. www.rutherford.org.

Wisnewski, Gerhard

2003 *Operation 9/11: Angriff auf den Globus*. München. Knaur Taschenbuch Verlag.

2004 *Mythos 9/11: Der Wahrheit auf der Spur*. München. Knaur Taschenbuch Verlag.

Wood, Allan & Paul Thompson

2003 "An Interesting Day: President Bush's Movements and

Actions on 9/11," Center for Cooperative Research. May.

Wood, Judy
2011 *Where Did the Towers Go? Evidence of Directed Free-Energy Technology on 9/11*. The New Investigation, www.drjudywood.com. The New Investigation.

Woods, Ian (editor)
2002- *Global Outlook: The Magazine of 9/11 Truth.* www.globaloutlook.ca.

Woodworth, Elizabeth
2022 "David Ray Griffin (1939-2022). The Man and His Work: A Synopsis," *Global Research*, www.globalresearch.ca, December 1.

Yoo, John
2001 "The President's Constitutional Authority to Conduct Military Operations Against Terrorists and Nations Supporting Them," September 25. [Memorandum to the president.] www.fas.org/irp/agency/doj/ok092501.html.

Zarembka, Paul (editor)
2006 *The Hidden History of 9-11-2001*. Amsterdam: Elsevier. New York: Seven Stories Press.

Zwicker, Barrie
2006 *Towers of Deception: The Media Cover-up of 9/11.* Gabriola Island, BC, Canada: New Society.

WEBSITES AND VIDEOS

Even more than the list of books and articles, this list of websites and videos is a work in progress. Items on it are those I found helpful in understanding what happened, but it's far from comprehensive.

Top Recommendation for an Introduction to the subject

The Anatomy of a Great Deception: How 9/11 Woke Me Up, by David Hooper (DVD, 99 minutes)
DVD is available from www.ae911truth.org. Also at: www.youtube.com/watch?v=bgZk4jGG50&t=5240s.

Films/Movies/Documentaries/Public Talks

9/11 (2002, 1 hr. 52 min.)
Directed by Jules and Gedeon Naudet and James Hanlon.

9/11 & American Empire—Intellectuals Speak Out (2006) (DVD, 2 hrs.)

9/11 The Big Bamboozle: Philip Marshall (60 min.)
Boeing 767 pilot Marshall examines the supposed flights on September 11.
www.youtube.com/watch?v=ag7tm8Kx5H4&t=259s.

9/11: Blueprint for Truth: The Architecture of Destruction
(DVD, 2 hrs.) With Richard Gage. Also at www.ae911truth.org.

9/11 Conspiracy Solved: Names, Connections & Details Exposed
By Ron Partain

911: Decade of Deception (2015) (DVD, 125 min.)
A summary of the strongest evidence presented over the four days of the Toronto Hearings.

9/11: Explosive Evidence – Experts Speak Out (2011) (DVD, 88 min.)
Also at: www.ae911truth.org and
www.youtube.com/watch?v=IYUYya6bPGw.

9/11 in the Academic Community (2020) (73 min.)
www. www.odysee.com/@911SpeakOut:8/9-11-in-the-Academic-Community:a.

9/11 Mysteries Part 1: Demolitions (DVD, 90 min.)
By Sofia Smallstorm. Also at:
www.youtube.com/watch?v=Z59XXi2Q8Fw&t=5s.

9/11: The Myth and the Reality (2006) (DVD, 78 min.)
A talk by David Ray Griffin.

9/11 National Security Alert
By Citizens Investigation Team

9/11 and Nationalist Faith (2007) (DVD, 87 min.)
A talk by David Ray Griffin in October, 2007.

9/11 and the Neo-Con Agenda (2006) (106 min.)
American Scholars Symposium held June 25, 2006 in Los Angeles. An Alex Jones Production. Includes James Fetzer, Steven Jones, Lt. Col. Bob Bowman, and Webster Tarpley. www.c-span.org/video/?193155-1/september-11th-terrorist-attacks.

911 in Plane Site: Director's Cut (72 min.)
Excellent examination of both planes hitting the towers.

9/11: Press for Truth (2006)
Ryko Distribution.

9/11 Ripple Effect
By Dave von Kleist

9/11: The Road to Tyranny (2004)
Alex Jones documentary.
www.archive.org/details/9-11-the-road-to-tyranny-by-alex-jones?utm_source=substack&utm_medium=email.

911 Truth – Experts Speak Out (95 min.)
Produced by Architects & Engineers for 9/11 Truth.
www.youtube.com/watch?v=kcd6PQAKmj4.

America Remembers: The Events of September 11 and America's Response (DVD, 112 min.)
A CNN tribute useful for much original images.

The Anatomy of a Great Deception: How 9/11 Woke Me Up, by David Hooper (DVD, 99 minutes)
At 38:55: many explosions visible in side of WTC 7 before collapse.
At 1:16:34: plane not visible in space between buildings as it supposedly passed behind them them.
www.youtube.com/watch?v=bgZk4jGG50&t=5240s.

The Best 9/11 Explainer Documentary You'll Ever See (87 min.)
Highlights Judy Wood's findings.
www.rumble.com/v4a8ixu-911-the-best-explainer-documentary-youll-ever-see.html?e9s=src_v1_ucp.

Calling Out Bravo-7

Collateral Damages (2011)
Documentary produced by Etienne Sauret.

Confronting the Evidence: A Call to Reopen the 9-11 Investigation (2005) Produced by Jimmy Walter.

Creating a New Path to Peace and Prosperity
(Empowering Citizens to End the 9/11 Wars and Restore Lost Liberties) With Senator Mike Gravel, Lt. Col. Bob Bowman, Richard Gage, Kathy McGrade.

Fahrenheit 9/11 (2004)
A film by Oliver Stone. Lions Gate Films.

Firefighters, Architects & Engineers Expose 9/11 Myths (DVD, 96 min.)

German Engineers Help the USA: What Had Happened Exactly on 9-11-2001?
www.web.archive.org/web/20030627205434/http://home.debitel.net/user/andreas.bunkahle/defaulte.htm.

The Great Conspiracy: The 9/11 News Special You Never Saw (2004), Barrie Zwicker, Producer/Host. DVD included with Zwicker's *Towers of Deception*.

Lifting the Fog: The Scientific Method Applied to the World Trade Center Disaster (2006)
A conference held at UC Berkeley, November 11, 2006.
www.liftingthefog.org.

Loose Change 9/11: An American Coup
Dylan Avery. Microcinema International.

www.loosechange911.com.
911 Loose Change: American Coup – 2007 Final Cut
www.youtube.com/watch?v=TjYQP0ly-lw.
Dylan Avery
www.loosechange911.com
The New Pearl Harbor (2013) (3 DVDs, 5 hours)
Documentary by Massimo Mazzucco.
Also at: www.youtube.com/watch?v=LgYNPaO1rNY.
Links to all 3 parts are at www.globalresearch.ca.
Also at: www.vimeo.com/353791767.
A Noble Lie: Oklahoma City, 1995 (2011)
Free Mind Films. Compares destruction of the towers in New York in 2001 with the destruction of the Federal Building in Oklahoma City in 1995.
Painful Deceptions: An Analysis of the September 11th Attack (2003)
By Eric Hufschmid. A video supplement to his book *Painful Questions*.
Gage, Richard
2023"The Astonishing Parallels of 9/11 & Covid," www.richardgage911.org/parallels-9-11-covid-the-video-you-want-to-watch
Paul Craig Roberts interviewed by James Corbett in 2010
"9/11 Ten Years After," www.GRTV.ca.
www.youtube.com/watch?v=hBOMSj0uNmw.
The Power of Nightmares: The Rise of the Politics of Fear, part 3: "Shadows in the Cave," BBC documentary.
Scientific & Ethical Questions / A New Standard for Deception
Steven E. Jones debunks the FEMA, NIST and other myths.
September Clues (91 min)
Simon Shack's analysis of all videos of the plane crash into the second tower broadcast on mainstream TV news.
www.archive.org/details/2008-Simon-Shack-September-Clues.
See also www.cluesforum.info.
Seven (DVD, 45 min.)
A film by Dylan Avery, narrated by Ed Asner.
Also at: www.ae911truth.org.
Solving the Mystery of WTC Building 7
From Architects & Eng. for 9/11 Truth, Narrated by Ed Asner.
Terrorstorm (2007) (Special Edition, 129 min.)
An Alex Jones documentary.
www.archive.org/details/20070711-terror-storm-second-edition?utm_source=substack&utm_medium=email.

The Unspeakable (DVD, 90 min.)
A film by Dylan Avery.
Also at: www.ae911truth.org.
Where Did the Towers Go? Implications of the Forensic Study and Its Cover Up (69 min.)
Examines Judy Wood's book and the evidence supporting destruction of the towers by free-energy technology.
www.youtube.com/watch?v=N6_aQQLYNw8.
Zero: An Investigation into 9/11
www.documentaryheaven.com/zero-an-investigation-into-911/.
Documentary by Italian journalist Giulietto Chiesa.

Top Eleven Websites

9/11 Facts: Events of September 11, 2001 – Evidence-Based Facts
www.911evidence.org.
Architects & Engineers for 9/11 Truth
www.ae911truth.org.
Consensus 9/11: The 9/11 Best Evidence Panel
www.consensus911.org.
Dr. Judy Wood
www.drjudywood.com
See also "The Best 9/11 Explainer Documentary You'll Ever See" (87 min.) A persuasive presentation of the evidence in Wood's book, *Where Did the Towers Go?*
www.rumble.com/v4a8ixu-911-the-best-explainer-documentary-youll-ever-see.html?e9s=src_v1_ucp.
Eric Hufschmid
www.hugequestions.com/Eric/index.html.
Painful Questions (book)
www.hugequestions.com/Eric/PainfulQuestionsTOC.html.
Painful Deceptions (video)
www.hugequestions.com/Eric/ThePainfulDeceptionsVideo.html
Global Outlook: The Magazine of 9/11 Truth
www.globaloutlook.ca.
Global Research: Centre for Research on Globalization
Ian Woods, editor. www.globalresearch.ca.
Journal of 9/11 Studies, The
www.journalof911studies.com.
No More Games.net
The official website of Morgan Reynolds.
www.nomoregames.net.
Rebekah Roth
www.readroth.com.

www.behindthegallerycurtain.com

Serendipity

www.serendipity.li.

Websites with Significant 9/11 Content

911 Blimp: Hijacker-Exculpatory Evidence

www.911blimp.net.

911 Blogger: Paying Attention to 9/11 Related News

www.911blogger.com.

9/11 Facts: Events of September 11, 2001 – Evidence-Based Facts

www.911evidence.org.

9-11 Research: An Attempt to Uncover the Truth about September 11

www.911research.wtc7.net.

9-11 Review: A Resource for Understanding the 9/11/01 Attack

www.911review.com.

9/11 Scholars Forum: Exposing Falsehoods and Revealing Truths

www.911scholars.ning.com.

9/11 Share the Truth

Gabriel Day.

www.911sharethetruth.com.

911 Speak Out

www.911speakout.org.

9/11 Truth

www.911truth.org.

911 Truth News

www.911truthnews.com.

9/11 TV: Video and More for the 9/11 Truth Movement

www.9-11tv.org.

Architects & Engineers for 9/11 Truth

www.ae911truth.org.

Assassination Science

Jim Fetzer's site. Also has September 11 material.

www.assassinationscience.com.

Center for Cooperative Research

www.cooperativeresearch.org.

Christopher Bollyn, Journalist without Frontiers

www.bollyn.com.

Colorado 9/11 Truth

www.colorado911truth.org.

Consensus 9/11: The 9/11 Best Evidence Panel

www.consensus911.org.

Counterpunch

www.counterpunch.org.

Daily Motion
www.dailymotion.com/video/x1ajanp.
David Chandler 911
www.911speakout.org.
Dr. Judy Wood
www.drjudywood.com.
See also "The Best 9/11 Explainer Documentary You'll Ever See" (87 min.) for a persuasive presentation of the evidence in her book, *Where Did the Towers Go?*
www.rumble.com/v4a8ixu-911-the-best-explainer-documentary-youll-ever-see.html?e9s=src_v1_ucp.
Eric Hufschmid
www.hugequestions.com/Eric/index.html.
Painful Questions (book)
www.hugequestions.com/Eric/PainfulQuestionsTOC.html.
Painful Deceptions (video)
www.hugequestions.com/Eric/ThePainfulDeceptionsVideo.html
Global Outlook: The Magazine of 9/11 Truth
www.globaloutlook.ca.
Global Research: Centre for Research on Globalization
Ian Woods, editor.
www.Globalresearch.ca.
Infowars
www.Infowars.com.
International Center for 9/11 Justice
www.ic911.org.
Journal of 9/11 Studies, The
www.journalof911studies.com.
Justice for 9/11
www.justicefor911.org.
Kevin's video with raw audio.
www.youtube.o6t31R4tI10.
Lawyers' Committee for 9/11 Inquiry
www.lawyerscommitteefor9-11inquiry.org/.
Lawyers for 9/11 Truth
www.lawyersfor911truth.blogspot.com.
Millennium Report
www.themillenniumreport.com.
Muslim-Jewish-Christian Alliance for 9/11 Truth
Founded by Kevin Barrett. The current site is not the original, and expresses views directly opposite to it.
www.mujca.com.

Naked Emperor's Newsletter
    www.nakedemperor.substack.com.
NIST 9/11 FOIA Release 37
    www.archive.org/details/NIST_9-11_Release_37/.
No More Games.net
    www.nomoregames.net.
    The official website of Morgan Reynolds.
Northern California 9/11 Truth
    www.sf911truth.org.
Paul Wellstone
    Wellstone: They Killed Him: A Preview
    www.youtube.com/watch?v=K-bmmpoDndw.
Pilots for 9/11 Truth
    www.pf911.org.
    The original Pilots for 9/11 Truth site was lost. This reconstruction by Jerry Russell restores 40,000 posts.
Political Leaders for 9/11 Truth
    www.pl911truth.com.
Religious Leaders for 9/11 Truth
    www.rl911truth.org.
Remember Building 7
    www.wtc7.net.
Reopen 911 – Jimmy Walter
    www.reopen911.org.
Richard Gage
    www.richardgage911.org.
Rethink 9/11
    www.rethink911.org.
Rebekah Roth
    www.readroth.com.
    www.behindthegallerycurtain.com.
Scholars for 9/11 Truth
    www.911scholars.org.
Scholars for 9/11 Truth and Justice
    www.stj911.org.
Scientists and Engineers for 9/11 Truth
    www.9-11tv.org/scientists-and-engineers-for-911-truth.
September 11
    www.septembereleventh.org.
Serendipity
    www.serendipity.li.
Snow Shoe Films
    www.snowshoefilms.com.

Steven Jones Paper: Why Indeed Did the WTC Buildings Collapse?
wtc7.net/articles/stevenjones_b7.html.
Veterans for 9/11 Truth
www.aneta.org/veterans911truth.com.
Visibility 9-11 Podcast
www.visibility911.org.
Voltaire Network
www.voltairenet.org/en.
What Really Happened
9/11 Index of what really happened by Michael Rivero.
www.whatreallyhappened.com/wrharticles/wrh_9-11_index.php.
WTC 7
www.wtc7.net.
The site of Professor Leroy Hulsey of the University of Fairbanks.

IMPORTANT SHORTER CLIPS

Planes hitting the WTC towers

United Airlines Flight 175 Crashes Into South Tower
Moment of impact shown in slow motion. The plane is dark and too big relative to the tower. It shows no vibrations or shaking from flying at high speed in the lower atmosphere, and that it disappears into the building with no damage to the building or the plane.
www.youtube.com/watch?v=Q6CderfTWlY.
911 Flight 175 Hitting the South Tower
www.youtube.com/watch?v=re6QX4DM214.
18 Views of Plane Impact in South Tower
The first six show the plane for only a second or two before impact on the far side.
#1 is ABC live chopper.
#7: Evan Fairbank video above coffee drinker. The plane disappears into building with no damage to either. Body of plane is thinner than stubbier planes in other videos.
#8: A "plane" disappears into the building, but a thin missile is shown exiting on the other side. The missile casts a shadow immediately.
#10: Michael Hezarkhani video: plane vanishes into building with no damage to either. The plane casts no shadow.
#12: NBC chopper 4 live: "Plane" doesn't look like a plane.

Too small and fuzzy.
#14: Park Foreman video: Plane is dark, no insignia, disappears into building with no damage to either.
www.youtube.com/watch?v=7YLm3pkAiJQ.

Setting the Record Straight about the Michael Hezarkhani Video
Analysis showing the Nezarkhani video to be fake.
www.mark-conlon.blogspot.com/2017/12/setting-record-straight-about-michael.html.

9/11: 2ND Plane Hit Collection
At :40, head of missile shown exiting the tower, but then screen goes blank for a second to hide it. Also at 6:00 and 6:39. News Anchor comments "completely in one side and out the other," recognizing that it went through solid concrete and steel twice.
www.youtube.com/watch?v=814rcm4KC5w.

9/11/01: The Towers are Hit
www.youtube.com/watch?v=9eTzV7HvKHU.

Destruction of the WTC towers

9/11 Rare Footage from Raspedine1
At 21:44 – close up of collapse of tower
www.youtube.com/watch?v=M1mcCBLU3tY.

The Inconvenient Facts (Must See) / 9/11 Was an Inside Job
High rise buildings with fires still standing and in use today.
www.youtube.com/watch?v=cUg9vwIfGJY. (40 min.)

World Trade Center Collapse on 9/11/2001
Video that surfaced in July, 2024.
www.youtube.com/watch?v=8TexFDMtomU&t=8s.

9/11: As Events Unfold
At 3:30 shows very clearly that at the moment of "collapse" the top block above the "crash" site disintegrates from the bottom up; no floors and no weight fall onto the tower below until almost all upper floors have disintegrated.
www.youtube.com/watch?v=EEogeIIOJzU.

9/11 – Clear Bomb Going Off in WTC Before First Plane Ever Hit (8 min.)
Interviews with people who heard, felt or saw bombs going off in subway under the towers before the first plane hit.
www.youtube.com/watch?v=NLlMXkWW_LM&t=174s.
www.youtube.com/watch?v=igX7Z8VstN4.

The North Tower Exploding, commentary by David Chandler
Chandler walks viewers through video showing explosions occurring floor by floor just before debris from explosions

on high floors covers them.

www.ae911truth.org.

Nearly 1 hour of Never-Before-Seen 9/11 World Trade Center Collapse Footage Surfaces after 23 Years

www.sgtreport.com/2024/07/new-nearly-1-hour-of-never-before-seen-9-11-world-trade-center-collapse-footage-surfaces-after-23-years-uploader-says-he-found-his-tapes-while-cleaning-closet/.

Shows buildings not collapsing but exploded from within.

WTC South Tower Falls – 52 clips.

www.youtube.com/watch?v=k_64RigP1Fk.

No Planes Hit the WTC Towers?

911 Planes Hoax

www.911planeshoax.com/2020/09/11/proof-that-no-real-planes-were-used-on-911/.

Believe Your Own Eyes – 9/11 – No Planes

Has good image of second plane before impact, from below, showing objects attached to the bottom of the plane.

www.youtube.com/watch?v=8W3y3Qh8R1s&t=56s.

Tower Explodes Without a Plane

Video from passing car captures the explosion in the second tower without hit from plane or missile. Yet "missile" exits on the far side.

www.rumble.com/vikbp3-tower-explodes-without-a-plane.-video-from-a-passing-car...html?e9s=src_v1_ucp.

No Plane in the Original Footage

Compares video with plane impacting the tower and with no plane. Explosion is the same in both.

www.rumble.com/vlh9mj-no-plane-on-the-original-footage.html?e9s=src_v1_ucp.

The Planes of 9/11 Were Crude CGI Graphics

www.rumble.com/vm1ruy-the-planes-of-911-were-crude-cgi-graphics.html?e9s=src_v1_ucp.

Tower Blows Up With No Plane

www.rumble.com/vikbnf-tower-blows-up-with-no-plane.html?e9s=src_v1_ucp.

Plane/No Plane Compilation

What's interesting to note in this video and some of the others is that although the image of the plane apparently inserted later does not cast a shadow on the building, the smoke and debris from the internal explosion do.

www.rumble.com/vik301-planeno-plane-compilation.html?e9s=src_v1_ucp.

As It Happened News, Coverage by WNYW Fox 5

News anchors express surprise at seeing no parts of a plane after impact of the towers, discuss explosions inside the tower.

www.youtube.com/watch?v=K5il18uy5Jc&list=PL11B566C52B060431&t=6s.

"Missile" Exiting the Far Side of the South Tower

The Window Cleaner of the World Trade Center (2001)

Dutch TV. At :40 shows head of missile exiting tower. WNYW 9-11. At 15:28 and at 22:12 shows missile exiting the tower. Reaction of anchorman confirms what we see.

www.youtube.com/watch?v=L2PMT3TdBxM.

As It Happened News, Coverage by WNYW Fox 5

At 15:45 nose of missile comes out other side of tower. Broadcast is then blacked out for a second to hide it.

www.youtube.com/watch?v=K5il18uy5Jc&list=PL11B566C52B060431&t=6s.

Jim Corbett – The People's Voice

www.thepeoplesvoice.org.

911: A Conspiracy Theory (2016)

5½ minute summary of what happened.

www.youtube.com/watch?v=Ikxb-wXUe90.

Also here:

www.corbettreport.com/911-a-conspiracy-theory.

www.thepeoplesvoice.org.

www.youtube.com/watch?v=Ikxb-wXUe90

www.themillenniumreport.com/2019/09/on-the-morning-of-9_11-the-truth_in-5-minutes-must-view-video/.

Based on text by Charles Burris?, which can be found at lewrockwell.com,

www.Corbettreport.com/911-a-conspiracy-theory.

911 Suspects – hour long documentary (2020)

Hour long documentary. Among those profiled are: Dick Cheney, Donald Rumsfeld, Larry Silverstein, Dov Zakheim, Paul Bremer, Richard Armitage, Rudy Giuliani, Christine Todd Whitman, Philip Zelikow, Robert Baer and General Ralph Eberhart.

www.Corbettreport.com/911suspects.

Trillions: Follow the Money. (2015)

www.corbettreport.com/911-rillions-follow-the-money-video.

War Games (2018)
911 Whistleblowers (2019) (127 min.)
www.corbettreport.com/911whistleblowers.

David Ray Griffin

9/11 and American Empire: Intellectuals Speak Out (DVD)
Talks given on September 24, 2006 by David Ray Griffin, Peter Dale Scott, Ray McGovern, Peter Phillips, Kevin Ryan.
Also on CSPAN.

The 9/11 Commission Report: Omissions and Distortions (2005)
Talk by David Ray Griffin, April 18, 2005.
www.c-span.org/person/?1014188/DavidRayGriffin.
www.youtube.com/watch?v=aEK2sp_EB7A.

9/11 Contradictions
"Cheney gave Stand Down Order."
www.youtube.com/watch?v=QIM8Sui6-X0.

9/11 Deception
Talk given at Drake University, Des Moines, Iowa, April 23, 2010.

9/11: The Myth and the Reality (2006) (DVD, 78 min.)
Talk given March 30, 2006.

9/11 and Nationalist Faith (DVD, 87 min.)
A talk given in October, 2007.

9/11 and the Neo-Con Agenda. American Scholars Symposium (2006, 106 min.) Held June 25, 2006 in Los Angeles. An Alex Jones Production. Includes James Fetzer, Steven Jones, Lt. Col. Bob Bowman, and Webster Tarpley. www.c-span.org/video/?193155-1/september-11th-terrorist-attacks

"Best Evidence of Truth on 9/11: Contradicting the Official Position on 9/11 (2022)
Based on *The 9/11 Report: Omissions and Distortions*.
www.youtube.com/watch?v=v6dkRa9pTNA.
www.globalresearch.ca.

Truth and Politics: Unanswered Questions about 9/11 (59 min.)
Griffin's talk in Santa Rosa, CA on October 3, 2004 based on The New Pearl Harbor.
www.youtube.com/watch?v=v6dkRa9pTNA.

"Was America Attacked by Muslims on 9/11?"
Griffin's talk at Bloomington, Indiana, Sept. 1, 2008. Based on *The New Pearl Harbor Revisited*. In two parts.
www.youtube.com/watch?v=7tjsCyglRk0. [Part 1]
www.youtube.com/watch?v=7tjsCyglRk0&t=7s. [Part 2]

Donald Trump live interview on September 11, 2001

Donald Trump Thought Bombs Exploded in the Towers
Live interview with WWOR/UPN 9 News on September 11, 2001. Comments are at 5:30.
www.nakedemperor.substack.com/p/donald-trump-thought-bombs-exploded?utm_source=publication-search.
Also at:
www.youtube.com/watch?v=poY5BQ49gf0.

Donald Trump Talks about Explosives Bringing Down the WTC Towers
www.infowars.com/posts/rare-video-watch-donald-trump-talks-about-explosives-bringing-down-world-trade-center-towers-plus-see-alex-jones-predict-9-11.

Flashback: Trump Interviewed on September 11, 2021
www.realclearpolitics.com/video/2017/09/11/flashback_trump_interviewed_on_september_11_2001_tours_damage_2_days_later.html.
www.rumble.com/vjpko9-donald-trump-on-911-bombs-must-have-been-used.html?mref=lzerp&mc=3ifeq.

Major General Albert Stubblebine talks about his awakening.

www.themillenniumreport.com/2014/09/911-must-see-i-can-prove-that-it-was-not-an-airplane-that-hit-the-pentagon-major-general-albert-n-stubblebine/.
www.winterwatch.net/2021/09/major-general-stubblebine-interview-911-was-a-false-flag/.

World Trade Center Building 7

The Anatomy of a Great Deception: How 9/11 Woke Me Up, by David Hooper (DVD, 99 minutes)
At 38:55, many flashes light throughout the building as explosives went off just prior to collapse.
www.youtube.com/watch?v=bgZk4jGG50&t=5240s.

Foreknowledge of the collapse of Building 7 in the Oral Histories – 26 testimonies
Transcripts of witness statements, with links to videos.
www.911blogger.com/node/21658.
www.911research.wtc7.net/wtc/evidence/oralhistories/b7foreknowledge.html

New Evidence that World Trade Center Was Not a Surprise
Shows many flashes of light throughout the building as explosives went off just prior to collapse.
www.armstrongeconomics.com/world-news/corruption/new-

evidence-that-world-trade-center-was-not-a-surprise-more-lies/.

WTC 7: Sound Evidence for Explosions.
www.youtube.com/watch?v=ERhoNYj9_fg.
David Chandler 911. Countdown to moment of demolition clearly audible at 1:10. Nine blasts in 2.5 seconds.

What happened at the Pentagon?

State of the Nation: Alternative News, Analysis & Commentary
Has footage from the air of the "missile" hitting the Pentagon, and much else of interest.
www.stateofthenation2012.com/?p=7381.

FBI Releases Never-Before-Seen Photos from 9/11 Pentagon Attack
Time Magazine. Shows piece of airplane that supposedly hit the Pentagon. The metal has been exposed to heat so intense that it's melted and bent, yet the label showing the flight number is completely undamaged.
www.time.com/4720770/fbi-911-pentagon-attack-photos/.

Plane Hits the Pentagon
Show the large ball of flame from an explosion at the Pentagon. It's all over within 10 seconds. The flames and thick black smoke observed later were from a fire in a dumpster.
www.youtube.com/watch?v=ZaPoD_7TmNc.

9/11 Truth
Pentagon eyewitness Bob Pugh tells his story.
www.youtuVe.com/watch?v=-xtEJ4zrIPM&t=498s.

The Pentagon Crash Site photos
By Peter Meyer. Close up of entrance hole. Note the foam on the glass in the windows above the impact point. Windows not broken. No sign of plane.
www.serendipity.li/wot/crash_site.htm.

Flight 93 – What happened in Pennsylvania?

On Second Thought, with William Wagner (90 minutes)
Draws on material from Pilots for 9/11 Truth to show that Flight 93 and one other flight were still airborne even after time of supposed crashes. Reporters at WCPO Channel 9 quoted then Cleveland Mayor Michael R. White as saying "a Boeing 767 out of Boston made an emergency landing due to a bomb threat." The airplane landed safely and moved to a secure location and was evacuated. The report went on to say that United Airlines verified the plane as Flight 93.
www.youtube.com/watch?v=zKiJC8e3yqw.

C-SPAN videos

9/11 and American Empire: Intellectuals Speak Out (DVD)

Talks given on September 24, 2006 by David Ray Griffin, Peter Dale Scott, Ray McGovern, Peter Phillips, Kevin Ryan. Also on DVD.

9/11 and the Neo-Con Agenda. American Scholars Symposium (2006) (106 min.) Held June 25, 2006 in Los Angeles. An Alex Jones Production. Includes James Fetzer, Steven Jones, Lt. Col. Bob Bowman, and Webster Tarpley. www.c-span.org/video/?193155-1/september-11th-terrorist-attacks.

"The 9/11 Commission Report: Omissions and Distortions. David Ray Griffin, April 18, 2005. www.c-span.org/person/?1014188/DavidRayGriffin.

Other important shorter clips

FOX 5 NY 9/11/2001 Breaking News 8:48

First tower: Reporters mention explosions and note lack of plane debris outside the building. Some witnesses say it was an explosion inside the building, others say it was a plane.

Second tower: Gives a wide view of the sky with no plane in sight before cutting to a close up of a plane visible for only a second before impacting the far side of the tower not visible to viewers. It also shows the head of a "missile" coming out the other side At 15:28 and at 22:12. Reaction of anchorman confirms what we see.

www.youtube.com/watch?v=K5il18uy5Jc&list=PL11B566C52B060431&t=1s.

48 Disturbing 9/11 Facts – 911 Was an Inside Job (35 min.)

48 reasons to doubt the official story, www.youtube.com/watch?v=pSG4XyJg9uY.

9/11 – Flight 175 was not a Commercial Aircraft?

Notes that all planes disappeared from radar for more than half an hour before reappearing.

At 3:00, shows bright flash from explosion just before plane hits the second tower.

At 7:00, shows an even more brilliant flash from explosion just before first plane hits the north tower.

At 12:00 notes that all planes turned around directly over air bases. The two from Boston that crashed in New York passed over the same airbase at exactly the same moment, yet hit the towers 17 minutes apart.

www.youtube.com/watch?v=o551CQFAMKI.

9/11 Miracles and the WTC Towers: Why Do Self-Styled "Skeptics" Believe in Their Own Brand of Miracles?
Petra Liverani. Globalresearch.ca, February 27, 2018.
www.globalresearch.ca/911-and-the-wtc-towers-why-do-self-styled-skeptics-believe-in-their-own-brand-of-miracles/5630813.

The Official ReThink911 Video (5 min.)
www.youtube.com/watch?v=rNR6Kbg5jJ8.

Pulverization and ejection of materials from the towers
4 minute video on pulverization of the towers at www.rethink911.org/evidence/twin-towers/pulverization-and-ejection-of-contents/#pagecontent . Gone, but see at www.youtube.com/watch?v=5G9KohEx9N4.

Jim Hoffman, co-author of Waking Up from Our Nightmare
www.wtc7.net.

The 9/11 Nuke's Total Energy, Part 1 of The Power Source of the 9/11 Event (24 min.)
One of three presentations.
www.youtube.com/watch?v=gxC_8Kuagcw&t=1044s.

9/11 – The Footage They Didn't Let You See Twice
Important witness testimony of bombs going off inside the towers, and much else.
www.themillenniumreport.com/2019/07/the-9-11-footage-they-dont-want-you-to-see-video/.
Also at www.youtube.com/watch?v=djKIlXz8WJs&t=16s.

Toasted Vehicles Outside WTC 7
Raw footage of the cars torched in usual and unusual ways.
www.youtube.com/watch?v=7IMZJk7b_VQ.

CIA Insider Tells 9/11 Truth – Time to Wake Up (24 minutes)
Trucks arrived at the towers from 3-5 a.m. from early August to early September. Air attacks were cover for bombs within the buildings, controlled demolition.
www.youtube.com/watch?v=i6eMq5Rit1w.

Unusual activities at the world trade center before 9/11
Discusses unusual activity at the WTC before September 11. Notes that 503 first responders described bombs going off, but none were mentioned in the 9/11 Commission Report.
www.youtube.com/watch?v=mB2fHqnqZaE&t=126s.

9/11 and the Laws of Physics (5 minutes)
www.youtube.com/watch?v=x7kGZ3XPEm4.
Good explanation of expulsion of building material.

Rare Footage of First "Plane" Impact
Photographs taken by Wolfgang Staehle.
www.youtube.com/watch?v=gKhfQDcDxUI.

IMPORTANT SITES NO LONGER AVAILABLE,
BUT PERHAPS RECOVERABLE.
Expanded from the list Russell Fletcher gave Jubal Jepson in Scene 51.

Websites (no longer available)
www.firefiightersfor911truth.org.
www.pilotsfor911truth.org, www.911pilots.org.
These sites and nearly all references to the organization have vanished from the web. Partially resurrected in summer 2024 at www.youtube.com/watch?v=AeVxnTO8Gu4&t=24s.
www.postmark911.com.
www.stl911truth.info.

Specific sites with titles (no longer available)
9/11: America Nuked
www.scribd.com/document/103906305/911- &
www.thepythoniccow.us/Jeff_Prager_pgs_163-247_911_America_Nuked.pdf.
911 Attack - 3D
www.youtube.com/watch?v=W70aGhJR7SM.
9/11 Contradictions
"Cheney gave Stand Down Order."
www.youtube.com/watch?v=QIM8Sui6-X0.
9/11 Deadly Fallout and Extreme Heat
Pictures of molten steel with GPS information on locations and temperatures weeks after September 11.
www.youtube.com/watch?v=mlMrrISxk9s.
9/11 Hard Facts
www.911hardfacts.com.
9/11 Hijackers were CIA plants.
www.youtube.com/watch?v=vB6k21Yyh7I.
9-11 Pinpoint Accuracy
At 3:08 shows first plane hitting the first tower.
www.youtube.com/watch?v=kB86WAsBj6Y.
9/11 3D Analysis reveals hidden technology
www.youtube.com/watch?v=rWXbjIusiaM.

9/11 Myths Exposed By Firefighters, Architects & Engineers"
    www.youtube.com/watch?v=57kdlbdYILM.

911 Revealing the Truth
    www.911revealingthetruth.org.

911 PlanesHoax.com
    Has Donald Trump phone interview.
    www.911planeshoax.com/tag/911-drone/.

9/11 Video & Radar Analysis of "Flight 175" – 2016 Update
    www.youtube.com/watch?v=sphUezUeiPI.
    www.youtube.com/watch?v=mhROd7Jt3-w.

Christopher Bollyn: The Man Who Solved 9/11
    Filled with brilliant observations.
    www.youtube.com/watch?v=pLWIV0TTcbI&t=675.s

CIA official confesses to blowing up WTC 7
    www.youtube.com/watch?v=hmx-DiWUqfs.

Falso Flag.
    In German, with subtitles in English.
    www.youtube.com/watch?v=zhnNy5EsebA.

Flight Manifests for AA 11 and other flights.
    As published by CNN. Other flights can be seen by changing that part of the URL.
    www.cnn.com/SPECIALS/2001/trade.center/victims/AA11.victims.html.

Flights of Fancy (2005)
    David Ray Griffin's talk.
    www.youtube.com/watch?v=aEK2sp_EB7A.

"I Blew Up WTC 7 on 9/11" CIA Agent Confesses
    www.youtube.com/watch?v=7-DoeFwBs3c.

JFK & 9/11: Insights Gained from Studying Both
    Peter Dale Scott talk at conference, November 18, 2006.
    www.youtube.com/watch?v=hBozfOm9ngV.

The Memory Hole
    Archives vital documents which it fears may be scrubbed from the web. No longer available.
    www.thememoryhole.org.

"The Missing Memorandum"
    Pilots for 9/11 Truth. Examines video fakery.
    At 9:03 shows some kind of ball approaching the tower.
    www.jameshfetzer.org/2018/07/pilots-for-9-11-truth-the-missing-memorandum/September Clues.
    www.youtube.com/watch?v=5QlWZQMYdfA&list=PLasMYrk3jHRTJkADhY831lh7tUZPwCe18.
    New version:

www.youtube.com/watch?v=vD_IgCKpNrY&list=PLasMYrk3jHRTJkADhY831lh7tUZPwCe18&index=2.

What Really Happened

Scientific Professionals Investigating 9/11 (physics911.net).

www.whatreallyhappened.com.

No planes? (no longer available)

9/11 Planes as Fake as Iraqi WMD

Shows tower exploding with and without plane image. If no plane, then flash at moment of impact came from within.

www.youtube.com/watch?v=VJMPN66FHwY&t=679s.

9/11 Was a Big Fake

Shows area of second plane impact, both with and without a plane visible before the explosion. At 41:51, shows a drone painted to look like an AA plane.

www.youtube.com/watch?v=tMqQfKj2c6c.

The No Planes Theory

Shows that CNN and other networks blacked out the moment of impact.

www.youtube.com/watch?v=zxLi577eyrE.

9/11 Planes – Impossible Physics

At 5:08, shows live footage of the explosion at the second tower hit. There is no plane at the time of the explosion. Must have been added later, so explosions came from within.

www.youtube.com/watch?v=lIHUVNgXAcQ.

Proving No Plane Crashes on 9/11 Vis Video

www.vimeo.com/156853233?fbclid=IwAR2IAUZM4xg2wUw-oDrfKv2f1KT65B-BBIsrJK4lhYqHQt7Es7iG0xD_CIo.

Pentagon (no longer available)

85 Reasons why the FBI won't release film it seized from 85 or so security cameras near the Pentagon.

www.youtube.com/watch?v=4uIsvJZqJtM.

Incoming Missile Striking the Pentagon.

www.youtube_scurl=http://www.youtube.com/watch?v=_wjOdhT3Yjg&w=560&h=315.

"No Boeing 757 Hit the Pentagon"

Pilots for 9/11 Truth. Lays out the many flaws in the official story.

www.globalresearch.ca/new-study-from-pilots-for-9-11-truth-no-boeing-757-hit-the-pentagon/6133.

The Pentagon on 9/11

www.youtube.com/watch?v=x779N003mHA.

Plane hit the Pentagon?
www.youtube.com/watch?v=JTJehfQkuyE.
What really happened at the Pentagon.
www.youtube.com/watch?v=puFkwR2DqH4.

Broadcasts and clips for which titles are not known (no longer available)

www.youtube.com/watch?v=YQBlv7sZGVE.
At WTC, four flight recorders were never found
Rubble 2,000 degrees months later

www.youtube.com/watch?v=in3vlyia8H4.
Six flights were supposed to have been involved. At least three Saudis with fake pilot IDs tried to board on Sept. 13.

www.vimeo.com/220124507.
View from helicopter of cruise missing hitting the Pentagon.

www.whatreallyhappened.com/osamatape.html.
Fake bin Laden video

www.whatreallyhappened.com/osamatape.html.
Fake bin Laden Video

www.youtube.com/watch?v=D4YbLihsehc.
Architect's point of view of destruction of the towers.

www.youtube.com/watch? v=D4YbLihsehc.
Thermite from an architect's perspective.

www.prisonplanet.com/011904wtc7.html.
Larry Silverstein saying "pull it" to order destruction of WTC 7.

www.youtube.com/watch?v=sq5UAx2zm_0.
Cockpit doors were never opened. Switch from plane to drone took place in radar hole.

www.youtube.com/watch?v=yli-if4F0DY.
Demolition flashes throughout the towers just before "collapse."

www.youtube.com/watch?v=ibW3pCWyqC0.
Shows flocks of "birds"(drones?) flying around holes in the towers.

www.prisonplanet.com/011904wtc7.html.
Larry Silverstein saying "pull it."

www.youtube.com/watch?v=q6alf9_xswA.
Mentioned in Paul Craig Roberts's 11th 09/11/2012 article.

www.youtube.com/watch?v=4fvJ8nFa5Qk.
Drone disguised as an American Airlines plane.

www.youtube.com/watch?v=8W3y3Qh8R1s.
Shows nose of "plane" emerging from far side of tower.

COUP #3: COVID-19
(and the United States as a colony)

BOOKS AND ARTICLES

Atlas, Scott

2021 *A Plague Upon Our House: My Fight at the Trump White House to Stop Covid from Destroying America*. New York: Post Hill Press.

Bawer, Bruce

2021 *That Year: Dispatches from 2020*. Swamp Fox Editions.

2022 *Peak Woke? Dispatches from 2021*. Swamp Fox Editions.

Berenson, Alex

2021 *Pandemia: How Coronavirus Hysteria Took Over Our Government, Rights, and Lives.* Washington, DC: Regnery Publishing.

Blaylock, Russell L.

2024 "Medical Science Has Changed with Covid," *Blaylock Wellness Report*, vol. 21, no. 7 (July): 1-6.

Block, Walter E.

2023 "Regulating Out Renters," Econolib: The Library of Economics and Liberty, November 25. www.econlib.org. Also at www.lewrockwell.com, December 15.

Breggin, Peter R. & Ginger R.

2021 *Covid-19 and the Global Predators: We Are the Prey*. Ithica: Lake Edge Press.

Canary House Publishing

2023 *Canary in a Covid World: How Propaganda and Censorship Changed Our (My) World: A Collection of Essays from 34 Contemporary Thought Leaders.*

Chan, Alina & Matt Ridley

2021 *Viral: The Search for the Origin of Covid-19*. New York: HarperCollins.

Chossudovsky, Michel

2023? *The Worldwide Corona Crisis: Global Coup d'Etat Against Humanity*. Global Research. www.globalresearch.ca.

2024 "Fear Campaign Resulting from Totally Invalid Covid-19 'Confirmed Cases'," March 16. www.michelchossudovsky.substack.com.

Cook, Jeffrey, Clayton Sandell & Jennifer Leong
2020 "Former Police Officer Arrested in Park for Throwing Ball with Daughter Due to Coronavirus Social Distancing Rules," April 8. www.sott.net.

Desmet, Mattias
2022 *The Psychology of Totalitarianism*. White River Junction, VT: Chelsea Green Publishing.

Dodsworth, Laura
2021 *A State of Fear: How the UK Government Weaponized Fear During the Covid-19 Pandemic*. London: Pinter & Martin, Ltd.

Doud, Edward
2022 *Cause Unknown: The Epidemic of Sudden Deaths in 2021 and 2022*. New York: Skyhorse Publishing.

Gage, Richard
2023 "The Astonishing Parallels of 9/11 & Covid," www.richardgage911.org/parallels-9-11-covid-the-video-you-want-to-watch.

Hollis, Laura
2024 "The West's Descent into Madness," March 21. www.townhall.com.

Humphries, Suzanne & Roman Bystrianyk
2023 *Dissolving Illusions: Disease, Vaccines and the Forgotten History*. Tenth Anniversary edition.

Jeffries, Donald
2023 *Masking the Truth: How Covid-19 Destroyed Civil Liberties and Shut Down the World*. Midnight Writer News.

Johnstone, Caitlin
2024 "You Only Need to Cage a Bird If It Knows that It Can Fly," February 28. www.caitlinjohnstone.com. Also at www.lewrockwell.com.

Kennedy, Robert F., Jr.
2021 *The Real Anthony Fauci: Bill Gates, Big Pharma and the Global War on Democracy and Public Health*. New York: Skyhorse Publishing.
2022 *A Letter to Liberals: Censorship and Covid*. New York: Skyhorse Publishing.
2023 *The Wuhan Cover-Up and the Terrifying Bioweapons Arms Race*. New York: Skyhorse Publishing.
2024 *Vax-Unvax: Let the Science Speak*. New York: Skyhorse Publishing.

Kheriarty, Aaron
2022 *The New Abnormal: The Rise of the Biomedical Security*

State. Washington, DC: Regnery Publishing.

Knightly, Kit
2021 "30 Facts You Need to Know: Your Covid Crib Sheet," Policy Research, September 22.

Kullander, James
2021 "A Letter to My Vaccinated Friend," www.lewrockwell.com, September 22.
2022 "Second Letter to My Vaccinated Friend," www.lewrockwell.com, January 14.
2022 "Third Letter to My Vaccinated Friend," www.lewrockwell.com, February 16.
2022 "Fourth Letter to My Vaccinated Friend," www.lewrockwell.com, June 29.
2022 "The Bodies of Others: The New Authoritarians, Covid-19 and the War Against the Human" [review of the book by Naomi Wolf], www.lewrockwell.com, July 14.
2022 "The Promise of Pleasure or the Threat of Pain," www.lewrockwell.com, July 28.
2023 "A Tale of Two Deaths," www.lewrockwell.com, March 4.
2023 "Small Town, Big Sleep," www.lewrockwell.com, May 11.
2024 "Create Dangerously: A Meditation on an Essay by Albert Camus," www.jameskullander.substack.com, August 14.
2024 "The Quest for Community: A Study in the Ethics of Order and Freedom," www.jameskullander.substack.com, September 27.
2024 "The Forest Passage: A Meditation on a Book by Ernst Jünger," www.jameskullander.substack.com, October 11.
2024 "The Captive Mind: A Meditation on a Book by Czeslaw Milosz," www.jameskullander.substack.com, December 5.

Leake, John
2023 "A Dictatorship Without Tears," Courageous Discourse, November 18. www.petermcculloughmd.substack.com.

Leake, John & Peter McCullough
2022 *The Courage to Face Covid-19: Preventing Hospitalization and Death While Battling the Bio-Pharmaceutical Complex*. Dallas: Counterplay Books.

Lerman, Debbie
2022 "Government's National Security Arm Took Charge During the Covid Response," Brownstone Institute,

November 3. www.brownstone.org.

2022 "Was There a Covid Response Plan? If So, Where Is It?" Brownstone Institute, November 7. www.brownstone.org,

Malone, Robert W.

2022 *Lies My Government Told Me and the Better Future Coming*. New York: Skyhorse Publishing.

McCarthy, Ken

2024 *What the Nurses Saw: Systemic Medical Murders*. Tivoli, NY: Brasscheck Press.

McDonald, Mark

2021 *United States of Fear: How America Fell Victim to a Mass Delusional Psychosis*. New York: Post Hill Press.

Mercola, Joseph & Ronnie Cummins

2021 *The Truth about Covid-19: Exposing the Great Reset, Lockdowns, Vaccine Passports, and the New Normal.* White River Junction, VT: Chelsea Green Publishing.

Miller, Ian

2022 *Unmasked: The Global Failure of Covid Mask Mandates*. New York: Post Hill Press.

Mosher, Steven W.

2022 *The Politically Incorrect Guide to Pandemics*. Washington, DC: Regnery Publishing.

Nehls, Michael

2023 *The Indoctrinated Brain: How to Successfully Fend Off the Global Attack on Your Mental Freedom*. New York: Skyhorse Publishing.

Nocera, Joe & Bethany McLean

2023 *The Big Fail: What the Pandemic Revealed about Who America Protects and Who It Leaves Behind*. New York: Penguin.

Paul, Rand

2023 *Deception: The Great Covid Cover-up*. Washington, D.C.: Regnery Publishing.

Ponesse, Julie

2024 *Our Last Innocent Moment*. Brownstone Institute.

Quinn, Jim

2024 "The Covid Experiment," The Burning Platform, March 13. www.theburningplatform.com.

Roberts, Paul Craig

2020 "The Main Threat from Covid is Not the Disease," Institute for Political Economy, November 13. www.paulcraigroberts.org.

2022 "The Government Also Taught Us to Lie," Institute for Political Economy, October 14. www.paulcraigroberts.org.

2021 "The Fake 'Covid Pandemic' was Orchestrated in Order to Impose Tyranny," Institute for Political Economy, November 23. www.paulcraigroberts.com.

2022 "Covid Roundup," Institute for Political Economy, November 27. www.paulcraigroberts.org.

2022 "In Honor of a Truth Teller," Institute for Political Economy, December 14. www.paulcraigroberts.org.

2023 *Empire of Lies*. Korsgaard Publishing, Inc.

2023 "In My Lifetime I Have Witnessed the Death of Independent Medicine and Fair Trials," Institute for Political Economy, January 18. www.paulcraigroberts.org.

2023 "All U.S. Regulatory Agencies are Protection Services and Marketing Agents for the 'Regulated' Industries," Institute for Political Economy, January 24. www.paulcraigroberts.org.

2023 "In America Democracy is a Veil Behind which the Oligarchy Rules," Institute for Political Economy, February 19. www.paulcraigroberts.org.

2023 "How Private Interests Seized Control of America," Institute for Political Economy, April 1. www.paulcraigroberts.org.

2023 "The American Population is Not Defending Our Liberty," Institute for Political Economy, May 8. www.paulcraigroberts.org.

2023 "Insouciant Americans Have Doomed America to Tyranny," Institute for Political Economy, May 25. www.paulcraigroberts.org.

2024 "Ivermectin Emerges as a Significant Aid in Cancer Treatment," Institute for Political Economy, April 9. www.paulcraigroberts.org.

2024 "America: Goodbye My Country," Institute for Political Economy, April 25. www.paulcraigroberts.org.

Roth, Carol

2021 *The War on Small Business: How the Government Used the Pandemic to Crush the Backbone of America.* New York: HarperCollins.

Shepherd, Igor

2021 "Covid-19: A Psychological Military Operation, Part 1," October 13. www.lewrockwell.com.

2021 "Covid-19: A Psychological Military Operation, Part 2," October 14. www.lewrockwell.com.

Simon, Roger L.

2022 "Has American Democracy Been a Hallucination for Nearly 60 Years?" Epoch Times, December 17. www.theepochtimes.com.

2023 "What Now for the Men and Women Without a Country?" Epoch Times, June 19. www.theepochtimes.com.

Stossel, John

2024 "A Ban on Freelance Work," Townhall, April 10. www.townhall.com.

Thomas, Jeff

2024 "When All Crimes are Those Against the State," Doug Casey's International Man, June 14. www.internationalman.com. Also at www.lewrockwell.com,.

Tucker, Jeffrey A.

2020 *Liberty or Lockdown.* American Institute for Economic Research.

2023 "Twenty Grim Realities Unearthed by Lockdowns," Brownstone Institute, June 5. www.brownstone.org.

2023 "Who Best Avoided the Covid Religion?" Brownstone Institute, August 21. www.brownstone.org.

2023 "Can We Handle the Truth?" Epoch Times, October 10. www.theepochtimes.com.

2023 "How to Restore Freedom," Brownstone Institute, November 7. www.brownstone,org.

2024 *Life After Lockdown*. Brownstone Institute.

2024 "A Coup Without Firing a Shot," Brownstone Institute, April 20. www.brownstone.org.

Unz, Ron

2022 "Prof. Jeffrey Sachs on the Covid Origins Cover-Up," Unz Review, August 29. www.unz.com.

2022 "American Pravda: The JFK Assassination and the Covid Cover-Up," Unz Review, December 19. www.unz.com.

Wade, Nicholas

2021 *Where Covid Came From*. New York: Encounter Books.

Walsh, Michael

2020 *Last Stands: Why Men Fight When All is Lost*. New York: St. Martin's Press.

Whitehead, John & Nisha

2019 "Betraying the Constitution: Who Will Protect Us from an Unpatriotic Patriot Act?" Rutherford Institute,

December 2. www.rutherford.org.
2023 "A State of Martial Law: America Is a Military Dictatorship Disguised as a Democracy," Rutherford Institute, June 29. www.rutherford.org.
2024 "Rule by Criminals: When Dissidents Become Enemies of the State," Rutherford Institute, March 27. www.rutherford.org.

Willis, Mikki
2021 *Plandemic: Fear is the Virus and Truth is the Cure*. New York: Skyhorse Publishing.

Wolf, Naomi
2021 *The End of America: Letter of Warning to a Young Patriot*. White River Junction, VT: Chelsea Green Publishing. [2007]
2022 *The Bodies of Others: The New Authoritarians, Covid-19 and the War Against the Human*. Fort Lauderdale, FL: All Seasons Press.
2023 *Facing the Beast: Courage, Faith and Resistance in a New Dark Age*. White-River Junction, VT: Chelsea Green Publishing.

Woods, Thomas
2023 *Diary of a Psychosis: How Public Health Disgraced Itself During Covid*. Austin: The Libertarian Institute.

WEBSITES AND VIDEOS

Videos

The "Covid Pandemic" was the Result of Extensive Media Propaganda: "Nobody is Safe, Be Afraid" (2023) (11.5 min.)
By Matt Orfalea. www.globalresearch.ca/covid-pandemic-was-entirely-product-propaganda-nobody-safe/5820225. Also at: www.youtube.com/watch?v=zI3yU5Z2adI&t=5s.

The Astonishing Parallels of 9/11 & Covid (2023)
Gage, Richard, www.richardgage911.org/parallels-9-11-covid-the-video-you-want-to-watch.

* * * * *

Made in the USA
Coppell, TX
07 February 2026

70959222R00371